Rick Steves®

WITHDRAWN
AMSTERDAM

& THE NETHERLANDS

Rick Steves & Gene Openshaw

D0089367

CONTENTS

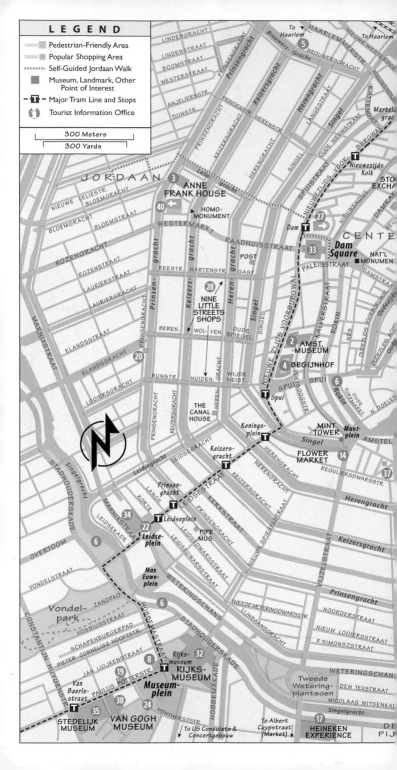

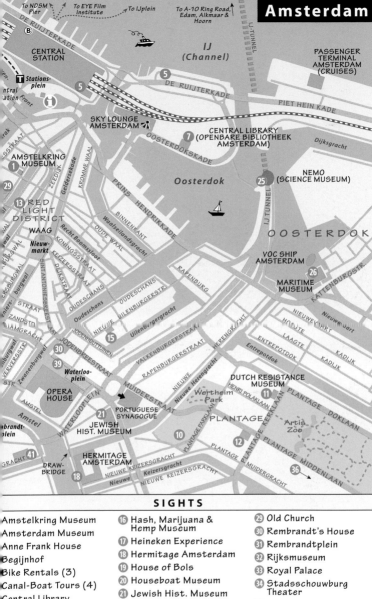

Amsterdam

IJ (Channel)

To NDSM Pier
To EYE Film Institute
To IJplein
To A-10 Ring Road, Edam, Alkmaar & Hoorn

DE RUIJTERKADE

CENTRAL STATION

PASSENGER TERMINAL AMSTERDAM (CRUISES)

Stations-plein

DE RUIJTERKADE

PIET HEIN KADE

Central Front

SKY LOUNGE AMSTERDAM

OOSTERDOKSKADE

7 CENTRAL LIBRARY (OPENBARE BIBLIOTHEEK AMSTERDAM)

Dijksgracht

AMSTELKRING MUSEUM **1**

29

Oosterdok

25 NEMO (SCIENCE MUSEUM)

13 RED LIGHT DISTRICT

WAAG

ZEEDIJK

KROMME WAAL

GELDERSKADE

PRINS HENDRIKKADE

BINNENKANT

Recht Boomssloot

WAALSEILANDSGRACHT

IJ-TUNNEL

OOSTERDOK

Nieuw-markt

KONINGSSTRAAT

OUDE WAAL

VOC SHIP AMSTERDAM

BURGWAL

SINT ANTONIESBREESTRAAT

ZANDST

NIEUWMARKT

 slers STRAAT

OUDESCHANS

OUDESCHANS

UILENBURGERSTR.

RAPENBURG

26 MARITIME MUSEUM

KATTENBURGSTR.

NIEUWEVAART

Nieuwe Vaart

HOUTT.

LAAGTE

KADIJK

burgwal

JODENBREESTRAAT

15

NIEUWE

Uilenburgergracht

ENTREPOTDOK

KADIJK

VERVERSSTR.

30

Zwanenburgwal

VALKENBURGERSTRAAT

RAPENBURGERSTRAAT

HERENGRACHT

Entrepotdok

39 Waterloo-plein

JODENBREESTRAAT

NIEUWE

Nieuwe Herengracht

11 DUTCH RESISTANCE MUSEUM

HENRI POLAKLAAN

PLANTAGE DOKLAAN

STR.

OPERA HOUSE

MUIDERSTRAAT

Wertheim Park

PLANTAGE

AMSTEL

21

PORTUGUESE SYNAGOGUE

JEWISH HIST. MUSEUM

10

PLANTAGE PARKLAAN

12

PLANTAGE KERKLAAN

Artis Zoo

rabrandt-plein

41

18

HERMITAGE AMSTERDAM

NIEUWE KEIZERSGRACHT

Keizersgracht

PLANTAGE P.

PLANTAGE MIDDENLAAN

GRACHT

DRAW-BRIDGE

Nieuwe

NIEUWE KEIZERSGRACHT

PLANTAGE P. MUIDERGRACHT

36

SIGHTS

Amstelkring Museum
Amsterdam Museum
Anne Frank House
Begijnhof
Bike Rentals (3)
Canal-Boat Tours (4)
Central Library
Coster Diamonds & Mus.
Damrak Sex Museum
De Hortus Botanical Garden
Dutch Resistance Mus.
Dutch Theater Memorial
Erotic Museum
Flower Market
Gassan Diamonds

16 Hash, Marijuana & Hemp Museum
17 Heineken Experience
18 Hermitage Amsterdam
19 House of Bols
20 Houseboat Museum
21 Jewish Hist. Museum
22 Leidseplein
23 Museum of Bags and Purses
24 Museumplein
25 NEMO (Science Museum)
26 Netherlands Maritime Museum
27 New Church
28 Nine Little Streets Shopping District

29 Old Church
30 Rembrandt's House
31 Rembrandtplein
32 Rijksmuseum
33 Royal Palace
34 Stadsschouwburg Theater
35 Stedelijk Museum
36 To Tropical Museum
37 Tuschinski Theater
38 Van Gogh Museum
39 Waterlooplein Flea Market
40 Westerkerk
41 Willet-Holthuysen Museum

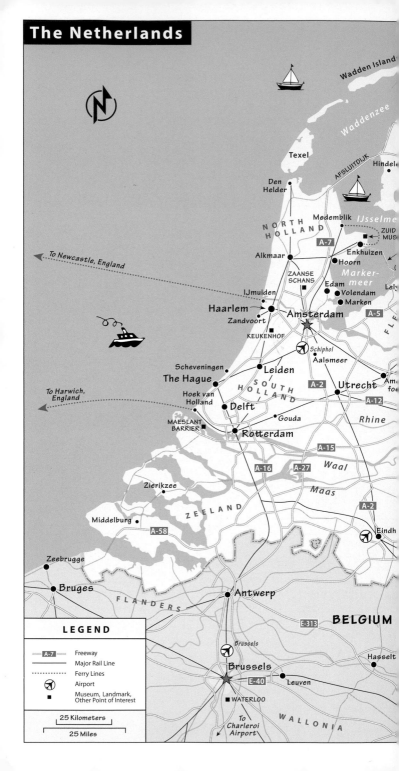

Rick Steves

AMSTERDAM

& THE NETHERLANDS

INTRODUCTION

Rattling your bike over cobbles, past a line of gabled houses reflected in a mirror-smooth canal...it's just like you imagined it.

This book presents the best of Amsterdam and the Netherlands—its great cities, small towns, fine food, rich history, and sensuous art. You'll experience both the quaintness of the countryside as well as the modern scene in the Netherlands' forward-thinking urban centers.

This book covers the predictable biggies while mixing in a healthy dose of Back Door intimacy. In Amsterdam you can see Vincent van Gogh's *Sunflowers*...and climb through Captain Vincent's tiny houseboat museum. Besides the city's many historic sights, you'll explore everyday neighborhoods, with their chiming carillons, cannabis coffeeshops, and one-of-a-kind fashion boutiques. Beyond Amsterdam, you'll discover the hidden charms of Haarlem, where a market bustles around a historic church. The Hague has Vermeer paintings in its top-notch museums, while placid Delft is a Vermeer painting come to life.

Because transportation is a snap, much of the country is an easy day-trip from anywhere. There's no end of cozy towns—Edam, Alkmaar, Hoorn, and on and on—as well as open-air folk museums. Along the way, you'll meet intriguing people who will show you how to swallow a pickled herring, paddle a canoe through polder waterways, or slice off a hunk of cheese from a giant wheel. It's as if the tourist clichés of the region—whirring windmills, Dutch Masters, dike hikes, and tulips—all come to life in the Netherlands.

Along with sightseeing, this book gives you tips on how to save money, plan your time, ride public transportation, and avoid lines at the busiest sights. You'll also get recommendations on hotels, restaurants, and entertainment.

This book is selective, including only the top sights. The best

Map Legend

⅃ Viewpoint	✈ Airport	Park
↑ Entrance	Ⓣ Taxi Stand	Pedestrian Zone
✚ Tourist Info	Ⓜ Metro Stop	Railway
WC Restroom	Ⓣ Tram Stop	Ferry/Boat Route
Church	Ⓑ Bus Stop	Tram
▪ Statue/Point of Interest	Ⓟ Parking	Stairs
◎ Fountain	⛴ Boat/Cruise Line	Walk/Tour Route

Use this legend to help you navigate the maps in this book.

is, of course, only my opinion. But after spending much of my life exploring and researching Europe, I've developed a sixth sense for what travelers enjoy.

Amsterdam and the Netherlands are ready for you. Sample a little, then a little more.

ABOUT THIS BOOK

Rick Steves Amsterdam & the Netherlands is a personal tour guide in your pocket. Better yet, it's actually two tour guides in your pocket: The co-author of this book is Gene Openshaw. Since our first "Europe through the gutter" trip together as high-school buddies in the 1970s, Gene and I have been exploring the wonders of the Old World. An inquisitive historian and lover of European culture, Gene wrote most of this book's self-guided museum tours and neighborhood walks. Together, Gene and I keep this book up-to-date and accurate (though for simplicity, from this point "we" will shed our respective egos and become "I").

This book is organized by destination. Each is a mini-vacation on its own, filled with exciting sights, strollable neighborhoods, affordable places to stay, and memorable places to eat.

The first half of this book focuses on Amsterdam, Haarlem, and Delft, and contains the following chapters:

The Netherlands offers an introduction to this fascinating land, including its long fight against the sea.

Orientation to Amsterdam includes specifics on public transportation, helpful hints, local tour options, easy-to-read maps, and tourist information. The "Planning Your Time" section suggests a schedule for how to best use your limited time.

Sights in Amsterdam describes the top attractions and includes their cost and hours.

Self-Guided Walks and **Tours** take you through characteristic neighborhoods and interesting museums. In Amsterdam, these

Key to This Book

Updates
This book is updated regularly—but things change. For the latest, visit www.ricksteves.com/update.

Abbreviations and Times
I use the following symbols and abbreviations in this book:
Sights are rated:

▲▲▲ Don't miss
▲▲ Try hard to see
▲ Worthwhile if you can make it
No rating Worth knowing about

Tourist information offices are abbreviated as **TI**, and bathrooms are **WCs**. To categorize accommodations, I use a **Sleep Code** (described on page 466).

Like Europe, this book uses the **24-hour clock**. It's the same through 12:00 noon, then keeps going: 13:00, 14:00, and so on. For anything over 12, subtract 12 and add p.m. (14:00 is 2:00 p.m.).

When giving **opening times**, I include both peak season and off-season hours if they differ. So, if a museum is listed as "May-Oct daily 9:00-16:00," it should be open from 9 a.m. until 4 p.m. from the first day of May until the last day of October (but expect exceptions).

If you see a ✪ symbol near a sight listing, it means that sight is described in far greater detail elsewhere—either with its own self-guided tour, or as part of a self-guided walk.

For **transit** or **tour departures**, I first list the frequency, then the duration. So a train connection listed as "2/hour, 1.5 hours" departs twice each hour, and the journey lasts an hour and a half.

include walks through the city center, Red Light District, and Jordaan neighborhood, plus tours of the Rijksmuseum, Van Gogh Museum, Anne Frank House, and more. In nearby Haarlem, tour the Grote Kerk and Frans Hals Museum. In Delft and Rotterdam, take the informative city walks.

Sleeping in Amsterdam describes my favorite hotels, from good-value deals to cushy splurges.

Eating in Amsterdam serves up a range of options, from inexpensive cafés to fancy restaurants.

Smoking covers Amsterdam's best "coffeeshops," which openly sell marijuana.

Amsterdam with Children includes my top recommendations for keeping your kids (and you) happy.

Shopping in Amsterdam gives you tips for shopping pain-

INTRODUCTION

lessly and enjoyably, without letting it overwhelm your vacation or ruin your budget.

Entertainment in Amsterdam is your guide to fun, including music, theater, comedy, movies, and more.

Amsterdam Connections outlines your options for traveling to destinations by train, bus, and plane (with information on getting to and from Amsterdam's Schiphol Airport).

Several chapters on **Haarlem** cover the highlights of this inviting Dutch town. If you'd rather base in a small town and daytrip to Amsterdam, Haarlem is a good choice.

The **Delft** chapters introduce you to the charms of this well-preserved city with a youthful atmosphere. Delft is another good home base, especially if you'll be day-tripping to The Hague and Rotterdam.

Day Trips, the second half of this book, has chapters on destinations to the north, south, and east of Amsterdam, ranging from cities—The Hague, Leiden, Rotterdam, and Utrecht—to sojourns into the Dutch countryside to see world-class art near Arnhem, quaint villages such as Edam and Marken, and open-air museums such as Enkhuizen.

The **History** chapter gives you a quick overview of Dutch history and a timeline of major events.

Practicalities is a traveler's tool kit, with my best travel tips and advice about money, sightseeing, sleeping, eating, staying connected, and transportation (trains, buses, car rentals, driving, and flights). There's also a list of recommended books and films.

The **appendix** has nuts-and-bolts information, including useful phone numbers and websites, a festival list, a climate chart, a handy packing checklist, and Dutch survival phrases.

Browse through this book, choose your favorite destinations, and link them up. Then have a *fantastisch* trip! Traveling like a temporary local, you'll get the absolute most out of every mile, minute, and dollar. As you visit places I know and love, I'm happy that you'll be meeting some of my favorite Dutch people.

Planning

This section will help you get started planning your trip—with advice on trip costs, when to go, and what you should know before you take off.

TRAVEL SMART

Your trip to the Netherlands is like a complex play—it's easier to follow and really appreciate on a second viewing. While no one does the same trip twice to gain that advantage, reading this book before your trip accomplishes much the same thing.

Design an itinerary that enables you to visit the various sights at the best possible times. Note festivals, holidays, specifics on sights (such as days when sights are closed or most crowded), and crowd-beating strategies. For example, to avoid the lines, you can reserve ahead for Amsterdam's major sights—the Rijksmuseum, Van Gogh Museum, and Anne Frank House. To get between destinations smoothly, read the tips in Practicalities on taking trains and buses, or renting a car and driving. A smart trip is a puzzle—a fun, doable, and worthwhile challenge.

When you're plotting your itinerary, strive for a mix of intense and relaxed stretches. To maximize rootedness, minimize one-night stands. It's worth taking a long drive after dinner (or a train ride with a dinner picnic) to get settled into a town for two nights. Every trip—and every traveler—needs slack time (laundry, picnics, people-watching, and so on). Pace yourself. Assume you will return.

Reread this book as you travel and visit local tourist information offices (abbreviated as TI in this book). Upon arrival in a new town, lay the groundwork for a smooth departure; get the schedule for the train or bus that you'll take when you depart. Drivers can find out the best route to their next destination.

Update your plans as you travel. You can carry a small mobile device (phone, tablet, laptop) to find out tourist information, learn the latest on sights (special events, tour schedules, etc.), book tickets and tours, make reservations, reconfirm hotels, research transportation connections, and keep in touch with your loved ones. If you don't want to bring a pricey device, you can use guest computers at hotels and make phone calls from landlines.

Enjoy the friendliness of the Dutch people. Connect with the culture. Set up your own quest to find the best salted herring or canal boat ride. Slow down and be open to unexpected experiences. Ask questions—most locals are eager to point you in their idea of the right direction. Keep a notepad in your pocket for planning your day and organizing your thoughts. Wear your money belt, learn the currency, and figure out how to estimate prices in dollars. Those who expect to travel smart, do.

TRIP COSTS

Five components make up your trip costs: airfare, surface transportation, room and board, sightseeing and entertainment, and shopping and miscellany.

Airfare: A basic, round-trip flight from the US to Amsterdam can cost, on average, about $1,000-2,000 total, depending on where you fly from and when (cheaper in winter). Consider saving time and money in Europe by flying into one city and out of another; for instance, into Amsterdam and out of Paris. If you're sticking

The Netherlands at a Glance

Best Home Bases
If you plan to stay in one of these cities for your whole trip, be sure to visit the other towns on day trips.

▲▲▲**Amsterdam** Progressive world capital with magnificent museums, wondrous waterways, Golden-Age architecture, diverse nightlife, and eye-opening Red Light District.

▲▲**Haarlem** Cozy, quiet burg with its own top attractions, plus easy access to big-city Amsterdam.

▲▲**Delft** Picturesque hometown of Vermeer and Delftware with college-town vibe—a good base for day-tripping to The Hague and Rotterdam.

Day Trips

North of Amsterdam
▲**Alkmaar and Zaanse Schans** Holland's tasty cheese capital—Alkmaar—with its Friday cheese market, and Zaanse Schans, an easy-to-reach though touristy folk museum.

▲▲**Edam**, **Volendam**, **and Marken** Postcard-perfect region with the adorable cheesemaking village of Edam, the tourist depot of Volendam, and the fascinating former fishing hamlet of Marken.

▲▲**Hoorn and Enkhuizen** Time-warp duo of the Golden-Age merchant's town of Hoorn and charming village of Enkhuizen, with an open-air museum that preserves lost Zuiderzee culture.

to the Netherlands, you're never more than about two hours from Amsterdam's airport. Overall, Kayak.com is the best place to start searching for flights on a combination of mainstream and budget carriers.

Surface Transportation: For getting around, you're best off enjoying the Netherland's excellent and affordable train system. Trains leave at least hourly between its major cities. It costs about $20 for a ticket from Amsterdam to Rotterdam. If you'll be renting a car, allow $200 per week, not including tolls, gas, and supplemental insurance. If you'll be keeping the car for three weeks or more, look into leasing, which can save you money on insurance and taxes. Car rentals and leases are cheapest if arranged from the US.

If you're staying within the Netherlands and relying on trains for transportation, you'll save money by simply buying tickets as

Flevoland Intriguing province reclaimed from the sea featuring Schokland, a former fishing village now surrounded by dry land.

South of Amsterdam
Keukenhof and Aalsmeer Flower-power destinations with fabulous tulip gardens (Keukenhof, open only in spring) and famous floral auction scene (Aalsmeer).

▲**Leiden** Historic, charming college town that was the Pilgrims' last stop before Plymouth Rock.

▲**The Hague** Governmental hub with excellent art museum (Mauritshuis), international courts, and nearby beach.

▲**Rotterdam** Europe's busiest port with soaring skyscraper architecture and 21st-century buzz.

East of Amsterdam
▲**Utrecht** Bustling university city with the Netherlands' largest medieval old town and its best railway museum.

▲▲**Museums near Arnhem** Two Dutch treats—the granddaddy of open-air museums (Netherlands Open-Air Folk Museum) and a world-class collection of Van Gogh masterpieces (Kröller-Müller Museum).

you go. But if you'll be traveling elsewhere in Europe, consider getting a rail pass (these normally must be purchased outside Europe) or taking a cheap flight, as budget airlines can be cheaper than taking the train (check www.skyscanner.com for intra-European flights).

For more on public transportation and car rental, see "Transportation" in Practicalities.

Room and Board: You can thrive in the Netherlands on $125 a day per person for room and board (more for Amsterdam). This allows $20 for lunch, $30 for dinner, and $70 for lodging (based on two people splitting the cost of a $140 double room that includes breakfast). That leaves you $5 for *friets* or chocolate. To live and sleep more elegantly, I'd propose a budget of $145 per day per person ($20 for lunch, $40 for dinner, and $80 each for a $160 hotel double with breakfast). Students and tightwads can enjoy the

Netherlands for as little as $60 a day ($30 per bed, $30 for meals and snacks).

Sightseeing and Entertainment: In big cities, figure about $15-20 per major sight (Rijks and Van Gogh museums); $6-10 for minor ones (climbing church towers or windmills); $10-18 for guided walks, boat tours, and bike rentals; and $30-60 for splurge experiences such as concerts, special art exhibits, big-bus tours, and guided canoe trips. An overall average of $25 a day works for most people. Don't skimp here. After all, this category is the driving force behind your trip—you came to sightsee, enjoy, and experience the Netherlands.

Shopping and Miscellany: Figure $1-2 per postcard, tea, or ice-cream cone, and $5 per beer. Shopping can vary in cost from nearly nothing to a small fortune. Good budget travelers find that this category has little to do with assembling a trip full of lifelong and wonderful memories.

SIGHTSEEING PRIORITIES

With affordable flights from the US, minimal culture shock, almost no language barrier, and a well-organized tourist trade, the Netherlands is a good place to start a European trip. Virtually every city I mention is within an hour (or so) train ride from centrally located Amsterdam. The best home-base cities are Amsterdam, Haarlem, and Delft.

So much to see, so little time. How to choose? Depending on the length of your trip, and taking geographic proximity into account, here are my recommended priorities:

2-3 days:	Amsterdam
4 days, add:	Delft
5-6 days, add:	Haarlem, The Hague, Rotterdam, and/or Leiden
7-9 days, add:	Towns north of Amsterdam such as Alkmaar, Edam/Waterland, Hoorn/Enkhuizen, and more
10-11 days, add:	Arnhem (with its Kröller-Müller and open-air folk museums), Utrecht, and possible overnight in Otterlo
12 days, add:	If you have a car, it's worth exploring Flevoland.

This includes nearly everything on the map on the next page. If you don't have time to see it all, prioritize according to your interests. With more time, add more Amsterdam, or dip down into Belgium (covered in my *Rick Steves Belgium: Bruges, Brussels, Antwerp & Ghent* guidebook).

INTRODUCTION

Top Destinations in The Netherlands

ENKHUIZEN

HOORN

ALKMAAR

EDAM

FLEVOLAND

HAARLEM

AMSTERDAM

AALSMEER

KEUKENHOF

LEIDEN

NETHERLANDS

THE HAGUE

UTRECHT

DELFT

ROTTERDAM

ARNHEM

WHEN TO GO

Although Amsterdam can be plagued by crowds, the long days, lively festivals, and sunny weather make summer a great time to visit. It's rarely too hot for comfort.

Peak Season: Amsterdam is surprisingly crowded—and hotel prices can be correspondingly high—in late March, April, and May, when the tulip fields are flowering in full glory. Seasonal conferences can also drive up prices in September in Amsterdam. July and August have typical summer crowds.

Shoulder Season: Late spring and fall are pleasant, with generally mild weather and lighter crowds (except during holiday weekends—see page 503).

Winter Season: Travel from late October through mid-March is cold and wet in this region, as coastal winds whip through these low, flat countries. It's fine for visiting Amsterdam, but smaller towns and countryside sights feel dreary and lifeless. Some sights

Rick Steves Audio Europe

If you're bringing a mobile device, be sure to check out **Rick Steves Audio Europe**, where you can download free audio tours and hours of travel interviews (via the Rick Steves Audio Europe app, www.ricksteves.com/audioeurope, Google Play, or iTunes).

My self-guided **audio tours** are user-friendly, easy-to-follow, fun, and informative, covering the major sights and neighborhoods in Amsterdam (an Amsterdam City Walk, Red Light District Walk, and Jordaan Walk). Compared to live tours, my audio tours are hard to beat: Nobody will stand you up, the quality is reliable, you can take the tour exactly when you like, and they're free.

Rick Steves Audio Europe also offers a far-reaching library of intriguing **travel interviews** with experts from around the globe. The interviews are organized by destination, including many of the places in this book.

close for lunch, TIs keep shorter hours, and some tourist activities (like English-language windmill tours) vanish altogether.

KNOW BEFORE YOU GO

Your trip is more likely to go smoothly if you plan ahead. Check this list of things to arrange while you're still at home.

You need a **passport**—but no visa or shots—to travel in the Netherlands. You may be denied entry into certain European countries if your passport is due to expire within three months of your ticketed date of return. Get it renewed if you'll be cutting it close. It can take up to six weeks to get or renew a passport (for more on passports, see www.travel.state.gov). Pack a photocopy of your passport in your luggage in case the original is lost or stolen.

Book rooms well in advance, especially if you'll be traveling during peak season (late March-May and Sept) or any major holidays (see page 503).

Call your **debit- and credit-card companies** to let them know the countries you'll be visiting, to ask about fees, request your PIN code (allow time for it to be mailed to you), and more. See page 459 for details.

Do your homework if you want to buy **travel insurance.** Compare the cost of the insurance to the likelihood of your using it and your potential loss if something goes wrong. Also, check whether your existing insurance (health, homeowners, or renters) covers you and your possessions overseas. For more tips, see www.ricksteves.com/insurance.

The big three **museums** in Amsterdam—Rijksmuseum, Van

INTRODUCTION

How Was Your Trip?

Were your travels fun, smooth, and meaningful? If you'd like to share your tips, concerns, and discoveries, please fill out the survey at www.ricksteves.com/feedback. To check out readers' hotel and restaurant reviews—or leave one yourself—visit my travel forum at www.ricksteves.com/travel-forum. I value your feedback—it helps shape the trips of travelers who follow in our footsteps.

Gogh, and Anne Frank—can come with long lines during high season. Consider buying tickets online from home (for details, see page 29).

If you plan to hire a **local guide,** reserve ahead by email. Popular guides can get booked up.

If you're bringing a **mobile device,** download any apps you might want to use on the road, such as translators, maps, and transit schedules. Check out **Rick Steves Audio Europe,** featuring audio tours of major sights, hours of travel interviews on the Netherlands, and more (described earlier).

Check the **Rick Steves guidebook updates** page for any recent changes to this book (www.ricksteves.com/update).

Because **airline carry-on restrictions** are always changing, visit the Transportation Security Administration's website (www.tsa.gov) for a list of what you can bring on the plane and for the latest security measures (including screening of electronic devices, which you may be asked to power up).

Traveling as a Temporary Local

We travel all the way to the Netherlands to enjoy differences—to become temporary locals. You'll experience frustrations. Certain

truths that we find "God-given" or "self-evident," such as cold beer, ice in drinks, bottomless cups of coffee, and bigger being better, are suddenly not so true. One of the benefits of travel is the eye-opening realization that there are logical, civil, and even better alternatives. A willingness to go local ensures that you'll enjoy a full dose of Dutch hospitality.

Europeans generally like Americans. But if there is a negative aspect to the Dutch image of Americans, it's that we are loud, wasteful, ethnocentric, too informal (which can seem disrespectful), and a bit naive.

My Dutch friends place a high value on speaking quietly in restaurants and on trains. Listen while on the bus or in a restaurant—the place can be packed, but the decibel level is low. Try to adjust your volume accordingly to show respect for their culture.

While the Dutch look bemusedly at some of our Yankee excesses—and worriedly at others—they nearly always afford individual travelers all the warmth we deserve.

Judging from all the happy feedback I receive from travelers who have used this book, it's safe to assume you'll enjoy a great, affordable vacation—with the finesse of an independent, experienced traveler.

Thanks, and have a *goede vakantie!*

Back Door Travel Philosophy

From *Rick Steves Europe Through the Back Door*

Travel is intensified living—maximum thrills per minute and one of the last great sources of legal adventure. Travel is freedom. It's recess, and we need it.

Experiencing the real Europe requires catching it by surprise, going casual…"through the Back Door."

Affording travel is a matter of priorities. (Make do with the old car.) You can eat and sleep—simply, safely, and enjoyably—anywhere in Europe for $120 a day plus transportation costs. In many ways, spending more money only builds a thicker wall between you and what you traveled so far to see. Europe is a cultural carnival, and time after time, you'll find that its best acts are free and the best seats are the cheap ones.

A tight budget forces you to travel close to the ground, meeting and communicating with the people. Never sacrifice sleep, nutrition, safety, or cleanliness to save money. Simply enjoy the local-style alternatives to expensive hotels and restaurants.

Connecting with people carbonates your experience. Extroverts have more fun. If your trip is low on magic moments, kick yourself and make things happen. If you don't enjoy a place, maybe you don't know enough about it. Seek the truth. Recognize tourist traps. Give a culture the benefit of your open mind. See things as different, but not better or worse. Any culture has plenty to share.

Of course, travel, like the world, is a series of hills and valleys. Be fanatically positive and militantly optimistic. If something's not to your liking, change your liking.

Travel can make you a happier American, as well as a citizen of the world. Our Earth is home to seven billion equally precious people. It's humbling to travel and find that other people don't have the "American Dream"—they have their own dreams. Europeans like us, but with all due respect, they wouldn't trade passports.

Thoughtful travel engages us with the world. In tough economic times, it reminds us what is truly important. By broadening perspectives, travel teaches new ways to measure quality of life.

Globetrotting destroys ethnocentricity, helping us understand and appreciate other cultures. Rather than fear the diversity on this planet, celebrate it. Among your most prized souvenirs will be the strands of different cultures you choose to knit into your own character. The world is a cultural yarn shop, and Back Door travelers are weaving the ultimate tapestry. Join in!

THE NETHERLANDS

THE NETHERLANDS

Nederland

In Holland's 17th-century Golden Age, Dutch traders sailed the seas to find exotic goods, creating a global economy. Tiny Holland was a world power—politically, economically, and culturally—with more great artists per square mile than any other country.

"Holland" is just a nickname for the Netherlands. North Holland and South Holland are the largest of the 12 provinces that make up the Netherlands. Today, the country is Europe's most densely populated and also one of its wealthiest and best organized. In 1944, the neighboring countries of Belgium, the Netherlands, and Luxembourg became the nucleus of a united Europe when they joined economically to form BeNeLux.

The average income in the Netherlands is higher than in the United States. Though only 8 percent of the labor force is made up of farmers, 70 percent of the land is cultivated—if you venture outside of Amsterdam, you'll travel through vast fields of barley, wheat, sugar beets, potatoes, and flowers.

The word *Nederland* means "lowland." The country occupies the low-lying delta near the mouth of three of Europe's large rivers, including the Rhine. In medieval times, inhabitants built a system of earthen dikes to protect their land from flooding caused by tides and storm surges. The fictional story of the little Dutch boy who saves the country—by sticking his finger in a leaking dike—summed up the country's precarious situation. (Many Americans know this story from a popular 19th-century novel, but few Dutch people have ever heard of it.)

In 1953, severe floods breached the old dikes, killing 1,800 and requiring a major overhaul of the system. Today's 350 miles of dikes and levees are high-tech, with electronic systems to monitor water levels. Dutch experts traveled to Louisiana after Hurricane Katrina to share their expertise with US officials after levee failure

The Netherlands

AFSLUITDIJK
(CLOSURE DIKE)

IJssel-
meer

Medemblik

ZUIDERZEE
MUSEUM

Enkhuizen

SCHOKLAND

**North
Sea**

Alkmaar

Hoorn

HOUTRIBDIJK
(N-302)

ZAANSE
SCHANS

Edam

*Marker-
meer*

Volendam

Lelystad

FLEVOLAND

Marken

Haarlem

Zandvoort

⊛**Amsterdam**

KEUKENHOF ✈ *Schiphol*

NETHERLANDS

Aalsmeer

Scheveningen

KRÖLLER-MÜLLER
MUSEUM

Leiden

Utrecht

The Hague

Hoge Veluwe
Nat'l Park

To Harwich,
England

NETH. OPEN-AIR
FOLK MUSEUM

Delft

Hoek Van
Holland

Rhine

Arnhem

Rotterdam

To Cologne

Waal

50 Miles

Maas

NETHER-
LANDS

GERMANY

25 Kilometers

25 Miles

BELGIUM

NETHERLANDS

caused massive flooding. And after Hurricane Sandy, American hydrology experts began looking to the Netherlands for models of how to protect vast areas from flooding.

Much of the Dutch landscape is reclaimed from the sea, rivers, and lakes. That's where Holland's famous windmills came in. After diking off large tracts of land below sea level, the Dutch used windmills to harness wind energy to lift the water up out of the enclosed area, divert it into canals, and drain the land. They cultivated hardy plants that removed salt from the soil, slowly turning marshy estuaries into fertile farmland. The windmills later served a second purpose for farmers by turning stone wheels to grind their grain.

The trifecta of Dutch reclamation technology is dikes, windmills...and canals. Picturesque waterways, big and small, course through both cities and the countryside. While we use the all-purpose term "canal," the Dutch recognize several variations, which

Netherlands Almanac

Official Name: Koninkrijk der Nederlanden (Kingdom of the Netherlands), or simply Nederland.

Population: 16.8 million people (1,200 people per square mile; 15 times the population density of the US). About 80 percent are Dutch; 5 percent hail from other EU countries; and the rest are mostly Indonesian, Turkish, Surinamese, or Moroccan. Less than a third are Catholic, 20 percent are Protestant, 5 percent are Muslim, and more than 40 percent have no religious affiliation.

Latitude and Longitude: 52 °N and 5 °E. The latitude is similar to Alberta, Canada.

Area: 16,000 square miles—about twice the size of New Jersey.

Geography: The Netherlands is located at the delta where three major European rivers empty into the North Sea: the Rhine from Germany and Switzerland; the Maas (Meuse) from Belgium and France; and the Waal (a short but mighty distributary of the Rhine). It shares borders with Belgium and Germany. The Dutch have been beating back the North Sea for centuries, forming polders—flat, low-lying reclaimed lands. The Netherlands has a mild marine climate; even hot, clear, and sunny days can come with surprise rain showers.

Biggest Cities: Amsterdam is the largest city, with 820,000 people, followed by Rotterdam (617,000), The Hague (500,000), and Utrecht (330,000).

Economy: The Netherlands is prosperous, with the planet's 23rd-largest economy ($700 billion), a per-capita GDP in the world's

can be helpful as you navigate place names: *singel* is a former moat, *gracht* is a dug-out waterway, *kanal* is for shipping, and *sloot* is a drainage canal (usually in the countryside).

Dutch reclamation projects are essentially finished (though a new province—Flevoland, near Amsterdam—has been drained, dried, and populated in the last 100 years; see the Flevoland chapter). But as the world's climate changes and sea levels rise, the Dutch are focusing more and more resources on upgrading their dikes and bulking up their beaches to hold back the sea. They also continue to innovate, building floatable homes and greenhouses (which rise with the tides) and relocating dikes farther back from the rivers (to create wider floodplains).

All this technological tinkering with nature—past and present—has brought about a popular local saying: "God made the Earth, but the Dutch made Holland."

Several Dutch icons came directly from the country's flat, reclaimed landscape: As mentioned, windmills and canals drained the land. Wooden shoes *(klompen)* allowed farmers to walk across

top 20 ($43,300), and one of Europe's lowest unemployment rates. Its port at Rotterdam is Europe's largest, and the country relies heavily on foreign trade. The nation's highly mechanized farms produce huge quantities of flowers, bulbs, and produce for export. The economy has also benefited from its many natural gas fields—including the huge Groningen field, one of the world's biggest.

Government: The Netherlands is a parliamentary democracy, with its seat of government at The Hague, although the country's official capital is Amsterdam. The ceremonial head of state is King Willem-Alexander, whose ascension to the throne in 2013 is celebrated each spring on King's Day—usually April 27. He is the first Dutch king in 123 years. The Dutch parliament consists of two houses: the 150-member, directly elected Second Chamber (or Lower House); and the 75-member First Chamber (or Upper House), elected by provincial assemblies. The government is led by a prime minister, currently Mark Rutte of the center-right People's Party for Freedom and Democracy (VVD).

Flag: The Netherlands' flag is composed of three horizontal bands of red (top), white, and blue.

The Dutch: They're among the world's tallest people—the average height for a man is 6'1" and for a woman, 5'6". The average age for both men and women is around 41 years old, and they'll live to be 81. They ride their bikes about 1.5 miles a day and smoke half as much marijuana as their American friends.

soggy fields. (They're also easy to find should they come off in high water because they float.)

Tulips and other flowers grew well in the sandy soil near dunes. In the 1630s, Holland was gripped with "tulip mania" (see sidebar on page 20). Financial speculators invested wildly in exotic varieties, causing prices to skyrocket. You could buy a house with just three tulip bulbs. In February of 1637, the bubble burst, investors were ruined, and the economic fallout helped contribute to the decline of the Dutch Golden Age.

The Netherlands' flat land also makes it a biker's dream. The Dutch, who average four bikes per family, have put small bike roads (with their own traffic lights) beside nearly every major highway. You can rent bikes at most train stations and drop them off at most others. And you can take bikes on trains (outside of rush hour) for €6 per day. But bikes can make things tricky for those on foot. You might expect the right-of-way pecking order to go pedestrians, then bikes, then cars. Not so. In practice, you should assume

Tulip Mania

A Dutch icon since the 17th century, the colorful flowers are actually native to central Asia ("tulip" comes from a Turkish word for "turban"). When the Holy Roman Emperor's ambassador to Constantinople first sent some bulbs westward in the mid-1500s, a few eventually wound up in the hands of a Dutch botanist—and thus began one of the oddest chapters in the Netherlands' history.

The region's harsh conditions turned out to be ideal for the hardy bulbs, which also benefited from good timing: They arrived in the Netherlands in the middle of the Dutch Golden Age, delighting a relatively affluent populace who were fond of beauty and able to pay for it. Within a generation the popularity of these then-exotic flowers—and for a few rare species in particular—grew from a trendy fad into an all-out frenzy. Prices shot skyward: Forty bulbs could fetch up to 100,000 florins (about $1.7 million in today's dollars); in the context of the times, an average laborer made around 150 florins a year. The most treasured variety was the Semper Augustus, with its distinctive red-and-white petals—just one bulb sold for 12 acres of land.

"Tulip mania" reached a fever pitch in late 1636, and for the next few months, frantic trading consumed the Dutch. Production of other goods declined as people dropped everything to get rich on the tulip exchange. Soon, instead of buying and selling actual bulbs, people began trading promissory vouchers—by that time, it wasn't really the flowers everyone was after, but the opportunity to resell them at a higher price. The number of potential buyers seemed endless...until it wasn't. In February of 1637, one of history's most famous speculative bubbles burst, leaving many tulip investors with empty contracts or bulbs worth only a tiny fraction of what they'd cost. But the demand for tulips never died out—a love of the flowers had been firmly planted in the Dutch psyche, and they continue to be an integral part of the culture as well as a major export.

it's bikes first...then everyone else. Watch very carefully for bikes before crossing (or even stepping into) the street.

The Dutch generally speak English, pride themselves on their frankness, and like to split the bill. Thriftiness, efficiency, and a dislike of wastefulness are longstanding Dutch traits. Traditionally, Dutch cities have been open-minded, loose, and liberal (to attract sailors in the days of Henry Hudson). And today, Amsterdam is a capital of alternative lifestyles—a city where nothing's illegal as long as nobody gets hurt. Coffeeshops serve cannabis (and sometimes cappuccinos), and prostitutes pose in government-licensed windows. The city is surprisingly diverse, housing many recent immigrants—a trend that, unfortunately, has resulted in tension in recent years. The Netherlands in general and Amsterdam in particular are gay-friendly. Some of the biggest festivals and parades on the social calendar bring out the LGBT crowd.

Although it expresses itself in a sometimes-jarring acceptance of drugs and sex, the Dutch passion for tolerance has deep historical roots: For generations, this part of Europe was a particularly fierce battleground between the Roman Catholic Church (backed primarily by Spain) and Reformation-era Protestants (Dutch nationalists). The Eighty Years' War and other conflicts flamed religious intolerance. But afterwards, the reaction against the Spanish Inquisition and the wealth of the Golden Age brought a new era of acceptance. Today—especially after the Nazi occupation's persecution of Jews and other minorities—the Dutch are determined to live and let live.

Another facet of this philosophy is Dutch humility. A popular saying here is, "The tree that grows the tallest gets blown by the strongest wind." While the Dutch have an affinity for Americans, they don't always quite know how to take our rugged individualism.

Wherever you roam, you'll find the Netherlands to be something of an eye-opener. Behind its placid exterior, it's a complex mix of modern technology, honored traditions, quaint countryside, outrageous architecture, and no-nonsense, globally minded people.

AMSTERDAM

ORIENTATION TO AMSTERDAM

Amsterdam still looks much like it did in the 1600s—the Dutch Golden Age—when it was the world's richest city, an international sea-trading port, and the cradle of capitalism. Wealthy, democratic burghers built a city upon millions of pilings, creating a wonderland of canals lined with trees and townhouses topped with fancy gables. Immigrants, Jews, outcasts, and political rebels were drawn here by its tolerant atmosphere, while painters such as young Rembrandt captured that atmosphere on canvas.

Today's Amsterdam is a progressive place of 820,000 people and almost as many bikes. It's a city of good living, cozy cafés, great art, street-corner jazz, stately history, and a spirit of live and let live.

Amsterdam also offers the Netherlands' best people-watching. The Dutch are unique, and observing them is a sightseeing experience all in itself. They're a handsome and healthy people, and among the world's tallest. They're also open and honest—I think of them as refreshingly blunt—and they like to laugh. As connoisseurs of world culture, they appreciate Rembrandt paintings, Indonesian food, and the latest French film—but with an un-snooty, blue-jeans attitude.

Be warned: Amsterdam, a bold experiment in freedom, may box your Puritan ears. For centuries, the city has taken a tolerant approach to things other places try to forbid. Traditionally, the city attracted sailors and businessmen away from home, so it was profitable to allow them to have a little fun. In the 1960s, Amsterdam became a magnet for Europe's hippies. Since then, it's become a world capital of alternative lifestyles. Stroll through any neighborhood and see things that are commonplace here but rarely found elsewhere. Prostitution is allowed in the Red Light District, while "smartshops" sell psychedelic drugs and marijuana is openly sold and smoked. (The Dutch aren't necessarily more tolerant or decadent than the rest of us—just pragmatic and looking for smart solutions.)

Approach Amsterdam as an ethnologist observing a strange culture. It's a place where carillons chime quaintly from spires towering above coffeeshops where yuppies go to smoke pot. Take it all in, then pause to watch the clouds blow past stately old gables—and see the Golden Age reflected in a quiet canal.

AMSTERDAM: A VERBAL MAP

Amsterdam's Central Station (Amsterdam Centraal), on the north edge of the city, is your starting point, with the TI, bike rental, and trams branching out to all points. Damrak is the main north-south axis, connecting Central Station with Dam Square (people-watching and hangout center) and its Royal Palace. From this main street, the city spreads out like a fan, with 90 islands, hundreds of bridges, and a series of concentric canals—named Singel (the original moat), Herengracht (Gentleman's Canal), Keizersgracht (Emperor's Canal), and Prinsengracht (Prince's Canal)—that were laid out in the 17th century, Holland's Golden Age. Amsterdam's major sights are all within walking distance of Dam Square.

To the east of Damrak is the oldest part of the city (today's Red Light District), and to the west is the newer part, where you'll find the Anne Frank House and the peaceful Jordaan neighborhood. Museums and Leidseplein nightlife cluster at the southern edge of the city center.

AMSTERDAM BY NEIGHBORHOOD

Amsterdam can feel like a big, sprawling city, but its major sights cluster in convenient zones. Grouping your sightseeing, walks, dining, and shopping thoughtfully can save you time.

Central Amsterdam—the historic core—runs north-south from Central Station along Damrak, passing through two major city squares (Dam and Spui) and ending at the Mint Tower. The central spine of streets (Damrak, Kalverstraat, Rokin) has some of the city's main department, chain, and tourist stores. Flanking Damrak on the east is the city's oldest area (today's Red Light District) and the revitalized waterfront around the train station.

West Amsterdam lies west of Damrak—from Dam Square to the Anne Frank House. This pleasant area is famous for its four grand canals (Singel, Herengracht, Keizersgracht, and Prinsengracht) that circle the historic core. West Amsterdam has tree-lined canals fronted by old, gabled mansions, as well as many of my recommended accommodations and restaurants. Within West Amsterdam is the boutique shopping district known as the Nine Little Streets. Farther west is the quieter, cozier Jordaan neighborhood, which is good for a stroll, though it's mostly residential. And

AMSTERDAM ORIENTATION

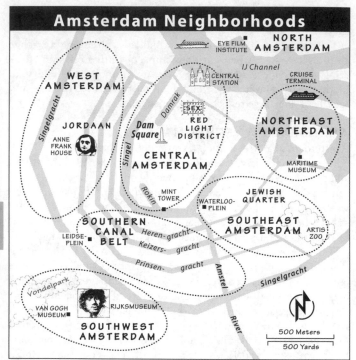

Amsterdam Neighborhoods

to the north is the old "Haarlem dike"—Haarlemmerstraat and Haarlemmerdijk—which is emerging as a trendy, youthful zone for shopping and eating.

The **Southern Canal Belt**—the next ring of canals south of the historic core—is spacious and dotted sparsely with a few intimate museums, art galleries, and antique shops along Nieuwe Spiegelstraat, plus recommended B&Bs. Rowdy Leidseplein anchors the lower corner.

Southwest Amsterdam is defined by two main features: museums and a city park. The city's major art museums (Rijksmuseum, Van Gogh, and Stedelijk) and other sights cluster together on an expansive square, Museumplein. The museums are just a short walk from Vondelpark, Amsterdam's version of a central park. While it's less central to stay in Southwest Amsterdam, I've recommended accommodations that are a quick, convenient walk to the area's tram lines.

Southeast Amsterdam contains the former Jewish Quarter and the Jewish Historical Museum. Several sights can be found around the square known as Waterlooplein (Rembrandt's House and a flea market). Additional sights are gathered in a park-dotted area called the Plantage (Dutch Resistance Museum, a theater-

Amsterdam Landmarks Guide

Dam (pronounced dahm)	Amsterdam's main square
Damrak (DAHM-rock)	main street between Central Station and Dam Square
Spui (spow, rhymes with now)	both a street and square
Rokin (roh-KEEN)	street connecting Dam Square and Spui
Kalverstraat (KAL-ver-straht)	pedestrian street
Leidseplein (LIDE-zuh-pline)	lively square
Jordaan (yor-DAHN)	neighborhood in West Amsterdam
Museumplein	square with top art museums
gracht (*hroht*, pronounce *h* gutturally)	canal
straat (straht)	street
plein (pline)	public square
huis (house)	house
kerk (kerk)	church

turned-Holocaust-memorial, a zoo, and a botanical garden). Rembrandtplein, another nightlife center, is a five-minute walk away. The short but appealing street called Staalstraat, which connects this area with Rokin in the center, is a delightful place to browse trendy shops.

Northeast Amsterdam has the Netherlands Maritime Museum, Amsterdam's Central Library, and a children's science museum (NEMO).

North Amsterdam, which sits across the very wide IJ (pronounced "eye") waterway, was long neglected as a sleepy residential zone. But recently it has sprouted some interesting restaurant and nightlife options, thanks partly to the construction of the EYE Film Institute and easy, free connections across the river on a public ferry just behind Central Station.

PLANNING YOUR TIME

Amsterdam is worth a full day of sightseeing on even the busiest itinerary. And though the city has a couple of must-see museums, its best attraction is its own carefree ambience. The city's a joy on foot—and a breezier and faster delight by bike. For a good walking overview, lace together my three Rick Steves Audio Europe walking tours (see page 10), all of which can be connected by Dam Square. They can be done in rapid succession—Amsterdam City Walk, Red Light District Walk, and Jordaan Walk—in as little as four hours...or take your time.

Amsterdam in One Day

9:00   Follow my self-guided Amsterdam City Walk, which takes you from the train station to Leidseplein (near the Rijksmuseum), with stops at the peaceful Begijnhof, the Amsterdam Museum, and the flower market. Break up the walk with a relaxing hour-long canal cruise (departs from opposite Central Station, Spui dock, or near Leidseplein).

14:00   Visit Amsterdam's two great art museums, located side by side: the Van Gogh Museum and the Rijksmuseum.

18:30   Tour the Anne Frank House (reserve online to skip long lines). Arrive earlier off-season, when it closes at 19:00.

19:30   Wander the Jordaan neighborhood, enjoying dinner by a canal or on a cobbled, quiet street.

21:30   Stroll the Red Light District for some of Europe's most fascinating window-shopping.

Amsterdam in Two or More Days
Day 1

9:00   Follow my self-guided Amsterdam City Walk, leading from the train station to Leidseplein, via the quiet Begijnhof, the Amsterdam Museum (make time to tour this), and the flower market.

12:00   Stop for lunch in the Spui neighborhood before completing the walk.

14:00   Visit Amsterdam's two outstanding art museums, located next to each other: the Van Gogh Museum and the Rijksmuseum.

18:00   Dinner.

20:00   Stroll the Red Light District for some memorable window-shopping.

Day 2

10:00   Start your day with a one-hour canal boat tour (boats leave across from train station).

11:00   Visit the sights of your choice around Rembrandtplein (Rembrandt's House, Waterlooplein flea market—closed Sun, Gassan

Diamonds polishing demo, Dutch Resistance
Museum).

13:30   Free time for lunch and to shop and explore.
17:00   Tour the Anne Frank House. (Reserve online...or
        waste an hour or two standing in line.)
18:30   Take my self-guided Jordaan Walk.
20:00   Dinner in the Jordaan neighborhood.

Day 3
Use this day to browse the wide variety of Amsterdam's museums—the Amstelkring, Royal Palace, Stedelijk, Bags and Purses,
Pipes, and Houseboat (see the Sights in Amsterdam chapter for
more ideas). Or visit the nearby town of Haarlem, only 20 minutes
away by train.

Day 4
Visit Delft (see the Delft chapters). Or side-trip by train to an open-
air folk museum; choose among Enkhuizen's, Zaandijk's (Zaanse
Schans Museum), or Arnhem's. Unless you're visiting far-flung
Arnhem, you could also easily fit in a short visit to nearby Edam.

With More Time
If you're staying longer, there are plenty more destinations awaiting
you in the Netherlands.

Amsterdam Overview

TOURIST INFORMATION
The Dutch name for a TI is "VVV," pronounced "fay fay fay." Amsterdam's main TI, located across the street from Central Station,
is centrally located, but it's crowded and inefficient, and the free
maps are poor quality (Mon-Sat 9:00-17:00, Sun 10:00-16:00). The
TI sells a good city map (€2.50), walking-tour brochures (€3), skip-
the-line museum tickets (though it's easier buying these online),
and the *Time Out Amsterdam* entertainment guide (€3).

More helpful is the call center (Mon-Fri 9:00-17:00, tel.
020/702-6000 in the Netherlands, from the US dial 011-31-20-
702-6000). Also helpful and less crowded are the TIs at Schiphol
Airport (daily 7:00-22:00) and in the town of Haarlem. Inside
Central Station, the GWK Currency Exchange offices (though not
officially TIs) can answer basic tourist questions, with shorter lines
(daily 9:00-22:00).

ADVANCE TICKETS AND SIGHTSEEING CARDS
You can avoid long ticket lines (common from late March-Oct) at
the Rijksmuseum, Van Gogh Museum, and Anne Frank House by
booking tickets in advance or getting a sightseeing pass. (If you're

AMSTERDAM ORIENTATION

Daily Reminder

The biggest Amsterdam sights—the Rijksmuseum, the Van Gogh Museum, and the Anne Frank House—are open daily year-round (the Anne Frank House until 22:00 July-Aug). The Westerkerk church and tower stay open late in summer (Mon-Sat until 20:00 May-Aug). The city's naughty sights, as you might expect, stay open late every day (the Hash, Marijuana, and Hemp Museum until 23:00, the Damrak Sex Museum until 23:00, and the Erotic and Red Light Secrets museums until 24:00).

Sunday: These sights have limited, afternoon-only hours today—the Amstelkring Museum (13:00-17:00) and Old Church (13:00-17:30). The Westerkerk church and tower and the Old Church tower are closed, as is the Waterlooplein flea market.

Monday: The Houseboat Museum, Canal House, the Old Church tower, and Tropical Museum are closed today. From September through May, NEMO is closed today (but open in peak season). Many businesses are closed Monday morning.

Tuesday: All recommended sights are open, except the Old Church tower.

Wednesday: All recommended sights are open, except the Old Church tower.

Thursday: All recommended sights are open. The Stedelijk Museum is open until 22:00.

Friday: During peak season, Westerkerk hosts a free organ concert most Fridays at 13:00 (May-Oct). The House of Bols is open until 22:00 year-round, while the Van Gogh Museum is open until 22:00 during peak season (March-Oct).

Saturday: The Anne Frank House is open late year-round (until 22:00 April-Oct, until 21:00 off-season), while the Van Gogh Museum is open until 22:00 during select months (July-Aug and Oct).

visiting off-season, it's less important to worry about line-skipping options, especially if you use my other crowd-beating tips.)

Since there's no single option that's best for every sight, here's the scoop:

Advance Tickets: It's easy to buy tickets online for the three major museums through each museum's website, generally with no extra booking fee. You just print out your ticket and bring it to the ticket-holder's line for a quick entry. You can also buy advance tickets at TIs (though lines there can be long). Because advance reservations for the Anne Frank House are limited, you should buy your ticket as soon as you're sure of your itinerary.

Museumkaart (€55): This sightseeing pass—which covers

many museums throughout the Netherlands for a year—can save money and time. Though the hefty price tag is daunting, museum lovers can easily make the pass pay for itself. For example, if you visit the Rijksmuseum, Van Gogh Museum, Anne Frank House, and Amsterdam Museum, the pass would almost pay for itself right there (adds up to €52.50). Other included Amsterdam sights are the Royal Palace, New Church, Hermitage, Jewish Historical Museum, Amstelkring, Willet-Holthuysen, Stedelijk, and more. Beyond Amsterdam, it covers Haarlem's Frans Hals and Teylers Museums, Delft's Prinsenhof Museum, the Kröller-Müller Museum near Arnhem, and Arnhem's Netherlands Open-Air Folk Museum, as well as many more.

Plus, the card lets you skip the ticket line at some sights, chiefly the Rijksmuseum. But you can't bypass the line at the Anne Frank House (to avoid waiting, you must make an online reservation), and at the Van Gogh Museum, you'll need to queue up, though at a much shorter line than ticket-buyers. At lesser sights, you may have to wait a bit at the ticket counter for them to issue you a paper ticket.

Bear in mind that an added bonus to the Museumkaart is that—once you bite the bullet—it opens up a whole new world of Amsterdam sights, letting you pop into small museums you'd otherwise pass on.

The Museumkaart is sold at participating museums. Buy it at a less-crowded one to avoid lines (e.g., the Royal Palace or New Church on Dam Square). For a full list of included sights, see www.amsterdam.info/museums/museumkaart.

I amsterdam Card: Though not as good a deal for most people, the I amsterdam Card covers many Amsterdam sights (including a canal boat ride) and includes a transportation pass. But it does not cover the Rijksmuseum, Anne Frank House, or any museums outside of Amsterdam, and it only lets you skip lines at the Van Gogh Museum (€47/24 hours, €57/48 hours, or €67/72 hours). You can check the list of sights at www.iamsterdamcard.com.

Another pass you'll see advertised, the **Holland Pass,** is not worth it.

If You Don't Have Advance Tickets or a Pass: If you end up visiting the Anne Frank House without a reservation, trim your wait in line by showing up the minute it opens, or late in the day; this works better in early spring and fall than in summer, when even after-dinner lines can be long. During peak season, you can visit the Van Gogh Museum on weekend evenings until 22:00—with no lines or crowds—on Fridays (March-Oct) and some Saturdays (only in July, Aug, and Oct).

ARRIVAL IN AMSTERDAM
By Train

The portal connecting Amsterdam to the world is its aptly named Central Station (Amsterdam Centraal). Through at least 2015, expect the station and the plaza in front of it to be a construction zone and therefore in a state of some flux.

Trains arrive on a level above the station. Go down the stairs or the escalator (at the "A" end of the platform). As you descend from the platforms, follow signs to *Centrum* to reach the city center. (Those wanting buses and river ferries should head in the opposite direction, to the north/*Noord* exit.)

The station is fully equipped. Helpful GWK Travelex counters are in both the east and west corridors (currency exchange, hotel reservations, phone cards, and basic tourist information, daily 9:00-22:00, tel. 020/624-6682). International train-ticket offices are near the *Centrum* exits. Luggage lockers are in the east corridor, under the "B" end of the platforms (€5-7/24 hours, depending on size of bag, always open, can fill up on busy summer weekends). The station has plenty of shops, eateries, and "to go" supermarkets. Platform 2 (at train level) is lined with eateries, including the tall, venerable, 1920s-style First Class Grand Café.

If you need to buy train tickets, remember that credit cards without an electronic chip won't work in the machines or with a live agent. (Sometimes even credit cards with a chip may not work.) Get ample cash for your tickets (ATMs nearby) before lining up at the ticket window. If you want to use cash at the ticket machines, be prepared—they only take coins.

Getting into Town: To get from the station to your hotel, you can walk, take a tram, hop on a rental bike, or catch a taxi.

Exiting the station, you're in the heart of the city. Straight ahead is Damrak street, leading to Dam Square (a 10-minute walk away). To your left are the TI, the GVB public-transit information office (see page 40), and two bike-rental places: MacBike (in the station building), and Star Bikes (a five-minute walk past the station), both listed on page 41.

To the right of the station lie the postcard-perfect neighborhoods of West Amsterdam; some of my recommended hotels are within walking distance. Also to your right are taxis—pricey, but can be worth it, when dealing with baggage, jet lag, and trying to find your hotel (see page 43 for taxi info).

Trams are easy. Trams #1, #2, and #5 all start here (in front of the station) and follow the same route through the center of town with stops within easy walking distance of most of my recommended hotels. Simply hop on, buy your ticket as you board, and you're on your way. For more on the transit system, see page 35.

By Plane

For details on getting from Schiphol Airport into downtown Amsterdam, see page 258.

HELPFUL HINTS

Theft Alert: Tourists are considered green and rich, and the city has more than its share of hungry thieves—especially in the train station, on trams, in and near crowded museums, at places of drunkenness, and at the many hostels. Wear your money belt. If there's a risk you'll be out late high or drunk, leave all valuables in your hotel. Blitzed tourists are easy targets for petty theft.

Emergency Telephone Number: Throughout the Netherlands, dial 112.

Street Smarts: Beware of silent transportation—trams, electric mopeds, and bicycles—when walking around town. Don't walk on tram tracks or pink/maroon bicycle paths. Before you step off any sidewalk, do a double- or triple-check in both directions to make sure all's clear.

Shop Hours: Most shops are open Tuesday through Saturday 10:00-18:00, and Sunday and Monday 12:00-18:00. Some shops stay open later (21:00) on Thursdays. Supermarkets are generally open Monday through Saturday 8:00-20:00 and have shorter hours or are closed on Sundays.

Busy Weekends: Every year, **King's Day** (Koningsdag, April 27) and **Gay Pride** (July 25-Aug 2 in 2015, July 26-Aug 7 in 2016) bring big crowds, fuller hotels, and inflated room prices. Also be prepared for **SAIL Amsterdam**, a festival featuring tall ships and other historic boats held every five years (Aug 19–23 in 2015).

Resources for Gay Travelers: A short walk from Central Station down Damrak is **GAYtic,** a TI specifically oriented to the needs of gay travelers. The office stocks maps, magazines, and brochures, and dispenses advice on nightlife and general sightseeing (Mon-Sat 11:00-20:00, Sun 12:00-20:00, Spuistraat 44, tel. 020/330-1461, www.gaytic.nl). **Pink Point,** in a kiosk outside Westerkerk and next to the Homomonument, is less of a resource, but has advice about nightlife (usually daily 10:00-18:00, tel. 020/428-1070).

Language Barrier: This is one of the easiest places in the non-English-speaking world for an English speaker. Nearly all signs and services are offered in two languages: Dutch and "non-Dutch" (i.e., English).

Cash Only: Thrifty Dutch merchants, who hate paying the unusually high fees charged by credit-card companies here, often refuse US credit cards (and cards without an electronic chip may not work anyway). Expect to pay cash in unexpected places, including grocery stores, cafés, budget hotels, train-station machines and windows, and at some museums.

Internet Access: It's easy at cafés all over town, but the best place for serious surfing and email is the towering **Central Library,** which has hundreds of fast terminals and Wi-Fi (€1/30 minutes, Openbare Bibliotheek Amsterdam, daily 10:00-22:00, an 8-minute walk from train station, described on page 67). The café across the street from Central Station (next to the TI) also has pay Internet access and Wi-Fi. "Coffeeshops," which sell marijuana, usually also offer Internet access—letting you surf with a special bravado.

English Bookstores: For fiction and guidebooks, try the **American Book Center** at Spui 12, right on the square (Mon 12:00-20:00, Tue-Sat 10:00-20:00, Sun 11:00-18:30, tel. 020/535-2575). The huge and helpful **Scheltema** is at Koningsplein 20 near the Leidsestraat (included in my Amsterdam City Walk; generally daily 10:00-19:00; lots of English novels, guidebooks, and maps; tel. 020/523-1411). **Waterstone's Booksellers,** a UK chain, also sells British newspapers (generally daily 9:30-18:30, near Spui at 152 Kalverstraat, tel. 020/638-3821). Expect shorter hours on Monday and Sunday.

Maps: Given the city's maze of streets and canals, I'd definitely get a good city map (€2.50 at Central Station TI). The free tourist maps can be confusing, except for *Amsterdam Museums: Guide to 44 Museums* (includes tram info and stops, ask for it at the big museums, such as the Van Gogh). I like the *Carto Studio Centrumkaart Amsterdam* map. Amsterdam Anything's virtual "Go Where the Locals Go" city map is also worth checking out, especially if you have mobile Internet access (www.amsterdamanything.nl). Also consider picking up any of the TI's walking-tour brochures (€3 each, including ones covering the city center, former Jewish Quarter, Jordaan, and funky De Pijp neighborhood).

Pharmacy: The shop named **DA** (Dienstdoende Apotheek) has all the basics—shampoo and toothpaste—as well as a pharmacy counter hidden in the back (Mon-Sat 9:00-22:00, Sun 11:00-22:00, Leidsestraat 74-76 near where it meets Keizersgracht, tel. 020/627-5351). Near Dam Square, there's **BENU Apotheek** (Mon-Fri 8:00-17:30, Sat 10:00-17:00, Sun 12:00-17:00, Damstraat 2, tel. 020/624-4331).

Laundry: Try **Clean Brothers Wasserij** in the Jordaan (daily 8:00-20:00 for €7 self-service, €9 drop-off—ready in an hour—Mon-Fri 9:00-17:00, Sat 9:00-18:00, no drop-off Sun, Westerstraat 26, one block from Prinsengracht, tel. 020/627-9888) or **Powders,** near Leidseplein (daily 8:00-22:00, €6-10 self-service, €13 drop-off available Mon-Fri 8:00-17:00, Sat 9:00-15:00, no drop-off Sun, Kerkstraat 56, one block south of Leidsestraat, mobile 06-8140-4069).

Best Views: Although sea-level Amsterdam is notoriously horizontal, there are a few high points where you can get the big picture. My favorite is the rooftop **Sky Lounge Amsterdam**, on the 11th floor of the DoubleTree by Hilton Hotel (daily until very late, 5-minute walk east of train station; see page 211). Other good choices are from the top-floor view café at the **Central Library** (Openbare Bibliotheek Amsterdam; see page 67), or nearby, the rooftop terrace—generally open to the public—at the **NEMO science museum.** The **Westerkerk**—a stop on my Jordaan Walk and convenient for anyone visiting the Anne Frank House—has a climbable tower with fine views. Other options are the tower of the **Old Church** (Oude Kerk) in the Red Light District, and the top-floor café at the Kalvertoren mall on Kalverstraat (see page 100).

Updates to This Book: For updates to this book, check www.ricksteves.com/update.

GETTING AROUND AMSTERDAM

Amsterdam is big, and you'll find the trams handy. The longest walk a tourist would make is an hour from Central Station to the Rijksmuseum. When you're on foot, be extremely vigilant for silent but potentially painful bikes, trams, and crotch-high bollards.

By Tram, Bus, and Metro

Amsterdam's public transit system includes trams, buses, and an underground metro. Of these, trams are most useful for most tourists.

Paper Tickets: Within Amsterdam, a single transit ticket (called a single-use or disposable OV-chipkaart) costs €2.80 and is good for one hour on the tram, bus, and metro, including transfers. Passes good for unlimited transportation are available for 24 hours (€7.50), 48 hours (€12), 72 hours (€16.50), and 96 hours (€21). Given how expensive single tickets are, think about buying a pass before you buy that first ticket.

The easiest way to buy a ticket or pass is to simply board a tram or bus and pay the conductor (whose station is usually at the rear of the tram; no extra fee). Tickets and passes are also available at metro-station vending machines (which take cash but not US credit cards unless they have a chip), at GVB public-transit offices, and at TIs.

Transit Card: If you're staying for several days or more, consider investing in the **Anonymous OV-chipkaart**, which brings down per-ride costs dramatically. With this electronic card, the

Amsterdam's Spine by Tram: Trams #1, #2, and #5 from Central Station to Leidseplein

Amsterdam becomes much easier to wrap your brain around when you master the tram #1/#2/#5 corridor. As if made for the sightseer, this main tram thoroughfare makes connecting the station, the Jordaan neighborhood, many of my recommended hotels, and the museum zone amazingly easy. The entire ride takes about 20 minutes, with trams zipping by every few minutes in peak times. Use these tram lines both for an overview and as a handy spine to lace together your sightseeing. At any point you can simply hop out, cross the street, and catch a tram heading back exactly where you came from. A single €2.80 ticket is good for an hour, and the trip is covered by an all-day or multi-day pass (all sold on the tram).

Starting at the train station, here are the stops and the landmarks near each one; if you want to go beyond Leidseplein (including the Rijksmuseum or Van Gogh Museum), be sure to take tram #2 or #5.

Centraal Station: Amsterdam's Central Station is the beginning of the line, so any of the trams #1, #2, or #5 that you catch here is headed in the right direction. This tram stop puts you near the Red Light District and at the start of Damrak (the city's main drag, and the beginning of my self-guided Amsterdam City Walk). This station is also Amsterdam's main transportation hub (trains, airport shuttle bus, bus station, many other trams, metro, and bike rental, plus the free ferry across the IJ waterway behind the station).

Martelaarsgracht: As you approach this first stop, notice how wide the street is. Wide streets are generally former canals filled in. (Hint: *Gracht* means canal.) Nearby: Haarlemmerstraat, with shops and eateries.

Nieuwezijds Kolk: Nothing of interest nearby.

Dam: You'll roll by the back side of the towering New Church and Royal Palace (on your left). Nearby: the Dam Square, Anne

tram ride between Central Station and the Rijksmuseum costs about €1.30—less than half the paper-ticket price. It also works on public transit anywhere in the Netherlands (such as the Rotterdam subway or the tram from Delft to The Hague). While it sounds like a deal, the card will cost you €10 in nonrefundable fees—€7.50 to buy the card and another €2.50 when you cash out at the end of your trip. Also, the cards aren't shareable for companions traveling

Frank House, and starting point for two of my self-guided walks—Jordaan and Red Light District.

Spui: Pronounced spow (rhymes with now) and means "spew," this is where water was once pushed away over a dike. Nearby: Amsterdam Museum, Begijnhof, recommended bookstore, the Nine Little Streets shopping zone.

Koningsplein: From here, the tram turns right and crosses four canals over the next few stops: Singel, Heren, Keizers, and Prinsen. To keep them straight, use this memory aid: A Single Hairy Kaiser's Prince really knows his canals. Nearby: Mint Tower, flower market.

Keizersgracht: Here the street fills with people and gets so narrow that trams share one set of rails, and bikers are required to walk their bikes. This is the vibrant shopping district of modern Amsterdam.

Prinsengracht: You'll roll past more shops and more pedestrians.

Leidseplein: This is the tourists' nightlife center, with the famous Bulldog Coffeeshop (a former police station that now sells marijuana), venerable edgy nightclubs and concert venues like the Milkweg and Paradiso, and the city theater (Stadsschouwburg).

From here, trams #2 and #5 leave the old town, cross the outermost canal, stop at the Rijksmuseum, and head for Vondelpark. (If you're on tram #1, transfer here at Leidesplein to trams #2 or #5 to continue to the museum and park.)

Rijksmuseum (tram #2 and #5 only): This is the start of the museum zone with the popular park (with the pond and much-photographed "I amsterdam" sign) and several great museums. Nearby: Rijksmuseum, House of Bols, and Coster Diamonds.

Van Baerlestraat (trams #2 and #5 only): Jump out here for the Van Gogh or Stedelijk museums.

Jacob Obrechtstraat (tram #2 only): Here you leave the commotion of the city and are in a district of high-end apartments. The inviting Café Gruter faces the tram stop and the entry to Vondelpark (with the recommended 'T Blauwe Theehuis—The Blue Tea House—a block away).

together. As a rough rule of thumb, figure on saving €1 to €1.50 per tram or bus trip by using this card. If you plan to take 10 or more trips on public transit in the Netherlands, it starts becoming worthwhile.

When you buy the card, it is automatically loaded with €10 of credit, which is deducted each time you take public transit. On

AMSTERDAM ORIENTATION

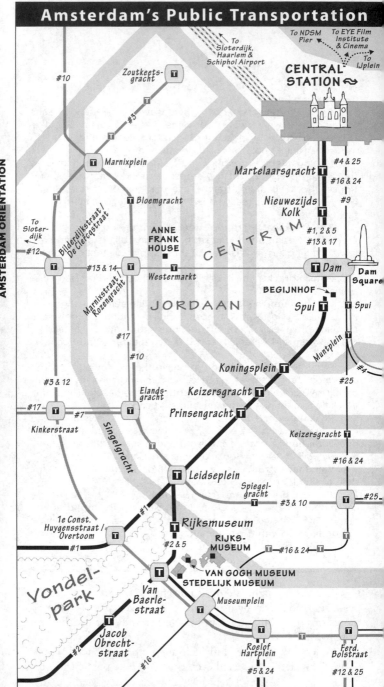

Amsterdam's Public Transportation

To Sloterdijk, Haarlem & Schiphol Airport

To NDSM Pier

To EYE Film Institute & Cinema

To IJplein

CENTRAL STATION

Zoutkeetsgracht

#10

#3

Marnixplein

Martelaarsgracht   #4 & 25

#16 & 24

Bloemgracht

Nieuwezijds Kolk   #9

To Sloterdijk

Bilderdijkstraat / De Clercqstraat

ANNE FRANK HOUSE

CENTRUM

#1, 2 & 5
#13 & 17

#12

#13 & 14

Westermarkt

Dam

Dam Square

Marnixstraat / Rozengracht

JORDAAN

BEGIJNHOF

Spui   Spui

#17

#10

Koningsplein

Muntplein

#4

#3 & 12

Elandsgracht

Keizersgracht

#25

#17   #7

Prinsengracht

Kinkerstraat

Singelgracht

Keizersgracht

#16 & 24

Leidseplein

Spiegelgracht

#3 & 10   #25

1e Const. Huygensstraat / Overtoom

#1

Rijksmuseum

#1

#2 & 5

RIJKS-MUSEUM   #16 & 24

Vondelpark

Van Baerlestraat

VAN GOGH MUSEUM
STEDELIJK MUSEUM

Museumplein

Jacob Obrechtstraat

#2

#16

Roelof Hartplein

Ferd. Bolstraat

#5 & 24

#12 & 25

AMSTERDAM ORIENTATION

IJ (Channel)

CRUISE TERMINAL

Muziekgebouw / Bimhuis

#26

Azart-plein

Central Station

Kotten-burger-straat

#22 & 48

#48

MARITIME MUSEUM

Nieuwmarkt

#26

RED LIGHT DISTRICT

#48

#22

Rietlandpark

#51

#53

#54

REMBRANDT'S HOUSE

#10

Not to Scale

Not all stations shown on map

Rembrandt-plein

JEWISH HIST. MUSEUM & DUTCH THEATER

#9

#14

Mr. Visserplein

#22

Waterlooplein

#4

Keizersgracht

Artis / Pln. Kerklaan

ARTIS ZOO

#9

Prinsengracht

Pln. Badlaan

#14

Frederiksplein

#3 & 10

Alexanderplein

Stadhouderskade

Weesperplein

#7

Amstel

#4 & 25

Van Woustraat

#25
#3

Wibautstraat

#3

River

#4

▬T▬	Tram #1, 2 & 5
T	Tram #4 & 25, 16 & 24, 9
T	Tram #13, 14 & 17
T	Tram #7 & 10, 3 & 12, 26
M	Metro #51, 53 & 54
--B--	Bus #22 & 48

trams or buses, the cards must be loaded with a minimum of €4; the card reader will show the remaining value when you exit.

Purchase OV-chipkaarts at the train station service desks, at certain train-station ticket machines, and at GBV public transit offices—they are not sold on board trams or buses. Cards can be reloaded at service desks with cash or at any train-station ticket machine with chip-and-PIN credit cards (some take coins). To cash out the card, you must go to a service desk.

With a higher deposit, the cards can also be used on domestic train trips; for more information, see the Practicalities chapter.

Information: For more on riding public transit, visit the helpful GVB public-transit information office in front of Central Station (Mon-Fri 7:00-21:00, Sat-Sun 10:00-18:00). Its free, multilingual *Public Transport Amsterdam Tourist Guide* includes a transit map and explains ticket options and tram connections to all the sights. Everything is also explained in English on their helpful website at www.gvb.nl.

Riding the Trams: Board the tram at any entrance not marked with a red/white "do not enter" sticker. If you need a ticket

or pass, pay the conductor (in a booth at the back); if there's no conductor, pay the driver in front. Whether you have a paper ticket or an OV-chipkaart, you must always "check in" as you board by scanning your ticket or pass at the pink-and-gray scanner, and "check out" by scanning it again when you get off. The scanner will beep and flash a green light after a successful scan. Be careful not to accidentally scan your ticket or pass twice while boarding, or it becomes invalid. Checking in and out is very important, as controllers do pass through and fine violators; if you have an OV-chipkaart and forget to check out, you'll be charged for a longer journey. To open the door when you reach your stop, press a green button on one of the poles near an exit.

If you get lost in Amsterdam, remember that most of the city's trams take you back to Central Station, and nearly all drivers speak English.

Buses and Metro: Tickets and passes work on buses and the metro just as they do on the trams—scan your ticket or pass to "check in" as you enter and again to "check out" when you leave. The metro system is scant—used mostly for commuting to the suburbs—but it does connect Central Station with some sights east

of Damrak (Nieuwmarkt-Waterlooplein-Weesperplein). The gla-
cial speed of the metro-expansion project is a running joke among
cynical Amsterdammers.

By Bike

Everyone—bank managers, students, pizza delivery boys, and police—uses this mode of transport. It's by far the smartest way to
travel in a city where 40 per-
cent of all traffic rolls on two
wheels. You'll get around town
by bike faster than you can by
taxi. On my last visit, I rented
a bike for five days, chained it
to the rack outside my hotel
at night, and enjoyed wonderful mobility. I highly encourage this for anyone who wants
to get maximum fun per hour
in Amsterdam. One-speed bikes, with *"brrringing"* bells, rent for
about €10 per day (cheaper for longer periods) at any number of
places—hotels can send you to the nearest spot.

Rental Shops: Star Bikes Rental has cheap rates, long hours,
and inconspicuous black bikes. They're happy to arrange an after-
hours drop-off if you give them your credit-card number and pre-
pay (€5/3 hours, €7/day, €9/24 hours, €12/2 days, €17/3 days, Mon-
Fri 8:00-19:00, Sat-Sun 9:00-19:00, requires ID but no monetary
deposit, 5-minute walk from east end of Central Station—walk
underneath tracks near Doubletree by Hilton Hotel and then turn
right, De Ruyterkade 127, tel. 020/620-3215, www.starbikesrental.
com).

MacBike, with thousands of bikes, is the city's bike-rental
powerhouse—you'll see their bright-red bikes all over town (they
do stick out a bit). It has a huge and efficient outlet at Central Station (€7.50/3 hours, €9.75/24 hours, €15.75/48 hours, €21.75/72
hours, more for 3 gears and optional insurance, 25 percent discount
with I amsterdam Card; either leave €50 deposit plus a copy of
your passport, or leave a credit-card imprint; free helmets, daily
9:00-17:45; at east end of station—on the left as you're leaving;
tel. 020/620-0985, www.macbike.nl). They have two smaller satellite stations at Leidseplein (Weteringschans 2) and Waterlooplein
(Nieuwe Uilenburgerstraat 116). Return your bike to the station
where you rented it. MacBike sells several pamphlets outlining
bike tours with a variety of themes in and around Amsterdam for
€1-2.

Frederic Rent-a-Bike, a 10-minute walk from Central Station, has quality bikes and a helpful staff (€8/3 hours, €15/24

Bike Theft

Bike thieves are bold and brazen in Amsterdam. Bikes come with two locks and stern instructions to use both. The wimpy ones go through the spokes, whereas the industrial-strength chains are meant to be wrapped around the actual body of the bike and through the front wheel, and connected to something stronger than any human. (Note the steel bike-hitching racks sticking up all around town, called "staples.") Follow your rental agency's locking directions diligently. Once, I used both locks, but my chain wasn't  around the main bar of my bike's body. In the morning, I found only my front tire (still safely chained to the metal fence). If you're sloppy, it's an expensive mistake and one that any "included" theft insurance won't cover.

hours—€10 if returned by 17:30, €25/48 hours, €60/week, 10 percent discount with this book, half-price for those renting a room through Frederic—see page 194, daily 9:00-17:30, no after-hours drop-off, no deposit but must leave a credit-card imprint, Brouwersgracht 78, tel. 020/624-5509, www.frederic.nl, Frederic and son Marne).

Tips: As the Dutch believe in fashion over safety, no one here wears a helmet. They do, however, ride cautiously, and so should you: Use arm signals, follow the bike-only traffic signals, stay in the obvious and omnipresent bike lanes, and yield to traffic on the right. Fear oncoming trams and tram tracks. Carefully cross tram tracks at a perpendicular angle to avoid catching your tire in the rut. Warning: Police ticket cyclists just as they do drivers. Obey all traffic signals, and walk your bike through pedestrian zones. Fines for biking through pedestrian zones are reportedly €30-50. Leave texting-while-biking to the locals. A handy bicycle route-planner can be found at www.routecraft.com (select "bikeplanner," then click British flag for English). For a "Do-It-Yourself Bike Tour of Amsterdam" and for bike tours, see "Guided Bike Tours," later in this chapter.

By Boat

While the city is great on foot, bike, or tram, you can also get around Amsterdam by boat. **Rederij Lovers** boats shuttle tourists on a variety of routes covering different combinations of the city's top sights. Their Museum Line, for example, costs €18 and stops near the Hermitage, Rijksmuseum/Van Gogh Museum, and Central Station (at least every 45 minutes, 6 stops, 2 hours). Sales booths in front of Central Station (and the boats) offer free brochures listing museum hours and admission prices. Most routes come with recorded narration and run daily 10:00-17:30 (tel. 020/530-1090, www.lovers.nl).

The similar **Canal Bus** is actually a hop-on, hop-off boat, offering 16 stops on three different boat routes (€24/24-hour pass, discounts when booking online, departures daily 9:45-18:30, until 20:45 on Fri-Sun April-Oct, leaves near Central Station and Rederij Lovers dock, tel. 020/217-0500, www.canal.nl).

If you're simply looking for a floating, nonstop tour, the regular canal tour boats (without the stops) give more information, cover more ground, and cost less (see "Tours in Amsterdam," later).

For do-it-yourself canal tours and lots of exercise, Canal Bus also rents "canal bikes" (a.k.a. paddleboats) at several locations: near the Anne Frank House, near the Rijksmuseum, near Leidseplein, and where Leidsestraat meets Keizersgracht (€8/1 hour, €11/1.5 hours, €14/2 hours, prices are per person, daily July-Aug 10:00-22:00, Sept-June 10:00-18:00).

If you're a confident boater, consider renting a serious vessel. **Sloep Delen Boat Rental** has a fleet of 12-seater boats with silent electric motors. Captaining your little ship is fun, and you're just minutes away from the idyllic canals of the Jordaan neighborhood. While it's designed for locals to book on the Web, for tourists it's easiest to call and pay an attendant who will meet you at the dock, give you a little map and suggestions, and set you free (€55/hour for up to 12 people, minimum 2 hours, €150 deposit, on far west side of Jordaan at Nassaukade 69 on Singelgracht canal, tel. 020/419-1007, www.sloepdelen.nl).

By Taxi

For short rides, Amsterdam is a bad town for taxis. Given the good tram system and ease of biking, I use taxis less in Amsterdam than in just about any other city in Europe. The city's taxis have a high drop charge (about €7) for the first two kilometers (e.g., from Central Station to the Mint Tower), after which it's €2.12 per kilometer. You can wave them down, find a rare taxi stand, or call one (tel. 020/777-7777). All taxis are required to have meters. You'll also see **bike taxis,** particularly near Dam Square and Leidseplein. Negotiate a rate for the trip before you board (no meter), and they'll wheel you wherever you want to go (estimate €1/3 minutes, no surcharge for baggage or extra weight, sample fare from Leidseplein to Anne Frank House: about €6).

By Car

If you've got a car, park it—all you'll find are frustrating one-way streets, terrible parking, and meter maids with a passion for booting cars parked incorrectly. You'll pay €60 a day to park safely in a central garage. If you must bring a car to Amsterdam, it's best to leave it at one of the city's supervised park-and-ride lots (follow *P&R* signs from freeway, €8/24 hours, includes round-trip transit into city center for up to five people, 4-day maximum).

Tours in Amsterdam

BY BOAT
▲▲Canal Boat Tours

These long, low, tourist-laden boats leave continually from several docks around town for a relaxing, if uninspiring, one-hour introduction to the city (with recorded headphone commentary). Some people prefer to cruise at night, when the bridges are illuminated. Select a boat tour based on your convenience: your proximity to its starting point, or whether it's included with your I amsterdam Card (which covers Blue Boat Company and Holland International boats). Tip: Boats leave only when full, so jump on a full boat to avoid waiting at the dock. Choose from one of these three companies:

Rederij P. Kooij is cheapest (€10, 3/hour in summer 10:00-22:00, 2/hour in winter 10:00-17:00, at corner of Spui and Rokin streets, about 10 minutes from Dam Square, tel. 020/623-3810, www.rederijkooij.nl).

Blue Boat Company's boats depart from near Leidseplein (€15; every half-hour April-Sept 10:00-18:00, hourly Oct-March 10:00-17:00; 1.25 hours, Stadhouderskade 30, tel. 020/679-1370, www.blueboat.nl). Their evening cruise includes the Red Light District (€17.50, nightly at 20:00, 1.5 hours, April-Sept also at 21:00 and 22:00, reservations required).

Holland International offers a standard one-hour trip and a variety of longer tours from the docks opposite Central Station (€15.50, 1-hour "100 Highlights" tour with recorded commentary, daily 4/hour 9:00-18:00, 2/hour 18:00-22:00; Prins Hendrikkade 33a, tel. 020/217-0500, www.hir.nl).

Canoe Tours near Amsterdam

If you want some exercise and a dose of the polder country and village life, consider the **Wetlands Safari** five-hour tour. Majel Tromp, a friendly villager who speaks great English, takes from 2 to 15 people per tour. The program: Meet Majel at the bus stop behind Central Station (leave the station from the west corridor and take the escalator up to the buses) at 9:30, catch a public bus, stop for coffee, take a 3.5-hour canoe trip with several stops, tour a village by canoe, munch an included canalside picnic lunch, then canoe and bus back into Amsterdam by 15:00 (€48, €29 for kids ages 7-16, €3 discount by showing this book, 2-3 people per canoe, daily May-mid-Sept, reservations required, mobile 06-5355-2669, www.wetlandssafari.nl, info@wetlandssafari.nl).

ON FOOT

Red Light District Tours

For a stroll through Amsterdam's most infamous neighborhood, consider my self-guided Red Light District Walk on page 106. But if you'd be more comfortable exploring with a group, a guided tour is a good way to go. **Randy Roy's Red Light Tours** consists of one expat American woman, Kimberley. She lived in the Red Light District for years and gives fun, casual, yet informative 1.5-hour walks through this fascinating and eye-popping neighborhood. Though the actual information is light, you'll walk through various porn and drug shops and have an expert to answer your questions. Call or email to reserve (€15 includes a drink in a colorful bar at the end, nightly at 20:00, Fri and Sat also at 22:00, no tours Dec-Feb, tours meet in front of Victoria Hotel—in front of Central Station, mobile 06-4185-3288, www.randyroysredlighttours.com, kimberley@randyroysredlighttours.com).

Free City Walk

New Europe Tours "employs" native, English-speaking students to give irreverent and entertaining three-hour walks (using the same "free tour, ask for tips, sell their other tours" formula popular in so many great European cities). While most guides lack a local's deep understanding of Dutch culture, not to mention professional training, they're certainly high-energy. This long walk covers a lot of the city with an enthusiasm for the contemporary pot-and-prostitution scene (free but tips expected, daily at 11:15 and 14:15, www.neweuropetours.eu). They also offer paid tours (Red Light District—€12, daily at 19:00; coffeeshop scene—€12, daily at 15:00; Amsterdam by bike—€18.50, includes bike, daily at 12:00). Their walking tours leave from the National Monument on Dam Square; the bike tour leaves from Central Station.

Adam's Apple Tours

Frank Sanders' walking tour offers a two-hour, English-only look at the historic roots and development of Amsterdam. You'll have a small group of generally 5-6 people and a caring guide, starting off at Central Station and ending up at Dam Square (€25; May-Sept daily at 10:00, 12:30, and 15:00 based on demand; call 020/616-7867 to confirm times and book, www.adamsapple.nl). Frank is happy to tailor a private walk to your interests.

Private Guide

Albert Walet is a likeable, hardworking, and knowledgeable local guide who enjoys personalizing tours for Americans interested in knowing his city. Al specializes in history, architecture, and water management, and exudes a passion for Amsterdam (€70/2 hours, €120/4 hours, up to 4 people, on foot or by bike, mobile 06-2069-7882, abwalet@yahoo.com). Al also takes travelers to nearby towns, including Haarlem, Leiden, and Delft.

Tour Packages for Students

Andy Steves (Rick's son) runs **WSA Europe**, offering three-day and longer guided and unguided packages—including accommodations, sightseeing, and unique local experiences—for budget travelers across 11 top European cities, including Amsterdam (from €99, see www.wsaeurope.com for details).

BY BIKE

Guided Bike Tours

Yellow Bike Guided Tours offers city bike tours of either two hours (€21, daily at 10:30) or three hours (€25, daily at 13:30), which both include a 20-minute break. They also offer a four-hour, 15-mile tour of the dikes and green pastures of the countryside (€31.50, lunch extra, includes 45-minute break, April-Oct daily at 10:30). All tours leave from Nieuwezijds Kolk 29, three blocks from Central Station (reservations smart, tel. 020/620-6940, www.yellowbike.nl). If you'd prefer a private guide, contact Albert Walet, listed earlier.

Joy Ride Bike Tours is a creative little company run by Americans Sean and Allison Cody. They offer group tours designed to show you all of the clichés—cheese, windmills, and clogs—as you pedal through the pastoral polder land in 4.5 hours (€30, April-Sept Thu-Mon, meet at 10:15 and depart precisely at 10:30, no tours Tue-Wed, groups limited to 15 people and no kids under 13 years). They also offer private tours tailored to your interests—options include a city tour, Jewish History, World War II, Outer Villages, Cannabis, and Culinary (tours offered mid-March-Nov, €125/2 people plus €25/person after that). Helmets, rain gear, and saddlebags are provided free. All tours must be booked in advance;

tours meet behind the Rijksmuseum next to the Cobra Café (mobile 06-4361-1798, www.joyridetours.nl).

Do-It-Yourself Bike Tour of Amsterdam

A day enjoying the bridges, bike lanes, and sleepy, off-the-beaten-path canals on your own bike is an essential Amsterdam experience. The real joys of Europe's best-preserved 17th-century city are the countless intimate glimpses it offers: the laid-back locals sunning on their porches under elegant gables, rusted bikes that look as if they've been lashed to the same lamppost since the 1960s, wasted hedonists planted on canalside benches, and happy sailors permanently moored, but still manning the deck.

For a good day trip, rent a bike at or near Central Station (see "By Bike" on page 41). Head west down Haarlemmerstraat, work-

ing your wide-eyed way down Prinsengracht (drop into Café 't Papeneiland at Prinsengracht 2) and detouring through the small, gentrified streets of the Jordaan neighborhood before popping out at the Westerkerk under the tallest spire in the city.

Pedal south to the lush and peaceful Vondelpark, then cut back through the center of town (Leidseplein to the Mint Tower, along Rokin street to Dam Square). From there, cruise the Red Light District, following Oudezijds Voorburgwal past the Old Church (Oude Kerk) to Zeedijk street, and return to the train station.

Then, you can escape into the countryside by hopping on the free ferry behind Central Station (described next). In five minutes, Amsterdam is gone, and you're rolling through your very own Dutch painting.

Taking Bikes Across the Harbor on a Free Ferry

Behind Central Station is a little commuter port where four ferries come and go constantly (free, bikes welcome, signs count down minutes until next departure), offering two quick little excursions.

EYE Film Institute: The middle two ferries (labeled *Buiksloterweg*) run immediately across the harbor (3-minute ride). The striking EYE Film Institute Netherlands complex is about 200 yards to the left of the ferry landing. And a bike path leads from the ferry landing directly ahead for a mile along the tree-lined North Holland Canal to a little windmill—biking there takes about 10 minutes—and eventually into the wide-open polder land and villages.

Industrial Port and Hipster Zone: Ferries leaving from the far-left "NDSM" wharf cruise 10 minutes across the North Sea Canal (2/hour, generally departing at :15 and :45). This gives a fun peek at the fifth-biggest harbor in Europe (nearby Rotterdam is number one); old wheat silos now renovated into upscale condos; and the shoreline of north Amsterdam, where the planned metro connection to the center is bringing growth, with lots of new apartments under construction. The ferry deposits you in an industrial wasteland (a vacant old warehouse just past the modern MTV headquarters building is filled with artist studios, wacky ventures, and a noisy skateboard hall). **IJ-Kantine** is a fine modern restaurant/café 30 yards from the ferry landing (daily from 9:00, tel. 020/633-7162).

SIGHTS IN AMSTERDAM

One of Amsterdam's delights is that it has perhaps more small specialty museums than any other city its size. From houseboats to sex, from marijuana to Old Masters, you can find a museum to suit your interests.

For tips on how to save time otherwise spent in the long ticket-buying lines of the big three museums—the Anne Frank House, Van Gogh Museum, and Rijksmuseum—see "Advance Tickets and Sightseeing Cards" on page 29. Admission prices are high: A sightseeing card such as the Museumkaart (or I amsterdam Card) can pay for itself quickly. Entry to most sights is free with a card (I've only noted those that *aren't* covered).

Most museums require baggage check—usually free (often in coin-op lockers where you get your coin back).

The following sights are arranged by neighborhood for handy sightseeing. When you see a ✪ in a listing, it means the sight is covered in much more depth in one of my walks or self-guided tours. This is why Amsterdam's most important attractions get the least coverage in this chapter—we'll explore them later in the book.

SOUTHWEST AMSTERDAM
▲▲▲Rijksmuseum

Built to house the nation's great art, the Rijksmuseum (RIKES-moo-zay-oom) owns several thousand paintings, including an incomparable collection of 17th-century Dutch Masters: Rembrandt, Vermeer, Hals, and Steen. Its vast collection also includes interesting

artifacts—such as furniture—that help bring the Golden Age to life.

Cost and Hours: €17.50, not covered by I amsterdam Card, daily 9:00-17:00, last entry 30 minutes before closing, audioguide-€5, tram #2 or #5 from Central Station to Rijksmuseum stop; info tel. 020/674-7047 or switchboard tel. 020/674-7000, www. rijksmuseum.nl. The entrance is off the passageway that tunnels right through the center of the building.

○ See the Rijksmuseum Tour chapter.

▲▲▲Van Gogh Museum

Near the Rijksmuseum, this remarkable museum features works by the troubled Dutch artist whose art seemed to mirror his life.

Vincent, who killed himself in 1890 at age 37, is best known for sunny, Impressionist canvases that vibrate and pulse with vitality. The museum's 200 paintings—which offer a virtual stroll through the artist's work and life—were owned by Theo, Vincent's younger, art-dealer brother. Highlights include *Sunflowers, The Bedroom, The Potato Eaters*, and many brooding self-portraits. The third floor shows works that influenced Vincent, from Monet and Pissarro to Gauguin, Cézanne, and Toulouse-Lautrec. The worthwhile audioguide includes insightful commentaries and quotes from Vincent himself. Temporary exhibits fill the new wing, down the escalator from the ground-floor lobby.

Cost and Hours: €15, more for special exhibits, daily 9:00-18:00; Fri until 22:00 in March-Oct, Sat until 22:00 in July-Aug and Oct—with no crowds in the evenings; audioguide-€5, kids' audioguide-€2.50, Paulus Potterstraat 7, tram #2 or #5 from Central Station to Van Baerlestraat or Rijksmuseum stop, tel. 020/570-5200, www.vangoghmuseum.com.

○ See the Van Gogh Museum Tour chapter.

▲▲Stedelijk Museum

The Netherlands' top modern-art museum is filled with a permanent collection of 20th-century classics as well as far-out, refreshing, cutting-edge temporary exhibits.

Cost and Hours: €15, daily 10:00-18:00, Thu until 22:00, top-notch gift shop, Paulus Potterstraat 13, tram #2 or #5 from Central Station to Van Baerlestraat, tel. 020/573-

2911, www.stedelijk.nl. The fine €5 audioguide covers both the permanent and temporary exhibits.

Avoiding Lines: As you enter, note that there are "Fast Lane" doors for visitors with advance tickets or a Museumkaart. (Museumkaart holders can then print out a paper ticket from machines in the lobby.)

Eating: Try the simple first-floor café or the ground-floor restaurant with outdoor seating, or visit the supermarket next door (ideal for a picnic in the adjacent park).

Ↄ Self-Guided Tour: Before entering, notice the architecture of the modern section (aptly nicknamed "the bathtub") abutting the original older building. Once inside, pick up the current map and envision the museum's four main sections: the permanent collection 1850-1950 (ground floor, right half), design (ground floor, left half), permanent collection 1950-2000 (first floor), and the various temporary exhibits (scattered about, usually some on each floor). Each room comes with thoughtful English descriptions. (And if you're into marijuana, I can't think of a better space than the Stedelijk in which to enjoy its effects.)

This tour focuses on the permanent collection, which is displayed roughly chronologically and always in the same rooms (though specific paintings rotate in and out).

Ground Floor (1850-1950): From the lobby, pass through the turnstiles, go straight ahead (up the six steps), then turn right into Room 0.2 to start the permanent collection. Working counterclockwise around the perimeter, you'll see modern art unfold (approximately) chronologically.

The collection starts where the Van Gogh Museum leaves off—works by Van Gogh and his mentors, the Impressionists (Monet) and Realists (Courbet). Continue on through the even-brighter colors and stronger emotions of the Expressionists (Kandinsky) and Fauves (Matisse). You'll see how artists (including cubists, Chagall, and Holland's own Piet Mondrian) broke up the real world into patterns and shapes. Note how Picasso explored many of the 20th century's main art trends. Amsterdam's Karel Appel weighs in with his dense canvases of swirling ultra-bright colors and ultra-thick paints.

From Room 0.15, you can continue on through the design wing of functional-but-beautiful everyday objects. Or go up the stairs, making a U-turn at the top to the left, and enter Room 1.15.

First Floor (1950-2000): Though less chronological than the ground floor, you'll see the major styles and artists. Appreciate the big, empty canvases of Abstract Expressionists, who "expressed" primeval emotions and ideas through simple "abstract" patterns of color and line. Netherlands-born Willem de Kooning often included glimpses of the human figure amid his densely patterned

Amsterdam at a Glance

▲▲▲**Rijksmuseum** Best collection anywhere of the Dutch Masters—Rembrandt, Hals, Vermeer, and Steen—in a spectacular setting. **Hours:** Daily 9:00-17:00. See page 49.

▲▲▲**Van Gogh Museum** More than 200 paintings by the angst-ridden artist. **Hours:** Daily 9:00-18:00, Fri until 22:00 March-Oct, Sat until 22:00 July-Aug and Oct. See page 50.

▲▲▲**Anne Frank House** Young Anne's hideaway during the Nazi occupation. **Hours:** April-Oct daily 9:00-21:00, Sat and July-Aug until 22:00; Nov-March daily 9:00-19:00, Sat until 21:00. See page 60.

▲▲**Stedelijk Museum** The Netherlands' top modern-art museum, recently and extensively renovated. **Hours:** Daily 10:00-18:00, Thu until 22:00. See page 50.

▲▲**Vondelpark** City park and concert venue. **Hours:** Always open. See page 55.

▲▲**Amsterdam Museum** City's growth from fishing village to trading capital to today, including some Rembrandts and a playable carillon. **Hours:** Daily 10:00-17:00. See page 65.

▲▲**Amstelkring Museum** Catholic church hidden in the attic of a 17th-century merchant's house. **Hours:** Mon-Sat 10:00-17:00, Sun and holidays 13:00-17:00. See page 66.

▲▲**Red Light District Walk** Women of the world's oldest profession on the job. **Hours:** Best from noon into the evening; avoid late at night. See page 66.

▲▲**Netherlands Maritime Museum** Rich seafaring story of the Netherlands, told with vivid artifacts. **Hours:** Daily 9:00-17:00. See page 68.

▲▲**Hermitage Amsterdam** Russia's Tsarist treasures, on loan from St. Petersburg. **Hours:** Daily 10:00-17:00. See page 74.

▲▲**Dutch Resistance Museum** History of the Dutch struggle against the Nazis. **Hours:** Tue-Fri 10:00-17:00, Sat-Mon 11:00-17:00. See page 79.

▲**Museumplein** Square with art museums, street musicians, crafts, and nearby diamond demos. **Hours:** Always open. See page 54.

▲**Leidseplein** Lively square with cafés and street musicians. **Hours:** Always open, best on sunny afternoons. See page 56.

▲**Royal Palace** Lavish city hall that takes you back to the Golden Age of the 17th century. **Hours:** Daily 11:00-17:00 when not closed for official ceremonies. See page 62.

▲**Begijnhof** Quiet courtyard lined with picturesque houses. **Hours:** Daily 8:00-17:00. See page 64.

▲**Hash**, **Marijuana, and Hemp Museum** All the dope, from history and science to memorabilia. **Hours:** Daily 10:00-23:00. See page 67.

▲**EYE Film Institute Netherlands** Film museum and cinema complex housed in a futuristic building. **Hours:** Exhibits open daily 11:00-18:00, Friday until 20:00; cinemas and bar open roughly 10:00-24:00. See page 70.

▲**Rembrandt's House** The master's reconstructed house, displaying his etchings. **Hours:** Daily 10:00-18:00. See page 73.

▲**Diamond Tours** Offered at shops throughout the city. **Hours:** Generally daily 9:00-17:00. See page 73.

▲**Willet-Holthuysen Museum** Elegant 17th-century house. **Hours:** Mon-Fri 10:00-17:00, Sat-Sun 11:00-17:00. See page 58.

▲**Jewish Historical Museum** The Great Synagogue and exhibits on Judaism and culture, with Portuguese Synagogue across the street. **Hours:** Daily 11:00-17:00. See page 76.

▲**Dutch Theater** Moving memorial in former Jewish detention center. **Hours:** Daily 11:00-17:00. See page 78.

▲**Tropical Museum** Re-creations of tropical-life scenes. **Hours:** Tue-Sun 10:00-17:00, closed Mon. See page 80.

Houseboat Museum Your chance to see one of these floating homes from the inside. **Hours:** March-Oct Tue-Sun 11:00-17:00, closed Mon; Nov-Dec and Feb Fri-Sun 11:00-17:00, closed Mon-Thu; closed most of Jan. See page 60.

Central Library Architecturally fun spot—with great view terrace—to take a breather among Amsterdam's bookworms. **Hours:** Daily 10:00-22:00. See page 67.

canvases. Besides paintings, enjoy other trends: everyday "found" objects presented as high art; installations (an entire room you walk into); and new interactive technology (lights, video, gizmos) to dazzle the eye and tickle your wonderbone.

Don't miss the groundbreaking installation (Room 1.15) by America's own Edward Kienholz—*The Beanery.* One person at a time is allowed to enter—and once you're in, you can't help but smile.

▲Museumplein

Bordered by the Rijks, Van Gogh, and Stedelijk museums, and the Concertgebouw (classical music hall), this park-like square is interesting even to art haters. Amsterdam's best acoustics are found underneath the Rijksmuseum, where street musicians perform everything from chamber music to Mongolian throat singing. Mimes, human statues, and crafts booths dot the square. Skateboarders careen across a concrete tube, while locals enjoy a park bench or a coffee at the Cobra Café (playground nearby). And the city's marketing brilliance—the climbable "I amsterdam" letters—awaits as mostly young visitors grab their selfies.

Nearby is **Coster Diamonds,** a handy place to see a diamond-cutting and polishing demo (free, frequent, and interesting 30-minute tours followed by sales pitch, popular for decades with tour groups, prices marked up to include tour guide kickbacks, daily 9:00-17:00, Paulus Potterstraat 2-6, tel. 020/305-5555, www. costerdiamonds.com). The end of the tour leads you straight into their Diamond Museum, which is worthwhile only for those who  have a Museumkaart (which covers entry) or feel the need to see even more diamonds (€8.50, daily 9:00-17:00, tel. 020/305-5300, www.diamantmuseumamsterdam.nl). The tour at **Gassan Diamonds** is free and better (see page 73), but Coster is convenient to the Museumplein scene.

House of Bols: Cocktail & Genever Experience

This leading Dutch distillery runs a slick, pricey little museum/marketing opportunity across the street from the Van Gogh Museum. If you feel like a good stiff drink after your museum-going, it's ideal. The "experience" is a self-guided walk through what is essentially an ad for Bols—"four hundred years of working on the art of mixing and blending...a celebration of gin"—with some fun sniffing opportunities and a drink at a modern, mirrored-out cocktail bar for a finale. The line of bottles with 36 different scents (with the answers identifying each odor hidden until you guess)  is fascinating. Your ticket includes two gin-tastings with a talkative expert guiding you and a design-your-own cocktail. It's fun to watch your barista mix up the cocktail of your dreams—based on what you learned during your sniffing.

Cost and Hours: €15, not covered by Museumkaart, daily 12:00-18:30, Fri until 22:00, Sat until 20:00, last entry one hour before closing, must be 18, Paulus Potterstraat 14, tel. 020/570-8575, www.houseofbols.com.

Heineken Experience

This famous brewery, having moved its operations to the suburbs, has converted its old headquarters into a slick, Disneyesque beer-fest—complete with a beer-making simulation ride. The self-guided "experience" also includes do-it-yourself music videos, photo ops that put you inside Heineken logos and labels, and no small amount of hype about the Heineken family and the quality of their beer. It's a fun trip—like an hour at a beer lover's amusement park—if you can ignore the fact that you're essentially paying for 60 minutes of advertising. Note that this place is a huge hit with twentysomething travelers.

Cost and Hours: €18, includes two drinks, daily 11:00-19:00, Fri-Sun until 20:30, longer hours July-Aug, last entry 90 minutes before closing; tram #16, #24, or #25 to Stadhouderskade; an easy walk from Rijksmuseum, Stadhouderskade 78, tel. 020/523-9222, www.heinekenexperience.com.

De Pijp District

This former working-class industrial and residential zone (behind the Heineken Experience, near the Rijksmuseum)—once notorious as a slum—is gentrified now and has emerged as a colorful, vibrant district. Its spine is Albert Cuypstraat, a street taken over by a long, sprawling produce/flea market packed with interesting people. With its many inviting cafés and edgy intellectual/artsy/working-class heritage, it's nicknamed the Latin Quarter of Amsterdam. Don't look for actual sights here. The charm is the fun, creative vibe.

▲▲Vondelpark

This huge, lively city park is popular with the Dutch—families with little kids, romantic couples, strolling seniors, and hipsters sharing blankets and beers. It's a favored venue for free summer concerts. On a sunny afternoon, it's a hedonistic scene that seems

AMSTERDAM SIGHTS

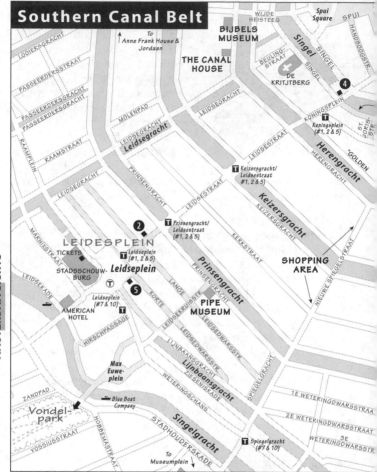

Southern Canal Belt

WIJDE HEISTEEG

Spui Square SPUI

HANDBOOGSTR

To Anne Frank House & Jordaan

BIJBELS MUSEUM

Singel SINGEL SINGEL

LOOIERSGRACHT

BEULING-STRAAT SINGEL

THE CANAL HOUSE

DE KRITJTBERG

❹

PASSEERDERSSTRAAT

LEIDSEGRACHT

KONINGSPLEIN

Koningsplein (#1, 2 & 5)

PASSEERDERSGRACHT

MOLENPAD

LEIDSEGRACHT

HERENGRACHT

'GOLDEN

PASSEERDERSGRACHT

T *Keizersgracht/ Leidsestraat #1, 2 & 5*

PRINSENGRACHT

Leidsegracht

LEIDSESTRAAT

RAAMSTRAAT

KEIZERSGRACHT

HERENGRACHT

KAMPERFOELIE

LEIDSEGRACHT

Keizersgracht KEIZERSGRACHT

PRINSENGRACHT

LEIDSESTRAAT

T *Prinsengracht/ Leidsestraat (#1, 2 & 5)*

❷

KERKSTRAAT

LEIDESPLEIN

TICKETS

T *Leidseplein (#1, 2 & 5)*

Leidseplein

SHOPPING AREA

Prinsengracht PRINSENGRACHT

NIEUWE SPIEGELSTRAAT

STADSSCHOUW-BURG

T

LANGE

KORTE

LEIDSEKRUISSTR.

LEIDSEDWARSSTR

MARNIXSTRAAT

LEIDSEKADE

❺

Leidseplein (#7 & 10)

AMERICAN HOTEL

T

PIPE MUSEUM

LEIDSEDWARSSTR

HIRSCHPASSAGE

LIJNBAANSGRACHT

SPIEGELGRACHT

Max Euwe-plein

LIJNBAANSGRACHT

ZIPSIKADE

1E WETERINGDWARSSTRAA

ZANDPAD

WETERINGSCHANS

2E WETERINGDWARSSTRAAT

Vondel-park

🚢 *Blue Boat Company*

STADHOUDERSKADE

Singelgracht SINGELGRACHT

3E WETERINGDWARSSTR

HOBBEMASTRAAT

T *Spiegelgracht (#7 & 10)*

VOSSIUSSTRAAT

To Museumplein

---

to say, "Parents...relax." The park's 'T Blauwe Theehuis ("The Blue Tea House") is a delightful spot to nurse a drink and take in the scene; see page 213.

SOUTHERN CANAL BELT
▲Leidseplein

Brimming with cafés, this peo-ple-watching mecca is an im-promptu stage for street artists, accordionists, jugglers, and unicy-clists. It's particularly bustling on sunny afternoons. After dark, it's a vibrant tourists' nightclub center. Stroll nearby Lange Leidsed-

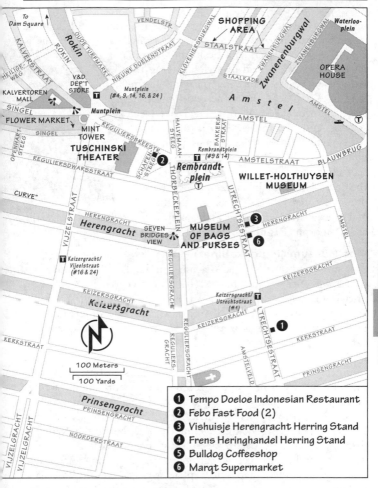

❶ Tempo Doeloe Indonesian Restaurant
❷ Febo Fast Food (2)
❸ Vishuisje Herengracht Herring Stand
❹ Frens Heringhandel Herring Stand
❺ Bulldog Coffeeshop
❻ Marqt Supermarket

warsstraat (one block north) for a taste-bud tour of ethnic eateries, from Greek to Indonesian.

Rembrandtplein and Tuschinski Theater

One of the city's premier nightlife spots is the leafy Rembrandt-plein (and the adjoining Thorbeckeplein). Rembrandt's statue stands here, along with a jaunty group of life-size statues giving us *The Night Watch* in 3-D—step into the ensemble for a photo-op. Several late-night dance clubs keep the area lively into the wee hours. Utrechtsestraat is lined with upscale shops and restaurants. Nearby Reguliersdwarsstraat (a street one block south of Rembrandtplein) is a center for gay and lesbian nightclubs.

The **Tuschinski Theater,** a movie palace from the 1920s (a half-block from Rembrandtplein down Reguliersbreestraat), glitters inside and out. Still a working theater, it's a delightful old place to see first-run movies (always in their original language—usually English—with Dutch subtitles). The exterior is an interesting hybrid of styles, forcing the round peg of Art Nouveau into the square hole of Art Deco. The stone-and-tile facade features stripped-down, functional Art Deco squares and rectangles, but is ornamented with Art Nouveau elements—Tiffany-style windows, garlands, curvy iron lamps, Egyptian pharaohs, and exotic gold lettering over the door. Inside (lobby is free), the sumptuous decor features fancy carpets, slinky fixtures,

and semi-abstract designs. Grab a seat in the lobby and watch the ceiling morph (Reguliersbreestraat 26-28).

Pipe Museum (Pijpenkabinet)

This small and quirky-yet-classy museum holds 300 years of pipes in a 17th-century canal house. (It's almost worth the admission price just to see the inside of one of these elegant homes.) You enter through the street-level shop, Smokiana, which is almost interesting enough to be a museum itself. It sells new and antique pipes, various smoking curiosities, and scholarly books written by the shop's owner. If you want more, pay to enter the museum, and a volunteer docent will accompany you upstairs through a tour of smoking history. You begin with some pre-Columbian terra-cotta pipes (from the discoverers of tobacco, dating from around 500 B.C.), followed by plenty of intricately carved Victorian smoking paraphernalia—long-stemmed Dutch pipes (the Dutch were the first importers of tobacco), meerschaum pipes (made from a soft white mineral), pipes carved into portraits, and so on. Ask questions—your guide is happy to explain why the opium pipes have their bowls in the center of the stem, or why some white clay pipes are a foot long.

Cost and Hours: €8, Wed-Sat 12:00-18:00 (though visits are sometimes possible on other days, when the shop itself is open), usually closed Sun-Tue, tel. 020/421-1779, just off Leidsestraat at Prinsengracht 488, www.pijpenkabinet.nl.

▲Willet-Holthuysen Museum
(a.k.a. Herengracht Canal Mansion)

This 1687 townhouse is a must for devotees of Hummel-topped sugar bowls and Louis XVI-style wainscoting. For others, it's a pleasant look inside a typical (rich) home with much of the original furniture and decor. Forget the history and just browse through a dozen rooms of beautiful saccharine objects from the 19th century.

Cost and Hours: €8, Mon-Fri 10:00-17:00, Sat-Sun 11:00-

17:00, audioguide–€4; take tram #4, #9, or #14 to Rembrandt-plein—it's a 2-minute walk southeast to Herengracht 605, tel.

020/523-1822, www.willetholthuysen.nl. The museum also hands out a free brochure that covers the house's history.

Visiting the Museum: Upon entering (through the servants' door under the grand entry), see photos of the owners during the house's heyday in the 1860s, and the 15-minute introductory video. In 1861, the wealthy heiress Louise Holthuysen and the art-collecting bon vivant Abraham Willet got married and became joined at the hyphen, then set out to make their home the social hub of Amsterdam. When the widow Louise died in 1895, she bequeathed the house to the city, along with its candelabras, snuff boxes, and puppy paintings.

In the kitchen, picture the couple's servants—before electricity and running water—turning meat on the spit at the fireplace or filtering rainwater.

Continue to the first floor, where the Willet-Holthuysens entertained. Several rooms are decorated in the Louis XVI style, featuring chairs with straight, tapering legs (not the heavy, curving, animal-claw feet of earlier styles). You'll see blue, yellow, and purple-themed rooms; wainscoting ("wallpaper" covering only the lower part of walls); and mythological paintings on the ceiling. Paintings introduce you to Abraham's artistic tastes, showing scenes of happy French peasants and nobles frolicking in the countryside.

The gilded ballroom—the house's most impressive space—contains a painting showing the room in its prime (and how little it's changed). Imagine Abraham, Louise, and 22 guests mingling here. Then they'd retire to the dining room to dine off the 275-piece Meissen porcelain set, or chat in the Blue Room by the canal. In the Garden Room they sipped tea while gazing out at symmetrically curved hedges and classical statues.

The top-floor bedroom is furnished with a canopy bed, matching oak washstand, and makeup table (and a chamber pot tucked under the bed). You can even browse the collection virtually using a computer terminal.

Museum of Bags and Purses (Tassenmuseum Hendrikje)

Runway models on their day off enjoy this quirky-but-elegant collection of purses crammed into a small 1664 canal house. The top floor quickly tells 500 years of bag and purse history—from before the invention of pockets—with a few choice and beautiful old pouches. Then you peruse the many varieties of the modern purse, from kitschy (shaped like a dog or a Coke can) to designer labels representing Paloma Picasso and beyond. The temporary exhibits, gift shop, and café bring added interest. Fans of handbags will love the place, and their partners might, too.

Cost and Hours: €9.50, daily 10:00-17:00, behind Rembrandtplein at Herengracht 573, tel. 020/524-6452, www.tassenmuseum.nl.

WEST AMSTERDAM
▲▲▲Anne Frank House

A pilgrimage for many, this house offers a fascinating look at the hideaway of young Anne during the Nazi occupation of the Netherlands. Anne, her parents, an older sister, and four others spent a little more than two years in a "Secret Annex" behind her father's business. While in hiding, 13-year-old Anne kept a diary chronicling her extraordinary experience. Acting on a tip, the Nazis arrested the group in August of 1944 and sent them to concentration camps in Poland and Germany. Anne and her sister died of typhus in March of 1945, only weeks before their camp was liberated. Of the eight inhabitants of the Secret Annex, only Anne's father, Otto Frank, survived. He returned to Amsterdam and arranged for his daughter's diary to be published in 1947. It was followed by many translations, a play, and a movie.

The thoughtfully designed exhibit offers thorough coverage of the Frank family, the diary, the stories of others who hid, and the Holocaust.

Cost and Hours: €9, not covered by I amsterdam Card; April-Oct daily 9:00-21:00, Sat and July-Aug until 22:00; Nov-March daily 9:00-19:00, Sat until 21:00; last entry 30 minutes before closing, often less crowded right when it opens or after 18:00, no baggage check, no large bags allowed inside, Prinsengracht 267, near Westerkerk, tel. 020/556-7100, www.annefrank.org.

❂ See the Anne Frank House Tour chapter.

Houseboat Museum (Woonbootmuseum)

In the 1930s, modern cargo ships came into widespread use—making small, sail-powered cargo boats obsolete. In danger of extinction, these little vessels found new life as houseboats lining the canals of Amsterdam. Today, 2,500 such boats—their cargo holds turned into classy, comfortable living rooms—are called home. For a peek into this *gezellig* (cozy) world, visit this tiny museum. Captain Vincent enjoys showing visitors around the houseboat, which feels lived-in because, until 1997, it was.

Cost and Hours: €4; March-Oct Tue-Sun 11:00-17:00, closed Mon; Nov-Dec and Feb Fri-Sun 11:00-17:00, closed Mon-

Thu; closed most of Jan; on Prinsengracht, opposite #296 facing Elandsgracht, tel. 020/427-0750, www.houseboatmuseum.nl.

Westerkerk

Located near the Anne Frank House, this landmark Protestant church has an appropriately barren interior, Rembrandt's body buried somewhere under the pews, and Amsterdam's tallest steeple. Built in the early 1600s, after the Reformation, it's very Dutch Reformed—plain, white walls, no statues, no stained glass—with the focus on the pulpit. The only ostentations: the church organ and the fancy gravestones of big-shot families. But even the organ (one of the top three in Amsterdam—free concerts most Fridays May-Oct at 13:00) had "modesty covers." The fine family tombstones lie on top of a chamber that held a coffin and six to eight bone boxes. When a leading family member would die, they'd pull up the tombstone, move the bones laying in the latest coffin into a bone box, and lay the body of the recently deceased family member to rest. This is the church that Anne Frank would gaze at out of

her hiding-place window...the church bells reminded her of the world outside.

While the church is free to visit, the Westerkerk tower is climbable only with a guided tour. The English-language, 30-minute tour takes you on a 185-step climb, rewarding you with a look at the carillon and grand city views. Tours are limited to six people; to reserve a spot, come in person on the same day or call.

Cost and Hours: Church entry free, generally April-Sept Mon-Sat 11:00-15:00, closed Sun and Oct-March; tower-€8 by tour only, April-Oct Mon-Sat 10:00-18:00, May-Aug until 20:00, closed Sun and Nov-March; tours leave on the half-hour, last tour leaves 30 minutes before closing; Prinsengracht 281, tel. 020/624-7766, www.westerkerk.nl.

Reypenaer Cheese Tasting Rooms

While essentially just a fancy cheese emporium, this place does a good job of showcasing Dutch cheese. You can pop into the delight-

ful shop any time for a few samples, or experience an hour-long cheese tasting in the basement (which has just 20 seats—it's smart to reserve ahead). The informative tasting session, run by Ron Peters and his staff, starts with a short video that's somewhere between an ad for cheese and dairy soft porn. Then, with an English-speaking guide, you guillotine six different cheeses and study, smell, and taste them with a wine accompaniment.

Cost and Hours: €15 for tasting; Mon-Tue at 13:00 and 15:00, Wed-Sun at 12:00, 13:30, 15:00, and 16:30; book by phone or online, near the Multatuli statue at Singel 182, tel. 020/320-6333, www.reypenaer.com.

The Canal House (Het Grachtenhuis)

This aggressively promoted museum sounds exciting and tells an interesting story—but, for most visitors, it's not worth the time or money. There aren't any artifacts on display, and as you shuffle through a series of rooms showing video presentations, you get no sense of the great canalside mansion you came to experience.

Cost and Hours: €12, not covered by Museumkaart, Tue-Sun 10:00-17:00, closed Mon, Herrengracht 386, www. hetgrachtenhuis.nl.

Nearby: Next door is the **Biblical Museum,** which, like its neighbor, has the potential to be fascinating. Instead, it's an old-school jumble of all things biblical, with temporary exhibits that'll disappoint most visitors (€8, Tue-Sat 10:00-17:00, Sun 11:00-17:00, closed Mon, Herrengracht 366, tel. 020/624-2436, www. bijbelsmuseum.nl).

CENTRAL AMSTERDAM, NEAR DAM SQUARE

▲Royal Palace (Koninklijk Huis)

This palace was built as a lavish city hall (1648-1655), when Holland was a proud new republic and Amsterdam was the richest city on the planet—awash in profit from trade. The building became a "Royal Palace" when Napoleon installed his brother Louis as king (1806). After Napoleon's fall, it continued as a royal residence for the Dutch royal family, the House of Orange. Today, it's one of King Willem-Alexander's official residences, with a single impressive floor open to the public. Visitors can gawk at a grand hall and stroll about 20 rooms branching off from it, all of them lavishly decorated with chandeliers, paintings, statues, and furniture that reflect Amsterdam's former status as the center of global trade.

Cost and Hours: €10, includes audioguide, daily 11:00-17:00 but often closed for official business, last entry 30 minutes before closing, tel. 020/620-4060, www.paleisamsterdam.nl.

Visiting the Palace: The huge, white central hall (Gallery or Citizens' Hall) is the palace's highlight—120 feet by 60 feet by 90 feet—and lit by eight big chandeliers. At the far end, a statue of Atlas holds the globe of the world, and the ceiling painting shows Amsterdam triumphant amid the clouds of heaven. On the floor, inlaid maps show the known world circa 1750 (back when the West

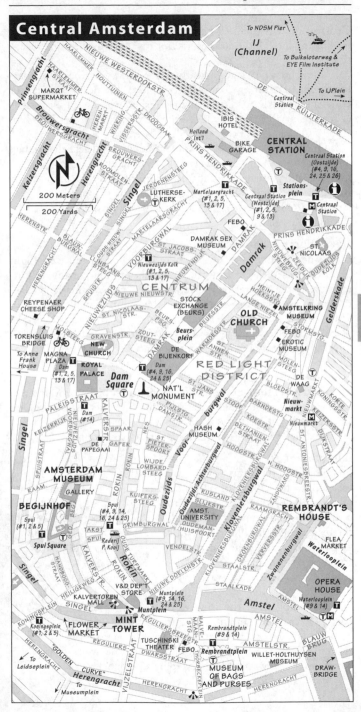

Central Amsterdam

To NDSM Pier

IJ (Channel)

To Buiksloterweg & EYE Film Institute

To IJPlein

Centraal Station

NIEUWE WESTERDOKSTR.

DE RUIJTERKADE

HOUTTUINEN

HAARLEMMER STRAAT

HAARLEMMER STR.

MARQT SUPERMARKET

HEREN-MARKT

WIERINGERSTR.

DROOGBAK

PRINS HENDRIKKADE

IBIS HOTEL

CENTRAL STATION

Holland Int'l

BIKE GARAGE

Stationsplein

Centraal Station

Centraal Station (Oostzijde) (#4, 9, 16, 24, 25 & 26)

Centraal Station (Westzijde) (#1, 2, 5, 9 & 13)

Prinsengracht

Brouwersgracht

Brouwersgracht

Keizersgracht

Herengracht

Singel

Singel

Singel

HERENSTR.

BLAUW. BURGWAL

HERENGRACHT

REYPENAER CHEESE SHOP

TORENSLUIS BRIDGE

To Anne Frank House

MAGNA PLAZA

ROYAL PALACE

Dam Square

AMSTERDAM MUSEUM

BEGIJNHOF

Spui (#1, 2 & 5)

Spui Square

Singel

KONINGSPLEIN

Koningsplein (#1, 2 & 5)

FLOWER MARKET

MINT TOWER

"GOLDEN CURVE" Herengracht

To Leidseplein

To Museumplein

LUTHER-KERK

Martelaarsgracht (#1, 2, 5, 13 & 17)

FEBO

NEW CHURCH

Dam (#1, 2, 5, 13 & 17)

Dam (#14)

DE PAPEGAAI

GALLERY

Spui (#4, 9, 14, 16, 24 & 25)

Rederij P. Kooij

V&D DEP'T STORE

KALVERTOREN MALL

Muntplein

TUSCHINSKI THEATER

MARTELAARSGRACHT

VOORBURGWAL

ST. JACOBS-STRAAT

Nieuwezijds Kolk (#1, 2, 5, 13 & 17)

LIJNBAANS-STEEG

SPUISTR.

ST. NICOLAAS-STR.

MOLSTEEG

GRAVENSTR.

ZOUT-STEEG

DAMRAK

DAMRAK

DE BIJENKORF

NAT'L MONUMENT

PIJLSTEEG

DAMSTR.

SPAAR

NES

ST. PIETER SPOORT

WIJDE LOMBARD-STEEG

ROKIN

ROKIN

KUIPERS-STEEG

Oudezijds

GRIMBURGWAL

OUDE TURFMARKT

ROKIN

ROKIN

NIEUWE DOELENSTR.

HALVE-MAAN

REGULIERSBREESTR.

REGULIERSBREESTR.

VIJZELSTRAAT

REGULIERS DWARSSTRAAT

CENTRUM

STOCK EXCHANGE (BEURS)

Beurs-plein

Damrak

NIEUWEZIJDS

NIEUWE NIEUWSTR.

ST. NICOLAAS-STR.

FEBO

Nieuwendijk

DAMRAK SEX MUSEUM

Damrak

HEINTJE HOEKSTEEG

LANGE NIEZEL

HASH MUSEUM

AMST. UNIVERSITY OUDEMAN-HUISPOORT

RUSLAND

SLIJKSTR.

BETHANIEN-STRAAT

HOOGSTR.

N. HOOGSTRAAT

Kloveniersburgwal

RAAMGRACHT

GROENBURGWAL

VERVERSTR.

STAALSTR.

STAALKADE

ST. NICOLAAS

OLD CHURCH

AMSTELKRING MUSEUM

RED LIGHT DISTRICT

EROTIC MUSEUM

MOLENSTEEG

DE WAAG

Nieuwmarkt

Nieuwmarkt

REMBRANDT'S HOUSE

FLEA MARKET

Waterlooplein

Waterlooplein (#9 & 14)

OPERA HOUSE

ZEEDIJK

WARMOESSTR.

OUDEZIJDS ACHTERBURGWAL

Kloveniersburgwal

Oudezijds Achterburgwal

ST. JANS STR.

STOOF STEEG

BARNDESTG.

KOESTR.

Gelderskade

OUDEZIJDS VOORBURGWAL

OUDEZIJDS KOLK

STORMSTG.

KONINGSSTR.

KORTE NIEUWMARKT

KEIZERSTR.

ST. ANTONIESBREESTR.

ZANDSTR.

Zwanenburgwal

Amstel

Amstel

AMSTEL

BLAUW BRUG

DRAW-BRIDGE

Rembrandtplein

Rembrandtplein (#9 & 14)

FEBO

AMSTELSTR.

WILLET-HOLTHUYSEN MUSEUM

MUSEUM OF BAGS AND PURSES

Herengracht

Muntplein (#9, 14, 16, 24 & 25)

200 Meters

200 Yards

AMSTERDAM SIGHTS

Coast of the US was still being explored). The hall is used today for hosting foreign dignitaries and for royal family wedding receptions.

The central hall leads directly to a room where Louis Bonaparte's throne once sat in front of the fireplace. The next room has his era's Empire Style furniture (high-polished wood with Neoclassical motifs). After that you'll see then-Princess Beatrix's bedroom (1939-80).

One room, which overlooks Dam Square, is where the council of ex-mayors would meet every year to elect the four new burgomasters, who governed the city. The paintings over the fireplace, by Rembrandt's pupils, show righteous Romans whom Golden Age Amsterdammers modeled themselves after (all well-explained by the audioguide).

New Church (Nieuwe Kerk)

Barely newer than the "Old" Church (located in the Red Light District), this 15th-century sanctuary has an intentionally dull interior, after the decoration was removed by 16th-century iconoclastic Protestants seeking to unclutter their communion with God. This is where many Dutch royal weddings and all coronations take place. A steep entrance fee is charged for admission to the church's popular temporary exhibits, but you can view the church itself for free from the landing above the shop (enter to left of main door and go up the stairs in the gift shop).

Cost and Hours: Free to view from gift-shop balcony, interior with special exhibits-€8-15, daily 10:00-17:00, audioguide-€3, on Dam Square, tel. 020/353-8168, www.nieuwekerk.nl.

See page 91 of the Amsterdam City Walk chapter.

▲Begijnhof

Stepping into this tiny, idyllic courtyard in the city center, you escape into the charm of old Amsterdam. (Please be considerate of the people who live around the courtyard, and don't photograph the residents or their homes.) Notice house #34, a 500-year-old wooden structure (rare, since repeated fires taught city fathers a trick called brick). Peek into the hidden Catholic church, dating from the time when post-Reformation Dutch Catholics  couldn't worship in public. It's opposite the English Reformed church, where the Pilgrims worshipped while waiting for their voyage to the New World—marked by a plaque near the door.

Cost and Hours: Free, daily 8:00-17:00, on Begijnensteeg lane, just off Kalverstraat between #130 and #132, pick up flier at office near entrance, www.ercadam.nl.

See page 96 of the Amsterdam City Walk chapter.

▲▲Amsterdam Museum

Housed in a 500-year-old former orphanage, this creative museum traces the city's growth from fishing village to world trade center to hippie haven. The key is to not get lost somewhere in the 17th century as you navigate the meandering maze of rooms. The museum tries hard to make the city's history engaging and fun (almost too hard—it dropped "history" from its name for fear of putting people off). But the story of Amsterdam is indeed engaging and fun, and this is the only museum in town designed to tell it.

Cost and Hours: €11, daily 10:00-17:00, one-hour audioguide-€4, pleasant restaurant, next to Begijnhof at Kalverstraat 92, tel. 020/523-1822, www.ahm.nl. This museum is a fine place to buy the Museumkaart (for details, see page 29).

Visiting the Museum: Start with the easy-to-follow **"DNA"** section, which hits the historic highlights from 1000-2000. The city was built atop pilings in marshy soil (the museum stands only four feet above sea level). By 1500, they'd built a ring of canals and established the sea trade. The Golden Age (1600s) is illustrated by fine paintings of citizens, including Rembrandt's portrait of his wife Saskia. The 1800s brought modernization and new technologies like the bicycle. After the gloom of World War II, Amsterdam emerged to become the "Capital of Freedom."

From the DNA section, move quickly through the next series of rooms (spanning the 17th to early 20th centuries), following these directions: Go downstairs to pass through the 17th-century rooms (paintings, sea trade). Then go upstairs to Floor 1 for the 18th century (curly wigs and tea in the piano parlor), 19th century (modernizing the city's port), and 20th century (housing issues).

From here, go upstairs to the 1940-2000 exhibits. Don't miss the small side-room (at the top of the stairs) featuring life under the Nazis ("Amsterdam 1940-45"). In "Amsterdam 1945-2000" you'll relive the liberating Sixties, the Provo people's movement with their free "white car" experiment, the Ajax football team, and legalized drugs. At the very end is a meticulous reconstruction of the historic, gay-friendly Café 't Mandje (see page 120), with its jukebox, cut-off ties, and an explanatory video about the owner. Your tour is over. (Now, if only that beer tap worked.)

The museum's free pedestrian corridor (described in the Amsterdam City Walk)—lined with old-time group portraits—is a powerful teaser.

RED LIGHT DISTRICT
▲▲Amstelkring Museum

Although Amsterdam has long been known for its tolerant attitudes, 16th-century politics forced Dutch Catholics to worship discreetly. At this museum near Central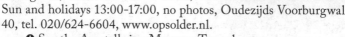
Station, you'll find a fascinating, hidden Catholic church filling the attic of three 17th-century merchants' houses. Don't miss the silver collection and other exhibits of daily life from 300 years ago.

Cost and Hours: €8, includes audioguide, Mon-Sat 10:00-17:00, Sun and holidays 13:00-17:00, no photos, Oudezijds Voorburgwal 40, tel. 020/624-6604, www.opsolder.nl.

✪ See the Amstelkring Museum Tour chapter.

▲▲Red Light District Walk

Europe's most popular ladies of the night tease and tempt here, as they have for centuries, in several hundred display-case windows around Oudezijds Achterburgwal and Oudezijds Voorburgwal, surrounding the Old Church (Oude Kerk, described later). Drunks and druggies make the streets uncomfortable late at night after the gawking tour groups leave (about 22:30), but it's a fascinating walk earlier in the evening.

The neighborhood, one of Amsterdam's oldest, has hosted prostitutes since 1200. Prostitution is entirely legal here, and the prostitutes are generally entrepreneurs, renting space and running their own businesses, as well as filling out tax returns and even paying union dues. Popular prostitutes net about €500 a day (for what's called "S&F" in its abbreviated, printable form, charging €30-50 per customer).

✪ See the Red Light District Walk chapter.

Sex Museums

Amsterdam has three sex museums: two in the Red Light District and another one a block in front of Central Station on Damrak street. While visiting one can be called sightseeing, visiting more than that is harder to explain. The one on Damrak is the cheapest and most interesting. Here's a comparison:

The **Damrak Sex Museum** tells the story of pornography from Roman times through 1960. Every sexual deviation is revealed in various displays. The museum includes early French pornographic photos; memorabilia from Europe, India, and Asia; a Marilyn Monroe tribute; and some S&M displays (€4, not covered by Museumkaart, daily 9:30-23:00, Damrak 18, a block in front of Central Station, tel. 020/622-8376).

The **Erotic Museum** in the Red Light District is five floors of uninspired paintings, videos, old photos, and sculpture (€7, not covered by Museumkaart, daily 11:00-24:00, along the canal at Oudezijds Achterburgwal 54, tel. 020/624-7303; see page 122).

Red Light Secrets Museum of Prostitution is a pricey look at the world's oldest profession. If you're wondering what it's like to sit in those red booths, watch the video taken from the prostitute's perspective as "johns" check you out. The exhibit is much smaller than the others (€7.50, not covered by Museumkaart, daily 12:00-24:00, Oudezijds Achterburgwal 60, tel. 020/662-5300; see page 122).

Old Church (Oude Kerk)
This 14th-century landmark—the needle around which the Red Light District spins—has served as a reassuring welcome-home symbol to sailors, a refuge to the downtrodden, an ideological battlefield of the Counter-Reformation, and, today, a tourist sight with a dull interior.

Cost and Hours: €7.50, Mon-Sat 10:00-18:00, Sun 13:00-17:30, free carillon concerts Tue and Sat at 16:00, tel. 020/625-8284, www.oudekerk.nl. It's 167 steps to the top of the church tower (€7, April-Sept Thu-Sat only 13:00-17:00, visits leave every half-hour).

See page 112 of the Red Light District Walk chapter.

Marijuana Sights in the Red Light District
Three related establishments cluster together along a canal in the Red Light District. The **Hash, Marijuana, and Hemp Museum,** worth ▲, is the most worthwhile of the three; it shares a ticket with the less substantial **Hemp Gallery.** Right nearby is **Cannabis College,** a free nonprofit center that's "dedicated to ending the global war against the cannabis plant through public education."

Cost and Hours: Museum and gallery–€9, daily 10:00-23:00, Oudezijds Achterburgwal 148, tel. 020/624-8926, www.hashmuseum.com. College entry free, daily 11:00-19:00, Oudezijds Achterburgwal 124, tel. 020/423-4420, www.cannabiscollege.com.

For more on these sights, see pages 123-124 of the Red Light District Walk chapter. For all the dope on Dutch dope, see the Smoking chapter.

NORTHEAST AMSTERDAM
Central Library (Openbare Bibliotheek Amsterdam)
This huge, striking, multistory building holds almost 1,400 seats—many with wraparound views of the city—and lots of Internet terminals, not to mention Wi-Fi (€1/30 minutes, buy vouchers at the

desk or use pay terminals). It's a classy place to check email. The library, which opened in 2007, demonstrates the Dutch people's dedication to a freely educated populace (the right to information, they point out, is enshrined in the UN's Universal Declaration of Human Rights). Everything's relaxed and inviting, from the fun kids' zone and international magazine and newspaper section on the ground floor to the organic cafeteria, with its dramatic view-terrace dining on the top (La Place, €10 meals, salad bar, daily 10:00-21:00). The library is a 10-minute walk from the east end of Central Station.

Cost and Hours: Free, daily 10:00-22:00, tel. 020/523-0900, www.oba.nl.

NEMO (National Center for Science and Technology)

This kid-friendly science museum is a city landmark. Its distinctive copper-green building, jutting up from the water like a sinking ship, has prompted critics to nickname it the *Titanic*. Designed by Italian architect Renzo Piano (known for Paris' Pompidou Center and Berlin's Sony Center complex on Potsdamer Platz), the building's shape reflects its nautical surroundings as well as the curve of the underwater tunnel it straddles.

Several floors feature permanent and rotating exhibits that allow kids (and adults) to explore topics such as light, sound, and gravity, and play with bubbles, topple giant dominoes, and draw with lasers. The museum's motto: "It's forbidden NOT to touch!" Whirring, room-size pinball machines reputedly teach kids about physics. English explanations are available.

Up top is a restaurant with a great city view, as well as a sloping terrace that becomes a popular "beach" in summer, complete with lounge chairs and a lively bar. On the bottom floor is a cafeteria offering €5 sandwiches.

Cost and Hours: €15, June-Aug daily 10:00-17:30, Sept-May generally closed Mon, tel. 020/531-3233, www.e-nemo.nl. The roof terrace—open until 19:00 in the summer—is generally free.

Getting There: It's above the entrance to the IJ tunnel at Oosterdok 2. From Central Station, you can walk there in 15 minutes, or take bus #22 or #48 to the Kadijksplein stop.

▲▲Netherlands Maritime Museum (Nederlands Scheepvaartmuseum)

This huge, kid-friendly collection of model ships, maps, and sea-battle paintings fills the 300-year-old Dutch Navy Arsenal (clev-

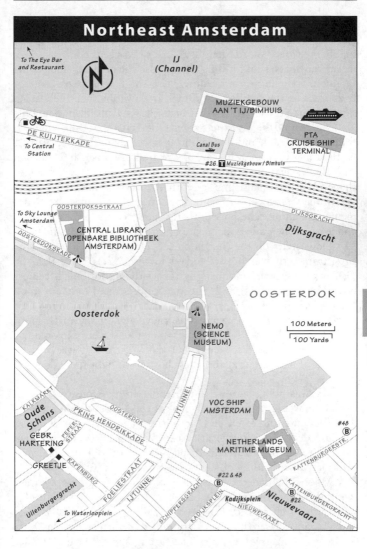

Northeast Amsterdam

To The Eye Bar and Restaurant

IJ (Channel)

MUZIEKGEBOUW AAN 'T IJ/BIMHUIS

PTA CRUISE SHIP TERMINAL

DE RUIJTERKADE

To Central Station

Canal Bus

#26 Muziekgebouw / Bimhuis

OOSTERDOKSSTRAAT

DIJKSGRACHT

Dijksgracht

To Sky Lounge Amsterdam

CENTRAL LIBRARY (OPENBARE BIBLIOTHEEK AMSTERDAM)

OOSTERDOKSKADE

OOSTERDOK

Oosterdok

NEMO (SCIENCE MUSEUM)

100 Meters
100 Yards

OOSTERDOK

IJTUNNEL

VOC SHIP AMSTERDAM

KALKMARKT

Oude Schans

PRINS HENDRIKKADE

PEPERSTRAAT

GEBR. HARTERING

KAPENBURG

GREETJE

#48 B

NETHERLANDS MARITIME MUSEUM

KATTENBURGERSTR.

#22 & 48 B

KATTENBURGERGRACHT

FOELIESTRAAT

IJTUNNEL

SCHIPPERSGRACHT

KADIJKSPLEIN

Kadijksplein

#22

NIEUWEVAART

Nieuwevaart

Uilenburgergracht

To Waterlooplein

erly located a little ways from the city center, as this was where they stored the gunpowder). The finale is a chance to explore below the decks of an old tall-masted ship. Given the Dutch seafaring heritage, this is an appropriately important and impressive place.

Cost and Hours: €15 covers both museum and ship, both open daily 9:00-17:00, bus #22 or #48 from Central Station to Kattenburgerplein 1, tel. 020/523-2222, www.scheepvaartmuseum.nl.

◐ Self-Guided Tour: Start in the **east wing** of the second floor. In the Paintings section, pause at the first big painting—*The Battle of Gibraltar, 1607*—which shows the Dutch navy's crowning moment. In this battle, 26 Dutch ships routed the seemingly invincible Spanish force. Notice that virtually all the ships in the painting fly the three-color Dutch flag. That's because the Spanish fleet has already been sunk, killing thousands. The painting depicts the infamous mopping-up procedure. (Use the touch-screen monitor to zoom in on the details.) The Dutch are lowering their lifeboats to save the Spaniards—or, as other historians say, to finish them off.

The rest of the Paintings rooms illustrate how ships changed from sail to steam, and how painting styles changed from realistic battle scenes to Romantic seascapes to Impressionism and Cubism.

The Navigational Instruments section has quadrants (a wedge-shaped tool you could line up with the horizon and the stars to determine your location), compasses, and plumb lines. In Ornamentation, admire the busty gals that adorned the prows of ships, and learn of their symbolic meaning for superstitious sailors.

Downstairs on the first floor, see Yacht Models through the ages, from early warships to today's luxury vessels. Note that the display case groups the boats by type—round-bottomed, centerboard, keel, etc. (Psst. Slide those monitor screens to zoom in on a particular model.) The section on Atlases (i.e., maps) shows how human consciousness expanded as knowledge of the earth grew. In 1482 only Europe, Africa, and some of Asia were explored. By 1579 America was discovered, but the West Coast was still an amorphous blob. (Psst again. Press buttons to light these dark exhibits.)

The **west wing** is more kid-oriented and less meaty, with an exhibit on whales and a friendly look at the Golden Age.

The museum often has **activities;** check the schedule at the info desk. The Voyage at Sea—a whimsical 25-minute walk through rooms of multimedia displays—is more for kids, and is not informative or thrilling enough to justify a long wait to enter.

Moored behind the museum is a replica of the ship *Amsterdam.* This type of ship (called an East Indiaman) had its heyday during the 17th and 18th centuries, sailing for the Dutch East India Company (see the abbreviation VOC—for Vereenigde Oost-Indische Compagnie—on insignias throughout the boat). Wander the decks, then duck your head and check out the captain and surgeon's quarters, packed with items they would have used. Don't forget to climb down into the hold. The ship is a little light on good historical information, but it's still shipshape enough to delight history buffs and *Pirates of the Caribbean* fans.

NORTH AMSTERDAM
▲EYE Film Institute Netherlands
The newest and most striking feature of the Amsterdam skyline is EYE, a film museum and cinema housed in an übersleek mod-

ern building immediately across the water from Central Station. Heralding the coming gentrification of the north side of the IJ waterway, EYE (a play on "IJ") is a complex of museum spaces and four theaters playing mostly art films (shown in their original language, with selections organized around various themes). Its many other offerings include a Sunday afternoon program of silent films with live musical accompaniment, special exhibits on film-related themes, a free permanent exhibit in the basement, a shop, and a

trendy terrace café with great waterside seating (daily 10:00-24:00). Helpful attendants at the reception desk can get you oriented.

Cost and Hours: General entry and basement exhibit are free, films cost €10, and seasonal exhibits cost around €9 (plus around €4 for special exhibits; no cash accepted, but standard US credit cards OK), exhibits open 11:00-18:00, Friday until 20:00, cinemas open daily at 10:00 until last screening (ticket office usually closes at 22:00 or 23:00), tel. 020/589-1400, www.eyefilm.nl.

Getting There: From the docks behind Central Station, catch the free ferry (labeled *Buiksloterweg*) across the river and walk left to the big white modern building.

SOUTHEAST AMSTERDAM

To reach the following sights from the train station, take tram #9 or #14. All of these sights (except the Tropical Museum) are close to one another and can easily be connected into an interesting walk—or, better yet, a bike ride. Several of the sights in southeast Amsterdam cluster near the large square, Waterlooplein, dominated by the modern opera house.

For an orientation, survey the neighborhood from the lamplined Blauwbrug ("Blue Bridge")—a modest, modern version of Paris' Pont Alexandre III. The bridge crosses the Amstel River. From this point, the river is channeled to form the city's canals.

Scan clockwise. The big, curved, modern facade belongs to the opera house, commonly called the "Stopera," as it's the combo City Hall *(stadhuis)* and opera. Behind the Stopera are these sights (not visible from here, but described next): the Waterlooplein flea market, Rembrandt's House, and Gassan Diamonds. To the right of the Stopera are the twin gray steeples of the Moses and Aaron Church, which sits roughly in the center of the former Jewish Quarter.

Several Jewish sights cluster to the right of the Moses and Aaron Church: the Jewish Historical Museum, the Portuguese

Southeast Amsterdam

① To Stayokay Stadsdoelen Hostel
② To Stayokay Zeeburg Hostel
③ Restaurant Gebr. Hartering
④ Restaurant Greetje
⑤ Café de Sluyswacht

Synagogue, and the dockworker statue (a Holocaust memorial). Just east of those is the De Hortus Botanical Garden.

The cute little drawbridge, while not famous, is certainly photogenic. (Its traditional counterbalance design is so effective that even a child can lift the bridge.) Beyond that is the Hermitage Amsterdam (it takes up an entire city block). Crossing the Amstel upstream is one of the city's romantic spots, the Magere Brug ("Skinny Bridge"). A block away is the city's best look at a Dutch Golden Age mansion, the Willet-Holthuysen Museum (a.k.a. Herengracht Canal Mansion).

Waterlooplein Flea Market

For more than a hundred years, the Jewish Quarter flea market has raged daily except Sunday (at the Waterlooplein metro station, behind Rembrandt's House). The long, narrow park is filled with stalls selling cheap clothes, hippie stuff, old records, tourist knickknacks, and garage-sale junk.

▲Rembrandt's House (Museum Het Rembrandthuis)

A middle-aged Rembrandt lived here from 1639 to 1658 after his wife's death, as his popularity and wealth dwindled down to

obscurity and bankruptcy. As you enter, ask when the next etching or painting demonstration is scheduled and pick up the excellent audioguide.

Start with the video on Rembrandt's life—his rise, peak, and fall—then tour the rooms. The house is reconstructed and filled with period objects (not his actual belongings) that re-create what his bankruptcy inventory of 1656 said he owned. You'll see his well-equipped kitchen and big entrance hall. His art cabinet is filled with odd curios collected by this eccentric genius—shells, books, classical busts, and a Baroque-era jackalope. In his large studio, imagine him at work, creating *The Night Watch*, *The Portrait of Maria Trip*, and numerous self-portraits (seen at the Rijksmuseum). You can attend an etching demonstration and ask the printer to explain the etching process (drawing in soft wax on a metal plate that's then dipped in acid, inked up, and printed). For the finale, enjoy several rooms of original Rembrandt etchings. You're not likely to see a single Rembrandt painting, but the master's etchings are marvelous and well-described. I came away wanting to know more about the man and his art.

Cost and Hours: €12.50, includes audioguide, daily 10:00-18:00, etching and painting demonstrations almost hourly between 11:00 and 15:00, Jodenbreestraat 4, tel. 020/520-0400, www.rembrandthuis.nl.

Nearby: If you'd like a scenic drink or snack after your museum visit, stop by **Café de Sluyswacht,** across the street (see page 216).

▲Diamonds

Many shops in this "city of diamonds" offer tours. These tours come with two parts: a chance to see experts behind magnifying glasses polishing the facets of precious diamonds, followed by a visit to an intimate sales room to see (and perhaps buy) a mighty shiny yet very tiny souvenir.

The handy and professional **Gassan Diamonds** facility fills a huge warehouse one block from Rembrandt's House. A visit here plops you in the big-tour-group fray (notice how each tour group has a color-coded sticker so they know which

guide gets the commission on what they buy). You'll get a sticker, join a free 15-minute tour to see a polisher at work, and hear a general explanation of the process. Then you'll have an opportunity to sit down and have color and clarity described and illustrated with diamonds ranging in value from $100 to $30,000. Before or after, you can have a free cup of coffee in the waiting room across the parking lot (daily 9:00-17:00, Nieuwe Uilenburgerstraat 173-175, tel. 020/622-5333, www.gassan.com, handy WC). Another company, **Coster,** also offers diamond demos. They're not as good as Gassan's, but convenient if you're near the Rijksmuseum (described on page 54).

▲▲Hermitage Amsterdam

The famous Hermitage Museum in St. Petersburg, Russia, loans art to Amsterdam for a series of rotating, and often exquisitely beautiful, special exhibits in the Amstelhof, a 17th-century former nursing home that takes up a whole city block along the Amstel River.

Why is there Russian-owned art in Amsterdam? The Hermitage collection in St. Petersburg is so vast that they can only show about 5 percent of it at any one time. Therefore, the Hermitage is establishing satellite collections around the world. The one here in Amsterdam is the biggest, filling the large Amstelhof. By law, the great Russian collection can only be out of the country for six months at a time, so the collection is always changing (check the museum's website to see what's on during your visit). Curators in Amsterdam make a point to display art that complements—rather than just repeats—what the city's other museums show so well. The one small permanent History Hermitage exhibit explains the historic connection between the Dutch (Orange) and Russian (Romanov) royal families.

Cost and Hours: Generally €15, but price varies with exhibit; daily 10:00-17:00, come later in the day to avoid crowds, audioguide-€4, mandatory free bag check, café, Nieuwe Herengracht 14, tram #9 from the train station, recorded info tel. 020/530-7488, www.hermitage.nl.

De Hortus Botanical Garden

This is a unique oasis of tranquility within the city (no mobile phones are allowed, because "our collection of plants is a precious community—treat it with respect"). One of the oldest botanical gardens in the world, it dates from 1638, when medicinal herbs were grown here. Today, among its 6,000 different kinds of plants—most of which were collected by the Dutch East India Company in the 17th and 18th centuries—you'll find medicinal herbs, cacti, several greenhouses (one with a fluttery butterfly house—a hit with kids), and a tropical palm house. Much of it is described in English: "A

Jews in Amsterdam

In 1940, one in ten Amsterdammers was Jewish, and most lived in the neighborhood behind Waterlooplein. Jewish trad-

ers had long been welcome in a city that cared more about business than religion. In the late 1500s, many Sephardic Jews from Spain and Portugal immigrated, fleeing persecution. (The philosopher Baruch Spinoza's ancestors were among them.) In the 1630s, Yiddish-speaking Eastern European Jews (Ashkenazi) poured in. By 1700, the Jewish Quarter was a bustling, exotic, multicultural world, with more people speaking Portuguese, German, and Yiddish than Dutch.

Despite their large numbers, for several centuries Jews were not first-class citizens. They needed the city's permission to settle here, and they couldn't hold public office (but then, neither could Catholics under Calvinist rule). Still, the Jewish Quarter was not a ghetto per se, as the segregation wasn't forced, and Jews faced no special taxes. Cosmopolitan Amsterdam was well-acquainted with all types of beliefs and customs.

In 1796, Jews were given full citizenship. In exchange, they were required to learn the Dutch language and submit to the city's legal system. Over the next century or so, the Jewish culture began assimilating into the Dutch.

In 1940, Nazi Germany occupied the Netherlands. On February 22, 1941, the Nazis began rounding up Jews and shipping them to extermination camps in Eastern Europe. By war's end, more than 100,000 of the country's 135,000 Jews had died.

Today, about 25,000 Jews live in Amsterdam, and the Jewish Quarter has blended with the modern city. For more information on Amsterdam's many Jewish sights, see www.jhm.nl.

Dutch merchant snuck a coffee plant out of Ethiopia, which ended up in this garden in 1706. This first coffee plant in Europe was the literal granddaddy of the coffee cultures of Brazil—long the world's biggest coffee producer."

Cost and Hours: €8.50, not covered by Museumkaart, daily 10:00-17:00, Plantage Middenlaan 2A, tel. 020/625-9021, www.dehortus.nl. The inviting Orangery Café serves tapas.

▲Jewish Historical Museum (Joods Historisch Museum)
This interesting museum tells the story of the Netherlands' Jews through three centuries, serving as a good introduction to Judaism and Jewish customs and religious traditions.

Originally opened in 1932, the museum was forced to close during the Nazi years. Recent renovations have joined four historic former synagogues together into one modern complex. Your ticket also includes the Portuguese Synagogue a half-block away.

Cost and Hours: €12, includes Portuguese Synagogue, more for special exhibits, ticket also covers Dutch Theater—see next listing; museum daily 11:00-17:00, Portuguese Synagogue daily 10:00-16:00, last entry 30 minutes before closing; free audioguides cover the Great Synagogue and Portuguese Synagogue, displays all have English explanations, children's museum, Jonas Daniel Meijerplein 2, tel. 020/531-0310, www.jhm.nl. The museum has a modern, minimalist, kosher café.

Visiting the Museum: Start in the impressive **Great Synagogue.** Have a seat in the high-ceilinged synagogue, surrounded by religious objects, and picture it during its prime (1671-1943). The hall would be full for a service—men downstairs, women above in the gallery. On the east wall (the symbolic direction of Jerusalem) is the Ark, where they keep the scrolls of the Torah (the Jewish scriptures, comprising the first five books of Old Testament of the Bible). The rabbi and other men, wearing thigh-length prayer shawls, would approach the Ark and carry the Torah to the raised platform in the center of the room. After unwrapping it from its drapery and silver cap, a man would use a *yad* (ceremonial pointer) to follow along while singing the text aloud.

Video displays around the room explain Jewish customs, from birth (circumcision) to puberty (the bar/bat mitzvah, celebrating the entry into adulthood) to Passover celebrations to marriage—culminating in the groom stomping on a glass while everyone shouts "Mazel tov!"

Next, head up the spiral staircase to the women's gallery, with exhibits tracing the **history** of Amsterdam's Jews from 1600 to 1900. This was a golden age, when Amsterdam and its Jewish population both thrived in relative harmony. (See the "Jews in Amsterdam" sidebar.) Next comes the 20th century (housed in the former New Synagogue) and the grim era of the Nazi occupation, which decimated the community. Personal artifacts—chairs, clothes—tell the devastating history in a very real way. Downstairs (in the

The Synagogue

A synagogue is a place of public worship, where Jews gather to pray, sing, and read from the Torah. Most synagogues have similar features, though they vary depending on the congregation.

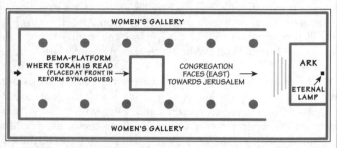

The synagogue generally faces toward Jerusalem. At the east end is an alcove called the **ark,** which holds the Torah. These scriptures (the first five books of the Old Testament) are written in Hebrew on scrolls wrapped in luxuriant cloth. The other main element of the synagogue is the **bema,** a platform from which the Torah is read aloud. In traditional Orthodox synagogues, the bema is near the center of the hall, and the reader stands facing the same direction as the congregation. (In other branches of Judaism, the bema is at the front, and the reader faces the worshippers.) Orthodox synagogues have separate worship areas for men and women, usually with women in the balcony.

The synagogue walls might be decorated with elaborate patterns of vines or geometric designs, but never statues of people (as that might be considered idol worship). A lamp above the ark is always kept lit, as it was in the ancient temple of Jerusalem. Candelabras called menorahs also recall the temple. Other common symbols are the two tablets of the Ten Commandments given to Moses, or a Star of David, representing the Jewish king's shield.

At a typical service, the congregation arrives at the start of Sabbath (Friday evening). As a sign of respect toward God, men don yarmulkes (small round caps). As the cantor leads songs and prayers, worshippers follow along in a book of weekly readings. At the heart of the service, everyone stands as the Torah is ceremoniously paraded, unwrapped, and placed on the bema. Someone—the rabbi, the cantor, or a congregant—reads the words aloud. The rabbi ("teacher") might give a commentary on the Torah passage.

Aanbouw Annex) are **temporary exhibits**, generally showing the work of Jewish artists from around the world.

Continue your visit by heading to the nearby **Portuguese Synagogue.** (As you exit the Jewish Museum, turn right and cross busy Weesperstraat.) This grand structure brings together both old and new—a historic synagogue that today serves a revived Jewish community. It was built in the 1670s (when Catholics were worshipping underground), to house a community of Sephardic (Iberian) Jews who fled persecution. At the time, it was the world's largest. The building survived World War II, though its congregation barely did.

Inside, it's majestic in its simplicity—a spacious place of worship with four Ionic columns supporting a wooden roof. There's no electric lighting, only candles and windows. Find the main features: the platform (near the back) where the cantor presides, the wood-columned niche at the far end for the Torah, the two ceremonial sofas for VIPs, the wood canopy where weddings take place...and the sand under your feet, which (may) symbolize the Israelites' sojourn through the desert.

Explore the rest of the Portuguese Synagogue complex. (Any unlocked door is yours for the visiting.) You can see the Ladies Gallery, the candle-storage room, and the ritual bath, where women purify after menstruation. Don't miss the downstairs Treasury, containing precious ceremonial objects, textiles, and rare books, plus a slideshow on the history of this beloved synagogue, known as the *Esnoga.*

▲Dutch Theater (Hollandsche Schouwburg)

Once a lively theater in the Jewish neighborhood, and today a moving memorial, this building was used as an assembly hall for local Jews destined for Nazi concentration camps.  On the wall, 6,700 family names pay tribute to the 104,000 Jews deported and killed by the Nazis. Some 70,000 victims spent time here, awaiting transfer to concentration camps. Upstairs is a small history exhibit with a model of the ghetto, plus photos and memorabilia (such as shoes and letters) of some victims, putting a human face on the staggering numbers. Television monitors show actual footage of the Nazis rounding up Amsterdam's Jews. You can also see a few costumes from the days when the building was a theater. While the exhibit is small, it offers plenty to think about. Back in the ground-floor courtyard, notice the hopeful messages that visiting school groups attach to the wooden tulips.

Cost and Hours: Covered by €12 Jewish Historical Museum ticket, daily 11:00-17:00, last entry 30 minutes before closing, Plantage Middenlaan 24, tel. 020/531-0380, www.hollandscheschouwburg.nl.

▲▲Dutch Resistance Museum (Verzetsmuseum)

This is an impressive look at how the Dutch resisted (or collaborated with) their Nazi occupiers from 1940 to 1945. You'll see propaganda movie clips, study forged ID cards under a magnifying glass, and read about ingenious and courageous efforts—big and small—to hide local Jews from the Germans and undermine the Nazi regime.

Cost and Hours: €10 includes audioguide; Tue-Fri 10:00-17:00, Sat-Mon 11:00-17:00, English descriptions, no flash photos, mandatory and free bag check, tram #9 from station or #14 from Dam Square, Plantage Kerklaan 61, tel. 020/620-2535, www.verzetsmuseum.org.

Visiting the Museum: The museum does a good job of presenting the Dutch people's struggle with a timeless moral dilemma:

Is it better to collaborate with a wicked system to effect small-scale change—or to resist outright, even if your efforts are doomed to fail? You'll learn why some parts of Dutch society opted for the former, and others for the latter. While proudly describing acts of extraordinary courage, it doesn't shy away from the less heroic side of the story (for example, the fact that most of the population, though troubled by the persecution of their Jewish countrymen, only became actively anti-Nazi after gentile Dutch men were deported to forced-labor camps). The exhibit is interspersed with riveting first-person accounts of what it was like to go underground, strike, starve, or return from the camps—with every tragic detail translated into English. And its excellent children's section (described on page 231) tells the story of four children who lived through the horrors of war.

The first dozen displays set the stage, showing peaceful, upright Dutch people of the 1930s living oblivious to the rise of fascism. Then—bam—it's May of 1940 and the Germans invade the Netherlands, pummel Rotterdam, drive Queen Wilhelmina into exile, and—in four short days of fighting—hammer home the message that resistance is futile. The Germans install local Dutch Nazis in power (the "NSB"), led by Anton Mussert.

Next, in the corner of the exhibition area, push a button to see photos of the event that first mobilized organized resistance. In February of 1941, Nazis start rounding up Jews from the neighborhood, killing nine protesters. Amsterdammers respond by shutting down the trams, schools, and businesses in a massive two-day strike. (This heroic gesture is honored today with a statue of a striking dockworker on the square called Jonas Daniel Meyerplein, where Jews were rounded up.) The next display makes it clear that this brave strike did little to save 100,000 Jews from extermination.

Turning the corner into the main room, you'll see numerous exhibits on Nazi rule (on topics including ID cards, propaganda, and the segregation of Jews) and the many forms of Dutch resistance: vandals turning Nazi V-for-Victory posters into W-for-Wilhelmina, preachers giving pointed sermons, schoolkids telling "Kraut" jokes, printers distributing underground newspapers (such as *Het Parool,* which became a major daily paper), counterfeiters forging documents, and ordinary people hiding radios under floorboards and Jews inside closets. As the war progresses, the armed Dutch Resistance becomes bolder and more violent, killing German occupiers and Dutch collaborators. In September of 1944, the Allies liberate Antwerp, and the Netherlands starts celebrating... too soon. The Nazis dig in and punish the country by cutting off rations, plunging West Holland into the "Hunger Winter" of 1944 to 1945, during which 20,000 die. Finally, it's springtime. The Allies liberate the country, and at war's end, Nazi helmets are turned into Dutch bedpans.

▲Tropical Museum (Tropenmuseum)

As close to the Third World as you'll get without lots of vaccinations, this imaginative museum offers wonderful re-creations of tropical life and explanations of Third World problems (largely created by Dutch colonialism and the slave trade). Ride the elevator to the top floor, and circle your way down through this immense collection, opened in 1926 to give the Dutch people a peek at their vast colonial holdings. Don't miss the display case where you can see and hear the world's most exotic musical instruments. The Ekeko cafeteria serves tropical food.

Cost and Hours: €12.50, Tue-Sun 10:00-17:00, closed Mon, tram #9 to Linnaeusstraat 2, tel. 020/568-8200, www.tropenmuseum.nl.

AMSTERDAM CITY WALK

From Central Station to Leidseplein (near the Rijksmuseum)

Amsterdam today looks much as it did in its Golden Age, the 1600s. It's a retired sea captain of a city, still in love with life, with a broad outlook and a salty story to tell.

Take a Dutch sampler walk from one end of the old center to the other, tasting all that Amsterdam has to offer along the way. It's your best single stroll through quintessentially Dutch scenes, hidden churches, surprising shops, thriving happy-hour hangouts, and eight centuries of history.

Orientation

Length of This Walk: Allow three hours.

When to Go: The walk is best during the day, when churches and sights are open.

Alert: Beware of silent transport—trams and bikes. Walkers should stay off the tram tracks and bike paths, and yield to bell-ringing bikers.

WCs: You can find public toilets at fast-food places (generally €0.50) and near the entrance to the Amsterdam Museum.

Royal Palace: €10, includes audioguide, daily 11:00-17:00 but often closed for official business, last entry 30 minutes before closing.

New Church: Free to view from gift-shop balcony, interior with special exhibits-€8-15, audioguide-€3, daily 10:00-17:00.

De Papegaai Hidden Church: Free, daily 10:00-16:00.

Civic Guards Gallery: Free, daily 10:00-17:00.

Amsterdam Museum: €11, one-hour audioguide-€4, daily 10:00-17:00.

Begijnhof: Free, open to visitors daily 8:00-17:00.

Accommodating the Amsterdam of the Future

For years now, anyone arriving to this grand city by train has been met by a cacophony of construction chaos, as the city works to extend its metro system. It's proven to be a huge challenge: Workers must tunnel under ancient buildings—which stand on pilings driven centuries ago into the mud below the city—without unsettling everything. While the project is now scheduled to wrap up in 2017, Amsterdammers are skeptical. The whole thing got underway in the "Golden '90s," when the economic climate was much sunnier than now. Since then the project has been riddled with delays, and many think it's bleeding the city economically. But most realize that the city's infrastructure needs to accommodate the tens of thousands of people living in North Amsterdam, the fast-growing suburb beyond the IJ. (The city is also planning a new bus hub across the IJ that'll serve destinations in northern Netherlands, hopefully moving congestion away from the Central Station area.)

If you're into engineering and/or urban design, pop into the **North-South Line Information Center**, where you'll learn about the 85-yard-long "mole" that's chewing a 23-foot-wide tunnel, and the futuristic vision for the station district (free; Wed, Fri, and Sun 12:00-16:00; otherwise closed; on the left as you leave the station, look for the blue-and-red sign next to MacBike; www.hierzijnwij.nu).

Rijksmuseum: €17.50, audioguide-€5, daily 9:00-17:00, last entry 30 minutes before closing.

Van Gogh Museum: €15, more for special exhibits, audioguide-€5, kids' audioguide-€2.50, daily March-Aug 9:00-18:00, Fri until 22:00; Sept-Feb 9:00-17:00, Fri until 22:00.

Audio Tour: You can download this chapter as a free Rick Steves audio tour (see page 10).

OVERVIEW

This walk starts at the central-as-can-be Central Station, and ends at Leidseplein, near the Rijksmuseum. The train station and art museum—designed by the same architect—stand like bookends holding the old town together. You'll walk about three miles, heading down Damrak to Dam Square, continuing south down Kalverstraat to the Mint Tower (Munttoren), then wafting through the flower market (Bloemenmarkt), before continuing south to Leidseplein. The route basically follows the central tramline, so to zip from any spot to anywhere else, simply hop on tram #1, #2, or #5. Trams #2 and #5 continue to the Rijksmuseum (and Van Gogh Museum).

The Walk Begins

❶ Central Station

Here, where today's train travelers enter the city, sailors of yore disembarked from seagoing ships. They were met by street musicians,

pickpockets, hotel-runners, and ladies carrying red lanterns. Central Station, built in the late 1800s, sits on reclaimed land at what was once the harbor mouth. The station, with warm red brick and prickly spires, is the first of several Neo-Gothic buildings we'll see from the late 1800s, built during Amsterdam's economic revival. One of the towers has a clock dial; the other tower's dial is a weather vane. Watch the hand twitch as the wind gusts in every direction—N, Z, O, and W.

Let's get oriented: *nord, zuid, ost,* and *vest.* Facing the station, you're facing north. Farther north, on the other side of the station, is the IJ (pronounced "eye"), the body of water that gives Amsterdam access to the open sea.

Now turn around 180 degrees and, with your back to the station, face the city, looking south. The city spreads out before you like a fan, in a series of concentric canals. Ahead of you stretches the street called Damrak, which leads to Dam Square a half-mile away. That's where we'll be heading.

To the left of Damrak is the city's old *(oude)* town. More recently, that historic neighborhood has become the Red Light District (for a tour of that neighborhood, ❍ see the Red Light District Walk chapter). The big church towering above the old part of town is St. Nicholas Church. It was built in the 1880s, when Catholics—after about three centuries of oppression—were finally free to worship in public. To your far left is the DoubleTree by Hilton Hotel, with its 11th-floor Sky Lounge Amsterdam offering perhaps the city's best viewpoint.

To the right of Damrak is the new *(nieuwe)* part of town, where you'll find the Anne Frank House and the peaceful Jordaan neighborhood.

The train station is the city's transportation hub. Many trams and taxis leave from out front. Beneath your feet are the beginnings of a new arm of the city's metro; as you can see, the mess from the construction has spilled above ground (see sidebar). Across the street from the station is the city's main TI, marked by the *VVV* sign.

On your far right, in front of Ibis Hotel, is a huge, multistory

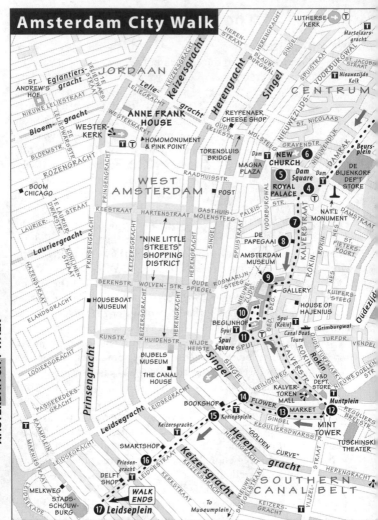

Amsterdam City Walk

parking garage. This is for bikes only. Biking in Holland is the way to go—the land is flat, distances are short, and there are designated bike paths everywhere. This bike parking garage is completely free, courtesy of the government, and intended to encourage this green and ultra-efficient mode of transportation.

• *Let's head out. With your back to Central Station, start walking south from the station into the city, to the head of Damrak.*

   Again, be careful crossing the street. Be aware of trams, bikes, and cars. When you reach the head of Damrak, keep going south straight along the right side of the street, following the crowds on...

To big Hotel & Bike Garage

Central Station · Stationsplein

CENTRAL STATION · **1**

WALK BEGINS

To IJ (Channel)

To Cruise Terminal

DE RUIJTERKADE

SKY LOUNGE AMSTERDAM

DAMRAK SEX MUSEUM · **2**

Z. PRINS HENDRIKKADE

WEEPERS' TOWER

ST. NICHOLAS

OOSTERDOKSSTR.

CENTRAL LIBRARY (OPENBARE BIBLIOTEEK AMSTERDAM)

Damrak

NIEUWEBRUGSTEEG

OUDEZIJDS KOLK

OOSTERDOKSKADE

KROMME WAAL

PRINS HENDRIKKADE

NEMO (SCIENCE MUSEUM)

STOCK EXCHANGE (BEURS) · **3**

LANGE NIEZEL

AMSTELKRING MUSEUM

GELDERSEKADE

STORMSTEEG

Oosterdok

WARMOESSTR.

OLD CHURCH

Voorburgwal

EROTIC MUSEUM

MOLEN

ST. ANNEN- STR.

RED LIGHT DISTRICT

BLOED- STR.

DE WAAG

Nieuwmarkt

Nieuwmarkt

HASH MUSEUM

Oudezijds

STOOF

BARNDESTEEG

KOESTRAAT

BETH. STR.

ST. ANTONIESBREESTR.

chterburgwal

HOOGSTR.

Kloveniersburgwal

RUSLAND

RAAMGRACHT

AMST. UNIVERSITY

REMBRANDT'S HOUSE

FLEA MARKET

GASSAN DIAMONDS

MOSES & AARON CHURCH

VALKENBURGER- STRAAT

SOUTHEAST AMSTERDAM

STR.

STAALSTR.

STAALKADE

Waterlooplein

OPERA HOUSE

Meester Visserplein

Waterlooplein

PORTUGUESE SYNAGOGUE

Jonas Daniel Meijerplein

BLUYSPAD

MIDDENLAAN

Amstel

AMSTEL

Canal Boat Tours

NIEUWE AMSTELSTRAAT

JEWISH HIST. MUSEUM

DOCK WORKER STATUE

De Hortus Botanical Garden

DUTCH THEATER

HALVEMAAN

BAKKERS STRAAT

AMSTEL

BLAUW BRUG

Rembrandtplein

AMSTELSTRAAT

WILLET- HOLTHUYSEN MUSEUM

DRAW- BRIDGE

HERMITAGE AMSTERDAM

NIEUWE HERENGRACHT

HORTUSPLANTSOEN

PLANTAGE MUIDERGRACHT

TASSEN MUSEUM

UTRECHTSESTRAAT

HERENGRACHT

Amstel

KEIZERSGRACHT

NIEUWE Nieuwe

KEIZERSGRACHT

WEESPERSTR.

KEIZERSGRACHT

200 Meters

200 Yards

1	Central Station
2	Damrak
3	Stock Exchange
4	Dam Square
5	Royal Palace
6	New Church
7	Kalverstraat
8	De Papegaai Hidden Church
9	Amsterdam Museum & Civic Guard Gallery
10	Begijnhof
11	Spui Square
12	Mint Tower
13	Flower Market
14	Koningsplein
15	Leidsestraat Canals
16	Shops
17	Leidseplein

❷ Damrak

This street was once a riverbed. It's where the Amstel River flowed north into the IJ, which led to a vast inlet of the North Sea called the Zuiderzee. It's this unique geography that turned Amsterdam into a center of trade. Boats could sail up the Amstel into the interior of Europe, or out to the North Sea, to reach the rest of the world.

As you stroll along Damrak, look left. There's a marina, lined with old brick buildings. Though these aren't terribly historic buildings, the scene still captures a bit of Golden Age Amsterdam.

Think of it: Back in the 1600s, this area was the harbor, and those buildings warehoused exotic goods from all over the world.

All along Damrak, you'll pass a veritable gauntlet of touristy shops. These seem to cover every Dutch cliché. You'll see wooden shoes, which the Dutch used to wear to get around easily in the marshy soil, and all manner of tulips; the real ones come from Holland's famed fresh-flower industry. Heineken fridge magnets advertise one of the world's most popular pilsner beers. You'll likely hear a hand-cranked barrel organ and see windmill-shaped saltshakers. And everything seems to be available in bright orange—because that's the official color of the Dutch royal family.

At the **Damrak Sex Museum** at Damrak 18, you'll find the city's most notorious commodity on display (described on page 66). As a port town catering to sailors and businessmen away from home, Amsterdam has always accommodated the sex trade.

Continue up Damrak (noting the **canal boats** on your right—see page 44) for more touristy delectables. Teasers (at #36) is the local Hooters. You'll also pass places selling the popular local fast food: french fries. Here they're called *Vlaamse friets* (Flemish fries), since they were invented in the Low Countries. The stand at Damrak 41 is a favorite. Locals dip their fries in mayonnaise, not ketchup.

All along Damrak, you'll pass many restaurants. It quickly becomes obvious that, here in cosmopolitan Amsterdam, international cuisine is almost like going local. Indonesian restaurants are especially popular, since that was a former Dutch colony. Here you can order *rijsttafel*, a sampler assortment of Indonesian dishes that's big enough for two. Also popular in Amsterdam are Argentinian steak houses. Amsterdammers on the go usually just grab a simple sandwich, called a *broodje* (BRODE-juh), or a pita-bread wrap, such as a *shoarma*, from a Middle Eastern take-out joint.

We're walking along what was once the Amstel River. Today, the Amstel is channeled into canals and its former mouth is covered by the Central Station. But Amsterdam still remains a major seaport. That's because, in the 19th century, the Dutch dug the North Sea Canal. These days, more than 100,000 ships a year dock on the outskirts of Amsterdam, making it Europe's fourth-busiest seaport (and those giant cruise ships have begun stopping here as well). For all of Amsterdam's existence, it's been a trading center.

• *The long brick building with the square clock tower, along the left side of Damrak, is the...*

❸ Stock Exchange (Beurs van Berlage)

This impressive structure, a symbol of the city's long tradition as a trading town, was built with nine million bricks. Like so many

buildings in this once-marshy city, it was constructed on a foundation of pilings—some 5,000 tree trunks hammered vertically into the soil. When the Beurs opened in 1903, it was one of the world's first modernist buildings, with a geometric, minimal, no-frills style. Emphasizing function over looks, it helped set the architectural tone for many 20th-century buildings.

Continuing along Damrak, make your way to the end of the long building. Though it's only a century old, Amsterdammers have gathered in this neighborhood to trade since medieval times. Back then, "trading stock" meant buying and selling any kind of goods that could be loaded and unloaded onto a boat—goats, chickens, or kegs of beer. Over time, they began exchanging slips of paper, or "futures," rather than actual goods. Traders needed moneychangers, who needed bankers, who made money by lending money. By the 1600s, Amsterdam had become one of the world's first great capitalist cities, loaning money to free-spending kings, dukes, and bishops.

When you reach the end of the building, detour left into the square called **Beursplein.** In 1984, the Beurs building was turned into a cultural center, and the stock exchange moved next door to the Euronext complex—a joint attempt by France, Belgium, and the Netherlands to compete with the power of Britain's stock exchange. See the stock price readout board. How's your Heineken stock doing? Green means it's going up, and red means it's losing value. Amsterdam still thrives as the center of Dutch business and is home to Heineken, Shell Oil, Philips Electronics, and Unilever.

Before leaving Beursplein, drop into **Café Beurs** and take in its minimalist 1930s interior. The optimistic art heralds a new age of worker-empowering technology, social democracy, and a hope for peace. It's also a nice place for a break.

• *Return to Damrak, and continue south along the busy boulevard until it opens into Dam Square. Make your way—carefully—across the street to the cobblestone pavement. Now, stand in the middle of the square and take it all in.*

Amsterdam's Story

Visualize the physical layout of this man-made city: built on trees, protected by dikes, and laced with canals in the marshy delta at the mouth of the Amstel River. Location, location, location. Boats could arrive here from Germany by riverboat down the Rhine, from England across the Channel and down the IJ, and from Denmark by entering the Zuiderzee inlet of the North Sea. No wonder that St. Nicholas, protector of water travelers, was the city's patron saint.

As early as 1300, Amsterdam was already an international trade center of German beer, locally caught herring, cloth, bacon, salt, and wine. Having dammed and canalized the Amstel and diked out the sea tides, the Dutch drained land, sunk pilings, and built a city from scratch. When the region's leading bishop granted the town a charter (1300), Amsterdammers could then set up law courts, judge their own matters, and be essentially autonomous. The town thrived.

By 1500, Amsterdam was a walled city of 12,000, with the Singel canal serving as the moat. The city had a midcentury growth spurt when its trading rival Antwerp fell to Spanish troops, and a flood of fellow Flemish headed north, fleeing chaos and religious persecution.

In 1602, hardy Dutch sailors (and Englishman Henry Hudson) tried their hand at trade with the Far East. When they returned, they brought with them valuable spices, jewels, luxury goods...and the Golden Age.

The Dutch East India Company (abbreviated as "VOC" in Dutch), a state-subsidized import/export business, combined nautical skills with capitalist investing. With 500 or so 150-foot ships cruising in and out of Amsterdam's harbor, it was the first great multinational corporation. Amsterdam's Golden Age (c. 1600-1650) rode the wave of hard work and good fortune. Over the next two centuries, the VOC would send a half-million Dutch people on

❹ Dam Square

This is the historic heart of Amsterdam. The city got its start right here in about the year 1250, when fishermen in this marshy delta settled along the built-up banks of the Amstel River. They built a *damme*, blocking the Amstel River, and creating a small village called "Amstel-damme." To the north was the *damrak* (meaning "outer harbor"), a waterway that eventually led to the sea. That's the street we just walked. To the south was the *rokin* (roh-KEEN,

business trips to Asia, broadening their horizons.

This city of the Golden Age was perhaps the wealthiest on earth, thriving as the "warehouse of the world." Goods came from everywhere. The VOC's specialties were spices (pepper and cinnamon), coffee and tea, Chinese porcelain (Delftware's Eastern inspiration), and silk. Meanwhile, the competing Dutch West India Company concentrated on the New World, trading African slaves for South American sugar. With its wealth, Amsterdam built in grand style, erecting the gabled townhouses we see today. The city expanded west and south, adding new neighborhoods.

But by 1650, Amsterdam's overseas trade was being eclipsed by new superpowers—England and France. Inconclusive wars with Louis XIV and England drained the economy, destroyed the trading fleet, and demoralized the people. Throughout the 1700s, Amsterdam was a city of backwater bankers rather than international traders, although it remained the cultural center of Holland. In early 1795, Napoleon's French troops occupied the country, and the economy was dismal.

A revival in the 1800s was spurred by technological achievements. The Dutch built a canal reconnecting Amsterdam directly with the North Sea (1824-1876), railroads laced the small country, and the city expanded southward by draining new land. The Rijksmuseum, Central Station, and Magna Plaza were built as proud monuments to the economic upswing.

The 1930s Depression hit hard, followed by five years of occupation under the Nazis, aided by pro-Nazi Dutch. The city's large Jewish population was decimated by Nazi deportations and extermination (falling from about 80,000 Jews in 1940 to just 16,000 in 1945).

With postwar prosperity, 1960s Amsterdam again became a world cultural capital as the center for Europe's hippies, who came here to smoke marijuana. Grassroots campaigns by young, artistic, politically active people promoted free sex and free bikes.

Today, Amsterdam is a city of 820,000 people jammed into small apartments (often with the same floor plan as their neighbors'). Since the 1970s, many immigrants have become locals. One in 10 Amsterdammers is Surinamese, and one in 10 prays toward Mecca.

AMSTERDAM CITY WALK

"inner harbor"), for river traffic. Nowadays, the Rokin is also a main street. With access to the sea, the fishermen were soon trading with German riverboats traveling downstream and with seafaring boats from Stockholm, Hamburg, and London. Land trade routes converged here as well, and a customs house stood in this spot. Dam Square was the center of it all.

Today, Dam Square is still the center of Dutch life, at least symbolically. The Royal Palace and major department stores face the square. Mimes, jugglers, and human statues mingle with locals and tourists. As Holland's most recognizable place, Dam Square is where political demonstrations begin and end.

Circling the Square: Pan the square clockwise, and take in the sights, starting with the Royal Palace—the large domed building on the west side. To its right stands the New Church (Nieuwe Kerk); it's located on the pedestrian-only shopping street called Nieuwendijk, which runs parallel to Damrak and stretches all the way to Central Station. Panning past Damrak, see the proud old De Bijenkorf ("The Beehive") department store. The store's cafeteria on the top floor is a great place to rise above it all for a light meal and pleasant views (see page 206).

Farther right, the Grand Hotel Krasnapolsky has a lovely circa-1900 Winter Garden. The white obelisk is the National Monument. A few blocks behind the hotel is the edge of the Red Light District. To the right of the hotel stretches the street called the Nes, lined with some of Amsterdam's edgy live-theater venues. Panning farther right, find Rokin street—Damrak's southern counterpart, continuing past the square. Next, just to the right of the touristy Madame Tussauds, is Kalverstraat, a busy pedestrian-only shoppers mall (look for *Rabobank* sign).

❺ Royal Palace (Koninklijk Huis)

Despite the name, this is really the former City Hall—and Amsterdam is one of the cradles of modern democracy. In medieval times, this was where the city council and mayor met. Amsterdam was a self-governing community that prided itself on its independence and thumbed its nose at royalty. In about 1650, the old medieval town hall was replaced with this one. Its style is appropriately Classical, recalling the democratic Greeks. The triangular

pediment features denizens of the sea cavorting with Neptune and his gilded copper trident—all appropriate imagery for sea-trading Amsterdam.

Today, the palace remains one of the four official residences of King Willem-Alexander and is usually open to visitors (see page 62).

• *A few paces away, to the right as you're facing the Royal Palace, is the...*

❻ New Church (Nieuwe Kerk)

Though called the "New" Church, this building is actually 600 years old—a mere 100 years newer than the "Old" Church in the Red Light District. The sundial above the entrance once served as the city's official timepiece.

While it's pricey to enter the church (which offers little besides the temporary exhibits), cheapskates can actually see much of the church for free. Enter the gift shop (through the "Museumshop" door to the left of the main church entrance), and climb the stairs to a balcony with a small free museum and great views of the nave.

The church's bare, spacious, well-lit interior (occupied by a new art exhibit every three months) looks quite different from the Baroque-encrusted churches found in the rest of Europe. In 1566, clear-eyed Protestant extremists throughout Holland marched into Catholic churches (including this one), lopped off the heads of holy statues, stripped gold-leaf angels from the walls, urinated on Virgin Marys, and shattered stained-glass windows in a wave of anti-Catholic vandalism.

This iconoclasm (icon-breaking) of 1566 started an 80-year war against Spain and the Habsburgs, leading finally to Dutch independence in 1648. Catholic churches like this one were converted to the new dominant religion, Calvinist Protestantism (today's Dutch Reformed Church). From then on, Dutch churches downplayed the "graven images" and "idols" of ornate religious art.

Take in the church's main highlights. At the far left end is an organ from 1655, still played for midday concerts. Opposite the entrance, a stained-glass window shows Count William IV giving the city its "XXX" coat of arms. And the window over the entrance portrays the inauguration of Queen Wilhelmina, who became the steadfast center of the Dutch Resistance during World War II. The choir, once used by the monks, was, after the Reformation, turned into a mausoleum for a great Dutch admiral.

This church is where many of the Netherlands' monarchs are married, and all are "inaugurated." (Dutch royals never actually wear the official crown.) While on the viewing balcony, imagine the church in action in April of 2013, when King Willem-Alexander—Wilhelmina's great-grandson—was paraded through this church to the golden choir screen. (There may be a video of this.) The king, wearing a tuxedo with an orange sash, is presented with the royal crown, scepter, orb, sword, and a copy of the Dutch constitution. With TV lights glaring and cameras flashing, he is sworn in as the new sovereign. He stands at the church altar with his wife by his side and addresses the assembled throngs. They announce "Long live the king!" (in Dutch), and the new king marches out and across Dam Square, waving to his happy subjects.

Leave the shop via the main church entrance. On your way out, look up to see stained-glass windows showing Dutch royals from 1579 to 1898.

Back outside, look at the **monument** standing tall in the middle of Dam Square. This white obelisk was built in 1956 as a WWII memorial. The Nazis occupied Holland from 1940 to 1945; in those years they deported 100,000 Jewish Amsterdammers, driving many—including young Anne Frank and her family—into hiding. Near the end of the war, the "Hunger Winter" of 1944-1945 killed thousands of Dutch and forced many to survive on little more than tulip bulbs. The national monument—with its carvings of the crucified Christ, men in chains, and howling dogs—remembers the suffering of that grim time. Now the structure is also considered a monument for peace.

• *From Dam Square, head south (at the* Rabobank *sign) on...*

❼ Kalverstraat

Kalverstraat (strictly pedestrian-only—even bikers need to dismount and walk) has been a traditional shopping street for cen-

turies. But today it's notorious among locals as a noisy, soulless string of chain stores. For smaller and more elegant stores, try the adjacent district called De Negen Straatjes ("The Nine Little Streets"). Only about four blocks west of Kalverstraat, it's where 200 or so shops and cafés mingle along tranquil canals.

• *About 100 yards along, keep a sharp eye out for the next sight (it's fairly easy to miss): On the right, just before and across from the McDonald's, at #58. Now pop into...*

❽ De Papegaai Hidden Church (Petrus en Paulus Kerk)

This Catholic church—with a simple white interior, nice carved

---

City on a Sandbar

Amsterdam sits in the marshy delta at the mouth of the Amstel River—a completely man-made city, built on millions of wooden pilings. The city was founded on unstable mud, which sits on stable sand. In the Middle Ages, buildings were made of wood, which rests lightly and easily on mud. But devastating fires repeatedly wiped out entire neighborhoods, so stone became the building material of choice. Brick is fire resistant, but was too heavy for a mud foundation, so for more support, pilings were driven 30 feet through the soggy soil and into the sand. The Royal Palace sits upon 13,000 such pilings—still solid after 350 years. (The wood survives if kept wet and out of the air.)

Since World War II, concrete, rather than wood, has been used for the pilings, with foundations driven 60 feet deep through the first layer of sand, through more mud, and into a second layer of sand. Today's biggest buildings have foundations that go down as much as 120 feet deep.

Many of the city's buildings, however, tend to lean this way and that as their pilings settle—and local landowners are concerned that the tunneling for the now metro line will cause their buildings to tilt even further. The snoopy-looking white cameras mounted on various building corners (such as on the Beurs) are monitoring buildings to check for settling.

wood, and Stations of the Cross paintings (try reading the Dutch captions)—is an oasis of peace amid crass 21st-century commercialism. It's not exactly a hidden church (after all, you've found it), but it still keeps a low profile. That's because it dates from an era when Catholics in Amsterdam were forced to worship in secret.

In the 1500s, Protestants were fighting Catholics all over Europe. As a center for trade, Amsterdam has long made an effort to put business above ideological differences, doing business with all parties. But by 1578 the division had become too wide to straddle, and Protestant extremists took political control of the city. They expelled Catholic leaders and bishops and outlawed the religion. Catholic churches were stripped of their lavish decoration and converted into Dutch Reformed churches. Simultaneously, the Dutch were rising up politically against their (Catholic) Spanish overlords, and eventually threw them out.

For the next two centuries, Amsterdam's Catholics were driven underground. While technically illegal here, Catholicism was tolerated (kind of like marijuana is, these days). Catholics could worship so long as they practiced in humble, unadvertised places, like this church. The church gets its nickname from a parrot *(papegaai)* carved over the entrance of the house that formerly stood on this site. Now, a stuffed parrot hangs in the nave to remember that original *papegaai*.

Today, the church asks visitors for a mere "15 minutes for God" (so says the sign: *een kwartier voor God*)—an indication of how religion has long been a marginal part of highly commercial and secular Amsterdam.

• *Return to Kalverstraat and continue south for about 100 yards. At #92, where Kalverstraat crosses Wijde Kapel Steeg, look to the right at an archway that leads to the entrance and courtyard of the Amsterdam Museum.*

❾ Amsterdam Museum and Civic Guard Gallery

Pause at the entrance to the museum complex to view the archway. On the slumping arch is Amsterdam's coat of arms—a red shield with three Xs and a crown. The X-shaped crosses represent the crucifixion of St. Andrew, the patron saint of fishermen. (And here you thought the three Xs referred to the city's sex trade.) They also represent the three virtues of heroism, determination, and mercy—symbolism that was declared by the queen after the Dutch experience in World War II. (Before that, they likely symbolized the three great medieval threats: fire, flood, and plague.) The crown dates from 1489, when Maximilian I—a Habsburg emperor—also ruled the Low Countries. He paid off a big loan with help from Amsterdam's city bankers and, as thanks for the cash, gave the city permission to use his prestigious trademark, the Habsburg crown, atop its shield.

Now check out the relief above the door, dated 1581. It shows boys around a dove, asking for charity, reminding all who pass that this building was once an orphanage. People would donate by putting a coin in the slot of a donation box (find the bronze, nipple-crowned box on the sidewalk).

Go inside. The pleasant café has a shaded courtyard with a pay toilet, and old lockers for the orphans' uniforms. The exhibit here helps you imagine life in the orphanage through the centuries.

The courtyard leads to the best city history museum in town, the **Amsterdam Museum** (described on page 65). Next to the museum's entrance is a free, glassed-in passageway lined with paintings. If it's closed, you'll need to backtrack to Kalverstraat to continue our walk (continue south, then turn right on Begijnensteeg, then look for the gate leading to the Begijnhof). Otherwise, step into the **Civic Guard Gallery** (Schuttersgalerij).

This hall features group portraits of Amsterdam's citizens, from the Golden Age to modern times. Giant statues of Goliath

and a knee-high David (from 1650) watch over the whole thing. Civic Guard paintings from the 1600s (featuring men and their weapons) established a tradition of group portraits that continues today.

Stroll around and gaze into the eyes of the hardworking men and women who made tiny Holland so prosperous and powerful. These are ordinary middle-class people, merchants, and traders, dressed in their Sunday best. They come across as good people—honest, businesslike, and friendly.

The Dutch got rich the old-fashioned way—they earned it. Dutch fishermen sold their surplus catch in distant areas of Europe, importing goods from these far lands. In time, fishermen became traders, and by 1600, Holland's merchant fleets ruled the waves. They had colonies as far away as India, Indonesia, and America (remember—New York was originally "New Amsterdam"). Back home, these traders were financed by shrewd Amsterdam businessmen on the new frontiers of capitalism. These people are clearly proud of their accomplishments.

The portraits show the men gathered with their Civic Guard militia units. These men defended Holland, but the Civic Guards were also fraternal organizations of business bigwigs—the Rotary Clubs of the 17th century. The weapons they carry—pikes and muskets—are mostly symbolic.

Many paintings look the same in this highly stylized genre. The men usually sit arranged in two rows. Someone holds the militia's flag. Later group portraits showed "captains" of industry going about their work, dressed in suits, along with the tools of their trade—ledger books, quill pens, and money.

Everyone looks straight out, and every face is lit perfectly. Each paid for his own portrait and wanted it right. It took masters like Rembrandt and Frans Hals to take the starch out of the collars and compose more natural scenes.

Now focus on some more modern portraits. They show today's city leaders, posing playfully as Golden Age bigwigs.

And don't miss the colorful patchwork carpet. Dutch society has long been a melting pot society and this—with a patch representing each country from where Dutch immigrants originated—

The Pilgrims in Holland

The Pilgrims—a group of English Protestants—split from England's Anglican Church in the early 1600s. They believed the Church hadn't gone far enough in its break from medieval Catholicism. This was highly illegal under English law. These "Separatists" (as they were called) were thrown in prison, persecuted, and fined.

In 1609, the Separatists decided to flee increasingly hostile England for the relatively tolerant Holland. But emigrating without permission was illegal. On their first attempt (in 1607), several were arrested, including the young William Bradford (who later became governor of the Plymouth Colony). Trying again (1608), they were betrayed by the ship's captain.

Finally, in 1609, they succeeded, landing in the safe harbor of **Amsterdam**. The Separatists lived in Amsterdam for a year, worshipping with fellow English ex-pats in (today's) English Reformed Church in the Begijnhof. Then they relocated south to **Leiden**, where they lived for more than a decade, making their homes near St. Peter's Church (see page 381.)

While in Leiden, Separatist leader William Brewster (who later wrote the Mayflower Compact—the document that governed the Plymouth Colony and a forerunner to the US Constitution) began publishing religious tracts and smuggling them back to England. Under pressure from England, the Dutch authorities arrested Brewster. Holland was no longer safe. Compounding things, the Separatists were having trouble finding work in Leiden's textile trade, and they worried that Holland would soon

celebrates today's multicultural reality. (A chart locates the various countries.)

• *The gallery offers a shortcut to our next stop, a hidden and peaceful little courtyard. To get there, exit out the far end of the Civic Guards Gallery. Once in the light of day, continue ahead one block farther south and find the humble gate on the right, which leads to the...*

⑩ Begijnhof

As you enter, keep in mind that this spot isn't just a tourist attraction; it's also a place where people live. Be considerate: Don't photograph the residents or their homes, and if you're here in the evening, be quiet and stick to the area near the churches.

This quiet courtyard, lined with houses around a church, has sheltered women since 1346 (and is

be at war with Spain. They decided they needed a fresh start—in America.

The cash-poor Separatists borrowed money from English investors, in return for whatever furs, timber, or other goods they could send back. Only the young and strong from the congregation would make the first journey, with the rest to follow once a colony was established. In the summer of 1620, they traveled to **Delfshaven** (near Rotterdam—see page 413). There they said their good-byes to loved ones, boarded a small ship called the *Speedwell*, and sailed to England. Once there, they met up with other colonists, recruited by the investors. So it was that on September 16, 1620, 102 passengers set sail from Plymouth (on England's south coast) and traveled across the Atlantic on their new, larger ship—the *Mayflower*.

After an arduous crossing, the *Mayflower* arrived in what is now Plymouth Harbor, Massachusetts on December 16, 1620. The rest is (grade-school) history: the Mayflower Compact, hardships and the first Thanksgiving, and the eventual success of the Plymouth Colony.

Governor William Bradford remembered the group's sad departure from Holland: "With mutual embraces and many tears, they took their leaves of one another, which proved to be the last leave to many of them...But they knew they were pilgrims." Over time, Bradford's words gave these brave people the name we know them by today—Pilgrims.

quite a contrast with the noisy Kalverstraat just steps away). This was for centuries the home of a community of Beguines—pious and simple women who removed themselves from the world at large to dedicate their lives to God. When it was first established, it literally was a "woman's island"—a circle of houses facing a peaceful courtyard, surrounded by water.

Begin your visit at the **statue** of one of these charitable sisters. You'll find it just beyond the church. The Beguines' ranks swelled during the Crusades, when so many men took off, never to return, leaving society with an abundance of single women. Later, women widowed by the hazards of overseas trade lived out their days as Beguines. Poor and rich women alike turned their backs on materialism and marriage to live here in Christian poverty. And though obedient to a mother superior, the members of the lay order of Beguines were not nuns. The Beguines were very popular in their communities for the lives they led—unpretentious, simple, with a Christ-like dedication to serving others. They spent their days deep in prayer and busy with daily tasks—spinning wool, making lace, teaching, and caring for the sick. In quiet seclusion, they provided a striking contrast to the more decadent and corrupt Roman Church, inspiring one another as well as their neighbors.

Now turn your attention to the brick-faced **English Reformed**

church (Engelse Kerk). The church was built in 1420 to serve the Beguine community. But then, in 1578, Catholicism was outlawed, and the Dutch Reformed Church took over many Catholic monasteries. Still, the Begijnhof survived; in 1607, this church became Anglican. The church served as a refuge for English traders and religious separatists fleeing persecution in England. Strict Protestants such as the famous Pilgrims found sanctuary in tolerant Amsterdam and worshipped in this church. They later moved to Leiden, where they lived for a decade before sailing to religious freedom in America (see sidebar). If the church is open, step inside, and head to the far end, toward the stained-glass window. It shows the Pilgrims praying before boarding the Mayflower. Along the right-hand wall is an old pew they may have sat on, and on the altar is a Bible from 1763, with lot∫of old-∫tyle ∫'s.

Back outside, find the **Catholic church,** which faces the English Reformed Church. Because Catholics were being persecuted when it was built, this had to be a low-profile, "hidden" church—notice the painted-out windows on the second and third floors. Step inside, through the low-profile doorway; you can pick up an English brochure near the entry. This church served Amsterdam's oppressed 17th-century Catholics, who refused to worship as Protestants. It's decorated lovingly, if on the cheap (try tapping softly on a "marble" column). Amsterdam's Catholics must have eagerly awaited the day when they were legally allowed to say Mass (that day finally came in the 19th century).

Today, Holland still has something of a religious divide, but not a bitter one. Amsterdam itself is, like many big cities in the West, pretty un-churched. But the Dutch countryside is much more religious, including a "Bible Belt" region where 98 percent of the population is Protestant. Overall, in the Netherlands, the country is divided fairly evenly between Catholics, Protestants, and those who see Sunday as a day to sleep in and enjoy a lazy brunch.

Step back outside. The last Beguine died in 1971, but this Begijnhof still thrives, providing subsidized housing to about 100 single women (mostly Catholic seniors). The Begijnhof is just one of a few dozen *hofjes* (little housing projects surrounding courtyards) that dot Amsterdam.

The statue of the Beguine faces a black **wooden house,** at #34. This structure dates from 1528, and is the city's oldest. Originally, the whole city consisted of wooden houses like this one. They were eventually replaced with brick houses, to minimize the fire danger of having so many homes packed together.

Stroll a few steps to the left of the house to find a display of colorfully painted carved gable stones. These once adorned housefronts and served as street numbers.

• *Near the wooden house and gables, find a little corridor leading you back into the modern world. Head up a few steps to emerge into the lively...*

⓫ Spui Square

Lined with cafés and bars, this square is one of the city's more popular spots for nightlife and sunny afternoon people-watching. Its name, Spui (spow, rhymes with "now" and means "spew"), recalls the days when water was moved over dikes to keep the place dry.

Head two blocks to the left, crossing busy Kalverstraat, to the bustling street called **Rokin.** A small black statue of Queen Wilhelmina (1880-1962) on the Rokin shows her riding daintily sidesaddle. Remember that in real life, she was the iron-willed inspiration for the Dutch Resistance against the Nazis.

Canal cruises depart from the Rondvaart Kooij dock across the water, in the yellow canal house (see "Canal Boat Tours" on page 44).

Turn left on the Rokin and walk up 50 yards to the **House of Hajenius** (at Rokin 92). This temple of cigars is a "paradise for the connoisseur" showing "175 years of tradition and good taste." To enter this sumptuous Art Deco building with painted leather ceilings is to step back into 1910. Don't be shy—the place is as much a free museum for visitors as it is a store for paying customers. The brown-capped canisters (under the wall of pipes, to the right) are for smelling fine pipe tobacco. Take a whiff. Sample three, and appreciate the differences between them. The personal humidifiers (read the explanation) allow locals (famous local names are on the cupboard doors) to call in an order and have their cigars waiting for them at just the right humidity. Above the street entry, check out the humidifier pipes pumping moisture into the room. Upstairs in back is a small, free museum. As you leave, read the legal notice on the door—establishing a strict age limit and limits on promotion—no discounts and no freebies. (If you ask me, this is a good, pragmatic "legalize, tax, and regulate" approach to the sale of a soft drug.)

In front of the cigar house is a red cage offering taxpayers (and tourists) an encouraging peek at the massive north-south metro line project. Descend 80 feet into a vast cave—a future metro stop—and get a sense of the work involved as they tunnel and build deep under the city.

From here, turn right and backtrack down the Rokin, past the statue of the queen. Stay on the right side of the street until you reach **Muntplein**. On your right, where Kalverstraat hits the square, are two department stores. **Vroom & Dreesman** has basic supplies (nothing fancy) and a handy, cheap, and cheery La Place cafeteria where shoppers and hungry tourists can grab an easy meal (see page 203). The **Kalvertoren** complex, across Kalverstraat from V&D, is a modern mall. Enter and go deeper within to find a slanting glass elevator. You can ride this to the top-floor café, where a €3 coffee buys you something that's rare in altitude-challenged Amsterdam—a nice view.

• *At the center of the square stands the…*

ⓘ Mint Tower (Munttoren)

This tower marked the limit of the medieval walled city, and served as one of its original gates. In the Middle Ages, the city walls were girdled by a moat—the Singel canal. Until about 1500, the area beyond here was nothing but marshy fields and a few farms on reclaimed land. The Mint Tower's steeple was added later—in the year 1620, as you can see written below the clock face.

Today, the tower is a favorite within Amsterdam's marijuana culture. Stoners love to take a photo of the clock and its 1620 sign at exactly 4:20 p.m. (On the 24-hour clock, 4:20 p.m. is 16:20...Du-u-u-ude!)

Before moving on, look left (at about 10 o'clock) down Reguliersbreestraat. Midway down the block, the twin green domes mark the exotic **Tuschinski Theater.** Here you can see current movies (subtitled in Dutch) in a sumptuous Art Deco setting. If you like, take a quick detour to check out its lobby, and imagine this place in the Roaring '20s (see page 57). Wa-a-ay at the end of the long block (where you see trees) is **Rembrandtplein,** another major center for nightlife.

• *Continue past the Mint Tower, first walking a few yards south along busy Vijzelstraat (keep an eye out for trams). Then turn right and walk west along the south bank of the Singel canal. The canal is lined with the greenhouse shops of the...*

⓭ Flower Market (Bloemenmarkt)

The stands along this busy block sell cut flowers, plants, bulbs, seeds, and garden supplies. Browse your way along while heading for the end of the block.

The Flower Market is a testament to Holland's long-time love affair with flowers. The Netherlands is by far the largest flower exporter in Europe, and a major force worldwide. If you're looking for a souvenir, note that certain seeds are marked as OK to bring back through customs into the US (the marijuana starter-kit-in-a-can is probably...not).

For more on the history of tulips in Holland, see page 20.

• *The long Flower Market ends at the next bridge, where you'll see a square named...*

⓮ Koningsplein

This pleasant square, with a popular outdoor *heringhandel* (herring shop), is a great place to choke down a raw herring—a fish that has

a special place in every Dutch heart. After all, herring was the commodity that first put Amsterdam on the trading map. It's also what Dutch sailors ate for protein on those long cross-global voyages. Even today, it's a specialty, and locals flock to this popular place. In season you'll see the sign—*Hollandse nieuwe*—alerting locals that the herring are "new" (fresh), caught during the May-June season. They eat it chopped up with onions and pickles, using the Dutch-flag toothpick as a utensil. Elsewhere in the Netherlands, people are more likely to eat the fish whole (a.k.a. Rotterdam style)—you grab it by the tail, tip your head back, and down she goes.

• *From Koningsplein, turn left, heading straight south to Leidseplein along Leidestraat.*

Amsterdam's Canals

Amsterdam's many canals are as pretty as they are practical. The city was founded in a marshy river delta, so its citizens needed to keep the water at bay. They built a dike, near where Central Station stands today, to keep out the sea-tide surge. Then they dammed the Amstel River. The excess water was channeled safely away into canals, creating pockets of dry land to build on. They used windmills to harness wind power to pump the excess water into the canals. The canals also functioned as part of the transportation infrastructure as merchants needed to move their goods efficiently. Today, the city has about 100 canals, most of which are

about 10 feet deep. They're crossed by some 1,200 bridges, fringed with 100,000 Dutch elm and lime trees, and bedecked with 2,500 houseboats. A system of locks (back near the Central Station) controls the flow. The locks are opened periodically to flush out the system.

The word *gracht* (pronounced, roughly, "*hroh*t," with guttural flair) can refer to a canal itself, or to the ensemble of a canal and the lanes that border it on each side. A *straat* is a street without a canal, though a few paved-over canals, such as Elandsgracht, have kept their old name.

Some of the boats in the canals look pretty funky by day, but Amsterdam is an unpretentious, anti-status city. When the sun goes down and the lights come on, people cruise the sparkling canals with an on-board hibachi and a bottle of wine, and even scows can become chick-magnets.

Learn the general order of the series of watery semi-circles that radiate out from the Central Station. There are four that will matter in your city navigating: Singel (the innermost, originally the fortified medieval town's defensive moat); Herengracht (named for the aristocrats, or *heren*, who built the Dutch East India Company and with their profits, their fancy mansions along here); Keizersgracht (named for the Holy Roman Emperor and also lined with fine mansions); and Prinsengracht (less swanky, lined with old warehouses and smaller homes, the liveliest of the canals).

Memorize this sentence to help you remember the order of the canals: A Single Hairy Kaiser's Prince really knows his canals.

⑮ Leidsestraat Canals and ⑯ Shops

At first, the street is just labeled *Koningsplein*. You'll pass by Amsterdam's leading bookstore, **Selexyz Scheltema,** just before reaching the first of several grand canals, Herengracht.

Looking left down Herengracht, you'll see the so-called **"Golden Curve"** of the canal. It's lined with townhouses sporting especially nice gables. Amsterdam has many different types of gables—bell-shaped, step-shaped, and so on. This stretch is best known for its "cornice" gables (straight across); these topped the Classical-looking facades of rich merchants—the *heren*. (For more on gables, see the sidebar on page 132.)

After the bridge, Koningsplein becomes Leidsestraat. It's a busy street, crowded with shoppers, tourists, bicycles, and trams (keep your wits about you along here, and don't walk on the tram tracks). Notice that, as the street narrows, trams must wait their turn to share a single track.

Cross over the next canal (Keizersgracht), then find the little **When Nature Calls Smartshop,** on the right at Kaisersgracht 508. While "smartshops" like this one are all just as above-board as any other in the city, they sell drugs—some of them quite strong, most of them illegal back home, and not all of them harmless. But since all these products are found in nature, the Dutch government considers them legal (for more on smartshops, see page 111). You can check out the window displays, or go on in and browse.

Where Leidsestraat crosses Prinsengracht, just over the bridge on the right (at Prinsengracht 440), you'll find **The Delft Shop.** This place sells good examples of the glazed ceramics known as Delftware, famous for its distinctive blue-and-white design (see the sidebar on page 314). It's traditionally made in Delft, a quaint town about 30 miles southwest of here (and described later in this book). Dutch traders learned the technique from the Chinese of the Ming dynasty, and many pieces have an Oriental look. The doodads with arms branching off a trunk are popular "flower pagodas," vases for displaying tulips.

• *Looking left, half a block down Prinsengracht, you can see the home of the* **Pipe Museum** *(at #488; see listing on page 58). Unless you're* *detouring to visit the museum, turn right on Leidsestraat and follow it to the big, busy square, called...*

⑰ Leidseplein

This is Amsterdam's liveliest square: filled with outdoor tables under trees; ringed with cafés, theaters, and nightclubs; bustling with tourists, diners, trams, mimes, and fire-eaters. No wonder locals and tourists alike come here day and night to sit under the trees and sip a coffee or beer in the warmth of the sun or the glow of lantern light.

Do a 360-degree spin: Leidseplein's south side is bordered by the huge Apple Store—sitting on what may be the city's most expensive piece of real estate. Nearby is the city's main serious theater, the **Stadsschouwburg.** The theater company dates back to the 17th-century Golden Age, and the present building is from 1890. Does the building look familiar, with its red brick and fanciful turrets? That's because this building, along with Central Station and the Rijksmuseum, were built by the same architect, Pierre Cuypers, who helped rebuild the city during its late 19th-century revival.

Tucked inside the theater is the **Last Minute Ticket Shop.** This handy box office sells tickets to all kinds of shows and concerts around town, including half-price, same-day tickets to select shows (see page 250).

Now look to the right of the Stadsschouwburg, down a lane behind the big theater. There you'd find the **Melkweg** ("Milky Way") nightclub. Back in the 1970s, this place was almost mythical—an entertainment complex entirely devoted to the young generation and their desires. Even today it offers an edgy array of new acts—step into the lobby or check out posters nearby to see what's on.

Continue panning. The neighborhood beyond Burger King is Amsterdam's **"Restaurant Row,"** featuring countless Thai, Brazilian, Indian, Italian, Indonesian—and even a few Dutch— eateries. Next, on the east end of Leidseplein, is the **Bulldog Café and Coffeeshop,** the flagship of several coffeeshops in town with the Bulldog name. (Notice the sign above the door: It once housed the police bureau.) A small green-and-white decal on the window indicates that it's a city-licensed "cof-feeshop," where marijuana is sold and smoked legally. Incredible as that may seem to visitors from the States, it's been going on here in Amsterdam for over 30 years—another Dutch cliché alongside windmill peppermills and wooden shoes.

• *Our walk is over. But those with more energy could get out their maps and make their way to Vondelpark or the Rijksmuseum (one stop away on tram #2 or #5). To return to Central Station (or to nearly anyplace along this walk), catch tram #1, #2, or #5 from Leidseplein.*

RED LIGHT DISTRICT WALK

Amsterdam's oldest neighborhood has hosted the world's oldest profession since the Middle Ages. Today, prostitution and public marijuana use still thrive here, creating a spectacle that's unique in all of Europe.

The Red Light District lies between Damrak and Nieuwmarkt. On our walk, we'll see history, sleaze, and cheese: transvestites in windows, drunks in doorways, cruising packs of foreign twentysomethings, cannabis being enjoyed, and sex for sale.

The sex trade runs the gamut from sex shops selling porn and accessories to blue video arcades, from glitzy nightclub sex shows featuring strippers and sex acts to the real deal—prostitutes in bras, thongs, and high heels, standing in window displays, offering their bodies. Amsterdam keeps several thousand prostitutes employed—and it's all legal.

Not for Everyone: The Red Light District seems to have something to offend everyone. Whether it's in-your-face images of graphic sex, exploited immigrant women, whips and chains, passed-out drug addicts, the pungent smells of pot smoke and urine, or just the shameless commercialism of it all, it's not everyone's cup of tea. And though I encourage people to expand their horizons—that's a great thing about travel—it's perfectly OK to say, "No, thank you."

Orientation

Length of This Walk: Allow two hours.

Photography: Consider leaving your camera in your bag. Avoid taking photos of ladies in windows—even with an inconspicuous camera phone—or a snarly bouncer may appear from out of nowhere to forcibly rip it from your hands. In this district, taking even seemingly harmless pictures of ordinary people is frowned upon by privacy-loving locals. Photos of landmarks like the Old Church and wide shots of distant red lights from the bridges are certainly OK, but remember that a camera is a prime target in this high-theft area.

When to Go: The best times to visit are afternoons and early evenings. Mornings are dead, but are also when you see more passed-out-drunk-in-a-doorway scenes. Avoid late nights (after about 22:30), when the tourists disappear and the area gets creepy. Earlier in the evening, the streets start filling with tourists, and the atmosphere feels safe, even festive.

Safety: Coming here is asking for trouble, but if you're on the ball and smart, you'll find that it's quite safe. While there are plenty of police on horseback keeping things orderly, there are also plenty of rowdy drunks, drug-pushing lowlifes, con artists, and pickpockets (not to mention extremely persuasive women in windows). Assume any fight or commotion in the streets is a ploy to distract innocent victims who are about to lose their wallets. As always, wear your money belt and keep a low profile.

Tours: This walk is enough for most visitors, but if you want a more in-depth visit with a guide and a group, consider Randy Roy's Red Light Tours (described on page 45). The Prostitution Information Center also offers tours (see below).

Old Church (Oude Kerk): €7.50, Mon-Sat 10:00-18:00, Sun 13:00-17:30, free carillon concerts Tue and Sat at 16:00.

Prostitution Information Center (PIC): €1, Wed-Fri 10:00-17:00 and Sat 10:00-19:00, closed Sun-Tue, €15 walking tours offered Sat at 17:00 and Wed at 18:30, tel. 020/420-7328, www.pic-amsterdam.com.

Amstelkring Museum (Our Lord in the Attic): €9, Mon-Sat 10:00-17:00, Sun and holidays 13:00-17:00, no photos.

Erotic Museum: €7, not covered by Museumkaart, daily 11:00-24:00.

Red Light Secrets Museum of Prostitution: €7.50, not covered by Museumkaart, daily 12:00-24:00.

Cannabis College: Free, daily 11:00-19:00.

Hemp Gallery and Hash, Marijuana, and Hemp Museum: €9, not covered by Museumkaart, daily 10:00-22:00.

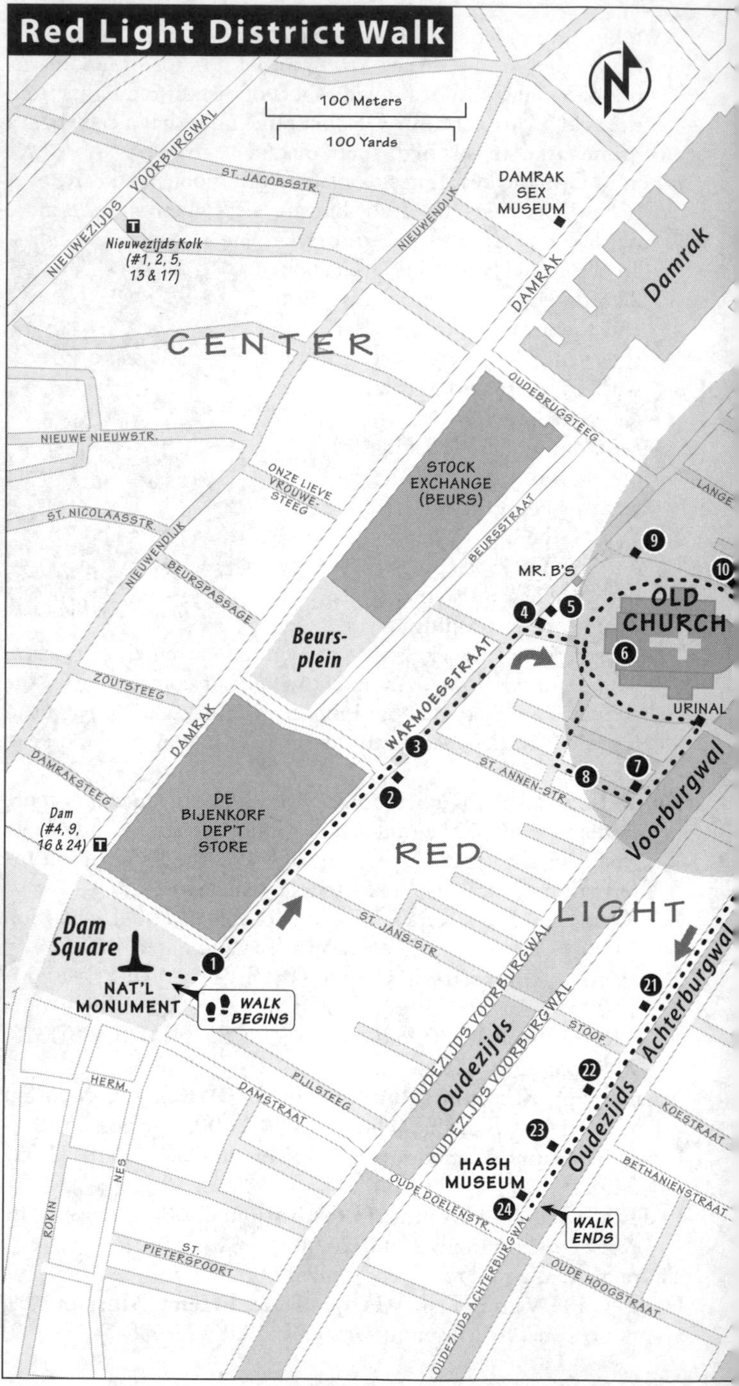

Red Light District Walk

RED LIGHT WALK

Map labels:

100 Meters
100 Yards

DAMRAK SEX MUSEUM

ST. JACOBSSTR.

NIEUWEZIJDS VOORBURGWAL

NIEUWENDIJK

Nieuwezijds Kolk
(#1, 2, 5, 13 & 17)

CENTER

DAMRAK

Damrak

NIEUWE NIEUWSTR.

OUDEBRUGSTEEG

ONZE LIEVE VROUWE-STEEG

STOCK EXCHANGE (BEURS)

LANGE

ST. NICOLAASSTR.

NIEUWENDIJK

BEURSPASSAGE

BEURSSTRAAT

MR. B'S

9

OLD CHURCH

10

ZOUTSTEEG

Beurs-plein

WARMOESSTRAAT

4   5

6

DAMRAK

URINAL

DAMRAKSTEEG

3

ST. ANNEN-STR.

Voorburgwal

Dam
(#4, 9, 16 & 24)

DE BIJENKORF DEP'T STORE

2

8   7

RED

LIGHT

ST. JANS-STR.

Dam Square

NAT'L MONUMENT

WALK BEGINS

1

OUDEZIJDS VOORBURGWAL

Achterburgwal

21

HERM.

NES

ROKIN

PIJLSTEEG

DAMSTRAAT

ST. JANS-STR.

Oudezijds Voorburgwal

STOOF

OUDEZIJDS VOORBURGWAL

22

KOESTRAAT

ST. PIETERSPOORT

OUDE DOELENSTR.

HASH MUSEUM

23

BETHANIENSTRAAT

OUDEZIJDS ACHTERBURGWAL

24

WALK ENDS

OUDE HOOGSTRAAT

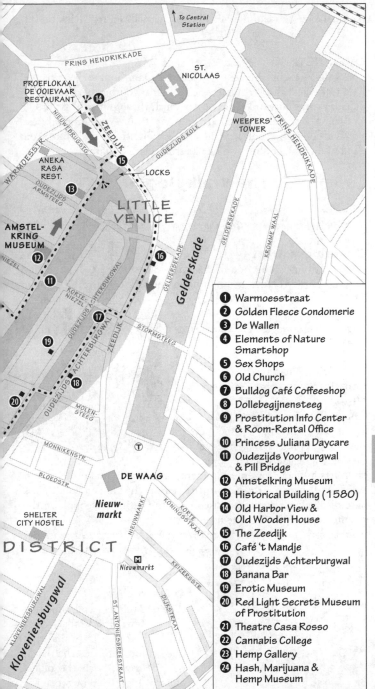

① Warmoesstraat

② Golden Fleece Condomerie

③ De Wallen

④ Elements of Nature Smartshop

⑤ Sex Shops

⑥ Old Church

⑦ Bulldog Café Coffeeshop

⑧ Dollebegijnensteeg

⑨ Prostitution Info Center & Room-Rental Office

⑩ Princess Juliana Daycare

⑪ Oudezijds Voorburgwal & Pill Bridge

⑫ Amstelkring Museum

⑬ Historical Building (1580)

⑭ Old Harbor View & Old Wooden House

⑮ The Zeedijk

⑯ Café 't Mandje

⑰ Oudezijds Achterburgwal

⑱ Banana Bar

⑲ Erotic Museum

⑳ Red Light Secrets Museum of Prostitution

㉑ Theatre Casa Rosso

㉒ Cannabis College

㉓ Hemp Gallery

㉔ Hash, Marijuana & Hemp Museum

Audio Tour: You can download this chapter as a free Rick Steves audio tour (see page 10).

OVERVIEW

The walk starts on the centrally located Dam Square. Two parallel streets with similar names—Oudezijds Voorburgwal and Oudezijds Achterburgwal—run north-south through the heart of De Wallen. You'll walk a big, long loop: north on Voorburgwal past the Old Church, hook around on Zeedijk street, and return on Achterburgwal, ending two blocks from Dam Square.

The Walk Begins

• *Start on Dam Square. Face the big, fancy Grand Hotel Krasnapolsky. To the left of the hotel stretches the long street called...*

❶ Warmoesstraat

You're walking along one of the city's oldest streets. It's the traditional border of the neighborhood tourists call the Red Light District.

• *Our first stop is the small shop with the large, yellow triangle sign, on the right at #141.*

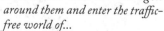

❷ Golden Fleece Condomerie (Het Gulden Vlies)

Located at the entrance to the Red Light District, this is the perfect place to get prepared. Besides selling an amazing variety of condoms, this

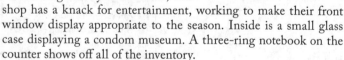

shop has a knack for entertainment, working to make their front window display appropriate to the season. Inside is a small glass case displaying a condom museum. A three-ring notebook on the counter shows off all of the inventory.

• *From here, pass the two little street barricades with cute red lights around them and enter the traffic-free world of...*

❸ De Wallen

Amsterdammers call this area De Wallen ("The Walls"), after the old retaining walls that once stood here. It's the oldest part of town, with the oldest church. It grew up between the harbor and the Dam Square, where the city was born. Amsterdam was a port town, located where the river met the sea. The city traded in all kinds of goods, including things popular with sailors and businessmen away from home—like sex and drugs.

According to legend, Quentin Tarantino holed up at the Winston Hotel for three months in 1993 to write *Pulp Fiction* (you'll pass the hotel on your right, at #129). It's clear that the area attracts many out-of-towners, especially Brits. Notice all the Irish pubs, advertisements for football (soccer) games, and British, Scottish, and Irish flags. From the British Isles, the Red Light District is just a cheap flight away. Brits come here in droves for "stag" (bachelor) parties or just a wild weekend—and the money-savvy Dutch know their best customers.

Farther down, also on the right, you'll come to an intersection with a small street called Wijde Kerksteeg, which leads to the Old Church (we'll go to the church in a moment). Standing here, note the gay rainbow flags and the S&M flags (black and blue with a heart). Also notice the security cameras and modern lighting. Freedom reigns in this quarter—under the watchful eye of the two neighborhood police departments.

• *Continue down Warmoesstraat a few more steps. At #97 is the...*

❹ Elements of Nature Smartshop

This "smartshop" is a little grocery store of mind-bending natural ingredients. Like the city's other smartshops, it's a clean, well-lit, fully professional retail outlet that sells powerful drugs, many of which are illegal in America. Products are clearly marked with prices, brief descriptions, ingredients, and effects. The knowledgeable salespeople can give you more information on their "100 percent natural products that play with the human senses."

Their "natural" drugs include harmless nutrition boosters (such as royal jelly), harmful but familiar tobacco, and herbal versions of popular dance-club drugs (such as herbal Ecstasy). Marijuana seeds, however, are the big sellers. You'll also see mind-bending truffles, a recent trend that caught on after the EU forbade the retailing of hallucinogenic mushrooms. (Truffles grow underground—so they're technically not mushrooms.)

Still, my fellow travelers, *caveat emptor!* We've grown used to thinking, "If it's legal, it must be safe. If it's not, I'll sue." Though perfectly legal and aboveboard in the Netherlands, some of these substances can cause powerful, often unpleasant reactions.

• *Continue a bit farther down Warmoesstraat, to an area filled with so-called...*

❺ Sex Shops

These places deal in erotic paraphernalia (dildos, S&M starter kits,

The History of Prostitution in Amsterdam

Today nearly a thousand prostitutes work in the Red Light District, sharing about 200 windows...and a very long history. The tolerance of this sex industry swings with the times. But, as usual, Amsterdam finds a way for tolerance to win out. Sex has always been for sale in De Wallen.

De Wallen is the oldest surviving residential neighborhood in town, built around 1400. (The Old Church that marks its center is even older, dating from the early 1200s.) Historically a port city, Amsterdam always had sailors in need of entertainment—and as far back as the 1400s, there were prostitutes walking with red lanterns and working mostly in inns. With the piety of the Reformation (late 1500s), there was a brief attempt to suppress the sex trade. But by the 1600s, a thousand prostitutes were working here, and sexually transmitted disease ran rampant—many customers enjoyed brief encounters, then paid with their lives.

With the age of Napoleon (early 1800s) came a pragmatic form of legal prostitution in an attempt to fight STDs. Sex workers were required to have permits and submit to twice-weekly checkups to certify they were disease-free. By mid-century, effective (rubber) condoms were readily available. Prostitution boomed, with an estimated 3,000 sex workers here.

The widespread prostitution was targeted by the more moralistic Victorian Age. But creative tolerance prevailed again, and

and kinky magazines). Browsers are welcome. Some shops have video booths playing porn films, charging by the minute. (Haven't these guys heard of the Internet?) While Amsterdam is notorious for its Red Light District, even small Dutch towns often have a sex shop and a brothel to satisfy their citizens' needs.

Farther down Warmoesstraat, at #93 and #96, you'll see several men-only leather bars, distinguished by their black doors and windows. These places come with a bar, a dance floor, and a dark back room.

A few steps along, at #89, is **Mr. B's Leather and Rubber Land,** proudly flying an S&M flag. This place takes macho to painful—and what seems like anatomically impossible—extremes. (Ouch.) Downstairs, you'll find some irresistible deals on whips and masks.

• *Let's go see the Old Church. Backtrack a few steps to the intersection, and head down Wijde Kerksteeg to the...*

❻ Old Church (Oude Kerk)

As the name implies, this was the medieval city's original church. Returning from a long sea voyage, sailors of yore would spy the steeple of the Old Church on the horizon and know they were

by about 1900, the streetwalkers were gone, replaced by the "window prostitution" limited to specific districts we know today.

In more recent times, prostitution has not been seen as a moral threat but as a practical one—bringing disease, human trafficking, and organized crime. Many sex workers are victims forced to work by pimps who use their children back home as hostages. To fight these threats, prostitution was officially legalized in 2000, and is now considered just another profession, with rules, regulations, and taxes. In 2007, city leaders introduced Project 1012 (named for De Wallen's postal code), an attempt to concentrate and normalize the trade while removing the criminal element.

Amsterdam's current city government is trying to rein in the sex trade by limiting it to De Wallen. It's also splicing in other "legitimate" businesses into a district that for centuries has relied on basically only one product. As many as half of the sex businesses here may close over the next few years—not because of prudishness, but to limit the encroachment of organized crime. A major Red Light District landlord was essentially given the option either to lease many of his booths to the city or be zoned out of business. The city picked up the leases, and windows that once showcased "girls for rent" now showcase mannequins wearing the latest fashions—lit by lights that aren't red.

home. Having returned safely, they'd come here to give thanks to St. Nicholas—the patron saint of this church, of seafarers, of Christmas, and of the city of Amsterdam.

Church construction began in the early 1200s—starting with a humble wooden chapel that expanded into a stone structure by

the time it was consecrated in 1306. It was added onto in fits and starts for the next 200 years—as is apparent in the building's many gangly parts. Then, in the 15th century, Amsterdam built the New Church (Nieuwe Kerk) on Dam Square. But the Old Church still had the tallest spire, the biggest organ, and the most side-altars, and remained the city's center of activity, bustling inside and out with merchants and street markets.

The **tower** is 290 feet high, with an octagonal steeple atop a bell tower (you can pay to climb to the top). This tower served as the model for many other Dutch steeples. The carillon has 47 bells, which can chime mechanically or be played by one of Amsterdam's three official carillonneurs. (For more on carillons, see page 135.)

While the church is historic, there's not much to see inside other than 2,500 gravestones in the floor (the most famous is for Rembrandt's wife, Saskia). Its stark plainness stems from the religious wars of the 16th century: Protestants gutted this Catholic church, smashing windows and removing politically incorrect statues they considered "graven images." One renowned girl threw her shoe at the Virgin statue. (Strict Calvinists at one point even removed the organ as a senseless luxury, until they found they couldn't stay on key singing hymns without it.) Atop the brass choir screen, an inscription *('t misbruyk in Godes...)* commemorates the iconoclasm: "The false practices introduced into God's church were undone here in 1578."

The church, permanently stripped of "pope-ish" decoration, was transformed from Catholic to Dutch Reformed, the name St. Nicholas' Church was dropped, and it became known by the nickname everyone called it anyway—the Old Church.

Nowadays, the church is the holy needle around which the unholy Red Light District spins. This marks the neighborhood's most dense concentration of prostitution.

Back outside, explore around the right side of the church. You'll see a **statue,** dedicated to the Unknown Prostitute. She's nicknamed Belle, and the statue honors "sexworkers around the world." Also nearby you might trip over a bronze breast sculpted into the pavement, being groped by bronze hands.

Attached to the church like barnacles are **small buildings.** These were originally used as homes for priests, church offices, or rental units. The house to the right of the entrance (at #25) is very tiny—32 feet by 8 feet. (An elderly lady lives here, so be discreet.)

Now check out the green metal **urinal** over by the canal. This one gets a lot of use. Consider that, on average, about 12 people drown in Amsterdam every year. When found, most of them turn out to be men with their zippers down. It's not hard to imagine the scene: Some guy is drunk as a skunk at 3 a.m., goes to the edge of the canal to take a pee...and falls in.

• *From the urinal, go half a block south along the canal toward the...*

❼ Bulldog Café Coffeeshop

The Bulldog claims to be Amsterdam's very first marijuana coffeeshop, established here in 1975. Now there's a chain of Bulldogs around the city. At "coffeeshops" like this one, customers start the

transaction by asking the bartender, "Can I see the cannabis menu?" (As it's illegal to advertise marijuana, buyers must ask to see a list of what's for sale.) Then the bartender pulls out a display case with different varieties of weed, sold in baggies or pre-rolled joints. It's all clearly priced, and available either to-go or to smoke on the premises. You'll see people at the Bulldog enjoying a joint while they sip a beer or a Coke.

As coffeeshops go, the Bulldog is considered pretty touristy. The staff is unintimidating, though, and timid first-timers are guided through the process. Connoisseurs, however, seek out smaller places with better-quality pot. While the Bulldog caters to a young crowd, other coffeeshops play Donovan and target an older, mellower clientele.

In recent years, various Dutch politicians have proposed new laws that would forbid sales of marijuana to nonresidents. Their big worry is European drug dealers who drive over the Dutch border, buy up large quantities of pot, and return home to sell it illegally. This law would be devastating for these Dutch businesses, who depend on out-of-towners to stay in business. The current mayor of Amsterdam is adamant that the city's coffeeshops will remain open—for the sake of the businesses, and because the city believes that the law would just drive business back into a black market, and cause an increase in street crime.

For more on the Dutch approach to pot, and how coffeeshops work, see the Smoking chapter.

• *Time to dive into the heart of the Red Light District—we're right around the corner from one of the neighborhood's main streets for legal prostitution. Immediately adjacent to the coffeeshop is a three-foot-wide entrance to a narrow alleyway, called...*

❽ Dollebegijnensteeg

You're right in the thick of high-density prostitution. Remember: Don't take any pictures, and watch for pickpockets if crowds jostle together. If you do both these things, you'll be fine.

As you pass window after window of women in panties and bras, notice how they wink at the horny men, rap on the

window to attract attention, text their friends, or look disdainfully at sightseers. You can take your time here and then explore deeper (or you can hurry to the end of the block and turn right to return to the Old Church).

This alleyway is just one of several in this area. You may notice that different zones feature prostitutes from different lands—Asia, Africa, Eastern Europe. This is to cater to customer tastes, as regulars know what they want.

• *Return to the Old Church and start to circle the church clockwise. Around the back (on Oudekerksplein), you'll see older, plumper (and cheaper) prostitutes. In the same area, at Enge Kerksteeg 3, is the...*

❾ Prostitution Information Center (PIC) and Room-Rental Office

This PIC exists solely to demystify prostitution, giving visitors matter-of-fact information on how the trade works and what it's like to be a sex worker. It doles out pamphlets, books, condoms, T-shirts, and other offbeat souvenirs, and offers a twice-weekly walking tour (see beginning of chapter for details). They have a map showing exactly where prostitution is legal, and sell a small, frank booklet (€1.50) answering the most common questions tourists have about Amsterdam's Red Light District. The center also offers a one-to-one workshop, for women only, on what it's like to be a sex worker in Amsterdam (must be booked in advance).

Next door is a **room-rental office** (labeled *Kamerverhuurbedrijf*). Prostitutes come here to rent window space and bedrooms to use for their work. Several of the available rooms for rent are just next door. The office also sells supplies—condoms by the case, lubricants, and soft drinks. The man at the desk does not arrange sex. The women who rent space from this business are self-employed, and negotiate directly with their customers.

In return for their rental fees, prostitutes get security. The man in the office keeps an eye on them by video surveillance—you can see the monitors inside. Looking down the street, you can see small cameras and orange alarm lights above the doors. If prostitutes have any trouble, they press a buzzer that swiftly unleashes not a pimp, but a burly bouncer or the police. The area sure looks rough, but, aside from tricky pickpockets, these streets are actually pretty safe.

• *Continue circling clockwise around the church. Amid prostitutes in windows, find the orange brick building on the left at Oudekerksplein 8. (Since it's low-profile and sealed up tight, it might be hard to find—look for the black-and-white photo of the princess near a gunmetal-gray door.) This is the...*

RED LIGHT WALK

Prostitution 101

The system is simple. A customer browses around. A prostitute catches his eye. If the prostitute is interested in his business

(prostitutes are selective for their own safety), she winks him over. They talk at the door as she explains her price and what she has to offer. Many are very aggressive at getting the man inside, where the temptation game revs up. A price is agreed on and paid in advance. A typical visit can cost €30-50 for a promised 20 minutes. The man goes in. The woman draws the curtain. Where do they actually do it? The rooms look tiny from the street, but these are just display windows. There's a bigger room behind or upstairs that comes with a bed, a sink, and not much else (or so I've heard). The average time for a visit: about 10 minutes.

Are there male prostitutes? Certainly—anything you might want is available somewhere in the Red Light District. But an experiment in the 1990s to put male prostitutes in windows didn't stand up. The district does, however, have plenty of "reconstructed women"—i.e., transvestites, many of them so gorgeous they need to (but don't necessarily) warn customers before they get a rude surprise. Blue lights (rather than red) mark where transvestites do business.

The prostitutes here are self-employed—entrepreneurs, renting space and running their own business. They usually work a four- to eight-hour shift. A good spot costs about €100 for a day shift, and €150 for an evening. Prostitutes are required to keep their premises hygienic, make sure their clients use condoms, and avoid minors.

Popular prostitutes can make about €500 a day. They fill out tax returns, and many belong to a loose union called the Red Thread. The law, not pimps, protects prostitutes. If a prostitute is diagnosed with HIV or AIDS, she loses her license. As shocking as legalized prostitution may seem to some, it's a good example of a pragmatic Dutch solution to a persistent problem.

Although some women choose prostitution as a lucrative career, others (likely most) are forced into it by circumstance—poverty, drug addiction, abusive men, and immigration scams. Since the fall of the Iron Curtain, many Eastern Europeans have flocked here, and Russian and East European crime syndicates have muscled in. While the hope here in the Netherlands is that sex workers are smartly regulated small-businesspeople, in reality the line between victim and entrepreneur is not always so clear.

⑩ Princess Juliana Daycare

De Wallen is also a residential neighborhood, where ordinary citizens go about their daily lives. Of course, locals need someplace to send their kids. The Princess Juliana Daycare is for newborns to four-year-olds. It was built in the 1970s, when the idea was to mix all dimensions of society together, absorbing the seedy into the decent. I don't know about you, but this location would be a tough sell where I come from.

• *Turn left at the canal and continue north along...*

⑪ Oudezijds Voorburgwal and Pill Bridge

Pause at Pill Bridge and enjoy the canal and all the old buildings with their charming gables. Back in the 1970s, this bridge was nicknamed for the retail items sold by the seedy guys who used to hang out here. Now it's a pleasant place for a photo op.

• *Just past the bridge, at Oudezijds Voorburgwal 40, is one of the city's most worthwhile museums.*

⑫ Amstelkring Museum (Our Lord in the Attic Church)

With its triangular gable, this building looks like just another townhouse. But inside, it holds a secret—a small, lavishly decorated place of worship hidden in the attic. Although Amsterdam has long been known for its tolerance, back in the 16th century there was one group they kept in the closet—Catholics. (For more, ✪ see the Amstelkring Museum Tour chapter.)

As we stroll up the canal, remember that this neighborhood is Amsterdam's oldest. It sits on formerly marshy land that was reclaimed by diking off the sea's tidal surge. That location gave Amsterdam's merchants easy access to both river trade and the North Sea. By the 1500s, Amsterdam was booming.

• *Near the next bridge, at #14, is a...*

⑬ Historical Building

This building dates from that very era—around 1580. At the time of its construction, Amsterdam's citizens were rising up in revolt to throw out their Spanish rulers. Now free to govern themselves, a group of energetic businessmen turned the city into a sea-trading hub. By 1600, brave Dutch sailors were traveling as far as Africa, America, and Asia. They returned with shiploads of exotic goods to sell to the rest of Europe.

The 1600s were Amsterdam's heyday. With its canals and fine townhouses, it became known as the "Venice of the North." The part of the canal we're walking along now is known as **"Little Venice"** (a term used Europe-wide for any charming neighborhood with canalside houses). Houses rise directly from the water here, with no quays or streets. Like Venice, the city was built in a marshy delta area, on millions of pilings. And, like Venice, it grew rich on sea trade.

You'll soon reach the end of the canal. Before you go on, notice the collection of fine gable stones embedded in the wall on the right.

• *Continue straight up a small inclined lane called Sint Olofssteeg. At the top, turn left onto a street called the Zeedijk. Walk along the Zeedijk about 100 yards to the end of the block, where it opens up to an...*

⓮ Old Harbor View and Old Wooden House

As you survey the marina, Damrak, and Central Station, imagine the scene in the 1600s. The **old wooden house**—now a café— was once a tavern, sitting right at what was then the water's edge (today's marina was the city's harbor). Boats sailed in and out of the harbor through an opening located where Central Station sits today. (The station was built on reclaimed land.) From there, they could sail along the IJ River out to the North Sea.

Amsterdam became home to the Dutch East India Company, the world's first multinational corporation. Goods from all over the world flowed into this harbor, and cargo could be transferred from there to smaller river-trade boats that sailed up the Amstel to Europe's interior. The city grew wealthier and larger, expanding beyond De Wallen to new neighborhoods to the west and south. In its Golden Age, Amsterdam was perhaps the wealthiest city on earth, known as the "warehouse of the world."

Picture a ship tying up in the harbor. The crew has just returned home from a two-year voyage to Bali. They're bringing home fabulous wealth—crates and crates of spices, coffee, and silk. Sailors are celebrating their homecoming, spilling onto the Zeedijk. Here they'll be greeted by swinging ladies swinging red lanterns. Their first stop might be St. Olaf's chapel to say a prayer of thanks—or perhaps they'll head straight to this tavern at Zeedijk 1 and drop anchor for a good Dutch beer. Ahh-hh!

• *But our journey continues on. Backtrack along the same street, to the crest of a bridge, to take in the...*

⓯ Zeedijk

See that green box by the railing? It's part of the city's system of **locks:** Once a day a worker opens up this box and presses a button. The locks open, and the tides flush out the city's canals. Look down—if the gate is open, you might see water flowing in or out.

The Zeedijk runs along the top of the "sea dike" that histori-

RED LIGHT WALK

cally protected sea-level Amsterdam from the North Sea tides. It also connected the harbor, bustling with ocean-going ships, with De Wallen.

In the early 1600s, Zeedijk street was thriving with overseas trade. But Amsterdam would soon lose its maritime supremacy to England and France, and by mid-century, its trading ships and economy had been destroyed by wars with these rivals. The city remained culturally vibrant, and banking flourished—but without all the ships, De Wallen never really recovered. For centuries, the area languished as Amsterdam's grimy old sailors' quarter. It wasn't until the 1960s that this neighborhood began the transformation to the place we see today.

As you continue down the Zeedijk and around the bend, you can see that the area has become fairly gentrified. Residents enjoy a mix of ethnic restaurants—Thai and Portuguese, for example—and bars like the Queen's Head (at #20, on the left) that draw a gay clientele. The apartment building at #30 (on the right) is new, built in "MIIM" (1998).

Back in the 1960s, it was a whole different story. Amsterdam was the world capital of experimental lifestyles, a wide-open city of sex and drugs. By the 1970s, the Zeedijk had become unbelievably sleazy. That's where I come into the story. When I made my first trip here, this street was nicknamed "Heroin Alley." Thousands of hard-drug addicts wandered the neighborhood and squatted in old buildings. "Pill Bridge" (which we passed earlier) became "Needle Bridge." It was a scene with little else besides sex, hard drugs, and wandering lonely souls. The area was a no-man's-land of junkies fighting among themselves, and the police just kept their distance.

But locals longed to take back this potentially wonderful corner of their city, and the Dutch eventually decided to do something about the problem. The first step was legalizing marijuana and allowing "coffeeshops" to sell small quantities of pot. Then they cracked down on hard drugs—heroin, cocaine, and pills. Almost overnight, the illicit drug trade dropped dramatically. Dealers got stiff sentences. Addicts got treatment. Four decades later, the policy seems to have worked. Pot-smoking has not gone up, hard drug use is down, and the Zeedijk belongs to the people of Amsterdam once again.

• *Pause at #63, on the left.*

⑯ Café 't Mandje

This was perhaps Europe's first gay bar. It opened in 1927, closed in 1985, and is now a working bar once again. It stands as a memo-

Social Control

De Wallen has pioneered the Dutch concept of "social control." In Holland, neighborhood security doesn't come from just the police, but from neighbors looking out for each another. If Geert doesn't buy bread for two days, the baker asks around if anyone's seen him. An elderly man feels safe in his home, knowing he's being watched over by the prostitutes next door. Unlike many big cities, there's no chance that anyone here could die or be in trouble and go unnoticed. Video-surveillance cameras keep an eye on the streets. So do prostitutes, who buzz for help if they spot trouble. As you stroll, watch the men who watch the women who watch out for their neighbors—"social control."

rial to the woman who ran it during its heyday in the 1950s and '60s: Bet van Beeren, "Queen of the Zeedijk." Bet was a lesbian, and her bar became a hangout for gay people. It still is, though all are welcome. If you go inside for a drink, you'll enjoy a tiny interior crammed with photos and memorabilia. Bet was the original Zee-dyke—you might see a picture of her decked out in leather, cruising the streets on her motorcycle. Neckties hang from the ceiling, a reminder of Bet's tradition of scissoring off customers' ties.

• *This tour veers right at the next intersection, back into the heart of the Red Light District. For a quick detour, however, you could continue straight ahead for a peek into the local Chinatown. Otherwise, make the next right and head a few steps down narrow Korte Stormsteeg street, back to the canalside red lights. Then go left, before the bridge, along the left side of the canal.*

⑰ Oudezijds Achterburgwal

We're back in the glitzy Red Light District. This beautiful, tree-lined canal is the heart of this neighborhood's nightlife, playing host to most of the main nightclubs.

• *Keep walking along the left side of the canal, making your way to the first bridge. Up ahead, at #78, is the...*

⑱ Banana Bar (Bananenbar)

This popular nightclub has an erotic Art Nouveau facade that's far classier than what's offered inside. Basically, this place is a strip club with a-peel: For €60 you get admission for an hour, drinks included. Undressed ladies serve the drinks, perched on the bar. Touching is not allowed, but you can order a banana, and the lady will serve it to you, any way you like. For a full description, step into the lobby.

• *At Molensteeg, cross the bridge to head to the right side of Oudezijds Achterburgwal. Once across the bridge, we'll be turning left. But first, pause and look to the right. At #54 is the...*

⑲ Erotic Museum

"Wot a rip-off!" said a drunk British lout to his mates as he emerged from the Erotic Museum. If it's graphic sex you seek, this is not the place. To put it bluntly, this museum is not very good (the Damrak Sex Museum is better; see page 66).

This museum, however, does offer a peek at some of the sex services found in the Red Light District. Besides the self-pleasuring bicycle girl in the lobby, displays include reconstructions of a prostitute's chambers, sex-shop windows, and videos of nightclub sex shows (on the third floor). There's also the S&M room, where S-mannequins torment M-mannequins for their mutual pleasure.

• *From the bridge, turn left, and walk south along Oudezijds Achterburgwal. At #60H is the...*

⑳ Red Light Secrets Museum of Prostitution

Though overpriced, this museum is an earnest and mildly educational behind-the-scenes look at those girls in the window. You'll walk through a typical (tiny) room where girls stand at the window, and a typical (tiny) back room with a bed and sink where the dirty deed takes place. There's a cheesy hot-tub room for the high rollers, a display of S&M paraphernalia, and several videos about daily life for prostitutes. Perhaps most thought provoking: a video giving you the point of view of a prostitute as browsers check you out. The place is small, and a visit takes about as long as a typical session with a prostitute.

Farther down Oudezijds Achterburgwal (at #78) is **The Love Boutique.** Part lingerie store, part soft-core sex shop, this place caters to all of your sensual needs.

• *Continuing south, you'll pass two Casa Rosso franchises a block apart. The larger, lined by pink elephants, is...*

㉑ Theatre Casa Rosso

This is the Red Light District's best-known nightclub for live sex shows. Unlike some strip clubs that draw you in to rip you off with hidden charges, the Casa Rosso is a legitimate operation. Audience members pay a single price that includes drinks and a show. Evening performances feature strippers, but the main event is naked people on stage engaging in sex acts—some simulated, some completely real (€40, €50 includes drinks, tickets cheaper online, nightly until 2:00 in the morning).

As you continue south along the canal, you gotta wonder, Why does Amsterdam embrace prostitution and drugs? It's not that the Dutch are any more liberal in their attitudes—they aren't. They're simply more pragmatic. They've found that when the sex trade goes underground, you get pimps, mobsters, and the spread of STDs. When marijuana is illegal, you get drug dealers, gangs, and violent turf wars. Their solution is to keep these markets legal, and minimize problems through strict regulation.

• *Had it with the sleaze? We're almost done. But first...more drugs. Along the right side of the next block, you'll find four cannabis-related establishments, starting with the Cannabis College, at #124.*

⓶ Cannabis College

This free, nonprofit public study center aims to explain the pros and cons (but mostly pros) of the industrial, medicinal, and recreational uses of the green stuff. You can read about practical hemp products, the medical uses of marijuana, and police prosecution/persecution of cannabis users. The pride and joy of the college is downstairs. For a €3 donation, you can visit the organic flowering cannabis garden, where, as the sign reads,

you can "see some real cannabis plants in all their glory." The garden is small—it fits the Dutch legal limit of three plants per person or five per household. And if you've brought your own pot, they'll let you try out their vaporizer, a device that lets you inhale without actually smoking, making it less damaging to your lungs.

• *Continue up the street to #130, the...*

⓶ Hemp Gallery

One ticket admits you to both the Hemp Gallery and the Hash, Marijuana, and Hemp Museum (described next). The gallery focuses mainly on extolling the wonders of industrial hemp, and isn't as meaty as the small, earnestly educational museum. If you have the patience to read its thorough displays, you'll learn plenty about how valuable the cannabis plant was to Holland during the Golden Age. The leafy, green cannabis plant was grown on large plantations. The fibrous stalks (hemp) were made into rope and canvas for ships, and even used to make clothing and lace.

Certain strains of the cannabis plant—particularly mature females of the species *sativa* and *indica*—contain the psychoactive alkaloid tetrahydrocannabinol (THC) that makes you high. The buds, flowers, and leaves (marijuana) can be dried and smoked. The brown sap/resin/pitch that oozes out of the leaves (hashish, a.k.a. hash) can also be dried and smoked. Both produce effects ranging from euphoria to paranoia to the munchies.

Throughout history, various peoples have used cannabis as a sacred ritual drug—from ancient Scythians and Hindus to modern Nepalis and Afghanis. Modern Rastafarians, following a Bible-based religion centered in Jamaica, smoke cannabis. To worship, they get high, bob to reggae music, and praise God. They love the Bible verse (Genesis 1:11-12) that says God created "every herb" and called them all "good." All over Amsterdam, you'll see the Rastafarian colors: green, gold, and red, mon.

• *Next is our last stop at #148, the...*

㉔ Hash, Marijuana, and Hemp Museum

The museum's highlight is the grow room, where you look through windows at live cannabis plants in various stages of growth, some as tall as I. These plants are grown hydroponically (in water, no soil) under grow lights. At a certain stage they're "sexed" to weed out the boring males and "selected" to produce the most powerful strains. Your ticket includes a souvenir guidebook about the exhibit and a fun photo op.

At the museum's exit you'll pass through the **Sensi Seed Bank Store,** which sells weed seeds, how-to books, and knickknacks geared to growers.

• *We've reached the end of our tour. Dam Square is just two blocks away. Continue a few steps farther up the canal to the big and busy Oude Doelen street. Look right, and you'll see the Royal Palace on Dam Square, two blocks away.*

Congratulations

We've seen a lot. We've peeked at locals—from prostitutes to drug pushers to the ghosts of pioneer lesbians to politically active heads with green thumbs. We've talked a bit of history, a little politics, and a lot of sleaze. Congratulations. You've survived. Now, go back to your hotel and take a shower.

JORDAAN WALK

This walk takes you from Dam Square—the Times Square of Amsterdam—to the Anne Frank House, and then deep into the characteristic Jordaan neighborhood. Cafés, boutiques, bookstores, and art galleries have gentrified the area. The walk is a cultural scavenger hunt, offering you a chance to experience the laid-back Dutch lifestyle and catch a few intimate details most busy tourists never appreciate. In the Jordaan (yor-DAHN) you'll see things that are commonplace in Amsterdam, but that you won't find in any other city in the world.

This is a short and easygoing walk—nice in the sleepy morning or en route to a Jordaan dinner in the evening. Bring your camera, as you'll enjoy some of Amsterdam's most charming canal scenes.

Orientation

Length of This Walk: Allow 90 minutes.

When to Go: For the best views, and to hit a few minor sights while they're open, do this walk in daylight (and before 18:00, when some of the minor sights along the way close). Sundays aren't ideal, as many shops (and St. Andrew's Courtyard, our last stop) are closed.

Westerkerk: Church—free, generally open April-Sept Mon-Sat 11:00-15:00, closed Sun and Oct-March. Tower—€8 for 30-minute tour—departures on the half hour April-Oct Mon-Sat 10:00-18:00, May-Aug until 20:00, last tour leaves 30 minutes before closing, closed Sun and Nov-March.

Anne Frank House: €9, April-Oct daily 9:00-21:00, Sat and July-Aug until 22:00; Nov-March daily 9:00-19:00, Sat until 21:00; last entry 30 minutes before closing.

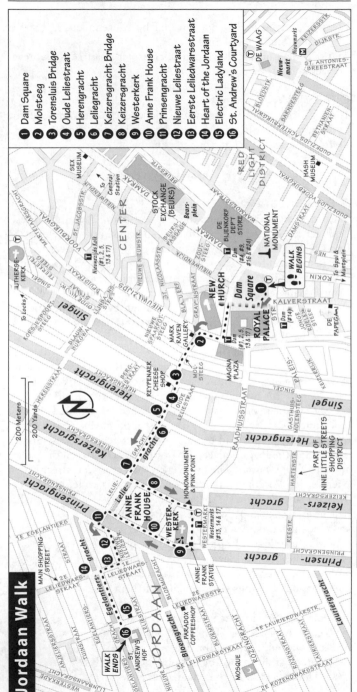

Jordaan Walk

1. Dam Square
2. Molsteeg
3. Torensluis Bridge
4. Oude Leliestraat
5. Herengracht
6. Leliegracht
7. Keizersgracht Bridge
8. Keizersgracht
9. Westerkerk
10. Anne Frank House
11. Prinsengracht
12. Nieuwe Leliestraat
13. Eerste Leliedwarsstraat
14. Heart of the Jordaan
15. Electric Ladyland
16. St. Andrew's Courtyard

Electric Ladyland: €5, not covered by Museumkaart, Tue-Sat 13:00-18:00, closed Sun-Mon.

Audio Tour: You can download this chapter as a free Rick Steves audio tour (see page 10).

OVERVIEW

The walk begins at Dam Square and ends at the center of the Jordaan, along the Egelantiersgracht canal. From there it's just a short, scenic walk back to your starting point.

The Walk Begins

❶ Dam Square

Start in Dam Square, where the city was born. The original residents settled east of here, in the neighborhood now known as the Red Light District. But as Amsterdam grew—from a river-trading village to a worldwide sea-trading empire—the population needed new places to live. Citizens started reclaiming land to the west of Dam Square, and built a "new church" (Nieuwe Kerk) to serve these new neighborhoods. Canal by canal, they created new neighborhoods of waterways lined with merchants' townhouses. This is the area we'll be walking through in the first half of our tour. By the 1600s—Amsterdam's Golden Age—they needed still more land. They opened up a new development farther west, the Jordaan. It was served by a new church to the west—the Westerkerk, which we'll pass on this walk. It was also in the 1600s that the Royal Palace was built here on Dam Square (described on page 62 and 90).

From Dam Square, leave the fast-food chains, mimes, and tourists behind, and head to the place where real Amsterdammers live. Facing the Royal Palace, slip (to the right) between the palace and the New Church (Nieuwe Kerk), then cross the street called Nieuwezijds Voorburgwal. If it seems like this wide, busy street doesn't really fit the city, that's because it's new—built over what had been a canal up until the 1880s. You'll soon see the facade of a red-brick building.

Magna Plaza Shopping Center: Built in 1899, the Magna Plaza was, like so many buildings in this soggy city, constructed atop a foundation of pilings—some 4,500 of them, in this case. In its day, it was ultra-modern, symbolizing the city's economic revival after two centuries of decline. The North Sea Canal had just opened, industrialization was on the rise, and it was all capped by a World's Fair in 1883. Until the 1980s, the Magna Plaza was

Amsterdam's main post office. Now, however, it's a mall, housing 40 stores.

• *Facing Magna Plaza, head right, walking 50 yards down the busy street to the corner of a tiny street called Molsteeg. Before turning left down Molsteeg, stand and survey this slice of Amsterdam.*

❷ Molsteeg

Scan the higgledy-piggledy facades across the busy street. Are you drunk, high...or just in Amsterdam, where the houses were built on mud? Check out the nice line of gables in this row of houses. We'll see more like this on our walk.

Before moving on, notice the T-shirt gallery on the corner. Decades ago, I bought a Mark Raven T-shirt from a street vendor.

Now this Amsterdam original has his own upscale shop, selling T-shirts and paintings featuring spindly lined, semi-abstract cityscapes. Raven works primarily with small etchings—as Rembrandt often did.

Now head down tiny Molsteeg street—but don't walk on the reddish pavement in the middle; that's for bikes. Keep to the side. A few steps along, on the left, find house #5: Just one window wide, it's typical of the city's narrow old merchants' houses, with a shop on the ground floor, living space in the middle, and storage in the attic. Look up to see the hooks above warehouse doors. Houses like this lean out toward the street on purpose: Attach a pulley to the hook, and you can hoist cargo without banging it against the house (or, these days, lift up a sofa and send it through a big upper-story window without lugging it up a steep, narrow staircase).

From here this tour's essentially a straight shot west, though the street changes names along the way.

At the intersection with Spuistraat, you'll likely see rows of **bicycles** parked along the street. Amsterdam's 820,000 residents own nearly that many bikes. The Netherlands' 17 million people own 17 million bikes, with many people owning two—a long-distance racing bike and a junky in-city bike, often deliberately kept in poor maintenance so it's less enticing to the many bike thieves in town. Locals are diligent about locking their bikes twice: They lock the spokes with the first lock, and then they use a heavy chain to attach the bike to something immovable, such as one of the city's U-shaped "staple" hitching racks.

Amsterdam is a great bike town—and indeed, bikes outnumber cars. Notice how 100 bikes might be parked along the road, yet they blend right in. Then imagine if each bike were a car. The efficient Dutch appreciate a self-propelled machine that travels five times faster than a person on foot, while creating zero pollution, noise, parking problems, or high fuel costs. On a *fiets* (bike), a speedy local can traverse the historic center in about 10 minutes. Biking seems to keep the populace fit and good-looking—people here say that Amsterdam's health clubs are more for networking than for working out.

• *After one more block, the street opens onto a small space (understandably nicknamed "Big Head Square") that's actually a bridge, straddling the Singel canal. It's called...*

❸ Torensluis Bridge

We haven't quite reached the Jordaan yet, but the atmosphere already seems miles away from busy Dam Square. With cafés, art

galleries, and fine benches for picnics, this is a great place to relax and take in a Golden Age atmosphere. Find a place to enjoy the scene. Belly up to the railing, take a seat on a bench, or even pause the tour for a drink at one of the **characteristic bars** that spill out onto the bridge. Café Van

Zuylen is famous for its variety of beers, and Café Villa Zeezicht is popular for its apple pie (both cafés described on page 210). Take in your surroundings.

The Singel canal was the original moat running around the old walled city. This bridge is so wide because it was the road that led to one of the original city gates. The area still looks much as it might have during the Dutch Golden Age of the 1600s. This was when Amsterdam's seagoing merchants ruled the waves, establishing trading colonies as far away as modern Indonesia. Fueled with this wealth, the city quickly became a major urban center, lined with impressive homes. Each proud merchant tried to outdo his neighbor. Pan 360 degrees and take in the variety of buildings.

The houses crowd together, shoulder-to-shoulder. They're built on top of thousands of logs hammered vertically into the marshy soil to provide a foundation. Over the years, they've shifted with the tides, leaving some

leaning this way and that. Notice that some of the brick houses have iron rods strapped onto the sides. These act like braces, binding the bricks to an inner skeleton of wood. Almost all Amsterdam houses have big, tall windows to let in as much light as possible.

Although some houses look quite narrow, most of them extend far back. The rear of the building—called the *achterhuis*—is often much more spacious than you might expect, judging from the facade. Real estate has always been expensive on this canal, and owners were taxed by the amount of street frontage. It was especially expensive for homes with a wide facade and minimum usable space in back. A local saying back then was, "Only the wealthy can live on the inside of a canal's curve."

Mingled among the old houses are a few modern buildings. These sleek, gray-metal ones are part of the university. Built in the less affluent 1970s, architecture like this wouldn't be allowed today. Though these buildings try to match the humble, functional spirit of the older ones, they're still pretty ugly. But the students they house inject life into the neighborhood.

The "big head" statue honors a writer known by his pen name: **Multatuli.** Born in Amsterdam in 1820, Multatuli (a.k.a. Eduard

Douwes Dekker) did what many young Dutchmen did back then: He sought his fortune in Indonesia, then a colony of the Netherlands. While working as a bureaucrat in the colonial system, he witnessed firsthand the hard life of Javanese natives slaving away on Dutch-owned plantations. His semi-autobiographical novel, *Max Havelaar* (1860), follows a progressive civil servant fighting to reform colonial abuses. He was the first author to criticize Dutch colonial practices—a very bold position back then. For his talent and subject matter, Multatuli has been dubbed "the Dutch Rudyard Kipling."

The Singel canal is just one of Amsterdam's many canals—all told, there are roughly 50 miles of them (see sidebar on page 102). In the distance, way down at the north end of Singel, beyond the dome, you can get a glimpse of one of this canal's **locks.** Those white-flagpole thingies, sprouting at 45-degree angles, are part of the apparatus that opens and shuts the gates. While the canals originated as a way to drain diked-off marshland, they eventually became part of the city's sewer system. They were flushed daily: Just open the locks, and let the North Sea tides come in and out.

The Dutch are credited with inventing locks in the 1300s. (Let's not ask the Chinese.) Locks are the single greatest innova-

Gables

Along the rooftops, Amsterdam's famous gables are false fronts to enhance roofs that are, generally, sharply pitched. Gables come in all shapes and sizes. They might be ornamented with animal and human heads, garlands, urns, scrolls, and curlicues. Despite their infinite variety, most belong to a few distinct types. See how many of these you can spot.

A simple "point" gable just follows the triangular shape of a normal pitched roof. A "bell" gable is shaped like...well, guess. "Step" gables are triangular in shape and lined with steps; these are especially popular in Belgium. The one with a rectangular protrusion at the peak is called a "spout" gable. "Neck" gables rise up vertically from a pair of sloping "shoulders." "Cornice" gables make pointed roofs look classically horizontal. (There's probably even a "clark" gable, but frankly, I don't give a damn.)

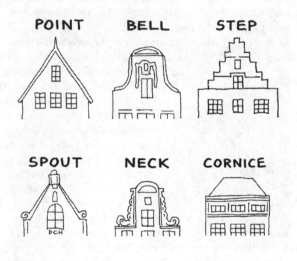

tion in canal-building. Besides controlling water flow in the city, they allow ships to pass from higher to lower water levels, and vice versa. It's because of locks that you can ship something by boat from here inland. Thanks to an extensive system of locks, from this very spot, you could hop a boat and go upriver, connect to the Rhine, and eventually—over the continental divide in Germany—connect to the Danube and then sail downstream, finally reaching Romania and the Black Sea.

The green copper dome in the distance marks the Lutheran church. To the left of the church is the new city—reclaimed in the

1600s and destined to be the high-rent district. To the right is the old town.

• *Continue west on...*

❹ Oude Leliestraat

On "Old Lily Street," consumers will find plenty of Amsterdam treats—Reypenaer's cheeses, Puccini's bonbons, Sukabumi's *rijst-tafel*, Grey Area's marijuana, California's burritos, sushi, and *shoarmas*—everything but lilies. (The Reypenaer cheese shop is especially worthwhile, as it offers tasty samples, and has a classroom in the basement for tasting sessions; see page 61.)

The Grey Area is a thriving coffeeshop; like Holland's other "coffeeshops," it sells marijuana. The green-and-white decal in the window identifies it as #092 in the city's licensing program. While smoking marijuana is essentially legal here, the café's name refers to the murky back side of the marijuana business—how coffeeshops get their supply from wholesalers. That's the "gray area" that Dutch laws have yet to sort out. (For more on this and other coffeeshops, see the Smoking chapter.)

This esteemed coffeeshop, which works with the best boutique growers in Holland, regularly wins big at Amsterdam's annual Cannabis Cup Awards—a "high" honor, to be sure.

• *The next canal is...*

❺ Herengracht

During the Dutch Golden Age boom in the 1600s, Amsterdam expanded, adding this canal. It's named for the *heren,* the wealthy

city merchants who lined it with their mansions. Because the city was anti-royalty, there was no blue-blooded class; these *heren* functioned as the town's aristocracy. Even today, Herengracht runs through a high-rent district. (Notice that zoning here forbids houseboats.)

Check out the house that's kitty-corner across the bridge, at Herengracht 150. It has features you'll find on many old Amsterdam buildings. On the roof, rods support the false-front gable (which originally supported only a rich

JORDAAN WALK

merchant's ego). Also, notice that, because this particular building is at the end of the block, you get a cutaway look of its entire depth—the long side of the building. Most Amsterdam buildings, like this one, are much bigger than they appear from the front.

Before moving on, notice the parking sign along Herengracht, on the left. The sign instructs motorists to put money in the meter at the end of the block. Parking is a major problem in a city like this, designed for boats, not cars.

• *Continue west, walking along...*

❻ Leliegracht

This is one of the city's prettiest small canals, lined with trees and crossed by a series of arched bridges. There are some 400 such bridges in Amsterdam. It's a pleasant street of trendy furniture shops and bookstores. Notice that some buildings have staircases leading down below the street level to residences. Looking up, you'll see the characteristic beams jutting out from the top with a cargo-hoisting hook on the end.

• *Continue on to the next canal, and pause on the...*

❼ Keizersgracht Bridge

Take in another fine row of gables.

• *After the bridge, we'll take a detour off our westward route, and veer left along...*

❽ Keizersgracht

Walk south about 100 yards along the canal with an eye toward

the church tower, rising above the rooftops and capped with a colorful crown. You'll reach a set of steps leading down to the water, where a triangular pink stone juts into the canal. This is part of the so-called **Homomonument**—Amsterdam's AIDS memorial. If you survey the square, you'll see that the pink triangle is just one of three triangles between here and the church. These are contained in a single large triangle that comprises the Homomonument. The pink-triangle design reclaims the symbol that the Nazis used in concentration camps to label homosexual men. It's also a reminder of the persecution gay people still experience today. You may see flowers or cards left here by friends and loved ones.

Near the monument, on Westermarkt square, is a souvenir kiosk called Pink Point. Here the volunteer staff gives out information on gay and lesbian Amsterdam, especially nightlife.

The green metal structure near the Homomonument is a public urinal. It offers just enough privacy. City trucks circulate around town on a regular basis, suds-ing them down.

From here, walk through the square called Westermarkt, between the church and busy Raadhuisstraat. Circle around the far end of the church to find two very Dutch kiosks. One sells french fries; when it's closed, the shutters feature funny paintings putting *friets* into great masterpieces of Western art. The other sells fresh herring. If you've yet to try a delicious Dutch herring, this is the perfect opportunity. For €2.75 you get a fresh herring with pickles and onion on a paper plate and instructions from the friendly merchant on how to eat it (for pointers, see page 210).

• *Keep walking toward the entrance to...*

❾ Westerkerk

Near the western end of the church, look for a cute little statue. It's of Anne Frank, who holed up with her family in a house just down the block from here (we'll pass it in a minute).

For now, look up at the towering spire of the impressive Westerkerk. The crown shape was a gift of the Habsburg emperor, Maximilian I. As a thanks for a big loan, the city got permission to use the Habsburg royal symbol. The tower also displays the symbol of Amsterdam, with its three Xs. The Westerkerk (Western Church) was built in 1631, as the city was expanding out from Dam Square. Rembrandt's buried inside...but no one knows where. You can pop into the church for free, or pay to climb to the tower balcony (just below the *XXX*) for a grand view (see page 61).

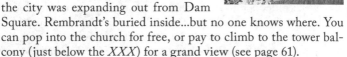

The church tower has a carillon that chimes every 15 minutes. At other times, it plays full songs. Invented by Dutch bellmakers in the 1400s, a carillon is a set of bells of different sizes and pitches. There's a live musician inside the tower who plays a keyboard to make the music. Mozart, Vivaldi, and Bach—all of whom lived during the heyday of the carillon—wrote music that sounds great on this unique instrument. During World War II, the Westerkerk's carillon played every day. This hopeful sound reminded Anne Frank that there was, indeed, an outside world.

• *Continue around the church, and walk north along the canal, past the long line of tourists marking the entrance to the ever-popular...*

⑩ Anne Frank House

This was where the Frank family hid from the Nazis for 25 months. With actual artifacts, the museum gives the cold, mind-boggling statistics of fascism the all-important intimacy of a young girl who lived through it and died from it. Even bah-humbug types find themselves caught up in Anne's story. ✪ See the Anne Frank House Tour chapter.

• *At the next bridge turn left. Stop at its summit, mid-canal, for a view of...*

⑪ Prinsengracht

The "Princes' Canal" runs through what's considered one of the most livable areas in town. It's lined with houseboats, some of the city's estimated 2,500. These small vessels were once cargo ships—but by the 1930s, they had become obsolete, replaced by more modern craft. They found a new use, as houseboats lining the canals of Amsterdam, where dry land was so limited and pricey. Today, their former cargo holds are fashioned into elegant, cozy living rooms. The once-powerful engines  have generally been removed to make room for more living space. Moorage spots are prized and grandfathered in, making some of the junky old boats worth more than you'd think. Houseboaters can plug hoses and cables into outlets along the canals to get water and electricity. (To learn more about houseboats, visit the charming Houseboat Museum, described on page 60.)

Notice the canal traffic. The official speed limit on canals is about four miles per hour. At night, boats must have running lights on the top, the side, and the stern. Most boats are small and low, designed to glide under the city's bridges. The Prinsengracht bridge is average height, with less than seven feet of headroom (it varies with the water level); some bridges have less than six feet. Boaters need good maps to tell them the height, which is crucial for navigating. Police boats roam on the lookout for anyone CUI (cruising under the influence).

Just across the bridge are several typical Jordaan cafés. The relaxed **Café de Prins** serves food and drink both day and night.

The old-timey **De Twee Zwaantjes** (a few doors to the right) occasionally features the mournful songs of a late local legend, balladeer Johnny Jordaan. Finally, there's the **Café 't Smalle**—it's not visible from here, but it's a half-block to the right. It has a deck where you can drink outside along a quiet canal (for details, see listing in the Eating in Amsterdam chapter)

• *Once you cross Prinsengracht, you enter what's officially considered the Jordaan neighborhood. Facing west (toward Café de Prins), cross the bridge and veer left down...*

⓬ Nieuwe Leliestraat

Welcome to the quiet Jordaan. Built in the 1600s as a working-class housing area, it's now home to artists and yuppies. The name Jordaan probably was not derived from the French *jardin*—but given the neighborhood's garden-like ambience, it seems like it should have been.

Have your ultra-sharp "traveler's eyes" trained on all the tiny details of Amsterdam life. Notice how the pragmatic Dutch deal with junk mail. On the doors, stickers next to mail slots say *Nee* or *Ja* (no or yes), telling the postman if they'll accept or refuse junk mail. Residents are allowed a "front-yard garden" as long as it's no more than one sidewalk tile wide. The red metal bollards known as *Amsterdammertjes* ("little Amsterdammers") have been bashing balls since the 1970s, when they were put in to stop people from parking on the sidewalks. Though many apartments have windows right on the street, the neighbors don't stare and the residents don't care.

• *At the first intersection, turn right onto...*

⓭ Eerste Leliedwarsstraat

Pause and linger awhile on this tiny lane. Imagine the frustrations of home ownership here. The ugly modern buildings you see date from the 1960s and '70s. This was before the gentrification of the 1980s, when the city started writing more restrictive building codes. Check out house #9. Here, a run-down historic home was torn down, replaced by a cheap and functional building with modern heating and plumbing. Now move ahead to #5. Its owners were probably stuck with rent control, so they didn't invest in the place. They missed the window of time when a cheap and functional rebuild was allowed, and now they can't get permission to renovate this home without making it prohibitively expensive. Across the street, #2A obviously had the cash to do a first-class sprucing up. Even newly renovated homes must preserve their funky leaning angles and original wooden beams. They're certainly nice to look at, but absolutely maddening if you own a building and aren't rich.

• *Just ahead, walk out to the middle of the bridge over the next canal (Egelantiersgracht). This is what I think of as...*

⓮ The Heart of the Jordaan

For me, this bridge and its surroundings capture the essence of the Jordaan. Take it all in: the bookstores, art galleries, working artists' studios, and small cafés full of rickety tables. Look down the quiet canal. It's lined with trees and old, narrow buildings with gables—classic Amsterdam.

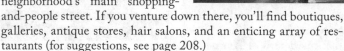

Look north, farther down the street beyond the bridge. This lane, called Tweede Egelantiersdwarsstraat, is the laid-back Jordaan neighborhood's main shopping-and-people street. If you venture down there, you'll find boutiques, galleries, antique stores, hair salons, and an enticing array of restaurants (for suggestions, see page 208.)

Now turn around and look south at the Westerkerk, and you'll see a completely different view of the church from the one that the tourists in line at the Anne Frank House get. Framed by narrow streets, crossed with streetlamp wires, and looming over shoppers on bicycles—to me, this is the church in its best light.

Backtrack to the base of the bridge, then turn right. As you walk west along Egelantiersgracht, check out the junky old boats that litter the canal. Some aren't worth maintaining and are left abandoned. As these dinghies fill with rainwater and start to rot, the city confiscates them and stores them in a big lot. Unclaimed boats are auctioned off three times a year. But most boats are well used, and even the funkiest scows can become cruising Love Boats when the sun goes down.

• *At the first intersection, turn left onto Tweede Leliedwarsstraat, and walk a few steps to #5.*

⓯ Electric Ladyland

This small shop, with a flowery window display, calls itself "The First Museum of Fluorescent Art." Its funky facade hides an illuminated wonderland within, with a tiny exhibit of black-light art (under the shop, down a very steep set of stairs). It's the creation of Nick Padalino—one cool cat who really found his niche in life. He enjoys personally demonstrating the fluorescence found in unexpected places—everything from minerals to stamps to candy to the tattoo on his arm. Nick seems to get an even bigger kick out of it than his customers. You can see the historic first fluorescent crayon from San Francisco in the 1950s. Wow. Its label says, "Use with black light for church groups." Wow.

About 100 yards farther down the street and across the canal, old hippies might want to visit the **Paradox Coffeeshop.** It's the perfect coffeeshop for the nervous American who wants a friendly, mellow place to go local (see listing in the Smoking chapter).

• *To reach our last stop, backtrack to the canal and turn left, then walk a few dozen yards to Egelantiersgracht #107, the entrance to...*

⓰ St. Andrew's Courtyard (Sint-Andrieshof)

The black door is marked *Sint-Andrieshof 107 t/m 145.* The doorway looks private, but it's the public entrance to a set of residences. It's

generally open during daytime hours, except on Sundays. Enter quietly; you may have to push hard on the door. Go inside and continue on into a tiny garden courtyard surrounded by a dozen or so residences. Take a seat on a bench. This is one of the city's scores of similar courtyards, called *hofjes*—subsidized residences built around a courtyard, and funded by churches, charities, and the city for low-income widows and pensioners.

• *And this is where our tour ends—in a tranquil world that seems right out of a painting by Vermeer. You're just blocks from the bustle of Amsterdam, but it feels like another world. You're immersed in the Jordaan, where everything's in its place, and life seems very good.*

RIJKSMUSEUM TOUR

At Amsterdam's Rijksmuseum ("Rijks" rhymes with "bikes"), Holland's Golden Age shines with the best collection anywhere of the Dutch Masters—from Vermeer's quiet domestic scenes and Steen's raucous family meals to Hals' snapshot portraits and Rembrandt's moody brilliance.

The 17th century saw the Netherlands at the pinnacle of its power. The Dutch had won their independence from Spain, trade and shipping boomed, wealth poured in, the people were understandably proud, and the arts flourished. This era was later dubbed the Dutch Golden Age. With no church bigwigs or royalty around to commission big canvases in the Protestant Dutch Republic, artists had to find different patrons—and they discovered the upper-middle-class businessmen who fueled Holland's capitalist economy. Artists painted their portraits and decorated their homes with pretty still lifes and unpreachy, slice-of-life art.

This delightful museum—recently much improved after a long renovation—offers one of the most exciting and enjoyable art experiences in Europe. As if in homage to Dutch art and history, the Rijksmuseum lets you linger over a vast array of objects and paintings, appreciating the beauty of everyday things.

Orientation

Cost: €17.50.
Hours: Daily 9:00-17:00, last entry 30 minutes before closing, café and gift shop open until 18:00.

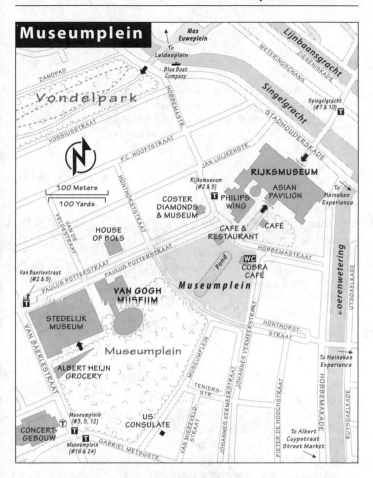

Museumplein

Avoiding Crowds: The museum is most crowded on weekends and holidays, and there's always a peak midday crush around noon. Avoid crowds by coming on Monday or Tuesday, and plan your visit for either first thing in the morning or later in the day (it's least crowded after 15:00). You can reserve tickets; see "Getting In," below.

Getting There: From Central Station, catch tram #2 or #5 to the Rijksmuseum stop. The museum entrance is just off the arched passage that cuts under the building at its center (watch out for bikes).

Getting In: You can skip the ticket-buying line by getting your ticket in advance at www.rijksmuseum.nl; you can print out your ticket or save your ticket barcode to your phone or tablet. Many hotels also sell tickets. The ticket is good any time (no entry time specified). A Museumkaart pass also lets you skip the line.

Information: The helpful information desk in the lower-level Atrium has free maps. Info tel. 020/674-7047, www.rijksmuseum.nl.

Videoguide: A multimedia videoguide (€5) offers both a 45-minute highlights tour and a more in-depth tour. Use this chapter to hit the highlights, then (if you choose) explore the rest of the collection with the videoguide.

Length of This Tour: Allow 1.5 hours.

Baggage Check: Leave your bag at the free checkroom in the Atrium.

Photography: Permitted but no flash.

Cuisine Art: The Rijksmuseum Grand Café, in the Atrium above the gift shop, is outside the ticketed entry, so you don't need a museum ticket to eat here. On the south side of the building, there's a café in the Philips Wing and a pleasant coffee-and-pastry café in the garden to the right.

Nearby on Museumplein, you'll find the Cobra Café (daily 10:00-18:00, tel. 020/470-0111), a number of take-out stands, and (at the far end, near the Stedelijk Museum), an Albert Heijn grocery. Museumplein and nearby Vondelpark are both perfect for a picnic.

Starring: Rembrandt van Rijn, Frans Hals, Johannes Vermeer, Jan Steen, and many interesting artifacts of the Golden Age.

OVERVIEW

Dutch art is meant to be enjoyed, not studied. It's straightforward, meat-and-potatoes art for the common man. The Dutch love the beauty of mundane things painted realistically and with exquisite detail. So set your cerebral cortex on "low" and let this art pass straight from the eyes to the heart, with minimal detours.

The Tour Begins

• *Enter the building. Those with advance tickets or a Museumkaart can use a special marked entrance. You'll descend into the lower-level Atrium, with all the tourist services: ticket sales, information desk, baggage check, café, gift shop, and WCs. After showing your ticket (and perhaps renting a videoguide), follow the crowds up the stairway to the top (second) floor,*

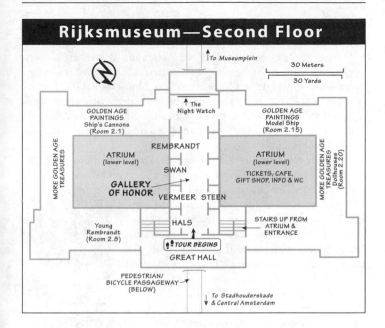

Rijksmuseum—Second Floor

To Museumplein

30 Meters
30 Yards

GOLDEN AGE
PAINTINGS
Ship's Cannons
(Room 2.1)

GOLDEN AGE
PAINTINGS
Model Ship
(Room 2.15)

↑ The
Night Watch

MORE GOLDEN AGE
TREASURES

ATRIUM
(lower level)

REMBRANDT

ATRIUM
(lower level)

MORE GOLDEN AGE
TREASURES
Dollhouses
(Room 2.20)

SWAN

GALLERY
OF HONOR

TICKETS, CAFE,
GIFT SHOP, INFO & WC

VERMEER STEEN

HALS

Young
Rembrandt
(Room 2.8)

STAIRS UP FROM
ATRIUM &
ENTRANCE

TOUR BEGINS

GREAT HALL

PEDESTRIAN/
BICYCLE PASSAGEWAY
(BELOW)

↓ To Stadhouderskade
& Central Amsterdam

*where you emerge into the **Great Hall**. With its stained-glass windows, vaulted ceiling, and murals of Golden Age explorers, it feels like a cathedral to Holland's middle-class merchants. Gaze down the long adjoining hall to the far end, with the "altarpiece" of this cathedral—Rembrandt's Night Watch. Now, follow the flow of the crowds toward it, into the...*

GALLERY OF HONOR

This grand space was purpose-built to hold the Greatest Hits of the Golden Age, by the era's biggest rock stars: Frans Hals, Vermeer, Jan Steen, and Rembrandt. The best of the era's portraits, still lifes, landscapes, and slice-of-life "genre scenes" give us a close-up look at daily life in this happy, affluent era. The smaller rooms surrounding the Gallery hold more treasures of the Golden Age.

Frans Hals

Frans Hals (c. 1582-1666) was the premier Golden Age portrait painter. Merchants hired him the way we'd hire a wedding photographer. With a few quick strokes, Hals captured not only the features, but also the personality.

A Militiaman Holding a Berkemeyer (a.k.a. *The Merry Drinker,* c. 1628-1630)

You're greeted by a jovial man in a black hat, capturing the earthy, exuberant spirit of the Dutch Golden Age. Notice the details—the happy, red face of the man offering us a *berkemeyer* drinking glass, the sparkle in his eyes, the lacy collar, the decorative belt buckle, and so on.

Now move in closer. All these meticulous details are accomplished with a few thick, messy brushstrokes. The beard is a tangle of brown worms, the belt buckle a yellow blur. His hand is a study in smudges. Even the expressive face is created with a few well-chosen patches of color. Unlike Dutch still-life scenes, this canvas is meant to be viewed from a distance, where the colors and brushstrokes blend together.

Rather than posing his subject, making him stand for hours saying "cheese," Hals tried to catch him at a candid moment. He often painted common people, fishermen, and barflies such as this one. He had to work quickly to capture the serendipity of the moment. Hals used a stop-action technique, freezing the man in mid-gesture, with the rough brushwork creating a blur that suggests the man is still moving.

Two centuries later, the Impressionists learned from Hals' messy brushwork. In the Van Gogh Museum, you'll see how Van Gogh painted, say, a brown beard by using thick dabs of green, yellow, and red that blend at a distance to make brown.

Portrait of a Couple, Probably Isaac Abrahamsz Massa and Beatrix van der Laen (c. 1622)

This likely wedding portrait of a chubby, pleasant merchant and his bride sums up the story of the Dutch Golden Age. Because

this overseas trader was away from home for years at a time on business, Hals makes a special effort to point out his patron's commitment to marriage. Isaac pledges allegiance to his wife, putting his hand on his heart. Beatrix's wedding ring is prominently displayed dead center between them (on her right-hand forefinger, Protestant-style). The vine clinging to a tree is a symbol of man's support and woman's dependence. And in the distance at right, in the classical love garden, are other happy couples strolling arm-in-arm amid peacocks, a symbol of fertility.

In earlier times, marriage portraits put the man and wife in separate canvases, staring out grimly. Hals' jolly side-by-side cou-

The Dutch Golden Age (1600s)

Who bought this art? Look around at the Rijksmuseum's many portraits, and you'll see ordinary middle-class people, merchants, and traders. Even in their Sunday best, you can tell that these are hardworking, businesslike, friendly, simple people (with a penchant for ruffled lace collars).

Dutch fishermen sold their surplus catch in distant areas of Europe, importing goods from these far lands. In time, fishermen became traders, and by 1600, Holland's merchant fleets ruled the waves with colonies as far away as India, Indonesia, and America (remember—New York was originally "New Amsterdam"). The Dutch slave trade—selling Africans to Americans—generated a lot of profit for luxuries such as the art you're viewing. Back home, these traders were financed by shrewd Amsterdam businessmen on the new frontiers of capitalism.

Look around again. Is there even one crucifixion? One saint? One Madonna? This art is made for the people, not for the church. In most countries, Catholic bishops and rich kings supported the arts. But the Dutch Republic, recently free of Spanish rule and Vatican domination, was independent, democratic, and largely Protestant, with no taste for saints and Madonnas.

Instead, Dutch burghers bought portraits of themselves and pretty, unpreachy, unpretentious works for their homes. Even poor people bought art—usually on smaller canvases, painted by no-name artists, and designed to fit their budgets and lifestyles. We'll see examples of their four favorite subjects—still lifes (of food and mundane objects), landscapes, portraits (often of groups), and scenes from everyday life.

ple reflects a societal shift from marriage as business partnership to an arrangement that's more friendly and intimate.

Hals didn't need symbolism to tell us that these two are prepared for their long-distance relationship—they seem relaxed together, but each looks at us directly, with a strong, individual identity. Good as gold, these are the type of people who propelled this soggy little country into its glorious Golden Age.

Johannes Vermeer

Vermeer (1632-1675) is the master of tranquility and stillness. He creates a clear and silent pool that is a world in itself. Most of his canvases show interiors of Dutch homes, where Dutch women engage in everyday activities, lit by a side window.

Vermeer's father, an art dealer, gave Johannes a passion for painting. Late in the artist's career, with Holland fighting draining wars against England, the demand for art and luxuries went sour

Shhh...Dutch Art

You're sitting at home late one night, and it's perfectly calm. Not a sound, very peaceful. And then...the refrigerator motor turns off, and it's really quiet.

Dutch art is really quiet art. It silences our busy world, so that every sound, every motion is noticeable. You can hear cows tearing off grass 50 yards away. Dutch art is still. It slows our fast-lane world, so we notice the motion of birds. We notice how the cold night air makes the stars sharp. We notice that the undersides of leaves and cats are always a lighter shade than the tops. Dutch art stills the world so we can hear our own heartbeat and reflect upon that most noble muscle that, without thinking, gives us life.

To see how subtle Dutch art is, realize that one of the museum's most exciting, dramatic, emotional, and extravagant Dutch paintings is probably *The Threatened Swan* (in the Gallery of Honor). It's quite a contrast to the rape scenes and visions of heaven of Italian Baroque paintings from the same time period.

in the Netherlands, forcing Vermeer to downsize—he sold his big home, packed up his wife and 14 children, and moved in with his mother-in-law. He died two years later, and his works fell into centuries of obscurity.

The Rijksmuseum has the best collection of Vermeers in the world—four of them. (There are only some 34 in captivity.) But each is a small jewel worth lingering over.

The Milkmaid (c. 1660)

It's so quiet you can practically hear the milk pouring into the bowl.

Vermeer brings out the beauty in everyday things. The subject is ordinary—a kitchen maid—but you could look for hours at the tiny details and rich color tones. These are everyday objects, but they glow in a diffused light: the crunchy crust, the hanging basket, even the rusty nail in the wall with its tiny shadow. Vermeer had a unique ability with surface texture, to show how things feel when you touch them.

The maid is alive with Vermeer's distinctive yellow and blue—the colors of many tra-

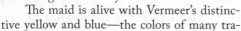

ditional Dutch homes—against a white backdrop. She is content, solid, and sturdy, performing this simple task as if it's the most important thing in the world. Her full arms are built with patches of reflected light. Vermeer squares off a little world in itself (framed by the table in the foreground, the wall in back, the window to the left, and the footstool at right), then fills this space with objects for our perusal.

Woman Reading a Letter (c. 1663)

Notice how Vermeer's placid scenes often have an air of mystery. The woman is reading a letter. From whom? A lover? A father on a

two-year business trip to Indonesia? Not even taking time to sit down, she reads intently, with parted lips and a bowed head. It must be important. (She looks pregnant, adding to the mystery, but that may just be the cut of her clothes.)

Again, Vermeer has framed a moment of everyday life. But within this small world are hints of a wider, wilder world—the light coming from the left is obviously from a large window, giving us a whiff of the life going on outside. The map hangs prominently, reminding us of travel, and perhaps of where the letter is from.

The Love Letter (c. 1669-1670)

There's a similar theme here. The curtain parts, and we see through the doorway into a doll-house world, then through the seascape on the back wall to the wide ocean. A woman is playing a lute when she's interrupted by a servant bringing a letter. The mysterious letter stops the music, intruding like a pebble dropped into the pool of Vermeer's quiet world. The floor tiles create a strong 3-D perspective that sucks us straight into the center of the painting—the woman's heart.

View of Houses in Delft
(a.k.a. The Little Street, c. 1658)

Vermeer was born in the picturesque town of Delft, grew up near its Market Square, and set a number of his paintings there. This may be the view from his front door.

The details in the painting actually aren't very detailed—the cobblestone street doesn't have a single individual stone in it. But Vermeer shows us the beautiful interplay of colored rectangles on the buildings. Our eye moves back and forth from shutter to gable to window...and then from front to back, as we notice the woman deep in the alleyway.

Jan Steen

Not everyone could afford a masterpiece, but even poorer people wanted works of art for their homes (like a landscape from Sears for over the sofa). Jan Steen (c. 1625-1679, pronounced "yahn stain"), the Norman Rockwell of his day, painted humorous scenes from the lives of the lower classes. As a tavern owner, he observed society firsthand.

Adolf and Catharina Croeser (a.k.a. *The Burgomaster of Delft and His Daughter*, 1655)

Steen's well-dressed burgher sits on his front porch, when a poor woman and child approach to beg, putting him squarely between the horns of a moral dilemma. On the one hand, we see his rich home, well-dressed daughter, and a vase of flowers—a symbol that his money came from morally suspect capitalism (the kind that produced the folly of 1637's "tulip mania," described on page 20). On the other hand, there are his poor fellow citizens and the church steeple, reminding him of his Christian duty. The man's daughter avoids the confrontation. Will the burgher set the right Christian example? This moral dilemma per-

plexed many nouveau-riche Dutch Calvinists of Steen's day.

This early painting by Steen demonstrates his mastery of several popular genres: portrait, still life (the flowers and fabrics), cityscape, and moral instruction.

The Feast of St. Nicholas (1665-1668)

It's Christmas time, and the kids have been given their gifts, including a little girl who got a doll. The mother says, "Let me see

it," but the girl turns away playfully. Everyone is happy except the boy, who's crying. His Christmas present is only a branch in his shoe—like coal in your stocking, the gift for bad boys. His sister gloats and passes it around. The kids laugh at him. But wait—it turns out the family is just playing a trick. In the background, the grandmother beckons to him, saying, "Look, I have your real present in here." Out of the limelight, but smack in the middle, sits the father providing ballast to this family scene and clearly enjoying his children's pleasure.

Steen has frozen the moment, sliced off a piece, and laid it on a canvas. He's told a story with a past, a present, and a future. These are real people in a real scene.

Steen's fun art reminds us that museums aren't mausoleums.

The Merry Family (1668)

This family—three generations living happily under one roof—is eating, drinking, and singing like there's no tomorrow. The broken

eggshells and scattered cookware symbolize waste and extravagance. The neglected proverb tacked to the fireplace reminds us that children will follow in the footsteps of their parents. The father in this jolly scene is very drunk—ready to topple over—while in the foreground his mischievous daughter is feeding her brother wine straight from the flask. Mom and Grandma join the artist himself (playing the bagpipes) in a lively sing-along, but the child learning to smoke would rather follow Dad's lead.

Dutch Golden Age families were notoriously lenient with their kids. Even today, the Dutch describe a rowdy family as a "Jan Steen household."

Rembrandt van Rijn

Rembrandt van Rijn (1606-1669) is the greatest of all Dutch painters. Whereas most painters specialized in one field—portraits, landscapes, still lifes—Rembrandt excelled in them all.

The son of a Leiden miller who owned a waterwheel on the Rhine ("van Rijn"), Rembrandt took Amsterdam by storm with his famous painting *The Anatomy Lesson of Dr. Nicolaes Tulp* (1632, currently in The Hague's Mauritshuis Royal Picture Gallery; see page 391). The commissions poured in for official portraits, and he was soon wealthy

and married (1634) to Saskia van Uylenburgh. They moved to an expensive home in the Jewish Quarter (today's Rembrandt House Museum), and decorated it with their collection of art and exotic furniture. His portraits were dutifully detailed, but other paintings explored strong contrasts of light and dark, with dramatic composition.

In 1642, Saskia died, and Rembrandt's fortunes changed, as the public's taste shifted and commissions dried up. In 1649, he hired an 18-year-old model named Hendrickje Stoffels, and she soon moved in with him and gave birth to their daughter.

Holland's war with England (1652-1654) devastated the art market, and Rembrandt's free-spending ways forced him to declare bankruptcy (1656)—the ultimate humiliation in success-oriented Amsterdam. The commissions came more slowly. The money ran out. His mother died. He had to auction off his paintings and furniture to pay debts. He moved out of his fine house to a cheaper place on Rozengracht. His bitter losses added a new wisdom to his work.

In his last years, his greatest works were his self-portraits, showing a tired, wrinkled man stoically enduring life's misfortunes. Rembrandt piled on layers of paint and glaze to capture increasingly subtle effects. In 1668, his lone surviving son, Titus, died, and Rembrandt passed away the next year. His death effectively marked the end of the Dutch Golden Age.

Isaac and Rebecca (a.k.a. The Jewish Bride, c. 1665-1669)

The man gently draws the woman toward him. She's comfortable enough with him to sink into thought, and she reaches up unconsciously to return the gentle touch. They're young but wizened. This uncommissioned portrait (its subjects remain unknown) is a truly human look at the relationship between two people in love. They form a protective pyramid of love amid a gloomy background. The touching hands form the center of this somewhat sad but peace-  ful work. Van Gogh said that "Rembrandt alone has that tenderness—the heartbroken tenderness."

Rembrandt was a master of oil painting. In his later years, he rendered details with a messier, more Impressionistic style. The red-brown-gold of the couple's clothes is a patchwork of oil laid on thick with a palette knife.

The Wardens of the Amsterdam Drapers' Guild (a.k.a. The Syndics, 1662)

Rembrandt could paint an official group portrait better than anyone. In the painting made famous by Dutch Masters cigars, he catches the Drapers Guild in a natural but dignified pose (dignified, at least, until the guy on the left sits on his friend's lap).

It's a business meeting, and they're all dressed in black with black hats—the standard power suit of the Dutch Golden Age. They gather around a table examining the company's books. Suddenly, someone (us) walks in, and they look up. It's as natural as a snapshot, though X-rays show Rembrandt made many changes in posing them perfectly.

The figures are "framed" by the table beneath them and the top of the wood paneling above their heads, making a three-part composition that brings this band of colleagues together. Even in this simple portrait, we feel we can read the guild members' personalities in their faces. (If the table in the painting looks like it's sloping a bit unnaturally, lie on the floor to view it at Rembrandt's intended angle.)

• At the far end of the Gallery of Honor is the museum's star masterpiece. The best viewing spot is to the right of center—the angle Rembrandt had in mind when he designed it for its original location.

The Night Watch (a.k.a. *The Militia Company of Captain Frans Banninck Cocq*, 1642)

This is Rembrandt's most famous—though not necessarily greatest—painting. Created in 1642, when he was 36, it was one of his

most important commissions: a group portrait of a company of Amsterdam's Civic Guards to hang in their meeting hall.

It's an action shot. With flags waving and drums beating, the guardsmen (who, by the 1640s, were really only an honorary militia of rich bigwigs) spill onto the street from under an arch in the back. It's "all for one and one for all" as they rush to Amsterdam's rescue. The soldiers grab lances and load their muskets. In the center, the commander (in black, with a red sash) strides forward energetically with a hand gesture that seems to say, "What are we waiting for? Let's move out!" His lieutenant focuses on his every order.

Rembrandt caught the optimistic spirit of Holland in the 1600s. Its war of independence from Spain was heading to vic-

Ruffs

I cannot tell you why men and women of the Dutch Golden Age found these fanlike collars attractive, but they certainly were all the rage here and elsewhere in Europe. It started in Spain in the 1540s, but the style really took off with a marvelous discovery in 1565: starch. Within decades, Europe's wealthy merchant class was wearing nine-inch collars made from 18 yards of material.

The ruffs were detachable and made from a long, pleated strip of linen set into a neck (or wrist) band. You tied it in front with strings. Big ones required that you wear a wire frame underneath for support. There were various types—the "cartwheel" was the biggest, a "double ruff" had two layers of pleats, and a "cabbage" was somewhat asymmetrical.

Ruffs required elaborate maintenance. First, you washed and starched the linen. While the cloth was still wet, hot metal pokers were painstakingly inserted into the folds to form the characteristic figure-eight pattern. The ruffs were stored in special round boxes to hold their shape.

For about a century, Europeans loved the ruff, but by 1630, Holland had come to its senses, and the fad faded.

---

tory and the economy was booming. These guardsmen on the move epitomize the proud, independent, upwardly mobile Dutch.

Why is *The Night Watch* so famous? Compare it with other, less famous group portraits nearby, where every face is visible and everyone is well-lit, flat, and flashbulb-perfect. These people paid good money to have their mugs preserved for posterity, and they wanted it right up front. Other group portraits may be colorful, dignified works by a master...but not quite masterpieces.

By contrast, Rembrandt rousted the Civic Guards off their fat duffs. By adding movement and depth to an otherwise static scene, he took posers and turned them into warriors. He turned a simple portrait into great art.

OK, some *Night Watch* scuttlebutt: First off, "night watch" is a misnomer. It's a daytime scene, but over the years, as the preserving varnish darkened and layers of dirt built up, the sun set on this painting, and it got its popular title. When the painting was moved to a smaller room, the sides were lopped off (and the pieces lost), putting the two main characters in the center and causing the work to become more static than intended. During World War II, the painting was rolled up and hidden for five years. In 1975, a madman attacked the painting, slicing the captain's legs, and in

1990, it was sprayed with acid (it was skillfully restored after both incidents).

The Night Watch, contrary to popular myth, was a smashing success in its day. However, there are elements in it that show why Rembrandt soon fell out of favor as a portrait painter. He seemed to spend as much time painting the dwarf and the mysterious glowing girl with a chicken (the very appropriate mascot of this "militia" of shopkeepers) as he did the faces of his employers.

Rembrandt's life darkened long before his *Night Watch* did. This work marks the peak of Rembrandt's popularity...and the beginning of his fall from grace. He continued to paint master-pieces. Free from the dictates of employers whose taste was in their mouths, he painted what he wanted, how he wanted it. Rembrandt goes beyond mere craftsmanship to probe into, and draw life from, the deepest wells of the human soul.

• *Backtrack a few steps to the Gallery of Honor's last alcove to find Rembrandt's...*

Self-Portrait as the Apostle Paul (1661)

Rembrandt's many self-portraits show us the evolution of a great painter's style, as well as the progress of a genius's life. For Rembrandt, the two were intertwined.

In this somber, late self-portrait, the man is 55 but he looks 70. With a lined forehead, a bulbous nose, and messy hair, he peers out from under several coats of glazing, holding old, wrinkled pages. His look is...skeptical? Weary? Resigned to life's misfortunes? Or amused? (He's looking at us, but not *just* at us—remember that a self-portrait is done staring into a mirror.)

This man has seen it all—success, love, money, fatherhood, loss, poverty, death. He took these experiences and wove them into his art. Rembrandt died poor and misunderstood, but he remained very much his own man to the end.

• *You'll find more Rembrandts, from his early years, just off the Great Hall in Room 2.8, which is dedicated to...*

The Young Rembrandt
Self-Portrait (c. 1628)

Here we see the young small-town boy about to launch himself into whatever life has to offer. Rembrandt was a precocious kid. His father, a miller, insisted that he become a lawyer. His mother hoped he'd be a preacher (you may see a portrait of her reading the Bible). Rembrandt combined the secular and religious worlds by becoming an artist, someone who can hint at the spiritual by showing us the beauty of the created world.

He moved to Amsterdam and entered the highly competitive art world. Amsterdam was a booming town and, like today, a hip and cosmopolitan city. Rembrandt portrays himself at age 22 as being divided—half in light, half hidden by hair and shadows—open-eyed, but wary of an uncertain future. Rembrandt's paintings are often light and dark, both in color and in subject, exploring the "darker" side of human experience.

Portrait of a Woman, Possibly Maria Trip (1639)

This debutante daughter of a wealthy citizen is shy and reserved—maybe a bit awkward in her new dress and adult role, but still self-assured. When he chose to, Rembrandt could dash off a commissioned portrait like nobody's business. The details are immaculate—the lace and shiny satin, the pearls behind the veil, the subtle face and hands. Rembrandt gives us not just a person, but a personality.

Look at the red rings around her eyes, a detail a lesser painter would have airbrushed out. Rembrandt takes this feature, unique to her, and uses it as a setting for her luminous, jewel-like eyes. Without being prettified, she's beautiful.

Young Woman in Fantasy Costume (1633)

It didn't take long for Amsterdam to recognize Rembrandt's great talent. Everyone wanted a portrait done by the young master, and

he became wealthy and famous. He fell in love with and married the rich, beautiful, and cultured Saskia, who is thought to be the sitter for this painting. (It's considered a "fantasy" because she's dressed in clothing from centuries before her day.)

By all accounts, the two were enormously happy, entertaining friends, decorating their house with fine furniture, raising a family, and living the high life. In this painting, Saskia's face literally glows, and a dash of white paint puts a sparkle in her eye. Barely 30 years old, Rembrandt was the most successful painter in Holland. He had it all.

Other "Rembrandts"

The Rijksmuseum displays real Rembrandts, paintings by others that look like his, portraits of Rembrandt by his students, and one or two "Rembrandts" that may not be his. A century ago, there were 1,000 so-called Rembrandt paintings in existence. Since then, a panel of five art scholars has declared most of those to be by someone else, winnowing the number of authentic Rembrandts to 300, with some 50 more that may one day be "audited" by the Internal Rembrandt Service. Most of the fakes are not out-and-out forgeries, but works by admirers of his distinctive style. The lesson? Be careful the next time you plunk down $15 million for a "Rembrandt."

Jeremiah Lamenting the Destruction of Jerusalem (1630)

The Babylonians have sacked and burned Jerusalem, but Rembrandt leaves the pyrotechnics (in the murky background at left) to Spielberg and the big screen. Instead,  he tells the story of Israel's destruction in the face of the prophet who predicted the disaster. Jeremiah slumps in defeat, deep in thought, confused and despondent, trying to understand why this evil had to happen. Rembrandt turns his floodlight of truth on the prophet's deeply lined forehead.

Rembrandt wasn't satisfied to crank out portraits of fat merchants in frilly bibs, no matter what they paid him. He wanted to experiment, trying new techniques and more probing subjects. Many of his paintings weren't commissioned and were never even intended for sale. His subjects could be brooding and melancholy, a bit dark for the public's taste. His technique set him apart—you can recognize a Rembrandt canvas by his play of light and dark. Most of his paintings are a deep brown tone, with only a few bright spots glowing from the darkness. This allowed Rembrandt to highlight the details he thought most important and to express moody emotions.

Light has a primal appeal to humans. (Dig deep into your DNA and remember the time when fire was not tamed. Light! In the middle of the night! This miracle separated us from our fellow animals.) Rembrandt strikes at that instinctive level.

• *Our tour is over, but you're free to browse. A good place to start (right in Room 2.8) is the large, colorful group portrait by Bartholomeus van der Helst,* The Banquet at the Crossbowmen's Guild, *which celebrates Holland's new era of peace after its war with Spain.*

MORE GOLDEN AGE TREASURES

The entire second floor of the Rijksmuseum is dedicated to the prosperous Dutch Golden Age. As you browse the rest of the exhibits, you'll see the following.

Group Portraits: The men in these "Civic Guard" and "Banquet" portraits helped make Amsterdam the richest city on earth in the 1600s. Though shown in military uniforms, these men were really captains of industry—shipbuilders, seamen, salesmen, spice tasters, bankers, and venture capitalists—all part of the complex economic web that planned and financed overseas trade.

Still Lifes: Savor the fruits of Holland's rich overseas trade—lemons from the south, pewterware from Germany, and spices from Asia.

Pick a still life, and get so close that the guard joins you. You'll swear you can see yourself reflected in the pewter vessels. Linger over the little things—the closer you get, the better they look. These carefully composed, photorealistic still-lifes capture the pride the Dutch had for their homes, which they cultivated like gardens to be immaculate, decorative, and in perfect order.

Artifacts: You'll see everyday items such as dollhouses (*poppenhuizen*, Room 2.20) but also seafaring ship's cannons (Room 2.1) and a big wooden model (Room 2.15) of a 74-gun Dutch man-of-war that would have escorted convoys of merchant ships loaded with wealth.

THE REST OF THE RIJKS

Most visitors are here to see the Golden Age art, but the museum has much, much more. The Rijks is dedicated to detailing Dutch history from 1200 until 2000, with upward of 8,000 works on display. There's everything from an airplane (third floor, in the 20th-century exhibit) to women's fashion and Delftware (lower level). The Asian Art Pavilion shows off 365 objects from Indonesia—a former Dutch colony—as well as items from India, Japan, Korea, and China. (The bronze Dancing Shiva, in Room 1 of the pavilion, is considered one of the best in the world.)

The newly renovated **Philips Wing** hosts temporary exhibits upstairs (with themes that complement the Rijksmuseum's strengths) and a rotating photography collection downstairs (admission covered by Rijksmuseum ticket).

VAN GOGH MUSEUM TOUR

The Van Gogh Museum (we say "van GO," the Dutch say "van *h*ock") is a cultural high even for those not into art. Located near the Rijksmuseum, the museum houses the 200 paintings owned by Vincent's younger brother, Theo. It's a user-friendly stroll through the work and life of one enigmatic man. If you like brightly colored landscapes in the Impressionist style, you'll like this museum. If you enjoy finding deeper meaning in works of art, you'll really love it. The mix of Van Gogh's creative genius, his tumultuous life, and the traveler's determination to connect to it makes this museum as much a walk with Vincent as with his art.

New Entrance: Because the museum is opening a new main entrance in 2015, expect some changes to the entry procedure and the exhibits.

Orientation

Cost: €17, more for special exhibits, free for those under 18 and for those with one ear.

Hours: Daily 9:00-18:00, Fri until 22:00 March-Oct, Sat until 22:00 July-Aug and Oct.

When to Go: Consider visiting on a Friday or Saturday evening, when crowds are sparse, and sometimes on Friday, there are musicians or a DJ and a wine bar in the lobby.

Avoiding Lines: Skip the wait in the ticket-buying line by purchasing advance tickets online (www.vangoghmuseum.nl) or at the TI. Museumkaart holders queue up at a shorter line than ticket buyers. The I amsterdam Card admits you immediately.

Getting There: It's the big, modern, gray-and-beige place a few blocks behind the Rijksmuseum. From Central Station, catch tram #2 or #5 to the Rijksmuseum or Van Baerlestraat stop.

Getting In: Visitors must pass through a security checkpoint.

Information: At the information desk, pick up a free floor plan. The bookstore has several good, basic "Vincent" guidebooks and lots of posters (with mailing tubes). The museum has free Wi-Fi. Tel. 020/570-5200, www.vangoghmuseum.nl.

Audioguides: The €5 multimedia guide gives insightful commentaries about Van Gogh's paintings and his technique, along with related quotations from Vincent himself. There's also a kids' audioguide (€2.50).

Length of This Tour: Allow one hour.

Baggage Check: Free and mandatory.

Cuisine Art: The museum has a cafeteria-style café (€5 sandwiches, €10 salads, €15 hot dishes). For more recommendations in the Museumplein area, see page 142.

Photography: No photos allowed.

OVERVIEW

The core of the museum is on the first floor (level 1) of the Rietveld building. Some paintings may be displayed on the ground floor (level 0) or second floor (level 2), so be flexible.

The galleries proceed roughly chronologically, through the changes in Vincent van Gogh's life and styles. The paintings are divided into five periods—the Netherlands, Paris, Arles, St-Rémy, and Auvers-sur-Oise—proceeding clockwise around the floor. Some background on Vincent's star-crossed life makes the museum even better, so I've included doses of biographical material for each painting. Also, the unattributed quotations in my tour below are all Vincent's own words. As you tour, don't bother so much about finding specific paintings. Read the story of Van Gogh's life, and watch his style unfold.

The Tour Begins

• *Enter the museum (a new glass-walled entrance is opening in 2015). Make your way to the permanent collection. The museum often displays self-portraits to introduce you to the artist.*

VINCENT VAN GOGH (1853-1890)

I am a man of passions...

You could see Vincent van Gogh's canvases as a series of suicide notes—or as the record of a life full of beauty...perhaps too full of beauty. He attacked life with a passion, experiencing highs and lows more intensely than the average person. The beauty of the world overwhelmed him; its ugliness struck him as only another dimension of beauty. He tried to absorb the full spectrum of experience, good and bad, and channel it onto a canvas. The frustration of this overwhelming task drove him to madness. If all this is a bit overstated—and I guess it is—it's an attempt to show the emotional impact that Van Gogh's works have had on many people, me included.

Vincent, a pastor's son from a small Dutch town, started working at age 16 as a clerk for an art dealer. But his two interests, art and religion, distracted him from his dreary work, and after several years, he was fired.

The next 10 years were a collage of dead ends as he traveled northern Europe pursuing one path after another. He launched into each project with incredible energy, then became disillusioned and moved on to something else: teacher at a boarding school, assistant preacher, bookstore apprentice, preacher again, theology student, English student, literature student, art student. He bounced around England, France, Belgium, and the Netherlands. He fell in love, but was rejected for someone more respectable. He quarreled with his family and was estranged. He lived with a prostitute and her daughter, offending the few friends he had. Finally, in his late twenties, worn out, flat broke, and in poor health, he returned to his family in Nuenen and made peace. He then started to paint.

• *The first-floor collection follows the main periods of Vincent's life. Start with his stark, dark early work.*

THE NETHERLANDS (1880-1885)
Poverty and Religion

These dark, gray canvases show us the hard, plain existence of the people and town of Nuenen, in the rural southern Netherlands. We

see simple buildings, bare or autumnal trees, and overcast skies—a world where it seems spring will never arrive. What warmth there is comes from the sturdy, gentle people themselves.

The style is crude—Van Gogh couldn't draw very well and would never become a great technician. The paint is laid on thick, as though painted with Nuenen mud. The main subject is almost always dead center, with little or no background, so there's a claustrophobic feeling. We are unable to see anything but the immediate surroundings.

The Potato Eaters (1885)

Those that prefer to see the peasants in their Sunday-best may do as they like. I personally am convinced I get better results by painting them in their roughness.... If a peasant picture smells of bacon, smoke, potato steam—all right, that's healthy.

In a dark, cramped room lit only by a dim lamp, poor workers help themselves to a steaming plate of potatoes. They've earned it. Their hands are gnarly, their faces kind. Vincent deliberately wanted the canvas to be potato-colored.

Vincent had dabbled as an artist during his wandering years, sketching things around him and taking a few art classes, but it wasn't until age 29 that he painted his first oil canvas. He soon threw himself into it with abandon.

He painted the poor working peasants. He knew them well, having worked as a lay minister among peasants and miners. He joined them at work in the mines, taught their children, and even gave away his own few possessions to help them. The church authorities finally dismissed him for "excessive zeal," but he came away understanding the poor's harsh existence and the dignity with which they bore it.

Still Life with Bible (1885)

I have a terrible need of—shall I say the word?—religion. Then I go out and paint the stars.

The Bible and Émile Zola's *La Joie de Vivre*—these two books dominated Van Gogh's life. In his art he tried to fuse his religious upbringing with his love of the world's beauty. He lusted after life with a religious fervor. The burned-out candle tells us of the recent death of his father. The Bible is open to Isaiah 53: "He was despised and rejected of men, a man of sorrows..."

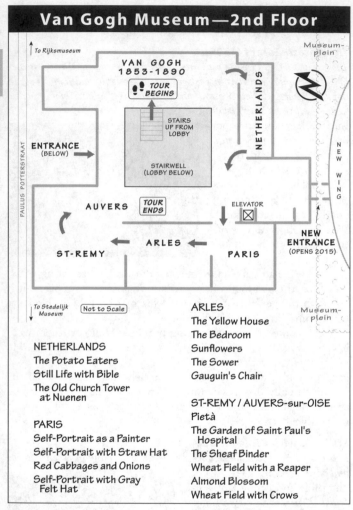

Van Gogh Museum—2nd Floor

To Rijksmuseum

VAN GOGH
1853-1890

👣 TOUR BEGINS

STAIRS UP FROM LOBBY

ENTRANCE (BELOW) →

STAIRWELL (LOBBY BELOW)

PAULUS POTTERSTRAAT

Museumplein

NETHERLANDS

NEW WING

AUVERS   TOUR ENDS

ELEVATOR ⊠

TOUR ENDS

ARLES ←

ST-REMY   PARIS

NEW ENTRANCE (OPENS 2015)

To Stedelijk Museum   Not to Scale

Museumplein

NETHERLANDS
The Potato Eaters
Still Life with Bible
The Old Church Tower
  at Nuenen

PARIS
Self-Portrait as a Painter
Self-Portrait with Straw Hat
Red Cabbages and Onions
Self-Portrait with Gray
  Felt Hat

ARLES
The Yellow House
The Bedroom
Sunflowers
The Sower
Gauguin's Chair

ST-REMY / AUVERS-sur-OISE
Pietà
The Garden of Saint Paul's
  Hospital
The Sheaf Binder
Wheat Field with a Reaper
Almond Blossom
Wheat Field with Crows

The Old Church Tower at Nuenen (a.k.a. *The Peasants' Churchyard*, 1885)

The crows circle above the local cemetery of Nuenen. Soon after his father's death, Vincent—in poor health and depressed—moved briefly to Antwerp. He then decided to visit his younger brother Theo, an art dealer living in Paris, the art capital of the world. Theo's support—financial and emotional—allowed Vincent to spend the rest of his short life painting.

Vincent moved from rural, religious, poor Holland to Paris, the City of Light. Vincent van Gone.

• *Continue to the room with work he did in…*

PARIS (MARCH 1886-FEB 1888)
Impressionism

The sun begins to break through, lighting up everything he paints. His canvases are more colorful and the landscapes more spacious, with plenty of open sky, giving a feeling of exhilaration after the closed, dark world of Nuenen.

In the cafés and bars of Paris' bohemian Montmartre district, Vincent met the revolutionary Impressionists. He roomed with Theo and became friends with other struggling young painters, such as Paul Gauguin and Henri de Toulouse-Lautrec. His health improved. He became more sociable, had an affair with an older woman, and was generally happy.

He signed up to study under a well-known classical teacher but quit after only a few classes. He couldn't afford to hire models, so he roamed the streets, sketch pad in hand, and learned from his Impressionist friends.

The Impressionists emphasized getting out of the stuffy studio and setting up canvases outside on the street or in the countryside to paint the play of sunlight off the trees, buildings, and water.

As you see in this room, at first, Vincent copied from the Impressionist masters. He painted garden scenes like Claude Monet, café snapshots like Edgar Degas, "block prints" like the Japanese masters, and self-portraits like…nobody else.

Self-Portrait as a Painter (1887-1888)

I am now living with my brother Vincent, who is studying the art of painting with indefatigable zeal.

—Theo van Gogh to a friend

Here, the budding young artist proudly displays his new palette full of bright new colors, trying his hand at the Impressionist technique of building a scene using dabs of different-colored paint. A whole new world of art—and life—opened up to him in Paris. Inspired by his fellow Dutchman Rembrandt, Vincent would explore himself through self-portraits for the rest of his life.

Self-Portrait with Straw Hat (1887)

You wouldn't recognize Vincent, he has changed so much.... The doctor says that he is now perfectly fit again. He is making tremendous strides with his work.... He is also far livelier than he used to be and is popular with people.

　　　　　　　—Theo van Gogh to their mother

In Paris, Vincent learned the Impressionist painting technique. The shimmering effect comes from placing dabs of different colors side by side on the canvas. At a distance, the two colors blend in the eye of the viewer to become a single color. Here, Vincent uses separate strokes of blue, yellow, green, and red to create a brown beard—but a brown that throbs with excitement.

Red Cabbages and Onions (1887)

Vincent quickly developed his own style: thicker paint; broad, swirling brushstrokes; and brighter, clashing colors that make even inanimate objects seem to pulsate with life. The many different colors are supposed to blend together, but you'd have to back up to Belgium to make these colors resolve into focus.

Self-Portrait with Gray Felt Hat (1887)

He has painted one or two portraits which have turned out well, but he insists on working for nothing. It is a pity that he shows no desire to earn some money because he could easily do so here. But you can't change people.

　　　　　　　—Theo van Gogh to their mother

Despite his new sociability, Vincent never quite fit in with his Impressionist friends. As he developed into a good painter, he became anxious to strike out on his own. He thought the social life of the big city was distracting him from serious work. And he'd been drinking too much absinthe, which alienated him from Theo. In this painting, his face screams out from a swirling background of molecular activity. He wanted peace and quiet, a place where he could throw himself into his work completely. He headed for the sunny south of France.

• *Travel to the next room to reach...*

ARLES (FEB 1888-MAY 1889)
Sunlight, Beauty, and Madness

Winter was just turning to spring when Vincent arrived in Arles, near the French Riviera. After the dreary Paris winter, the colors of springtime overwhelmed him. The blossoming trees inspired him to paint canvas after canvas, drenched in sunlight.

The Yellow House (a.k.a. The Street, 1888)

It is my intention...to go temporarily to the South, where there is even more color, even more sun.

Vincent rented this house with the green shutters. (He ate at the pink café next door.) Look at that blue sky! He painted in a frenzy, working feverishly to try and take it all in. For the next nine months, he produced an explosion of canvases, working very quickly when the mood possessed him. His unique style evolved beyond Impressionism—thicker paint, stronger outlines, brighter colors (often applied right from the paint tube), and swirling brushwork that makes inanimate objects pulse and vibrate with life.

The Bedroom (1888)

I am a man of passions, capable of and subject to doing more or less foolish things—which I happen to regret, more or less, afterwards.

Vincent was alone, a Dutchman in Provence. And that had its downside. Vincent swung from flurries of ecstatic activity to bouts of great loneliness. Like anyone traveling alone, he experienced those high highs and low lows. This narrow, trapezoid-shaped, single-room apartment (less than 200 square feet) must have seemed like a prison cell at times. (Psychologists have pointed out that most everything in this painting comes in pairs—two chairs, two paintings, a double bed squeezed down to a single—indicating his desire for a mate. Hmm.)

He invited his friend Paul Gauguin to join him, envisioning a sort of artists' colony in Arles. He spent months preparing a room upstairs for Gauguin's arrival. He painted *Sunflowers* to brighten up the place.

Sunflowers (1889)

The worse I get along with people, the more I learn to have faith in Nature and concentrate on her.

Vincent saw sunflowers as his signature subject, and he painted a half-dozen versions of them, each a study in intense yellow. He said he wanted the colors to shine "like stained glass." If he signed the work (look on the vase), it means he was proud of it.

Even a simple work like these sunflowers bursts with life. Different people see different things in *Sunflowers*. Is it a happy painting, or is it a melancholy one? Take your own emotional temperature and see.

The Sower (1888)

A dark, silhouetted figure sows seeds in the burning sun. It's late in the day. The heat from the sun, the source of all life, radiates out in

thick swirls of paint. The sower must be a hopeful man, because the field looks slanted and barren. Someday, he thinks, the seeds he's planting will grow into something great, like the tree that slashes diagonally across the scene—tough and craggy, but with small, optimistic blossoms.

In his younger years, Vincent had worked in Belgium sowing the Christian gospel in a harsh environment (see Mark 4:1-9). Now in Arles, ignited by the sun, he cast his artistic seeds to the wind, hoping.

Gauguin's Chair (1888)

Empty chairs—there are many of them, there will be even more, and sooner or later, there will be nothing but empty chairs.

Gauguin arrived. At first, he and Vincent got along great. They journeyed to the countryside and set up their easels, working side by side and critiquing each other's paintings. At night, they hit the bars, carousing and talking into the night.

But then things went sour. They clashed

over art, life, and their prickly personalities. On Christmas Eve 1888, Vincent went ballistic. Enraged during an alcohol-fueled argument, he pulled out a razor and waved it in Gauguin's face. Gauguin took the hint and quickly left town. Vincent was horrified at himself. In a fit of remorse and madness, he mutilated his own ear and presented it to a prostitute.

• *Continue into the next room. Just a reminder—if you're looking for a specific painting and you don't see it, try on the second floor when our tour's done.*

ST-REMY (MAY 1889-1890)
The Mental Hospital

The people of Arles realized they had a madman on their hands. A doctor diagnosed "acute mania with hallucinations," and the local vicar talked Vincent into admitting himself to a mental hospital. Vincent wrote to Theo: "Temporarily I wish to remain shut up, as much for my own peace of mind as for other people's."

In the mental hospital, Vincent continued to paint whenever he was well enough. He often couldn't go out, so he copied from books, making his own distinctive versions of works by Rembrandt, Delacroix, Millet, and others.

We see a change from bright, happy landscapes to more intro-spective subjects. The colors are less bright and more surreal, the brushwork even more furious. The strong outlines of figures are twisted and tortured.

Pietà, after Delacroix (1889)

It's evening after a thunderstorm. Jesus has been crucified, and the corpse lies at the mouth of a tomb. Mary, whipped by the cold wind, holds her empty arms out in de-spair and confusion. She is the tender mother who receives us all in death, as though saying, "My child, you've been away so long—rest in my arms." Christ has a Vincent-esque red beard.

At first, the peace and quiet of the asylum did Vincent good, and his health improved. Occasionally, he was allowed outside to paint the gardens and land-scapes. Meanwhile, the paintings he had been sending to Theo began to attract attention in Paris for the first time. A woman in Brussels bought one of his canvases—the only painting he ever sold during his lifetime. In 1987, one of his *Sun-flowers* sold for $40 million. Three years later a portrait of Vincent's doctor went for more than $80 million.

The Garden of Saint Paul's Hospital (a.k.a. *Leaf Fall*, 1889)

...a traveler going to a destination that does not exist...

The stark brown trees are blown by the wind. A solitary figure (Vincent?) winds along a narrow, snaky path as the wind blows leaves on him. The colors are surreal—blue, green, and red tree trunks with heavy black outlines. A road runs away from us, heading nowhere.

The Sheaf Binder, after Millet (1889)

I want to paint men and women with that something of the eternal which the halo used to symbolize...

Vincent's compassion for honest laborers remained constant following his work with Belgian miners. These sturdy folk, with their curving bodies, wrestle as one with their curving wheat. The world Vincent sees is charged from within by spiritual fires, twisting and turning matter into energy, and vice versa.

Wheat Field with a Reaper (1889)

I have been working hard and fast in the last few days. This is how I try to express how desperately fast things pass in modern life.

The harvest is here. The time is short. There's much work to be done. A lone reaper works uphill, scything through a swirling wheat field, cutting slender paths of calm. Vincent saw the reaper—a figure of impending death—as the flip side of the sower.

The fits of madness returned. During these spells, he lost all sense of his own actions. He couldn't paint, the one thing he felt driven to do. He wrote to Theo, "My surroundings here begin to weigh on me more than I can say—I need air. I feel overwhelmed by boredom and grief."

AUVERS-SUR-OISE (MAY-JULY 1890)
Flying Away

The bird looks through the bars at the overcast sky where a thunderstorm is gathering, and inwardly he rebels against his fate. 'I am caged, I am caged, and you tell me I have everything I need! Oh! I beg you, give me liberty, that I may be a bird like other birds.' A certain idle man resembles this idle bird...

Almond Blossom (1890)

Vincent moved north to Auvers, a small town near Paris where

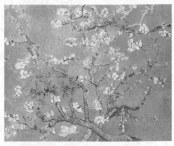

he could stay under a doctor friend's supervision. On the way there, he visited Theo. Theo's wife had just had a baby, whom they named Vincent. Brother Vincent showed up with this painting under his arm as a birthday gift. Theo's wife later recalled, "I had expected a sick man, but here was a sturdy, broad-shouldered man with a healthy color, a smile on his face, and a very resolute appearance."

In his new surroundings, he continued painting, averaging a canvas a day, but was interrupted by spells that swung from boredom to madness. His letters to Theo were generally optimistic, but he worried that he'd soon succumb completely to insanity and never paint again. The final landscapes are walls of bright, thick paint.

• *An example—the following painting—often hangs a few steps away, on a wall facing the atrium.*

Wheat Field with Crows (1890)

Since my illness, loneliness takes hold of me in the fields.... This new attack...came on me in the fields, on a windy day, when I was busy painting.

On July 27, 1890, Vincent left his room, walked out to a nearby field, and put a bullet through his chest. He stumbled back to his room, where he died two days later, with Theo by his side.

This is one of the last paintings Vincent finished. We can try to search the wreckage of his life for the black box explaining what happened, but there's not much there. His life was sad and tragic, but the record he left is one not of sadness, but of beauty—intense beauty.

The windblown wheat field is a nest of restless energy. Scenes like this must have overwhelmed Vincent with their incredible beauty—too much, too fast, with no release. The sky is stormy and dark blue, almost nighttime, barely lit by two suns boiling through the deep ocean of blue. The road starts nowhere, leads nowhere, disappearing into the burning wheat field. Above all of this swirling beauty fly the crows, the dark ghosts that had hovered over his life since the cemetery in Nuenen.

THE REST OF THE MUSEUM

You'll find more paintings by Van Gogh on the second floor (level 2). The third floor has work by fellow painters, those who influenced Vincent and those who were influenced by him: Academy painters and their smooth-surfaced canvases, Impressionists Claude Monet and Camille Pissarro, and fellow Post-Impressionists Paul Gauguin, Paul Cézanne, and Henri de Toulouse-Lautrec. In the basement auditorium (level -1), a 15-minute video gives a basic introduction to Van Gogh. Temporary exhibitions are found in the Kurokawa Wing.

ANNE FRANK HOUSE TOUR

Anne Frank Huis

ANNE FRANK
TAGEBUCH

On May 10, 1940, Germany's Luftwaffe began bombing Schiphol Airport, preparing to invade the Netherlands. The Dutch army fought back, and the Nazis responded by leveling Rotterdam. Within a week, the Netherlands surrendered, Queen Wilhelmina fled to Britain, and Nazi soldiers goose-stepped past the Westerkerk and into Dam Square, where they draped huge swastikas on the Royal Palace. A five-year occupation began. The Netherlands had been neutral in World War I, and Amsterdam—progressive and modern, but a bit naive—was in for a rude awakening.

The Anne Frank House immerses you, in a very immediate way, in the struggles and pains of the war years. Walk through rooms where, for two years, eight Amsterdam Jews hid from Nazi persecution. You'll see actual artifacts: the secret bookcase entry, Anne's movie-star cutouts on the wall, and her diaries.

Though the eight Jews were eventually discovered, and all but one died in concentration camps, their story has an uplifting twist—the diary of Anne Frank, an affirmation of the human spirit that cannot be crushed.

Orientation

Cost: €9 on-site or €9.50 online.

Hours: April-Oct daily 9:00-21:00, Sat and July-Aug until 22:00; Nov-March daily 9:00-19:00, Sat until 21:00; last entry 30 minutes before closing. Unlike many of Amsterdam's museums, the Anne Frank House is open on most holidays, although it does close for Yom Kippur (Sept 23 in 2015, Oct 12 in 2016).

Avoiding Lines: Expect long ticket-buying lines from opening to closing during summer months, and during midday hours off-season. If you don't have a ticket, try arriving right when the museum opens or after 18:00.

To skip the lines, book a timed-entry ticket online (€9.50, www.annefrank. org) as soon as you're sure of your itinerary. With your ticket in hand, you can by-pass the line and ring the buzzer at the low-profile door marked *Entrance: Reservations Only*.

Museumkaart holders (who get in free) can pay €0.50 to reserve an entry time online. Even if you don't have the card yet, choose the Online Ticket Sales option to select a time, then present your confirmation at the "reservations only" door. If you haven't purchased your Museumkaart yet, you can buy one right there.

Getting There: It's at Prinsengracht 267, near Westerkerk and about a 20-minute walk from Central Station. You can also take tram #13, #14, or #17—or bus #170, #172, or #174—to the Westermarkt stop, about a block south of the museum's entrance.

Information: The museum has excellent information in English, including a pamphlet at the door and good descriptions with excerpts from the diary throughout. Use this chapter as back-ground, and then let the displays and videos tell you more. Note that the house has many steep, narrow stairways. Tel. 020/556-7100, www.annefrank.org.

Length of This Tour: Allow one hour.

Baggage Check: The museum has a strict no-big-bags policy—but doesn't offer you a place to check them.

Eating: The museum café serves simple fare and has good views (daily 9:30-18:00).

The Tour Begins

We'll walk through the rooms where Anne Frank, her parents, her sister, and four other Jews hid for 25 months. The front half of the building, facing the canal, remained the offices and warehouses of

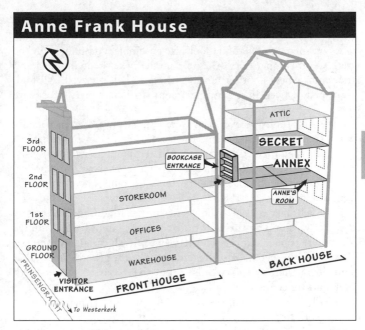

Anne Frank House

an operating business. The back half, where the Franks and others lived, was the Secret Annex, its entrance concealed by a bookcase.
• *After the ticket desk, enter the ground-floor exhibit. After viewing the important five-minute video, go upstairs to the offices/warehouses of the front half of the building.*

First Floor: Offices
From these offices, Otto Frank ran a successful business called Opekta, selling spices and pectin for making jelly. When the Nazis gained power in Germany in 1933, Otto moved his family from Frankfurt to tolerant Amsterdam, hoping for a better life.

Photos and displays show Otto with some of his colleagues. During the Nazi occupation, while the Frank family hid in the back of the building, these brave people kept Otto's business running, secretly bringing supplies to the Franks. Miep Gies, Otto's secretary (see her in the video), brought food every few days, while bookkeeper Victor Kugler cheered up Anne with the latest movie magazines.
• *Go upstairs to the...*

Second Floor: Warehouse
Two models show the two floors where Anne, her family, and four others lived. Dollhouse furniture helps you envision life in the now-bare living quarters. In the first model, find the swinging

bookcase that hid the secret entrance leading to Anne's parents' room (with wood stove). Anne's room is next to it, with a blue bed, a brown sofa, a table/chair/bookcase ensemble, and photos on the wall. On the upper floor (the next model) was the living area and the rooms where another family—the Van Pels—stayed. All told, eight people lived in a tiny apartment smaller than 1,000 square feet.

At first the Nazi overlords were lenient toward, even friendly with, the vanquished Dutch. But soon they began imposing restrictions that affected one in ten Amsterdammers—that is, Jews. Jews had to wear yellow-star patches and register with the police. They were banned from movie theaters and trams, and even forbidden to ride bikes.

In February of 1941, the Nazis started rounding up Amsterdam's Jews, shipping them by train to "work camps," which, in reality, were transit stations on the way to death camps in the east. Outraged, the people of Amsterdam called a general strike that shut down the city for two days...but the Nazis responded with even harsher laws.

In July of 1942, Anne's sister, Margot, got her call-up notice for a "work-force project." Otto handed over the keys to the business to his "Aryan" colleagues, sent a final postcard to relatives, gave the family cat to a neighbor, spread rumors that they were fleeing to Switzerland, and prepared his family to "dive under" (*onderduik,* as it was called) into hiding.

Photos of the people in hiding put faces on the eight inhabitants of the Secret Annex. First was the Frank family—Otto and Edith and their daughters, 13-year-old Anne and 16-year-old Margot. A week later, they were joined by the Van Pels (called the "Van Daans" in her diary), with their teenage son, Peter. A few months later, Fritz Pfeffer (called "Mr. Dussel" in the diary) was invited in.

• *It's now time to enter the hiding place. At the back of the second floor warehouse is the clever hidden passageway into the Secret Annex.*

SECRET ANNEX
The Bookcase Entrance

On a rainy Monday morning, July 6, 1942, the Frank family—wearing extra clothes to avoid carrying suspicious suitcases—breathed their last fresh air, took a long look at the Prinsengracht canal, and disappeared into the back part of the building, where they spent the next two years. Victor Kugler concealed the entrance to the annex with this swinging bookcase, stacked with business files.

Though not exactly a secret (since it's hard to hide an entire building), the annex was a typical back-house *(achterhuis),* a com-

Anne Frank House: Secret Annex

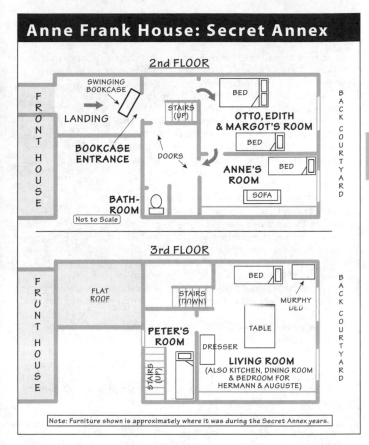

2nd FLOOR

SWINGING BOOKCASE

LANDING

STAIRS (UP)

BED

OTTO, EDITH & MARGOT'S ROOM

BED

BOOKCASE ENTRANCE

DOORS

ANNE'S ROOM

BED

SOFA

BATH-ROOM

Not to Scale

FRONT HOUSE

BACK COURTYARD

3rd FLOOR

FLAT ROOF

STAIRS (DOWN)

BED

MURPHY BED

PETER'S ROOM

TABLE

DRESSER

STAIRS (UP)

LIVING ROOM
(ALSO KITCHEN, DINING ROOM & BEDROOM FOR HERMANN & AUGUSTE)

FRONT HOUSE

BACK COURTYARD

Note: Furniture shown is approximately where it was during the Secret Annex years.

ANNE FRANK HOUSE

mon feature in Amsterdam buildings, and the Nazis had no reason to suspect anything on the premises of the legitimate Opekta business.

• *Pass through the bookcase entrance into...*

Otto, Edith, and Margot's Room

The family carried on life as usual. Otto read Dickens' *Sketches by Boz*, Edith read from a **prayer book** in their native German, and the children continued their studies, with Margot taking **Latin lessons** by correspondence course. They avidly followed the course of the war through radio broadcasts and news from their helpers. As the tides of war slowly turned and it appeared they might one day be saved from the Nazis, Otto tracked the Allied advance on a **map** of Normandy.

The room is very small, even without the furniture. Imagine yourself and two fellow tourists confined here for two years.

Life in the Annex

By day, it's enforced silence, so no one can hear them in the offices. They whisper, tiptoe, and step around squeaky places in the floor. The windows are blacked out, so they can't even look outside. They read or study, and Anne writes in her diary.

At night and on weekends, when the offices close, one or two might sneak downstairs to listen to Winston Churchill's BBC broadcasts on the office radio. Everyone's spirits rise and sink with news of Allied victories and setbacks.

Anne's diaries make clear the tensions, petty quarrels, and domestic politics of eight people living under intense pressure. Mr. Van Pels annoys Anne, but he gets along well with Margot. Anne never gets used to Mr. Pfeffer, who is literally invading her space. Most troublesome of all, pubescent Anne often strikes sparks with her mom. (Anne's angriest comments about her mother were deleted from early editions of the published diary.)

Despite their hardships, the group feels guilty: They have shelter, while so many other Jews are being rounded up and sent off. As the war progresses, they endure long nights when the house shakes from Allied air raids, and Anne cuddles up in her dad's bed.

Boredom tinged with fear—the existentialist hell of living in hiding is captured so well in Anne's journal.

Pencil lines on the wall track Margot's and Anne's heights, marking the point at which these growing lives were cut short.

Anne Frank's Room

Pan the room clockwise to see some of the young girl's idols in photos and clippings she pasted there herself: American actor Robert Stack, the future Queen Elizabeth II as a child, matinee idol Rudy Vallee, figure-skating actress Sonja Henie, and, on the other wall, actress Greta Garbo, actor Ray Milland, Renaissance man Leonardo da Vinci, and actress Ginger Rogers.

Out the window (which had to be blacked out) is the back courtyard, which had a chestnut tree and a few buildings. (In 2010, the tree, which Anne had greatly enjoyed, toppled in a storm.) These things, along with the Westerkerk bell chiming every 15 minutes, represented the borders of Anne's "outside world." Imagine Anne sitting here at a small desk, writing in her diary.

In November of 1942, the Franks invited a Jewish neighbor to join them, and Anne was forced to share the tiny room. Fritz Pfeffer was a middle-aged dentist with whom Anne didn't get along. Pfeffer wrote a farewell letter to his German fiancée, who lived nearby and continued to receive news of him from Miep Gies without knowing his whereabouts.

The Bathroom

The eight inhabitants shared this bathroom. During the day, they didn't dare flush the toilet.

• *Ascend the steep staircase—silently—to the...*

Common Living Room

This was also the kitchen and dining room. Otto Frank was well off, and early on, the annex was well-stocked with food. Miep Gies would dutifully take their shopping list, buy food for her "family" of eight, and secretly lug it up to them. Buying such large quantities in a coupon-rationed economy was highly suspect, but she knew a sympathetic grocer (a block away on Leliegracht) who was part of a ring of Amsterdammers risking their lives to help the Jews.

The menu for a special dinner lists soup, roast beef, salad, potatoes, rice, dessert, and coffee. Later, as war and German restrictions plunged Holland into poverty and famine, they survived on canned foods and dried kidney beans.

At night, the living room became sleeping quarters for Hermann and Auguste van Pels.

Peter van Pels' Room

On Peter's 16th birthday, he got a Monopoly-like board game called "The Broker" as a present.

Initially, Anne was cool toward Peter, but after two years together, a courtship developed, and their flirtation culminated in a kiss.

The **staircase** (no visitor access) leads up to where they stored their food. Anne loved to steal away here for a bit of privacy. At night they'd open a hatch to let in fresh air.

One hot August day, Otto was in this room helping Peter learn English, when they looked up to see a man with a gun. The hiding was over.

• *From here we leave the Secret Annex, returning to the Opekta storeroom and offices in the front house. As you work your way downstairs, you'll see a number of exhibits on the aftermath of this story.*

THE AFTERMATH
Arrest, Deportation, and Auschwitz Exhibits

They went quietly. On August 4, 1944, a German policeman accompanied by three Dutch Nazis pulled up in a car, politely entered the Opekta office, and went straight to the bookcase entrance. No one knows who tipped them off. The police gave the surprised hiders time to pack. They demanded their valuables and stuffed them into Anne's briefcase...after dumping her diaries onto the floor.

Taken in a van to Gestapo headquarters, the eight were processed in an efficient, bureaucratic manner, then placed on a train to Westerbork, a concentration camp northeast of the city (see their 3-inch-by-5-inch **registration cards**).

From there they were locked in a car on a normal passenger train and sent to Auschwitz, a Nazi extermination camp in Poland (see the **transport list,** which includes "Anneliese Frank"). On the platform at Auschwitz, they were "forcibly separated from each other" (as Otto later reported) and sent to different camps. Anne and Margot were sent to Bergen-Belsen.

Don't miss the **video** of one of Anne's former neighbors, Hannah Goslar, who, by chance, ended up at Bergen-Belsen with Anne. In English she describes their reunion as they talked through a barbed-wire fence shortly before Anne died. She says of Anne, "She didn't have any more tears."

Anne and Margot both died of typhus in March of 1945, only weeks before the camp was liberated. The other Secret Annex residents—except Otto—were gassed or died of disease.

The Franks' story was that of Holland's Jews. The seven who died were among the more than 100,000 Dutch Jews killed during the war years. (Before the war, 135,000 Jews lived in the Netherlands.) Of Anne's school class of 87 Jews, only 20 survived.

• *The next room is devoted to Anne's father.*

The Otto Frank Room
Listen to a 1967 video of Anne's father talking about how the diaries were discovered in the annex. The case holds a rotating display: You may find notebooks that Otto kept during the hiding period, or letters he wrote after the war as he tried to get Anne's diaries published.

• *Downstairs you come to...*

The Diaries
See Anne's three diaries, which were published after the war. Anne received the first diary (with a red-plaid binding) as a birthday present when she turned 13, shortly before the family went into hiding. She wrote her diary in the form of a letter to an imaginary friend named Kitty. The other two diaries

were written in school-exercise books. Also on display are a book of Anne's short stories, a notebook she kept of favorite quotes, and some loose-leaf pages on which she rewrote and revised parts of her diary.

Otto decided to have the diaries published, and in 1947, *De Achterhuis (The Back-House)* appeared in Dutch, soon followed by many translations, a play, and a movie. While she was alive, Anne herself had recognized the uniqueness of her situation and had been in the process of revising her diaries, preparing them to one day be published.

• *Continue downstairs to the ground-floor exhibits.*

The Moral

These displays tell the story of those who helped the Franks, those who survived, and the Anne Frank legacy.

A video of Miep Gies—who passed away in 2010 at the age of 100—describes how she found Anne's diaries in the Secret Annex following the arrest and gave them to Otto after the war. You'll learn of Otto's struggles to save the house from demolition and to turn it into a museum. Though the annex's furniture was ransacked during the arrest, the rooms remained virtually untouched, and we see them today much as they were. Otto wanted the Anne Frank House to be, in his words, "more than a museum."

An interactive exhibit called **Free2choose** helps fulfill his wish. Brief video clips present real-life situations in which human-rights values—democracy, equality, tolerance, multiculturalism, religious freedom, and free speech—have come into conflict with one another. At the end of each segment, you can vote your opinion on the dilemma, then see how others have responded. You may be surprised. The point? To keep visitors from leaving the museum with pat feelings of easy moral clarity.

The Anne Frank Foundation is obviously concerned that we learn from Europe's Nazi nightmare. The thinking that made the Holocaust possible still survives. Even today, some groups promote the notion that the Holocaust never occurred and contend that stories like Anne Frank's are only a hoax. It was Otto Frank's dream that visitors come away from the Anne Frank House with an indelible impression—and a better ability to apply these lessons to our contemporary challenges. He wrote: "The task that Anne entrusted to me continually gives me new strength to strive for reconciliation and for human rights all over the world."

AMSTELKRING MUSEUM TOUR

Ons' Lieve Heer op Solder

For two centuries (1578-1795), Catholicism in Amsterdam was illegal but tolerated (like pot in the 1970s). When hard-line Protestants took power in 1578, Catholic churches were vandalized and shut down, priests and monks were rounded up and kicked out of town, and Catholic kids were razzed on their way to school. The city's Catholics were forbidden to worship openly, so they gathered secretly to say Mass in homes and offices. In 1663, a wealthy merchant built Our Lord in the Attic (Ons' Lieve Heer op Solder), one of a handful of places in Amsterdam that served as a secret parish church until Catholics were once again allowed to worship in public. This unique church—embedded within a townhouse in the middle of the Red Light District—comes with a little bonus: a rare glimpse inside a historic Amsterdam home straight out of a Vermeer painting.

Renovation: The church museum, known as the Amstelkring, is undergoing an extensive renovation (due to wrap up in late 2015) that will eventually double the tourable space. Expect some changes to this tour.

Orientation

Cost: €8, includes audioguide.

Hours: Mon-Sat 10:00-17:00, Sun and holidays 13:00-17:00.

Getting There: It's at Oudezijds Voorburgwal 40, a seven-minute walk from either Central Station or Dam Square.

Information: Be warned that the museum has several steep, narrow staircases. Tel. 020/624-6604, www.opsolder.nl.

Photography: No photos allowed.

Length of This Tour: Allow one hour.

The Tour Begins

Exterior

Behind the attic windows of this narrow townhouse sits a 150-seat, three-story church the size of a four-lane bowling alley. Be-

neath it is the home of the wealthy businessman who built the church. This 17th-century townhouse, like many in the city, also has a back house *(achterhuis)* that was rented out to another family. On this tour we'll visit the front house, then the church, then the back house. Before entering, notice the emergency-exit door in the alley. This was once the hidden church's main entrance.

• *Step inside. Buy your ticket and climb the stairs to the first floor, where we begin touring the front house. The first stop is a room with a big fireplace, the...*

Parlor

By humble Dutch standards, this is an enormous, highly ornate room. Here, in the largest room of the house, the family received guests and hosted parties. The decor is the Dutch version of classical, where everything comes in symmetrical pairs—corkscrew columns flank the fireplace, the coffered ceiling mirrors the patterned black-and-white marble floor, and a fake exit door balances the real entrance door.

Over the fireplace is the coat of arms of Jan Hartman (1619-1668), a rich Catholic businessman who built this house for his family and the church for his fellow Catholics in the neighborhood. The family symbol, the crouching hart (deer), became the nickname of the church—*Het Hert.*

The painting over the fireplace *(The Presentation in the Temple)* has hung here since Hartman's time and shows his taste for Italian, Catholic, Baroque-style beauty. On the wall opposite the windows, the family portrait is right out of the Dutch Golden Age, showing a rich businessman and his family of four (though it's not Hartman).

• *Now head straight out the parlor door and ascend the small staircase on the left, leading to the...*

Canal Room

Unlike the rather formal parlor, this was where the family hung out, staring out the windows or warming themselves at the stove. The furnishings are typical of a wealthy merchant's home at the time. The wood stove and the textiles on the walls are re-creations but look like the originals. In the Dutch custom (still occasionally seen today), the family covered tables with exotic Turkish rugs imported by traders of the Dutch East India Company. You may spot a Delftware vase, which would have been filled with tulips, back then still an exotic and expensive transplant from the East. The tall ceramic doodad is a multi-armed tulip vase. Its pagoda shape reminds us that Delftware's designs and techniques originated in China.

Despite the family's wealth, space was tight. In the 1600s, entire families would often sleep together in small bed cabinets, like the one to the left of the entrance. They sat up to sleep because they believed reclining would cause blood to pool in their heads and kill them.

The black ebony knickknack cabinet is painted with a scene right out of the 1600s Red Light District. On the right door, the Prodigal Son spends his inheritance, making merry with barebreasted, scarlet-clothed courtesans—high-rent prostitutes who could entertain educated, cello-loving clients. On the left door, the Prodigal Son has spent it all. He can't pay his bill, and is kicked out of a cheap tavern—still half-dressed—by a pair of short-changed prostitutes.

• *Backtrack down the stairs and turn right to go up the spiral staircase to the church. As you climb, you can look through a window into the small Chaplain's Room, which shows how humbly the church chaplain lived in the 1800s. Then continue up into the actual hidden church.*

Our Lord in the Attic Church

The church is long and narrow, with an altar at one end, an organ at the other, and two balconies overhead to maximize the seating in this relatively small space. While Amsterdam's Protestant churches were white-washed and austere, this Catholic church has touches of elaborate Baroque decor, with statues of saints, garlands, and baby angels. The balconies are suspended from the ceiling and held in place by metal rods.

This attic church certainly is hidden, but everyone knew it was here. In tolerant (and largely Catholic) Amsterdam, Protestant authorities rarely made an issue of Catholic worship as long as it was kept from public view. Hartman was a respected businessman who used his wealth and influence to convince the city fathers to look the other way as the church was built. Imagine the jubilation when the church opened its doors in 1663, and Catholics could gather together and worship (if secretly) in this fine space.

The **altar** is flanked by classical columns and topped with an

Anti-Catholic = Anti-Spanish

Protestants imposed anti-Catholic laws in the 16th century partly as retribution for the Catholics' own oppressive rule and partly from a desire to reform what was seen as a corrupted religion...but mostly they did it for political reasons.

By a quirk of royal marriage, Holland was ruled from afar by Spain, Europe's most militantly Catholic country, home of the Inquisition, the Jesuits, and the pope's own Counter-Reformation army. In 1578, Amsterdam's hard-line Protestants staged the "Alteration"—a coup kicking out their Spanish oppressors and allying the city with the Prince of Orange's rebels.

Catholics in the city—probably a majority of the population—were considered guilty by association. Viewed as potential enemies, they were suspected to be puppets of the pope, spies for Spanish kings, or subverters of the social order. In addition, Catholics were considered immoral worshippers of false idols, bowing down to graven images of saints and the Virgin Mary.

In Amsterdam, Catholic churches were seized and looted, and prominent Catholics were dragged to Dam Square by a lynch mob, before being freed, unharmed, outside the city gates. Protestant extremists gave Catholics a taste of their own repressive medicine, passing laws that prohibited open Catholic worship (although few were actually arrested or prosecuted). Still, many families over many generations were torn apart by the religious and political strife of the Reformation.

arch featuring a stucco God the Father, a dove of the Holy Spirit, and trumpeting angels.

The **base of the left column**—made of wood painted to look like marble—is hollow. Inside is a foldout wooden pulpit that could be pulled out for the priest to preach from—as shown in photos on the wall opposite.

The **altarpiece painting** (Jacob de Wit's *Baptism of Jesus*) is one of four (three survive) that could be rotated with the feast days. Step into the room behind the altar to see the two spares.

• *Behind the altar is a room called the...*

Lady Chapel

A 400-year-old altar dedicated to Our Lady—the Virgin Mary, the mother of Christ—contains more of the images that so offended and outraged hard-line Protestants. See her statue with Baby Jesus and find her symbols, the rose and crown, in the blue damask altar cloth.

Calvinism

Holland's Protestant movement followed the stern French reformer John Calvin more than the beer-drinking German Martin Luther. Calvin's French followers, called Huguenots, fled religious persecution in the 1500s, finding refuge in tolerant Amsterdam. When Catholic Spain began persecuting them in Holland, they entered politics and fought back.

Calvin wanted to reform the Catholic faith by condemning corruption, simplifying rituals, and returning the faith to its biblical roots. Like other Protestants, Calvinists emphasized that only God's grace—and not our good works—can get us to heaven.

He went so far as to say that God predestined some for heaven, some for hell. Later, some overly pious Calvinists even claimed to be able to pick out the lucky winners from the unlucky, sinful losers. Today, the Dutch Reformed Church, as well as some other Reformed and Presbyterian churches, carry on Calvin's brand of Christianity.

Catholics have traditionally honored Mary, addressing prayers to her or to other saints, asking them to intercede with God on their behalf. To Calvinist extremists, this was like bowing down to a false goddess. They considered statues of the Virgin to be among the "graven images" forbidden by the Ten Commandments (Exodus 20:4).

The **collection box** (*voor St. Pieter*, on the wall by the staircase down) was for donations sent to fund that most Catholic of monuments, the pope's own church, the Basilica of St. Peter in Rome—to Calvinists, the center of corruption, the "whore of Babylon."

• *Later, we'll head down the stairs here, but first climb the stairs to the first balcony above the church.*

Lower Balcony

The window to the left of the altar (as you face it) looks south across ramshackle rooftops (note the complex townhouse-with-back-house design of so many Amsterdam buildings) to the steeple of the Old Church (Oude Kerk). The Old Church was the main Catholic church until 1578, when it was rededicated as Dutch Reformed (Protestant), the new official religion of the Netherlands. For the next hundred years, Catholics had no large venue to gather in until Our Lord in the Attic opened in 1663.

The 1749 **organ** is small, but more than adequate. These days, music lovers flock here on special evenings for a *Vondelkonzert* (wandering concert). They listen to a few tunes here, have a drink,

then move on to hear more music at, say, the Old Church or the Royal Palace.

Next to the organ, the **painting** *Evangelist Matthew with an Angel* (*De Evangelist Mattheus*, c. 1625, by Jan Lievens) features the wrinkled forehead and high-contrast shadings used by the artist's more famous colleague, Rembrandt.

• *Stairs next to the organ lead you to the...*

Upper Balcony

Looking down from this angle, the small church really looks small. It can accommodate 150 seated worshippers. From here the tapering roofline creates the "attic" feel that gives the church its nickname.

• *At the back of the upper balcony is the...*

Canalside Room

The religious hardware displayed here is standard in Catholic church services—elaborate silver-and-gold monstrances (ornamental holders in which the Communion wafer is displayed), chalices (for the Communion wine), ciboria (chalices with lids for holding consecrated wafers), pyxes (for storing unconsecrated wafers), candlesticks, and incense burners. "Holy earth boxes" were used for Catholics denied burial in consecrated ground. Instead, they put a little consecrated dirt in the box and placed it in the coffin.

While you admire these beautiful pieces, remember that it was this kind of luxury, ostentation, and Catholic mumbo-jumbo that drove thrifty Calvinists nuts.

Looking out the window, you can see that you're literally in the attic. Straight across the canal is a house with an ornate gable featuring dolphins. This street was once the city's best address.

• *Back down on the lower balcony, circle around to the window just to the right of the altar for a...*

Northern View

Look north across modern junk on rooftops to the impressive dome and twin steeples of St. Nicholas Church, near Central Station. This is the third Amsterdam church to be dedicated to the patron saint of seafarers and of the city. The first was the Old Church (until 1578), then Our Lord in the Attic (1663). Finally, after the last anti-Catholic laws were repealed (1821), St. Nicholas was built as a symbol of the faith's revival.

When St. Nicholas Church was dedicated in 1887, Our Lord in the Attic closed up shop. The next year, wealthy Catholics saved it from the wrecking ball, turning it into one of Amsterdam's first museums.

• *Head back downstairs, passing through the room behind the altar with the Lady Chapel, and taking the stairs (past the offering box) down to the...*

Confessional

The confessional dates from 1740. The priest sat in the left half, while parishioners knelt in the right to confess their sins through a grilled window. Catholic priests have church authority to forgive sins, whereas Protestants take their troubles directly to God.

The sociologist Max Weber theorized that frequently forgiven Catholics more easily accept the status quo, whereas guilt-ridden Protestants are driven to prove their worth by making money. Hence, northern Protestant countries—like the Netherlands—became capitalist powerhouses, while southern Catholic countries remained feudal and backward. Hmm.

• *Go down another flight and turn right, into the...*

Jaap Leeuwenberg Room

We've now left the church premises and moved to the back-house rooms that were rented out to other families. This room's colors are seen in countless old homes—white walls, ocher-yellow beamed ceiling, oxblood-red landing, and black floor tiles. The simple colors, lit here by a light shaft, make small rooms seem bright and spacious.

• *Some very steep stairs lead down to the...*

17th-Century Kitchen

This reconstructed room was inhabited as-is until 1952. Blue-tiled walls show playful scenes of kids and animals. Step into the small pantry, then open a door to see the toilet.

• *Climb the rope back up the stairs and turn left to find exhibits on Amsterdam's other Catholic churches (known to Protestants as "Papist meeting places"). Then descend a different set of stairs just one floor (not all the way down to the basement) into the...*

19th-Century Kitchen

This just looks so Dutch, with blue tiles, yellow walls, and Vermeer-esque lighting from a skylight. When the last resident of this house died, in 1953, she willed it to the museum.

Think of how her age overlaps our age...of all the change since she was born. Consider the contrast of this serene space with the wild world that waits just outside the door of this hidden church. And plunge back into today's Amsterdam.

SLEEPING IN AMSTERDAM

Contents

Greeting a new day by descending steep stairs and stepping into a leafy canalside scene—graceful bridges, historic gables, and bikes clattering on cobbles—is a fun part of experiencing Amsterdam. But Amsterdam is a tough city for budget accommodations, and any hotel room under €140 (or B&B room under €100) will have rough edges. Still, you can sleep well and safely in a great location for €100 per double.

I've grouped my hotel listings into four neighborhoods, each of which has its own character.

West Amsterdam (which includes the Jordaan) has Old World ambience, with quiet canals, traditional Dutch architecture, and candlelit restaurants. It's also just minutes on foot to Dam Square. Many of my hotels are charming, friendly gabled mansions. The downside here is that you'll pay more and likely have lots of stairs to climb.

The **Southern Canal Belt** is walkable (or an easy tram ride) to the center of town and bustling Leidseplein restaurants, tourist

Sleep Code

Abbreviations   (€1 = about $1.40, country code: 31)
S = Single, **D** = Double/Twin, **T** = Triple, **Q** = Quad, **b** = bathroom, **s** = shower only.
Price Rankings
 $$$ Higher Priced—Most rooms €140 or more.
  $$ Moderately Priced—Most rooms between €90-140.
   $ Lower Priced—Most rooms €90 or less.
Nearly everyone speaks English. Unless otherwise noted, credit cards are accepted, breakfast is included, and Wi-Fi is generally free. Rates may not include the city's 6 percent room tax. Prices change; verify current rates online or by email. For the best prices, always book directly with the hotel.

buzz, and nightlife—and it also delivers canalside charm and B&B coziness.

Staying in **Central Amsterdam** is ideal for people who like shopping, tourist sights, and easy access to public transportation (including Central Station). On the downside, the area has traffic noise, concrete, and urban grittiness, and the hotels can lack character.

Southwest Amsterdam, farther afield in the quieter semi-suburban neighborhood around Vondelpark and Museumplein, is close to the Rijks and Van Gogh museums, and you'll find good hotel values. However, it's a half-hour walk (or 10-minute tram ride) to Dam Square.

Some national holidays merit making reservations far in advance (see "Holidays and Festivals" on page 503). Amsterdam is jammed during tulip season (late March-mid-May), conventions, festivals, and on summer weekends. During peak season, some hoteliers won't take weekend bookings for those staying fewer than two or three nights.

Around just about every corner in downtown Amsterdam, you'll see construction: cranes for big transportation projects and small crews of bricklayers repairing the wobbly, cobbled streets that line the canals. Canalside rooms can come with great views—and early-morning construction-crew noise. If you're a light sleeper, ask the hotelier for a quiet room in the back. Smoking is illegal in hotel rooms throughout the Netherlands. Parking in Amsterdam is even worse than driving—if you must park a car, ask your hotelier for advice.

Canal houses were built tight. They have steep stairs with narrow treads; almost none have elevators. If steep stairs are potentially problematic, book a hotel with an elevator.

If you'd rather trade away big-city action for small-town coziness, consider sleeping in Haarlem, 20 minutes away by train (see Haarlem chapters).

West Amsterdam

STATELY CANALSIDE HOTELS

These hotels, a half-mile apart, both face historic canals. They come with lovely lobbies (some more ornate than others) and rooms that can feel like they're from another century. This area oozes elegance and class, and it is fairly quiet at night.

$$$ The Toren is a chandeliered, historic mansion with a pleasant, canalside setting and a peaceful garden for guests out back. Run by Eric and Petra Toren, this smartly renovated, super-romantic hotel is classy yet friendly, with 38 rooms in a great location on a quiet street two blocks northeast of the Anne Frank House. The capable staff is a great source of local advice. The gilt-frame, velvet-curtained rooms are an opulent splurge (tiny Sb-€115, Db-€200, deluxe Db-€250, third person-€40, prices bump way up during conferences and decrease in winter, breakfast buffet-€14, air-con, elevator, guest computer, Wi-Fi, Keizersgracht 164, tel. 020/622-6033, www.thetoren.nl, info@thetoren.nl). To get the best prices, check their website for the "daily rate," book direct, and in the "remarks" field, ask for the 10 percent Rick Steves cash discount.

$$$ Hotel Ambassade, lacing together 59 rooms in a maze of connected houses, is elegant and fresh, sitting aristocratically on Herengracht. The staff is top-notch, and the public areas (including a library and a breakfast room) are palatial, with antique furnishings and modern art (Sb-€220, Db-€280, more expensive deluxe canal-view doubles and suites, Tb-€245-325, extra bed-€60, ask for Rick Steves discount when booking, see website for specials, breakfast-€17.50, air-con, elevator, guest computer, Wi-Fi, Herengracht 341, tel. 020/555-0222, www.ambassade-hotel.nl, info@ambassade-hotel.nl, Roos—pronounced "Rose").

SIMPLER CANALSIDE HOTELS

These places have basic rooms—some downright spare, none plush—and most do without an elevator or other extras. Each of them, however, offers a decent night's sleep in a lovely area of town.

$$$ Wiechmann Hotel's 37 pricey rooms are sparsely furnished with just the dark-wood essentials, but they're spacious, and the *gezellig* public areas are chock-full of Old World charm (Sb-€70-115, Db-€155-175, Tb-€215, Qb-€225, Db suite-€270, check online for best price, 15 percent cheaper for 3 or more nights if booking through their website, some canal views, back rooms are quiet, guest computer, Wi-Fi, nicely located at Prinsen-

West/Central Amsterdam Hotels

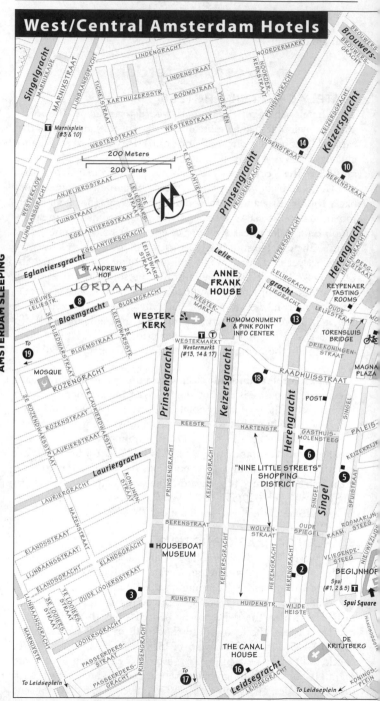

AMSTERDAM SLEEPING

Singelgracht

Marnixkade

Marnixstraat

Lijnbaansgracht

Tichelstraat

LINDENGRACHT

LINDENSTRAAT

KARTHUIZERSSTR

BOOMSTRAAT

WESTERSTRAAT

WESTERSTRAAT

NOORDERMARKT

NOORDER-
KERKSTRAAT

Prinsengracht

Keizersgracht

BROUWERS-
GRACHT

Brouwers-
gracht

VIOLETTEN

PRINSENSTRAAT

T Marnixplein
(#3 & 10)

WESTERSTRAAT

1E EGELANTIERS

ANJELIERSSTRAAT

TUINSTRAAT

1E LELIEDWARSSTR

LELIEDWARSSTR

EGELANTIERSSTRAAT

EGELANTIERSGRACHT

PRINSENSTRAAT

14

Keizersgracht

HERENSTRAAT

10

200 Meters

200 Yards

Westerkade

Lijnbaansgracht

Lijnbaansgracht

Nieuwe
Leliestr.

2E LELIEDWARSSTR

3E LELIEDWARSSTR

Eglantiersgracht

ST. ANDREW'S
HOF

JORDAAN

8

Bloemgracht

Bloemgracht

ROZENGRACHT

BLOEMGRACHT

1

Lelie-
gracht

ANNE
FRANK
HOUSE

LELIEGRACHT

LELIEGRACHT

Keizersgracht

Keizersgracht

LELIEGRACHT

OUDE
LELIESTRAAT

13

Herengracht

HERENGRACHT

HERENBERG-
STRAAT

REYPENAER
TASTING
ROOMS

TORENSLUIS
BRIDGE

DRIEKONINGEN-
STRAAT

MAGNA
PLAZA

MU

MOSQUE

2E ROZENDWARSSTR

1E LAURIERDWARSSTR

ROZENSTRAAT

LAURIERSTRAAT

Lauriergracht

WESTER-
KERK

WESTER-
MARKT

T T

Westermarkt
(#13, 14 & 17)

HOMOMONUMENT
& PINK POINT
INFO CENTER

Prinsengracht

Keizersgracht

REESTR.

HARTENSTR.

RAADHUISSTRAAT

18

POST

Herengracht

GASTHUIS-
MOLENSTEEG

6

"NINE LITTLE STREETS"
SHOPPING
DISTRICT

Singel

PALEIS-

Singel

KEIZERRIJK

Keizergracht

SPUISTRAAT

5

ROSMARIJN-
STEEG

2E LAURIERDWARSSTR

Lauriergracht

HAZENSTRAAT

KONINGENSTRAAT

ELANDSSTRAAT

LIJNBAANSSTRAAT

ELANDSGRACHT

1E LOOIERSSTRAAT

2E LOOIERS-
STRAAT

Marnixstr.

ELANDSGRACHT

OUDE LOOIERSGRACHT

3

Prinsengracht

Keizersgracht

BERENSTRAAT

HOUSEBOAT
MUSEUM

RUNSTR.

WOLVEN-
STRAAT

OUDE
SPIEGEL

HUIDENSTR.

WIJDE
HEISTE

Herengracht

Herengracht

2

VLIEGENDE-
STEEG

BEGIJNHOF

Spui
(#1, 2 & 5)

T

Spui Square

DE
KRITJTBERG

HANDBOOGSTR

LOOIERSGRACHT

PASSEERDERS-
STRAAT

PASSEERDERS-
GRACHT

To Leidseplein

To

17

THE CANAL
HOUSE

16

Leidsegracht

To Leidseplein

KONINGS-
PLEIN

To

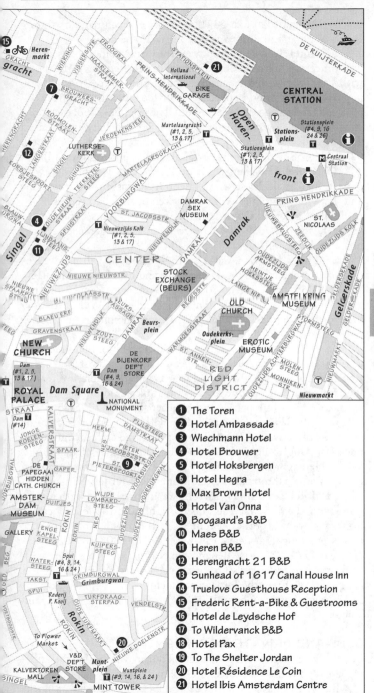

1. The Toren
2. Hotel Ambassade
3. Wiechmann Hotel
4. Hotel Brouwer
5. Hotel Hoksbergen
6. Hotel Hegra
7. Max Brown Hotel
8. Hotel Van Onna
9. Boogaard's B&B
10. Maes B&B
11. Heren B&B
12. Herengracht 21 B&B
13. Sunhead of 1617 Canal House Inn
14. Truelove Guesthouse Reception
15. Frederic Rent-a-Bike & Guestrooms
16. Hotel de Leydsche Hof
17. To Wildervanck B&B
18. Hotel Pax
19. To The Shelter Jordan
20. Hotel Résidence Le Coin
21. Hotel Ibis Amsterdam Centre

gracht 328, tel. 020/626-3321, www.hotelwiechmann.nl, info@hotelwiechmann.nl, John and Taz the welcome dog).

$$ Hotel Brouwer—woody and old-time homey—has a tranquil yet central location on the Singel canal. Renting eight rooms with canal views, old furniture, and soulful throw rugs, it's so popular that it's often booked three or four months in advance—reserve as soon as possible (Sb-€78, Db-€128, Tb-€160, cash only, small elevator, guest computer, Wi-Fi, located between Central Station and Dam Square, near Lijnbaanssteeg at Singel 83, tel. 020/624-6358, www.hotelbrouwer.nl, akita@hotelbrouwer.nl).

$$ Hotel Hoksbergen is well-run and welcoming, with a peaceful canalside setting. Helpful, hands-on owners Tony and Jay rent 14 rooms with newly remodeled bathrooms (Db-€105, Tb-€143, five Qb apartments-€165-198, fans, Wi-Fi, Singel 301, tel. 020/626-6043, www.hotelhoksbergen.com, info@hotelhoksbergen.nl).

$$ Hotel Hegra is cozy, with nine rooms filling a 17th-century merchant's house overlooking the canal (Db-€80-€160, Tb-€119-165, breakfast-€6.50, some rooms with canal view, pay guest computer, Wi-Fi, bike rentals, just north of Wolvenstraat at Herengracht 269, tel. 020/623-7877, www.hotelhegra.nl, info@hotelhegra.nl, Robert).

$$ Max Brown Hotel, the flagship hotel of a boutique-style chain, has a trendy, urban design geared toward a hipster clientele. Located in a quiet neighborhood near Central Station, it offers 25 modern rooms and public areas with funky-chic details. Rooms with canal views are pricier and breezier (Sb-€65-125, Db-€125-185, Tb loft-€250; rates vary wildly with demand, check online and book directly with hotel for best price; free coffee, continental breakfast, tangled floor plan connecting three canalside buildings, Wi-Fi, Herengracht 13, tel. 020/522-2345, www.maxbrownhotels.com, hello@maxbrownamsterdam.com, manager Jan Nijman).

$$ Hotel Van Onna has 41 simple, industrial-strength rooms, some with canal views. The price is right, and the leafy location makes you want to crack out your easel. The popular top-floor attic rooms are snug hideaways (Sb-€45-75, Db-€80-130, Tb-€125-180, Qb-€170-220, price depends on season, 5 percent more with credit card, cot-like beds are sufficient, no phones or TVs, guest computer, Wi-Fi, in the Jordaan at Bloemgracht 104, tel. 020/626-5801, www.hotelvanonna.nl, info@hotelvanonna.nl, Leon and Tsibo).

B&BS AND PRIVATE-ROOM RENTALS

B&Bs offer a chance to feel like a local during your visit, while paying less than you would for a hotel room.

Boogaard's has a busy and central location, a couple of blocks southeast of Dam Square. The following B&Bs lie between the Anne Frank House and Central Station: Maes, Heren, Sunhead of 1617 Canal House Inn, and Herengracht 21 (in the quietest location yet nearest the station). The last two listings—Truelove and Frederic—are services that manage and rent many apartments and rooms in West Amsterdam.

$$ Boogaard's B&B has three comfortable rooms with complimentary minibars and a rooftop terrace. Peter, an American expat opera singer who clearly enjoys hosting Americans in his home, provides royal treatment—and his fresh-baked goodies at breakfast. As his place is popular with my readers, it's smart to book as soon as possible—even as much as six months in advance (Db-€130, 2-night minimum, air-con, Wi-Fi, DVD library, free laundry, loaner cell phones and laptops, Pieter Jacobszstraat 21, tel. 064/358-6835, www.boogaardsbnb.com, info@boogaardsbnb.com).

$$ Maes B&B (pronounced "mahss") and **Heren B&B** are a dynamite value, with a total of nine cozy rooms plus nine thoughtfully appointed apartments in two buildings, within a three-minute walk of each other. Located where the restaurant-lined Herenstraat meets the picturesque Herengracht and Singel canals, the B&Bs are handy to the train station and Jordaan area and are well-run by Ken and Vlad, who offer a warm welcome, a delectable breakfast at a convivial shared table, and a wealth of sightseeing and dining advice. Regardless of where you're staying, check in at Maes B&B (B&B rooms: Sb-€105, Db-€125, extra bed-€20; apartments: Sb-€135, Db-€155; guest computer, Wi-Fi, if street noise bothers you ask for room in back, Maes at Herenstraat 26, Heren at Singel 95, tel. 020/427-5165, www.bedandbreakfastamsterdam.com, maesinfo@xs4all.nl).

$$ Herengracht 21 B&B has two stylish, intimate rooms in a canal house filled with art and run by lovely Loes Olden (2-floor Db-€125, canal-view Db-€135, air-con, Wi-Fi, Herengracht 21, tel. 020/625-6305, mobile 06-2812-0962, www.herengracht21.nl, loes@herengracht21.nl).

$$ Sunhead of 1617 Canal House Inn has four thoughtfully decorated, flower-filled rooms in a restored 17th-century townhouse. Charming Carlos hosts a daily happy hour for his guests (Db-€109-139, canal-view Db-€129-159, Wi-Fi, mobile 06-2865-3572, Herengracht 152, www.sunhead.com, carlos@sunhead.com).

$$ With Truelove Guesthouse, a room-rental service, you'll feel like you're staying at your Dutch friends' house while they're out of town. Sean and Paul—whose tiny antique store on Prinsenstraat doubles as the reception desk for their rental service—have 15 rooms and apartments in houses sprinkled throughout the northern end of the Jordaan neighborhood. The apartments are stylish and come with kitchens and pull-out beds (Db-€105-125, Db apartment-€115-180, prices soft in off-season and midweek, 10 percent more with credit card, 2-night minimum on weekends, no breakfast, pick up keys in store at Prinsenstraat 4, store tel. 020/320-2500, mobile 06-2480-5672, www.cosyandwarm-amsterdam.com, trueloveantiek@zonnet.nl).

$ Frederic Rent-a-Bike & Guestrooms, with a bike-rental shop as the reception, is a collection of private rooms on a gorgeous canal just outside the Jordaan, a five-minute walk from Central Station. Frederic has amassed about 100 beds, ranging from dumpy €75 doubles behind the bike-rental shop to spacious and elegant apartments (from €46/person; these places require a 2-night minimum, occasionally more). Some places are ideal for families and groups of up to eight. He also rents houseboat apartments. All are displayed on his website (phone bookings preferred, book with credit card but pay with cash, no breakfast, Brouwersgracht 78, tel. 020/624-5509, www.frederic.nl, info@frederic.nl, Frederic, Marjolijn, and their son Marne). His excellent bike shop is open daily 9:00-17:30 (€15/24 hours). My readers who rent an apartment get a 50 percent discount on Frederic's 24-hour bike rentals.

Charming B&Bs in Southern Canal Belt

The area around Amsterdam's rip-roaring nightlife center (Leidseplein) is colorful, comfortable, and convenient. These canalside mom-and-pop places are within a five-minute walk of rowdy Leidseplein, but generally are in quiet and typically Dutch settings. Within walking distance of the major museums, and steps off the tram line, this neighborhood offers a perfect mix of charm and location.

$$ Hotel de Leydsche Hof, a hidden gem located on a canal, doesn't charge extra for its views. Its four large rooms are a symphony in white, some overlooking a tree-filled backyard, others a canal, but be prepared for lots of stairs. Frits and Loes give their big, elegant, old building a stylish air. Breakfast is served in the grand canal-front room (Db-€130-150, cash only, 2-night minimum, guest computer, Wi-Fi, Leidsegracht 14, tel. 020/638-2327, mobile 06-3099-2744, www.freewebs.com/leydschehof, loespiller@planet.nl).

$$ Wildervanck B&B, run by Helene and Sjoerd Wildervanck with the help of their three girls, offers two tastefully decorated rooms in an elegant 17th-century canal house (big Db on first floor-€140, Db with twin beds on ground floor-€125, extra bed-€35, 2-night minimum, breakfast in their pleasant dining room,

Wi-Fi, just west of Leidsestraat at Keizersgracht 498, tel. 020/623-3846, www.wildervanck.com, info@wildervanck.com).

Central Amsterdam

You won't get a warm welcome at the first two hotels, but if you're looking for a no-nonsense room that's convenient to plenty of tram lines, these two fit the bill. The third listing is an inexpensive, well-worn hotel on the convenient but noisy and unromantic main drag, Raadhuisstraat. See the map on page 190 for locations.

$$$ Hotel Résidence Le Coin has 42 larger-than-average rooms complete with small kitchenettes. Located near the Mint Tower, this hotel is a two-minute walk to the Flower Market and a five-minute walk to Rembrandtplein (Sb-€126, small Db-€146, bigger Db-€161, Qb-€237, extra bed-€37, breakfast-€12, Wi-Fi, by the University at Nieuwe Doelenstraat 5, tel. 020/524-6800, www.lecoin.nl, hotel@lecoin.nl).

$$$ Hotel Ibis Amsterdam Centre, located next door to Central Station, is a modern, efficient, 363-room place. It offers a central location, comfort, and good value, without a hint of charm (Db-€141-160 Nov-Aug, Db-€200 Sept-Oct, breakfast-€16, check website for deals, book long in advance—especially for Sept-Oct, air-con, elevators, pay guest computer, Wi-Fi; facing Central Station, go left toward the multistory bicycle garage to Stationsplein 49; tel. 020/721-9172, www.ibishotel.com, h1556@accor.com). When business is slow, usually in mid-summer, they occasionally rent rooms to same-day drop-ins for around €110.

$ Hotel Pax has 11 large, plain, but airy rooms with Ikea furniture up several flights of very steep steps—a lot like a European dorm room (S-€35-45, D-€65, Db-€85, T-€100, Tb-€140, prices drop dramatically in winter, no breakfast, five rooms share two showers and two toilets but all have in-room sinks, Wi-Fi, Raadhuisstraat 37, tel. 020/624-9735, hotelpax@telfort.nl, run by go-getters Philip and Pieter).

Southwest Amsterdam, near Vondelpark and Museumplein

These options cluster around Vondelpark in a safe neighborhood. Though they don't have a hint of Old Dutch or romantic canalside flavor, they're reasonable values and only a short walk from the action. Unless noted, the places below have elevators. Many are in a pleasant nook between rollicking Leidseplein and the park, and most are a 5- to 15-minute walk to the Rijks and Van Gogh museums. They are easily connected with Central Station by trams #2 or #5.

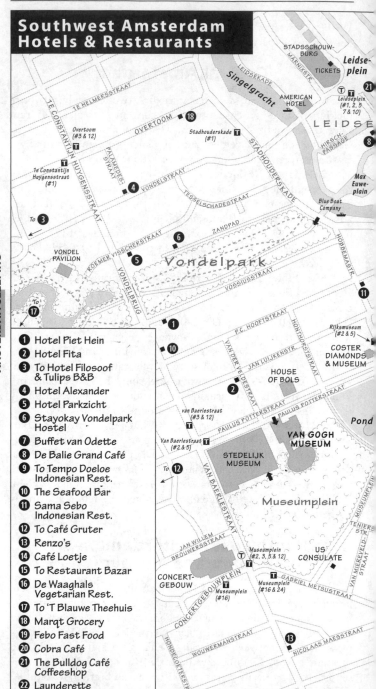

Southwest Amsterdam Hotels & Restaurants

1 Hotel Piet Hein
2 Hotel Fita
3 To Hotel Filosoof & Tulips B&B
4 Hotel Alexander
5 Hotel Parkzicht
6 Stayokay Vondelpark Hostel
7 Buffet van Odette
8 De Balie Grand Café
9 To Tempo Doeloe Indonesian Rest.
10 The Seafood Bar
11 Sama Sebo Indonesian Rest.
12 To Café Gruter
13 Renzo's
14 Café Loetje
15 To Restaurant Bazar
16 De Waaghals Vegetarian Rest.
17 To 'T Blauwe Theehuis
18 Marqt Grocery
19 Febo Fast Food
20 Cobra Café
21 The Bulldog Café Coffeeshop
22 Launderette

Labels on map:

STADSSCHOUW-BURG
Leidse-plein
TICKETS
LEIDSEKADE
MARNIXSTR
Singelgracht
AMERICAN HOTEL
Leidseplein (#1, 2, 5 7 & 10)
LEIDSE
1E HELMERSSTRAAT
1E CONSTANTIJN HUYGENSSTRAAT
Overtoom (#3 & 12)
OVERTOOM
Stadhouderskade (#1)
STADHOUDERSKADE
HIRSCH-PASSAGE
1e Constantijn Huygensstraat (#1)
VONDELSTRAAT
PACHEDESSTRAAT
Max Euwe-plein
Blue Boat Company
To 3
TESSELSCHADESTRAAT
ROEMER VISSCHERSTRAAT
ZANDPAD
VONDEL PAVILION
Vondelpark
VONDELBRUG
JOSSIUSSTRAAT
ROBBEMASTR.
To 17
P.C. HOOFTSTRAAT
Rijksmuseum (#2 & 5)
COSTER DIAMONDS & MUSEUM
VAN DER JEDESTRAAT
JAN LUIJKENSTR.
HONTHORSSTRAAT
HOBBEMASTRAAT
van Baerlestraat (#3 & 12)
HOUSE OF BOLS
Van Baerlestraat (#2 & 5)
PAULUS POTTERSTRAAT
VAN GOGH MUSEUM
Pond
STEDELIJK MUSEUM
To 12
VAN BAERLESTRAAT
Museumplein
MUSEUMPLEIN
TENIERS STR.
JAN WILLEM BROUWERSSTRAAT
Museumplein (#2, 3, 5 & 12)
US CONSULATE
VAN MIERELVELD STRAAT
CONCERT-GEBOUW
CONCERTGEBOUWPLEIN
Museumplein (#16 & 24)
GABRIEL METSUSTRAAT
Museumplein (#16)
HONDECOETERSTR.
WOUWERMANSTRAAT
NICOLAAS MAESSTRAAT

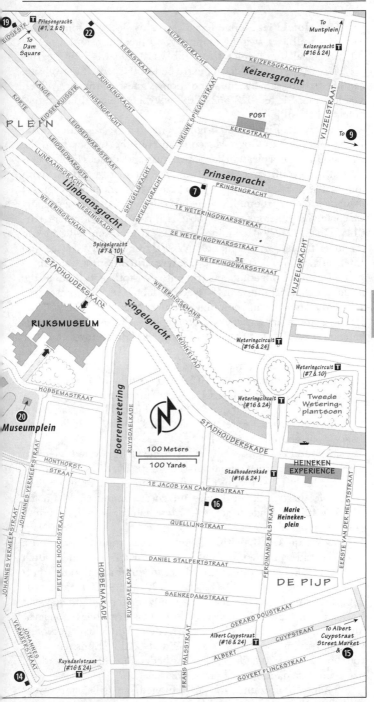

$$$ Hotel Piet Hein offers 81 stylishly sleek yet comfortable rooms as well as a swanky lounge, good breakfast, and a peaceful garden, all on a quiet street (Sb-€110, Db-€145-160, extra-posh Db-€180-250, Tb-€200, extra bed-€30, specials on website, breakfast-€9.50, air-con in some rooms, guest computer, Wi-Fi, Vossiusstraat 51, tel. 020/662-7205, www.hotelpiethein.nl, info@hotelpiethein.nl).

$$$ Hotel Fita has 20 bright rooms in a great location—100 yards from the Van Gogh Museum, an even shorter hop from the tram stop, and on a pleasant corner with a grade school's lively recess yard filling a traffic-free street. The style is modern yet rustic, with minimalist plywood furniture and nice extras, including espresso machines in every room. It's well-run by Roel, who offers a friendly welcome and generous advice (Sb-€115, two small basement Db-€149, Db-€149-179 depending on size, extra person-€40, air-con on upper floors, guest computer, Wi-Fi, free laundry service, Jan Luijkenstraat 37, tel. 020/679-0976, www.fita.nl, info@fita.nl).

$$ Hotel Filosoof greets you with Aristotle and Plato in the foyer and classical music in its spacious lobby. Its 45 rooms, some across the street from reception, are decorated with themes; the Egyptian room has a frieze of hieroglyphics. Philosophers' sayings hang on the walls, and thoughtful travelers wander down the halls or sit in the garden, rooted in deep discussion. The rooms are small, but the hotel is endearing (Db-€110-130 weeknights, €130-150 Fri-Sat, bigger "deluxe" rooms-€30 extra, suites-€60 extra, prices depend on season; breakfast-€15, guest computer, Wi-Fi, 3-minute walk from tram line #1, get off at Jan Pieter Heijestraat, Anna van Den Vondelstraat 6, tel. 020/683-3013, www.hotelfilosoof.nl, reservations@hotelfilosoof.nl).

$$ Hotel Alexander is a modern, newly renovated 34-room hotel on a quiet street. Some of the rooms overlook the garden patio out back (Db-€135, prices soft in winter—call or check their website for best deal, breakfast-€10, guest computer, Wi-Fi, tel. 020/589-4020, Vondelstraat 44, www.hotelalexander.nl, info@hotelalexander.nl).

$$ Tulips B&B, with a bunch of cozy rooms—some on a canal—is run by a friendly Englishwoman, Karen, and her Dutch husband, Paul. Rooms are clean, white, and bright, with red carpeting, plants, and flowers (D-€85, Db-€120, suite-€150, extra bed-€30, discounts for longer stays, cash only, prefer 3-night stays on weekends, includes milk-and-cereal breakfast, no shoes, no elevator but not a lot of stairs, Wi-Fi, south end of Vondelpark at Sloterkade 65, 7-minute walk from trams #1 and #2, directions sent when you book, tel. 020/679-2753, www.bedandbreakfastamsterdam.net, rooms@bedandbreakfastamsterdam.net).

$ Hotel Parkzicht, an old-fashioned, no-frills, dark-wood place with extremely steep stairs, rents 13 big, plain, and somewhat frayed rooms on a street bordering Vondelpark (S-€59, Sb-€69, Db-€79-98, Tb-€120-155, closed Nov-March, no elevator, Wi-Fi, some noise from neighboring youth hostel, Roemer Visscherstraat 33, tel. 020/618-1954, www.parkzicht.nl, hotel@parkzicht.nl).

Hostels

Amsterdam has a world of good, cheap hostels located throughout the city. Most are designed for the party crowd, but here are a few quieter options. They all offer dorm beds and charge for towels. Stayokay Vondelpark and The Shelter City also have some basic doubles.

In the Jordaan: $ The Shelter Jordan is a scruffy, friendly, Christian-run, 90-bed place in a great neighborhood. Although most of Amsterdam's hostels are pretty wild, this place is drug- and alcohol-free, with boys on one floor and girls on another. These are Amsterdam's best budget beds (bunks in dorms-€15-37, higher prices for 4-5-bed rooms, includes sheets and breakfast, guest computer in lobby, Wi-Fi, near Anne Frank House at Bloemstraat 179, tel. 020/624-4717, www.shelter.nl, jordan@shelter.nl). The Shelter serves hot meals, offers free lockers, leads nightly Bible studies, and runs a snack bar in its big, relaxing lounge.

In the Red Light District: $ The Shelter City is Shelter Jordan's sister—similar, but definitely not preaching to the local choir. And though its 180 beds are buried in the heart of the red lights, it feels very well-run and perfectly safe (same prices as Shelter Jordan, bunks in Qb-€3 extra, D-€50-78 for spouses or single-sex; same amenities, rules, and Bible study; Barndesteeg 21, see map on page 108, tel. 020/625-3230, www.shelter.nl, city@shelter.nl).

In Vondelpark: $ Stayokay Vondelpark (IYHF), with 536 beds in 130 rooms, is one of Amsterdam's top hostels for the under-25 set—but over-25s will feel comfortable here too (€24-42/bed in 4- to 20-bed dorms, D-€68-115—most with bunk beds, higher prices are for March-Oct, members save €2.50, price depends on demand—cheapest when booked in advance, family rooms, lots of school groups, lockers, laundry, pay guest computer, Wi-Fi, bike rental, right on Vondelpark at Zandpad 5, tel. 020/589-8996, www.stayokay.com, vondelpark@stayokay.com). Though Stayokay Vondelpark and Stayokay Stadsdoelen (listed next) are generally booked long in advance, occasionally a few beds open up each day at 11:00.

Near Waterlooplein: $ Stayokay Stadsdoelen (IYHF), small-er and simpler than its Vondelpark sister (listed above), has only large dorms and no private bathrooms, but is free of large school groups. Because of the lower prices, this one caters mostly to twentysomethings (€18-35/bed with sheets and breakfast in 10-bed dorms, members save €2.50, price depends on demand—cheapest when booked in advance, lockers, guest computer, Wi-Fi, bike rental, Kloveniersburgwal 97, see map on page 72, tel. 020/624-6832, www.stayokay.com, stadsdoelen@stayokay.com).

Farthest East: **$ Stayokay Zeeburg (IYHF)** is a 500-bed hostel with all the modern services. While it's pretty far from the center, by tram or bike you're just 15 minutes from Damrak street. Oldsters fit in here with the youngsters (€20-42/bed in 4- to 9-bed dorms, price depends on demand—cheapest when booked in advance, pay guest computer, Wi-Fi, lockers, games, restaurant, bike rental, tram #14 to Timorplein 21, tel. 020/551-3190, www.stayokay.com, zeeburg@stayokay.com).

EATING IN AMSTERDAM

Contents

Amsterdam has a thriving restaurant scene. In this international city, there's something for every taste. While I've listed options, one good strategy is simply to pick an area and wander.

Along the main tourist spine, the sloppy food ghetto thrives around Leidseplein; if you want to eat with a bunch of rowdy Aussies in a very touristy zone, wander along Leidseplein's "Restaurant Row" (on Leidsedwarsstraat). The area around Spui Square and that end of Spuistraat is also trendy, though not as noisy. For fewer crowds, better food and service, and far more charm, head a few blocks west into the Jordaan district, which has its own, more authentically Dutch "Restaurant Row" (on Tweede Egelantiersdwarsstraat).

Most hoteliers keep a list of reliable eateries for their neighborhood and know which places keep their travelers happy. For a local take on restaurants, check out this food blog: www.dutchgrub.com.

Note that many of my listings are lunch-only (usually termed "café" rather than "restaurant")—good for a handy bite near major sights. Similarly, many top restaurants serve only dinner. Before trekking across town to any of my listings, check the hours.

Before you leave Amsterdam, be sure to have a filling *rijsttafel* dinner (see page 214), a herring snack at a fish stand (page 218), and a drink at a brown café (page 219).

Central Amsterdam

You'll likely have lunch at some point in the city's core, but you'll find a better range of more satisfying dinner choices in the Jordaan area of West Amsterdam (described later). For the locations of these eateries, see the "West/Central Amsterdam Restaurants" map on page 205.

ON AND NEAR SPUI

Gartine is a hidden gem, filling a rustic and relaxed but border-line-elegant little space tucked just off the tourist-thronged Spui and Rokin zones. It's a calm and classy spot for a good lunch (€6-9 open-faced sandwiches, €16-20 high tea, Wed-Sun 10:00-18:00, closed Mon-Tue, Taksteeg 7, tel. 020/320-4132).

Restaurant Kantjil en de Tijger is a lively, modern place with a plain and noisy ambience, full of happy, youthful eaters who know a good value. The food is purely Indonesian; the waiters are happy to explain your many enticing options. Their three *rijsttafels* (traditional "rice tables" with about a dozen small courses) range from €25 to €33 per person. Though they are designed for two people, three people can make a meal by getting a *rijsttafel* for two plus a soup or light dish (daily 12:00-23:00, reservations smart, mostly indoor with a little outdoor seating, Spuistraat 291, tel. 020/620-0994, www.kantjil.nl). Before you dig in, read the *rijsttafel* sidebar on page 214.

Kantjil to Go is a tiny take-out bar serving up inexpensive Indonesian fare. Their printed menu explains the mix-and-match plan (€6 for medium, €7.50 for large, daily 12:00-21:00, a half-block off Spui Square at Nieuwezijds Voorburgwal 342, behind the restaurant listed above, tel. 020/620-3074). Split a large box, grab a bench on the charming Spui Square around the corner, and you've got perhaps the best cheap, hot meal in town.

Pannenkoekenhuis Upstairs is a tight, tiny (just four tables), characteristic perch up some extremely steep stairs, where Arno and Ali cook and serve delicious €6-12 pancakes throughout the afternoon. They'll tell you that I discovered this place long before Anthony Bourdain did (Tue-Fri 12:00-19:00, closed Mon, Grimburgwal 2, tel. 020/626-5603).

Restaurant d'Vijff Vlieghen, in spite of being called "The Seven Flies," is a dressy Dutch museum of a restaurant with an interior right out of a Rembrandt painting. It's a romantic splurge, offering Dutch, French, and international cuisine (€23-27 main courses, €36 three-course dinner, nightly 18:00-22:00, Spuistraat 294, tel. 020/530-4060).

Singel 404, just across the Singel canal from Spui and near the Nine Little Streets, is a popular café serving €4-7 sandwiches on bread, bagels, and flatbread (daily 10:30-19:00, food served until 18:00, Singel 404, tel. 020/428-0154).

Café 't Gasthuys, a brown café, is a good canalside choice in this part of town (Grimburgwal 7, described on page 220).

Atrium University Cafeteria feeds travelers and students from Amsterdam University for great prices, but only on weekdays (€7 meals, Mon-Fri 11:00-15:00 & 17:00-19:30, closed Sat-Sun; from Spui, walk west down Landebrug Steeg past recommended Café 't Gasthuys three blocks to Oudezijds Achterburgwal 237, then go through arched doorway on the right; tel. 020/525-3999).

Café Luxembourg is a venerable old bistro with a very tired interior and tables (some in a heated veranda) looking right out on Spui Square. The food's basic, but it's easy and friendly with nice Belgian beer on tap. If it's a burger you want, try their Luxem burger (€10-15 salads and sandwiches, €16-20 main dishes, daily 9:00-23:00, Spui 24, tel. 020/620-6264).

NEAR ROKIN AND THE MINT TOWER

De Jaren Café ("The Years") is chic yet inviting, and clearly a favorite with locals. Upstairs is a minimalist restaurant with a top-notch salad bar and canal-view deck (serving €16-20 dinners after 17:30, prices include salad bar plus fish, meat, and veggie dishes; €14 for salad bar only). Downstairs is a modern café, great for light lunches (soups, salads, and sandwiches served all day and evening) or just coffee over a newspaper. On a sunny day, the café's canalside patio is a fine spot to nurse a drink; this is also a nice place to go just for a drink in the evening and to enjoy the spacious Art Deco setting (daily 9:30-24:00, a long block up from Muntplein at Nieuwe Doelenstraat 20, tel. 020/625-5771).

La Place Cafeteria, on the ground floor of the V&D depart-

ment store, has an abundant, colorful array of fresh, appealing, self-serve food. A multi-story eatery that seats 300, it has a small outdoor terrace upstairs. Explore before you make your choice. This bustling spot has a lively market feel, with everything from made-on-the-spot stir-fry, to fresh juice, to veggie

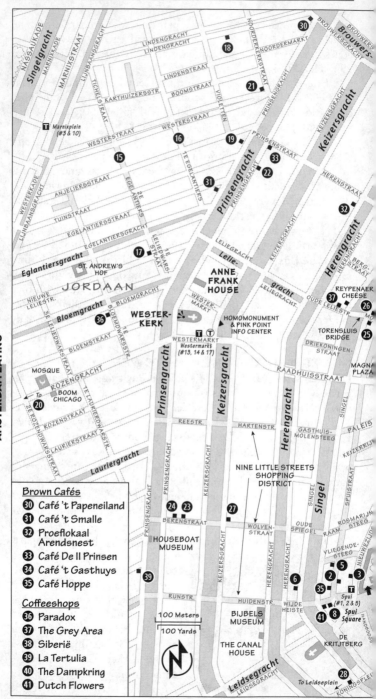

AMSTERDAM EATING

Brown Cafés

30 Café 't Papeneiland
31 Café 't Smalle
32 Proeflokaal Arendsnest
33 Café De II Prinsen
34 Café 't Gasthuys
35 Café Hoppe

Coffeeshops

36 Paradox
37 The Grey Area
38 Siberië
39 La Tertulia
40 The Dampkring
41 Dutch Flowers

100 Meters
100 Yards

West/Central Amsterdam Restaurants

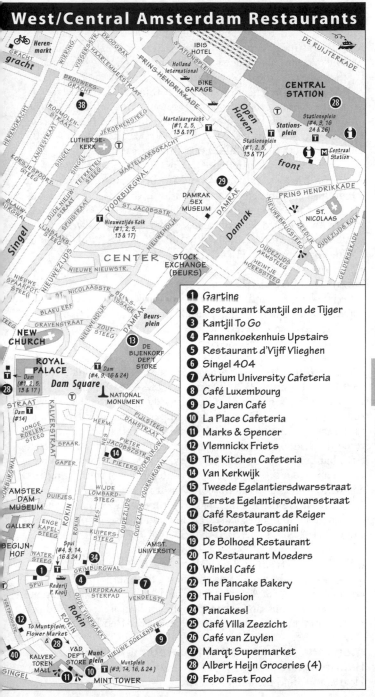

AMSTERDAM EATING

1. Gartine
2. Restaurant Kantjil en de Tijger
3. Kantjil To Go
4. Pannenkoekenhuis Upstairs
5. Restaurant d'Vijff Vlieghen
6. Singel 404
7. Atrium University Cafeteria
8. Café Luxembourg
9. De Jaren Café
10. La Place Cafeteria
11. Marks & Spencer
12. Vlemnickx Friets
13. The Kitchen Cafeteria
14. Van Kerkwijk
15. Tweede Egelantiersdwarsstraat
16. Eerste Egelantiersdwarsstraat
17. Café Restaurant de Reiger
18. Ristorante Toscanini
19. De Bolhoed Restaurant
20. To Restaurant Moeders
21. Winkel Café
22. The Pancake Bakery
23. Thai Fusion
24. Pancakes!
25. Café Villa Zeezicht
26. Café van Zuylen
27. Marqt Supermarket
28. Albert Heijn Groceries (4)
29. Febo Fast Food

soups, and much more (€5 pizza and sandwiches, Sun-Mon 11:00-19:00, Tue-Wed 10:00-19:30, Thu-Sat 10:00-21:00, at the end of Kalverstraat near Mint Tower, tel. 020/622-0171). For fast and healthy take-out food (such as sandwiches, yogurt, and fruit cups), try the bakery on the department store's ground floor.

Marks and Spencer, up the street from V&D's La Place, has an enticing mini-grocery on the ground floor selling packaged sandwiches, salads, and other prepared meals with an upscale-English flair (€4-6 meals, Mon 10:00-20:00, Tue-Sat 9:00-20:00, Thu until 21:00, Sun 11:00-20:00, Kalverstraat 226).

Fries: While Amsterdam has no shortage of *Vlaamse friets* ("Flemish fries") stands, locals and in-the-know visitors head for **Vlemnickx,** an unpretentious hole-in-the-wall *friets* counter hiding just off the main Kalverstraat shopping street. They sell only fries, with a wide variety of sauces—they call themselves *"de sausmeesters"* (Sun-Mon 12:00-19:00, Tue-Sat 11:00-19:00, Thu until 20:00, Voetboogstraat 31).

NEAR DAM SQUARE

Eateries along Damrak are touristy, overpriced, and dreary. But if you need a meal in this area, these listings are good options.

The Kitchen Cafeteria at De Bijenkorf fills the top floor of Amsterdam's swankiest department store with delightful, tasty self-service options, from Dutch to Asian to salads and burgers. It's modern and spacious, with a great outdoor terrace (daily 10:00-19:30, Thu-Fri until 20:30, Dam 1, tel. 088-245-9080).

Along the Nes: The narrow, relatively quiet street called Nes, running south from Dam Square and paralleling Rokin one block to the east, is fun to browse. It's home to several small theaters and restaurants, among them the popular **Van Kerkwijk,** an unpretentious but quirky eatery that has a loyal following. There's no written menu—your server relays the day's offerings of freshly prepared and reasonably priced international dishes. They don't take reservations and there's often a line; pass the time with a drink in the bar (€6 lunches, €8 lunch salads, €11-20 main courses at dinner, daily 11:00-23:00, Nes 41, tel. 020/620-3316).

NEAR THE TRAIN STATION

These two neighborhoods are close to the train station, in the northern part of central Amsterdam. The Haarlemmerdijk/Haarlemmerstraat area runs along the top of the Jordaan area; the Zeedijk is more central but less appealing, bordering the Red Light District.

Along the Haarlem Dike: Haarlemmerdijk and Haarlemmerstraat

Haarlemmerdijk, the long, high street running west from the train station (once the top of a dike and Amsterdam's harborfront), used to be one of the city's more dismal areas. But a recent rejuvenation brought in creative new restaurants. While locals lament that high rents are closing down a few of the more colorful places along here, it's worth scouting. (For more on this area—including a self-guided stroll—see page 245 in the Shopping in Amsterdam chapter.)

Bistrot Neuf, a chic, wine-focused French eatery, is the "destination" restaurant along Haarlemmerdijk—and worth reserving ahead (especially on weekends). You'll pass the busy kitchen as you squeeze through the narrow entrance. Sleek black tables fill the dimly lit, sophisticated interior, walled with exposed brick (€8-16 lunches, €26-28 *plats du jour,* €32 three-course dinner, 60 wines by the glass, daily 12:00-22:30, Haarlemmerstraat 9, tel. 020/400-3210, www.bistrotneuf.nl).

Toscana Italian Restaurant is a favorite for good, inexpensive meals, served in a woody, Dutch-beer-hall setting (€7-10 pizza and pastas, €18-20 main courses, daily 16:00-23:30, fast service, Haarlemmerstraat 130, tel. 020/622-0353).

Along Zeedijk and in the Red Light District

Skirting the heart of the Red Light District, the crowded pedestrian street, Zeedijk, is lined with dozens of mostly cheap, family-run, hole-in-the-wall Asian eateries. While packed with rowdy tourists, this is a convenient place to survey several options in one go.

Aneka Rasa Indonesian Restaurant is weirdly bright, spacious, and peaceful at the edge of this otherwise unappetizing zone. It's a good place for budget *rijsttafel*, and although the menu states that an order requires a minimum of two people, in practice they'll serve it to one (€20 *rijsttafel*, price is per person—no sharing, daily 17:00-22:30, Warmoesstraat 25, tel. 020/626-1560). For a primer before you eat, see the sidebar on page 214; for the location, see page 108.

West Amsterdam, in the Jordaan District

Even if you're not sleeping in West Amsterdam, it's a fun area to explore. Nearly all of these places are within a few scenic blocks of the Anne Frank House, providing handy lunches and atmospheric dinners in the city's most charming neighborhood—perfect for a break during my Jordaan Walk or while browsing the shops. For locations, see the map on page 205.

JORDAAN'S "RESTAURANT ROW": TWEEDE (2ND) EGELANTIERSDWARSSTRAAT

The Jordaan's trendiest street (sometimes spelled Anjeliersd-warsstraat) is home to a variety of tempting places to eat. This is a youthful and exuberant scene, with high-energy eateries that spill out into lively brick-sidewalk seating. Stroll its length from Egelantiers Canal to Westerstraat to survey your options: Japanese pancakes, Italian trattoria, fancy burgers, ice cream, and a classic Dutch *eetcafé,* **Café Sonneveld** (which serves basic €10-20 meals, but has great tables facing the most delightful intersection in Jordaan—at the very start of the street). Many of these places are quite popular; as you stroll, consider reserving a spot for a return dinner visit.

La Oliva is a very well-regarded tapas bar that lays out a tantalizing array of Northern Spanish (Basque and Cantabrian) *pintxos* in a hip environment. As you'll likely share several small plates, your bill can add up fast (€11-16 small plates, €23-27 big plates, daily 13:00-24:00, at #122, tel. 020/320-316).

La Perla has a big, busy wood-fired oven surrounded by a few humble tables, with a more formal dining room across the street and—best of all—sidewalk tables on one of the liveliest intersections in the Jordaan (€12-14 pizzas, daily 12:00-24:00, locations face each other at #14 and #53—take your pick, tel. 020/624-8828).

Eerste (1st) Egelantiersdwarsstraat: This smaller street, one block parallel to "Restaurant Row," has a few more choices but lacks the main drag's bustle. The block just before Westerstraat has the highest concentration of good choices—Indian, tapas, and more. **Kinnaree Thai Restaurant,** with a modern ambience, features delicious, freshly prepared Thai cuisine served by an attentive waitstaff (€15 dishes, daily 17:30-22:00, at #14). **Los Pilones** next door, owned by a pair of brothers, serves surprisingly authentic Mexican food (€18 meals, at #6).

ELSEWHERE IN THE JORDAAN

Café Restaurant de Reiger must offer the best cooking of any *eetcafé* in the Jordaan. Famous for its fresh ingredients, ribs, and delightful bistro ambience, it's part of the classic Jordaan scene. The daily specials (€18-20) on the chalkboard always include a meat, fish, and vegetarian dish. They're proud of their fresh fish and French-Dutch cuisine. The café, which is crowded late and on weekends, takes no reservations. Come early and have a drink at the bar while you wait (€10 starters, €20 main courses, Tue-Sun 17:00-24:00, closed Mon, Nieuwe Leliestraat 34, tel. 020/624-7426).

Café 't Smalle, a recommended brown café, is also a good place for a light lunch (Egelantiersgracht 12, described on page 220).

Ristorante Toscanini is an upmarket Italian place that's always packed. With a lively, spacious ambience and great Italian cuisine, this place is a treat—if you can get a seat. Reservations are essentially required. Eating with the local, in-the-know crowd and the busy open kitchen adds to the fun energy (€10-14 first courses, €16-25 main courses, Mon-Sat 18:00-22:30, closed Sun, deep in the Jordaan at Lindengracht 75, tel. 020/623-2813, http://restauranttoscanini.nl).

De Bolhoed Vegetarian Restaurant has serious vegetarian and vegan food in a colorful setting that Buddha would dig, with a clientele that appears to dig Buddha. Just inhaling here brings you inner peace (big splittable portions, €17 dinners, light lunches, daily 12:00-22:00, dinner starts at 17:00, Prinsengracht 60, tel. 020/626-1803).

Restaurant Moeders is a celebration of motherhood with a homey menu and a mismatched world of tables, chairs, plates and silverware—all donated by neighbors at the grand opening. The tight interior feels like a family rec room, and tables spill out onto the street overlooking a canal. The fun, accessible menu features Dutch and international home cooking. Make a reservation before taking the long walk out here (€8 starters, €15-20 main courses, every day is Mothers' Day from 17:00, Rozengracht 251, tel. 020/626-7957, www.moeders.com).

Winkel, the North Jordaan's canalside hangout, is a sloppy and youthful favorite serving simple bar food. It has a borderline-hipster vibe, with a rustic interior and great casual tables on the big open square. It's busy on Monday mornings, when the Noordermarkt flea market is underway. But Amsterdammers come from across town all week for the *appeltaart*. Rather than eat a meal here, I'd come to enjoy the square and a slice of pie (€11-14 plates, Mon-Sat 8:00-late, Sun 10:00-late, Noordermarkt 43, tel. 020/623-0223).

BETWEEN DAM SQUARE AND THE JORDAAN

Herenstraat, between Keizersgracht and Herengracht, has a fine cluster of more subdued, pricier options, including the next two recommendations.

Max Restaurant offers an intriguing menu of upscale Indonesian food fused with French influences. With its refreshing international twist, it's understandably popular. The prices are high and the service is brisk, but the quality is good. Their formula is to let you choose from a short list to assemble a two-course (€29) or three-course (€37) meal. They also offer a €35 *rijsttafel* tasting menu. Sit at one of their few tables on the charming street, or in their simple no-frills interior (dinner Tue-Sun from 18:00, closed Mon, reservations recommended, Herenstraat 14, tel. 020/420-0222, www.maxrestaurant.nl).

Prego Restaurant is an elegant, modern-yet-invitingly-Dutch place with a tight split-level dining room, an open kitchen, and warm, attentive service. The menu is not Italian (as the name suggests), but features tasty French and international dishes (€10-13 starters, €19-25 main courses, nightly from 18:00, Herenstraat 25, tel. 020/638-0148).

The Pancake Bakery has long been a favorite of backpackers, youth hostelers, and people who just want a pancake for dinner. They offer a fun and creative menu with lots of hearty €10-15 savory pancakes (including a rainbow of international-themed options—kind of like a pizza place, but with pancakes) and €7-10 dessert pancakes. The scene feels like a bar, with a quieter zone upstairs (daily 9:00-21:30, American breakfasts until noon, two blocks north of the Anne Frank House at Prinsengracht 191, tel. 020/625-1333).

In the Nine Little Streets District: This popular shopping zone also has several appealing eateries. Comparison-shop for what looks best, or try one of my recommendations. **Thai Fusion,** despite the name, serves straight-up, top-quality Thai food in a sleek black-and-white room wedged neatly in the middle of the Nine Little Streets action (€14-18 main courses, daily 16:30-22:30, good veggie options, Berenstraat 8, tel. 020/320-8332). **Pancakes!** is a fresh and modern-feeling little eatery serving up savory and sweet pancakes from an inviting location in the heart of the Nine Little Streets (€6-10 pancakes, daily 10:00-18:30, Berenstraat 38, tel. 020/528-9797).

On "Big Head Square" (Torensluis Bridge): Two cafés face the atmospheric, canal-spanning "Big Head Square" (with the landmark statue of Multatuli's massive noggin—explained on page 131 of the Jordaan Walk). While neither is as atmospheric as a true brown café, they compensate with particularly scenic outdoor tables and longer menus. **Café Villa Zeezicht** has the better interior, with all the romantic feel of a classic Old World café. The interior is crammed with tiny tables topped by tall candlesticks, and wicker chairs outside gather under a wisteria-covered awning. The menu is uninventive—decent pastas, burgers, and salads for €10-15. Come here instead for their famous *appeltaart* and for the great people-watching on Torensluis bridge (daily 9:00-21:30, Torensteeg 7, tel. 020/626-7433). Across the street, **Café van Zuylen** is bigger and feels more upscale. It owns the most scenic outdoor tables, right out on the bridge. In bad weather you can sit in the glassed-in front room or the cozier and classier back room (farther down Toren-

Dining with a View

This low-slung, flat city doesn't offer many high-altitude views, but here are a few options near the Central Station.

Sky Lounge Amsterdam crowns the DoubleTree by Hilton hotel, a five-minute walk east of Central Station. Ride the elevator to the 11th floor, where you'll find a chic indoor bar (best views) and an amazing open roof terrace with a trendy crowd enjoying the scene. Scan the horizon to see how Amsterdam's building code protects the downtown core, where spires still stand high (daily 11:00 until late, DJ from 21:00 nightly, €5 beer, €13 cocktails, €15-30 plates, way more drinks than food, Oosterdoksstraat 4, tel. 020/530-0875).

Central Library's La Place Cafeteria is on the top floor of Amsterdam's slick library with a commanding view terrace. Browse the various islands to assemble a tasty, fresh, appealing meal (about €10, salad bar, daily 10:00-21:00, Oosterdokskade 143, tel. 020/523-0900).

Across the River: **The Eye Bar and Restaurant**, directly across the water from Central Station, serves upscale Dutch and international fare on their sprawling view terrace or in their spacious modern interior (€6-11 lunches; dinners with €10 starters, €20 main dishes; daily 10:00-23:00, IJpromenade 1, tel. 020/589-1402). From the back side of the train station, ride the free ferry across the IJ and walk to the far-out white building to the left of the landing.

steeg). They have Dutch and Belgian beers on tap (open long hours daily, Torensteeg 4, tel. 020/639-1055).

Southern Canal Belt

Stroll through the colorful cancan of eateries on Lange Leidsedwarsstraat, the "Restaurant Row" just off Leidseplein, and choose your favorite (but don't expect intimacy or good value). Nearby, busy Leidsestraat has plenty of starving-student options (between Prinsengracht and Herengracht) offering fast and fun food for around €5 a meal. To escape the crowds without too long a walk from Leidseplein, wander a few blocks away from the hubbub to one of these options. To locate the first two restaurants, see the map on page 196.

Buffet van Odette, an elegant little restaurant with a feminine twinkle, serves Mediterranean and Italian cuisine with lots of farm-fresh, seasonal vegetables. It seems just perfect: healthy, unpretentious, very romantic, and peaceful. They have a few tables outside facing a picturesque canal (€10-15 lunch plates, €12 buffet salad at lunch, dinner-€8-14 starters and €15-19 main courses, always vegetarian option and fish, Wed-Mon 10:00-21:00, closed Tue, two blocks past Pipe Museum at Prinsengracht 598, tel. 020/423-6034).

De Balie Grand Café is a venerable ground-floor eatery in part of a former prison complex—now home to galleries and concert venues. While just a block off the touristy Leidseplein, you'll feel as if you're in a parallel, tourist-free world. They serve salads, sandwiches, and simple plates, and your bill helps support culture and progressive thinking—peruse the program of events at your table. Dinner (€8 starters, €18 mains) is served from 17:30-21:30 (open daily for lunch and dinner, great local beers, free Wi-Fi, Kleine-Gartmanplantsoen 10, tel. 020/553-5130).

South of Rembrandtplein: **Tempo Doeloe Indonesian Restaurant**, proudly and purely Indonesian, is renowned. Tourists pack their 50 seats, so it can be hot and crowded (€32 *rijsttafel*, €38 giant *rijsttafel*, price is per person, Mon-Sat 18:00-22:00, closed Sun, several blocks south of Rembrandtplein at Utrechtsestraat 75, reservations smart, tel. 020/625-6718, www.tempodoeloerestaurant. nl). For more on Indonesian food, see the sidebar on page 214.

Southwest Amsterdam

The area surrounding Amsterdam's museum quarter is one of the city's most upscale, with swanky broad boulevards, the top-of-the-line fashion street (P. C. Hooftstraat), and exclusive homes. While a few eateries are within just a few steps of the big museums, my less-touristy picks are generally within a 10-minute walk and have better food and service. These restaurants are good for a lunch or early dinner combined with museum-going—none is worth going out of your way for. See the map on page 196 for locations.

The Seafood Bar—modern, slick, and extremely popular—features a tasty array of seafood. The decor is white-subway-tile trendy, and the food focuses on fresh and sustainable dishes with a Burgundian flair. You can try dropping by, but it's best to reserve during mealtimes (€8-12 sandwiches, €13-18 fish-and-chips, €15-23 main courses and oysters, daily 12:00-22:00, Van Baerlestraat 5, between the Rijksmuseum and Vondelpark, tel. 020/670-8355, www.theseafoodbar.nl).

Sama Sebo Indonesian Restaurant is considered one of the best Indonesian restaurants in town. It's a venerable local favorite for *rijsttafel*, with a waitstaff that seems to have been on board since Indonesia was still a colony. I prefer the energy in the casual "bodega" to the more formal restaurant (and only in the bodega will they serve the smaller €18 lunch plate for dinner). Their 17-dish, €32 classic *rijsttafel* spread is as good as any. At lunch the €18 *bami goreng* or *nasi goreng* (fried noodles or rice) is a feast of its own (Mon-Sat 12:00-15:00 & 17:00-22:00, closed Sun, reservations smart for dinner, P.C. Hooftstraat 27, between the Rijksmuseum and Vondelpark, tel. 020/662-81460, www.samasebo.nl). For pointers on enjoying your *rijsttafel* feast, see the sidebar.

Café Gruter, with a classic brown café interior and great seating on a little square, is a neighborhood hangout—away from the center's tourism in a ritzy residential zone with fashion boutiques and leafy squares (lunch daily 11:00-16:00, also serves dinner, open very late, Willemsparkweg 73, tel. 020/679-6252). Ride tram #2 to the Jacob Obrechtstraat stop—one tram stop beyond the Van Gogh Museum—near a gateway to Vondelpark.

Renzo's is a tempting Italian delicatessen, where you can buy good sandwiches or prepared pasta dishes and *antipasti* (priced by weight, can be heated up; about €5-7 for a meal). Get your food to go, or pay a bit more to sit at one of the tables in the tiny interior, with more seating upstairs (house wine-€2.50/glass, or buy a bottle for the takeaway price to enjoy with your meal, daily 11:00-21:00, Van Baerlestraat 67, between the Rijksmuseum and Vondelpark, tel. 020/763-1673).

Café Loetje has a rollicking neighborhood beer-hall feel. Of the three dining zones, the interior is least interesting; head instead for the glassed-in winter garden (in bad weather) or the sprawling outdoor tables (in good weather). In addition to beer, they slam out good, affordable pub grub (€9-16 meals, daily 11:00 until late, Johannes Vermeerstraat 52, several blocks southeast of Museumplein, tel. 020/662-8173).

In De Pijp: This neighborhood—southeast of the Rijksmuseum—is best known for its thriving Albert Cuyp market (described on page 242). And although the market stalls are typically wrapped up by about 17:00, the restaurants in this area stay busy late into the evening. **Restaurant Bazar,** right in the center of the market action, offers a memorable and fun budget eating experience. Converted from a church, it has spacious seating and mod belly-dance music, and is filled with young locals enjoying good, cheap Middle Eastern and North African cuisine (€8.50 daily plate, delicious €13 couscous, €16 main dishes, daily 11:00 until late, reservations smart if eating after 20:00, Albert Cuypstraat 182, tel. 020/675-0544, http://bazaramsterdam.nl).

Frans Halsstraat: This pleasant tree-and-restaurant-lined street connects the De Pijp market action and the Rijksmuseum. Browse along here to see what looks good. **De Waaghals Vegetarian Restaurant** is a local favorite for its top-quality organic produce and appealing dining room, where red tables lead to peek-a-boo views of the back garden (€12-18 main courses, daily 17:00-21:30, Frans Halsstraat 29, tel. 020/679-9609).

In Vondelpark: **'T Blauwe Theehuis** ("The Blue Tea House")

Rijsttafel: **The Indonesian Rice Table**

Indonesia was a Dutch colony from 1602 through World War II, and reminders of that heritage persist—especially in the food. Spice was key to Indonesian cuisine and trade; after all, the archipelago was home to the famous "Spice Islands." The essential Indonesian dining experience is the *rijsttafel* ("rice table")—a spread of many different dishes and sauces. *Rijsttafel* is not really an indigenous dish, but a Dutch creation to showcase an extravagant array of food and spices from the colony.

My four favorite spots in Amsterdam for *rijsttafel* are **Sama Sebo,** near the Rijksmuseum; **Tempo Doeloe,** in the Southern Canal Belt; **Kantjil en de Tijger,** near Spui in the center of town; and **Aneka Rasa** at the north edge of the Red Light District. All are described in this chapter.

If you order a *rijsttafel* (and you should), begin with a mound of rice, then take a bit of chicken, beef, lamb, or vegetable with the accompanying sauce. (Vegetarian versions are always available.) Start with mild and work up to spicy. Try to keep your rice clean—to cleanse your palate between each dish. Sample as many different combinations as you can, enjoying the variety of flavors and textures.

One *rijsttafel* is plenty for two. Budget diners can ask to share one (with one person ordering just a soup or salad), though some restaurants require a minimum of two people paying the entire per-person cost. If you have a smaller appetite, order à la carte, or ask for *nasi rames*—a cheaper, one-plate version of a *rijsttafel*. Or try *bami goreng*, a plate of stir-fried noodles (or *nasi goreng*, fried rice) served with *rijsttafel* items.

Experiment with the different sauces. *Sambal* is a chutney-like hot paste that comes in hundreds of varieties, usually made by mixing peppers with other ingredients. (*Atjar tjampoer* are sweet-and-sour mixed pickles that help cool down your tongue.) Other common sauces and flavors are peanut (*kacang*), dark soy (*kecap*), sour tamarind (*asam*), and coconut (*lodeh*).

For dessert (as if you need it), it's *spekkoek*—a cake with thin layers of pungent spices.

is a venerable meeting point where, since the 1930s, all generations have come for drinks and light meals. The setting, deep in Vondelpark, is like a Monet painting. Sandwiches are served at tables outside, inside, and on the rooftop from 11:00 to 16:00, drinks and apple pie are served all day, and pot smoking—while discreet—is as natural here as falling leaves (daily 9:00-22:00 in summer, Vondelpark 5, tel. 020/662-0254). **Café Gruter,** listed earlier, is just outside Vondelpark.

Rijsttafel Menu Decoder

ayam	chicken
bakar	baked
goreng	fried
bami (or mie)	noodles
bami goreng	fried noodles
gado-gado	steamed veggies and hard-boiled eggs with peanut sauce
kacang	peanut
kecap	dark soy sauce
krupuk	deep-fried shrimp chips
lodeh	coconut
nasi	rice
nasi goreng	fried rice
nasi kuning	turmeric rice
nasi pedang (or nasi putih)	steamed rice
nasi rames	small rijsttafel on a plate
nasi uduk	sweet coconut rice
pisang goreng	battered-and-fried bananas
sambal	hot paste, comes in many varieties
sambal goreng	stir-fried veggies with a spicy sauce
sayur lodeh	veggies in a spicy coconut sauce
sapi	beef
spekkoek	spiced cake

East Amsterdam

These eateries are worth seeking out. See the map on page 72 for locations.

If you're in the area and hoping for a *rijsttafel*, the nearest recommended place is Tempo Doeloe Indonesian Restaurant, several long blocks south of Rembrantplein (listed under "Southern Canal Belt," earlier).

"Foodie Corner": This pair of upscale eateries in northeast Amsterdam is a magnet for gourmands who've done their homework. They face each other next to a drawbridge at an inviting corner in a sleepy residential zone a short walk from more touristy areas and the Netherlands Maritime Museum. These ambitious, inventive spots are worth the stroll—but reserve ahead to avoid disappointment.

At **Gebr. Hartering,** the namesake brothers—Paul and Niek Hartering—apply the trendy "nose-to-tail" philosophy to Dutch cooking, assembling an interesting array of old and new flavors. Come here with a spirit of adventure, and put yourself in the hands of creative chefs serving items you might not ordinarily try. Most diners opt for the fixed-price meals (€40/4 courses, €65/7 courses on weekdays; they add a couple of courses and charge €10 more on weekends); if you arrive after about 19:30, you'll be limited to the quite short list of à la carte choices. The tight rustic-chic dining room surrounds the open kitchen, and the outdoor seating on the barge down below is unpretentiously romantic (Tue-Sun 18:00-24:00, closed Mon, Peperstraat 10, tel. 020/421-0699, www. gebrhartering.nl).

Greetje features generous sidewalk seating and a classic interior, where steps by the old-fashioned bar lead to a split-level, blue-tiled dining zone. Their goal is to elevate classic Dutch recipes—including some very traditional home-cooking choices not often served in restaurants—into fine dining, often by giving them a fresh spin (€12-16 starters, €23-28 main courses, €39 and €49 fixed-price meals, daily from 18:00, Peperstraat 23, tel. 020/779-7450, www.restaurantgreetje.nl).

Near Waterlooplein: **Café de Sluyswacht**, great for drinks and snacks with a view, is just across the street from Rembrandt's House. This "Lockkeeper's House" dates from 1695. Their outdoor terrace, idyllically looking out over wide canals, has one of Amsterdam's best views. If the weather's bad, head upstairs and hunker down in the cozy painted-wood room. This place is mostly about the drinks, but they serve €6 bar snacks that you could turn into a light—and very scenic—meal (Dutch and Belgian beers on tap, Mon-Sat 13:00-24:00, Sun 13:00-19:00, Jodenbreestraat 1, tel. 020/625-7611).

Cheap and Fast Eats

To dine cheaply yet memorably alongside the big spenders, grab a meal to go, then find a bench on a lively neighborhood square or along a canal. Sandwiches *(broodjes)* of delicious cheese on fresh bread are cheap at snack bars, delis, and *broodjes* shops. Ethnic restaurants—many of them Indonesian or Surinamese, and seemingly all named with varying puns on "Wok"—serve inexpensive, split-table carryout meals. Middle Eastern fast-food stands and diners abound, offering a variety of meats wrapped in pita bread. Easy to buy at grocery stores, yogurt in the Netherlands is tasty and often drinkable right out of its plastic container. For cheap herring sandwiches, see "Amsterdam Experiences," next.

Supermarkets: To stock up on picnic items, you'll find mini-markets all around town. For the location of the following chains, see the maps on pages 196 and 205.

I like **Marqt,** an elegant picnicker's dream, with the freshest organic produce and plenty of prepared foods. This chain is making a bold step into a cashless future and accepts only credit cards. It's worth a look even if you're just browsing (your magnetic-strip card will work fine, daily 9:00-21:00). You'll find locations in the Nine Little Streets district (along Keizersgracht, at Wolvenstraat 34) and in the emerging Haarlemmerdijk zone west of the train station (Haarlemmerstraat 165). Another Marqt is several blocks from Vondelpark and Leidseplein (Overtoom 21). And there's one south of Rembrandtplein (Utrechtsestraat 17).

Albert Heijn grocery stores are more traditional, cheaper, take cash, and are all over town (daily 8:00-22:00). They have great deli sections with picnic-perfect takeaway salads and sandwiches. Helpful, central locations are near Dam Square behind the Royal Palace (Nieuwezijds Voorburgwal 226), near the Mint Tower (Koningsplein 4), on Leidsestraat (at Koningsplein, on the corner of Leidsestraat and Singel), and inside Central Station (at the far end of the passage under the tracks). Be aware that none of their stores accept US credit cards: Bring cash, and don't get in the checkout lines marked *PIN alleen*.

Dutch Fried Fast Food: Febo is an Amsterdam junk-food institution, catering mainly to late-night drinkers looking for greasy fried foods to soak up the booze. A wall of self-service, coin-op windows provides piping-hot gut bombs: fried cheese, burgers, croquettes, and so on (change machine on wall). While many diners turn up their noses, a certain breed of locals swears by their slogan—*De lekkerste!* (The tastiest!). You'll find branches all over town, including a handy one at Leidsestraat 94, just north of Leidseplein; another at Damrak 6; in the Red Light District (facing the Old Church across the canal at Oudezijds Voorburgwal 33); and another near Rembrandtplein and the Tuschinski Theater (Reguliersbreestraat 38).

Amsterdam Experiences

While in Amsterdam, make it a point to partake in these quintessential Dutch experiences: scarfing a whole herring at a fish stand, and relaxing in a cozy "brown café."

TRADITIONAL HERRING STANDS

Amsterdam's old-fashioned fish stands *(heringhandel)* sell €4 herring sandwiches and other salty and fishy treats, usually from easy photo menus. Most stands are open all day, until 17:00 or 18:00.

Herring thrive in the shallow North Sea waters surrounding the Netherlands, so it's logical they've become a delicacy here. While it seems the Dutch eat herring "raw," the fish is actually cured in salt (soaked for five days in an oak cask filled with a mild brine solution). Herring is caught fresh during the May/June fishing season, and immediately preserved. The government sets the date (usually during the second week in June) when the new catch is allowed to be sold; you'll see that date along with the words *Hollandse nieuwe* or *nieuwe haring* ("new"). This also means that, as summer turns to fall and winter, the herring gets older (though still preserved and perfectly edible). Locals claim that the herring tastes best in years with a warm and sunny spring (more sunlight means more plankton...and fatter fish).

When ordering herring, you have a few choices. The easiest for novices is the sandwich (***broodje***, tucked into a soft roll with pickles and raw onions), while purists prefer their herring unadulterated. If you go with straight herring, your big decision is **Rotterdam-style** (pick it up by the tail, dredge it in chopped raw onions, and lower it into your mouth, all in one go) or **Amsterdam-style** (cut up in toothpick-friendly hunks, also with onions... between the raw fish and the onion, herring ought to come with breath mints). The Rotterdam style is more common nationwide; the Amsterdam style evolved when herring was scarce and a complete fish was harder to come by. Yet another variation (though less

common at fish stands) is *rollmops*—herring rolled around a filling, fastened with a toothpick.

Fish stands sell other types of seafood (sometimes deep-fried and/or in sandwiches). *Garnalen* (shrimp) come in two types: little, grayish *hollandse garnalen* or big, pink *noorse garnalen*. Other options are *zalm* (salmon), *makreel* (mackerel), *anguille* (eel), and *krabsalade* (crab salad).

To sample Dutch herring, try these handy outposts (listed from north to south). The first three locations are on the map on page 205; the second two are on the map on page 56.

Near Central Station, on Singel Canal: **Stubbe's Haring,** where the Stubbe family has been selling herring for 100 years, is well-established, a few blocks from Central Station (Tue-Sat 10:00-18:00, closed Sun-Mon, at the locks on Singel canal). Grab a sandwich and have a canalside picnic (benches nearby).

Near Dam Square: **De Zeevang** sits just behind the Royal Palace, at a busy tram-and-traffic intersection (closed Sun-Mon, corner of Nieuwezijds Voorburgwal and Raadhuisstraat, tel. 020/423-1283)

On Spui Square: **Volendammer Heringhandel** is central, at the Rokin end of Spui Square (daily, mobile 06-1419-1750).

Near the Flower Market and Mint Tower: **Frens Heringhandel** enjoys a particularly good location right along my Amsterdam City Walk (daily, Singel 468 at Koningsplein).

South of Rembrandtplein: **Vishuisje Herengracht** sits a block south of the square along Utrechtsestraat, on the bridge over Herengracht (closed Sun, Herengracht 560, tel. 020/423-0098).

AMSTERDAM'S CHARACTERISTIC BROWN CAFÉS: *GEZELLIG* PLACES FOR A DRINK OR SNACK

Be sure to experience the Dutch institution of the *bruin* café (brown café)—so called for the typically hardwood decor and nicotine-stained walls. (While smoking was banned several years ago—making these places even more inviting to nonsmokers—the prior pigmentation persists.) Exemplifying the *gezellig* (cozy) quality that the Dutch hold dear, these are convivial hangouts, where you can focus on conversation while slowly nursing a drink. Like a British pub, the corner brown café is the neighborhood's living room. Some brown cafés specialize in beer, while others focus on the Dutch gin, *jenever;* most also serve wine (for more on drinks, see page 476). Non-drinkers can enjoy a soft drink or coffee. While you could come here for a light meal, the food menu (if they have one) is usually very short, often limited to bar snacks (mostly deep-fried goodies, called *hapjes;* for some options, see page 474).

Admittedly, the line separating a brown café from a plain old bar is blurry, but below I've recommended my favorites. While some brown cafés are jammed with noisy drinkers, others are a bit more sleepy and mellow.

In the North Jordaan: **Café 't Papeneiland** is a classic brown café with Delft tiles, an evocative old stove, and a stay-awhile perch overlooking a canal with welcoming benches. It's been the neighborhood hangout since the 17th century. It feels a little exclusive; patrons who come here to drink and chat aren't eager to see it overrun by tourists. The café's name means "Papists' Island," since this was once a refuge for Catholics; there used to be an escape tunnel here for priests on the run (daily 10:00-24:00, drinks but almost no food—€3.50-cheese or liverwurst sandwiches, €4.30-apple pie, overlooking northwest end of Prinsengracht at #2, tel. 020/624-1989).

Buried Deep in the Jordaan: **Café 't Smalle** is extremely charming, with three zones where you can enjoy a light lunch or a drink: canalside (literally—on a little barge in the canal), inside around the bar, and up some steep stairs in a quaint little back room. The café is open late, and serves simple meals from 11:00 to 17:30 (salads, soup, and fresh sandwiches; plenty of fine €3-4 Belgian beers on tap, interesting wines by the glass; at Egelantiersgracht 12—where it hits Prinsengracht, tel. 020/623-9617).

Between Central Station and the Jordaan: **Proeflokaal Arendsnest** is the ideal brown café experience for beer lovers. Awash in wonderful old-fashioned decor, it displays the day's 30 rotating Belgian beers "on tap/on draft" on a big chalkboard. They also have more than a hundred bottled beer choices, as well as *jenever* (daily 14:00-24:00, Herengracht 90, tel. 020/421-2057). **Café De II Prinsen,** dating from 1910, feels more local. It's relaxed and convivial, with a few outdoor tables facing a particularly pretty canal and a lively shopping street (Dutch beers on tap, daily 12:00-24:00, Prinsenstraat 27, tel. 020/428-4488).

Near Central Station: Fittingly for this neighborhood at the edge of the Red Light District, **Proeflokaal de Ooievaar** ("Pelican") feels like a grubby sailors' tavern—which is exactly what it was. Although it dates from the Golden Age of Dutch seafarers (1782), today its tight nautical-themed interior is crammed with tourists coming up for air from the crowded Red Light District streets (open long hours daily, at the corner of the Red Light District facing Central Station at Sint Olofspoort 1—see map on page 108 for location, look for the pelican on the sign, tel. 020/420-9004).

Near Rokin: **Café 't Gasthuys** offers a long bar, a lovely secluded back room, peaceful canalside seating, and sometimes slow service. I'd come here to eat outside on a quiet canal in the city center. The busy dumbwaiter cranks out light lunches, sandwiches, and reasonably priced basic dinners (€6-10 lunch plates, €11-

15 main courses, cheeseburgers are a favorite, daily 12:00-16:30 & 17:30-22:00, Grimburgwal 7—from the Rondvaart Kooij boat dock, head down Langebrugsteeg, and it's one block down on the left, tel. 020/624-8230).

On Spui Square: **Café Hoppe** is a classic drinking bar that's as brown as can be. This is a good choice if you want to hang out with locals and drink hard. They have a good selection of traditional drinks and *jenevers*, sandwiches at lunch (€6-7, 12:00-17:00), a packed interior, and fun stools outside to oversee the action on Spui (Mon-Thu 14:00-24:00, Fri-Sun 12:00-24:00, Spui 18, tel. 020/420-4420).

Other Brown Cafés and Similar Places: Elsewhere in this chapter, I've recommended some places that aren't quite "brown cafés," but offer similar ambience. These include **Winkel** (at the north end of the Jordaan); **Café Gruter** (just past the Rijks/Van Gogh museum neighborhood, at an entrance to Vondelpark); **Café Villa Zeezicht** and **Café van Zuylen** (a pair of cafés with a longer menu than most and a sterling location right on "Big Head Square"); and **Café de Sluyswacht** (with perhaps the best view in Amsterdam, overlooking a wide canal near Rembrandt's House).

SMOKING

The Dutch have a long (and complicated) relationship with smoking, whether marijuana or tobacco. This chapter considers Dutch tobacco habits, explains the current Dutch laws regarding marijuana, and offers advice both on how marijuana-selling "coffeeshops" work and which ones in Amsterdam may be worth a visit.

TOBACCO

A quarter of Dutch people smoke tobacco. Holland has a long tradition as a smoking culture, being among the first to import the tobacco plant from the New World. (For a history of smoking, visit the fascinating Pipe Museum, described on page 58.)

Tobacco shops, such as the House of Hajenius (described on page 99), glorify the habit, yet the Dutch people are among the healthiest in the world. Tanned, trim, firm, sixtysomething Dutch people sip their beer, take a drag, and ask me why Americans murder themselves with Big Macs.

Still, the Dutch version of the Surgeon General is speaking out loud and clear about the health risks of smoking. Warning stickers bigger than America's are required on cigarette packs, and some of them are almost comically blunt—for example, "Smoking will make you impotent...and then you die."

Since 2008, a Dutch law has outlawed smoking tobacco almost everywhere indoors: trains, hotel rooms, restaurants, bars... and even marijuana-dealing coffeeshops.

MARIJUANA (A.K.A. CANNABIS)

For tourists from lands where you can do hard time for lighting up, the open use of marijuana here can feel either somewhat disturbing, or exhilaratingly liberating...or maybe just refreshingly sane.

Several decades after being legalized in the Netherlands, marijuana causes about as much excitement here as a bottle of beer.

Marijuana Laws and "Coffeeshops"
Throughout the Netherlands, you'll see "coffeeshops"—cafés selling marijuana, with display cases showing various joints or baggies for sale.

Rules and Regulations: The retail sale of marijuana is strictly regulated, and proceeds are taxed. The minimum age for purchase

is 18, and coffeeshops can sell up to five grams of marijuana per person per day. It's also illegal for these shops (or anyone) to advertise marijuana. In fact, in many places, the prospective customer has to take the initiative and ask to see the menu. In some coffeeshops, you actually have to push and hold down a button to see an illuminated menu—the contents of which look like the inventory of a drug bust.

Shops sell marijuana and hashish both in pre-rolled joints and in little baggies. Joints are generally sold individually (€3-5, depending on the strain you choose), though some places sell only small packs of three or four joints. Baggies generally contain a gram and go for €8-15. The better pot, though costlier, can actually be a better value, as it takes less to get high—and it's a better high. But if you want to take it easy, as a general rule, cheaper is milder.

Each coffeeshop is allowed to keep an inventory of about a pound of pot in stock: The tax authorities don't want to see more than this on the books at the end of each accounting cycle, and a shop can lose its license if it exceeds this amount. A popular shop—whose supply must be replenished five or six times a day—simply has to put up with the hassle of constantly taking small deliveries. A shop can sell a ton of pot with no legal problems, as long as it maintains that tiny stock and just refills it as needed. The reason? Authorities want shops to stay small and not become export bases.

Smoking Tips: Shops have loaner bongs and inhalers, and dispense rolling papers like toothpicks. While it's good style to ask first, as long as you're a paying customer (e.g., you buy a cup of coffee), you can generally pop into any coffeeshop and light up, even if you didn't buy your pot there.

Tourists who haven't smoked pot since their college days are famous for overindulging in Amsterdam. Coffeeshop baristas nickname tourists about to pass out "Whitey"—the color their faces turn just before they hit the floor. They warn Americans (who aren't used to the strength of the local stuff) to try a lighter leaf. If you do overdo it, the key is to eat or drink something sweet to avoid getting sick. Cola is a good fast fix, and coffeeshop staff keep sugar tablets handy. They also recommend trying to walk it off.

Don't ever buy pot on the street in Amsterdam. Well-established coffeeshops are considered much safer, and coffeeshop owners have an interest in keeping their trade safe and healthy. They're also generally very patient in explaining the varieties available.

Types of Cannabis: The Dutch sell several forms of the cannabis plant: They smoke both hashish (the sap of the cannabis plant) and the leaf of the plant (which they call "marihuana" or "grass"). While each shop has different brands, it's all derived from two types of marijuana plant: *Cannabis indica* and *Cannabis sativa*. *Indica* gets you a stoned, heavy, mellow, "couch-weed" high. *Sativa* is light, fun, uplifting, and more psychedelic. *Sativa* makes you giggle.

Most of the pot sold in Dutch coffeeshops is grown locally, as coffeeshops know it's much safer to deal with Dutch-grown plants than to import marijuana (the EU, as you might imagine, prohibits any international drug trade). Technological advances have made it easier to cultivate exotic strains. You may see joints described as if they'd come from overseas, e.g. "Thai"—and indeed the strain in that joint may have originated elsewhere—but it's still Dutch-grown. "Netherlands weed" is now refined, like wine. Most shops get their inventory from the pot equivalent of local home- or microbrewers. Shops with better "boutique suppliers" develop a reputation for having better-quality weed. (These are the places that proudly display a decal announcing them as winners at Amsterdam's annual Cannabis Cup Awards.)

Tobacco and Marijuana: While most American pot-smokers like their joints made purely of marijuana, the Dutch (like most Europeans) are accustomed to mixing tobacco with marijuana. Back in the 1970s, most "pot-smokers" here smoked hash, which needs to be mixed with something else (like tobacco) to light up. Today, more Dutch prefer "herbal cannabis"—the marijuana bud common in the US—but they still keep the familiar tobacco in their joints. Tobacco-mixed joints also go back to hippie days, when pot was expensive and it was simply wasteful to pass around a pure marijuana joint. Mixing in tobacco allowed poor hippies to be generous without going broke. And since the Dutch don't dry and cure their marijuana, it's simply hard to smoke without tobacco.

The Netherlands' indoor-smoking ban pertains to tobacco smoke, not pot smoke. It might seem strange to an American, but these days, if a coffeeshop is busted, it can be for tobacco. Coffeeshops with a few outdoor seats have a huge advantage, as their customers can light up outside. Shops without the outdoor option are in for an extra challenge, as many local smokers would rather get their weed to go than smoke it without tobacco at their neighborhood coffeeshop. Prerolled joints are now sold three ways: pure, with the nontobacco "hamburger helper" herb mix, or with tobacco. Any place that caters to Americans will have joints without tobacco, but you have to ask specifically for a "pure" joint.

The Dutch Approach to Marijuana

To foreign visitors, the Netherlands can seem frighteningly comfortable with—even nonchalant about—drug use. But the Dutch are well aware of the problems associated with drugs, especially addictive ones. (The Dutch word for addiction is "enslavement.") Most also believe that the concept of a "victimless crime" is a contradiction in terms: Any drug-related behavior that affects others is taken seriously. Drive under the influence of anything and you're toast. Because of their wide-reaching social costs, heroin and cocaine are strictly illegal in the Netherlands, and the police stringently enforce laws prohibiting their sale and use.

The Dutch are not even necessarily pro-marijuana; most people here simply believe that outlawing marijuana creates more problems than it solves—and statistics indicate they may be right. No one here would say that smoking pot was healthy. It's a drug. It's dangerous, and it can be abused. But the Dutch have chosen to allow marijuana's responsible adult use as a civil liberty, and treat its abuse as a health-care and education challenge rather than a crime.

Many Dutch believe that America's long-standing "War on Drugs" is based on fear, misinformation, and electoral politics. After several decades of not arresting pot-smokers, the Dutch can point to studies showing that they smoke less than the European average—and fewer than half as many Dutch smoke pot, per capita, as Americans do. (My Dutch friends also enjoy pointing out that, while the three most recent US presidents admitted or implied that they had smoked marijuana, no Dutch prime minister ever has.) The Dutch have found that strict regulation of the soft-drug trade has helped minimize many of the problems associated with it, such as street crime, gang warfare, and hard-drug use.

So what am I? Pro-marijuana? Let's put it this way: I agree with the Dutch people, who remind me that a society either has to allow some room for drug use on the less-harmful end of the spectrum...or build more prisons. About 800,000 Americans are arrested every year for simple possession of marijuana. While a wide variety of Americans smoke pot, the people prosecuted for possessing it are disproportionately poor and/or black or Latino.

If you'd like to learn more about marijuana (and don't feel like Googling "Rick Steves marijuana"), drop by Amsterdam's Canna-

New Pressure to Re-Criminalize Marijuana

Dutch pot-smokers complain that the generation that ran naked on acid around Amsterdam's Vondelpark during the '60s is now threatening the Netherlands' well-established, regulated marijuana trade.

Responding to international pressure and conservatives in rural and small-town Holland, the federal government is cracking down on coffeeshops. While they're still allowed to sell marijuana, many aspects of these businesses' operations exist in a legal limbo, with certain restrictions usually going unenforced—until now.

Neighboring countries (France and Germany) have complained that it's too easy for citizens to make drug runs across the border, returning home with lots of pot. In response, some Dutch border towns implemented a "weed pass" system, allowing pot sales only to registered Dutch citizens. But the independent-minded Dutch (especially young people) don't want to be registered as pot users, so they're buying it on the street—rekindling the black market, and, many fear, the crime and social problems associated with it.

In 2012, marijuana tourists—and the businesses that rely on them—panicked when it was announced that a similar "weed pass" would go into effect nationwide. But a newly elected national government withdrew the plan, leaving the weed-pass decision up to each individual city. Amsterdam's coffeeshops remain open to the general public.

In general, Amsterdam city leaders recognize that legalized marijuana and the Red Light District's prostitution are part of the city's edgy charm; the mayor wants to keep both, but get rid of the accompanying sleaze. Amsterdam recognizes the pragmatic wisdom of its progressive policies and is bucking the federal shift to the right. Locals don't want shady people pushing drugs in dark alleys; they'd rather see marijuana sold in regulated shops.

A 2011 law sought to close coffeeshops near schools, including the landmark Bulldog Café on Leidseplein (it's still open). And coffeeshop licenses are not being renewed in some neighborhoods—the number of coffeeshops in Amsterdam has fallen from a peak of more than 700 (in the mid-1990s) to about 200 today. But Amsterdam's mayor has vowed to keep its central coffeeshops open...and with all the talk of new restrictions, coffeeshops are on their best behavior (and are being very careful to nurture good relations with their neighbors).

A 2013 law allows individual coffeeshops to ban foreigners, if they choose (a shop-by-shop variation on the "weed pass"). By the time you visit, new developments will surely have taken place—stay tuned.

SMOKING

bis College or the Hash, Marijuana, and Hemp Museum (both located on Oudezijds Achterburgwal street—see pages 123-124). Back home, if you'd like to support an outfit dedicated to taking the crime out of pot, read up on the National Organization for the Reform of Marijuana Laws (www.norml.org).

COFFEESHOPS IN AMSTERDAM

Most of downtown Amsterdam's coffeeshops feel grungy and foreboding to American travelers who aren't part of the youth-hostel crowd. The neighborhood places (and those in small towns around the countryside) are much more inviting to people without piercings, tattoos, and favorite techno artists. I've listed a few places with a more pub-like ambience for Americans wanting to go local, but within reason. For locations, see the map on page 205 in the Eating in Amsterdam chapter.

Paradox is the most *gezellig* (cozy) coffeeshop I found—a mellow, graceful place. The managers, Ludo and Wiljan, and their staff are patient with descriptions and happy to walk you through all your options. This is a rare coffeeshop that serves light meals. The juice is fresh, the music is easy, and the neighborhood is charming (single tobacco-free joints-€3, loaner bongs, games, Wi-Fi, daily 10:00-20:00, two blocks from Anne Frank House at Eerste Bloemdwarsstraat 2, tel. 020/623-5639).

The Grey Area—a hole-in-the-wall spot with three tiny tables—is a cool, welcoming, and smoky place appreciated among local aficionados as a perennial winner of Amsterdam's Cannabis Cup awards. Judging by the autographed photos on the wall, many famous Americans have dropped in (say hi to Willie Nelson). You're welcome to just nurse a bottomless cup of coffee. It's run by friendly American Jon, with helpful Coen and George. They even have a vaporizer if you want to try "smoking" without smoking (daily 12:00-20:00, they close relatively early out of consideration for their neighbors, between Dam Square and Anne Frank House at Oude Leliestraat 2, tel. 020/420-4301).

Siberië Coffeeshop is a short walk from Central Station, but feels cozy, with a friendly canalside ambience. Clean, big, and bright, this place has the vibe of a mellow Starbucks and plays host to the occasional astrology reading (daily 11:00-23:00, Fri-

SMOKING

Sat until 24:00, Wi-Fi for customers, helpful staff, English menu, Brouwersgracht 11, tel. 020/623-5909).

La Tertulia is a sweet little mother-and-daughter-run place with pastel decor and a cheery terrarium atmosphere (Tue-Sat 11:00-19:00, closed Sun-Mon, sandwiches, brownies, games, Prinsengracht 312).

The Bulldog Café is the high-profile, leading touristy chain of coffeeshops. These establishments are young but welcoming,

 with reliable selections. They're pretty comfortable for green tourists wanting to just hang out for a while. The flagship branch, in a former police station right on Leidseplein, is very handy, offering alcohol upstairs, pot downstairs, and fun outdoor seating on a heated patio. It's the rare place where you can have a beer while you smoke and watch the world skateboard by (daily 10:00-24:00, later on weekends, Leidseplein 17—see map on page 56, tel. 020/625-6278). Their original café still sits on the canal near the Old Church in the Red Light District (see page 114).

The Dampkring is a rough-and-ready constant party. It's a high-profile, busy place, filled with a young clientele and loud music, but the owners still take the time to explain what they offer. Scenes from the movie *Ocean's Twelve* were filmed here (daily 10:00-24:00, close to Spui at Handboogstraat 29, tel. 020/638-0705).

Dutch Flowers, conveniently located near Spui Square on Singel canal, has a very casual "brown café" ambience, with a mature set of regulars. A couple of tables overlooking the canal are perfect for enjoying the late-afternoon sunshine (daily 10:00-23:00, on the corner of Heisteeg and Singel at Singel 387, tel. 020/624-7624).

SMOKING

AMSTERDAM WITH CHILDREN

Amsterdam is a great destination for families. From vibrant street life to peaceful pond-filled parks, engaging and interactive museums to sit-back-and-relax canal cruises, Amsterdam (and the Netherlands in general) has something fun for every age.

Trip Tips

EATING

Try these tips to keep your kids content throughout the day.

• Make sure to start with a good breakfast (at hotels and B&Bs, breakfast is nearly always included).

• Picnic lunches or dinners work well. Try large grocery stores, like the popular Albert Heijn supermarket chain. Having snacks on hand can avoid meltdowns.

• As a treat, stop for *friets* (fries), *pannekoeken* (pancakes), or *stroopwafels* (a delicious cookie-waffle hybrid). You can typically find any of these Dutch specialties at street stands around the city.

• Kids will have fun choosing their meal from a Febo. This wall of coin-op windows features rows upon rows of warmed up (though not necessarily healthy) food, such as burgers and fried chicken sticks (see page 216). Also, department-store cafeterias are centrally located and a safe bet for kid-friendly food.

SIGHTSEEING

The key to a successful family vacation is to slow down. Take extended breaks when needed.

• Have a "what if" procedure in case something goes wrong. Give each child a business card from your hotel, along with your contact information and taxi fare, to use if you get separated. If they have

Books and Films for Kids

To prepare your kids for the trip, get them into the Dutch spirit with these books and movies:

Anne Frank: The Diary of a Young Girl (Anne Frank, 1947). Kids can read this book or watch the 1959 film to learn a little bit about the Netherlands during World War II. If you're visiting Haarlem, consider a similar account of the Nazi occupation, Corrie ten Boom's *The Hiding Place.*

The Fault in Our Stars (John Green, 2012). Two teens diagnosed with cancer make it their dying wish to travel to Amsterdam and meet their favorite author. Read the book or see the 2014 film adaptation, which includes beautiful shots of the city.

Girl With a Pearl Earring (Tracy Chevalier, 1999). This fictional story is based on Vermeer's famous painting, which is exhibited in the Mauritshuis Royal Picture Gallery in The Hague (see listing on page 391).

Ocean's Twelve (2004). In this popular sequel, the gang hits Amsterdam to pull off a heist. Look for George Clooney outside the renowned Pulitzer Hotel or Brad Pitt strolling by the canals.

Any art book on Van Gogh. Many young people (and adults) find his swirling colorful art compelling.

a mobile phone, make sure they know how to use it in the Netherlands.

• Incorporate your child's interests into each day's plans. Let your kids make some decisions: choosing lunch spots, deciding which shops to visit, or navigating the maze of Amsterdam's back streets. Deputize your child to lead you on my self-guided walks and museum tours.

• Give your child a money belt and an expanded allowance; you are on vacation, after all. Let your children budget their funds by comparing and contrasting the dollar and euro.

• Buy your kids a trip journal and encourage them to write down their observations, thoughts, and favorite memories. This journal could end up being their favorite souvenir.

• Seek out museums with kid appeal and interactive exhibits, such as the NEMO science museum or Tropenmuseum Junior. If you're visiting art museums with younger children, hit the gift shop first so you can buy postcards; then hold a scavenger hunt to find the pictured artwork.

• Public WCs are hard to find: Try museums, bars, and fast-food restaurants.

• Follow this book's crowd-beating tips. Kids dislike long lines even more than you do.

CHILDREN

Top Sights and Activities

MUSEUMS

NEMO (National Center for Science and Technology)

This waterfront science museum for children offers a world of hands-on explorations, from building a bridge to conducting historical experiments to sending a package halfway around the world. See listing on page 68.

Cost and Hours: €15 for ages 4 and up, daily 10:00-17:30, generally closed on Mon Sept-May, tel. 020/531-3233, www.e-nemo.nl.

Netherlands Maritime Museum (Nederlands Scheepvaartmuseum)

This comprehensive collection of model ships and instruments also includes several exhibitions geared toward children, such as a virtual simulation of a sea battle and an exhibit on whales. At the museum's dock is the *Amsterdam*, a replica of an 18th-century sailing ship. See page 68 for more information.

Cost and Hours: €7.50 for ages 5-17, €15 for adults, daily 9:00-17:00, Kattenburgerplein 1, tel. 020/523-2222, www.scheepvaartmuseum.nl.

Dutch Resistance Museum (Verzetsmuseum)

Both educational and interactive, the excellent junior section of this WWII museum lets kids follow the stories of four children who lived through the war. Kids can wander through different homes, exploring hidden rooms and playing games where they make decisions based on wartime scenarios. This section makes a great introduction to some of the heavier content in the museum. For more on the museum, see page 79.

Cost and Hours: €5 for ages 7-15, €10 for adults, family tickets available, includes audioguide, Tue-Fri 10:00-17:00, Sat-Mon 11:00-17:00, Plantage Kerklaan 61, tel. 020/620-2535, www.verzetsmuseum.org.

Tropical Museum Junior (Tropenmuseum Junior)

Part of the Tropenmuseum (see listing on page 80), this interactive section geared for children focuses on a different country every three years. Open only on weekends, the rotating 1.5-hour programs let kids participate in dance, music, and arts and crafts (usually in Dutch, English upon request). Programs start at various times and space is limited, so reserve in advance by phone or email.

Cost and Hours: €8 for ages 4-18, €12.50 for adults, Sat-Sun

11:00-17:00 and on school holidays, Linnaeusstraat 2, tel. 020/568-8300, www.tropenmuseumjunior.nl, reserveren@tropenmuseum.nl.

Van Gogh Museum

The artist's swirling, colorful, emotional work can be easier for kids to appreciate than dark Rembrandts. Van Gogh's relatively simple subjects (self-portraits, bedroom furniture, sunflowers, sowers in fields) can be taken in at a glance. His work is child-like in a way—his broad, vibrant strokes resemble children's drawings with color crayons. For older, more discerning children, it's a good experience to be in a museum focused on one artist's work, allowing them to see the evolution in an artist's style over time. For a self-guided tour, ✪ see the Van Gogh Museum Tour chapter.

Cost and Hours: €15, free for those under 18, €2.50 for kids' audioguide, good gift shop, daily 9:00-18:00, Fri until 22:00 March-Oct, Sat until 22:00 July-Aug and Oct.

Rijksmuseum

The Rijksmuseum is a must-see destination in Amsterdam, but it can be challenging to keep kids' interest here. To make things a little more interactive, the museum offers a one-hour "multimedia mystery" tour. Rent an audio device (€2.50) or download the free app to your mobile device, then set the kids loose to solve eight mysteries within the exhibits. The museum's outdoor gallery features a kids' area with playground equipment and a playful water fountain. For a self-guided tour, ✪ see the Rijksmuseum Tour chapter.

Cost and Hours: Free for ages 18 and under, €17.50 for adults, daily 9:00-17:00, last entry 30 minutes before closing, tel. 020/674-7047, www.rijksmuseum.nl.

Anne Frank House

A visit to the place where Anne Frank and her family hid for two years can be a powerful experience, especially for children who have read her journal or watched the movie. The museum's website offers tips about how to prepare your children for the visit: Go to www.annefrank.org and click on "Museum," then look under "Practical Information." ✪ See the Anne Frank House Tour chapter.

Cost and Hours: €4.50 for ages 10-17, €9 for adults; April-Oct daily 9:00-21:00, Sat and July-Aug until 22:00; Nov-March daily 9:00-19:00, Sat until 21:00; last entry 30 minutes before closing, Prinsengracht 267, tel. 020/556-7100, www.annefrank.org.

PARKS AND PLAYGROUNDS

Amsterdam is filled with great parks that are fun for kids, especially Vondelpark, Amstelpark, and Woeste Westen (covered more fully next). Other good outdoor spaces include:

• Museumplein, with a playground adjacent to the Cobra Café, big 3-D "I amsterdam" letters to climb on, and a fountain to play in on a sunny day.

• Oosterpark, south of the zoo, with a pond, wading pool, and free Wi-Fi.

• The waterfront park next to the EYE Film Institute Netherlands (see page 70).

• Rembrandtplein, with life-size sculptures of Rembrandt's *Night Watch* to pose among (see page 57).

• Outdoor markets, for kids who enjoy browsing: Check out the Waterlooplein flea market (see page 246), or explore the Albert Cuyp street market (see page 242) and head to Sarphatipark for a picnic afterwards.

Vondelpark

Vondelpark is the largest and most famous park in Amsterdam. It's great for people-watching and has plenty of space for kids to run free, including several fun playground areas (such as the delightful treehouse structure nearly hidden in the woods, about mid-park). Cycling through
Vondelpark on one of its many bike paths makes for a great family outing (see page 55).

Amstelpark

Located at the southern edge of the city, Amstelpark has plenty of gardens and green space, along with extra entertainment for kids, including a train ride, small amusement park, petting zoo, playground, and miniature golf.

Cost and Hours: Free to enter but fee for some of the activities; attractions have different hours but generally open daily between 10:00 and 11:00 and close between 16:00 and 18:00; take tram #4 or the metro to RAI Station, then walk 10 minutes; tel. 20-644-1744, www.speeltuin-amstelpark.nl.

Woeste Westen

At this "adventurous nature playground," located in the northwest corner of Westerpark, kids 13 and under are welcome to climb logs, wade across streams, paddle rafts, play with sand, and tread through the tall grass and trees. Just make sure to bring a change of clothes, as this place can get messy.

Cost and Hours: Free; always open but playground supervi-

CHILDREN

sor and main building are accessible during certain hours, starting daily between 11:00 and 13:00 and closing at 18:00; Overbrakerpad 3, www.woestewesten.nl.

OTHER KID-CENTRIC ATTRACTIONS
Canal Cruises

A canal boat ride is a great way to view the city from a new perspective, especially after a long day of walking on little feet. Cruises

last about an hour and leave from various docks around the city (for details, see page 44). For a longer outing, join **Wetlands Safari** for a canoe trip through the beautiful Dutch countryside (€29 for ages 7-16, €48 for adults, €3 discount by showing this book—see page 45 for details).

The **Pancake Cruise** (De Pannenkoekenboot) takes a 1.25-hour glide through the canals of Amsterdam while families indulge in an all-you-can-eat pancake buffet (€13 for ages 3-12, €18 for adults, generally 3-4/day, tel. 020/636-8817, www.pannenkoekenboot.nl).

Artis Royal Zoo (Natura Artis Magistra)

The Artis is a convenient escape from the bustle of Amsterdam. Besides legions of plants and animals, these historical grounds also feature a planetarium, aquarium, insectarium, and butterfly pavilion. Kids can wander through the petting zoo or learn about animal training and care in one of the daily programs.

Cost and Hours: €16.50 for ages 3-9, €20 for ages 10 and up; daily April-Oct 9:00-18:00, off-season until 17:00; Plantage Kerklaan 38—take tram #9 (from Amsterdam Central Station) or #14 (from Dam Square) and get off at Artis stop; toll tel. 900-278-4796, www.artis.nl.

Nearby: The **botanical gardens** (Hortus Botanicus) are a couple of blocks away, offering a lovely butterfly greenhouse (see page 74). Oosterpark, with a pond and wading pool, is south of the zoo, connected by tram #9.

Amsterdam Marionette Theatre

Beautiful wooden marionettes come to life in shows based on classics from opera and musical theater. Though performances are in Dutch, kids should still find the visuals and music entertaining regardless of the language barrier. Bonus: A playground is located just outside the theater.

Cost and Hours: Typically €7.50 for ages 7-14 and €16 for adults, performances generally on weekends at 14:30 with occasional Saturday shows at 20:00, Nieuwe Jonkerstraat 8, tel. 020/620-8027, www.marionettentheater.nl.

Wind n' Wheels

Try land sailing on a go-cart. Each person sits in his or her own "land yacht" (like a sailboat on wheels), but two-seaters are also available for parents with younger kids or those who prefer to ride with an instructor (must be at least 11 years old to drive). If there's not enough wind to keep these vehicles sailing (check wind speeds on their website), you can try other adrenaline-pumping activities such as electric skateboarding, trampolining, and acro bungee (think trampolining while tethered to a bungee).

Cost and Hours: €29.50 for 1.5-hour sailing clinic; Mon-Fri 12:00-19:00, Sat-Sun 10:00-19:00; Zuiderzeeweg 1—take tram #26 from Central Station (direction: IJburg) to the Zuiderzeeweg stop; tel. 020/752-1790, www.windnwheels.nl.

Miniportworld

At Miniportworld, kids get the chance to captain an electric boat around a semi-scenic lake. They can pick the boat they'd like to drive (police boat, lifeboat, etc.), and at the end, they'll receive an official "captain's diploma." Ages 12 and up can sail alone; younger kids must be accompanied by an adult.

Cost and Hours: €10 for 15 minutes, €15 for 30 minutes; open Easter-mid-Oct Sat-Sun 11:00-18:00 and Wed 12:00-18:00, closed Mon-Tue and Thu-Fri, hours subject to weather conditions; Duizendmeterweg 4, tel. 062/162-3836, www.miniportworld. com. Another location is in Haarlem.

SIGHTS OUTSIDE AMSTERDAM

Railway Museum (Spoorwegmuseum)

Just 30 minutes by train from Amsterdam, Utrecht is home to the Railway Museum. It's a fun mix of exhibits, historic locomotives, and rides, including a roller coaster and miniature train. See page 429 for more information.

Cost and Hours: Free for ages 3 and under, otherwise €16, Tue-Sun 10:00-17:00, closed Mon, at east edge of town in old-fashioned Maliebaanstation, tel. 030/230-6206, www. spoorwegmuseum.nl.

Scheveningen

What kid doesn't like a beach? This popular beach, near The Hague and Delft, is great on a sunny day. Expect cafés, shops, a boardwalk, bungee-jumping fun, wide beach, and sun worshippers. See page 395 for more information.

Madurodam

With replicas of ships, canals, windmills, and the airport, this miniature theme park in The Hague makes even the smallest kids feel like giants. See page 395.

Cost and Hours: Free for ages 3 and under, otherwise €15.50, family tickets available, daily April-June 9:00-20:00, March and Sept-Oct 9:00-18:00, Nov-Dec and Feb 11:00-17:00, closed Jan, last entry one hour before closing, George Maduroplein 1, tel. 070/416-2400, www.madurodam.nl.

Open-Air Folk Museums

These outdoor museums provide a first-hand glance into traditional Dutch lifestyles. With old structures to explore (farmhous-

es, schools, windmills), fun interactive activities, and workers dressed up in period costumes, they're great for kids of all ages. The excellent **Enkhuizen Zuiderzee**, an hour north of Amsterdam, is a re-creation of an early 1900s fishing village, where kids can get candy samples from the pharmacist and craft a ship out of old wooden shoes (see page 359); if you have extra time, spend it in the pleasant town of Enkhuizen. Holland's first folk museum (and one of its finest) is found in **Arnhem,** an hour southwest from Amsterdam (see page 415); although the museum is great, the town has little to offer tourists. If you prefer a museum closer to Amsterdam, **Zaanse Schans** is handy, though also more touristy and commercial (charging separate prices for most exhibits rather than one overall admission fee). Its main attractions include a clock museum, cookie factory, and an abundance of windmills (about 15 minutes by train from Amsterdam, plus a 15-minute walk; see page 337).

De Adriaan Windmill

For kids, a trip to the Netherlands would not be complete without visiting a windmill. Haarlem's town windmill offers nice views from the top, along with exhibits, videos, and demonstrations on how it all works. See page 271.

Cost and Hours: €1 for ages 5-12, €3.50 for adults; March-Nov Mon and Wed-Fri 13:00-17:00, Sat-Sun 10:30-17:00, closed Tue; Dec-Feb Fri-Mon 13:00-16:30, closed Tue-Thu; Papentoren-vest 1, tel. 23/545-0259, www.molenadriaan.nl.

Zandvoort

The coastal town of Zand-
voort makes for a fun fam-
ily outing, with its large
sandy beach, pedestrian
promenade, and abun-
dance of ice-cream shops.
It's easy to reach by train
(about 10 minutes from
Haarlem and 30 minutes
from Amsterdam), and the
beach is only 150 yards from the station. If you're staying in Haarlem, consider renting bikes and cycling to the shore—it's a flat ride
that takes less than an hour (but consider the wind factor). For
more information, see page 271.

SHOPPING IN AMSTERDAM

Amsterdam brings out the browser even in those who were not born to shop. Amsterdam has lots of one-of-a-kind specialty stores, street markets, and specific streets and neighborhoods worthy of a browse. Poke around and see what you can find. For information on shopping, pick up the TI's *Shopping in Amsterdam* brochure.

Ten general markets, open six days a week (generally 9:30-17:00, closed Sun), keep folks who brake for garage sales pulling U-turns. Markets include Waterlooplein (the flea market), the huge Albert Cuyp street market, and various flower markets (such as the Singel canal Flower Market near the Mint Tower).

Store Hours: Most shops in the center are open 10:00-18:00 (later on Thu—typically until 20:00 or 21:00); the businesslike Dutch know no siesta, but many shopkeepers take Sundays and Monday mornings off. Supermarkets are generally open Monday-Saturday 8:00-20:00, with shorter hours on Sunday; most Albert Heijn grocery stores, however, are open until 22:00 every day.

Tax Refunds, Shipping, and Red Tape: To find out how to get a VAT (Value-Added Tax) refund on merchandise, see page 462. While the Netherlands has closed most of its post offices, you can still mail your purchases home (ask your hotelier for the nearest ersatz post office, or use Service Point, a shipping service at Schiphol Airport—see page 257). If you want to bring home edibles and drinkables, see page 463 for restrictions.

Souvenir Ideas: Good consumable souvenirs include **cheese** (many travel well—see the "Dutch Cheeses" sidebar on page 472 for types of cheese, and places to buy it), **chocolates**, or a bottle of *jenever* (Dutch gin made from juniper berries, sold in traditional stone bottles and carefully wrapped in your checked luggage). Art lovers enjoy packing home a postcard or print of their favorite **art-work** from the Van Gogh or other museums. For something higher-end, consider **Delftware** or **diamonds**. The city's many small shops are fun for browsing for items of unique **design** (both clothes and housewares) and **vintage**. If you're seeking Dutch clichés (**wooden shoes, flower seeds, or bulbs,** and so on), make a surgical strike at any souvenir stand, or at the shops at the airport.

Bad Idea: Do not try to bring home anything drug-related—smartshop supplements, marijuana, or even bongs or marijuana pipes (yes, even to Colorado and Washington). American laws are written in a way that—technically—even importing an unused pipe could get you arrested. But if you want to take that chance, make sure the pipe is clean and unused, because even a little residue can get you busted at US Customs.

Shops

DEPARTMENT STORES

When you need to buy something but don't know where to go, two chain stores are handy for everything from inexpensive clothes and notebooks to food and cosmetics. **Hema** is at Kalverstraat 212, in the Kalvertoren mall (Mon-Sat 9.00-19:00, Thu until 21:00, Sun 11:00-18:30) and at Central Station (similar hours). **Vroom & Dreesmann (V&D),** with its great La Place cafeteria, is at Kalverstraat 203 (Sun-Mon 12:00-19:00, Tue-Wed 10:00-19:30, Thu 10:00-21:00, Fri-Sat 10:00-20:00, cafeteria on ground floor has longer hours—see page 203).

The **De Bijenkorf** department store, towering high above Dam Square, is Amsterdam's top-end option and worth a look even if you're not shopping. It sparkles with name brands, which are actually independent stores operating under the Bijenkorf roof. The entire fifth floor is a ritzy self-service cafeteria with a fine rooftop terrace (see page 206; store open daily 10:00-20:00).

Dutch Design

Like their Belgian neighbors, the Dutch have a knack for practical and eye-pleasing design. Think Piet Hein, the 20th-century jack-of-all-trades known for everything from scientific theory to designing housewares to creating beloved games. Amsterdam has a variety of worth-a-detour shops that showcase both established and emerging designers in the Dutch tradition. Here are a couple of favorites:

Droog, one of the top design shops in town, is described in the "Staalstraat Shopping Stroll," later—and offers a good excuse to explore that pleasant neighborhood.

The Frozen Fountain, another institution of Dutch design, is an extremely fun warehouse of innovative creations, from kitchen gadgets and furniture to textiles and bold wallpaper. Drop in here

AMSTERDAM SHOPPING

Shopping in Amsterdam

To Haarlem 15 To Haarlem

HAARLEMMERSTR NIEUWE WESTERDOKSTR Oper

LINDENGRACHT 17 Prinsengracht Brouwers- Gracht BROUWERSGRACHT NIEUWENDIJK KATTENG HEKELVEL

LINDENSTRAAT KARTHUIZERSSTR

NASSAUKADE MARNIXSTRAAT BOOMSTRAAT WESTERSTRAAT PRINSENGRACHT KEIZERSGRACHT Herengracht LANGESTRAAT Singel VOORBURGWAL

ANJELIERSSTR TUINSTR PRINSENSTR HERENSTE OUDE NIEUWEZIJDS STOCK EXCHANGE

Egelantiers- dwarsstraat 2e Egelantiers- 21 dwarsstraat 20 Eglantiersgracht

TUINSTRAAT EGELANTIERSSTR EGELANTIERSGRACHT

JORDAAN 9 Lelie- gracht ANNE FRANK HOUSE NIEUWEZIJDS NEW CHURCH DAMRA BEURSST

NIEUWE LELIESTR BLOEMGRACHT WESTERKERK HOMO- MONUMENT 13 24 CENTER

BLOEMGRACHT WESTERMARKT RAADHUISSTRAAT ROYAL PALACE Dam Square 2 DAMSTR

BLOEMSTRAAT 18 gracht POST PALEISSTRAAT NAT'L MONUMENT

ROZENGRACHT Prinsen- Keizers- gracht Heren- gracht KALVERSTRAAT RAMSTRAAT

ROZENSTRAAT KEESTR HARTENSTR GAST ROKIN NES

LAURIERSTRAAT BEREN WOL-VEN- OUDE SPIEGEL NIEUWE ZIJDS VOORBURGWAL OUDEZIJDS VOORBURGWAL

LAURIERGRACHT 14 AMST. MUSEUM 22 OUDEZIJDS ACHTERBURG

HAZEN STRAAT ELANDSSTRAAT HUIDEN- BEGIJNHOF 10

ELANDSGRACHT HOUSEBOAT MUSEUM KUNSTR WIJDE HEIST SPUI

19 LIJNBAANSGRACHT THE CANAL HOUSE Rokin N. DOELENSTR

4 Singelgracht Leidsegracht LEIDSEGRACHT MINT TOWER 6 Munt- plein 8 AMSTEL

STADHOUDERSKADE STADSSCHOUWBURG THEATER 7 KORTE LANGE Singel REGULIERSDWARSSTR

MARNIXSTRAAT LEIDSEKADE Leidseplein i KERKSTRAAT MUSEUM OF BAGS & PURSES Herengracht

OVERTOOM PIPE MUS. PRINSENGRACHT LEIDSEDWARSSTRAAT NIEUWE SPIEGELSTRAAT 23 Keizersgracht

VONDELSTRAAT Max Euwe- plein WETERINGSCHANS Prinsengracht

CONSTANTIJN HUYGENSTR Vondel- park ZANDPAD STADHOUDERSKADE TWEEDEWETERINGDWARSSTR LIJNBAANSGRACHT NOORDERSTRAAT

YSSIUSSTRAAT 25 NIEUW LOOIERSSTRAAT F SIMONSZSTRAAT

SCHAPENBURGERPAD PIETER CORNELISZ HOOFTSTR HOBBEMASTRAAT WETERINGSCHANS

JAN LUIJKENSTRAAT 12 RIJKS- MUSEUM Tweede Wetering- plantsoen DEN TEXSTRAAT

PAULUS POTTERSTRAAT HOUSE OF BOLS Museum- plein HOBBEMAKADE NICOLAAS WITSENKADE Singelgracht

STEDELIJK MUSEUM VAN GOGH MUSEUM To Albert Cuypstraat Market & 5 HEINEKEN EXPERIENCE DE PIJP

To US Consulate & Concertgebouw

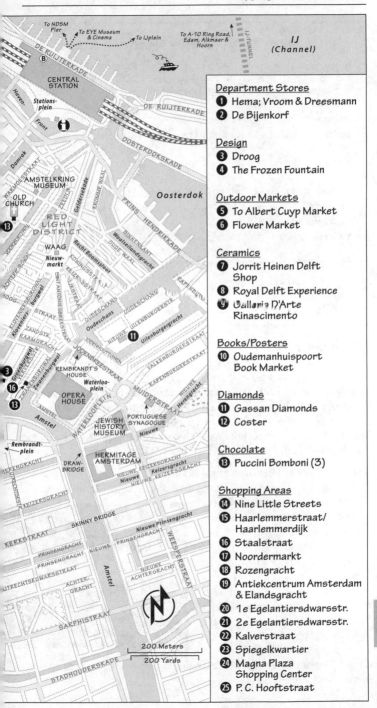

To NDSM Pier

To EYE Museum & Cinema

To IJplein

To A-10 Ring Road, Edam, Alkmaar & Hoorn

IJ-TUNNEL

IJ (Channel)

DE RUIJTERKADE

CENTRAL STATION

Stations-plein

Haven-front

DE RUIJTERKADE

OOSTERDOKSKADE

Damrak

WARMOESSTRAAT

AMSTELKRING MUSEUM

OLD CHURCH

RED LIGHT DISTRICT

Gelderskade

KROMME WAAL

Oosterdok

PRINS HENDRIKKADE

BINNENKANT

Woofseilandsgracht

Recht Boomssloot

OUDE WAAL

WAAG

Nieuwmarkt

KONINGSSTR

ST ANTONIE BREESTRAAT

OUDESCHANS

NIEUWE UILENBURGERSTR.

Uilenburgergracht

RAPENBURG

JODENHOUTTUINEN

JODENBREESTRAAT

REMBRANDT'S HOUSE

Waterloo-plein

VALKENBURGERSTRAAT

RAPENBURGERSTRAAT

MUIDERSTRAAT

NIEUWE Herengracht

OPERA HOUSE

WATERLOOPLEIN

Amstel

JEWISH HISTORY MUSEUM

PORTUGUESE SYNAGOGUE

Nieuwe

Rembrandt-plein

DRAW-BRIDGE

HERMITAGE AMSTERDAM

NIEUWE KEIZERSGRACHT

Nieuwe Keizersgracht

HERENGRACHT

KEIZERSGRACHT

KERKSTRAAT

SKINNY BRIDGE

Nieuwe Prinsengracht

PRINSENGRACHT

NIEUWE PRINSENGRACHT

PRINSENGRACHT

UTRECHTSEDWARSSTRAAT

ACHTER-GRACHT

Amstel

NIEUWE ACHTERGRACHT

WEESPERSTRAAT

SARPHISTRAAT

STADHOUDERSKADE

200 Meters

200 Yards

N

Department Stores
- **1** Hema; Vroom & Dreesmann
- **2** De Bijenkorf

Design
- **3** Droog
- **4** The Frozen Fountain

Outdoor Markets
- **5** To Albert Cuyp Market
- **6** Flower Market

Ceramics
- **7** Jorrit Heinen Delft Shop
- **8** Royal Delft Experience
- **9** Galleria D'Arte Rinascimento

Books/Posters
- **10** Oudemanhuispoort Book Market

Diamonds
- **11** Gassan Diamonds
- **12** Coster

Chocolate
- **13** Puccini Bomboni (3)

Shopping Areas
- **14** Nine Little Streets
- **15** Haarlemmerstraat/ Haarlemmerdijk
- **16** Staalstraat
- **17** Noordermarkt
- **18** Rozengracht
- **19** Antiekcentrum Amsterdam & Elandsgracht
- **20** 1e Egelantiersdwarsstr.
- **21** 2e Egelantiersdwarsstr.
- **22** Kalverstraat
- **23** Spiegelkwartier
- **24** Magna Plaza Shopping Center
- **25** P. C. Hooftstraat

AMSTERDAM SHOPPING

Market Days in the Netherlands

If you're day-tripping, keep in mind that most open-air markets are held only in the morning (e.g., 10:00-12:30), though in bigger cities such as Rotterdam, markets bustle throughout the day.

Alkmaar: Friday (cheese, early April-early Sept).

Delft: Thursday (general & flower) and Saturday (general & flea).

Edam: Wednesday (general year-round, plus cheese July-Aug).

Haarlem: Monday (clothing) and Saturday (general).

Leiden: Wednesday and Saturday (bigger).

Rotterdam: Daily.

Utrecht: Wednesday, Friday, and Saturday.

to explore, and don't miss the upstairs (Mon 13:00-18:00, Tue-Sat 10:00-18:00, Sun 12:00-17:00, just south of the Nine Little Streets shopping zone—described later—at Prinsengracht 645, tel. 020/638-3041, www.frozenfountain.nl).

Albert Cuyp Market

Amsterdam's biggest open-air market, stretching for several blocks along Albert Cuypstraat, bustles daily (roughly 9:00-17:00) except Sunday. You'll find fish, exotic vegetables, bolts of fabric, pantyhose, bargain clothes, native Dutch and ethnic food stands (especially *stroopwafels* and Surinamese *rotis*), and great people-watching. It's located a 10-minute walk east of Museumplein and a block south of the Heineken Experience (tram #16 or #24).

Flower Market (Bloemenmarkt)

While flower shops are scattered around the city, the most enjoy-able browsing is at the **Flower Market,** which stretches luxuriously along the Singel canal between the Mint Tower and Koningsplein. Actually situated on a row of barges, this floating market boasts a well-stocked cornucopia of pretty petals tucked under tents. Buy a bouquet for your hotel room, or stock up on seeds and bulbs to bring home—  look for ones that are packed with a seal that promises they are US Customs-friendly.

Delftware Galleries

Ceramic plates, vases, and tiles decorated with a fake Chinese blue-and-white design were all the rage in the 1600s. Only a few licensed places sell the real stuff (expensive) and antiques (very expensive). You can find fireplace tiles (cheap) at most gift shops.

Pricey, authentic Delftware shouldn't be an impulse buy, so do your homework before committing. Ideally, you'd hop on the train to the town of Delft (an hour away), where you can tour two Delftware factories—the official Royal Dutch Delftware Manufactory, and the smaller but still top-quality Delftse Pauw—and buy directly from their shops (for details, see the Delft chapter). In Amsterdam, reputable vendors include **Jorrit Heinen Delft Shop,** between the museum neighborhood and Rokin (Prinsengracht 440, www.jorritheinen.com); the official **Royal Delft Experience** at the Mint Tower (also offers tours on a lesser scale than the ones in Delft proper, Muntplein 12, www.royaldelftexperience.nl); and **Galleria D'Arte Rinascimento,** in the Jordaan (Prinsengracht 170, www.delft-art-gallery.com).

Oudemanhuispoort Book Market

Book lovers will want to seek out this rustic book market, tucked down a hidden corridor between two big university buildings (Mon-Sat 9:00-17:00, closed Sun). On the canalside Oudezijds Achterburgwal, just east of Rokin, find the stone gate marking a passage next to #229. (You can also enter through the other end, next to Kloveniersburgwal 82.) The gallery is lined with stalls and tables stacked high with secondhand books (many in English), all surrounded by university bustle. Vendors at the Kloveniersburgwal end specialize in prints and posters. The tranquil courtyards just off of this hallway are jammed with students enjoying a sunny escape from the classrooms and clogged streets.

Diamond Shops

Diamonds have been a big Dutch commodity ever since Golden Age traders first exploited the mines of Africa. In Amsterdam, you can get them cut or uncut, expensive or really expensive. Diamond dealers offer free cutting and polishing demos at their shops. **Gassan Diamonds**, near Rembrandt's House, is best (page 73); **Coster** is on Potterstraat, behind the Rijksmuseum (page 54).

Chocolate Shops

While neighboring Belgium is famous for its chocolates, the Dutch dabble as well. Dutch Verkade or Droste cocoa are sold in tins. Or you can stop by a branch of the premium Dutch chocolatier **Puccini Bomboni,** which sells an enticing array of pralines in various flavors, all made on the premises. While extremely expensive (€17 for a selection of 6-8 bonbons), this can be a tasty souvenir or a splurgy gift—especially if you're not also going to Belgium (locations at Staalstraat 17; between Dam Square and the Jordaan at Singel 184; and in the Red Light District at Oudekerksplein 17; all open daily, www.puccinibomboni.com).

Museum Shops

The shops at major museums (such as the **Rijksmuseum** and **Van Gogh Museum**) are well-stocked with posters, postcards, and gorgeous glossy books showing off masterpieces. They also sell protective mailing tubes for carrying or shipping your posters home.

Amsterdam's Top Shopping Zones

This section focuses on four of the city's top shopping areas—all equally good, but each with a different flavor: The **Nine Little Streets** (touristy, tidy, and central); **Haarlemmerstraat/Haarlemmerdijk** (emerging, borderline-edgy neighborhood of creative, unpretentious shops); **Staalstraat** (postcard-cute, short-and-sweet street tucked just away from the tourist crowds); and the **Jordaan** (mellow residential zone with a smattering of fine shops). While I've mentioned some specific shops in each area, remember that—like anywhere—stores come and go every day.

THE NINE LITTLE STREETS (DE NEGEN STRAATJES)

This handy central zone—hemmed in by a grid plan between Dam Square and the Jordaan—is home to a diverse array of shops mixing festive, inventive, nostalgic, practical, and artistic items. Trendy cafés dot the area. While not quite as artsy or funky as it once was, this zone remains a very convenient place to browse. Walking west from the Amsterdam Museum/Spui Square or south from the Anne Frank House puts you right in the thick of things. For a preview, see www.theninestreets.com.

The cross streets make a tic-tac-toe with a couple of canals and bicycle-friendly canalside streets just west of Kalverstraat. Because each street changes names when it crosses a canal, this small area really does include nine separate little streets (hence the name). Here are a few pointers on what you can expect to find on each street, from south to north (but visit them in any order you like):

South Strip: Starting from Spui and heading west, **Wijde Heisteeg** is the shortest of the little streets, with a fun old sign shop, a deli, and some clothes shops. **Huidenstraat** is even more clothes-oriented, from fancy fashion boutiques to bags, jewelry, and shoes, as well as some home decor. **Runstraat** has yet more clothes (including Banksy-style street-art T-shirts at Moku, #2) and an excellent, well-stocked cheese shop (De Kaaskamer van Amsterdam, ideal for stocking a memorable picnic, at #7), along with cosmetics, shoes, and flowers. From where Runstraat hits the Prinsengracht canal, it's a short stroll south to The Frozen Fountain design shop (see page 239).

Center Strip: In general, this zone feels a bit more yuppie/ posh than the others. From east to west, first you'll come to **Oude Spiegelstraat,** a short stretch with some fashion boutiques and the atmospheric Evenaar travel bookshop—with a room in back that has antique travel books (at the corner, Singel 348). **Wolvenstraat** has some upscale clothing shops (international chains such as Filippa K) and several eateries (plus a branch of the recommended Marqt upscale supermarket). **Berenstraat** is a bit younger and more dynamic, with some artsy clothes stores.

North Strip: Gasthuismolensteeg is the funkiest of the nine streets, with vintage shops and a hole-in-the-wall selling world folk art. **Hartenstraat** is loaded with upscale clothes, shoes, and accessories shops, as well as a game shop and hip home decor (at DR Wonen, #27). **Reestraat** has yet more clothing stores, as well as a bit more variety—including vintage shops, watches, and eclectic home decor at De Weldaad (#1).

North of the Nine Little Streets: The area just north of the Nine Little Streets and Anne Frank House—particularly the Herenstraat/Prinsenstraat corridor between Damrak and the Jordaan—is another fine place to browse. If you're looking for jewelry, accessories, trendy clothing, and fancy delicatessens, this may be an expensive but rewarding stroll. **Herenstraat** feels relatively local-oriented, with upscale clothes, home decor, and shops that ooze creativity and charm; Tangram (#9) has fun design, including stuff for kids; Niels (#15c) displays engaging home decor and accessories. **Prinsenstraat** is a bit more youthful, with more fashion galleries and eateries.

HAARLEMMERSTRAAT/HAARLEMMERDIJK

A bit grotty until recently, the area just west of Central Station has morphed into a thriving and trendy string of shops, cafés, and restaurants. Tagged as "emerging" and "gentrifying," this area is home to a spirited mix of older, grungier residents and creative young hipsters. It's edgier and more in-your-face than the sleepy Jordaan, but still more accessible than the Red Light District. It's the kind of place where you'll see "coffeeshops" (selling green "coffee" to tourists) mixed in with coffee shops (selling gour-

met black coffee to residents). And it has arguably the most inspired and eclectic assortment of shops in Amsterdam—a browse here is a fun chance to spot new trends, and maybe to pick up some local clothes and goods (vintage and casual young fashions abound). The former dike along what was Amsterdam's harborfront provides the high spine of this neighborhood. From the Singel canal near Central Station, this lively drag leads a half-mile west along a colorful string of lanes, all the way to Haarlem Gate, a triumphal arch built in the 1840s.

From the train station, follow the canal west, then use the underpass to go beneath the busy traffic bridge. Emerging, turn right across the smaller bridge (passing my favorite herring stand—Stubbe's Haring, on the bridge—then a cluster of coffee shops on the left) and continue straight down **Haarlemmerstraat.** Near the start of the street on the left (at #9) is the recommended Bistrot Neuf, the neighborhood's foodie destination restaurant, tucked amid a rainbow of international eateries. A few doors down is Wini Vintage (at #29), with well-curated finds that may tempt even those turned off by their hometown Salvation Army. This boutique sets the tone for this street—with secondhand shops, ironic T-shirts, young and casual fashion, ethnic takeaway joints, ethnics taking away joints, hair salons, nail parlors, launderettes, and more, all under leaning gables. Enjoy the browsing for a few blocks, and if you need a snack or drink, notice the recommended Marqt organic supermarket on the left just before the canal.

After crossing the canal, you'll continue on **Haarlemmerdijk.** Things get even more artsy and eclectic along here, and it feels a bit less seedy (more urbane/Jordaan, less touristy/Red Light District). Store Without a Home (on the left, at #26) showcases creative design and home decor (closed Sun). As you browse, keep an eye out for some beautiful Art Nouveau facades (on the left, at #39, #43, and #51) shuffled among the brick gables. You'll see gourmet coffee and tea shops, Finnish-design eyeglass frames, a letterpress gallery, kitchenware, frozen yogurt, and Concrete Matter (at #127), with classy gifts for men (shaving gear, pocketknives, desk toys, leather wallets, dapper hatchets, etc.). The street ends at The Movies, an art-house cinema with a built-in *eetcafé.* You'll pop out at the relaxing Haarlemmerplein, with its wannabe-Brandenburg Gate.

STAALSTRAAT SHOPPING STROLL

This lively street, boasting more than its share of creative design shops, is tucked in a youthful area just east of the university zone. While it's good for shopping, it's also wonderful just for a relaxing stroll, away from the throngs of drugged-out tourists. It's a quick walk from the bustling Rokin zone.

From where the canal hits Rokin (by the boat tour kiosk),

head east (with the canal at your back, turn right) down Lange-brugsteeg/Grimburgwal. At the second canal you cross, when you dead-end at the university buildings, jog left and go through the stone arch of the **Oudemanhuispoort Book Market** (described on page 243). Halfway through the market, duck through the student-filled courtyard on the right; when you pop out onto Vendelstraat, turn left, then jog right to go over the bridge. This marks the start of Staalstraat.

On this first stretch of Staalstraat, you'll pass an eclectic variety of shops. **Retro & Chic** (#2) sells vintage, while the **Juggle** shop across the street (#3) is a fun spot to browse for all of your juggling needs. **Tatanka** (next door, at #5) is a smartshop selling intense, sometimes mind-bending, herbal supplements (for more on smartshops, see page 111). Farther down on the left, at #7b, is **Droog**—which, despite a name that evokes controlled substances, is actually a "destination" design store. Half gallery (with cutting-edge installations) and half shop (selling a bumper crop of clever kitchen and household gadgets you never knew you desperately wanted), this design mecca also has a café and rents a single hotel room. It's a fascinating browse, even for those who don't think they care about design (closed Mon, www.droog.com). Just across the street from Droog, at #20, is the easy-to-miss (but don't) **Het Hanze Huis**. This cramped little shop sells a very classy array of carefully curated imports—food, candies, soaps, lotions, and so on—from all over the world. Most products have their own little leaflet (in English) describing their history and uses—ask for it when you check out (www.hethanzehuis.nl).

Continuing over the white drawbridge, you'll reach another fun batch of shops—more vintage and design, a wine shop, and so on. **Puccini Bomboni** (#17) is an outpost of the top-of-the-line local chain selling varied and expensive Belgian-style pralines (described on page 243), while **O Shop** (#26) sells stylish rubber hand-bags and watches (cooler than they sound, www.oshop.nu). You'll end at yet another drawbridge (with Frenzi Café).

Crossing this and turning left (at the "Stopera" music center), you'll follow the canal up to the bustling **Waterlooplein flea market**. The somewhat sketchy-feeling streets just north of Waterlooplein—past the colorful tattoo parlors—are fertile breeding grounds for smart young designers; poking around here you'll discover some shops on the cutting edge of Amsterdam's young fashion scene. For example, at Houtkopersdwarsstraat 3 (on the right) is **290 sq m,** a fancy boutique filling a basement space with youthful international fashion and bags (closed Mon, www.290sqm.com).

THE JORDAAN

Once a working-class district, this colorful old neighborhood is now upscale—a veritable wonderland of funky shops. But they're not as concentrated in the Jordaan as they are along Staalstraat, Haarlemmerdijk, or the Nine Little Streets (described earlier). Here are a few areas to focus on:

On Mondays, you'll find the busy **Noordermarkt** market at the end of Westerstraat and spilling onto the neighboring street, **Lindengracht.**

Rozengracht, the wide street just southwest of the Anne Frank House, has several eclectic shops (though the busy traffic makes lingering in the area less enticing). Kitsch Kitchen, near the big canal, has a fun, colorful collection of mostly Latin American-themed kitsch (at #8).

Antiekcentrum Amsterdam isn't just an antique mall—it's a sprawling warren of display cases crammed with historic bric-a-brac (including lots of smaller items, easily packed home), and all of it for sale. You'll find everything from old helmets and medals to vintage blue tiles (Mon and Wed-Fri 11:00-18:00, Sat-Sun 11:00-17:00, closed Tue, Elandsgracht 109, tel. 020/624-9038). While you're in the neighborhood, browse **Elandsgracht's** many specialty food stores (high-end butcher, bakery, and so on). The cross-street **Hazenstraat** has a fine assortment of art galleries and other shops.

Eerste and **Tweede Egelantiersdwarsstraat**, both lined with great restaurants and recommended in the Eating in Amsterdam chapter, also have some fun shops mixed in.

OTHER SHOPPING AREAS
Kalverstraat-Heiligeweg-Spui

This is the busiest shopping corridor in town. Kalverstraat, a pedestrian street, is a human traffic jam of low-end shoppers. It's clogged with cheap and midrange international chains—Forever 21, Pull and Bear, Desigual, Pimkie, Urban Outfitters, Mango, Claire's, Zara, Bershka, and so on, along with the big Hema and Vroom & Dreesmann department stores (described earlier). It feels soulless, but if you explore the fringes, there are some interesting places.

Spiegelkwartier

Located between the Rijksmuseum and the city center, this is *the* place for art and antiques. You'll find 70 dealers offering 17th-century furniture, old Delftware, Oriental art, clocks, jewelry, and Art Nouveau doodads. Wander down Spiegelgracht and Nieuwe Spiegelstraat. **Leidsestraat**, just to the west, is a tourist artery clogged with pedestrians, bikes, trams, and some trendy international shops.

Magna Plaza Shopping Center

Formerly the main post office, this grand 19th-century building has been transformed into a stylish mall with 40 boutiques. You'll find fashion, luxury goods, and gift shops galore. It's just behind the Royal Palace a block off Dam Square (Mon 11:00-19:00, Tue-Sat 10:00-19:00, Thu until 21:00, Sun 12:00-19:00; see page 128).

P. C. Hooftstraat

The city's most expensive shopping street, with a storefront for nearly every top-name designer, is between Museumplein and Vondelpark.

ENTERTAINMENT IN AMSTERDAM

Many Amsterdam hotels serve breakfast until 11:00 because so many people—visitors and locals—live for nighttime in this city.

On summer evenings, people flock to the main squares for drinks at outdoor tables. Leidseplein is the liveliest square, surrounded by theaters, restaurants, and nightclubs. The slightly quieter Rembrandtplein (with adjoining Thorbeckeplein and nearby Reguliersdwarsstraat) is the center of gay clubs and nightlife. Spui features a full city block of bars. And Nieuwmarkt, on the east edge of the Red Light District, is a bit rough, but is probably the least touristy.

The Red Light District (particularly Oudezijds Achterburgwal) is less sleazy in the early evening, and almost carnival-like as the neon lights come on and the streets fill with tour groups. But it starts to feel scuzzy after about 22:30 (✪ see the Red Light District Walk chapter).

The **brown cafés** recommended on page 219 are ideal after-hours hangouts. Peruse those listings for pre- or post-dinner drink ideas.

INFORMATION

The TI's website, www.iamsterdam.com, has good English listings for upcoming events (click on "What to do," then "What's on"). Newsstands sell *Time Out Amsterdam* and Dutch newspapers (Thu editions generally list events). *Uitkrant* is in Dutch, but it's just a calendar of events, and anyone can figure out the name of the event and its date, time, and location (available at TIs, bars, and bookstores).

Box Office: The **Last Minute Ticket Shop** at Stadsschouwburg Theater is the best one-stop-shopping box office for theater, classical music, and major rock shows. The Last Minute window sells half-price, same-day tickets to certain shows; half-price sales start at noon (Mon-Sat 10:00-18:00, closed Sun, Leidseplein 26, tel. 0900-0191—€0.40/minute, www.lastminuteticketshop.nl). Tickets are also available from the Central Station TI and at the library.

MUSIC

You'll find classical music at the **Concertgebouw** (free 12:30 lunch concerts on Wed except in July and Aug; arrive at 12:00 for best first-come, first-serve seating; at far south end of Museumplein, tel. 0900-671-8345, www.concertgebouw.nl). For chamber music and contemporary works, visit the **Muziekgebouw aan 't IJ,** a mod concert hall on the waterfront, near the train station (Piet Heinkade 1, tel. 020/788-2000, www.muziekgebouw.nl). For opera and dance, try the **opera house** in the Stopera building (Amstel 3, tel. 020/625-5455, www.operaballet.nl). In the summer, Vondelpark hosts open-air concerts.

Three of Amsterdam's historic churches have extensive music programs. In summer, the **Westerkerk** has free lunchtime concerts most Fridays at 13:00 (May-Oct), plus an annual Bach organ concert cycle in August (Prinsengracht 281, tel. 020/624-7766, www. westerkerk.nl). The **New Church** offers periodic organ concerts and a religious music festival in June (included in €8-15 church entry, covered by Museumkaart, Dam Square, tel. 020/626-8168, www. nieuwekerk.nl). The Red Light District's **Old Church** (Oude Kerk) has carillon concerts Tuesday and Saturday at 16:00, and holds an organ-music competition in early September (Oudekerksplein 23, tel. 020/625-8284, www.oudekerk.nl).

Jazz has a long tradition at the **Bimhuis** nightclub, now housed in a black box jutting out from the Muziekgebouw performance hall, right on the waterfront. Its great bar has citywide views, and is open to the public after concerts (Piet Heinkade 3, tel. 020/788-2188, www.bimhuis.com).

The nearby town of Haarlem offers free pipe-organ concerts on Tuesday evenings in summer at its 15th-century church, the **Grote Kerk** (at 20:15 mid-May-mid-Oct, additional concerts Thu at 16:00 July-Aug, see page 268).

COUNTERCULTURE HISTORY

If you're a child of the 1970s, you may have a warm spot for Melkweg and Paradiso—the granddaddies of Amsterdam clubs. Today, the beat goes on at these two rock music (and hip-hop) clubs, just off Leidseplein.

Paradiso was once the church of a former prison complex that was taken by squatters (artists and musicians) in the 1960s. The city allowed it because of the creative work the squatters contributed to local culture. But, not surprisingly, the scene attracted drug users. The first pot-selling coffee shops were here at Paradiso, which was also the venue for rising (and falling) counterculture stars. Today they still present big-name acts that you might recognize...if you're younger than me (Weteringschans 6, tel. 020/626-4521, www. paradiso.nl).

Melkweg has a similar history going back to the 1960s, and offers a comparable lineup to Paradiso's (Lijnbaansgracht 234a, tel. 020/531-8181, www.melkweg.nl).

COMEDY

Boom Chicago, an R-rated comedy improv act, was started 15 years ago by a group of Americans on a graduation tour. They have been entertaining tourists and locals ever since, and some of their alums (Seth Meyers, Jason Sudeikis, Jordan Peele) have gone on to great fame among stateside comedy fans. The two-hour English-only show is a series of rude, clever, and high-energy sketches mixed with improv games, all offering a raucous look at both Dutch culture and local tourism. The big, boxy, 300-seat Rozentheater has small tables for drinks and Domino's pizza (€22-27, generally Sun and Tue-Fri at 20:30, Sat at 20:00; all-improv show Sat at 22:30 is €14; no shows Mon, ticket office open daily from 15:00 until 15 minutes after curtain time, in the Jordaan a couple of long blocks past Westerkerk at Rozengracht 117, tel. 020/217-0400, www.boomchicago.nl).

When sales are slow, ticket-sellers on the street out front offer steeply discounted tickets, with a drink included. Drop by that afternoon and see what's up.

THEATER

Amsterdam is one of the world centers for experimental live theater (much of it in English). Many theaters cluster around the street called the Nes, which stretches south from Dam Square, paralleling the wide street named Rokin. Along here you'll find theaters big and small, as well as cafés and eateries catering to the pre- and post-theater crowd. Most of the shows are oriented to Dutch audiences, but some are in English (or work in any language). You can browse the offerings on the theaters' websites: **Vlaams Culturhuis de Brakke Grond** (at #45, creative and artistic performances from cutting-edge Flanders/Belgium, options suitable for an "international audience" listed on their website, www.brakkegrond. nl), **Frascati** (at #63, off-Broadway-style experimental theater by mostly Dutch artists, www.frascatitheater.nl), **Tobacco Theater** (at #75, cabaret and dinner shows in an industrial space, www.tobacco. nl), and **Comedy Theater in de Nes** (at #110, comedy troupes and stand-up comedians, www.comedytheater.nl).

MOVIES

In the Netherlands, most movies are subtitled, rather than dubbed, so English-only speakers have plenty of cinematic options. It's not unusual for movies at many cinemas to be sold out—consider buying tickets during the day. Catch modern movies in the 1920s setting of the classic **Tuschinski Theater** (between Muntplein and Rembrandtplein, described on page 57).

The splashy **EYE Film Institute Netherlands,** across the water from Central Station, is a very memorable place to see a movie (described on page 70).

MUSEUMS

Several museums stay open late. The **Anne Frank House** always stays open until at least 19:00 year-round; it's open daily until 22:00 in July and August and closes late on Saturday year-round (22:00 peak-season, 21:00 off-season). The **Stedelijk Museum's** collection of modern art is on view until 22:00 on Thursday. The **Van Gogh Museum** is open until 22:00 on Fridays from March through October (when it sometimes has music and a wine bar in the lobby), and on Saturdays in July, August, and October.

The **Hash, Marijuana, and Hemp Museum** is open daily until 23:00. And the **sex museums** always stay open late (Damrak Sex Museum until 23:00, Erotic Museum until 24:00).

SKATING AFTER DARK

Amsterdammers get their skating fix every Friday night in summer and early fall in Vondelpark. Huge groups don inline skates and meet at the round bench near the Vondel Pavilion (around 20:15, www.fridaynightskate.com). Anyone can join in. Ask your hotelier about the nearest place to rent skates, or try SkateDoktor, though it's 1.5 miles north of the park (€10/day, valid ID for deposit, Tue-Fri 10:00-17:30, closed Sun-Mon, Jan van Galenstraat 161, tel. 020/260-0055).

AMSTERDAM CONNECTIONS

The Netherlands is so small, level, and well-covered by trains and buses that transportation is a snap. Buses take you where trains don't go, and bicycles take you where buses don't go. Bus stations and bike-rental shops cluster around train stations. The easy-to-navigate airport is well-connected to Amsterdam and other destinations by bus and train. Use the comprehensive transit website www.9292.nl to plan connections inside the Netherlands by train, bus, or both. For tips on how to buy train tickets (it can be complicated for tourists) and information on tickets, deals, and rail passes, see page 488.

By Train

Amsterdam is the country's hub, but all major cities are linked by speedy trains that come and go every 15 minutes or so. Dutch rail schedules are online at www.ns.nl (domestic) and www.nshispeed.nl (international).

AMSTERDAM CENTRAL STATION

Amsterdam's Central Station is being renovated—a messy construction project that's expected to last at least through 2015 (see "Arrival in Amsterdam" on page 32 for more details on the station). The station's train-information center can require a long wait. Save lots of time by getting international train tickets and information at a small-town station (such as Haarlem), the airport upon arrival (wonderful service), or a travel agency. If you need domestic train tickets, buy these on the day you'll travel; you can't purchase them in advance.

If you have a rail pass, it's quicker to validate it when you arrive at Schiphol Airport than in Amsterdam's Central Station, but keep

in mind that you don't need to actually start using your rail pass the same day; you could buy an inexpensive point-to-point ticket into Amsterdam, and save your flexi-days for a longer journey.

Budget travelers and rail-pass holders heading to Brussels or Antwerp should avoid the pricey Thalys train, and take an Inter-City (IC) train instead.

Thalys has a monopoly on direct trains between Amsterdam and Paris. For passholders, Thalys trains can be a bit of a hassle (since you have to prebook your seat reservation, which can sell out quite early), but can save time.

From Amsterdam Central Station by Train to Domestic Destinations: Schiphol Airport (4-6/hour, 15 minutes, €5, have coins handy to buy from a machine to avoid lines),

Haarlem (8/hour, 20 minutes; see page 272 for a train-window tour of the countryside), **Keukenhof** (catch train to Leiden—4/hour, 35 minutes; then bus #854, called Keukenhof Express, to garden—4/hour, 30 minutes), **Aalsmeer** (take bus instead; see next page), **Zandvoort** (2/hour, 30 minutes), **Leiden** (4/hour, 35 minutes), **Delft** (4/hour, 1 hour, more with transfer in Leiden or The Hague), **The Hague/Den Haag** (4/hour, 50 minutes, more with change in Leiden or Hoofddorp), **Rotterdam** (4/hour on express ICD train, 45 minutes; slower options make several stops along the way and take 1.25 hours), **Arnhem** (3/hour, 1 hour, half with transfer in Utrecht), **Kröller-Müller Museum/Hoge Veluwe National Park** (get off at Ede-Wageningen—4/hour, 1 hour, half with transfer in Utrecht; from Ede-Wageningen, take bus to Otterlo near park entrance—1-2/hour, 20 minutes), **Utrecht** (5/hour, 30 minutes), **Edam/Volendam/Marken** (take bus; see next page), **Hoorn** (2/hour, 30 minutes; more with change in Zaandam, 45 minutes), **Enkhuizen/Zuiderzee Museum** (2/hour, 1 hour), **Alkmaar** (4/hour, 40 minutes), **Zaanse Schans Open-Air Museum** (get off at Koog-Zaandijk; train direction: Uitgeest; 4/hour, 15 minutes).

By Train to International Destinations: Bruges (hourly, 3-4.5 hours; easiest connection requires one change in Antwerp; fastest connection changes in Brussels, but the first leg is on an expensive Thalys train; otherwise change in Antwerp and Ghent), **Brussels** (hourly, 2 hours direct by pricey Thalys to Midi/Zuid/South Station; otherwise hourly, 3.5 hours direct on cheaper IC train to all three Brussels stations), **Antwerp** (every 1-2 hours, 1.25 hours by pricey Thalys; otherwise hourly, 2.5 hours by cheaper IC trains), **London** (6/day, 4.75-5.5 hours, with transfer to Eurostar train in Brussels; Eurostar plans direct trains to London taking 4 hours and starting in Dec 2016; Eurostar discounted with rail pass, www.eurostar.com), **Copenhagen** (3/day, 11.25 hours, multiple transfers), **Bacharach/St. Goar** (roughly every 2 hours, 4.5-6 hours), **Frankfurt** (every 2 hours, 4 hours direct), **Berlin** (5/day, 6.25 hours), **Munich** (roughly hourly, 7.5-8.75 hours, 1-2 transfers; one direct night train, 10.5 hours), **Bern** (5/day, 8.5-10.5 hours, fastest trains change once in Frankfurt), **Paris** (nearly hourly, 3.25 hours direct on fast Thalys train or 4.75 hours with change to Thalys train in Brussels, www.thalys.com). When booking Thalys trains, even rail-pass holders need to buy a seat reservation. If your rail pass covers France but not Benelux, the reservation will cost more. Save money by taking a bus to Paris—described on the next page.

By Bus

The biggest companies serving towns near Amsterdam include Arriva (www.arriva.nl) and Connexxion (www.connexxion.nl).

From Amsterdam by Bus to: Edam/Volendam (EBS bus #314 or #316, 2/hour, 30 minutes), **Marken** (bus #311, 2/hour, 40 minutes), **Aalsmeer Flower Auction** (Connexxion bus #172, 4/hour, 1 hour). Buses depart from just north of Amsterdam's Central Station (exit station through the back of the west passageway, and head up the escalator).

To Paris by Bus: If you don't have a rail pass, the cheapest way to get to Paris is by Eurolines bus (about 6/day, 8 hours, about €46 one-way, €70-86 round-trip; price depends on demand—nonrefundable, advance-purchase one-way tickets as cheap as €17 and round-trip as cheap as €28, check online for deals, Julianaplein 5, Amstel Station, five stops by metro from Central Station, tel. 020/560-8788, www.eurolines.com).

By Plane

SCHIPHOL AIRPORT

Schiphol (SKIP-pol) Airport is located about 10 miles southwest of Amsterdam's city center. Like most of Holland, it is user-friendly and below sea level. With an appealing array of shops, eateries, and other time-killing opportunities, Schiphol is a fine place to arrive, depart, or change planes. A truly international airport, Schiphol has done away with Dutch—signs are in English only.

Information: Schiphol flight information can give you flight times and your airline's contact info (airport code: AMS, toll tel. 0900-0141, from other countries dial +31-20-794-0800, www.schiphol.nl).

Orientation: Though Schiphol officially has four terminals, it's really just one big building. You could walk it end to end in about 20 minutes (but allow some time to pass through security checkpoints between certain terminals). All terminals have ATMs, banks, shops, bars, and free Wi-Fi. An inviting shopping and eating zone called Holland Boulevard runs between Terminals 2 and 3.

Arrival at Schiphol: Baggage-claim areas for all terminals empty into the same arrival zone, called Schiphol Plaza. Here you'll find a busy **TI** (near Terminal 2, daily 7:00-22:00), a train station, and bus stops for getting into the city.

Services: The ABN/AMRO **banks** around the airport offer fair exchange rates. **Service Point,** in Schiphol Plaza at the end of the shopping mall near Terminal 4, is a useful all-purpose service counter that sells SIM cards, has an ATM, and ships packages. Convenient **luggage lockers** are at various points around the airport—allowing you to leave your bag here on a lengthy layover (both short- and long-term lockers, credit card only; biggest bank of lockers near the train station at Schiphol Plaza). To get train information, buy a ticket, or validate your rail pass, take advantage of the **"Train Tickets and Services" counter** (Schiphol Plaza ground level, just past Burger King). They have an easy info desk and generally short lines—so transactions here tend to be much quicker than at Amsterdam's Central Station ticket desks. While you're here, consider validating your rail pass, booking future international train tickets, making seat reservations for later in your trip, or handling any other time-consuming tasks.

Time-Killing Tips: If you have extra time at Schiphol, check out the **Rijksmuseum Amsterdam Schiphol,** a little art gallery and museum store on Holland Boulevard, the lively shopping/ eating zone between Lounges 2 and 3. The Rijksmuseum loans a dozen or so of its minor masterpieces from the Dutch Golden Age to this unique airport museum, including actual Dutch Masters by Rembrandt, Vermeer, and others (free, daily 7:00-20:00). Or, to escape the airport crowds, follow signs for the **Panorama Terrace** to the third floor of Terminal 2, where you'll find a quieter, full-of-locals cafeteria, a kids' play area, and a view terrace where you can watch planes come and go while you nurse a coffee. If you plan to visit the terrace on arrival, stop there before you pass through customs.

From Schiphol Airport to Amsterdam

To get between Schiphol and downtown Amsterdam, you have several options:

By Train: This is your fastest and cheapest option. Direct trains to Amsterdam's Central Station run frequently from Schiphol Plaza (4-6/hour, 15 minutes, €5). You can buy tickets at the ticket windows—expect to pay cash unless your credit card has a chip (there are ATMs nearby). The ticket machines accept coins and credit cards with a chip (start the no-brainer transaction by pressing "I want to go to Amsterdam Centraal"). Schiphol's train station also serves other destinations (see next page). When traveling *from* Amsterdam Central to Schiphol, trains generally leave every 15 minutes from track 14a.

By Shuttle Bus: The Connexxion shuttle bus departs from lane A7 in front of the airport and takes you directly to most hotels. There are three different routes, including one to the Westerkerk (near some of my recommended hotels). Ask the attendant which one works best for you (2/hour, 20 minutes, €17 one-way, €27 round-trip, some routes may cost a couple euros more). For trips from Amsterdam to Schiphol, reserve at least two hours ahead (tel. 088-339-4741, www.airporthotelshuttle.nl).

By Public Bus: Bus #197 (departing from lane B9 in front of the airport) is handy for those going to the Leidseplein district (€5, buy ticket from driver).

By Taxi: Allow about €60-70 to downtown Amsterdam. But many hotels have cabs offering a fixed-price airport deal for €45; ask your hotelier for details.

From Schiphol Airport to Haarlem: The big red #300 **bus** is direct, stopping at Haarlem's train station and near the Grote Markt/Market Square (4-10/hour, 40 minutes, €4—buy ticket from driver, departs from lane B6 in front of airport). The **train** is just as quick, but you'll have to transfer at the Amsterdam-Sloterdijk station (6/hour, 30-40 minutes, €5.80). Figure about €30-40 to Haarlem by **taxi.**

From Schiphol Airport by Train to: Delft (4/hour, 45 minutes, some with transfer in Leiden), **The Hague/Den Haag** (4/hour, 30-40 minutes, more with change in Leiden), **Rotterdam** (3/hour, 30 minutes), **Bruges** (10/day, 2.75-3.5 hours, change in Antwerp or Brussels), **Brussels** (hourly, 3 hours on IC to Brussels' three main stations; hourly, 1.5 hours on pricey Thalys to Midi/Zuid/South Station).

From Schiphol Airport by Bus to: Keukenhof (bus #858, 8/hour, 40 minutes), **Aalsmeer** (Connexxion bus #198, 4/hour, 18 minutes).

By Cruise Ship

Things here are simple for cruisers: The Passenger Terminal Amsterdam (PTA) is just a 15-minute walk or three-minute tram ride along the water east of Central Station. There's an ATM (with poor rates) inside the terminal, and many better ones at the train station.

To ride the **tram,** simply exit the cruise terminal, follow the *Town Center* sign, cross the busy portside street, and look for the stop for tram #26. Buy a ticket from the driver (either a single ticket or a day pass, pay cash) and ride it one stop to Central Station. To **walk,** head out the same door, turn right, and stroll with the water on your right for about 15 minutes toward the station's glass-and-steel arch. You'll pass between the station and the river, then turn left at the major crosswalk to enter the lower level of Central Station. Once you've reached Central Station—by tram or by foot—turn to the arrival instructions on page 32.

From the cruise terminal, a **taxi** to the Rijksmuseum or Van Gogh Museum should cost about €16. The **Canal Bus** red line stops at the Passenger Terminal (for details, see page 42). The nearest **bike rental** is AmsterBike, in the parking garage under the

Mövenpick Hotel next door (daily 9:00-18:00 except closed Wed in winter, tel. 020/419-9063, www.amsterbike.eu); more bike-rental options are near Central Station.

A few ships dock at the **Felison Terminal** in IJmuiden if Amsterdam's terminal is full. Connexxion buses run to Amsterdam (bus #82) and Haarlem (bus #75); see www.felisonterminal.nl.

HAARLEM

HAARLEM ORIENTATION AND SIGHTS

Cute and cozy, yet authentic and handy to the airport, Haarlem is a good home base, giving you small-town warmth overnight, with easy access (20 minutes by train) to wild-and-crazy Amsterdam during the day.

Bustling Haarlem gave America's Harlem its name back when New York was New Amsterdam, a Dutch colony. For centuries Haarlem has been a market town, buzzing with shoppers heading home with fresh bouquets, nowadays by bike.

Enjoy the market on Monday (clothing) or Saturday (general), when the town's atmospheric main square bustles like a Brueghel painting, with cheese, fish, flowers, and families. Make yourself at home; buy some flowers to brighten your hotel room.

If it's a sunny day and you need a beach, head to nearby Zandvoort.

Haarlem Overview

TOURIST INFORMATION

Haarlem's TI (VVV), in the Town Hall building on Grote Markt, is friendlier, more helpful, and less crowded than Amsterdam's, so ask your Amsterdam questions here (April-Sept Mon-Fri 9:30-17:30, Sat 9:30-17:00, Sun 12:00-16:00; Oct-March Mon 13:00-17:30, Tue-Fri 9:30-17:30, Sat 10:00-17:00, closed Sun; tel. 023/531-7325, www.haarlem.nl, info@vvvhaarlem.nl).

The TI offers a good selection of maps and sightseeing- and walking-tour brochures, and sells discounted tickets (€1 off) for the Frans Hals Museum and the Teylers Museum, and a €15 combo-ticket that covers both (saving €8.50).

ARRIVAL IN HAARLEM

By Train: Lockers are available at the station at the very end of platform 3A (€3.70/day, no coins—use a credit card or buy a "Chipknip" prepaid debit card at a ticket window). Two parallel streets flank the train station (Kruisweg and Jansweg). Head up either street, and you'll reach the town square and church within 10 minutes. If you need help, ask someone to point you toward Grote Markt (Market Square). If you're arriving by train from Amsterdam, see the end of this chapter for a description of sights you'll see out the train window along the way.

By Bus: Buses from Schiphol Airport stop both in the center (Centrum/Verwulft stop, a short walk from Grote Markt) and at the train station.

By Car: Parking is expensive on the streets (€3.25/hour). It's cheaper (€2.20/hour; €2.80 overnight—19:00-8:00) in these central garages: at the train station, at the southern end of Gedempte Oude Gracht (the main thoroughfare), near the recommended Die Raeckse Hotel, and near the Frans Hals Museum. The most central garage, near the Teylers Museum is pricier (€1.50 every 40 minutes—essentially, €2.75/hour).

By Plane: For details on getting from Schiphol Airport to Haarlem, see page 258.

HELPFUL HINTS

Blue Monday and Early Closures: Most sights are closed on Monday, except the Grote Kerk (the big church on the main square), De Adriaan Windmill, and History Museum Haarlem. The **Corrie ten Boom House**, which is closed on Sunday on Monday, closes early the rest of the week (15:00).

Internet Access: Try **Suny Telecom** (€2/hour, daily 8:30-22:00, near train station at Kruisweg 42, tel. 023/532-3757) or **High Times Coffeeshop** (free if you buy some pot, Lange Veerstraat 47—see sidebar on page 301).

Post Office: There isn't one. To buy stamps, head to a newsstand with the orange *TNT* logo; if you need to send a package, ask your hotelier for help.

Laundry: My Beautiful Launderette is handy and fairly central (€6 self-service wash and dry, daily 8:30-20:30, €9 full service available Mon-Fri 9:00-17:00, near V&D department store at Boter Markt 20).

Bike Rental: You can rent bikes from **Pieters Fietsverhuur** inside the train station (fixed-gear bike-€6.50/day, 3-speed bike-€10/day, €50 deposit and passport number required, Mon-Sat 6:00-24:00, Sun 7:30-24:00, Stationsplein 1, tel. 023/531-7066, www.rijwielshoppieters.nl). They have only 50 fixed-gear bikes to rent and often run out by midmorning—especially when the weather's good. **Rent a Bike Haarlem** charges more, but is friendly and efficient, and carries plenty of new, good-quality bikes. If you're renting for less than a full day, negotiate a cheaper price (fixed-gear bike-€10/day, 3-speed bike-€13.50/day, mountain bikes available, after-hours drop-off possible, ID required for deposit—if you don't want to leave ID, there's a €150 cash deposit; April-Sept daily 9:30-17:30; Oct-March Mon-Sat 10:00-17:00, closed Sun; near station at Lange Herenstraat 36, tel. 023/542-1195, www.rentabikehaarlem.nl).

Taxi: The drop charge of €7.50 gets you a little over a mile.

Local Guide: Consider hiring **Walter Schelfhout,** a bearded repository of Haarlem's historical fun facts. If you're into beer lore, Walter's your guy (€91/2 hours, also leads a beer walk sponsored by the Jopenkerk brewpub, tel. 023/535-5715, mobile 06-1258-9299, schelfhout@dutch.nl).

Best View: At **La Place** cafeteria, you get wraparound views of the city as you sip your €2 self-serve tea (top floor of V&D department store—see page 300).

Best Ice Cream: Gelateria Bartoli, on the south side of the church, is the local favorite (daily March-Sept 10:00-22:00, Oct-Dec 12:00-17:30 in good weather, closed Jan-Feb).

Sights in Haarlem

▲▲GROTE MARKT (MARKET SQUARE)

Haarlem's Grote Markt, where 10 streets converge, is the town's delightful centerpiece...as it has been for 700 years. To enjoy a coffee or beer here, simmering in Dutch good living, is a quintessential European experience. Observe. Sit and gaze at the church, appreciating essentially the same scene that Dutch artists captured centuries ago in oil paintings that now hang in museums.

Until the 1990s, trolleys ran through the square, and cars were parked everywhere. But now it's a pedestrian zone, with market stalls filling the square on Mondays and Saturdays, and café tables dominating on other days.

This is a fun place to build a picnic with Haarlem finger foods and enjoy great seating on the square. Look for pickled herring (takeaway stand on the square), local cheese (Gouda and Edam—tasty shop a block away on Barteljorisstraat), french fries with mayonnaise (recommended old-time fries place behind the church on Warmoesstraat), and, in the summer, *stroopwafels* (waffles with built-in syrup) and *poffertjes* (little sugar doughnuts, cooked on the spot).

As you enjoy a snack, take this simple spin tour of the square.
• *Overseeing the square is the...*

L. J. Coster Statue: Forty years before Gutenberg invented movable type, this man carved the letter *A* out of wood, dropped it into some wet sand, and saw the imprint it left. He got the idea of making movable type out of wood (and later, he may have tried using lead). For Haarlemmers, that was good enough, and they credit their man, Coster, with inventing modern printing. In the statue, Coster (c. 1370-1440) holds up a block of movable type and points to himself, saying, "I made this." How much Coster did is uncertain, but Gutenberg trumped him by building a printing press, casting type in metal, and pounding out the Bible.

• *Coster is facing the...*

Town Hall: Whereas most of medieval Europe was ruled by kings, dukes, and barons, Haarlem has been largely self-governing since 1425. This building—built from a royal hunting lodge in the mid-1200s, then rebuilt after a 1351 fire—has served as Haarlem's Town Hall since about 1400. The facade dates from 1630.

The town drunk used to hang out on the bench in front of the Town Hall, where he'd expose himself to newlyweds coming down the stairs. Rather than arresting the man, the townspeople simply moved the bench (a typical Dutch solution to the problem).

• *Next to the church is the...*

Meat Market (Vleeshal), 1603: The fine Flemish Renaissance building nearest the cathedral is the old meat hall, built by the rich butchers' and leatherworkers' guilds. The meat market was on the ground floor, the leather was upstairs, and the cellar was filled with ice to preserve the meat. It's decorated with carved bits of early advertising—sheep and cows for sale. Today, rather than meat, the hall shows off temporary modern art exhibits in the Museum De Hallen (€7.50, Tue-Sat 11:00-17:00, Sun 12:00-17:00, closed Mon, Grote Markt 16, tel. 023/511-5775, www.dehallen.nl) and bits of

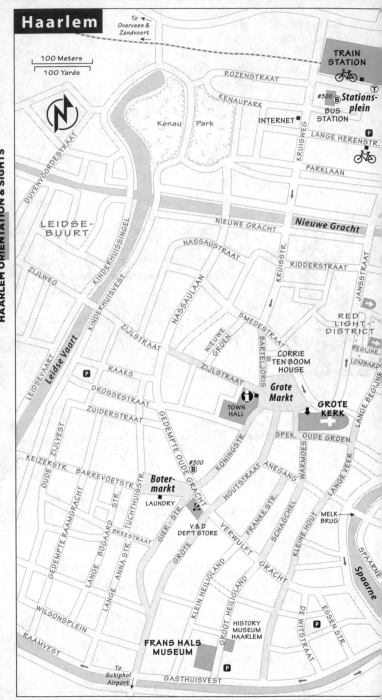

Haarlem

To Overveen & Zandvoort

100 Meters
100 Yards

ROZENSTRAAT

TRAIN STATION

#300 B Stations-plein
BUS STATION

KENAUPARK

INTERNET

LANGE HERENSTR.

KENAU PARK

PARKLAAN

DUYENYOORDESTRAAT

LEIDSE-BUURT

NIEUWE GRACHT

Nieuwe Gracht

ZIJLWEG

NASSAUSTRAAT

RIDDERSTRAAT

KRUISSTR.

JANSSTRAAT

KINDERHUISSINGEL

KINDERHUISVEST

ZIJLSTRAAT

NASSAULAAN

SMEDESTRAAT

RED LIGHT DISTRICT

Leidse Vaart

NIEUWE GROEN.

BARTELJORIS

CORRIE TEN BOOM HOUSE

BEGIJNE

LOMBARD

LANGE BEGIJNE

ZIJLSTRAAT

RAAKS

Grote Markt

GROTE KERK

LEIDSEVAART

DROSSESTRAAT

TOWN HALL

ZUIDERSTRAAT

SPEK. OUDE GROEN.

KEIZERSTR.

OUDE ZIJLVEST

BARREVOETESTR.

GEDEMPTE OUDE GRACHT

KONINGSTR.

ANEGANG

WARMOES

LANGE VEER

#300 B

Boter-markt

HOUTSTRAAT

FRANKE STR.

SCHAGCHEL

MELK BRUG

GEDEMPTE RAAMGRACHT

LANGE BOGAARD STR.

TUCHTHUISSTR.

GIER. STR.

LAUNDRY

V & D DEP'T STORE

VERWULFT

GRACHT

KLEINE HOUT

Spaarne

WILSONGPLEIN

LANGE ANNA STR.

BREESTRAAT

GROTE

KLEIN HEILIGLAND

GROOT HEILIGLAND

DE WITSTRAAT

ESSEN STR.

RAAMVEST

FRANS HALS MUSEUM

HISTORY MUSEUM HAARLEM

To Schiphol Airport

GASTHUISVEST

To Schiphol Airport

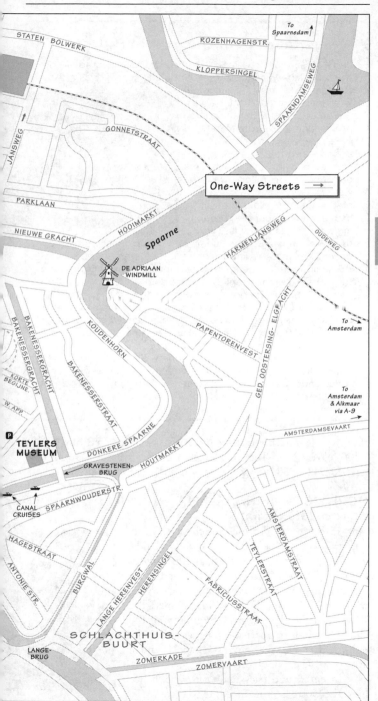

Haarlem of the Golden Age

Parts of Haarlem still look like they did four centuries ago, when the city was a bustling commercial center rivaling Amsterdam. It's easy to imagine local merchants and their wives dressed in black with ruff collars, promenading on Grote Markt.

Back then, the town was a port on the large Haarlemmer Lake, with the North Sea only about five miles away. As well as being the tulip capital of the country, Haarlem was a manufacturing center, producing wool, silk, lace, damask cloth, furniture, smoking pipes (along with cheap, locally grown tobacco), and mass quantities of beer. Haarlemmers were notorious consumers of beer—it was a popular breakfast drink, and the average person drank six pints a day.

In 1585, the city got an influx of wealthy merchants when Spanish troops invaded the culturally rich city of Antwerp, driving Protestants and Jews north. Even when hard-line, moralistic Calvinists dominated Haarlem's politics, the city remained culturally and religiously diverse.

In the 1700s, Haarlem's economy declined, along with that of the rest of the Netherlands. In the succeeding centuries, industry—printing, textiles, ship building—once again made the city an economic force.

the town's past in the Archaeology Museum (free, Wed-Sun 13:00-17:00, closed Mon-Tue, in the cellar of the Museum De Hallen, tel. 023/542-0888, www.archeologischmuseumhaarlem.nl).

MORE SIGHTS IN HAARLEM
▲Church (Grote Kerk)

This 15th-century Gothic church (now Protestant) is worth a look, if only to see Holland's greatest pipe organ (from 1738, 100 feet high). Its more than 5,000 pipes impressed both Handel and Mozart. Note how the organ, which fills the west end, seems to steal the show from the altar. Quirky highlights of the church include a replica of Foucault's pendulum, the "Dog-Whipper's Chapel," and a 400-year-old cannonball.

To enter, find the small *Entrée* sign behind the Coster statue on Grote Markt.

Cost and Hours: €2.50, not covered by Museumkaart, Mon-Sat 10:00-17:00, closed Sun to tourists, tel. 023/553-2040, www.bavo.nl.

Concerts: Consider attending—even just part of—a **concert** to hear the Oz-like pipe organ (regular free concerts Tue at 20:15 mid-May-mid-Oct, additional concerts Thu at 16:00 July-Aug; bring a sweater—the church isn't heated).

For a self-guided tour, ✪ see the Grote Kerk Tour chapter.

▲▲Frans Hals Museum

Haarlem is the hometown of Frans Hals, the foremost Dutch portrait painter of the 17th-century Golden Age. This refreshing museum, once an almshouse for old men back in 1610, displays many of Hals' greatest paintings, crafted in his nearly Impressionistic style. You'll see group portraits and paintings of old-time Haarlem.

Cost and Hours: €12.50, €15 combo-ticket with Teylers Museum (purchase at TI), sometimes more with special exhibits, includes audioguide, Tue-Sat 11:00-17:00, Sun 12:00-17:00, closed Mon, Groot Heiligland 62, tel. 023/511-5775, www.franshalsmuseum.nl.

For a self-guided tour, ✪ see the Frans Hals Museum Tour chapter.

History Museum Haarlem

This small museum, across the street from the Frans Hals Museum, offers a glimpse of old Haarlem. Request the English version of the 10-minute video, low-key Haarlem's version of a sound-and-light show. Study the large-scale model of Haarlem in 1822 (when its fortifications were still intact), and wander the three rooms without English descriptions.

Cost and Hours: Overpriced at €7, Sun-Mon 12:00-17:00, Tue-Sat 11:00-17:00, Groot Heiligland 47, tel. 023/542-2427, www.historischmuseumhaarlem.nl. The adjacent architecture center (free) may be of interest to architects.

▲Corrie ten Boom House

Haarlem was home to Corrie ten Boom, popularized by her inspirational 1971 book (and the 1975 movie that followed), *The Hiding Place*. Both tell about the Ten Boom family's experience protecting Jews from the Nazis. Corrie ten Boom gives the other half of the Anne Frank story—the point of view of those who risked their lives to hide Dutch Jews during the Nazi occupation (1940-1945).

The Ten Boom House is open only for English tours—check the sign on the door for the next start time. The gentle and loving one-hour tours come with a little evangelizing that some may find objectionable.

Cost and Hours: Free, but donations accepted; April-Oct

Tue-Sat first tour at 10:00, last tour at 15:00; Nov-March Tue-Sat first tour at 11:00, last tour around 15:00; closed Sun-Mon year-round; 50 yards north of Grote Markt at Barteljorisstraat 19; the clock-shop people get all wound up if you go inside—wait in the little side street at the door, where tour times are posted; tel. 023/531-0823, www.corrietenboom.com.

Background: The clock shop was the Ten Boom family business. The elderly father and his two daughters—Corrie and Betsy, both in their 50s—lived above the store and in the brick building attached in back (along Schoutensteeg alley). Corrie's bedroom was on the top floor at the back. This room was tiny to start with, but then the family built a second, secret room (less than a yard deep) at the very back—"the hiding place," where they could hide six Jews at a time. Devoutly religious, the family had a long tradition of tolerance, having hosted prayer meetings here in their home for both Jews and Christians for generations.

The Gestapo, tipped off that the family was harboring Jews, burst into the Ten Boom house. Finding a suspicious number of ration coupons, the Nazis arrested the family, but failed to find the six Jews (who later escaped) in the hiding place. Corrie's father and sister died while in prison, but Corrie survived the Ravensbrück concentration camp to tell her story in her memoir.

▲Teylers Museum

Famous as the oldest museum in Holland, Teylers is a time-warp experience, filled with all sorts of fun curios for science buffs: fossils, minerals, primitive electronic gadgetry, and examples of 18th- and 19th-century technology (it also has two lovely painting galleries and hosts good temporary exhibits).

The science-oriented sections of this place feel like a museum of a museum. They're serious about authenticity here: The presentation is perfectly preserved, right down to the original labels. Since there was no electricity in the olden days, you'll find little electric lighting...if it's dark outside, it's dark inside. The museum's benefactor, Pieter Teyler van der Hulst, was a very wealthy merchant who willed his estate, worth the equivalent of €80 million today, to a foundation whose mission was to "create and maintain a museum to stimulate art and science." The museum opened in 1784, six years after Teyler's death (his last euro was spent in 1983—now it's a national museum). Add your name to the guest book, which goes back to before Napoleon's visit here. The freshly renovated oval room—a temple of science and learning—is the core of the museum; in the art salons paintings are hung in the old style.

Cost and Hours: Overpriced at €11, better €15 combo-ticket with Frans Hals Museum (purchase at TI), includes excellent (and I'd say, essential) audioguide, Tue-Sat 10:00-17:00, Sun

12:00-17:00, closed Mon, Spaarne 16, tel. 023/531-9010, www.
teylersmuseum.eu. The museum's modern café has good prices and
faces a delightful garden.

▲De Adriaan Windmill

Haarlem's old-time windmill, located just a 10-minute walk from
the station and Teylers Museum, welcomes visitors with a short
video, a little museum, and fine town views.

Cost and Hours: €3.50, not covered by Museumkaart;
March-Nov Mon and Wed-Fri 13:00-17:00, Sat-Sun 10:30-17:00,
closed Tue; Dec-Feb Fri-Mon 13:00-16:30, closed Tue-Thu; Pa-
pentorenvest 1, tel. 023/545-0259, www.molenadriaan.nl.

Canal Cruise

Making a scenic 50-minute loop through and around Haarlem
with a live guide who speaks Dutch and sometimes English, **Post
Verkade Cruise**'s little trips are more relaxing than informative
(€11; April-Oct daily departures at the top of the hour 12:00-
16:00; Nov-March same hours Wed-Sun, reservations required;
also evening cruises, across canal from Teylers Museum at Spaarne
11a, tel. 023/535-7723, www.postverkadecruises.nl). **Haarlem
Canal Tours** runs similar but longer tours, and uses an open boat.
You'll find them farther down Spaarne, across from #17 (€13.50,
online reservations smart, 70-75 minutes, leaves every 1.5 hours
daily 10:00-19:00, may not run in bad weather and off-season,
www.haarlemcanaltours.com).

▲Red Light District

Wander through a little Red Light District that's as precious as a
Barbie doll—and legal since the 1980s (2 blocks northeast of Grote
Markt, off Lange Begijnestraat, no senior or student discounts).
Don't miss the mall on Begijnesteeg marked by the red neon sign
reading *'t Steegje* ("free"). Just beyond that, the nearby 't Poortje
("office park") costs €6 to enter. Jog to the right to pop into the
much more inviting "Red Lantern" (window-shopping welcome, at
Korte Begijnestraat 27). As you wander through this area, remember that the people here don't condone prostitution any more than
your own community back home probably does; they just find it
practical not to criminalize it and drive it underground, but instead
to regulate it and keep the practice as safe as possible.

NEAR HAARLEM: ZANDVOORT

For a quick and easy look at the windy coastline in a shell lover's
Shangri-la, visit the beach burg of Zandvoort. This pretty, manicured resort has plenty of cafés, ice-cream parlors, *Vlaamse friet*
stands, restaurants, and boutiques. Just beyond the town is the vast
and sandy beach, lined with cafés and rentable chairs. Above it all

is a pedestrian promenade and a line of high-rise hotels. South of the main beach, sunbathers work on all-over tans. Come to Zandvoort if the weather's hot and you want a taste of the sea and sun, if you want to see how Dutch and German holidaymakers have fun, or if you just want an excuse for a long bike ride from Haarlem.

Tourist Information: The helpful TI is on Bakkerstraat 2 (Mon-Fri 9:00-17:00, Sat 10:00-17:00, Sun 11:00-16:00, tel. 023/571-7947, www.vvvzandvoort.nl).

Getting There: It's easy to reach by train, and the station is just around the corner from the beach (4/hour from Haarlem in summer, 10 minutes; 2/hour, 30 minutes from Amsterdam). By bike, it's a breezy 45-minute ride from Haarlem, heading west and following road signs for *Bloemendaal,* then *Zandvoort.*

AMSTERDAM TO HAARLEM TRAIN TOUR

Since you'll probably take the train from Amsterdam to Haarlem, here's an out-the-window tour to keep you entertained while you travel. Departing from Amsterdam, grab a seat on the right (with your back to Amsterdam, top deck if possible). Everything is on the right unless I say it's on the left.

You're riding the oldest train line in Holland. Leaving Amsterdam, you'll see the cranes and ships of its harbor—sizable, but nothing like Europe's biggest in nearby Rotterdam.

On your left, a few minutes out of Amsterdam, you should be able to see an old **windmill** (you can visit a similar one in Haarlem). In front of it, the little garden plots and cottages are escapes for big-city people who probably don't even have a balcony.

Coming into the **Sloterdijk Station** (where trains connect for Amsterdam's Schiphol Airport), you'll see huge office buildings, such as Dutch telecom giant KPN. These sprouted after the station made commuting easy. On the horizon, sleek and modern windmills whirl.

Passing through a forest and by some houseboats, you enter a *polder*—an area of reclaimed land. This is part of an ecologically sound farm zone, run without chemicals. Cows, pigs, and chickens run free—they're not raised in cages. The train tracks are on a dike, which provides a raised foundation less susceptible to flooding, so the transportation system generally keeps running, even in bad weather. Looking out at another dike in the distance (visible on

The Haarlemmermeer

The land between Haarlem and Amsterdam—where trains speed through, cattle graze, and 747s touch down—was once a lake the size of Washington, DC called the Haarlemmermeer.

In the 1500s, a series of high tides and storms caused the IJ River to breach its banks, flooding this sub-sea-level area and turning a bunch of shallow lakes into a single one nearly 15 feet deep, covering 70 square miles. By the 1800s, floods were licking at the borders of Haarlem and Amsterdam, and the residents needed to act. First, they dug a ring canal to channel away water (and preserve the lake's shipping business). Then, using steam engines, they pumped the lake dry, turning marshy soil into fertile ground. The Amsterdam-Haarlem train line that soon crossed the former lakebed was the country's first.

clear days), consider that you're actually in the most densely populated country in Europe.

On the right, just after the Ikea building, find a big beige-and-white building. This is the **mint,** where currency is printed (top security, no advertising). This has long been a family business—see the name: Joh. Enschedé.

As the train slows down, you pass a giant, silvery structure (the Netherlands' biggest train-car-maintenance facility), and enter Haarlem. Look left. The domed building is a **prison,** built in 1901 and still in use. The **De Adriaan Windmill** that you see was rebuilt in 2002, after the original burnt down in 1932 (the windmill is open for visits—see listing earlier).

When you cross the Spaarne River, you'll see the great **church spire** of the Grote Kerk towering over Haarlem, as it has since medieval times, back when a fortified wall circled the town. Notice the white version of the same spire capping the smaller church (between the prison and the big church): This was the original sandstone steeple that stood atop the big church. However, structural problems forced its move to another church, and a new spire was built for the big church.

Exit the train into one of Holland's oldest stations, adorned with Art Nouveau decor from 1908. Welcome to Haarlem.

GROTE KERK TOUR

Haarlem's impressive Grote Kerk (Great Church), one of the best-known landmarks in the Netherlands, is visible from miles around, rising above the flat plain that surrounds it. From the Grote Markt (Market Square), you see the church at a three-quarters angle, emphasizing both its length (240 feet) and its height (260 feet).

Orientation

Cost: €2.50, not covered by Museumkaart.

Hours: Mon-Sat 10:00-17:00, closed Sun to tourists, Sun service at 10:00 (May-Oct). The church also holds a daily 15-minute prayer service at 12:45 (May-Oct). Occasionally, the church is closed for a wedding or a funeral; if you see a closed sign when it's supposed to be open, return in a couple of hours.

Getting There: The church is on the main square, a 10-minute walk south of the train station.

Information: The leaflet at the ticket desk offers basic information in English. Tours are offered on Saturdays, by request (€5). Tel. 023/553-2040, www.bavo.nl.

Music: Consider attending even just part of a concert to hear Holland's greatest pipe organ. Free concerts generally are offered throughout the summer (Tue at 20:15 mid-May-mid-Oct, additional concerts Thu at 16:00 July-Aug; concerts last about one hour). In even years, an organ competition is held here in July, bringing nearly nightly performances at 20:15. If you're coming for a concert, bring a sweater—the thick stone walls keep the church cool, even during summer. Entrance to the evening concerts is through the south transept, around the back of the church.

Length of This Tour: Allow 45 minutes.

WC: Nice WCs are inside, just after the ticket desk.

OVERVIEW

After a fire destroyed the old church (1328), the Grote Kerk was built over a 150-year period (c. 1390-1540) in the late Gothic style of red-and-gray brick, topped with a slate-covered wood roof and a stacked tower bearing a golden crown and a rooster weathervane.

Originally Catholic, the church was named after St. Bavo, a local noble who frequented seventh-century Red Light Districts during his youth. After his conversion, he moved out of his castle and into a hollow tree, where he spent his days fasting and praying. In the late 1500s, the St. Bavo Church became Protestant (Dutch Reformed) along with much of the country. From then on, the anti-saint Protestants simply called it the Great Church.

The Tour Begins

• *Before entering, take a few minutes to walk around this incredible building.*

EXTERIOR

Notice the rough buttress anchors, which were never needed. Money ran out, and the planned stone ceiling (which would have

required these buttresses) was replaced by a lighter wooden one. Some windows are bricked up because the organ fills the wall.

The original stone tower crowned the church from 1522 until 1530, when the church began sinking under its weight. The tower was removed and replaced by the lighter, lead-covered-wood version you see today. (The frugal Dutch recycled the old tower, using it to cap the Bakenesser church, a short walk away.)

Because the tower was used as a lookout by Napoleon, it was classified as part of the town's defense. As a result, the tower (but not the rest of the church) became city property, and, since Haarlem's citizens own it, they must help pay to maintain it.

The base of the church is encrusted, barnacle-like, with shops—selling jewelry, souvenirs, haircuts, and artwork in the colonnaded former fish market—harkening back to medieval times, when religion and commerce were more intertwined. The little shops around the cathedral have long been church-owned, rented out to bring in a little cash.

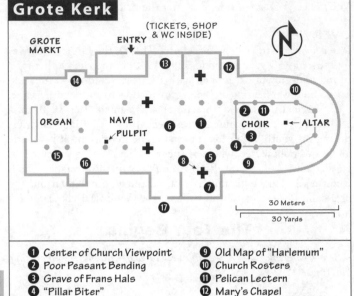

Grote Kerk

(TICKETS, SHOP & WC INSIDE)

GROTE MARKT

ENTRY

GROTE MARKT

ORGAN

NAVE

PULPIT

CHOIR

ALTAR

30 Meters

30 Yards

1. Center of Church Viewpoint
2. Poor Peasant Bending
3. Grave of Frans Hals
4. "Pillar Biter"
5. Three Little Ships
6. Memorial to Hydraulic Engineers
7. Brewers' Chapel & Café
8. Giant & Dwarf Marks
9. Old Map of "Harlemum"
10. Church Rosters
11. Pelican Lectern
12. Mary's Chapel
13. Foucault's Pendulum
14. Dog-Whipper's Chapel
15. Model of the Church
16. Cannonball
17. Evening Concert Entrance

During the day, a machine plays music on the bells of the Grote Kerk's carillon (live carillonneurs play occasionally). If you're in Haarlem at night, you'll hear the carillon chiming a simple "de dong dong, de dong dong" ("Don't worry, be happy") at 21:00. In days gone by, this used to warn citizens that the city gates would soon close for the night.

• *Enter the church on the Grote Markt side, near the north transept (look for the small* Entrée *sign). Walk to the* **center of the church** *and take it all in.*

INTERIOR

Simple white walls, a black floor, a brown ceiling, and a mahogany-colored organ make this spacious church feel vast, light, and airy. Considering it was built over a span of 150 years, its architecture is surprisingly homogenous. Originally, much of the interior was painted in bright patterns, similar

to the carpet-like frescoes on some columns near the center of the church. But in 1566, Protestant extremists stripped the church of its graven images and ornate Catholic trappings, leaving it relatively stark, with minimal decoration. They whitewashed everything. The few frescoes you see today were restored when the whitewash was removed in the 1980s.

Look up to see the fan-vaulted cedar ceiling from 1530. Look down to see tombstones paving the floor. And look midway up the walls to catch squatting characters supporting the pilasters. The three-story organ fills the west wall.

• *We'll circle the church, but first stand at the candle-lined, fence-like brass barrier and look into an enclosed area of wooden benches ("stalls") and the altar, known as the...*

Choir

After the church's foundation was laid, the choir was built first and used for worship for more than a century while the rest of the building was completed.

Today, the brass-and-wood barrier keeps tourists from entering the most sacred area, just as peasants were kept out in medieval times. While the commoners had to stand during services, local big shots got to perch their heinies on the little ledg-

es (called misericords, carved in 1512) of the **wooden stalls** that line the choir; the eighth stall along the left-hand side shows a poor peasant bending over to bear a rich guy's bum on his back. The stalls are also decorated with the coats of arms of noble families, whose second sons traditionally became priests.

The choir's floor holds a simple slab marked with a lantern—the **grave of Frans Hals** *(graf van Frans Hals),* Haarlem's own master artist of the Golden Age. When he was a child, Hals' family moved to Haarlem, and he lived and worked here all his life, worshipping in the Grote Kerk. A friend of mayors and preachers, he chronicled middle-class citizens and tavern life, producing hundreds of masterpieces...and 10 kids.

GROTE KERK

At both ends of the brass barrier, look for the endearing knee-level carvings of the **"pillar biter."** The message of these carvings,

aimed at those who were "more Catholic than even the pope," was this: Don't go overboard on devotion.

More than a thousand wealthy people are buried under the church's pavement stones. Only those with piles of money to give to the church could be buried in a way that gave them an advantage in the salvation derby. But even though the dead bodies were embalmed, they stunk. Imagine being a peasant sitting here, trying to think about God...and thinking only of the stench of well-fed bodies rotting below. Here is where the phrase "stinking rich" was born.

• *To your right (as you face the choir), suspended between columns, are...*

Three Little Ships

Sailing under the red-white-and-blue Dutch flag and the flag of a rearing lion, ships like these helped make Holland the world's number-one sea-trading nation in the 1600s.

The biggest model ship of the three is a frigate. These fast, heavily armed, three-masted, fully rigged ships rode shotgun for merchant vessels, protecting them from pirates in their two-year journey to the Far East and back. This one has a flat-bottomed hull, which was necessary to ply Amsterdam's shallow harbor. It could fire a 21-gun salute from each side, and extra cannons on the poop deck and forecastle made it more powerful than the average frigate. The keel has an iron saw, a Dutch military specialty for slicing through the chains that commonly blocked harbors (see the chain between two towers near the bow).

• *At the next column down, just to the right, is the...*

Memorial to Hydraulic Engineers

The marble relief shows Neptune in his water chariot. In low-lying Holland of the 1800s, when flooding could mean life or death, hydraulic engineers were heroes, specifically the two commemorated here.

• *Behind the columns, set into the wall of the church, is the...*

Brewers' Chapel (Brouwerskapel)

This chapel, with its humble café, marks the long and short of the city's 750-year history—literally. On the chapel's central pillar, black lines on the column show the height of Haarlem's shortest citizen, thigh-high (33 inches) Simon Paap, who supposedly died in a dwarf-tossing incident, and—wow!—8-foot-8-inch-tall Daniel Cajanus.

• *On the wall to the left of the café hangs an...* ·

Old Map of "Harlemum"

The map shows the walled city in 1688, with ramparts and a moat. Surrounding panels showcase Haarlem's 750-year history. The

lower-left panel shows the 1572-1573 Siege of Haarlem, as brave Haarlem women join their men-folk in battle—bombs exploding around them—to fight off invading Spanish troops.

The lower-right panel shows knights kneeling before a king in the 12th century, while in the distance, ships sail right along the city walls. Up until the 1840s, when it was drained and reclaimed, there was a large lake (the Haarlemmermeer) standing between Haarlem and Amsterdam. The Grote Kerk, when viewed by distant travelers, seemed to float like a stately ship on the lake, as seen in the landscape along the bottom of the map.

• *From here, circle the church counterclockwise, heading around the altar. Just after rounding the bend, on the wall, you'll see the first of the church's many lists of prominent church members, dating back to 1577, when the church became Protestant. The first* **roster**, *from 1770, has mesmerizingly ornate calligraphy. Opposite this list, inside the choir, is the...*

Pelican Lectern

According to medieval lore, pelicans are so attentive to their chicks that mothers, when necessary, feed their young with their own blood. Because of this myth, the pelican became a symbol of Christ's self-sacrifice. This lectern from 1499 has a brass bird that looks just like other symbolic pelicans—shown stabbing itself with its own beak—except for one important difference: It looks like an eagle. Apparently, its creator had never come across an actual pelican.

• *Just past the end of the choir is...*

Mary's Chapel (Maria Kapel)

Inside the iron cage on the chapel's back wall is an old wood-and-iron chest that served as a safe for the church's cash and precious documents—such as those papers granting the power to sell forgiveness. See the board of keys for the many doors in this huge complex. Notice also the sarcophagi. Once filled with the "stinking rich," boxes like this were buried five deep below the church floor. Such high-density burying maximized the revenue generated by selling burial spots.

Foucault's Pendulum

In the north transept, a ball on a wire hangs from the ceiling (see the brass sphere in the far-right corner). When set in motion (by a church tour guide, mostly on Saturdays), it swings across a dial on the floor, re-creating physicist Léon Foucault's pendulum experiment in Paris in 1851. If it's swinging, stand here patiently and watch the earth rotate on its axis.

As the pendulum swings steadily back and forth, the earth rotates counterclockwise underneath it, making the pendulum appear to rotate clockwise around the dial. The earth rotates once every 24 hours, of course, but at Haarlem's latitude of 52 degrees, it makes the pendulum (appear to) sweep 360 degrees every 30 hours, 27 minutes (to knock over the bowling pin). Stand here for five minutes, and you'll see the earth move one degree.

As the world turns, find several small relief statues (in a niche on the right-hand wall) with beheaded bodies and defaced faces—victims of the 1566 Iconoclastic Fury, when angry Protestant extremists vandalized Dutch Catholic churches (as this once was).

• *Ten yards farther on, the shallow niche is the...*

Dog-Whipper's Chapel

In a sculpted relief (top of column at left end of chapel, above eye level), an angry man whips an angry dog while striding over another angry dog's head. Back when churches served as rainy-day marketplaces, this man's responsibility was to keep Haarlem's dogs out of the church.

The Organ

Even when silent, this organ impresses. Finished in 1738 by Amsterdam's Christian Muller, it features a mahogany-colored casing with tin pipes and gold trim, studded with statues of musicians and an eight-piece combo of angels. Lions on the top hold Haarlem's coat of arms—a sword, surrounded by stars, over a banner reading *Vicit Vim Virtus* ("Virtue Conquers Violence"). There are larger pipe organs in the world, but this is one of the best.

With three keyboards, a forest of pedals, and 65 stops (the knobs on either side of the keyboards), this magnificent organ produces an awesome majesty of sound. Picture 10-year-old Mozart at the controls of this 5,000-pipe sound machine. In 1766, he played Haarlem at the tail end of his triumphant, three-year whirlwind tour of Europe. He'd just returned from London, where he met J. C. Bach, the youngest son of Johann Sebastian Bach (1685-1750), the grandfather of organ music. Mozart had recently written several pieces inspired by Bach, and he may have tried them out here.

"Hal-le-lu-jah!" That famous four-note riff may have echoed around the church when Handel played here in 1740, the year before his famous oratorio, *Messiah,* debuted. The 20th-century organist/humanitarian Albert Schweitzer also performed here.

The organist sits unseen amid the pipes, behind the section that juts out at the bottom. While the bellows generate pressurized air, the organist presses a key, which opens a valve, admitting forced air through a pipe and out its narrow opening, producing a tone. An eight-foot-long pipe plays middle C. A four-foot-long pipe plays C exactly one octave up. A 20-foot pipe rumbles the rafters. With 5,068 pipes ranging from more than 20 feet tall to just a few inches, this organ can cover eight octaves (a piano plays seven), and each key can play a variety of sounds. By pulling one of the stops (such as "flute" or "trumpet"), the organist can channel the air into certain sets of pipes tuned to play together to mimic other instruments. For maximum power, you "pull out all the stops."
• *Cross in front of the organ to find the glass box holding a...*

Model of the Church

A hundred times smaller than the church itself, this model still took a thousand work-hours to build. See if you can spot the matchsticks, washers, screens, glue, wire, and paper clips used to make it.
• *Just beyond the model, to the left of the chapel with the green metal gate and above eye level, is...*

A Cannonball in the Wall

Duck! Placed here in 1573, this cannonball commemorates the city's finest hour: the Siege of Haarlem.

In the winter of 1572-1573, Holland rebelled against its Spanish oppressors. Haarlem proclaimed its alliance with William of Orange (and thus, independence from Spain). In response, the angry Spanish governor—camped in Amsterdam—laid siege to Haarlem. The winter was cold, food ran low, and the city was bombarded by Spanish cannons. Inside huddled 4,000 cold, hungry Calvinists. At one point, the city's women even joined the men on the barricades, brandishing kitchen knives.

But Spain had blockaded the Haarlem Lake (the Haarlemmermeer), and by June 12, 1573, Haarlem had to surrender. The Spanish rounded up 1,500 men (three-quarters of Haarlem's able-bodied male population) and executed them to send a message to the rest of the country. Still, Haarlem's brave seven-month stand against overwhelming odds became a kind of Dutch Alamo, inspiring their countrymen to fight on.

Following Haarlem's brave lead, other Dutch towns rebelled, including Amsterdam (see page 447). Though Holland and Spain would skirmish for another five decades, the battles soon moved southward, and Spanish troops would never again seriously penetrate the country's borders.

• *Back in the middle of the nave, returning to where you began, you'll pass the impressive wooden...*

Pulpit

Elaborately carved from oak in 1679, the pulpit is topped with a tower-shaped roof. Brass handrails snake down the staircase—serpents fleeing the word of God. In this simply decorated Protestant church, the pulpit is perhaps the most ornate element, directing worshippers' eyes to the speaker. During the Reformation, Protestants changed the worship service. As teaching became more important than ritual, the pulpit was given a higher profile.

• *This ends our tour—complete with pillar biters, dwarves and giants, a towering wall of organ pipes, and hanging ships. Who said, "When you've seen one Gothic church, you've seen them all"?*

FRANS HALS MUSEUM TOUR

Frans Hals (c. 1582-1666) is Haarlem's most famous son. He was a bold humanist who painted everyday people in their warts-and-all glory, a forerunner of Impressionist brushwork, a master of composition, and an articulate visual spokesman for his generation—the generation of Holland's Golden Age.

Stand eye-to-eye with life-size, lifelike portraits of Haarlem's citizens—brewers, preachers, workers, bureaucrats, and housewives. Take a close look at the people who built the Dutch Golden Age, and then watched it start to fade.

Orientation

Cost: €12.50, €15 combo-ticket with Teylers Museum (purchase at TI), sometimes more with special exhibits, includes audioguide.

If you are visiting more museums in the Netherlands, consider buying the €55 Museumkaart pass here. It covers entry to both the Frans Hals and Teylers museums in Haarlem, and lets you skip the ticket-buying line at some bigger sights, such as the Van Gogh Museum in Amsterdam (for more on sightseeing passes, including the Museumkaart, see page 29).

Hours: Tue-Sat 11:00-17:00, Sun 12:00-17:00, closed Mon.

Getting There: The museum is at Groot Heiligland 62, a delightful five-minute stroll from the main square.

Information: Frans Hals' masterpieces never leave Room 14 (and nearby rooms), but the other paintings can rotate—ask a guard if you can't locate them easily. The entire museum is thoughtfully described in English. Tel. 023/511-5775, www.franshalsmuseum.nl.

Length of This Tour: Allow one hour.

Cuisine Art: The Frans Hals Museum Café serves sandwiches and other simple food (daily 12:00-16:30, only drinks and dessert served after 15:30).

OVERVIEW

Frans Hals' paintings are just one part of the collection. The museum fancies itself as *the* museum of the Dutch Golden Age, offering you the rare opportunity of enjoying 17th-century art in a 17th-century building. Well-described exhibits unfold as the rectangular museum wraps around a peaceful central courtyard. The building's layout makes sense when you realize it was built as subsidized housing for poor old men (in 1610).

The Tour Begins

Your visit starts with an exhibit called "Haarlem in the 17th Century," showing Dutch slice-of-life paintings alongside short background stories on the issues and items that concerned everyday Dutch Golden Agers: tulips, trading, linen-weaving, militias, "women power," and beer. For those of us who weren't Dutch tradesmen in the 1600s, this well-done exhibit puts the rest of the museum's artwork in an interesting context.

• *From this room, find your way to Room 14. Circle the museum counterclockwise, through the art of Hals' predecessors and colleagues, to the back of the complex. Don't be shy about opening a door to the next wing; because of a new climate-control system, there are lots of closed doors here. You'll know you've arrived in the right place when you find yourself well-guarded by canvases full of companies of uniformed men. We'll start with the men in the bright red sashes.*

Banquet of the Officers of the St. George Civic Guard (1616)

In 1616, tiny Holland was the richest country on earth, and these Haarlem men are enjoying the fruits of their labor. The bright red sashes, the jaunty poses, the smiles, the rich food, the sweeping tilt of the flags...the exuberant spirit of the Dutch Golden Age. These weekend warriors have finished their ceremonial parade through town and hung their weapons on the wall, and now they sit down for a relaxed, post-show party.

The man in the middle (next to the flag-bearer, facing us) is about to carve the chicken, when the meal is interrupted. It's us, arriving late through the back door, and heads turn to greet us. Rosy-cheeked Nicolaes Woutersz van der Meer (see his portrait on page 290), hand on hip, turns around with a friendly look, while

Frans Hals Museum—Room 14

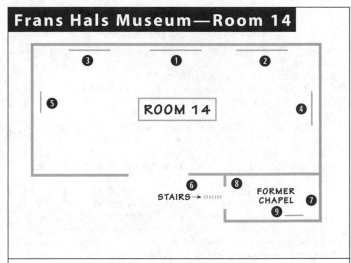

- ❶ Banquet of the Officers of the St. George Civic Guard (1616)
- ❷ Banquet of the Officers of the St. George Civic Guard (1627)
- ❸ Banquet of the Officers of the Civic Guard of St. Adrian (1627)
- ❹ Meeting of the Officers and Subalterns of the Civic Guard of St. Adrian (1633)
- ❺ Officers and Subalterns of the St. George Civic Guard (1639)
- ❻ Still Lifes
- ❼ Dollhouse
- ❽ Bed Curtain
- ❾ Flemish Proverbs

FRANS HALS MUSEUM

the man to the right, the colonel in charge, waves us in. Frans Hals knew these men well as friends and colleagues, since he himself was a lifelong member of this Civic Guard company.

This band of brothers is united by common gestures—two men have hands on hips, three turn their palms up, two plant their

Frans Hals (c. 1582-1666)

At age 10, Frans Hals, the son of a weaver, moved with his family to Haarlem. He would spend the rest of his life there, rarely traveling even to nearby Amsterdam.

His early years are known to us only through his paintings of taverns and drunks, musicians and actors, crafted in a free and colorful style (like the Rijksmuseum's *The Merry Drinker* on page 143). In 1610, he married and joined Haarlem's St. Luke's Guild of painters. In 1612, he was admitted to the prestigious St. George Civic Guard. In 1617, widowed Hals married again, producing (altogether) ten children, five of whom took up painting.

Hals' group portrait of the St. George Civic Guard (1616) put him on the map as Haarlem's premier portrait painter. For the next five decades, he abandoned the lighthearted slice-of-life scenes of his youth and dedicated himself to chronicling Haarlem's prosperous, middle-class world of businessmen and professionals—people he knew personally, as well as professionally.

Despite his success, Hals had trouble with money. In 1654, he had to sell his belongings to pay debts, and he fought poverty for the rest of his life. Commissions became scarce, as the public now preferred more elegant, flattering portraits. His final works (1650-1666) are dark and somber, with increasingly rough and simple brushwork.

In 1664, the city granted him a pension for his years of service. When he died two years later, his work quickly passed out of fashion, dismissed as mere portraiture. In the 1800s, the Impressionists rediscovered him, and today he's recognized for his innovations, craftsmanship, and unique style.

FRANS HALS MUSEUM

hands downward, three clutch wine glasses. But mostly, they're joined by the uniform sashes. The red sashes slant both left and right, perfectly forming opposing diagonals.

With this painting, Frans Hals broke the mold of stuffy group portraits. He relegates the traditional symbolic weapons to the shelf (upper right) and breaks up the traditional chorus line of soldiers by placing the men naturally around a table. Van der Meer sticks his elbow in our faces (another Hals trademark) to define a distinct foreground, while the flag-bearer stakes out the middle ground, and a window at the back opens up to a distant, airy background.

Then Hals sets the scene in motion. A guy on the left leans over to tell a joke to his friend. The dashing young flag-bearer in the middle turns back to listen to the bald-headed man. An ensign (standing, right side) enters and doffs his cap to Captain Van der Meer. And then we barge in, interrupting the banquet, but welcomed as one of the boys.

Banquet of the Officers of the St. George Civic Guard (1627)

A decade later, Hals painted the same militia again. Familiar faces appear (Captain Van der Meer is in the upper left), but most of the old men have been replaced by a crop of younger, battle-tested officers. These men had recently seen action in the Battle of Breda (1625), fighting for Dutch independence from Spain. The man in the center—facing us and turning his empty glass down to show he needs a refill—was a well-known Haarlem pub owner. (Find him again, in the same tan coat with blue sash, in the 1639 painting described later.)

The banquet looks spontaneous, but the men's poses were carefully planned. Hals painted the bodies first, then brought in the men one by one for their portraits. As colorful as these Civic Guard paintings appear, much of the canvas is black, white, or gray. Van Gogh marveled at Hals' ability to capture "27 shades of black."

Banquet of the Officers of the Civic Guard of St. Adrian (1627)

The men are bunched into two symmetrical groups, left and right, with a window in the back. The figures form a Y, with a tilted flag marking the right diagonal (echoed by several tilted ruffs), and a slanting row of heads forming the left diagonal (echoed by several slanting sashes). The diagonals meet at the back of the table, marking the center of the composition, where the two groups of men exchange food, drink, and meaningful eye contact.

Meeting of the Officers and Subalterns of the Civic Guard of St. Adrian (1633)

Six years later, Hals painted many of these same men gathered around an outdoor table. The horizontal row of faces is punctuated by three men standing sideways, elbows out. Again, the men are united by sashes that slant in (generally) the same direction and by repeated gestures—hands on hips, hands on hearts, and so on.

Civic Guard Portraits

The fathers of the men pictured in this room fought, suffered imprisonment, and died in the great Siege of Haarlem (1572-1573), which helped turn the tide against Spanish oppression. But their sons were bankers, merchants, traders, and sailors, boldly conquering Europe on the new frontier of capitalism. The Civic Guards became less of a militia, and more a social club for upwardly mobile men. Their feasts—huge eating and drinking binges, punctuated by endless toasts, poems, skits, readings, dirty limericks, and ceremonial courses—could last for days on end.

Standard Civic Guard portraits (like many of those in the Rijksmuseum in Amsterdam) always showed the soldiers in the same way—two neat rows of men, with everyone looking straight out, holding medieval weapons that tell us their ranks. It took master artists like Hals and Rembrandt to turn these boring visual documents into art.

Officers and Subalterns of the St. George Civic Guard (1639)

When 57-year-old Frans Hals painted this, his last Civic Guard portrait, he included himself among his St. George buddies. (Find Frans in the upper left, second from left, under the faint gray—number 19.)

As he got older, Hals refined and simplified his group-portrait style, using quieter colors, the classic two horizontal rows of soldiers, and the traditional symbolic weapons.

A decade after this was painted, Holland officially ended its war with Spain (Treaty of Munster, 1648), the Civic Guards lost their military purpose, businessmen preferred portraits showing themselves as elegant gentlemen rather than crusty soldiers, and the tradition of Civic Guard group portraits quickly died.

• *Backtrack and pause to enjoy the exquisite* **still lifes** *in Room 13. These lush paintings give us a sense of how good life is, and how important it is to embrace it before it all rots and falls away. Just after this room, look on your left for the five steps leading up to the...*

Former Chapel

Take a look inside. You'll find a **fancy dollhouse** *(poppenhuis)*, the hobby of the lady of the house (her portrait is on the left). Hand-

Frans Hals' Style

- Hals' forte is portraits. Of his 240 paintings, 195 are individual or group portraits, mostly of Haarlem's citizens.
- His paintings are life-size and realistic, capturing everyday people—even downright ugly people—without airbrushing out their blemishes or character flaws.
- Hals uses rough, Impressionistic brushwork, where a few thick, simple strokes blend at a distance to create details. He works quickly, often making the rough sketch the final, oil version.
- His stop-action technique captures the sitter in mid-motion. Aided by his rough brushwork, this creates a blur that suggests the person is still moving.
- Hals adds 3-D depth to otherwise horizontal, widescreen canvases. (Men with their elbows sticking out sometimes serve to define the foreground.)
- His canvases are unified by people wearing matching colors, using similar poses and gestures, and gathered in symmetrical groups.
- His paintings have a relaxed, lighthearted, even comical atmosphere. In group portraits, the subjects interact with one another. Individual portraits meet your eyes as if meeting an old friend.
- His works show nothing religious—no Madonnas, Crucifixions, angels, or Bible scenes. If anything, he imbues everyday objects with heavenly beauty and grants ordinary people the status of saints.

made by the finest local craftsmen, this delicately crafted dollhouse offers a glimpse of wealthy 18th-century living.

The exquisite **bed curtain,** brought back from New England, decorated the bed of a wealthy Dutch family who lived in colonial America. It's embroidered with bulb flowers known during the 17th century—and well-described in English.

On the wall is *Flemish Proverbs (Vlaamse Spreekwoorden),* a fun  painting that shows 72 charming Flemish scenes representing different folk sayings. (It's a copy of a 17th-century work by Pieter Brueghel the Younger.) Pick up the chart to identify these clever bits of everyday wisdom. True to form, this piece of Flemish art isn't preachy religious art or political propaganda; rather, it shares the simple, decent morals of these hardworking people.

• *Continue counterclockwise around the museum. When you reach the hallway that is Room 17, look for the...*

Portrait of Jacobus Zaffius (1611)

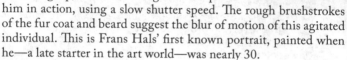

Arr-r-r-r-rh! This fierce, intense, rough-hewn man is not a pirate, but a priest, the rogue leader of an outlawed religion in Haarlem—Catholicism. In the 1600s, Haarlem was a Protestant town in the midst of a war against Catholic Spain, and local Catholics were guilty by association. But Zaffius refused to be silenced. He turns to glare and snarl at the Protestant town fathers. He was so personally imposing that the city tolerated his outspokenness.

The face jumps out from a background of neutral gray-brown-black. His features are alive—head turning, mouth twisting, face wrinkling up, beard bristling. Hals captures him in action, using a slow shutter speed. The rough brushstrokes of the fur coat and beard suggest the blur of motion of this agitated individual. This is Frans Hals' first known portrait, painted when he—a late starter in the art world—was nearly 30.

• *Make a left into Room 18 to see the...*

Portraits of Nicolaes Woutersz van der Meer and his wife, Cornelia Claesdr Vooght (1631)

Hals knew Nicolaes van der Meer, a fellow Civic Guard lodge member, personally. Van der Meer was a brewer, an important post in a city where average beer consumption was six pints a day per person (man, woman, and child). He was also the mayor, so his pose is official and dignified, larger than life-size. But the face is pure Dutch Golden Age—red-cheeked and healthy, confident and intelligent, his even gaze tinged with wisdom. This mayor kept a steady hand on the tiller of Haarlem's ship of state.

The face is the focus of this otherwise messy painting. The ruffled collar is a tangle of simple, figure-eight swirls of white paint; the brocaded coat is a patchwork of white lines; and the lace cuffs are a few broad outlines. But out of the rough brushwork and somber background, Van der Meer's crystal-clear eyes meet ours. The finely etched crow's-feet around his eyes suggest that Hals had seen this imposing man break into a warm smile. Hey, I'd vote for him as my mayor.

The companion painting shows Van der Meer's companion,

his wife, **Cornelia.** Husband-and-wife portraits were hung together—notice that they share the same background, and the two figures turn in toward each other. Still, both people are looking out at us, not clinging to each other, suggesting mature partners more than lovey-dovey newlyweds. Married couples in Golden Age Holland divvied up the work—men ran the business, women ran the home—and prided themselves on their mutual independence. (Even today, in progressive Holland, fewer women join the workforce than in many other industrial nations.) Cornelia's body is as imposing as her husband's, with big, manly hands and a practical, slightly suspicious look. The intricate work in her ruff collar tells us that Hals certainly could sweat the details when it suited his purpose.

Regents of the St. Elisabeth Hospital of Haarlem (1641)

These aren't the Dutch Masters cigar boys, though it looks like Rembrandt's famous (and later) *De Staalmeesters* (described in the Amsterdam Rijksmuseum Tour chapter). It's a board meeting, where five men in black hats and black suits with lace collars and

cuffs—the Dutch Golden Age power suit—sit around a table in a brown room.

Pretty boring stuff, but Hals was hired to paint their portraits, and he does his best. Behind the suits, he captures five distinct men (this photo shows three of them). The man on the far left is pondering the universe or raising a belch. The man on the right (facing us) looks like the classic Dutch Golden Age poster boy, with moustache, goatee, ruddy cheeks, and long hair. The middle guy is nearly clean-shaven. Hals links these unique faces with one of his trademark techniques—similar poses and gestures. The burping man and the goateed man are a mirror image of the same pose—leaning on the table, hand on chest. Several have cupped hands; several have hands laid flat, or on their chests, or on the table. And the one guy keeps working on that burp.

• *Continue to Room 19. On the wall straight ahead are the...*

Regents of the Old Men's Almshouse (1664)

These men look tired. So was Holland. So was Hals. At 82, Hals, despite years of success, was poor and dependent on the charity of the city, which granted him a small pension.

He was hired to paint the board of directors of the Old Men's

Almshouse, located here in the building that now houses the Frans Hals Museum. Though Hals himself never lived in the almshouse, he fully understood what it was to be penniless and have to rely on money doled out by men like these.

The portrait is unflattering, drained of color. Somber men dressed in black peer out of a shadowy room. These men were trying to administer a dwindling budget to house and feed an aging population. Holland's Golden Age was losing its luster.

The style is nearly Impressionistic—collars, cuffs, and gloves rendered with a few messy brushstrokes of paint. Hands and faces are a patchwork of light and dark splotches. Despite the sketchiness, each face captures the man's essence.

Historians speculate that this unflattering portrait was Hals' revenge on tightwad benefactors, but the fact is that the regents were satisfied with their portrait. By the way, the man just to the right of center isn't drunk, but suffering from facial paralysis. To the end, Hals respected unvarnished reality.

• *Directly behind you, find the...*

Regentesses of the Old Men's Almshouse (1664)

These women ran the women's wing of the almshouse, located across the street. Except for a little rouge on the women's pale faces, this canvas is almost a study in gray and black, as Hals pared his palette down to the bare essentials. The faces are subtle variations on old age. Only the woman on the right resolutely returns our gaze.

The man who painted this was old, poor, out of fashion, in failing health, perhaps bitter, and dying. In contrast with the lively group scenes of Hals' youth, these individuals stand forever isolated. They don't look at one another, each lost in her own thoughts, perhaps contemplating mortality (or stifling belches). Their only link to one another is the tenuous, slanting line formed by their hands, leading to the servant who enters the room with a mysterious message.

Could that message be...death? Or just that this tour is over?

HAARLEM SLEEPING, EATING & MORE

Contents

Jet-lagged travelers arriving in the Netherlands should consider Haarlem a convenient home base: There's fast-and-easy access to Amsterdam or Schiphol Airport, and other side-trips are a quick train trip away. This chapter describes Haarlem's best places to sleep, eat, and relax at night, along with transportation connections.

Sleeping in Haarlem

The helpful Haarlem TI can nearly always find you a €32 bed in a private home, and their website (www.haarlem.nl) has a booking system with good last-minute deals on hotels (€5.50/person fee, plus a cut of your host's money, two-night minimum; you may get a better price by booking directly with accommodations). Nearly every Dutch person you'll encounter speaks English.

Haarlem is most crowded in April, particularly on Easter weekend (April 3-6 in 2015, March 25-28 in 2016), during the flower parade (April 22-26 in 2015, check with TI or http://bloemencorso-bollenstreek.nl for 2016 dates), on King's Day (April 27), and in May, July, and August (especially during Haarlem's jazz festival on the third weekend of August). Also see the list of holidays in the appendix.

Sleep Code

Abbreviations   **(€1 = about $1.40, country code: 31)**
S = Single, **D** = Double/Twin, **T** = Triple, **Q** = Quad, **b** = bathroom, **s** = shower only.
Price Rankings
  $$$ Higher Priced—Most rooms €95 or more.
   $$ Moderately Priced—Most rooms between €60-95.
    $ Lower Priced—Most rooms €60 or less.
Nearly everyone speaks English. Unless otherwise noted,
credit cards are accepted, breakfast is included, and Wi-Fi is
generally free. Rates may not include the €3 per person, per
night hotel tax. Prices change; verify current rates online or by
email. For the best prices, always book directly with the hotel.

To avoid excessive street noises, forgo views for a room in the back. Hotels and the TI have a useful parking brochure.

IN THE CENTER
Hotels and B&Bs

$$$ Stempels Hotel, modern yet elegant, is located in a renovated 300-year-old building. With bare floors, comfy high-quality beds, and minimalist touches in its 17 rooms, what it lacks in warmth it makes up for in style and value. Double-paned windows help keep down the noise—it's just a block east of Grote Markt, with a bustling brasserie and bar downstairs (standard Sb-€98, standard Db-€112-150, pricier rooms and suites available, breakfast-€12.50, guest computer, Wi-Fi, elevator, Klokhuisplein 9, tel. 023/512-3910, www.stempelsinhaarlem.nl, info@stempelsinhaarlem.nl).

$$$ Hotel Lion D'Or, across from the train station, is a classy 34-room business hotel with all the professional comforts and pleasingly posh decor (Db-€135-150, Fri-Sat Db-€110-125, extra bed-€15, check website for special deals, 8 percent Rick Steves discount with 2-night stay if you book directly with hotel, air-con, elevator, guest computer, Wi-Fi, Kruisweg 34, tel. 023/532-1750, www.hotelliondor.nl, reservations@hotelliondor.nl, friendly Dirk Pauw).

$$$ Brasss Haarlem rents upscale suites in a turn-of-the-century building once home to Haarlem's first department store. Each cushy room is named after a fish and has an open-floor plan with a see-through bathroom (standard Db-€100-150, deluxe Db-€175-195, largest suite with in-room sauna-€275, in-room espresso machine, air-con, Wi-Fi, Korte Veerstraat 40, tel. 023/542-7804, www.brassshaarlem.nl, info@brassshaarlem.nl). They also run the nearby **$$$ Haarlem Hotelsuites**, offering cozy apartment-style units with kitchens (Db-€100-120, Qb-€145, Wi-Fi, check-in at

Brasss Haarlem, www.haarlem-hotelsuites.nl, haarlemhotelsuites@gmail.com).

$$$ Ambassador City Centre Hotel, with 46 comfortable rooms in a big plain hotel, is located just behind the Grote Kerk. If you're willing to trade some street noise for amazing church views, ask for a room in the front (Db-€100, often less off-season, breakfast buffet-€13.50, guest computer, Wi-Fi, Oude Groenmarkt 20, tel. 023/512-5300, www.acc-hotel.nl, info@acc-hotel.nl). They also run **$$ Hotel Joops,** with 32 rooms, a block away (rooms are €10 cheaper; studios and apartments with kitchenettes for 2-4 people-€110-140 depending on season and number of people).

$$ Hotel Amadeus, on Grote Markt, is charming and has 15 small, bright, and basic rooms. Front rooms with views of the square are noisy, while the back rooms are relatively quiet. Breakfast is served in a trendy restaurant overlooking the main square—a great place to watch the town greet a new day. Mike and Inez take good care of their guests (Sb-€60, Db-€85, check website for special deals, 6 percent Rick Steves discount when booking online with discount code RS1516, Wi-Fi, Grote Markt 10—from square it's a steep climb to lounge, check in at ground-floor restaurant where there's an elevator accessible during open hours, tel. 023/532-4530, www.amadeus-hotel.com, info@amadeus-hotel.com).

$$ Hotel Malts rents 14 modern, bright, and fresh rooms in a central location for a good price. Owners Henk and Annemarie have a wealth of Haarlem knowledge and sit with each guest over coffee to share the town's secrets (small Db-€79-85, standard Db-€95, big Db with sleeper sofa-€105, check website for best prices, honor bar, no elevator, Wi-Fi, Zijlstraat 58, tel. 023/551-2385, www.maltshotel.nl, info@maltshotel.nl).

Rooms in Restaurants

These places are all run as sidelines by restaurants, and you'll know it by the style of service and rooms. Lobbies are in the restaurant, and there are no public spaces. Still, they are handy and—for Haarlem—inexpensive.

$$ Hotel Carillon overlooks the town square and comes with bell-tower chimes and a little traffic. With run-down public spaces and st-e-e-e-p stairs, it's an old-school, over-the-restaurant place. The rooms themselves, however, are freshly updated and pleasant. The front rooms come with more street noise and great town-square views (tiny loft S-€42, Sb-€60, D-€65, Db-€80-90, Tb-€120, Qb-€150, 5 percent Rick Steves discount if you ask when you reserve and show book on arrival, no elevator, Wi-Fi, Grote Markt 27, tel. 023/531-0591, www.hotelcarillon.com, info@hotelcarillon.com, owners Ja Qing and Chien Yu).

$$ Die Raeckse Hotel, family-run and friendly, is not as cen-

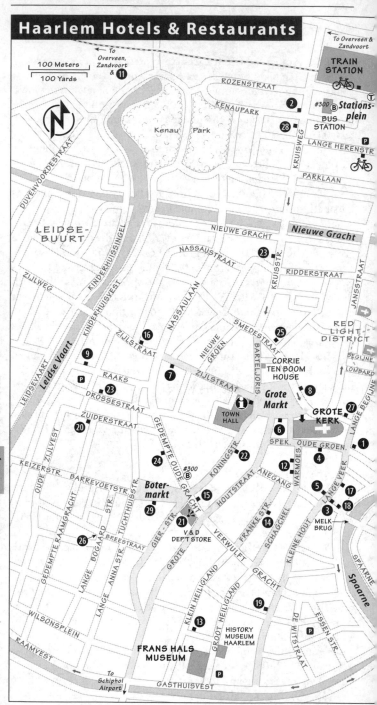

Haarlem Hotels & Restaurants

To Overveen & Zandvoort

TRAIN STATION

To Overveen, Zandvoort & ⑪

100 Meters
100 Yards

ROZENSTRAAT

KENAUPARK

②

#500 Ⓑ Stations-plein

BUS STATION

Kenau Park

㉘

LANGE HERENSTR

KRUISWEG

PARKLAAN

DUVENVOORDESTRAAT

LEIDSE-BUURT

NIEUWE GRACHT

Nieuwe Gracht

ZIJLWEG

KINDERHUISSINGEL

KINDERHUISVEST

NASSAUSTRAAT

㉓

RIDDERSTRAAT

JANSSTRAAT

KRUISSTR.

Leidse Vaart

LEIDSEVAART

ZIJLSTRAAT

⑯

NASSAULAAN

NIEUWE GROEN

SMEDESTRAAT

㉕

RED LIGHT DISTRICT

BEGIJNE

ZIJLSTRAAT

BARTELJORIS

CORRIE TEN BOOM HOUSE

LOMBARD

⑨

⑦

Grote Markt

⑧

GROTE KERK

LANGE BEGIJNE

㉗

RAAKS

㉓

DROSSESTRAAT

ZUIDERSTRAAT

GEDEMPTE OUDE GRACHT

TOWN HALL

⑥

SPEK.

OUDE GROEN.

①

⑳

KONINGSTR.

㉒

WARMOES

⑫

ANEGANG

④

OUDE ZIJLVEST

KEIZERSTR.

BARREVOETSTR.

TUCHTHUISSTR.

#500 Ⓑ

Boter-markt

㉔

⑮

HOUTSTRAAT

FRANKE STR.

SCHAGCHEL

KLEINE HOUT

⑤

⑰

LANGE VEER

③

⑱

MELK BRUG

Spaarne

GIER-STR.

BREESTRAAT

LANGE BOGAARD STR.

㉙

㉑

V & D DEP'T STORE

⑭

GEDEMPTE RAAMGRACHT

㉖

LANGE ANNA STR.

GROTE

VERWULFT

GRACHT

DE WITSTRAAT

ESSEN STR.

Spaarne

WILSONSPLEIN

KLEIN HEILIGLAND

GROOT HEILIGLAND

⑲

⑬

HISTORY MUSEUM HAARLEM

RAAMVEST

FRANS HALS MUSEUM

To Schiphol Airport

GASTHUISVEST

HAARLEM SLEEPING, EATING & MORE

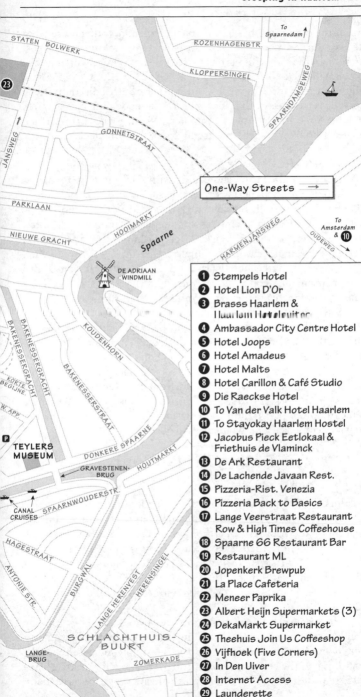

One-Way Streets →

1 Stempels Hotel
2 Hotel Lion D'Or
3 Brasss Haarlem & Haarlem Hotelsuites
4 Ambassador City Centre Hotel
5 Hotel Joops
6 Hotel Amadeus
7 Hotel Malts
8 Hotel Carillon & Café Studio
9 Die Raeckse Hotel
10 To Van der Valk Hotel Haarlem
11 To Stayokay Haarlem Hostel
12 Jacobus Pieck Eetlokaal & Friethuis de Vlaminck
13 De Ark Restaurant
14 De Lachende Javaan Rest.
15 Pizzeria-Rist. Venezia
16 Pizzeria Back to Basics
17 Lange Veerstraat Restaurant Row & High Times Coffeehouse
18 Spaarne 66 Restaurant Bar
19 Restaurant ML
20 Jopenkerk Brewpub
21 La Place Cafeteria
22 Meneer Paprika
23 Albert Heijn Supermarkets (3)
24 DekaMarkt Supermarket
25 Theehuis Join Us Coffeeshop
26 Vijfhoek (Five Corners)
27 In Den Uiver
28 Internet Access
29 Launderette

HAARLEM SLEEPING, EATING & MORE

tral as the others and has less character and more traffic noise—but its 21 rooms are decent and comfortable. Quiet rooms in back cost more than the noisy rooms on the street—but they're worth it (Sb-€60, smaller Db-€75-85, big Db-€85-95, Tb-€120, Qb-€155, €5/night discount for 2-night stay, ask for Rick Steves discount if you book direct and show this book on arrival—good only Nov-March, free but time-limited guest computer, Wi-Fi, Raaks Straat 1, tel. 023/532-6629, www.die-raeckse.nl, info@hoteldieraeckse.com).

NEAR HAARLEM
$$ Van der Valk Hotel Haarlem, with 315 modern rooms, is sterile but a good value for drivers. It sits in an industrial zone a 20-minute walk from the center, on the road to the airport (Db-€70-140, Tb-€85, higher rates for renovated rooms and suites, breakfast-€13, elevator, Wi-Fi, free parking, laundry service, free fitness center, reasonable hotel restaurant, Toekanweg 2, tel. 023/536-7500, www.hotelhaarlem.nl, haarlem@valk.com). Bus #300 conveniently connects the hotel with the train station, Grote Markt, and the airport (every 10 minutes, stop: Europaweg).

   $ Stayokay Haarlem Hostel, completely renovated and with all the youth-hostel comforts, has some simple doubles for €49-80 (also €20-30 beds in 4- and 6-bed dorms, €2.50 less for members, includes sheets and breakfast, save by booking on their website, pay guest computer, Wi-Fi, laundry service, reception open 8:00-23:00, Jan Gijzenpad 3, two miles from Haarlem station—take bus #2 from station, direction: Haarlem-Noord; or a 10-minute walk from Santpoort Zuid train station, tel. 023/537-3793, www.stayokay.com/haarlem, haarlem@stayokay.com).

Eating in Haarlem

RESTAURANTS
Jacobus Pieck Eetlokaal is popular with locals for its fine-value "global cuisine," good salads, and unpretentious flair. Sit in the peaceful garden courtyard, at a sidewalk table, or in the romantically cozy interior. The Oriental Peak Salad is a perennial favorite, and the dish of the day (*dagschotel,* €12.50) always sells out (great €7 sandwiches at lunch, Tue-Sat 11:00-16:00 & 17:00-22:00, closed Sun-Mon, cash only, Warmoesstraat 18, behind church, tel. 023/532-6144).

   De Ark Restaurant, a neighborhood bar, has been run by Frank for 40 years. There's nothing fancy here, just good-quality Dutch and French cuisine at fair prices—simply review the blackboard. Eat at the convivial bar for fun, or upstairs for more privacy (€15-18 plates, €19 three-course meal, always veggie options, daily

17:00-22:00, Nieuw Heiligland 3, around corner from Frans Hals Museum, tel. 023/531-1078).

De Lachende Javaan ("The Laughing Javanese") is a long-established Indonesian place serving a memorable *rijsttafel* (€23-28, Tue-Sun 17:00-22:00, closed Mon, Frankestraat 27, tel. 023/532-8792). For tips on Indonesian food and enjoying a *rijsttafel*, see page 214.

Pizzeria-Ristorante Venezia, run for 25 years by the same Italian family from Bari, is *the* place to go for pizza or pasta (€8-14 choices, daily 13:00-23:00, facing V&D department store at Verwulft 7, tel. 023/531-7753). Sit outdoors for quality people-watching, or indoors at a well-worn table.

Pizzeria Back to Basics serves a small menu of authentic wood-fired pizza and pasta. *Maestro* Francesco and his family from Naples use all-organic ingredients (€9-15 pizzas and pastas, €4/ glass organic wine, Tue-Sun 11:30-15:00 & 17:00-23:00, closed Mon, Zijlstraat 35, tel. 023/202-5125).

Lange Veerstraat Restaurant Row: If you don't know what you want to eat, stroll the delightful Lange Veerstraat behind the church and survey a fun range of restaurants (from cheap falafels to Cuban, and much more), including these favorites:

Visrestaurant Barend, run by chef and owner Barend, serves traditional seafood in a warm, inviting dining room with a few streetside tables. Try the chowder—an old family recipe—followed by the *sliptong* (sole) prepared as the chef's grandfather made it (€7-10 starters, €16-20 main courses, Wed-Sun 17:30-21:00, Fri-Sat until 22:00, closed Mon-Tue, Lange Veerstraat 15, tel. 023/532-8694).

Mr. and Mrs. Food and Wine—where Mark churns out thoughtful, locally sourced €9-12 small plates while his wife Corina tends to the wine list—has a rustic-modern dining space and a few outdoor tables. Wines are just €5 a glass, and Corina will help find a perfect pairing (Tue-Sat 17:00-22:00, closed Sun-Mon, Lange Veerstraat 4, tel. 023/531-5935).

La Plume Restaurant steakhouse is noisy, with a happy, local, and carnivorous crowd enjoying the candlelit scene. The relaxing outdoor seating faces the church and a lively pedestrian street (€20-25 meals, daily 17:00-23:00, *satay* and ribs are favorites, Lange Veerstraat 1, tel. 023/531-3202, www.la-plume.nl).

On the Spaarne River Canal: Haarlem seems to turn its back on its river with most of the eating energy a couple of blocks away. To enjoy a meal with a nice canal view, consider the **Spaarne 66 Restaurant Bar.** The Lemmers girls (a mom and her daughters) run this cozy eatery, with a woody, old-time interior and fine outdoor canalside seating (light €8 lunches, €20 Mediterranean/ Dutch dinner plates, €31.50 three-course fixed-price meal, daily in summer 10:00-23:45, closed Mon-Tue in winter, Spaarne 66, tel. 023/551-3800).

Dressy Splurge: At **Restaurant ML,** expert chef Mark Gratama serves chichi French-fusion cuisine in an elegant 17th-century dining room. This Michelin-rated restaurant offers four- to seven-course tasting menus starting at about €60 (€25 starters, €35 main courses, Tue-Sat 18:00-22:00, Wed-Fri also 12:00-14:00, closed Sun-Mon, enter through nondescript door at Kleine Houtstraat 70, tel. 023/534-5343).

Trendy Brewpub: While beer-drinking is a religion in Belgium, it's also getting that way in Haarlem, where the Jopen brewery has converted a church into a flashy, popular gastropub called **Jopenkerk.** With 18 brews on tap, including a *Hoppenbier* from a 1501 recipe, this is a beer lover's mecca. Budget pub grub is served on the ground floor, or try the upstairs restaurant for more elegant fare (€8-10 burgers, salads, and quiche in the pub, €15-23 main dishes in the restaurant, daily 10:00-24:00, Gedempte Voldersgracht 2, tel. 023/533-4114).

BUDGET OPTIONS

La Place is a snazzy chain cafeteria that dishes up fresh, healthy budget food. Sit on the top floor or the roof garden of the V&D department store with Haarlem's best view. If you're too hungry to ride six floors of escalators, they offer similar food in the ground-floor café (Mon 12:00-19:00, Tue-Sat 10:00-19:00, Thu until 21:00, Sun 12:00-18:00, Grote Houtstraat 70, on corner of Gedempte Oude Gracht, tel. 023/515-8700).

Friethuis de Vlaminck is your best bet for a cone of old-fashioned, fresh Flemish-style fries (€2, daily 11:00-19:00, until 21:00 on Thu, Warmoesstraat 3, behind church, tel. 061/271-1618). Ali offers a dazzling array of sauces. With his help, you can be adventurous.

For Families: **Meneer Paprika** ("Mr. Pepper") is a fun toy store with a little café (serving snacks and sandwiches), an inviting play area, and rental bikes with child seats available (café open Sun 12:00-17:00, Mon-Sat 9:00-17:00, shop usually open one hour later than café, Koningstraat 19, about halfway between main square and V&D department store, tel. 023-202-3268, www.meneerpaprika.nl).

Supermarkets: **Albert Heijn** has three convenient locations; all are cash only. One is in the train station (Mon-Fri 6:30-21:00, Sat 10:00-21:00, Sun 9:00-21:00); another is at Kruisstraat 10 (Mon-Sat 8:00-22:00, Sun 12:00-18:00); and their largest store is near the river and recommended Jopenkerk pub at Drossestraat 11 (Mon-Sat 7:00-22:00, Sun 12:00-18:00). The **DekaMarkt** is a few blocks west of Grote Markt (Mon-Sat 8:00-20:00, Thu-Fri until

Marijuana in Haarlem

Haarlem is a laid-back place for observing the Dutch approach to recreational marijuana. The town is dotted with about a

dozen coffeeshops, where pot is sold and smoked by relaxed, noncriminal types. These easy-going coffeeshops are more welcoming than they may feel—bartenders understand that Yankee travelers might feel a bit out of their element and are happy to answer questions.

If you don't like the smell of pot, avoid places sporting wildly painted walls; plants in the windows; or Rastafarian yellow, red, and green colors. The following two shops are inviting and particularly friendly to American visitors:

The tiny **Theehuis Join Us**, which feels like a hippie teahouse, was Haarlem's first coffeeshop (c. 1984). Along with a global selection of pot, it has 50 varieties of tea on the menu and a friendly staff. The staff is happy to roll you a €2.50-3.50 joint of your choice (daily 13:00-22:00, Fri-Sat until 24:00, a block off Grote Markt at Smedestraat 25).

High Times, with a living-room ambience and loaner bongs, offers smokers 12 varieties of joints in racks behind the bar (neatly pre-packed in trademarked "Joint Packs," €3-4.50, Mon-Fri 8:00-23:00, Sat from 9:00, Sun from 11:00, free Internet access for customers, Lange Veerstraat 47, www.coffee-shophightimes.nl). Across the street, at Crackers Pub, you can see what too much alcohol does to people.

21:00, Sun 12:00-18:00, Gedempte Oudegracht 54, near V&D department store).

Nightlife in Haarlem

Haarlem's evening scene is great. Consider four basic zones: Grote Markt in the shadow of the Grote Kerk; Lange Veerstraat; Boter Grote Markt; and Vijfhoek (Five Corners).

Grote Markt is lined with trendy bars that seem made for nursing a drink—**Café Studio** is generally the hot spot for a drink here (at Grote Markt 25); I'd also duck into the dark interior of **In Den Uiver** (near the Grote Kerk entry at Riviervischmarkt 13, live jazz on Tue twice a month). Lange Veerstraat (behind the Grote Kerk) is colorful and bordered with lively spots. Boter Grote Markt is more convivial and local, as it's less central and away from the tourists—try the nearby **Jopenkerk** brewpub (described earlier). Vijfhoek, named for the five lanes that converge here, is incredibly charming, although it has only one pub (with plenty of drinks, bar snacks, a relaxed crowd, and good indoor or outdoor seating). Also worth exploring is the area from this cutest corner in town to the New Church (Nieuwe Kerk), a couple of blocks away. If you want a more high-powered scene, Amsterdam is just 20 minutes away by train.

Haarlem Connections

For general tips about public transportation in the Netherlands—including types of trains, reading timetables, and how and where to buy tickets—see the appendix. If you take the train from Amsterdam to Haarlem, see page 272 for a train-window tour of the countryside.

From Haarlem by Train to: Zandvoort (2/hour, 10 minutes), **Amsterdam** (8/hour, 20 minutes), **Leiden** (4/hour, 20 minutes), **The Hague/Den Haag** (4/hour, 40 minutes), **Delft** (2/hour, 40 minutes), **Rotterdam** (6/hour, 1 hour, some with transfer in Amsterdam), **Utrecht** (4/hour, 50 minutes, transfer in Amsterdam), **Hoorn** (2/hour, 1 hour, more with change in Amsterdam Sloterdijk), **Alkmaar** (2/hour, 35 minutes), **Brussels** (hourly, 3.25 hours, transfer in Rotterdam), **Bruges/Brugge** (hourly, 3.5-4 hours, 2-3 changes—avoid Thalys connections if traveling with a rail pass).

From Haarlem by Bus to Aalsmeer: Connexxion bus #140 connects Haarlem to bus #172, which goes to the flower auction in Aalsmeer (4/hour, 1 hour, see "Getting There" on page 372).

To Schiphol Airport: Your best option is the **bus** (4-10/hour, 40 minutes, €4—buy ticket from driver, bus #300). For most of the trip, this bus travels on its own limited-access roadway—what transit wonks call a "busway." To catch the bus from the middle of Haarlem, head to the Centrum/Verwulft stop, near the V&D department store. To catch it from the train station, look for the "A" bus stop marked *R Net*. You can also get there by **train** (6/hour, 30-40 minutes, transfer at Amsterdam-Sloterdijk station) or **taxi** (about €30-40).

DELFT

DELFT ORIENTATION AND SIGHTS

Peaceful as a Vermeer painting and as lovely as its porcelain, Delft has a special soul. It feels like an idyllic mini-Amsterdam...urban Holland with training wheels. Enjoy this typically Dutch, "I could live here" town best by simply wandering around, munching syrup waffles, people-watching, and daydreaming on the canal bridges. If you're eager for some sightseeing, visit a pair of churches, learn more about favorite son Vermeer, or tour the famous porcelain factory.

Think of Delft as an alternative to Haarlem: a low-key, mid-sized city with fast and easy connections to big cities (Rotterdam or The Hague). And, laced with tranquil and picturesque canals, Delft would easily win the cuteness contest. If you love Vermeer's quiet, exquisite paintings, you understand why it's said that the painter's muse was his hometown of Delft.

PLANNING YOUR TIME

Delft works wonderfully as a side-trip by train from Amsterdam (one hour) or Haarlem (40 minutes), or as an overnight stop. If you spend the night anywhere in the Netherlands outside the capital, make it Delft.

Strategically located along the train line between Amsterdam and Belgium, Delft is within very easy side-tripping distance of both The Hague (30 minutes by tram) and Rotterdam (15 minutes by train)—and its canalside charm makes it a far more pleasant place to stay than those two bustling cities.

Whether side-tripping or home-basing, for a busy day of contrasts, visit both Delft and one of its big neighboring cities. In the morning, take in The Hague's impressive Mauritshuis collection (with a world-famous Vermeer) or Rotterdam's modern architecture, busy harbor, and urban vibrancy. Then continue to Delft to visit its churches, Vermeer Center, and Royal Dutch Delftware Manufactory (closes at 17:00)...or to simply mellow out by a canal.

Delft Overview

Delft feels much smaller than its population of 95,000. Squeezed between the two giant cities of Rotterdam and The Hague, locals describe Delft as a "small town."

Nearly everything of interest (except the porcelain factories) is contained within Delft's almost perfectly oval-shaped, canal-laced historic core. The vast Markt (Market Square), with the tall and skinny spire of the New Church, marks the center of the Old Town. A couple of blocks to the southeast is the lively, restaurant-lined Beestenmarkt. You could walk from one end of the Old Town to the other in about 15 minutes.

TOURIST INFORMATION

This TI is a tourist's dream. Pick up the good free brochure, which includes a map, or just get the map separately (daily 10:00-16:00, sometimes later, free Internet access and Wi-Fi, tucked around the right side of the New Church and the Markt at Kerkstraat 3, tel. 015/215-4051, www.delft.com); they'll store baggage for free for day-trippers if the lockers at the train station are closed. If you plan to visit the Royal Dutch Delftware Manufactory, pick up a discount coupon here (may also be available at your hotel).

Walking Tours: The TI sells a brochure describing a pleasant self-guided walking tour (€4); it also has a €2 "Vermeer Trail" pamphlet. In the summer, the TI offers a €12.50 deal that includes a one-hour walking tour and a one-hour canal-boat trip (Easter-Sept Sun-Fri at 11:30; on Sat it's just the one-hour walk—no boat trip—at 12:30 for €6.50).

ARRIVAL IN DELFT

By Train: Delft's train station has been undergoing an extensive reconstruction and is scheduled to be fully open sometime in 2015. If the work's still in progress when you visit, just follow signs to make your way into town. Lockers may be unavailable because of the construction—if so, you can leave bags for free at the TI.

DELFT

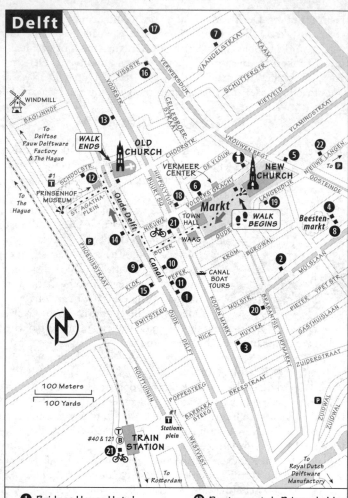

Delft

WINDMILL

To Delftse
Pauw Delftware
Factory
& The Hague

WALK
ENDS

OLD
CHURCH

VERMEER
CENTER

NEW
CHURCH

Markt

WALK
BEGINS

Beesten-
markt

#1
PRINSENHOF
MUSEUM

To The
Hague

TOWN
HALL

WAAG

CANAL
BOAT
TOURS

100 Meters
100 Yards

#40 & 121

TRAIN
STATION

#1
Stations
plein

To
Rotterdam

To
Royal Dutch
Delftware
Manufactory

❶ Bridges House Hotel
❷ Hotel Johannes Vermeer
❸ Hotel Leeuwenbrug
❹ Hotel de Koophandel
❺ Hotel de Emauspoort
❻ Jorplace City Hostel
❼ Hotel de Plataan
❽ Spijshuis de Dis Rest.
❾ Kleyweg's Stads Koffyhuis
❿ Restaurant Matties
⓫ Rossio Restaurant
⓬ Restaurant de Prinsenkelder
⓭ De V Pub
⓮ Burgerz
⓯ Frito Misto
⓰ Café de Pelicaan
⓱ Eetcafé de Verbeelding
⓲ Van der Eyk Visbanken
⓳ Daily Wok
⓴ Supermarket
㉑ Bike Rentals (2)
㉒ Laundry

DELFT

Track 1 typically serves northbound trains (toward The Hague, Leiden, Haarlem, and Amsterdam), while track 2 serves southbound trains (Rotterdam, Belgium). From the train station, it's about a 15-minute walk to the Markt at the center of the Old Town: Exit through the construction mess, walk across the canal, then continue into town, following yellow signs for *Centrum*.

If your primary interest in Delft is the famous Royal Dutch Delftware porcelain factory, it's more direct to catch bus #40 or #121 straight there from the station rather than heading downtown first (as there's no good public-transit connection from downtown): Find the bus stop on the far (west) side of the tracks, away from the construction. Or walk to the factory (about 20 minutes).

For now, the taxi stand is also located on the west side of the station.

By Car: Drivers take the Delft exit #9 off the A-13 expressway. Don't attempt to park within the Old Town; that's only allowed with a permit. Instead, use one of the three parking garages that ring the old town—Marktgarage (east end, at Willem Naghelstraat 1), Phoenixgarage (west end, at Phoenixstraat 29), and Zuidpoortgarage (south end, at Zuidwal 14). They're each about equidistant from the Markt (€14/24 hours, higher per-hour rates for shorter time periods, www.parkingdelft.nl/en).

HELPFUL HINTS

Laundry: Rein-Tex offers fast and affordable full-service laundering just off of the Markt, beyond the New Church (€12 wash, dry, and fold, same-day service usually possible if you drop it off in the morning, self-serve a few euros less, Mon-Fri 9:00-18:00, Sat 9:00-17:00, closed Sun, Nieuwe Langendijk 4a, tel. 015/214-5439).

Bike Rental: Delft—a low-impact mini-Amsterdam with pretty canals and very little car traffic—is an easy place to ride a bike. But since most sights are within walking distance, you won't really need a bike. Still, if you just enjoy biking, want to explore the countryside, or even pedal to The Hague or Rotterdam, you have two good options. The **train station** bike-rental office has reasonable prices and very long hours, but you may have to hunt for it until the station construction project wraps up (it's likely behind the station). More central, **Halfords** sits right behind the Town Hall at the bottom of the Markt (€7.50/day, Mon 11:00-18:00, Tue-Thu 9:30-18:00, Fri 9:30-21:00, Sat 9:30-17:00, Sun may be open 12:00-17:00, Wijnhaven 17, tel. 015/213-8558).

DELFT

Tours in Delft

Local Guides
Private tours led by licensed guides can be booked through the local guide bureau (€120/2 hours, mobile 062-242-9010, www.delftguidedtours.com, bureau@delft-guide.nl). I enjoyed a walk led by Sybrand de Jong.

Canal Boat Tour
Rondvaart Delft offers a 45-minute boat tour of the Old Town (€7.25, April-Oct daily 11:00-17:00, boats depart hourly from along Koornmarkt canal, tel. 015/212-6385, www.rondvaartdelft.nl). They also rent paddleboats (€12.50/hour).

Bike/Rickshaw Tour
Bryan, a hardworking young man with a funky bicycle-rickshaw, pedals visitors around town while delivering commentary. He's no historian, but he offers a quirky glimpse at the city. It's a fun before-dinner activity: He'll meet you at your hotel and drop you at the restaurant of your choice at the end of the tour (1-2 people: €10/half-hour, €20/hour, these special prices for my readers with this book, tel. 061/886-1552, info@fietsdienstdelft.com). He also provides bike taxi service.

Sights in Delft

IN THE OLD TOWN
My self-guided Delft Old Town Walk, in the next chapter, starts on the Markt and links many of the following sights.

Markt (Market Square)
The historic center of Delft, the rectangular Markt is bookended by the 14th-century New Church at one end (with a statue of legal scholar Hugo Grotius out front) and the 15th-century Town Hall at the other. The Markt is bordered by characteristic buildings—a mix of shops, cafés, and homes. For more on the Markt, see page 316.

▲New Church (Nieuwe Kerk)
Delft has two grand churches that hold tombs of prominent local residents. The can't-miss-it New Church rockets up from the Markt: It's the needle around which Delft spins, and holds the most important tombs of Dutch royalty. The more modest Old Church (described

later) sits along a canal a few blocks away. Both are covered by the same ticket; when you buy it, be sure to pick up the well-explained, illustrated brochure, which locates and describes all points of interest in both churches.

Cost and Hours: €3.50 for both churches (not covered by Museumkaart); same hours for both: April-Oct Mon-Sat 9:00-18:00; Nov-Jan Mon-Fri 11:00-16:00, Sat 10:00-17:00; Feb-March Mon-Sat 10:00-17:00; closed to tourists Sun year-round, tel. 015/212-3025, www.oudeennieuwekerkdelft.nl.

Visiting the New Church: The giant, Gothic New Church boldly presides over the town from its prominent position overlooking the Markt. Inside are buried the beloved Dutch ruler William I of Orange and the Dutch royalty that succeeded him.

Construction on the New Church, with its Late Gothic lines, began in 1393 and took 100 years to complete. The stone tower you see today houses a carillon, proudly considered the Stradivarius of carillons by locals. Its chimes, played on request by the town bell ringer, are in demand with couples getting married at Town Hall.

The church has been through a lot. It was devastated by a fire in 1536 and ransacked by iconoclasts in the 1560s. The first "re-formed" service was held here in 1572. After a nearby gunpowder depot exploded and ruined its windows in 1654, the church was rebuilt, giving it the look you see today. Until 1829, city leaders were buried under the floor stones. Because of the "stinking rich" problem, only royals have been buried here since then. The chandeliers, produced in 1981 in traditional 17th-century style, marked the 600th birthday of the church.

Head inside. Walk to the ornate, canopied **tomb of William of Orange,** which dominates the choir area at the far end of the church. William I was the founder of the House of Orange, the dynasty that still (in name) rules the Netherlands. It was William who rallied the Dutch to begin their revolt against the Spanish Habsburg rulers. That's why he's considered the father of the country. This canopied monument to his greatness features two representations of William: one of white marble, reclining peacefully; and a strong, armored king in bronze, sitting royally. The sweet dog at reclining William's feet symbolizes loyalty. Above the pooch, the angel of Fame blows a trumpet (notice that this whole bronze statue is supported by just one slender ankle). At the corners of his monument are female statues representing Liberty, Justice, Religion, and Fortitude. Unfortunately, all these fine virtues could not save William from being gunned down

DELFT

by an assassin's bullet right here in Delft. The assassin had hoped to collect a reward offered by Spanish King Philip II for killing William of Orange (but the assassin was soon caught and killed).

Most of William I's descendants of the House of Orange are also buried in this church. A few paces in front of William (near the transept), a large stone slab marks the entrance to the sprawling underground labyrinth that holds crates of Oranges. (The crypt is strictly off-limits for anyone unrelated.) In the transept, look for TV monitors showing the last few royal burials here.

Besides ruling Holland, the Orange family had owned the independent principality of Orange in the south of France since medieval times. The royal family's official color is—what else?—orange, which is why today's Dutch wear orange to soccer matches and consider it their national color (despite having a flag that's red, white, and blue).

If you want to work off your *pannenkoeken*, you can climb the New Church's **tower** (€3.50, three levels and 376 steps in a very narrow staircase). This is a particularly dizzying tower climb, one of Europe's more dramatic. On a clear day you can see the towers of The Hague and, in the other direction, Rotterdam.

From the New Church, you can walk a few blocks up pretty Hippolytus-buurt street (or follow my self-guided town walk, in the next chapter), to find the smaller Old Church.

▲Old Church (Oude Kerk)

The Old Church, with its leaning spire, is Dutch Reformed (English service Sun at 12:00) and has been around for a long time: The names of its ministers, going back to 1592, fill the wall on your right as you enter. Nearby, the wooden cano-pied pulpit—which dates from 1548—is con-sidered one of the finest in the Netherlands, thanks to the fine carvings on its sides, which demonstrate a mastery of perspective.

The church interior is sober and clean be-cause of iconoclastic riots, in 1566 and 1572, that made a violent point of destroying all hints of Roman Catholicism and its imag-ery. The Old Church holds the tombs of two local boys done good: the inventor of the mi-croscope, Anton van Leeuwenhoek (the tall, pyramid-shaped monument at the very back of the left nave); and the painter Johannes Vermeer. Vermeer's ac-tual tombstone is just a simple stone plaque in the floor (in the left transept, across from the pulpit). The grander Vermeer monument, installed in 2007 (and also in the floor), is a reflection of his greater popularity now than in previous generations.

Cost and Hours: Same as the New Church, described earlier.

Johannes Vermeer (1632-1675)

The great Dutch Golden Age painter Johannes Vermeer was born in Delft, grew up near the Markt, and set a number of his paintings here. His father, an art dealer, gave Johannes a passion for painting. Late in the artist's career, with Holland fighting draining wars against England, the demand for art and luxuries went sour in the Netherlands, forcing Vermeer to downsize—he sold his big home, packed up his wife and 14 children, and moved in with his mother-in-law. He died two years later.

Vermeer painted some 37 surviving works (though experts debate whether all of them were actually his). Although Vermeer painted landscapes and scenes from mythology and the Bible, he specialized in depicting the everyday actions of regular people. And though his scenes are usually still and peaceful, he artfully conveys deep tension, and suggests a complicated story with subtle body language (the subject glances at something out of view) or the inclusion of a small item (a letter that seems pregnant with significance). Vermeer also was a master of light, capturing it with an artistry that would make the Impressionists jealous two centuries later.

After centuries of relative obscurity—we still know very little about him—Vermeer and his paintings are now appreciated. Delft owns none of his works (you'll have to visit Amsterdam's Rijksmuseum, with four masterpieces, or The Hague's Mauritshuis museum). However, the town's Vermeer Center pays tribute to this great artist and his talent.

▲Vermeer Center (Vermeercentrum)

Although it doesn't have any Vermeer originals, this intelligent exhibit does a good job of tracing the career and unique creative mind of Delft's favorite resident. Everything is well-described in English.

Begin in the basement, where a short movie orients you to Vermeer and his ties to Delft. Then view copies of all 37 known Vermeer paintings, arranged chronologically and accompanied by brief and interesting commentary. The top floor hosts an exhibit explaining the hidden symbols of love found in many of Vermeer's paintings. On the middle floor, a mock-up of Vermeer's studio thoughtfully analyzes and explains some of Vermeer's techniques.

Cost and Hours: €8, includes essential audioguide, not covered by Museumkaart, daily 10:00-17:00, a block from the Markt—through the gap where Vermeer's house used to be—at Voldersgracht 21, tel. 015/213-8588, www.vermeerdelft.nl.

DELFT

Prinsenhof Museum

This former convent where William of Orange sought refuge and was ultimately assassinated is now a museum focusing on the life of that great statesman. It also displays a fine collection of blue Delftware and a spirited exhibit about Dutch innovation. Interesting to historians, but overpriced and underwhelming for the layperson, it's a decent rainy-day activity. While basic English information is posted, the €2.50 audioguide offers dry, thorough commentary on several specific items.

Cost and Hours: €10, daily 11:00-17:00 except closed Mon late Oct-late May, Sint Agathaplein 1, tel. 015/260-2358, www.prinsenhof-delft.nl.

Visiting the Museum: The ground floor uses old paintings, video projections, and other displays to tell the story of William of Orange, including a room about his descendants all the way to today's king (for more about William, see page 448). At the base of the stairs, you'll see the two actual bullet holes from his assassination, embedded in the wall. (The shooting is continuously re-enacted with silhouettes projected on the wall.)

Upstairs are two more exhibits: on Dutch innovation (an important resource for this little country cursed with marshy land) and on blue Delftware pottery, with a small but impressive selection of fine pieces. If you don't want to make the trip out to the Royal Dutch Delftware Manufactory, this is a good chance to see examples of this town's most famous product. The exhibit ends with a wraparound, fairly hokey film about the highlights and lowlights of Delft history.

Across the courtyard, the **Prinzenquartier** building is slated for renovation, and will someday house temporary exhibits, art galleries, and a café.

Markets

Various all-day markets are held on Thursdays (general market on the Markt, flower market on Hippolytusbuurt Square) and on Saturdays (general market on Brabantse Turfmarkt and Burgwal, flea market at Hippolytusbuurt Square in summer, and sometimes an art market at Heilige Geestkerkhof).

DELFTWARE FACTORIES

The Markt is jammed with shops selling Delft's famous blue-hued pottery. Those with a passing interest in Delftware can peruse a few window displays on the main square and call it good. But to delve deeper, consider visiting one of these two factories, at opposite ends of town. The first one is famous, slick, and pricey; it has a fine museum and a big reputation, but it's a headache to reach from the Old Town. The second place is a humbler, more intimate Back Door alternative that's free and easier to reach.

Royal Dutch Delftware Manufactory

The Delft Blue earthenware made at this factory (known as the Koninklijke Porceleyne Fles in Dutch) is famous worldwide, mak-ing this the biggest tourist attraction in town. The Dutch East India Company, partly headquartered in Delft, imported many exotic goods from the Far East, including Chinese porcelain. The Chinese designs became trendy and were copied by many local potters. Three centuries later, their descendants are still going strong, and you can see them at work in this factory—the only one left of an original 32. While some may think this is just an excuse to shop for Delftware, it's a worthwhile stop for those who enjoy porcelain.

Cost and Hours: €12.50, 25 percent discount with coupon available at TI and many hotels, not covered by Museumkaart, daily 9:00-17:00 except closed Sun Nov-March, Rotterdamsweg 196, tel. 015/251-2030, www.royaldelft.com.

Getting There: It's a pain **from the Old Town,** since there's no handy public-transit option. Get help from the TI or your hotelier to either call a taxi for you (about €10) or to give you detailed directions on how to get there on foot. It's a 25-minute walk south of the Old Town, on Rotterdamsweg (just off map on page 306); because of the canal crossings and railroad construction, the route can be confusing. Or you can take a bike-taxi (€5/person one-way, see "Bike/Rickshaw Tour," earlier). In the summer, you can take a canal boat (€16 includes factory admission, July-Aug at 13:00 and 14:00, 2.5-hour round-trip, catch along Koornmarkt canal, more expensive "full-service" tour includes lunch, tel. 015/212-6385, www.rondvaartdelft.nl).

To get **from the train station** to the factory, catch bus #40 or #121 (€2.50, 2/hour, 5 minutes, buy ticket from driver, get off at the second bus stop: Julianalaan, continue walking in the same direction as the bus to the next street—Jaffalaan, then turn right and walk one long block to Rotterdamsweg). Or you could simply walk to the factory from the station—figure about 20 minutes.

Visiting the Factory: There's an included audioguide, but it's not essential, as English descriptions are posted throughout. At the beginning you'll watch two short videos—the first on the history of Royal Delft and the second on the production process. Then comes the highlight of the tour: a chance to watch the artists as they paint

Delft Blue Manufacturing Process

Delft Blue earthenware is made from a soupy mix of clay (imported from England and Germany) and water. To make plates, the glop is rotated on a spinning disk until it looks like a traditional Dutch pancake. This "pancake" is then placed in a plate mold, where a design is pressed into it.

To make vases, pitchers, cups, and figurines, the liquid clay is poured into hollow plaster molds. These porous molds work like a sponge, sucking the water out of the clay to leave a layer of dry clay along the mold walls. Once the interior walls have reached the correct thickness, the excess clay within is poured off and recycled.

After the clay object is removed from the mold and allowed to dry completely, it's fired in the kiln for several hours, turning from gray to white. The pottery removed from the kiln is called "biscuit." Next, painters trace traditional decorations with sable-hair pencils onto the biscuit pottery; these are then painted with a black paint containing cobalt and copper oxide. The biscuit immediately soaks up the paint, making it a very unforgiving medium for mistakes.

Finally, the objects are dipped into an opaque white glaze and then fired a second time. A chemical reaction transforms the black paint into the famous Delft Blue, and the white glaze melts into a translucent, glass-like outer layer.

the designs on the fired pottery "biscuit." After rather kitschy exhibits that reconstruct Vermeer's dining room (with Royal Delft china, of course) and trace the firm's connections with the Dutch royal family, you'll see the company's priceless collection. Along with tableware and vases, there are gorgeous pictures made from tiles (including a life-size replica of Rembrandt's *The Night Watch* that took two artists a year to paint) and outdoor architectural elements (such as chimneys). After the museum, you'll walk through part of the factory, past racks upon racks of unfired pieces. Take some time to watch artisans at work—and feel free to stop and chat with them.

The tour ends in the gift shop. For bargain hunters, the factory store offers a bonus—"seconds" with slight blemishes for 20-40 percent off. The clerks can also prepare VAT refund documents for you (see page 462).

Delftse Pauw Delftware Factory
While it lacks the storied past of its rival, this much smaller facility makes up for it in spunk and personal attention. Walk-in visitors

are welcomed with a free 10-minute tour and explanation of the process (they're hoping you'll consider buying something in their well-stocked showroom). On the top floor, you'll see craftspeople hand-painting each piece (though you may not see them on weekends). Although less famous than the royal factory, this endearing, family-run business turns out high-quality products.

Cost and Hours: Free, April-Oct daily 9:00-16:30, Nov-March Mon-Fri 9:00-16:30, Sat-Sun 11:00-13:00, Delftweg 133, tel. 015/212-4920, www.delftpottery.com.

Getting There: It sits about a 30-minute walk north of the Markt. However, unlike the Royal Dutch, this factory is easily reachable by public transportation. From the train station (or the stop on Phoenixstraat in front of the Prinsenhof Museum), take tram #1 toward The Hague and get off at the Brasserskade stop. From the stop, walk a few steps farther in the same direction, then turn left on Pauwhof; from here, you'll zigzag right, then left, through a residential zone until you pop out at the big canal—turn left and you'll see the factory in 100 yards.

DELFT OLD TOWN WALK

Lace together many of Delft's sights with this pleasant stroll through the heart of town. The proud churches, spires, and memorials attest to Delft's once-bustling economy during the Golden Age of the 1600s. But this walk also meanders past the placid canals, windmills, and pockets of greenery of the postcard village that Delft has become.

Orientation

Length of This Walk: Allow about 30 minutes—more if you go inside the sights along the way.

New Church (Nieuwe Kerk): €3.50, includes Old Church entry, not covered by Museumkaart; April-Oct Mon-Sat 9:00-18:00; Nov-Jan Mon-Fri 11:00-16:00, Sat 10:00-17:00; Feb-March Mon-Sat 10:00-17:00; closed to tourists Sun year-round.

Prinsenhof Museum: €10, daily 11:00-17:00 except closed Mon late Oct-late May.

Old Church (Oude Kerk): Same ticket and hours as New Church.

The Walk Begins

• *Stand in the center of Delft's market square—the Markt—and face the towering New Church. You can trace the route of this walk using the map on page 306.*

The Markt

This is clearly a city with a rich history and a wealthy past. Its look today was defined in 1536, when lightning struck the spire of the **New Church** (Nieuwe Kerk; described in detail on page 308), starting a fire that destroyed two-thirds of the town. While all the buildings that ring the square have cellars dating from before the fire, what you see above ground made of brick was built after 1536.

Delft recovered well from the fire. In the 17th century, its Golden Age, this was a thriving market town, with an economy stoked by textiles and breweries. (With 200 breweries, the city exported 80 percent of its beer.) Then, in the 18th century, the economy collapsed. Without the infrastructure of a trading city—there's no river, local harbor, or major roads—Delft was left behind. It became a sleeping-beauty town, cocooned in an intact medieval structure, awaiting awakening.

The **square** has never really been renovated, perhaps because it must always be ready, on a day's notice, to host a royal funeral. In

1584, William I of Orange (b. 1533), leader of the Dutch revolt against Spain, was assassinated in Delft. Under normal circumstances, he would have been buried in his family's hometown of Breda, but the Spanish had occupied the city. So William was laid to rest in Delft, and to this day, the house of Orange—the Dutch royal family—buries its nobility in the New Church (if you pay to visit the interior, you'll see his elaborate tomb inside).

The statue dominating the square honors **Hugo Grotius.** Born in Delft in 1583, Grotius was the first to establish international rules of the sea, putting forth the idea that all the oceans were free-trade territory, open to every nation. That didn't go over so well with the rival English, who claimed dominion over all the sea around Britain. The controversy went on for nearly a century, during which the two nations fought a two-year war over it. (The eventual agreement—the sea within the range of a cannonball fired from your shore is yours; any waters beyond that are open to all nations—forms the basis for today's maritime laws.)

Part of Delft's economic heritage is in printing. At #57 (above the Subway sandwich shop) a Bible on the building's upstairs corner recalls the first printed Dutch Bible, produced here in 1477.

Opposite the New Church stands the **Town Hall,** rebuilt in 1620 in the Renaissance style after a fire. It's a law court, with Lady Justice and her scales prominently positioned on the facade. Of the 17 states in the Spanish Netherlands, seven seceded and created the Dutch Republic—the United Provinces of the Netherlands.

DELFT WALK

Holland was one of these; above Lady J, look for the coat of arms with the red lion. The independent Netherlands were dominated by Holland (which contained Amsterdam and drove 85 percent of the country's economy). The lower banner (under the stone canopy, above the door) is Delft's—it features a canal, which is what "Delft" means.

• *Walk around behind the Town Hall, where you'll find the Waag. It's the building with the Greek-style pediment roof decorated with a set of scales, facing the back of the Town Hall.*

The Waag

The city's medieval trading center, the Waag, was the weighing or **customs house,** with workspaces for goldsmiths and silversmiths

upstairs. Look up and down the street that runs in front of the Waag: To the left is the Stadsboterhuis, where butter was traded in barrels. At the far right, the Vleeshal, or meat market, is decorated with cow heads above its doors. Fish was traded in the Visbanken (left of the meat market).

The old sturdy tower around which the Town Hall is built was originally a **prison.** For security, the prison needed to be built of weighty stone—a potential problem in this naturally marshy place. The builders chose this spot, on a clay foundation, as the best place for the structure. It just made sense that the county seat—Delft—would be here, too.

• *With your back to the Town Hall, walk down Waagsteeg lane, a narrow alley to the right of the Waag, to reach Boterbrug.*

Boterbrug to the Oude Delft Canal

At the back side of the Waag, down below, is the **water gate** where produce was off-loaded from boats to be weighed and taxed. Continue walking straight down Boterbrug (literally, "butter bridge"), a wide street that once was the approach canal to the customs house. Merchants knew the drill for all their goods: Before you traded, first you weighed, then you paid. During Spanish rule, taxation got so out of hand that the Dutch revolted—much as high British taxes angered American colonists during the same period.

Boterbrug leads one block to the 11th-century **Oude Delft canal,** the town's first and major trading canal. On the black iron fence on the corner, facing the canal, is a memorial to Anton van Leeuwenhoek (1632-1723), who invented the microscope and then used it to discover bacteria. He's buried in the Old Church, visible in the distance (to the right; look for the tilting spire).

• *Turn right and walk along the Oude Delft canal toward the Old Church.*

Oude Delft Canal

In the past, boats passing the town used this waterway. Barges are now allowed to line the canal from April through September. Historically barges like these brought in the goods and produce that fueled Delft's economy—but today they provide the city's restaurants with sunny outdoor tables. For dining suggestions, see "Eating in Delft" in the next chapter.

• *Cross left over the first bridge (Nieuwstraat) and continue on to the ornate facade at #167.*

This building is the headquarters of the **water authority,** responsible for keeping waterways dredged and managing water

levels in towns and *polders* (lowlands). The colorful coats of arms of the various 17th-century water authority directors decorate the exterior wall.

Water levels are a big deal here. Turn around and look at the yardstick across the canal; the red *NAP* marking—"normal Amsterdam point"—is the average sea level in Amsterdam. The wide-open Dutch countryside plots reclaimed from the sea, known as *polders*, are generally three yards below this point. According to the NAP, we're above sea level and the canal is below, so we're standing on what was an island.

• *Keep walking along this side of the canal. Across from the Old Church, find the photo cube recalling the painter Vermeer, who's buried in the church. Turn left from the photo cube and church into a tiny, covered, brick lane (look for the cursive* Entree—Museum *sign). You'll pop out into a very long, wide courtyard called the...*

Prinsenhof

This was once the convent of St. Agatha. William of Orange took refuge here after the king of Spain put a bounty on his head in 1580 for his role in the revolt of the Netherlands. Figuring the convent was a safe place in a safe city, William stayed here until 1584, when an assassin finally killed him. Today this building houses the Prinsenhof Museum, with exhibits on William of Orange—including the chance to see the bullet holes from his assassin's gun, still embedded in the wall—and other facets of Delft history (for more about visiting this museum, see page 312).

• *Step into the tranquil green park, an old herb garden.*

The statue here honors William, considered the founder of the Netherlands (for more about William, see page 448). When the provinces broke away from Spain, they also broke from the Roman Catholic Church. The Dutch became "reformed" and dissolved the Catholic convents and monasteries. Although they had declared their freedom in 1579, a treaty ending the war for Dutch independence (which formally established their freedom) didn't come until 1648.

Back out in the main courtyard, notice the three blue-and-white lampposts; these were made in Delft's Chinese sister city and serve as reminders of the 400-year relationship between porcelain makers in China and Delft. The only color that could survive the extremely hot fire of the Chinese porcelain technique was blue, and that's the color of Delftware. In the far-left corner, you'll see the **Winkeltje Kouwenhoven** old-timey candy shop, where candies are still made the traditional way (Tue-Sun 13:00-17:00, closed Mon).

• *A few steps farther take you to...*

Phoenixstraat

You've arrived at the edge of the old town. Along this street (to the right) you'll see a tower and windmill. Twenty such structures once stood on the 11th-century city wall. The **windmills,** which ground the city's grain, date back to the 13th century. Tram line #1 heads (right) along Phoenixstraat to the Delftse Pauw Delftware Factory, The Hague, and the beach at Scheveningen.

• *Turn around and finish this walk by retracing your steps, through the Prinsenhof, to the Old Church (with the tilting spire).*

Old Church (Oude Kerk)

The Old Church—while smaller and less impressive (inside and out) than the New Church—feels more lived-in. For 150 years, its spire was the tallest in Delft; it leans because it's built on an unstable foundation, over a filled-in canal. (For more on touring the interior, which is covered by your New Church ticket, see the listing on page 310).

Standing in front of the Old Church is a statue of **Geertruyt van Oosten** (1330-1358), a particularly devout nun whose deep faith is meant to inspire worshippers. Supposedly Geertruyt was so moved by the power of Christ that she began to lactate during the Christmas season, and the stigmata (Crucifixion wounds) appeared on her hands and feet during the Easter season.

DELFT SLEEPING, EATING & MORE

Contents

Delightful Delft works well as a home-base for visits to The Hague and Rotterdam. This chapter provides suggestions for the best places to sleep and eat, and a rundown of connections to points throughout the Netherlands and beyond.

Sleeping in Delft

Delft's accommodations aren't cheap, but the ones listed here are well-run and offer good value for the money. If I don't mention an elevator, expect lots of stairs. For locations, see the map on page 306.

SOUTH OF THE MARKT

$$$ Bridges House Hotel, with 11 rooms around the corner from the Markt, was once the home of painter Jan Steen. Energetic Robbert Willemse brings class and charm to this lovely canalside splurge (Sb-€99, Db-€119, spacious junior suite—Sb-€139/Db-€149, prices can be lower in winter, extra bed-€20, air-con, guest computer and Wi-Fi, Oude Delft 74, tel. 015/212-4036, www.bridges-house.com, info@bridges-house.com).

$$$ Hotel Johannes Vermeer, a lesser value than others listed here, owns a fine location in an old cigar factory facing a canal. The lobby/bar/breakfast room gilds the lily, while the 30 rooms

---

Sleep Code

Abbreviations   (€1 = about $1.40, country code: 31)
S = Single, **D** = Double/Twin, **T** = Triple, **Q** = Quad, **b** = bathroom, **s** = shower only.

Price Rankings

 $$$ **Higher Priced**—Most rooms €115 or more.

  $$ **Moderately Priced**—Most rooms between €70-115.

   $ **Lower Priced**—Most rooms €70 or less.

Nearly everyone speaks English. Unless otherwise noted, credit cards are accepted, breakfast is included, and Wi-Fi is generally free. Rates may not include the €2.40 per person, per night hotel tax. Prices can change without notice; verify current rates online or by email. For the best prices, book directly with the hotel.

---

try hard to be elegant but feel slightly dated (Db-€125, Db suite-€175, Wi-Fi, Molslaan 20, tel. 015/212-6466, www.hotelvermeer.nl, info@hotelvermeer.nl).

$$ Hotel Leeuwenbrug, a former warehouse and now a business-class hotel, has 32 classic Dutch rooms (some with canal views), Old World atmosphere, a generous breakfast buffet, and a helpful staff (very small Sb-€55, standard Sb-€69-78, deluxe Sb-€125, standard Db-€75-88, deluxe Db-€95-125, price depends on demand, may be cheaper July-Aug—check website for best rates, elevator, guest computer and Wi-Fi, Koornmarkt 16, tel. 015/214-7741, www.leeuwenbrug.nl, sales@leeuwenbrug.nl, Mr. Wubben).

$$ Hotel de Koophandel has 25 painting-over-the-bed, dated-feeling rooms right on the charming, lively, tree-and-restaurant-lined Beestenmarkt. Request either a view room on the square, or a quieter room in the back (Sb-€99, Db-€115, Tb-€145, extra bed-€30, 3 ground-floor rooms, reception closed 23:00-7:00, guest computer and Wi-Fi, rental bikes, Beestenmarkt 30, tel. 015/214-2302, www.hoteldekoophandel.nl, info@hoteldekoophandel.nl).

JUST OFF THE MARKT

$$ Hotel de Emauspoort, picture perfect and family-run, is relaxed, friendly, and ideally located one block from the Markt. The 26 rooms, decorated with pleasantly old-fashioned wooden furniture and named for sea heroes and Delft artists, overlook a canal or peek into the courtyard. Romantics can stay in one of their two "Gypsy caravans"—wooden trailers in the courtyard (Sb-€98, Db-€108, stunning "Vermeer Room" Db-€150, Tb-€142, Qb-€185, caravan-€99—sleeps two, Wi-Fi, behind New Church at Vrouwenregt 9, tel. 015/219-0219, www.emauspoort.nl, info@emauspoort.nl, Jeroen and Desiree).

$ Jorplace City Hostel, just off the Markt, is a crowded slumbermill renting about 100 beds in dorm rooms that sleep 6, 12, or 24 (bunk-€20-30 depending on number of beds and season, breakfast extra, Wi-Fi, kitchen, terrace, next to the Vermeer Center at Voldersgracht 17, tel. 015/887-5088, www.jorplace.nl, delft@jorplace.nl).

NORTH OF THE MARKT

$$ Hotel de Plataan has an imaginative spirit and artistic flair. Its ground floor is a big, high-ceilinged-yet-rustic, inviting bar that faces a lively, leafy square that's filled with al fresco tables in good weather. About half of its 29 rooms are larger and dramatically themed, with outlandish decor (Sb-€105, Db-€115, themed rooms-€35 extra; the square can get noisy, especially on weekends—request a quieter back room; air-con in some rooms, elevator, Wi-Fi, Doelenplein 10, tel. 015/212-6046, www.hoteldeplataan.nl, info@hoteldeplataan.nl).

Eating in Delft

As Delft is a university town, lively and affordable eateries abound. Most places have outdoor seating, sometimes on an inviting square or on a little barge floating in the canal out front. For locations, see the map on page 306.

ON BEESTENMARKT

Spijshuis de Dis is driven by the creative energy of chef Jan Boheemen, who cooks Dutch with attitude. With an open kitchen, inviting menu, friendly service, a characteristic interior, and great food, the entire eating experience is a delight. Reservations are smart (€17 vegetarian plates, €19-23 main courses, kitchen opens at 17:00, closed Sun-Mon, Beestenmarkt 36, tel. 015/213-1782, www.spijshuisdedis.com). They serve fine Belgian Westmalle beer.

ON AND NEAR THE OUDE DELFT CANAL

Kleyweg's Stads Koffyhuis is a local institution that's won prizes for its sandwiches (see the trophies above the counter). This is a great spot for an affordable bite, either in the country-cozy interior or out on a canal barge (€7-10 sandwiches and hamburgers, €6-13 savory or sweet pancakes, big €13 salads, Mon-Fri 9:00-20:00, Sat 9:00-18:00, closed Sun, shorter hours off-

season, just down the canal from the Old Church at Oude Delft 133, tel. 015/212-4625).

Restaurant Matties—tight, small, and stylish—serves modern Dutch dishes and has a few nice canalside tables (€17-25 main dishes, Mon-Tue 17:00-22:00, Wed-Sun 13:30-22:00, Oude Delft 92, tel. 015/215-9837).

Rossio, in a bright, high-energy, inviting brasserie slathered with trendy subway tile, cooks up Mediterranean dishes from Spain, Portugal, France, and Italy. The upstairs—overlooking one of Delft's prettiest canal bridges—is also appealing. This place feels classy and a bit dressy (€6-10 lunches, €15-17 main dishes at dinner, Tue-Sun 12:00-23:00, closed Mon, Oude Delft 78, tel. 015/212-0950, www.rossio.nl).

Restaurant de Prinsenkelder, set in a candlelit cellar, offers French cuisine with formal service. Their outdoor courtyard is equally elegant (€12-20 starters, €21-28 main dishes, Mon-Sat 17:30-21:30, closed Sun, near the Prinsenhof at Schoolstraat 11, tel. 015/212-1860, www.de-prinsenkelder.nl).

Burgerz sells exactly that—beef, lamb, chicken, or veggie burgers—all made with locally sourced ingredients. While they do have takeaway, you'll have to wait a bit since everything is made to order. Most people opt to sit in the modern interior (€11-16 burgers, Tue-Fri 17:00-21:00, Sat-Sun 12:00-21:00, closed Mon, Oude Delft 113, tel. 015/212-3010).

Frito Misto is Delft's best fry shop. It combines an unhealthy snack food—french fries and other deep-fried goodies—with a fresh, healthy-for-fried-food outlook: Their ingredients are organic and locally sourced, and they offer gluten-free options. Burgers, soups from scratch, and homemade dipping sauces round out the menu. Get your cone of fries or other snacks to go, or linger in the bright interior (Tue-Sat 11:30-21:00, Sun 12:30-20:00, closed Mon, Oude Delft 105, tel. 015/214-6488).

NORTH OF THE OLD CHURCH

Café de Pelicaan, with candles and well-worn tables, is a favorite of students, who eat well on classic Italian food—no pizza. On balmy evenings, tables move out onto their canal barge (€6-12 pastas, €12-16 main dishes, Tue-Sun 18:00-22:00, closed Mon, Verwersdijk 47, tel. 015/213-9309, www.depelicaan.nl).

Eetcafé de Verbeelding ("The Imagination") serves Dutch pub grub in an intimate, woody, library-like setting that feels distinguished but not stuffy. Choose their dark, candlelit interior or take a spot outside on their canal barge. Their steak and shrimp are very popular (€15 plates, €27 three-course fixed-price meal, daily 17:00-22:00, Verwersdijk 128, tel. 015/212-1328, www. eetcafedeverbeelding.nl).

De V is a lively pub with a pleasantly cozy ambience and a local following loyal to its straightforward and well-priced food—from ribs and burgers to Asian. Sit in the crowded area near the bar, elbow your way up top to the glassed-in patio, or enjoy the barge tables on the canal (€8.50 daily specials, €11-14 main dishes, daily 16:00-24:00, food served 18:00-22:00, just past the Old Church along the canal at Voorstraat 9, tel. 015/214-0916).

AROUND THE MARKT

Delft's giant Markt, under the looming tower of the New Church, is a scenic spot for a meal. Most of the places around here are interchangeable, but tucked behind the Town Hall (across the square from the church) are some good options with outdoor seating.

Herring and Other Fish: **Van der Eyk Visbanken,** overlooking a canal a few steps from the bottom of the Markt (look for the long green awning), is the handiest place in town to sample the Dutch delicacy of herring (for more information, see page 218). The long display case shows off a variety of options: deep-fried, raw, smoked, or in a sandwich. This place is fun for its scenic setting and for the chance to actually see all of your options spread out before you. Pick what you like, then choke it down at one of the stand-up counters (€3 meals, daily 9:00-18:00, Cameretten 2, tel. 015/361-2014).

Asian: For a break from flapjacks, try **Daily Wok,** a mod Asian-fusion chain just off the Markt. It serves up affordable, good fare—either take-out or fast-food sit-down (€4-7 meals, daily 12:30-21:30, Oude Langendijk 23, tel. 015/213-7222).

Supermarket: A well-stocked **Albert Heijn** supermarket is a short walk south of the Markt, along a canal at Brabantse 41 (Mon-Sat 8:00-20:00, Fri until 21:00, closed Sun).

Delft Connections

FROM DELFT TO ROTTERDAM

It's very simple: From Delft's train station, trains run every 15 minutes for the 15-minute journey to the Rotterdam Central Station.

FROM DELFT TO THE HAGUE

It's easy and cheap to travel to The Hague by train or tram.

Tram #1 leaves from in front of the Delft train station and clatters through residential neighborhoods to The Hague. This connection is frequent, comes with nice urban scenery, and delivers you right into the center of The Hague's tourist zone (€3 regardless of how far you go, €6.50 day pass—sold at TI—covers the round-trip and any other public transit in the area all day). The tram runs every 10 minutes on weekdays and every 15 minutes on weekends (direction: Scheveningen Noorderstrand; get off after about 30 minutes at The Hague's Centrum stop for TI, parliament area, and most sights). You can continue on this tram directly to the Peace Palace (Vredespaleis stop, about 5 minutes beyond Centrum stop) or go all the way to the beach at Scheveningen (Kurhaus stop, about 15 minutes beyond Centrum stop).

Regular **trains** depart from Delft's station for The Hague (€3.70 one-way, €7.40 round-trip, 4/hour, 15 minutes). Get off at The Hague's Central Station (CS), not the Hollands Spoor station (HS). The train appears to be faster than the tram, but from The Hague's Central Station it's still a 15-minute walk or a 5-minute tram ride to reach the tourist zone (for details, see "Arrival in The Hague" on page 389).

For more information on trams and buses, call toll tel. 0900-486-4636, consult www.htm.net, or use the Netherlands' slick public-transit site, www.9292.nl.

FROM DELFT BY TRAIN TO OTHER POINTS

From Delft, trains go to **Amsterdam**'s Central Station (4/hour, 1 hour, more with transfer in Leiden or The Hague), **Haarlem** (2/hour, 40 minutes), **Leiden** (4/hour, 20 minutes), **Utrecht** (6-7/hour, 1 hour, change in Rotterdam or The Hague), **Arnhem** (2-4/hour, 1.75 hours, transfer in The Hague or Rotterdam, then Utrecht), **Antwerp** (hourly, 1.5 hours, change in Rotterdam), **Brussels** (hourly, 2.5 hours, change in Rotterdam), **Ghent** (hourly, 2.75 hours, change in Rotterdam and Antwerp), and **Bruges** (hourly, 3.25 hours, change in Rotterdam, Antwerp, and Ghent).

DAY TRIPS

Day Trips

25 Kilometers

25 Miles

Leeuwarden

Texel

Harlingen

AFSLUITDIJK
(CLOSURE DIKE)

Hindeloopen

Den
Helder

Medemblik

IJsselmer

North
Sea

ZUIDERZEE
MUSEUM

Alkmaar

NORTH

Enkhuizen

Urk

SCHOKLAND

Hoorn

HOUTRIBDIJK
(N-302)

ZAANSE
SCHANS

Volendam

Lelystad

Edam

Marken

FLEVOLAND

Haarlem

Zandvoort

Amsterdam

To Hanover
& Berlin

KEUKENHOF

Aalsmeer

Leiden

KRÖLLER-
MÜLLER
MUSEUM

Scheveningen

Otterlo

Utrecht

The Hague

SOUTH

NETH.
OPEN-AIR
MUSEUM

Delft

EAST

To
Harwich/
England

Rotterdam

Arnhem

To Cologne
& Rhine

To Brussels
& Paris

NORTH OF
AMSTERDAM

While cities sprawl to the south, the idyllic area north of Amsterdam is wonderfully dotted with Dutch clichés: cutesy cobbled villages, gently spinning windmills, and locals whom you can imagine will actually wear wooden shoes from time to time. This region holds some of the quaintest easy day trips from the city. (While you could stay the night in some of these towns—Edam is the most tempting, for its village cuteness—side-tripping from Amsterdam is so simple that I wouldn't bother.)

Some of these northern destinations once fronted the Zuiderzee ("South Sea"), but generations of land reclamation reshaped this part of the country, converting the stormy inlet into a pair of tame, freshwater lakes: the Markermeer and the IJsselmeer. To deepen your understanding of these places, be sure to read the "Taming the Zuiderzee" sidebar (see page 364).

DESTINATIONS

Each of these is reachable from Amsterdam by public transportation: train, bus, or boat. But if you want to explore Flevoland, it's much easier by car.

Alkmaar and Zaanse Schans

Allow a half-day for either destination. Alkmaar is liveliest on Friday mornings.

▲**Alkmaar:** This likeable town is jammed with gawking tour groups on Fridays, when it holds its ye olde traditional cheese market (early April-early Sept only, 10:00-12:30).

Zaanse Schans Open-Air Museum: Packed with windmills (and greedy shops), this sight is just a quick 15-minute train ride (plus a 15-minute walk) from central Amsterdam. Or you can visit it on your way back from Alkmaar (40 minutes by train, then a 15-minute walk).

Edam, Volendam, and Marken

Figure on a day (leaving Amsterdam by 10:00) to visit these picturesque villages, in the region aptly called Waterland. If you have only a half-day, choose Edam. (Edam's museum is closed Mon and its market is held Wed morning.)

▲▲**Edam:** In this quiet town, you can mellow out like a hunk of aging cheese. There are no real sights, but its tiny main square and peaceful canals may win you over.

Volendam: A transit hub for the Waterland region, this workaday town has an extremely touristy seafront promenade and a boat across to Marken.

Marken: Once an island, and now connected by a causeway to the mainland, this time-warp fishing village preserves traditional buildings and lifestyles.

Hoorn, Enkhuizen, and the Historic Triangle

The two towns of Hoorn and Enkhuizen, on the former Zuidersee, combine for a day of fascinating sightseeing (leave Amsterdam in the morning for a train to Hoorn, explore that town and its museum, then train over to Enkhuizen for the Zuiderzee Museum).

▲▲**Hoorn:** This strollable town boasts the fascinating Westfries Museum—a creaky old house crammed with an engaging collection from the Dutch Golden Age.

▲▲**Enkhuizen:** This town is worth a visit for its excellent open-air Zuiderzee Museum, with an emphasis on seaside lifestyles.

Historic Triangle: To slow things down even more, you can connect Hoorn and Enkhuizen with this time-consuming but quaint loop trip via historic steam train and boat.

Flevoland

Worthwhile only by car, you could spend the day just joyriding through the reclaimed polder land around the former Zuiderzee—crossing the sea on the Houtribdijk road, getting a dose of the youngest (1986) province of Flevoland (its capital, Lelystad, is home to some land-reclamation museums), and visiting Schokland, an old fishing island left high and dry by the draining of the Zuiderzee.

ALKMAAR AND ZAANSE SCHANS

Two handy day trips line up north of Amsterdam: Alkmaar is a famous cheesemaking town with a charming square and a bustling cheese market; Zaanse Schans, while the least interesting of Holland's open-air museums, is also its most convenient—offering a taste of traditional life a stone's throw from the capital. Consider combining the two destinations for a full day of sightseeing, ideally on a Friday in spring or summer, when Alkmaar's festive cheese market enlivens the town.

Alkmaar

Alkmaar is Holland's cheese capital (and, perhaps, the unofficial capital of high cholesterol). In addition to being an all-around delightful city, Alkmaar has a rich history and a zesty cheese-loving spirit. And though it's enjoyable to visit any time, it's most colorful, lively—and crowded—during its bustling Friday-morning cheese market (early April-early Sept). On your train ride here, you can study up by reading the "Dutch Cheeses" sidebar on page 472.

Orientation to Alkmaar

Once a stoutly walled city, Alkmaar (pop. 95,000) now has a tidy Old Town laced by canals. The main square, Waagplein, is named for Alkmaar's cheese-weighing. The mighty Weigh House, containing the TI and Cheese Museum, is at one end of the square, and the Beer Museum is at the other. (Think of it as "Holland's Wisconsin.") From this area, the main pedestrian drag, Langestraat, leads visitors to the Grote Kerk and Stedelijk Museum.

TOURIST INFORMATION

Alkmaar's TI, in the old Weigh House, sells a €2.50 town walking tour brochure (April-Oct Mon-Sat 10:00-17:00, Fri opens at 9:00; Nov-March Mon 13:00-17:00, Tue-Sat 10:00-17:00; closed Sun year-round, Waagplein 2, tel. 072/511-4284, www.vvvalkmaar.nl).

ARRIVAL IN ALKMAAR

From the train station, it's a 15-minute walk to the town center. The route is well-marked (just follow signs for *Centrum*): Exit the station to the right and veer left with the arterial down Stationsweg, then turn left (onto Scharlo) when the street dead-ends. Soon you'll cross a canal and see the big church (Grote Kerk), with the modern Stedelijk Museum to the left. From the church, walk straight up the main pedestrian street (Langestraat). When you reach the next canal, turn left and walk one more block to the main square and TI.

Sights in Alkmaar

▲▲Cheese Market (Kaasmarkt)

Tellingly, Alkmaar's biggest building isn't the church or the town hall, but the richly decorated **Weigh House** (Waaggebouw), used

since the 16th century for weighing cheese. (It was converted from an old chapel.) The right to weigh, sell, and tax cheese is what put Alkmaar on the map in the Middle Ages, and it's still what the town is celebrated for today.

Think about the udder importance of cheese to this culture—wheying the fact that it has long kept the Dutch economy moo-ving. If you travel through the Dutch countryside, you'll pass endless fields filled with cows, which are more reliable producers than crops in this marshy landscape. Because cheese offers similar nutritional value to milk, but lasts much longer without refrigeration, it was a staple on long sea voyages—and Holland was the first country to export it. Today the Netherlands remains the world's biggest cheese exporter.

There's no better time to sample a sliver of this proud wedge of Dutch culture than during Alkmaar's **cheese market,** which takes place on Fridays in the spring and summer (early April-early Sept, 10:00-12:30). Early in the morning, cheesemakers line up their giant orange wheels in neat rows on the square. Prospective buyers (mostly wholesalers) examine and sample the cheeses and make their selections. Then the cheese is sold off with much fanfare, as an emcee narrates the action (in Dutch and English). To close the deal, costumed cheese carriers run the giant wheels back and forth to the Weigh House just as they have for centuries: They load a wheel onto a "cheese-barrow"—kind of a wooden stretcher—then sling each end over their shoulders on ropes and run it to and fro. The cheese carriers' guild has four "fraternities" of seven carriers each: red, yellow, blue, and green (with color-coded hats, cheese-

barrows, and scales). Each fraternity is headed by a "cheese father," who enforces the strict rules and levies fines on carriers who show up late or drink beer before carrying cheese (which is strictly forbidden).

On cheese-market days, the town erupts in a carnival atmosphere, becoming one big street fair with festive entertainers and vendors selling souvenirs, snacks...and, of course, cheese. It can get crowded—especially midmorning—but the Cheese Museum (described below) is surprisingly empty, and its windows allow great unobstructed views of the action below.

▲Cheese Museum (Het Hollands Kaasmuseum)

This is probably the Netherlands' best cheese museum...and in this country, that's saying something. With displays on two floors above the TI in the Weigh House, the museum explains both traditional and modern methods of cheesemaking. You'll learn that as the economy evolved, cheesemaking went from being the work of farmers' wives to factory workers. You'll find old equipment (much of it still used for today's cheese market), such as big scales, wagons, cheese-barrows, and (upstairs) old presses for squeezing the last bit of whey out of the cheese molds. Ask for an English showing of the 15-minute movie that traces the history and traditions of Alkmaar cheesemaking. (You'll find out what a "cheesehead" really is, and the technical difference between Gouda and Edam cheeses.) Other, smaller screens around the museum show informative movies—press the flag for English subtitles.

Cost and Hours: €4; April-Oct Mon-Sat 10:00-16:00, Fri from 9:00 during cheese market, closed Sun; closed Nov-March except open Sat 10:00-16:00; enter TI at Waagplein 2 and walk up stairs to museum, tel. 072/515-5516, www.cheesemuseum.com.

Beer Museum (Nationaal Biermuseum De Boom)

This hokey old museum, in a former brewery, shows off an endearing collection about beer production across the centuries—from the days of barrels to the earliest bottling plants. The 1700s-era replica bar has sand on the floor, from a time when men were men and didn't have to aim into a spittoon. While interesting, the museum's explanations are scant (pick up the English descriptions as you enter). If you're not a beer lover or a backyard brewer, I'd skip it.

Cost and Hours: €4, May-Aug Mon-Sat 10:30-16:30; Sept-April Mon-Sat 13:00-16:00, Fri from 10:30-16:30 during cheese market, closed Sun year-round, across Waagplein from Weigh House at Houttil 1, tel. 072/511-3801, www.biermuseum.nl.

Grote Kerk

Alkmaar's "Great Church" is similar to others in Holland (such as Haarlem's and Delft's). Visit if you want to see a typically austere Dutch interior.

Cost and Hours: Free, April-early Sept Tue-Sat 10:00-17:00, Sun 12:00-17:00, closed Mon; closed off-season to sightseers. The church hosts frequent concerts (for schedules, call 072/514-0707 or see www.grotekerk-alkmaar.nl).

Stedelijk Museum Alkmaar

The Stedelijk, which has its primary collection in Amsterdam, also runs this worthwhile branch in little Alkmaar (next to Grote Kerk). The museum has two parts: a permanent collection about the history of Alkmaar and a space for temporary exhibits. The 15-minute movie in the town history section is excellent, enlivened by props and sound effects (ask to see it in English). But the rest of the history exhibit—with stiff group portraits, other paintings, and artifacts from the town's illustrious past—is only in Dutch and difficult for tourists to appreciate. Visit here only if the temporary exhibit intrigues you.

Cost and Hours: €10, Tue-Sun 10:00-17:00, closed Mon, Canadaplein 1, tel. 072/548-9789, www.stedelijkmuseumalkmaar.nl.

Alkmaar Connections

Alkmaar is connected by frequent fast trains to **Amsterdam** (4/hour, 40 minutes). However, these trains do not stop at the Zaanse Schans museum. To visit the **Zaanse Schans** museum (see next) on your way back to Amsterdam, take a train from Alkmaar to Uitgeest or Zaandam (2/hour), where you can transfer to a slower regional train (typically just across the platform) to Koog-Zaandijk (sometimes abbreviated as "Koog Z"; trip takes 40 minutes total). On busy days, the info desk in the tunnel of the Alkmaar train station hands out schedules for this connection.

Zaanse Schans Open-Air Museum

This re-created 17th-century town puts Dutch culture—from chee-semaking to wooden-shoe carving—on a lazy Susan. Located on the Zaan River in the town of Zaandijk, the museum is devoted to the traditional lifestyles along the Zaan— once lined with hundreds of windmills, used for every imaginable purpose, and today heavily industrialized (including a giant corporate

chocolate factory you'll pass on the way). In the 1960s, houses from around the region were transplanted here to preserve traditional culture. Most of the exhibits are run by quirky locals who've found their niche in life, and do it with gusto.

Zaanse Schans (ZAHN-zeh shahns), a hodgepodge of loosely related attractions in a pretty park with old houses, feels less like a museum than Arnhem's or Enkhuizen's open-air museums. And, since each attraction charges a separate entry fee (and those that are free are either selling or promoting something), it also feels more crassly commercial...you'll be nickel-and-dimed for your cultural education. But it's undeniably handy, just 15 minutes by train (plus a 15-minute walk) from downtown Amsterdam. Two of the at-tractions here—the Dutch Clock Museum and the tourable, work-ing windmills—are unique and genuinely interesting. Because it's the easiest one-stop look at the Netherlands' traditional cul-ture, Zaanse Schans can be flooded at midday by busloads of tour groups. To avoid the hordes, come early or late.

Orientation

Cost: Entry is free, but it costs money to visit each historical pre-sentation. If you'll be visiting the main Zaans Museum and at least one windmill, you'll save a little money with the €10 **Zaanse Schans Card** (also gives you discounts at some shops and cafés).

Hours: The grounds are open all the time because people actually live here. During the spring and summer (April-Sept), most of the building interiors are open daily 10:00-17:00 (though some are closed Mon, and individual opening and closing times can vary by up to an hour, as noted in each listing). After about

16:30, things get really quiet. In the off-season (Oct-March), only some of the buildings are open (roughly 9:00-17:00 on Sat-Sun, shorter hours or closed entirely Mon-Fri; specific month-to-month hours listed at www.zaanseschans-museum. nl).

Getting There: From Amsterdam, catch a slow **train** going toward Uitgeest (4/hour), ride for about 15 minutes, then hop out at Koog-Zaandijk (or "Koog Z"). Reaching Koog-Zaandijk from Alkmaar requires a change in Uitgeest or Zaandam (see "Alkmaar Connections," earlier).

Once at the Koog-Zaandijk station, it's about a 15-minute walk to the museum (well-marked, just follow the signs...and the other tourists). Go through the underpass and exit straight ahead, watching on your left for a TI machine where you can pull the crank to get a map. Then continue straight until the road forks. (If this area seems surprisingly sweet-smelling for an industrial district, thank the nearby chocolate factory.) From the fork, follow *Zaanse Schans* signs. Turn left, then right across the river, which puts you at the "back entrance" to the park, near the Clock Museum (signs to *Ned. Uurwerkmuseum*).

If **driving** from Amsterdam, take A-8 (direction: Zaanstad/Purmerend), turn off at *Purmerend A-7*, then follow signs to *Zaanse Schans* (parking—€8).

Information and Services: The visitors center, located in the Zaans Museum building, has a good, free map of the grounds. Ask if any events are scheduled for that day (daily 9:00-17:00, lockers, free WCs in museum, otherwise €0.50 in park, tel. 075/681-0000, www.zaanseschans-museum.nl).

Sights at Zaanse Schans

I've arranged these sights in order from the train station. Drivers should park at the Zaans Museum and then visit these in reverse order, or walk five minutes to the Dutch Clock Museum and begin there.

▲Dutch Clock Museum (Museum van het Nederlandse Uurwerk)

More interesting than it sounds, this collection is brought to life by its curator, clock enthusiast Pier van Leeuwen. If he's not too busy, Pier can show you around and will lovingly describe his favorite pieces. (Or pick up the free brochure and explore seven centuries' worth of timepieces on your own.) Upstairs is a big, bulky, crank-wound turret clock from around 1520. Back then, the length of an "hour" wasn't fixed—there were simply 12 of them between sunrise and sunset, so the clock's weights could be adjusted to modify the length of an hour at different times of year. Also up here are the museum's prized possessions: two of the world's four surviving, original 17th-century pendulum clocks, which allowed for more precision in timekeeping. Downstairs, appreciate the fine craftsmanship of the Zaans clocks (one clock is wound by being pushed up on a rack, rather than pulling a chain) and Amsterdam clocks.

Cost and Hours: €10; April-Oct daily 11:00-17:00; Nov-March Sun only 11:00-17:00, closed Mon-Sat; tel. 075/617-9769, www.mnuurwerk.nl.

• *Next door is the...*

Albert Heijn Grocery "Museum" (Museumwinkel)

Little more than a thinly veiled advertisement for the Dutch supermarket chain, this replica grocery store from the 1880s re-creates the first shop run by Albert Heijn. The scant exhibits lead you to a room promoting Heijn coffee.

Cost and Hours: Free, get English description sheet; Easter-Oct Tue-Sun 10:30-13:00 & 14:00-16:00, closed Mon; Nov-Easter Sat-Sun only 12:00-16:00, closed Mon-Fri; tel. 075/616-9619.

• *A few doors up the street is the recommended De Hoop op d'Swarte Walvis restaurant. Just beyond is the dock for the...*

Boat Cruise (Rederij de Schans Rondvaarten)

This 45-minute boat tour floats visitors through the park and adjacent town.

Cost and Hours: €6; departs on the hour; July-Aug daily 11:00-16:00; April-June and Sept Tue-Sun 12:00-15:00, closed Mon in April, June, and Sept; closed Oct-March; tel. 065/329-4467, www.rederijdeschans.nl.

• *From here, enjoy a lovely view of the windmills. But before you go on to visit them, poke into the little village area across from the boat landing. First you'll pass an adorable curiosity shop that's a pack rat's heaven. Then you'll encounter the...*

Bakery Museum (Bakkerijmuseum)

This fragrant and very modest "museum" displays old bakery equipment (including cookie molds) and sells what it bakes. Borrow the English descriptions to navigate the slapdash exhibit.

Cost and Hours: Free to enter museum, various treats available—most around €2.50, March-Oct Tue-Sun 10:00-17:00; Nov-Feb Sat-Sun only 11:00-17:00, closed Tue-Fri; closed Mon year-round, tel. 075/617-3522.

• *Now head for the...*

▲Windmills (Molens)

The very industrious Zaan region is typified by these hardworking windmills, which you'll see everywhere. Mills are built with sturdy oak timber frames to withstand the constant tension of movement. To catch the desired amount of wind, millers—like expert sailors—know just how much to unfurl the sails. When the direction of the wind shifts, the miller turns the cap of the building, which weighs several

tons, to face the breeze. You can tour several of Zaanse Schans' old-fashioned windmills, each one used for a different purpose.

Cost and Hours: €3 per mill, hours vary, tel. 075/621-5148, www.zaanschemolen.nl).

Visiting the Windmills: De Gekroonde Poelenburg is a sawmill, where stout logs are turned into building lumber (open

sporadically). **De Kat** ("The Cat") grinds dyes. Watch its gigantic millstones rolling over the colored dust again and again, as wooden chutes keep it on its path. Climb the steep steps (practically a ladder) for a closer look at the wooden gears and the fine views out over the museum grounds (July-Aug daily 9:00-17:00; March-June and Sept-Oct Tue-Sun 9:00-17:00, closed Mon; closed Nov-Feb). **De Zoeker** ("The Seeker") crushes oil from seeds and nuts, a drop at a time—up to an incredible 100 quarts

per day (March-Oct daily 9:30-16:30, closed Nov-Feb). Other mills may also be open for your visit. If deciding which mill to visit, choose one that's spinning—you'll see more action inside. And though these structures appear graceful, and even whimsical from the outside, on a windy day you can really experience the awesome power of the mills by getting up close to their grinding gears.

• *After exploring the windmills, cross the little canal to the big...*

De Catharina Hoeve Cheese Farm (Kaasmakerij)

Essentially a giant cheese shop, this is worthwhile only if you catch one of their presentations. A movie shows how cheese is made, and periodically a costumed Dutch maiden explains the process in person (about five quarts of milk are used to make about a pound of cheese) and dispenses samples...followed by a confident sales pitch.

Cost and Hours: Free entry, daily 8:00-18:00, tel. 075/621-5820, www.cheesefarms.com.

• *Walk past the mini-windmill to a shopping zone, which includes the...*

Wooden Shoe Workshop (Klompenmakerij)

More engaging than the park's other free attractions, this shoe store features a well-presented display of clogs from different regions of the Netherlands. You'll see how clogs were adapted for various purposes, including wooden clogs with boot-like leather to the knee, frilly decorative bridal clogs, high-heel clogs, roller-skate clogs, and spiky clogs for ice fishing. Watch the videos, and try to catch the live demonstration that sends wood chips flying as a machine carves a shoe. Your visit ends—where else?—in the vast clog shop.

Cost and Hours: Free entry, daily April-Sept 8:00-18:30, Oct-March 9:00-17:00, tel. 075/617-7121, www.woodenshoeworkshop. nl.

• *Nearby is the recommended De Kraai restaurant, and just across the big parking lot is the final attraction, the...*

▲Zaans Museum and Verkade Pavilion

This museum, with a modern structure that evokes both the hull of a ship and the curved body of a whale, is the focal point of the complex.

In addition to housing the visitors center, the museum has a fresh, modern multimedia presentation that explains Holland's industrial past and present with the help of a good, included audioguide. The exhibit, with some English descriptions, is thematically divided into four parts: life, work, wind, and water.

The other half of the building is given over to Verkade, a beloved Dutch brand of cookie (translations here use the British term "biscuit"). The pavilion is essentially a very slick version of several other "museums" around the park—thinly disguised branding opportunities for major Dutch companies. Nonetheless, this re-created cookie factory is a fun treat, thanks to the free samples, well-written explanations, and clever computer-based games. Don't miss your chance to make like Lucy and Ethel and try to see how many virtual cookies you can pick off a speeding conveyor belt and into a box—my score: 1,253.

Cost and Hours: €9, daily 10:00-17:00, tel. 075/681-0000, www.zaanseschans-museum.nl.

Eating at the Zaanse Schans Open-Air Museum

Pannenkoeken Restaurant de Kraai, across from the Wooden Shoe Workshop, is a self-service eatery offering traditional sweet and savory pancakes (€7-13 pancakes; March-Oct daily 9:00-18:00; Nov-Dec and Feb daily 10:00-17:00; Jan Sat-Sun only 10:00-17:00, closed Mon-Fri; on slow days may close earlier, indoor and outdoor seating, tel. 075/615-6403).

De Hoop op d'Swarte Walvis ("The Hope of the Black Whale") is the park's splurge, with a white-tablecloth interior, outdoor seating, and an ambitiously priced menu (€6-7 sandwiches, €28-32 main dishes at dinner, daily 11:00-22:00 except closed Sun in Feb, dinner served 18:00-21:30, tel. 075/616-5629, www. dewalvis.eu).

EDAM, VOLENDAM & MARKEN

The aptly named region of Waterland (VAH-ter-lahnd), just north of Amsterdam on the west shore of the IJsselmeer, is laced with canals and sprinkled with picturesque red-brick villages. Two in particular—the homey cheesemaking village of Edam and the trapped-in-a-time-warp hamlet of Marken—offer visitors an enticing peek at rural Holland. To travel between the two towns, you'll pass through the touristy waterfront town of Volendam.

If choosing just one Waterland town, make it Edam—and consider spending the night. Because of its charm and its proximity to Amsterdam, this region is popular. But if you'd like to get a taste of traditional Dutch living, it's worth joining the crowds.

PLANNING YOUR TIME

The most efficient way to see this area is as a one-day loop trip by public transportation from Amsterdam (or Haarlem); to have enough time for the whole loop, get started by 10:00. Begin with a bus from Amsterdam to Edam. Then, after enjoying Edam, continue by bus to Volendam for a stroll and to catch the boat across to Marken. Leave Edam by around 14:00 in order to have sufficient time in Volendam (you'll want at least an hour there), and to be able to reach Marken before its museum and shops close at 17:00. Poke around salty Marken before taking the bus back to Amsterdam.

All of the bus rides in this loop are covered by the €10 "Waterland Ticket" (sold by EBS bus company, located at rear of Central Station, catch buses here, localbus.nl; routes not covered by Amsterdam transit passes). The Volendam-Marken boat costs extra and doesn't take cars. The drive from Volendam to Marken is a delight.

Edam

This adorable cheesemaking village is sweet but not saccharine, and is just 30 minutes by bus from Amsterdam. It's mostly the terrain of day-trippers, who can mob the place on summer weekends. For the ultimate in cuteness and peace, make your home in tiny Edam (ay-DAHM) and stay overnight.

Although Edam is known today for cheese, it was once an industrious shipyard and port. But having a canal to the sea caused such severe flooding in town—cracking walls and spilling into homes—that one frustrated resident even built a floating cellar (which you can visit in what's now Edam's oldest house). To stop the flooding, the harbor was closed off with locked gates (you'll see the gates at Dam Square next to the TI). Eventually the harbor silted up, forcing the decline of the shipbuilding trade.

Edam's Wednesday market is held year-round, but it's best in July and August, when the focus is on cheese. You, along with piles of other tourists, can meet the cheese traders and local farmers.

Orientation to Edam

Edam is a very small town—you can see it all in a lazy 20-minute stroll. It's so nice, though, that you may be tempted to stay longer. Dam Square, with the City Hall and its TI, is right along the big canal called Spui (rhymes with "cow"); the town's lone museum is just over the big bridge.

TOURIST INFORMATION

The TI, often staffed by volunteers, is in City Hall on Dam Square. Pick up a free simple map and consider the €2.50 *A Stroll Through Edam* brochure outlining a self-guided walking tour (mid-March-Oct Mon-Sat 10:00-17:00, closed Sun except July-Aug open Sun 11:00-16:00; Nov-mid-March Mon-Sat 10:00-15:00, closed Sun; WC and ATM just outside, free Wi-Fi, tel. 0299/315-125, www.vvv-edam.nl).

ARRIVAL IN EDAM

The bus "station"—really just a parking lot for buses—is a five-minute walk from Dam Square and the TI. At the canal by the bus lot, turn right and walk along the water (on Schepenmakersdijk). Cross the next bridge (Kwakelbrug; a white bridge just wide enough for two people), and head straight up the street toward the gray-and-gold bell tower. Hook right around the church, pass one bridge, and you'll wind up across the canal from Dam Square.

HELPFUL HINTS

Cheese Market: From July to mid-August, farmers bring their cheese by boat and horse to the center of town on Wednesday mornings (10:30-12:30), where it's weighed and traded by Edamers in traditional garb.

Internet Access: The TI on Dam Square has free Wi-Fi.

Services: Free WCs are located behind City Hall near the canal.

Bike Rental: Tiny Edam has two bike shops full of friendly folks. **Ronald Schot** is near the cheese market, between Dam Square and the Grote Kerk (€7/half-day, €8.50/day, €14/24 hours; Tue-Fri 8:30-18:00, Sat 8:30-16:00, closed Sun-Mon except by appointment; sells regional maps with bike routes, Grote Kerkstraat 7/9, tel. 0299/372-155, www.ronaldschot.nl). **Ton Tweewielers** is between Dam Square and the bus station (€9/day, tandem-€19/day, April-Oct daily 8:00-18:00, closed Nov-March, free maps, Schepenmakersdijk 6, tel. 0299/371 922, www.tontweewielers.nl, Friet).

Sights in Edam

▲Edam's Museum: Edam's Oldest House

This 400-year-old historical home, across the bridge from Dam Square, provides a fun peek at what all these old canal houses once looked like inside. This house is particularly interesting for its floating cellar, designed to accommodate changes in water level without destabilizing the house. A classic town map shows how Edam would have been a mighty sight in 1698. Exhibits on the town's history and how people lived are invigorated by the included and essential audioguide. The top floor has an exhibit on the locally produced Fris art pottery. An extension of this museum with a few (lackluster) exhibits is across the bridge in City Hall (covered by the same ticket).

Cost and Hours: €4, Easter-Oct Tue-Sat 10:00-16:30, Sun 13:00-16:30, closed Mon and Nov-Easter, Dam Square 8, tel. 0299/372-644, www.edamsmuseum.nl.

▲Take a Stroll

The best thing to do in Edam is to just wander its storybook lanes and canals. Consider taking the short walking tour outlined in the TI's booklet, *A Stroll Through Edam*.

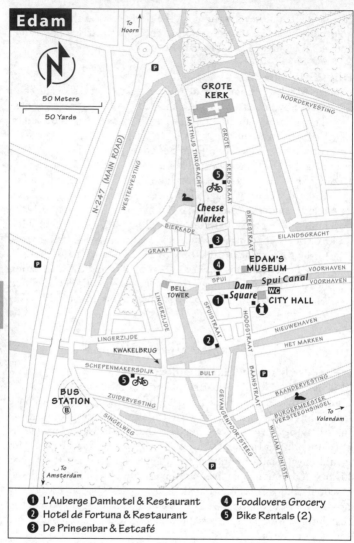

Edam

To Hoorn

GROTE KERK

NOORDERVESTING

50 Meters
50 Yards

N-247 (MAIN ROAD)

WESTERVESTING

MATTHIJS TINXGRACHT

GROTE KERKSTRAAT

Cheese Market

BIERKADE

GRAAF WILL.

BREESTRAAT

EILANDSGRACHT

EDAM'S MUSEUM

VOORHAVEN

SPUI

Spui Canal

VOORHAVEN

BELL TOWER

Dam Square

WC

CITY HALL

LINGERZIJDE

SPUISTRAAT

HOOGSTRAAT

NIEUWEHAVEN

LINGERZIJDE

HET MARKEN

KWAKELBRUG

SCHEPENMAKERSDIJK

BULT

BAANSTRAAT

BAANDERVESTING

BUS STATION

ZUIDERVESTING

GEVANGENPOORTSTEEG

BURGERMEESTER VERSTEEGHSINGEL

To Volendam

SINGELWEG

WILLIAM PONTSTR.

To Amsterdam

❶ L'Auberge Damhotel & Restaurant
❷ Hotel de Fortuna & Restaurant
❸ De Prinsenbar & Eetcafé
❹ Foodlovers Grocery
❺ Bike Rentals (2)

Grote Kerk

Perched on the edge of town, the Grote Kerk (Big Church) feels surprisingly huge for tiny Edam. Like other fine churches in Holland, it was built around 1500, then gutted by iconoclasts during the tumult that came with the Reformation; it's been Dutch Reform since 1566.

The church's vast interior is covered by a ceiling constructed just like a stone vault—but built of wood, because heavier stone would have made the building sink into the wet ground. The wood-

---

Sleep Code

Abbreviations   **(€1 = about $1.40, country code: 31)**
S = Single, **D** = Double/Twin, **T** = Triple, **Q** = Quad, **b** = bathroom, **s** = shower only.
Price Rankings
   $$ Higher Priced—Most rooms €125 or more.
   $ Lower Priced—Most rooms less than €125.
Unless otherwise noted, credit cards are accepted, breakfast is included, Wi-Fi is generally free, and hoteliers speak English. Prices can change without notice; verify current rates online or by email. For the best prices, book directly with the hotel.

---

en catwalks are original. Near the pulpit, find the massive "cabinet organ," dating from 1640, interesting for the big painted side panels that can swing around like shutters to cover it. Many 19th-century Dutch homes had one of these, cleverly disguised to evade a tax on organs. Pick up the church's €2 booklet for more on the church's interior, including some good background on the stained-glass windows. If you haven't landed in Edam on cheese-market day, look for the TV tucked in the side wall on the right, which plays a 12-minute loop video of scenes around town, including the cheese market. The church has a cute café corner and free WCs.

Cost and Hours: Free, daily April-Sept 13:30-17:00, www.grotekerkedam.nl.

Getting There: From Dam Square, walk over the bridge, turn left, then head right down Prinsenstraat to Nieuwenhuizenplein, the traditional cheese-market square. Find the "cheese weigh house" on the left—the one with the cheese frieze—and peek inside if it's open (tasty samples). Continue through the square to the canal, which leads to the church.

Sleeping in Edam

These two hotels are both distinctive and classy. For cheaper rooms in private homes, check www.vvv-edam.nl or ask at the TI.

$$ L'Auberge Damhotel, centrally located on a canal across the street from City Hall, has 11 overpriced rooms with over-the-top plush decor that doesn't quite seem to fit (Db-€125-165, Tb-€175, Qb-€195, air-con, Wi-Fi, Keizersgracht 1, tel. 0299/371-766, www.damhotel.nl, info@damhotel.nl).

$ Hotel de Fortuna is a canalside wonderland with flowers and the sounds of ducks and other birds. It offers steep stairs and 23 low-ceilinged rooms in a cozy collection of five ancient buildings in the old center of Edam. A fine value, it's been run by

the Dekker family for more than 30 years (Sb-€88-98, Db-€110-117, luxury Db-€160, Wi-Fi, Spuistraat 3, tel. 0299/371-671, www.fortuna-edam.nl, fortuna@fortuna-edam.nl).

Eating in Edam

Considering how close it is to Amsterdam, coming to Edam for a romantic dinner in the countryside and then heading back to your hotel in the big city can be a fine plan. The restaurant at **L'Auberge Damhotel** (listed earlier) dominates the main square with outdoor seating and a dressy interior, and Edam's lanes are lined with tourist-friendly restaurants (within a block or two of Dam Square).

Hotel de Fortuna, listed earlier, has a lovely restaurant, with a romantic dining room and seating in a gorgeous garden alongside a picturesque canal (€20-25 main dishes, three-course "Fortuna *menu*" for €35, pricier fixed-price meals also available, daily 12:00-15:00 & 18:00-21:30, www.fortuna-edam.nl).

De Prinsenbar and Eetcafé is a good bet for a light lunch or a midday snack. Their €8 *Portie gemengde Hollandse Kaas* is a

sampler of five regional cheeses with bread—a nibbler plate that goes well with a little Belgian beer (€4 soups, €5 salads, €7 pancakes, €6-10 pub grub meals, pub open nightly until at least 24:00, food served all day June-Aug but only Sat-Sun 10:30-16:00 in off-season, Prinsenstraat 8, tel. 0299/372-911). The pub offers darts and stay-awhile stools.

Picnickers can stock up on gourmet groceries or pick up a sandwich at **Foodlovers** (daily 8:30-18:00, until 17:00 on weekends, next door to cheese shop overlooking Spui canal across from Dam Square, tel. 0299/373-069). Ask them to heat up a handmade pizza for you.

Edam Connections

EBS runs frequent buses between Edam and **Amsterdam.** From Amsterdam, buses leave from the bus platforms behind Central Station (from the station's west corridor, exit the station and take escalators up to the bus stops). Bus #314 and #316 are the most direct options (2/hour, 30-minute trip, less after 18:30 and on weekends). For bus schedules, see www.9292ov.nl. The €10 all-day transit pass covers everything between Amsterdam and Hoorn.

By Bus to Volendam on the "Waterland Loop": Buses #110 and #316 zip you from Edam to Volendam in about 12 minutes (2/ hour daily). Hop off at the Zeestraat/Centrum stop (other buses also go to Volendam, but not to this handy town-center stop).

Volendam

Less cute and more functional than the other two Waterland towns, Volendam enjoys some workaday charm of its own—including a lively dike-top walkway stretching along a shimmering bay, and a fun town museum.

Tourist Information: Stop by the TI to pick up a free Volendam/Marken map (mid-March-Oct Mon-Sat 10:00-17:00, Sun 11:00-16:00; Nov-mid-March Wed-Mon 10:00-15:00, closed Tue; tel. 0299/363-747, www.vvv-volendam.nl).

Arrival in Volendam: If arriving by bus from Edam, get off at the Zeestraat/ Centrum stop. The museum and TI are within a block, in the modern part of town. To reach the boat to Marken, walk straight from the bus stop toward the water, then turn left and walk along the dike.

Volendams Museum: The town's lone sight is located in the same building as the TI. Its hokey but endearing little collection oozes local pride. You'll wander through displays of traditional costumes, replica house and shop interiors, scenes from village life, and nostalgic old grainy black-and-white movies that are worth watching even if you don't speak Dutch. The corner display showing Waterland life during World War II is worth a look, but the museum's highlight is the Cigarband House, where a local artist glued 11 million cigarbands to big boards to create giant images—from Dutch windmills to Venice to a sour-looking Statue of Liberty (€3, borrow English descriptions at entry, mid-March-Oct daily 10:00-17:00, generally closed Nov-mid-March, but may be open Fri-Sun 10:00-17:00, Zeestraat 41, tel. 0299/369-258, www. volendamsmuseum.nl).

To reach the waterfront from the museum, walk two blocks down Zeestraat to Europaplein, head left, cross the dark-green bridge, turn right, then zigzag back across the next bridge and follow the brick steps up to the harbor.

Along the Waterfront: Volendam's extremely touristy **promenade** has a lively boardwalk appeal and is lined with souvenir shops, indoor/outdoor eateries, and Dutch clichés. The walls inside **Hotel Spaander** (eight houses down from the northern end of the harbor, on the right) are decorated with paintings by starving artists who slept or ate there. Don't miss the maze of sleepy residential courtyards below sea level just behind the promenade, with an adorable dollhouse charm and fewer crowds.

"Marken Express": This boat connects Volendam with Marken (€7.50 one-way, €9.95 round-trip, bike-€1 extra each way, mid-March-Oct daily about 11:00-17:30, departs every 30-45 minutes, in March and Oct sails only if there's enough passengers, by appointment only Nov-mid-March, 30-minute crossing, leaves from northern corner of harbor, no outside food allowed on board, tel. 0299/363-331, www.markenexpress.nl).

Marken

Famous as one of the Netherlands' most traditional fishing communities, Marken is a time-passed hamlet in a bottle—once virtually abandoned, now revived but kept alive solely as a tourist attraction.

This island town once had a harbor for whaling and herring fishing, but when the Zuiderzee began to silt up in the late 17th century, it became more and more difficult to eke out a living here, and many people from Marken fled to easier conditions on the mainland. When the Zuiderzee was diked off in 1932 to become a giant freshwater lake (the IJsselmeer), it forced saltwater fishermen to adapt or find a new calling (which most did). Marken became a virtual ghost town. But in 1957, a long causeway was constructed from the mainland to the island hamlet, which allowed easy access for visitors—who today come in droves to walk its tiny lanes and marvel at its cuteness.

Arrival in Marken: From the boat dock at the little harbor, follow signs to the museum in the town center. Marken has no TI; the nearest one is in Volendam.

Sights: The village of Marken has two districts connected by counterweight bridges. The famously conservative village, which is historically both very religious and royalist, named its bridges after Dutch queens. Arriving by boat, you'll first wander through the colorful Havenbuurt ("Harbor Neighborhood"), then head for the charming Kerkbuurt ("Church Neighborhood") to get a taste of Marken's old-time charm.

Land is tight on Marken and so are its lanes. They may appear private, but they actually are public and you're welcome to explore them. As you walk, notice the unique architecture, adapted to survive the challenging local conditions. Because the tides could be so temperamental, Marken's houses tend to huddle together on manmade hills called *werven*. Homes in lower locations were built on pilings to keep them high and dry. After the Zuiderzee was diked and tamed, the pilings were boxed in to create basements. Traditional Marken homes, while dull and black-tarred outside, are painted a cheerful yellow and blue inside.

The delightful harbor dates to 1837. At its peak in 1890, the fishing fleet here boasted about 200 vessels. But when the big flood of 1916 spurred construction of the massive dike 50 miles north of here, the saltwater fishing industry dried up.

The town's main attraction, located in the cute Kerkbuurt neighborhood, is the modest **Marker Museum,** celebrating the 16th-century costumes (hand-sewn and still worn for special events) and traditional lifestyles of the people of Marken. As you enter, ask for an English showing of the good eight-minute movie (€2.50, April-Oct Mon-Sat 10:00-17:00, Sun 12:00-16:00, closed Nov-March, tel. 0299/601-904, www.markermuseum.nl). The church is generally closed, but if it's open, peek in. In this very Protestant town (unlike Volendam, which is Catholic), the church posts a list of pastors next to the altar that goes back in an unbroken line to 1579, when the Reformation came.

For sustenance, enjoy some *kibbeling* (local fish-and-chips) at an idyllic eatery on the harbor.

Just outside town, on the way to the parking lot and the bus stop, you'll pass Marken's raised **cemetery.** Open the black iron gates and step in. Because of the very limited land (so high and dry), plots are shared. That's why the graves are marked with numbers rather than names. With more time, you can walk (about 40 minutes) out to the **lighthouse,** picturesquely situated at the far end of the island, at the tip of a sandy spit.

At the far end of town is a parking lot where you'll find the bus stop, bike rental (from the ice-cream wagon), and a wooden shoe factory that is just a touristy shop unless a bus tour stops by (when they demonstrate the traditional way to carve a set of shoes).

Marken Connections: Bus #311 connects Marken with **Amsterdam's** Central Station (2/hour, 40 minutes, leaves at :15 and :45 past the hour until midnight). In Marken, catch the bus along the main road that skirts the town, a little past the south end of the harbor and just past the big parking lot. For info on the boat to Volendam, see "Marken Express," page 350.

Driving to and from Marken, you'll enjoy a scenic road taking you under majestic modern windmills along a four-mile spit. Bikers have their own lane running along the top of the dike. You'll notice lots of cows and sheep but no fences separating the farms. As the animals can't pole-vault, the canals keep them from roaming.

HOORN, ENKHUIZEN & THE HISTORIC TRIANGLE

Two towns in North Holland, each conveniently located on the same speedy train line, make this side-trip from Amsterdam a great day out. Hoorn, with its Westfries Museum, offers the best look I've seen at Golden Age Dutch East India Company heritage. And Enkhuizen has the Zuiderzee Museum, Holland's most complete and interactive open-air folk museum for traditional Dutch culture. For a more lazy day out, take the Historic Triangle loop, which combines the two towns with countryside scenery via steam train, vintage boat, and modern-day train.

PLANNING YOUR TIME

From Amsterdam, trains connect both towns easily (Amsterdam to Hoorn, 2/hour, 30 minutes; Hoorn to Enkhuizen, 2/hour, 25 minutes; Enkhuizen to Amsterdam, 2/hour, 60 minutes). Each town is easy to explore on foot and can keep you busy for a good three to four hours of sightseeing. For a full day out, combine both into one big loop.

In **Hoorn**, spend an hour at the Westfries Museum, an hour on the little tour bus, and an hour to wander and enjoy the town and its harbor.

In **Enkhuizen**, you can spend an hour in the sweet little town, but the big attraction is the Zuiderzee Museum, which merits at least three hours.

Another option is to do the **Historic Triangle** loop—a combination steam train, 1920s-era ship, and regular train circuit from Hoorn—which gives a fun and memorable look at the countryside. However, the one-day loop doesn't leave you enough time to fully appreciate the sights in Hoorn and Enkhuizen (with more time, you could add an overnight stop and spread the trip over two days). If you're contemplating the Historic Triangle, read that section carefully and confirm schedules before committing, as it requires a bit more planning.

Hoorn

Hoorn, with 70,000 people, is a big enough city that it has 21st-century urban problems and unsightly sprawl around the old core. But when you walk from the train station into the center, you go back in time and find yourself surrounded by the facades and cobbles of a day when New York City was called New Amsterdam and the Dutch really were masters. With a major harbor, Hoorn was a prosperous trade center during Holland's Golden Age in the 1600s. The town's merchant ships sailed to exotic corners of the globe to stuff their holds with precious commodities. Hoorn was the birthplace of Jan Pieterszoon Coen, an officer of the Dutch East India Company who became a brutal colonial governor-general of what is now Indonesia. Another local boy, Willem Schouten, sailed around South America's stormy southernmost point in 1616 and named it after his hometown—Kaap Hoorn (Cape Horn).

Orientation to Hoorn

ARRIVAL IN HOORN

The Hoorn train station is about a half-mile from the old center. Drop by the TI near the station to pick up a free city map and list of sights, and to review your sightseeing plan.

To **walk** into town, head south down Veemarkt (a TI is at Veemarkt 44), turn right on Gedempte Turfhaven, then take a left on Grote Noord—the big, bustling main commercial drag. Follow Grote Noord straight to Roode Steen, the main square (where there's another TI). The harbor is just a bit beyond that (down Grote Havensteeg).

Though it's only a 15-minute walk from the station to the main square and harbor, you could instead take the cute little hop-on, hop-off minibus service run by **Rondje Hoorn City Tours,** which does an hour-long tour of the town (€6, departs hourly, daily 10:00-18:00, tel. 061-277-5698, www.hoorncitytours.nl).

TOURIST INFORMATION

The helpful TI, located in the Hart van Hoorn gift shop, is a two-minute walk from the train station across the park to the street corner (Tue-Sat 9:30-17:00, Thu until 21:00, Sun 12:00-17:00, closed Mon, Veemarkt 44, tel. 0229/241-575, www.vvvhoorn.nl). Another TI is in the Westfries Museum on Roode Steen, the main square of the old center (Mon-Fri 11:00-17:00, Sat 13:00-17:00, closed Sun, shorter hours off-season).

Sights in Hoorn

Grote Noord

Stroll the bustling main drag of Hoorn just to feel the pulse of the city today. You'll pass Koepel Kerk on the right, with a big dome indicating that it's the Catholic church. Stepping inside you see a church filled with statues, colored glass, and decoration—definitely not Protestant.

▲De Roode Steen

Hoorn's small main square, literally "The Red Stone," is named for the blood that once flowed from the gallows here. It was a tough heritage. The statue in the center is of Jan Pieterszoon Coen, an officer of the Dutch East India Company and the ruthless governor-general of the Dutch East Indies in the early 1600s. He was so cruel to people in lands the Dutch colonized that even honoring the mean sonofabitch with this statue has become controversial. The old building with the brightly colored facade is the Westfries Museum (described next). Opposite from it is the delightful weigh house (Waag) sporting a unicorn, the symbol of the city. Dating from the 1600s, today it houses a popular café and restaurant, d'Oude Waegh, serving serves traditional dishes and providing a great place to just sip a drink and enjoy the scene at the center of Hoorn.

▲▲▲Westfries Museum

This museum—with a curiosity cabinet, still lifes, devotional art, city bigwig group portraits, and elegantly furnished living rooms and a kitchen—takes the art and heritage of the Rijksmuseum and the Dutch Masters and puts it in the context of a real town and Golden Age community. The building that houses the museum is perfectly suited for its task, dating from the 1630s, with a distinctive, ornate facade.

Stepping inside, you're engulfed in the 17th-century Golden Age, when the Dutch ruled the waves. From the cellar to the attic, via creaky spiral staircases and upon floorboards recycled from old ships, you'll explore lavish period rooms filled with actual artifacts of the age. Enjoying the riches and painted canvases inside, you can feel it was an age when local tycoons divvied up their world. Don't miss the basement model of Hoorn in 1650, complete with high-tech theatrical videos featuring a cast of historical characters talking about Hoorn in their time. The audio is in Dutch, but between the English subtitles and dramatic gesturing, you'll get the gist. There are English pages in each room, but the audioguide is available only in Dutch (request an English version as you enter, as they hope to produce one soon).

Cost and Hours: €8, Mon-Fri 11:00-17:00, Sat-Sun 13:00-17:00, Nov-March closes on Mon, Roode Steen 1, tel. 0229/280-022, www.wfm.nl.

Hoorn Harbor

The town harbor, ringed by leaning Golden Age merchants' houses and still guarded by its "half a castle," is an evocative scene. The old locks, once they were shut, protected the fleet from changing tides. That was before the Zuiderzee was controlled and made into a vast lake with the 1932 completion of a big dike, the Afsluitdijk. The great merchant ships are gone, replaced by seaworthy recreational boats. But under the half-castle, the charming statues of three boys still gaze out to sea, dreaming of salty adventures back when the Zuiderzee really was a sea and great ships sailed from here for the East Indies.

Museum Stoomtram

Train enthusiasts will enjoy the steam-train museum at the Hoorn station. Just across the tracks are an old-time station, a workshop where steam trains are maintained, and the departure point from where a historical steam train journeys 14 miles each way to Medemblik and back (€21 round-trip, €12.40 one-way, 1.25-hour trip, www.museumstoomtram.nl/en). This ride is part of the Historic Triangle loop (described later).

Hoorn Connections

From the main train station, trains zip back to **Amsterdam** (2/hour, 35 minutes) or on to **Enkhuizen** (2/hour, 25 minutes).

To Enkhuizen: The direct train is the quickest way to reach Enkhuizen, if you're trying to squeeze maximum sightseeing into one day. But another option is via the sleepy loop trip called the **Historic Triangle:** Take a steam train to Medemblik, then a vintage boat to Enkhuizen. While this takes much longer than the direct train (and connections run far less frequently), it's a relaxing way to soak up the Dutch scenery.

The Historic Triangle

This three-part journey designed for tourists makes for an interesting trip out from Hoorn (or from Amsterdam, connecting via Hoorn). If you're interested in steam trains, the pastoral countryside, and a little IJsselmeer cruise rather than the museums in Hoorn or Enkhuizen, it's a great way to spend a day.

De Historische Driehoek, as it's called in Dutch, consists of these three segments:

1. The cute steam train from Hoorn to Medemblik (€21 steam train/vintage boat combo-ticket, 1.25 hours, 1-2/day).

2. A cruise from Medemblik on the 1920s-era boat *MS Friesland* to Enkhuizen (1.25 hours, usually 1/day, stopping at the open-air Zuiderzee Museum).

3. A ride on a regular train from Enkhuizen back to Hoorn (€4, buy ticket at train station, 2/hour, 25 minutes).

The schedule can be frustrating, as most days there's just one steam-train departure from Hoorn (midmorning, typically around 10:45) connecting to one daily boat at Medemblik, leaving you in Enkhuizen without enough time to do the Zuiderzee Museum properly before it closes. (With more time, you could overnight in Hoorn and/or Enkhuizen.)

For a shorter trip, you could just take the steam train round-trip between Hoorn and Medemblik (all the way or do a quicker hour-long round-trip). For details, see www.museumstoomtram.nl/en.

If you want to do the entire Historic Triangle in a day, here's a sample schedule (confirm all times carefully first): 9:39—Train from Amsterdam to Hoorn; 10:15—Arrive in Hoorn; 10:45—Take steam train from Hoorn; 12:00—Arrive in Medemblik, with one hour free in Medemblik; 13:15—Boat sails from Medemblik; 14:30—Boat arrives at Zuiderzee Museum in Enkhuizen; 14:30-17:00—Enjoy Zuiderzee Museum; 17:00-18:00—Free time in Enkhuizen; 18:00—Catch the train to Amsterdam, and by 19:00, you're back home in Amsterdam.

STEAM TRAIN FROM HOORN TO MEDEMBLIK

The train departs from the Museum Stoomtram historical depot behind the main train station (across the tracks from the main arrivals hall; described earlier, under "Sights in Hoorn").

After you choose a seat inside the train, you can get up and walk around.

The best views (farthest from the engine) are standing on the train balcony at the very back of the train. You'll feel like a whistle-stop presidential candidate as the train plods through the Dutch countryside.

Enjoy the purely Dutch scenery on this serene, old-fashioned joyride. Count sheep. Moo at cows. Watch horses playfully run alongside the train. Look for ducks in the canals and pheasants in the fields. Go ahead, order the *poffertjes* (puffy mini-pancakes). If you see Dutch kids waving to the train from their backyards, wave back. The modern white windmills in the distance jolt you back into the 21st century, just in time to arrive at...

MEDEMBLIK

If connecting the steam train with the vintage boat ride, you'll have about an hour in this pleasant town before boarding the boat (confirm the exact departure time at station). One of the oldest ports in the area, it has a Hanseatic League heritage and characteristic lanes and fortified buildings huddled around its old harbor. Medemblik has three main sights: a bakery museum, the Kasteel Radboud (former castle, now a fortified mansion), and the Stoommachine Museum (an old pump station turned steam-engine museum just outside of town). Exit the station and bear left, then right, to walk up the main drag—a pretty market street lined with cafés, bakeries, shops, and postcard stands. If you're hungry, you could grab a quick sandwich at an outdoor café, but you likely won't have time for a full meal. Basic food is available on the boat.

Shortcut Back to Hoorn: If you skip the boat trip, you can ride back to Hoorn on the steam train, or catch the bus (bus #239, at least hourly, 40 minutes, €4.05, buy ticket from driver). There's no direct overland connection from Medemblik to Enkhuizen—if you miss the boat, you'll have to take the bus back to Hoorn, then the train or bus from there to Enkhuizen.

BOAT FROM MEDEMBLIK TO ENKHUIZEN

Catch the *MS Friesland* to Enkhuizen just over the dike from the Medemblik station (you'll see the boat moored there as your train pulls in, tel. 0229/214-862, www.msfriesland.nl). It's a 75-minute putter along the coast to the Zuiderzee Museum in Enkhuizen. You can grab a bite in the boat's surprisingly comfortable dining room. If you've brought a picnic, grab a wicker  chair and enjoy the peaceful, windswept deck. Kids can safely run around on the open spaces of the top deck, or play wooden board games in the lounge. In good weather, you'll pass small pleasure craft—little sailboats and windsurfers—close enough to shake hands.

Enkhuizen

Enkhuizen, while a sleepy town of about 20,000 today, was once a mighty harbor home to the Dutch merchant fleet. The modern age left it behind, and today it's home only to holiday yachts and sailboats. Towns like Enkhuizen were hit hard by the great reclamation projects that tamed the sea, landlocked once-vital ports, and destroyed hearty fishing traditions by turning the fertile sea into a big freshwater lake. From Enkhuizen, a 17-mile dike, the Houtribdijk (route N-302), stretches east toward Lelystad in Flevoland, disappearing into the lake called IJsselmeer (see the Flevoland chapter). The only real reason to stop in Enkhuizen is for its excellent Zuiderzee Museum, an open-air collection of traditional Dutch life.

Sights in Enkhuizen

▲▲▲Enkhuizen Zuiderzee Museum

With the devastation of the traditional culture resulting from the taming of the Zuiderzee (diked off and made into a lake in 1932),

it was clear that the age-old lifestyles were embattled and would likely not survive long. There needed to be an open-air folk museum to help preserve them. That was the purpose of the Zuiderzee (ZOW-der-zay) Museum. (For more on the Dutch land reclamation projects that closed off the Zuiderzee, see page 364.)

The museum's original buildings were collected from around the Zuiderzee. You'll meet people who do a convincing job of role-playing no-nonsense 1905 villagers. You're welcome to take their picture, but they won't smile—no one said, "Have a nice day," back then. On weekends, children enjoy trying out old-time games, playing at the dress-up chest, and making sailing ships out of old wooden shoes.

Cost and Hours: €14.50, kids 4-12-€8.70, free for kids under 4, family ticket-€40 includes two adults and two kids; tickets are sold at the town TI, at the parking lot, and at either end of the museum; April-Oct daily 10:00-17:00, closed Nov-March, tel.

0228/351-111, www.zuiderzeemuseum.nl. Upon arrival, pick up the sheet listing all the events and activities on for the day.

Tourist Office: In the small square to the right of the train station, a helpful TI sells tickets to the museum, allowing visitors to hop on the shuttle boat just next to the office and skip the 15-minute hike to the museum (April-Oct daily 8:00-17:00, shorter winter hours, tel. 0228/313-164).

Getting There: Whether you're arriving by **train** from Amsterdam (2/hour, 1-hour trip) or Hoorn (2/hour, 25 minutes), it's a 15-minute walk from Enkhuizen's train station to the museum, or you can buy a museum ticket and take the shuttle boat (details below).

If you're taking the **Historic Triangle** trip, you'll arrive by boat from Medemblik and dock directly at the museum.

Drivers pay €5 to park at the museum lot (near the bridge at the start of the N-302 dike road—from there, it's a short, scenic, and free shuttle boat ride to the actual museum).

The Museum Shuttle Boat: A shuttle boat circles counterclockwise constantly (parking lot, west end of Zuiderzee Museum, Enkhuizen train station, parking lot, repeat, free with museum ticket, 15-minute circuit, 3-4/hour). There are three possibilities to consider:

If arriving by train, you have two options. Your first option: Catch the boat from the station for the views from the water, kill a few minutes while it waits at the parking lot, and cruise over to the west end of the museum from where you'll tour the museum from west to east, and finish by walking through the town to the station. Your second option: Walk from the station along the harbor, tour the museum from east to west, and catch the boat at the west end of the museum back to the Enkhuizen train station.

If arriving by car, you have no choice: Pay €5 to park and take the 10-minute cruise to the west end of the museum. Walk the length of the museum, finishing at the museum building on the east end. Then explore the town itself, and walk to the train station where you catch the boat back to the parking lot (note when the last boat departs—normally around 17:30).

۞ Self-Guided Museum Tour (West to East): The Zuiderzee Museum is a delight to explore, with something for all the senses— smell the wood fires and tanning vats, savor a bite of aged cheese and old-fashioned licorice, watch a windmill turn, hold a lump of coal, and catch the sound of wooden clogs on a brick road. Follow this tour, but don't be afraid to poke into houses and backyards (the curious get a lot more out of this experience—any open door is open for you). While I've listed stops here going from west to east, you can easily turn this book upside down and do it from east to west. The museum has two sections: the outdoor part (Buitenmuseum) with more than 100 historic buildings from around the Zuiderzee relocated right here, and, 200 yards away, the indoor museum (Binnenmuseum), filling a fine old merchant's home and warehouse. Regardless of which direction you go, the museum is laid out in a nice meandering flow with one section leading to the next.

West Dock and Museum Welcome: A museum attendant greets you at the dock where the shuttle boat arrives. If you don't have a museum ticket, buy one here. A nature preserve lies to the right. Head to the left. The first building to the left (the brick-maker's place) functions as an information center where you can get oriented to the museum. It's organized into sections (e.g., the Church District). Every building has a little plaque with a brief English description and a map showing the building's original location in the Zuiderzee region.

Fishing Village: The first section, the fishing village, includes many fun-to-explore homes. Dressed-up locals populate

the ramshackle village street from Urk—once a remote island across the Zuiderzee, now high and dry with a seemingly over-sized fishing fleet.

Polder Land: Head to the polder area, near the windmill. Windmills harness the power of the wind to turn Archimedes' screws, which, by rotating in a tube, pump water up over a dike and into the sea—continuing to drain reclaimed polder land. (Try it.) Nearby are vats used to cure fishing nets and a smokehouse where you can buy a tasty snack of smoked herring or eel.

The Urban Canal: Circle around to the urban canal zone (near the pavilion), lined with shops—such as a bakery and a cheese shop where 15,000 clumps of Gouda could be aged. Don't miss the pharmacy (marked *Apotheke "De Groote Gaper,"* under the queen with her mouth hanging open). Past the counter where the pharmacist weighs out little bottles of camphor—and hands out candy samples—you'll find a room full of open-mouthed giant heads. Traditionally, Dutch pharmacies were marked by a head with a gaping mouth (opening wide to say "aaaah" for the doctor, or for taking a pill). Many of these original heads are dark-skinned—

medicine, like people from the east or south of Europe, was considered mysterious and magical. A nearby theater may be showing a dramatic film that includes some grainy black-and-white footage of traditional Zuiderzee life (with English subtitles). As you curl around along the little canal, you'll pop into a rich sailor's home from the 18th century and find other trades represented, such as a barber and a sailmaker.

The Church District: Next, head into the church district, surrounding a reconstructed church dating from the 15th century. Because local builders were more familiar with boats than buildings, standing inside this church feels like being under an overturned boat (a common feeling in many Dutch village churches). Around the church are more shops, including the blacksmith and the fascinating cooper shop, where you can watch barrels being made. Don't miss the schoolhouse, with two period classrooms: one from 1905 and another from 1930. Just across the canal from the church area is a big self-service restaurant, with indoor and outdoor seating (€3 sandwiches, €10 meals).

Harbor: Now walk toward the cute, enclosed harbor, filled with Zuiderzee watercraft from ages past (just beyond it is a modern harbor, filled with pleasure boats). The little cluster of houses just beyond the harbor (where you may be able to catch a rope-making demonstration) is based on the island village of Marken (for info on visiting the real Marken, see the previous chapter).

Indoor Museum (200 yards from the outdoor section): Finally, as you leave the park through the main entrance, head for the indoor museum (same ticket and hours). As you exit, turn left and walk two blocks, watching for the museum on your right. This space shows off temporary exhibits (some of which relate to the Zuiderzee), as well as an impressive hall filled with nine old Zuiderzee boats. Notice that many of them have big, flat fins on the sides. Because the Zuiderzee could be very shallow, these boats didn't have a keel; the fins could be extended down into the water to provide more stability.

BACK TO AMSTERDAM

From the indoor museum, it's a scenic 15-minute walk, mostly along the water, through the bricks-and-canals town to the Enkhuizen train station: Exit the indoor museum to the right, follow the wall, and cross three bridges (watching for *Station* directional signs). If you finish the visit on the east end, hop on a shuttle boat to ride back to the train station. Drivers can hitch a shuttle-boat ride back to the parking lot either from the east-end shuttle stop or the one near the station (last boat at 17:30).

FLEVOLAND

About a sixth of the Netherlands is reclaimed land—much of it a short drive northeast of Amsterdam. To appreciate the Dutch quest to show the sea who's boss (and what the sea did to deserve it), visit the youngest Dutch province, Flevoland. The area is worthwhile only with a car, and far less charming than most other day-trip options. But it offers a fascinating drive for engineers or anyone else who wants to understand how the Dutch have confidently grabbed the reins from Mother Nature. It combines well with a visit to the town of Marken or Enkhuizen's Zuiderzee Museum.

Sights in Flevoland

On a day's drive out from Amsterdam, I'd start by heading north to Enkhuizen. (For insight into the traditional lifestyles laid high and dry by the diking of the Zuiderzee, consider detouring to Marken for a stroll, or tour Enkhuizen's Zuiderzee Museum.) Drive over the Houtribdijk (N-302) to Lelystad, and then—if time allows—continue up to the Schokland Museum. Figure about an hour from Amsterdam to Enkhuizen, a half-hour across the dike to Lelystad, a half-hour from Lelystad north to Schokland, and about an hour from Schokland back to Amsterdam (depending on traffic).

DIKE ROAD (HOUTRIBDIJK, N-302)
This 17-mile dike, built in 1975 as part of the Markerwaard reclamation project, is a reminder of the audacity of the Dutch vision to block off and pump out the entire inland sea. While the plan to reclaim all of the land south of the dike (the floor of the Markermeer, to your right) was abandoned, this road remains a handy transportation link connecting North Holland and Flevoland and the East. While there's little to actually see, driving over it is a novel

Taming the Zuiderzee

Look at a map of the Netherlands. The big expanse of water in the middle was once the Zuiderzee—literally the "South Sea." The Dutch have always had a love/hate relationship with this tempestuous sea. While it provided the Dutch with a convenient source of fish and trade—and an outlet to the Atlantic—the unpredictable bay also made life challenging. Over the centuries, entire towns were gradually eroded off the map.

But in 1918, the Dutch fought back and began to ingeniously tame the sea and reclaim their land with the Zuiderzee Works. The vision: to carve up what was the South Sea, bit by bit, drain it out, and turn it into dry and fertile land.

First, in 1932, they completed a sturdy dike (the Afsluitdijk) across the mouth of the sea—stretching 20 miles from Den Oever to Friesland and the northern Netherlands. This enclosed a body of water a bit smaller than Rhode Island, and succeeded in turning a dangerous, raging sea into a mild puddle.

After the Zuiderzee was diked off, the Dutch began to partition pieces of the sea floor, dike them off, and drain the water. The Noordoostpolder (185 square miles) and Flevopolder (375 square miles) were created; together, these became (in 1986) the 11th governmental province of Flevoland, with about 400,000 inhabitants—many of them older than the land they live on. An area that was once a merciless sea is now dotted with tranquil towns. The salty new seabed soil was treated organically and eventually became fertile farmland. The roads, commercial centers, and neighborhoods—made affordable to the masses—are all carefully planned and as tidy as can be.

Over time, the remaining salty water of the Zuiderzee became fresh, and in 1975, it was further divided in the middle with

experience. At the start (near Enkhuizen), ships float in a channel (hydroduct) above the road. The stone monument midway marks the joining of North Holland with Flevoland.

At the other end, a bridge deposits you in Flevoland, the only entirely reclaimed province in the Netherlands. It's filled with bedroom communities famous for being nondescript. But it allows the residents of a densely inhabited country the option of owning a freestanding home, big garage, and piece of yard. The commute to Amsterdam is long for working parents, so Flevoland kids are bored, and often have drug problems and need counseling. These planned communities create an almost "Stepford Wives"-style contentment, a community designed to make Dutch suburban dreams come true—at the expense of the Dutch free spirit.

the 17-mile-long Houtribdijk, connecting Enkhuizen and Lelystad. This created two bodies of water: the IJsselmeer in the north, and the Markermeer in the south. The eventual plan was to drain almost the entire Markermeer to create a third big polder, called the Markerwaard (160 square miles), to use for farming, residential zones, and a new airport. However, by this time, public opinion about the need for polder land had swayed. There were ecological concerns: Fishermen in villages like Urk and Marken reported that they could no longer harvest the increasingly unsalty lake, dismantling the local economy. (Nowadays, these old fishing towns host more pleasure craft than serious fishing boats.) Also,

people enjoyed the Markermeer as a recreation zone, and viewed it as a useful reservoir in case of drought. The Markerwaard was never built.

There are several places in the Netherlands to appreciate the greatness of the Zuiderzee Works. Driving over either of the big dikes—the Afsluitdijk (A-7) in the north, or the Houtribdijk (N-302), between Enkhuizen and Lelystad—gives you a sense of the scale of these projects. And actually driving around Flevoland drives home how a little country worked hard to create new land; Flevoland's Schokland Museum and the museums in Lelystad are particularly evocative.

LELYSTAD

The capital of Flevoland, Lelystad is named for the statesman who originally proposed the Zuiderzee Works. Driving around the town, it's clear that everything was planned. The residential neighborhoods feel computer-generated and were all built at the same time. There are speed bumps on all roads, and the layout is a winding maze making it easy to get lost. The business district attempts to spice things up with wacky modern design elements.

On Lelystad's harbor are two interesting sights: a ship and an exhibit about reclaiming the land.

Batavia Yard (Bataviawerf)

Tour a replica of a 17th-century sailing ship built for the Dutch East India Company, the *VOC Batavia*, and see how workers currently are building a second vessel—a replica of the 17th-century Dutch battleship *De 7 Provinciën*, one of the largest historical naval reconstructions in the world. Your visit includes peeks into a wood-carving workshop, a rigging workshop, and a blacksmith's foundry.

Cost and Hours: €11, combo-ticket with Nieuw Land Museum–€16, does not accept Museumkaart, daily 10:00-17:00, Bataviaplein 2, tel. 0320/261-409, www.bataviawerf.nl.

Nieuw Land Museum

This museum covers the largest reclamation project in history—the "taming" of the Zuiderzee (see sidebar). The story of the struggle against the water is told through historic films, sound bites, models, and interactive displays. Exhibits also explore the geological evolution of Flevoland and the prehistoric people—hunters, fishermen and gatherers—who lived here 6,000 years ago. The unusual building consists of two superimposed blocks, symbolizing the region's interconnections between land and water.

Cost and Hours: €8, combo-ticket with Batavia Yard–€16, Tue-Fri 10:00-17:00, Sat-Sun 11:30-17:00, closed Mon, Oostvaardersdijk 113, tel. 0320/225-900, www.nieuwlanderfgoed.nl.

▲▲SCHOKLAND MUSEUM

Once a long, skinny island with a few scant villages, Schokland (about a half-hour drive northeast of Lelystad) was gradually enveloped by the sea, until the king condemned and evacuated it in 1859.

But after the sea around it was tamed and drained, Schokland was turned into a museum of Dutch traditions...and engineering prowess.

Cost and Hours: €6; July-Aug daily 10:00-17:00; April-June and Oct Tue-Sun 11:00-17:00, closed Mon; Nov-March Fri-Sun 11:00-17:00, closed Mon-Thu; Middelbuurt 3, tel. 0527/251-396, www.schokland.nl.

Getting There: From Amsterdam, it's about an hour's **drive** north (assuming there's no traffic), but the trip offers travelers an insightful glimpse at Dutch land reclamation. Leave Amsterdam's ring freeway, following signs for *Almere*—first southeast on A-1, then northeast on A-6. You'll drive the length of the very flat reclaimed island of Flevoland—past the towns of Almere and Lelystad—and pass a striking line of power-generating windmills spinning like gigantic pinwheels as you cross out of Flevoland and into Noordoostpolder, the reclaimed "Northeast Polder" that includes Schokland. Take the Urk exit (#13), turn right, and follow blue signs for *Schokland*.

FLEVOLAND

❍ **Self-Guided Tour:** After buying your ticket, you'll watch a 15-minute **film** (press button to start in English) about the history of the town, its loss to the sea, and its reclamation.

Then tour the exposition called **Schokland: An Island in Time,** which explains how Schokland was reclaimed as part of what would become the Northeast Polder, beginning in 1936. After being enclosed by a sturdy dike, a yearlong project drained this area of water in 1942 (while the Netherlands was occupied by the Nazis). Various Allied bombers were shot down and crashed into this area (including one whose mangled propeller is displayed just outside the museum), joining the dozens of shipwrecks that already littered the seafloor.

A model shows the full territory of the Northeast Polder, which is carefully planned in concentric circles around the central town of Emmeloord (with Schokland and another former island, Urk, creating a pair of oddball bulges in the otherwise tidy pattern).

The exhibit explains that this isn't the first time this area has been dry land. From prehistoric times through the Middle Ages, much of what is today the Northeast Polder was farmed (many old tools have been discovered). In 1100, medieval engineers even attempted a primitive (and ultimately unsuccessful) effort to reclaim the land. Other remains from former residents include bones from mammoths and other prehistoric mammals, and a primitive 2,450-year-old canoe.

Then you'll head into the **Schokkerhuisje** to learn about the people who lived here (called *Schokkers*) until they were evacuated in 1859. Up to 650 people at a time lived on Schokland, residing in settlements on hills called *terpen* while they farmed the often-flooded land below. Like the rest of the Netherlands, this little island was divided in half by religion: part Catholic, part Protestant. This museum holds artifacts from the former town of Middelbuurt. You'll see traditional *Schokker* costumes (abandoned when they left the island) and a map of the entire island.

Back outside, go into the former **town church,** with a ceiling like the hull of a ship, a pulpit like a crow's nest, and a model ship hanging from the ceiling—appropriate for the seafaring residents of a once nearly submerged island.

Finally, follow the path (below the church) to walk around the base of the former island—now surrounded by **farm fields.** When farmers first tilled their newly reclaimed soil a half-century ago, they uncovered more than just muck and mollusks. You'll see a pair of rusty anchors and a giant buoy that used to bob in the harbor—now lying on its side and still tethered to the ground. Examine the stone dike and black wooden seawall built by residents in a futile attempt to stay above water. The post with the long blue measuring strip helped residents keep an eye on the ever-rising water level.

SOUTH OF AMSTERDAM

Most of the Netherlands' most historic and interesting cities—as if purposefully arranged by the tourist board—line up along a single train line that runs south from Amsterdam.

With trains running at least every 15 minutes, it takes just over an hour to conveniently lace together Amsterdam, Haarlem, Leiden, The Hague, Delft, and Rotterdam. A couple of flowery destinations off the main train line—the Keukenhof garden show and the Aalsmeer flower auction—are also worth a visit.

As you travel through the countryside, make a point to look out the window for a glimpse of the Netherlands both past and present. Overstuffed cows moo contentedly in pastures, canals big and small turn pristine fields into graph paper, old-fashioned windmills spin, sleek modern bike paths trace canals and train tracks, idyllic pea patches burst with produce watched over by little potting sheds, and so on. The trip is a sightseeing treat in itself.

The towns themselves are so different, yet all unmistakably Dutch. Familiarize yourself with your options so you can hop out at whichever place intrigues you...and enjoy. In most cases, the train drops you right in the heart of town, or just a short and scenic stroll away.

The towns in this section are neatly bookended by a pair of home-base cities: Haarlem (to the north, near Amsterdam) and Delft (to the south, near Rotterdam). From either of these bases—or from Amsterdam itself—you can reach any of these destinations in a quick hop.

Notice that sleepy, accessible Delft—with its mellow pace, postcard-perfect canals, and generous selection of hotels and restaurants—is sandwiched between the big cities of The Hague and Rotterdam (both interesting, but less appealing to stay in). Delft is basically a bedroom community for both cities—close enough that you could make the connection on bicycle rather than on rails.

If you need a beach fix, try Scheveningen (near The Hague, listed on page 395) or Zandvoort (near Haarlem, described on page 237).

DESTINATIONS

One of the best destinations in this region—**Delft**—is covered earlier in this book.

Keukenhof and Aalsmeer

Flower lovers have two very different choices:

▲▲▲ **Keukenhof:** The can't-miss-it garden show, in the town of Lisse, is open for only two months every spring (mid-March through mid-May).

▲▲ **FloraHolland Aalsmeer Flower Auction:** This fast-paced auction, held in a vast warehouse near Schiphol Airport, shows you the business side of the Netherlands' beautiful flower scene (weekday mornings year-round).

▲Leiden

With its prestigious university, this pleasant small city—which was also the birthplace of Rembrandt—is the Netherlands' answer to Cambridge or Oxford. It offers visitors a low-impact, fun-to-explore cityscape of canals and old ivy-covered university buildings, as well as more and better museums than other Dutch cities of its size. Leiden's American Pilgrim Museum is closed Sunday through Tuesday, and its other museums are closed Monday.

▲The Hague

This big-city seat of Dutch government is a sleepy, modern-feeling town with the tourable parliament complex and a smattering of good museums. But the reason most visitors come is to tour the excellent Mauritshuis Royal Picture Gallery, with a remarkable collection of Dutch Masters art—including Vermeer's *Girl with a Pearl Earring*.

▲Rotterdam

Europe's largest port is built for trade much mightier than tourism, and its lack of cutesy wooden-shoe culture makes for a harsh contrast with most other Dutch towns. Still, it's a mighty city, bombed after World War II and rebuilt with a gleaming skyline. A bike ride through its towering skyscrapers and a sightseeing harbor cruise provide a dose of honest Holland you'll find nowhere else.

KEUKENHOF AND AALSMEER

Of all the day trips mentioned in this book, these are all about flowers: a lovely garden show (open only in spring) and a business-like flower auction (open weekday mornings year-round). Both are an easy half-day trip from Amsterdam or Haarlem.

▲▲▲KEUKENHOF

This is the greatest bulb-flower garden on earth, open for only two months in spring. Each spring, seven million flowers, enjoy-

ing the sandy soil of the Dutch dunes and polder land, conspire to thrill even the most horti-culturally challenged. Along with flowers, you'll enjoy all the Dutch icons, with a work-ing windmill, gaily playing carillons, warm-off-the-griddle syrup waffles, and wooden shoes galore. Get the map to be sure to get in on all the thrills. It's flat-out fun.

This 80-acre park is packed with tour groups daily; for the least crowds and the best light, go late in the day. Keukenhof is located at the northern tip of the town of Lisse, at the center of the "Dune and Bulb Region."

Cost and Hours: €16, not covered by Museumkaart, open mid-March through mid-May, daily 8:00-19:30, last entry at 18:00, tel. 0252/465-555, www.keukenhof.nl.

Combo-Ticket: €23.50 combo-ticket covers park entry and round-trip bus transport from Leiden, Schiphol Airport, or Haarlem; €28.50 from Amsterdam (available on Keukenhof website).

Getting There: From Amsterdam's Leidseplein, take bus #197 to Schiphol and change to bus #858 (2/hour, 1.25 hours). From Haarlem, take bus #50 to Lisse (4/hour, 1 hour). From Schiphol Airport, catch bus #858 (8/hour, 40 minutes). From Amsterdam or Haarlem you can also take a train to Leiden, then bus #854 (Keukenhof Express). Drivers will find Lisse well-marked from the A-6 expressway south of Amsterdam.

▲▲FLORAHOLLAND AALSMEER FLOWER AUCTION (BLOEMENVEILING)

Get a bird's-eye view of the huge Dutch flower industry in this cavernous building where the world's flower prices are set. You'll wander on elevated walkways (through what's claimed to be the biggest commercial building on earth) over literally trainloads of freshly cut flowers. About half of all the flowers exported from Holland are auctioned off here, in four huge auditoriums. The flowers are shipped here overnight (for maximum freshness), auctioned at the crack of dawn, and distributed as quickly as possible.

Cost and Hours: €6, not covered by Museumkaart, Mon-Wed and Fri 7:00-11:00, Thu 7:00-9:00, closed Sat-Sun, gift shop, cafeteria, tel. 0297/393-939, www.floraholland.com.

Getting There: By bus, you can reach the flower auction from Amsterdam (Connexxion bus #172 from Central Station, 4/hour, 1 hour, get off at "BVFH Hoofdingang" stop) or from Haarlem (take bus #140 to the town of Aalsmeer, transfer to bus #172, 4/hour, 1 hour).

Aalsmeer, which is close to the airport, makes a handy last fling for drivers before dropping off your car at the airport and catching a late-morning weekday flight out (bus #198 also runs between the auction and the airport; 4/hour, 20 minutes). From the A-6 expressway south of Amsterdam, drivers take the Aalsmeer exit (#3) and follow signs for *Aalsmeer*, then *Bloemenveiling*. Once you reach the complex, carefully follow the *P Tourist* signs to park on top of the garage, then take the elevator downstairs and follow *Tourist* signs to the visitors center.

Visiting the Flower Auction: For the best floral variety and auction action, the earlier, the better (best before 9:30, and the auction closes down by 11:00).

Standing above all those blooms, take a deep, fragrant breath and hold it in. As you wander, keep an eye out for tulip-shaped "listening posts," and press the English button for on-the-spot information. Peering into the auction halls, you'll see that clocks are projected on two big screens. This is a "Dutch auction," meaning that the price starts high and then ticks down, until buyers push the button at the price they're willing to pay. Think about the high stakes and the need for decisiveness...there's no time to think things over as the auctioneer calls, "Going once, going twice..."

Most of the flowers are purchased by wholesalers and exporters. You'll see the busy beehive of the distribution process as workers scurry to load carts of flowers onto little tractors to zip to awaiting buyers. Up along the ceiling, look for the suspended orange trams. This "Aalsmeer Shuttle" zips loads of flowers over the workers' heads to the distribution center across the street, far more quickly and efficiently than trucks.

You'll wind up at the even more elaborate Rose Market, where 450 buyers keep their eyes peeled on three different auction clocks as they jostle to buy the auction's most popular item. As you circle back to the entrance, you'll see the company's testing lab, where they actually create and test new varieties of flowers.

LEIDEN

Leiden (LIE-den) is the Oxford of Holland. Its prestigious university imbues the town with an upscale aura—and with 20,000 students, who keep otherwise hoity-toity Leiden firmly rooted on the ground. The birthplace of Rembrandt, the final European home of the Pilgrims before they set sail for America, and a manufacturing center famous in the Golden Age for its top-quality textiles—Leiden has many claims to fame. But perhaps most enticing of all is that it's simply a pleasant, relatively low-key Dutch city that's fun to explore...and happens to have more than its fair share of great sights and museums.

PLANNING YOUR TIME

Often-overlooked Leiden is tucked between Amsterdam and The Hague on Holland's busy north-south rail line. If you have only a few hours to spare, hop out at the station, throw your bag in a locker, and take a walk through town. The pretty and historic core can be appreciated in a three-hour stroll; with more time, you can dip into some of Leiden's fascinating museums. Note that the American Pilgrim Museum is closed Sunday through Tuesday, and Leiden's other museums are closed Monday. Market days are Wednesday and Saturday (bigger).

Orientation to Leiden

With about 120,000 residents, Leiden is slightly bigger than Haarlem or Delft. The neatly oblong old center is lassoed by its former moat *(singel)*, and the two branches of the Rhine River merge at its center—creating an inviting network of canals big and small. The train

station sits at its northwestern corner, a short walk from the town center.

TOURIST INFORMATION

The TI on the plaza directly in front of the train station—just look left as you walk out the door (free maps, self-guided walking tour brochures for sale, Mon-Fri 7:00-19:00, Sat 10:00-16:00, Sun 11:00-15:00, Stationsweg 41, tel. 071/516-6000, www.leiden.nl).

Local Guide: Marike Hoogduin-Berkhout is an excellent local guide who leads tours of her hometown of Leiden, as well as The Hague or Amsterdam (€125/up to 2 hours, tel. 071/361-7793, mobile 0653-773-808, info@zephyrart.nl).

ARRIVAL IN LEIDEN

Leiden's manageable train station has **lockers** (up the escalator just inside the main entrance, by tracks 1/2) and **bike rental** (exit out the back of the station and turn right; €7.50/day, €50 deposit, open long hours daily). To reach the center of town, simply head out the main doors and proceed straight down Stationsweg for five minutes, following my self-guided walk.

Leiden Walk

This 2.5-mile self-guided walk begins at the train station, curls through the center of the city to reveal its university and Rembrandt connections, climbs up to Leiden's historic castle, then loops right back to where you started. I'd give it about three hours, at a leisurely pace, not counting any sightseeing stops.

• *Walk out the front door of the train station. In the plaza out front, notice the TI on your left. To begin our walk, continue straight ahead down Stationsweg one block to the bridge. Find a viewpoint on the left side of the bridge, and look out over the canal known as the...*

Singel

Like many Dutch towns, historically Leiden was surrounded by a

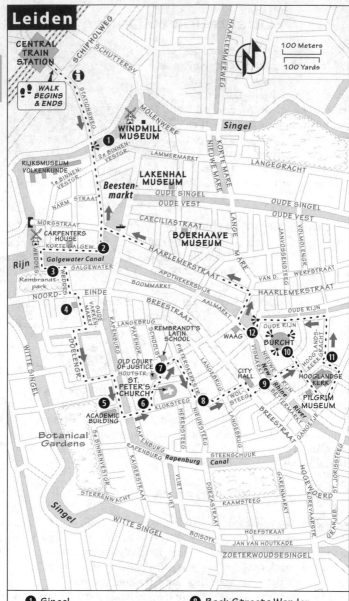

Leiden

CENTRAL TRAIN STATION

WALK BEGINS & ENDS

WINDMILL MUSEUM

RIJKSMUSEUM VOLKENKUNDE

Beestenmarkt

LAKENHAL MUSEUM

CARPENTERS HOUSE

Rijn

Galgewater Canal

Rembrandt-park

NOORD-

BOERHAAVE MUSEUM

Rembrandt's Latin School

WAAG

OLD COURT OF JUSTICE

ST. PETER'S CHURCH

ACADEMIC BUILDING

Botanical Gardens

Rapenburg Canal

Steenschuur Canal

BURCHT

CITY HALL

HOOGLANDSE KERK

PILGRIM MUSEUM

New Rhine River

100 Meters

100 Yards

① Singel
② Galgewater
③ Rembrandtplein
④ Loridanshofje
⑤ Leiden University
⑥ St. Peter's Church Square
⑦ Gerecht
⑧ Back-Streets Wander
⑨ Rhinefront Market & Corn Bridge
⑩ Burcht
⑪ Hooglandse Kerkgracht
⑫ Hoogstraat

LEIDEN

singel (moat). But Leiden's is unusually well-preserved. Much of the moat was built in the late 16th and early 17th centuries—after the Spanish siege, when Leiden was booming. The jagged zigzags of its serrated city wall and moat are still evident in the city's footprint.

Originally the moat ran in front of a fortified wall. That wall is long gone, but the windmill in the distance suggests how tall it was. The higher a windmill is situated, the better it's able to capture the wind—so, logically, windmills were often built on top of the town walls. This one is a "platform mill" (*stellingmolen*)—the miller lived in the house below, and could rotate only the windmill's head (with the wings) to face the wind. After our walk, you can climb up there to tour the fascinating **Windmill Museum** that fills its many funhouse floors (described later, under "Sights in Leiden").

Turn around to face the opposite direction. On the riverbank is the **Rijksmuseum Volkenkunde** (Royal Museum of Ethnology), with fine exhibits on world cultures; their display of art from the former Dutch colony of Indonesia is especially good. This is one of several major museums in this small town. As the Netherlands' traditional seat of learning, Leiden seems to have more than its share of culture.

• *Continue straight across the bridge. After another block, you pop out at the market square called* **Beestenmarkt** *(where animals—beesten—were traditionally traded). Continue to the end of the square. The big bridge on the left leads to* **Haarlemmerstraat***, the city's main shopping drag and a good place to browse for lunch (we'll return this way later, after our walk). In the opposite direction, the similarly shop-lined* **Morsstraat** *leads to the Morspoort gate. And* **canal cruises** *leave from the little house at the top of the bridge.*

For now, pass up these temptations and keep going straight along the canal. When you hit the wider canal, turn right and walk toward the windmill along...

Galgewater

The morbidly named "Gallows Water" is named for the field at the far end of the canal, where the corpses of executed criminals were put on public display to bully people into compliance.

Stroll along the canal. On your left, notice the fine collection of historic **houseboats** from the 1880s through the 1920s. Locals still live in these, paying about €200,000 for this cramped, if waterfront, "property" (near the dock, see the bank of mailboxes for residents).

After one block, look for the tall

Leiden History

The Romans built a settlement in the lowlands here along the Rhine River as early as the fifth century A.D. Later, a medieval town sprouted where the two Rhine branches meet, marked by an artificial mound with a bailey on top (today's fortified Burcht). Leiden became part of the realm of the Counts of Holland, achieving city rights in 1266. Throughout the Middle Ages, Leiden steadily produced cloth that was sold across Europe, as well as beer and pewter. By 1500, it was Holland's biggest and most important city.

With the arrival of the religious wars of the 1500s, Leiden's strategic location made it a target. Beginning in October of 1573, during the Eighty Years' War, pro-Catholic Spanish troops invaded rebellious, Protestant Holland. They laid siege to Leiden for the better part of a year, hoping to overtake the city. Completely surrounded and cut off from resources, Leiden's population was halved by starvation and the plague.

Finally, William of Orange raised an army to come to Leiden's aid. William's army breached the dikes near Rotterdam, flooding the low-lying territory all the way to Leiden. Then they waited for prevailing winds to push their flat-bottomed boats north, to advance on terrified Spanish troops and, eventually, to liberate Leiden. The boats also brought bread and herring to feed the starving townspeople. On October 3, 1574, the city gave thanks for "The Relief of Leiden" by feasting on foods that are still eaten ceremonially on that date each year: herring on white bread and *hutspot* (a pot of stew that the Spaniards left

"Carpenters House" building on the right (at #21, just after the little lane). Appreciate this quintessentially Dutch house: stripes of red and white bricks, shutters with the town colors of red and white, and a classic stepped-gable design. Built in 1612, as Leiden was booming, this building housed architects, carpenters, and bricklayers who were hard at work expanding the city. Since 1988, it has been a subsidized housing complex for local seniors—who must negotiate a very old building with no elevators. Walk a few steps past the front door and discreetly duck through the gate into the garden courtyard to see how the crenellated facade hides a much larger complex. (The former warehouse along the back of the courtyard once held building supplies.)

Continuing along the canal, you'll reach another **windmill**. A different style than the one we saw earlier, this is a "post mill" *(standerdmolen)*, which means that the entire structure rotates on its base. On weekends, you may be able to go inside to see the gears.

Turn left at the windmill and cross the bridge. Notice the **poem** written high on the wall on your right—one of over a hundred such

simmering as they beat a hasty retreat).

Following the siege, Leiden boomed. Over the next 50 years, the town's population tripled, buoyed by immigrants from lands where Protestants were still persecuted (including Huguenots from France and Belgium). These new arrivals brought know-how and a desire to work, and Leiden's textile trade again brought it wealth and fame. Its specialty was a flannel-like fabric called *laken*, coveted by bourgeois merchants and wealthy aristocrats. (In most famous Dutch Golden Age portraits of stuffy-looking people, the subjects wear suits of Leiden-made *laken*.) The material was so prized that outfits were passed down from parent to child.

During Leiden's post-siege Golden Age (late 16th and early 17th centuries), several other events helped put it on the map. As a sign of appreciation for the city's determined resistance, William of Orange founded Holland's first university in Leiden in 1575. In 1606, a Leiden miller's wife gave birth to a boy named Rembrandt, who would grow up and move to Amsterdam, and eventually become one of the world's greatest painters. And a small group of religious refugees from across the English Channel spent 12 years here before setting sail for the New World—the Pilgrims.

Leiden continues to be a center of learning, trade, and the arts...and a pleasant, low-impact place to stop off for an engaging visit between Amsterdam and the big Dutch and Belgian cities farther south.

verses scrawled on buildings all over highly literate Leiden. While this one's in the Frisian dialect, others are in English.

• *Once across the bridge, continue straight a few more steps down Weddesteeg, and pause at the pebbled square.*

Rembrandtplein

Leiden's favorite son was born in 1606, in a house that faced this square (find the plaque on the modern building that replaced that one, in 1978). Rembrandt van Rijn was the son of a miller who manned a windmill "on the Rhine" (as the name implies; you can faintly see the footprint of his former mill by the boat-rental place at the far corner of the square). His family owned a lot of property and  was well-to-do enough to send young Rembrandt to Latin school (like today's prep schools), and later to Leiden University. Rembrandt enrolled at Leiden U., but never actually attended any classes—even at age 14, he was only interested in painting. At age 17, he decided that he'd make more money in Amsterdam than here... and with that, he was gone. (For more on his life and career after that point, see page 149.)

On the little mound in the pebbled park, a life-size statue of a young Rembrandt appreciates his later self-portrait. Leiden savors the idea that this world-famous artist spent his formative years right here. Exploring town today, imagine li'l Rembrandt poking his way through Leiden's tight courtyards and zipping across its tranquil canals, finding inspiration for his later artistic life.

• *Continue down Weddesteeg, and turn left at the cross-street (Noordeinde). After one block, turn right down the wide, tree-lined Oude Varkenmarkt ("Old Pig Market"). In the middle of the long, brick building near the start of this street (on the right, across from #10), check to see if the door under the yellow arch is unlocked. If it's open, go inside. (Don't be shy, but do be discreet.)*

Loridanshofje

Leiden has 35 *hofjes*—residential courtyards—like this one. Similar to a *begijnhof*, this was a building funded by wealthy, churchgoing donors to house poor people in exchange for prayer. Today, many *hofjes* are used for student housing. The layout of this one is typical: 12 houses (symbolic of the 12 Apostles) in a U-shape, ringing a central courtyard with a well in the middle and a covered gallery on the far side. We'll walk through another *hofje*  later on this walk, and a TI brochure locates all of them. These are public property, but since people do live in them, try to keep a low profile.

• *Keep going down Oude Varkenmarkt. You'll pop out at a canal crossroads. Continue straight, under the **St. George Gate** (Sint Jorispoort, from 1645, marking the former headquarters of the local civic guard—like the gang in Rembrandt's* Night Watch*). The two red crossed keys on the gate are Leiden's city symbols (locals joke: "One key is St. Peter's, and the other is a spare.") Continue along the lily-padded canal, with a social-housing project on your right. Turn left over the next bridge (under the brick arch) and continue one block along Doelensteeg, surrounded by modern university faculties. You'll pop out at the wide canal called Rapenburg, with some of the finest homes in Leiden. Turn right and walk along the canal toward the next bridge. But before you reach* *that bridge, duck through the gate of the big, stately, striped-brick building on your right.*

Leiden University

William of Orange founded the Netherlands' first university in Leiden in 1575. Albert Einstein taught here, and its students have included Rembrandt, philosopher René Descartes, painter Jan Steen, novelist Henry Fielding, US President John Quincy Adams, scientist Enrico Fermi, and filmmaker Paul Verhoeven, as well as multiple Dutch prime ministers and the last three Dutch monarchs (including the current king, Willem-Alexander). Today, one in every six Leiden residents is a student. There's no unified campus; instead, students live scattered around the city center (including at *hofjes* like the one we saw earlier). Because Delft is home to the technical university, and Leiden U. has more of a liberal arts bent, locals half-joke that male students ride the train in from Delft to find a wife in Leiden.

As you stand in the entry courtyard, the big building on your left is the main **Academic Building** (Academiegebouw). This former nunnery was repurposed after the Reformation, and now hosts university events (unfortunately, it's not open to visitors—but you can peek through the windows).

Straight ahead at the end of the corridor, step out into the impressive **botanical gardens.** This historic complex was founded in the 1590s—back when understanding plant life went hand-in-hand with the medical sciences. They say that a Flemish professor, recently returned from a trip to Turkey, planted the first tulip bulb in Dutch soil right here. Scientists like those at Leiden University found that tulips thrive in Holland, and before long...tulip mania. Those who pay admission can explore the sprawling grounds, with an extensive collection of Japanese plants, a fine rose garden, and a complex of restored old greenhouses (€7, buy ticket and enter on the right, daily 10:00-18:00, www.hortusleiden.nl).

• *Head back out to the big Rapenburg canal, turn right, continue to the bridge at the corner, cross it, and head up charming Kloksteeg. In one block, you emerge at...*

St. Peter's Church Square (Pieterskerkhof)

The huge church itself is worth a peek, though it isn't an active church—it's used mostly for events and concerts (€2, not covered by Museumkaart, daily, www.pieterskerk.com). But for American visitors, this site is most significant for its role in Pilgrim history. In 1609, a large community of Pilgrims fled religious persecution in England, coming first to Amsterdam, then settling here in Leiden, concentrated in the square around this church. The building on the right, at #21 (an almshouse marked *Anno 1683*), was the site of the home and church of John Robinson, the Pilgrims' minister. Directly across the street, giant plaques embedded in the rounded corner of the church explain some Pilgrim history.

The Pilgrims were forced to thread a theological needle: While extremely rigid in their faith, they needed a relatively tolerant, progressive social context to thrive. When Holland's truce with Spain expired, the Pilgrims feared that the peace they found here wasn't to last. In the summer of 1620, they set out for the New World.

Leiden residents feel proud of their connection to American history. While at sea, the Pilgrims outlined rules for their planned society, the Mayflower Compact. Many of these tenets, which later formed the basis for the US Constitution, were inspired by the tolerant policies of William of Orange, which the Pilgrims became familiar with here. And the American Thanksgiving—celebrated in the autumn by the Pilgrims and their new Native American neighbors—seems partly inspired by the "Relief of Leiden" ceremonial meal that takes place here each October 3 (see the "Leiden History" sidebar, earlier).

For more about the Pilgrims, see page 96.

• *Circle clockwise around the left side of the church. From the back of the building, head up the narrow lane called Muskadelsteeg to...*

Gerecht

This tranquil, leafy square—whose name literally means "Justice"—is dominated by a large, turreted building that housed the 17th-century prison and court of justice (see Lady Justice holding her scales up top). Parts of the building are much older—from the 12th century—and the justice meted out here was medieval in every sense. Prisoners would be put to work: men dyeing cloth, women spinning wool. Many were tortured and executed right on this square. They'd be drawn and quartered, or their bones crushed on a wheel. Then their corpses were taken out to display at the park at the end of the "Gallows Water" (Galgewater) we saw earlier.

Before leaving the square, find the stepped-gabled house at the start of the tiny lane called Schoolsteeg, at the opposite corner of the square from the justice tower. This building was the young **Rembrandt's Latin school** (so we've basically been retracing his daily walk to school). Peek in the window to see a little Rembrandt, hard at work at his desk.

• *Head past the house up Lokhorststraat, turning right down Pieterskerkstraat. This takes you past the apse of the church, and a fun...*

Leiden Back-Streets Wander

Enjoy this atmospheric little courtyard. Notice the houses that huddle up against the apse, which the church rented out as a source of income.

Circling most of the way around the apse—but just before you hit the lane called Kloksteeg—look behind the tree with benches on your left, where you'll find a small doorway. Duck through this and down the lane into another, adorable, whitewashed *hofje*. Rather than students, these four homes house seniors. Continue through the far end of the *hofje*, then angle left through the grass yard and up the lane. You'll pop out at the street called **Langebrug.** Just to your right, at #93, was a residence of the painter Jan Steen; to the left lived Rembrandt's teacher.

Continue straight across Langebrug and up the little lane called Wolsteeg. You'll emerge at the busy and aptly named Breestraat ("Broadway")—busy with buses, bikes, and taxis. You're face-to-face with Leiden's late 16th-century **City Hall**, whose carillon tower jangles happy tunes.

• *Cross Breestraat (carefully) and jog a bit to the right to curl around the side of City Hall (following* Burcht *signs up Koornbrugsteeg). You'll run into...*

Leiden's Rhinefront Market

This is the New Rhine (Nieuwe Rijn), which meets up with the Old Rhine (Oude Rijn) about a hundred yards to your left—we'll be there later. From here, the Rhine River heads to the North Sea. While we've passed a few smaller market squares (basically wide streets) on this walk, Leiden lacked the "Grote Markt" (Great Market) of some Dutch towns, like Haarlem or Delft. So merchants would simply unload their wares at the wide wharf along  this river—today made even wider with restaurant-table-loaded barges. **Koornbrug**—the covered "Corn Bridge"—was built in 1825 to provide grain merchants protection from the rain. Leiden still hosts a thriving market here: Saturday is the big market day, while Wednesday hosts a smaller assortment. This area is fun to explore and browse for a meal.

• *Head across the covered Koornbrug and proceed straight up Burgsteeg (lined with nice shops—kitchenwear, home decor, and so on). You'll dead-end at Nieuwstraat. Turn left through the gate, and head up the steep stairs to the...*

Burcht

Let me guess—huffing and puffing, are we? This hike is a rude awakening if you've gotten used to the near-total lack of hills here in the Netherlands. This artifi-cial mound, built in the eighth or ninth century, is part of a system of castle construction called "motte and bailey"—that is, a fort (bailey) sitting upon a mound (motte). A castle has stood here since around 1150—first made of wood, later of stone. Climbing up into today's

version, you enter what feels like an empty shell. But there was never a big fortress here—just a walled courtyard where residents could safely set up tents in times of siege. And their siege resis-tance relied upon the well you see in the middle of the courtyard, which is still attached via a network of pipes to a wellhead down on the market canal. Climb up to the top of the wall and stroll all the way around for 360-degree views over Leiden, with key land-marks identified by orientation boards. Examining the wall you're standing on, notice the porous gray stone, which formed part of the original wall and was scavenged from Roman ruins.

• *Head back down the way you came, and proceed straight up Nieuw-straat, toward the big Hooglandse Kerk. On your right, at the corner of Beschuitsteeg opposite the church, is the oldest house in Leiden—which is also home to the unique and excellent* **American Pilgrim Museum** *(highly recommended, but open only a few afternoons each week; for de-tails, see "Sights in Leiden," next page).*

  Consider stepping into the church's vast, whitewashed interior (free entry). Then circle around to the far side of the church, and head up the tree-lined...

Hooglandse Kerkgracht

This gracefully arcing strip passes (on the left) the beautiful build-ing that once housed the **Holy Ghost Orphanage** (Heilige Geest of Arme Wees en Kinderhuis). Notice the colorful but wretched orphans topping the ceremonial gateway. Step into its courtyard to appreciate the enormous scale of this building, which—from the 16th century until 1961—housed up to 700 orphans at once.

• *Emerging at the canal, turn left. The next part of this walk follows the Old Rhine to the point where it meets the New Rhine.*

Hoogstraat and Back to the Station

Surrounded by lively café tables and general market bustle, take in the liveliness of Leiden. The light gray, highly ornamented building on your left (as you face the confluence) is the **Waag**—a weigh-house from 1658, where merchants would traditionally weigh their goods (in the relief above the door, notice the burly stevedores doing some heavy lifting). If it's market day, consider hooking left back down the embankments to browse the wares.

When you're ready to head back to the station, pass in front of the Waag and cross the adjacent Waaghoofdbrug footbridge. Continue up one block (to the ornate church), where you can turn left and follow the lively **Haarlemmerstraat** pedestrian shopping zone for several blocks. About halfway up the street, you could detour a block up Sionsteeg (on your right) to visit the **Boerhaave Museum**, with its bizarre and fascinating collection of historical science exhibits (see "Sights in Leiden," later). The **Lakenhal Museum** (master painters)—which is closed for renovation until at least mid-2017—is a few blocks farther north. Otherwise, continue straight ahead until you hit the canal. From here, you could turn right to walk up to the **Windmill Museum** (see "Sights in Leiden"); or you could continue over the bridge, turn right along the left side of Beestenmarkt, and retrace your steps back to the station.

Sights in Leiden

▲▲American Pilgrim Museum

Worth ▲▲▲ for historians, this quirky and engaging sight is Leiden's hidden treasure. Dr. Jeremy Bangs, an American histo-

rian, has filled the oldest house in Leiden (from the late 1360s, including the original fireplace and floors) with an eclectic collection of historical items. No Pilgrims actually lived here, but the collection offers an intriguing glimpse at early 17th-century lifestyles. This isn't just a "museum"—it's an experience, as Dr. Bangs tells you (with his entertainingly dry wit) the complete story behind any item that interests you. It's very hands-on (mostly *his* hands), as he demonstrates how various antique items were used. Be careful as you explore the house's two delightfully creaky rooms—many items are as fragile as they are priceless, and there are essentially no barriers between you and the collection.

Cost and Hours: €5, not covered by Museumkaart, Wed-Sat 13:00-17:00, closed Sun-Tue, Beschuitsteeg 9, tel. 071/512-2413, www.leidenamericanpilgrimmuseum.org.

▲Boerhaave Museum

Fun, fascinating, and appropriate for this very academic town, the modern, well-presented Boerhaave Museum traces the evolution of science. You'll follow the one-way, loosely chronological loop through the exhibit, focusing on medical science but also including astronomy and other disciplines. You'll see a replica of an operating theater with a wraparound movie (ask for an English showing), lots of old scientific equipment and textbooks, antique exercise equipment and doctors' tools, and the gruesome, larger-than-life anatomical models of Dr. Louis Auzoux. Everything is in English.

Cost and Hours: €9.50, Tue-Sun 10:00-17:00, closed Mon, Lange Sint Agnietenstraat 10, tel. 071/521-4224, www. museumboerhaave.nl.

▲Windmill Museum (Molenmuseum De Valk)

Worth ▲▲ for fit engineers, this is a fun chance to climb—steeply and claustrophobically—through the guts of a huge, working

windmill (named De Valk—"The Falcon"). You'll begin by walking through the miller's house on the ground floor, then climb up to view an excellent 10-minute film about Dutch windmills. As you work your way up, up, up through the cramped structure (with ladder-like stairs), at each level you can browse exhibits about the Netherlands' tradition for harnessing the wind's power. At the top, you'll enjoy fine views over the rooftops of Leiden.

Cost and Hours: €4, Tue-Sat 10:00-17:00, Sun 13:00-17:00, closed Mon, Tweede Binnenvestgracht 1, tel. 071/516-5353, molendevalk.leiden.nl.

▲▲Lakenhal Museum (Museum De Lakenhal)

Leiden's leading museum, with art treasures from the 16th century to the present as well as a fine collection of local history, is closed at least through mid-2017. But if it has reopened for your visit, be sure to drop by.

Cost and Hours: When it reopens, likely €7.50, Tue-Fri 10:00-17:00, Sat-Sun 12:00-17:00, closed Mon, Oude Singel 32, tel. 071/516-5360, www.lakenhal.nl.

Visiting the Museum: The prized possession of its **Dutch Masters collection** is an exquisitely detailed *Last Judgment* triptych (three-part altarpiece) by local engraver and painter Lucas van Leyden. Painted in 1527 and originally displayed in St. Peter's Church, its bright colors and energy-charged composition represent the arrival of the Renaissance in the Low Countries. Rembrandt's *Spectacles-Seller* (from 1623) was one of his earliest compositions; with its poorly painted hands, awkward profile, and clashing colors, it lacks the mastery of his later Amsterdam heyday. Rembrandt's pupil Gerrit Dou kicked off a school called the Leiden Fijnschilders, which specialized in small, extremely detailed scenes with a strong light/dark contrast—a fine collection of which is displayed here. Also represented is Jan Steen, with dynamic, borderline-erotic scenes; *Merry Couple* (1650), depicting a man playfully throwing himself at a smiling woman, is loaded with sexually charged symbols.

Upstairs are **historical rooms**, including an explanation of the prized *laken* cloth produced in Leiden that brought the city wealth and fame. This museum fills the cloth hall *(lakenhal)* used to store this precious cargo. A large painting illustrates how Mayor Pieter van der Werf offered to sacrifice himself during the Spanish siege so the starving people of Leiden could eat his left arm (keeping his right arm intact to defend the town with his sword). They declined...but appreciated the gesture.

Leiden Connections

Trains depart from Leiden at least every 15 minutes and head north to **Haarlem** (20 minutes) and **Amsterdam** (35 minutes); and south to **The Hague** (15 minutes), **Delft** (20 minutes), and **Rotterdam** (35 minutes). There are also two direct trains each hour to **Utrecht** (45 minutes). With a change in Roosendaal, you can also reach **Antwerp** (about 2 hours) and **Brussels** (2.5-3 hours, some require additional change in Antwerp; both are faster with transfer to pricey Thalys train in The Hague or Rotterdam). For **Ghent** or **Bruges**, transfer in Antwerp.

THE HAGUE

Den Haag

The Dutch constitution may identify Amsterdam as the official "capital," but The Hague has been the Netherlands' seat of government since 1588. It's home both to the country's parliament and to international organizations such as the International Court of Justice (at the tourable Peace Palace, where nations try to settle their disputes without bloodshed) and the UN International Criminal Tribunal for the Former Yugoslavia (not tourable).

From a sightseeing perspective, The Hague is a one-trick pony...and it's a fine trick. The excellent Mauritshuis art gallery boasts perhaps the Netherlands' best collection of homegrown art outside of the Rijksmuseum, including its masterpiece, Vermeer's *Girl with a Pearl Earring*. Beyond that museum, The Hague's appeal diminishes quickly, aside from a smattering of other museums and a fairly sterile, upscale, businesslike vibe. Although urban and manageable, it's far from charming. It's bigger and less cozy than Delft, Leiden, or Haarlem, and smaller and less architecturally thrilling than Rotterdam. But it's worth a few engaging hours of sightseeing. It's a particularly easy day trip from Delft—so close it's practically a neighborhood of this city.

Orientation to The Hague

Though it has a half-million residents (the Netherlands' third-largest city), The Hague feels manageable for a sightseer. On a quick visit, begin at the Centrum tram stop, between the TI and the parliament complex; most worthwhile museums are nearby.

The Hague

To
Panorama Mesdag,
Peace Palace,
Madurodam &
Scheveningen

100 Meters
100 Yards

ESCHER
IN THE
PALACE

HIST.
MUSEUM

MAURITSHUIS
ROYAL PICTURE
GALLERY

Stations-
plein

#8, 9, 10 & 16   CENTRAL
TRAIN
STATION

#22 & 24   B

NOORD-
EINDE
PALACE

Hofvijver

PRISON
TOWER
MUSEUM

BINNENHOF
PARLIAMENT
COMPLEX

Plein

PRODEMOS
VISITORS
CENTER

OUDE
KERK

Centrum   CITY
HALL

Spuiplein

To
Hollands
Spoor Station

To
Delft

TOURIST INFORMATION

The TI is in City Hall (Stadhuis); it's nearest the Centrum stop on tram #1 (two stops after the Station HS stop). Pick up the free map; the better €3 map isn't worth it, but the free information guide—while heavy on glossy promotion—is helpful for a longer visit (Mon 12:00-20:00, Tue-Fri 10:00-20:00, Sat 10:00-17:00, Sun 12:00-17:00, Spui 68, tel. 070/361-8860, www.denhaag.com).

ARRIVAL IN THE HAGUE

The major sights in The Hague are well-signed—just look for the black-and-gold directional arrows.

By Tram: If coming on tram #1 from Delft, get off at the Centrum stop.

By Train: The Hague has two train stations: Central Station ("CS," "Den Haag CS," or just "Centraal Station") and Hollands Spoor ("HS" or "Den Haag HS," used by more international trains). Central Station is closer to the tourist area.

To get from **Central Station** to the TI, follow Rijnstraat (which parallels the tram tracks that pass the station, to your left as you leave the station), walking back under the train tracks to where

Rijnstraat ends. Turn right through the imposing glass building, and follow Turfmarkt for five minutes to the City Hall (Stadhuis), near the corner of Turfmarkt and Spui. To get from the station to the main sights, exit toward the sign for *Uitgang Centrum* (to the left with your back to the tracks, near the Burger King). Here you can catch tram #16 (direction: Wateringen) and take it two stops to the Centrum stop. Or, for a 15-minute walk, turn right and walk past the big bike-parking lot, then turn left, cross the tram tracks, and head up Bezuidenhoutseweg. After the road changes names a few times, it leads you to Hofweg; the Binnenhof parliament complex will be on your right.

To get from the **Hollands Spoor Station** to the TI, turn right as you leave the station and backtrack along the tram tracks on Spui to find Spuiplein, home of the TI and City Hall (Stadhuis). To reach the main sights, walk out in front of the station and take tram #1 (direction: Scheveningen Noorderstrand) to the Centrum stop.

Sights in The Hague

▲▲MAURITSHUIS ROYAL PICTURE GALLERY

The Hague's top art museum features Dutch Golden Age art, including top-notch pieces by Vermeer (his famous *Girl with a Pearl Earring* lives here), Rembrandt, Rubens, and many others. This so-called "mini-Rijksmuseum" is well worth a visit.

Cost and Hours: €14, not covered by Museumkaart; Tue-Sun 10:00-18:00, Thu until 20:00, Mon 13:00-18:00; audioguide-€3.50 or free if you download the Mauritshius app in advance or by using the museum's free Wi-Fi (headphones available at ticket desk); café, free bag check, Plein 29, tel. 070/302-3456, www.mauritshuis.nl.

Getting There: The Mauritshuis gallery is on the far side of the parliament, a three-minute walk from the TI; cut straight through the Binnenhof courtyard and look left when you pop out on the other side.

Collection Highlights

This list covers the basics; if you have more time, take advantage of the excellent audioguide. Some of the following artworks may be out on tour when you visit.

Room 3

Peter Paul Rubens, *Old Woman and a Boy with Candles* (c. 1616-1617): In this touching scene, the elderly woman passes her light to the boy—encouraging him to enjoy life in a way that she perhaps hasn't. Her serene smile suggests her hope that he won't have the same regrets she does.

Rooms 9 and 10

Rembrandt, *The Anatomy Lesson of Dr. Nicolaes Tulp* (1632): Notice Rembrandt's uniquely engaging version of a (typically dull) group portrait—inquisitive faces lean in, hanging on the doctor's every word. The cadaver resembles a notorious criminal of the day. For more on Rembrandt, see page 149.

Rembrandt, *Portrait of an Elderly Man* (1667): Painted when Rembrandt was 61, this portrait is typical of his style: The clothes are painted lightly, but the face is caked on. Look closely at his ruddy cheeks, built up by layer after layer of paint, carefully slathered on by the master.

Room 14

Frans Hals, *Laughing Boy* (c. 1625): This loveable painting depicts an exuberant scamp grinning widely despite his decaying teeth and rat's-nest hair. Like *Girl with a Pearl Earring*, this is a character study, rather than a portrait of an important person. For more on Hals, see page 286.

Jan Steen, *Girl Eating Oysters* (c. 1658-1660): This seemingly innocent scene—a still life combined with a portrait, on the smallest canvas Steen ever painted—is loaded with 17th-century sexual innuendo. Oysters were considered a powerful aphrodisiac, and behind the subject, peeking through the curtains, we can see a bed. The girl's impish grin suggests that she's got more than shellfish on her mind.

Carel Fabritius, *The Goldfinch* (c. 1654): Made famous by Donna Tartt's 2013 novel of the same title, this luminous, simple painting shows a pet goldfinch perched on its feeder, shackled by a slender chain. Fabritius was Rembrandt's pupil and Vermeer's teacher, and this painting shows traces of both masters' styles. Get close to see how the artist rendered the wing by painting bold yellow strokes over the black and then scratching the paint off with the back of his brush.

Room 15

Vermeer, *Girl with a Pearl Earring* (c. 1665): Sometimes called "the Dutch *Mona Lisa*" for its enigmatic qualities, this canvas became a sensation in recent years as the subject of a popular book and film. This is a "tronie"—a type of picture in which the painter's goal is not to depict an individual person, but to capture mood or character by focusing on the expression of the subject. In fact, we don't even know who this mysterious girl is. Wearing a blue turban and with a gigantic pearl dangling from her earlobe, she glances over her shoulder and catches the viewer's gaze expectantly, maybe even seductively. Vermeer's portrayal subtly implies a much more complicated story than we'll ever know. The artist was a master of color and at suggesting shape with light—look closely and you'll see that the famous pearl is essentially formed by two simple brush-strokes. For more on Vermeer, see page 311.

Vermeer, *View of Delft* (c. 1660-1661): If this were a photograph, it'd be a bad one—you'd want to wait for the clouds to pass to snap another one with the entire scene bathed in light. But Vermeer, an expert at capturing light effects on canvas, uses the cloudy/sunny contrast to his advantage, illuminating the foreground and the distant, inner part of town instead of the more predictable middle ground. This makes your eye probe deep into the canvas, subconsciously immersing you in Vermeer's world.

And Lots More: These paintings are just the beginning. Look around to find works by Jan Brueghel the Elder (a painting of the Garden of Eden, done jointly with Rubens), Hans Holbein, Anthony van Dyck, Hans Memling, and many other famous painters.

OTHER MUSEUMS IN THE CITY CENTER

These attractions are all within a 10-minute walk of the TI (most are even closer).

Binnenhof Parliament Complex

The castle-like Binnenhof complex, overlooking a giant pond right in the center of The Hague, is the seat of Dutch political power. The prime minister's office is here, and it's also the meeting place of the two-house parliament, or Staten-Generaal. The power resides in the directly elected Second Chamber (a.k.a. House of Representatives), whereas the mostly figurehead First Chamber (a.k.a. Senate, but actually more like the UK's House  of Lords) meets once weekly to harrumph their approval.

It's surprisingly easy to dip into the low-key parliament complex (just saunter through the brick gateway across the street from the TI). In the inner courtyard—surrounded by orange-and-white-striped awnings—you'll find a golden fountain depicting the recently retired Queen Beatrix, a reminder that the respectful Dutch parliamentarians govern with the monarch's symbolic approval. Dominating the middle of the complex is the historic Knights' Hall (Ridderzaal), where the two houses meet jointly on special occasions.

Tours: Guided tours of the complex are given in Dutch (English audioguide available) through the ProDemos Visitors Center, across the street from the Binnenhof (tours-€5-10, not covered by Museumkaart, Mon-Sat 9:30-17:00, none on Sun). Tours depart from the lobby of the visitors center, next to Café Brasserie

Dudok at Hofweg 1 (tel. 070/757-0200, www.prodemos.nl, tours@prodemos.nl).

Prison Tower Museum (Gevangenpoort)

This torture museum, in a 13th-century gatehouse that once protected a castle on the site of today's parliament, shows you the me-

dieval mind at its worst. You'll get the full story on crime and punishment here from 1420 to 1823. You can wander around by yourself or tour the sight on a free 30-minute tour.

Cost and Hours: €7.50, Tue-Fri 10:00-17:00, Sat-Sun 12:00-17:00, closed Mon, across from parliament at Buitenhof 33, tel. 070/346-0861, www.gevangenpoort.nl.

Tours: Tours run once a week in English (Sun at 14:15) and hourly in Dutch (at :45 after the hour, also at :15 during busy times, last tour usually leaves at 15:45; use the free English guidebook to follow along).

Panorama Mesdag

For an overpriced look at the 19th century's attempt at virtual reality, stand in the center of this 360-degree painting of nearby Scheveningen in the 1880s, with a 3-D, sandy-beach foreground. As you experience this nostalgic attraction, ponder that this sort of "art immersion" experience was once mind-blowingly cutting-edge.

Cost and Hours: €10, Mon-Sat 10:00-17:00, Sun 12:00-17:00, last entry 15 minutes before closing, a few blocks east of the parliament area at Zeestraat 65, tel. 070/310-6665, www.panorama-mesdag.com.

Escher in the Palace (Escher in Het Paleis)

Compared with The Hague's other museums, this place is just a trifle...but an entertaining one. (Think of it as "art museum lite.") Celebrating Dutch optical illusionist M. C. Escher (1898-1972), the exhibit displays replicas of many of his works and traces his artistic evolution—from the Mediterranean landscapes of his beloved Italy, to shapes that melt into one another, to mind-bending experiments in angles and perspective. Hands-on displays on the top floor let you step right into an Escher engraving. The entry price is worth it, given the museum's extras: fun temporary exhibits, far-out chandeliers by Dutch artist Hans van Bentem, and the chance to stroll the former winter palace of Queen Emma, who lived here for three decades—it remained a royal residence until 1991. I'm guessing the skull-and-crossbones chandelier wasn't around then.

Cost and Hours: €9, cash only, not covered by Museumkaart, Tue-Sun 11:00-17:00, closed Mon, last entry 30 minutes before closing, mandatory bag check-€1 deposit, Lange Voorhout 74, tel. 070/427-7730, www.escherinhetpaleis.nl.

Historical Museum of The Hague (Haagshistorischmuseum)

This museum's eclectic collection includes landscapes of The Hague in the Golden Age, portraits of its movers and shakers, dollhouses, tile panels, and the well-preserved tongue and finger of a 17th-century murderer.

Cost and Hours: €7.50, Tue-Fri 10:00-17:00, Sat-Sun 12:00-17:00, closed Mon, across the pond from parliament at Korte Vijverberg 7, tel. 070/364-6940, www.haagshistorischmuseum.nl.

OUTSIDE THE CITY CENTER

The following sights lie north of the main tourist zone. Though worthwhile for the thorough sightseer, they're more difficult to reach than the previous sights.

▲Peace Palace (Vredespaleis)

The palace houses the International Court of Justice and the Permanent Court of Arbitration. These two Peace Palace courts attempt to reach amicable settlements for international disagreements, such as border disputes. While the judicial process is interesting, the building itself is the big draw. A gift from American industrialist Andrew Carnegie, it's filled with opulent decorations (donated by grateful nations who found diplomatic peace here), from exquisite Japanese tapestries, to a Hungarian tile fountain, to French inlay floors.

A free visitors center offers modest multimedia exhibits about the building and international courts. There's also a persuasive video about the history of the Peace Palace and the role of international law. However, if you want to see the inside of the building itself, you must book a weekend tour in advance (see next page). You'll see the judicial chambers and the grandly decorated halls, and learn how modern nations attempt to resolve their disputes here instead of on the battlefield.

Cost and Hours: Visitors center—free, plus a free audioguide; Tue-Sun 10:00-17:00, closes at 16:00 in winter, closed Mon year-round, Carnegieplein 2, tel. 070/302-4242, www.vredespaleis.nl.

Tours: €8.50, not covered by Museumkaart; Sat-Sun 11:00-16:00 only, 30-45 minutes; most tours offered in English, you must reserve in advance online and bring your passport (required to enter), due to court schedules you can only book about six weeks in advance (www.vredespaleis.nl). It is possible to attend a hearing (conducted in English or French) of the International Court of Justice; see www.icj-cij.org for details.

Getting There: Take tram #1 directly from Delft, or tram #10 or bus #24 from The Hague's Central Station, and get off at the Vredespaleis stop (right in front of the palace).

Scheveningen

This Dutch Coney Island, with its broad sandy beach, is at its liveliest on sunny summer afternoons (but is dead when the weather cools).

Its biggest appeal is watching urbanites from The Hague and Delft enjoy a day at the seashore. Dominating the scene is the long double-decker pleasure pier, with shops down below, a boardwalk up top, and a bungee-jumping pavilion at the far end. A café-lined promenade stretches along the sand.

By the way, if you can't pronounce this tongue-twisting name (roughly SK*H*EH-veh-ning-ehn), you're not alone. In World War II, Dutch soldiers would quiz suspicious visitors on how to pronounce this name as a test to determine who was Dutch-born and ferret out potential German spies.

Getting There: Take northbound tram #1 from Delft or from Hofweg/Spui (the street in front of the Binnenhof and The Hague's TI), or take tram #9 from The Hague's Central Station. Get out at Kurhaus (one stop before the end of the line) and follow signs for *Boulevard/Strand* and *Pier*.

Madurodam

This mini-Holland amusement park, with miniature city buildings that make you feel like Godzilla, is fun for kids.

Cost and Hours: Adults-€15.50, not covered by Museumkaart, daily April-June 9:00-20:00, March and Sept-Oct 9:00-18:00, Nov-Dec and Feb 11:00-17:00, closed Jan, last entry one hour before closing, George Maduroplein 1, tram #8 and #9 or bus #22 from Central Station, tel. 070/416-2400, www.madurodam.nl.

The Hague Connections

The Hague's Central Station (CS) is handier for sightseers; the Hollands Spoor Station (HS) is used mostly by international trains.

From The Hague's Central Station by Train to: Delft (4/hour, 15 minutes), **Leiden** (4/hour, 15 minutes), **Rotterdam** (4/hour, 20 minutes), **Amsterdam** (4/hour, 50 minutes, more with change in Leiden or Hoofddorp), **Haarlem** (4/hour, 40 minutes), **Arnhem** (4/hour, 1.5 hours, transfer in Utrecht).

From The Hague's Hollands Spoor Station by Train to: Bruges (hourly, 3.75 hours, change in Brussels).

By Tram to Delft: Take tram #1 from any stop (€3, €6.50 day pass, every 10 minutes on weekdays, 4/hour on weekends, direction: Delft Tanthof, about 30 minutes). If you're headed to the Markt in Delft, get off at the Prinsenhof stop (a little north of the Markt) or at Binnenwatersloot (the next stop south). The tram also stops at the train station.

THE HAGUE

ROTTERDAM

The Dutch say that money is made in Rotterdam, divvied up in The Hague, and spent in Amsterdam. The country's second-biggest city (with 617,000 in the center, and over one million in the metropolitan area), Rotterdam has a long history as the Netherlands' muscular moneymaker. Its strategic position at the delta of several major European rivers has made it a lucrative trading point for centuries. Today, it's home to Europe's busiest port (the third-biggest in the world). They say that in Rotterdam, shirts are sold with the sleeves already rolled up.

The city had a particularly tumultuous 20th century. Its highly strategic port earned it complete destruction—down to its very foundations—during World War II. When the time came to rebuild, Rotterdammers decided to leave their salty old town as a memory, and started from scratch to build a boldly modern city. Ever since, the city has been—and remains—a petri dish of architectural experimentation, with buildings big and small designed by a *Who's Who* of contemporary architects. You'll see wildly creative and futuristic train stations, libraries, market halls, office towers, bridges, subway stations, and apartment complexes that push the envelope of science fiction. But the city also respects its past, with a few historic buildings mixed in, and lots of stories to be told.

Strolling Rotterdam's sleek pedestrian malls, ogling its fantastical skyline, browsing for a meal on its eclectic shopping streets, or cruising its busy harbor, you'll experience another slice of the Netherlands. A visit to Rotterdam makes it clear: For many Dutch urbanites, the days of milkmaids and wooden shoes are long gone.

PLANNING YOUR TIME

Big, intense Rotterdam works well as a side-trip from Delft (or even from Amsterdam or Haarlem): Ride the train in and poke around for a few hours, following my self-guided walk. With more time, take a harbor cruise (to see the busy port) or an architectural bike tour (to appreciate its rich array of modern buildings), or—if you're desperate for cute canals—ride the metro to the historic Delfshaven quarter. A half-day is enough for a good first look, but the more time you have, the more of Rotterdam you'll see.

Orientation to Rotterdam

Rotterdam sprawls along both banks of the Maas River. But the central zone—on the north bank, with most of the important sights and architectural landmarks—is fairly compact. A loop from the train station to the river and back again is a long-but-doable walk or an easy bike ride.

TOURIST INFORMATION

The handiest TI branch is in a small, blocky structure inside the Central Station's cavernous main hall (as you leave the tracks, look for it on your left, beneath the huge video screen; daily 9:00-17:30). The main branch is downtown at Coolsingel 195 (daily 9:30-18:00, tel. 0900-403-4065, www.rotterdam.info). Their €1 map is good enough to get you around for the day.

Bike Tours: In this spread-out city, a bike tour is a smart choice. **Rotterdam By Cycle** offers a variety of custom tours. Their ArchiGuides tours, with a focus on Rotterdam's architectural heritage, are led by trained architects; their Rotterdam By Cycle tours are more general. They may have regularly scheduled tours in summer, or you may have to arrange your own (figure €100-150/2-hour tour for a small group, www.rotterdambycycle.nl or www.rotterdam-archiguides.nl, tel. 010/465-2228).

ARRIVAL IN ROTTERDAM

In Rotterdam's cutting-edge Central Station, a wide concourse crosses beneath the train platforms. Lockers are at the "back" end of the train station (follow signs for *Proveniersplein*; they're on the right, between tracks 15 and 16). To head into the city center, you'll go in the opposite direction, toward *Centrum*. When you pop out into the main hall, look for the TI kiosk on the left, just before the main doors. My self-guided walk begins inside this hall.

GETTING AROUND ROTTERDAM

If you want to **rent a bike,** head out into the main plaza directly in front of the station and look for the angled glass pavilion (on your right) that leads to the underground bike parking garage. Ride the bike escalator down and ask at the desk (€7.50-11.50/day depending on quality of bike, €50 cash deposit, open long hours daily, tel. 010/412-6220). If biking in this busy metropolis, stick to the red pavement (designated for cyclists), obey the many *no bikes* signs (you'll have to walk your bike through strictly controlled pedestrian zones), use hand signals...and remember you're in a congested city with more car traffic than Amsterdam or Delft.

While I've designed this chapter in the order of a long loop walk through the city, **public transit** can help you zip directly to an attraction of your choice (such as the harbor cruise or Delfshaven). As you exit the station, look left for a row of **tram** platforms (#7 zips you to the harbor cruise dock at Erasmus Bridge, direction: Willemsplein, ride to end of line; #4 and #8 go to Delfshaven). There's also an entrance to the **metro** in the plaza in front of the main entrance (the trip to Delfshaven requires a change at Beurs). Public transportation is covered by an OV-chipkaart (see page 35) by a paper ticket (€3 buys you a one-hour ride); or by a day pass (€7.10).

Rotterdam is also served by **water taxis** that shuttle between Leuvehaven, Veerhaven, and the skyscraper zone's Hotel New York (€2.90 one-way, every 10 minutes, www.watertaxirotterdam.nl).

Rotterdam Walk

This four-mile self-guided walk takes you through the shopping zone of Rotterdam and past some of its most dynamic architectural treasures to the river, then loops you back to the landmark Erasmus Bridge (where you can catch the harbor cruise) before heading back up to the station. You could do it at a brisk pace in about four hours (without stops for sightseeing or taking the harbor cruise), but it's also a useful spine for spending the entire day in the city. If four miles is too much, I list several places where you can head back early—at the Maas Riverfront/Williams Bridge, Erasmus Bridge (tram stop), and Rotterdam Centre tower (metro stop).

Bike Variation: Rotterdam is spread out, and this walk is lengthy. To speed things up, consider renting a bike at the station (see "Getting Around Rotterdam," earlier). You can link most of the stops on this walk by bike, but will need to vary the route to avoid pedestrian-only zones. Following the "Bike Tour" outlined on the map on page 400, at the start, skip the Lijnbaan shopping zone (where you'd have to walk your bike for several blocks) and instead zip east along the huge Weena boulevard and straight through the huge roundabout, then turn right down Haagseveer to St. Lawrence Church. From here, walk your bike through the Hoogstraat market zone and Blaak housing complex, then ride down to—and along—the river. On two wheels, a brisk and even more scenic route to the Erasmus Bridge is to pedal across the red Williams Bridge (Willemsbrug), then head to the southwestern tip

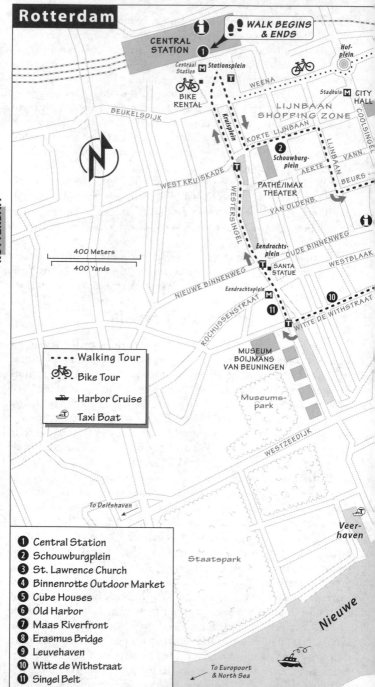

Rotterdam

WALK BEGINS & ENDS

CENTRAL STATION ①

Centraal Station Stationsplein

Hofplein

WEENA

Stadhuis CITY HALL

LIJNBAAN SHOPPING ZONE

BIKE RENTAL

BEUKELSDIJK

Kruisplein

KORTE LIJNBAAN

② Schouwburgplein

AERTE VANN.

WEST KRUISKADE

WESTERSINGEL

PATHÉ/IMAX THEATER

VAN OLDENB.

BEURS

N

400 Meters

400 Yards

Eendrachtsplein

OUDE BINNENWEG

SANTA STATUE

WESTBLAAK

NIEUWE BINNENWEG

Eendrachtsplein

⑩

ROCHUSSENSTRAAT

⑪

WITTE DE WITHSTRAAT

MUSEUM BOIJMANS VAN BEUNINGEN

Museumspark

WESTZEEDIJK

To Delfshaven

Veerhaven

· · · · Walking Tour

🚲 Bike Tour

⛴ Harbor Cruise

🛥 Taxi Boat

Staatspark

Nieuwe

To Europoort & North Sea

① Central Station
② Schouwburgplein
③ St. Lawrence Church
④ Binnenrotte Outdoor Market
⑤ Cube Houses
⑥ Old Harbor
⑦ Maas Riverfront
⑧ Erasmus Bridge
⑨ Leuvehaven
⑩ Witte de Withstraat
⑪ Singel Belt

ROTTERDAM

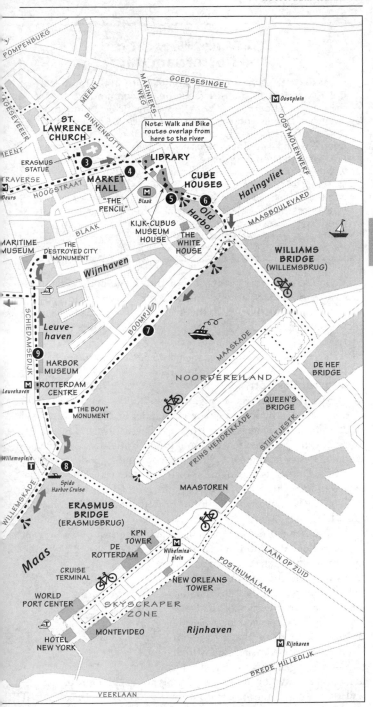

Old City, New City: The Rotterdam Blitz

Hitler invaded the Netherlands on May 10, 1940. He quickly grew impatient at the resistance he encountered, so to get the Dutch on board, on May 14 he systematically bombed the country's heavily industrialized second city: Rotterdam. As Rotterdam had already been evacuated, fewer than 1,000 people were killed—but the city was, quite literally, flattened. Following the bombing, a fire raged for three days, consuming what was left of the city. Photos of post-WWII Rotterdam are startling: A scant few historic buildings still stand—barely— and the outlines of the streets around them are barely visible. Hitler's methods proved successful. When the Nazis threatened to similarly destroy Utrecht the next day, the Dutch government surrendered immediately.

of Noordereiland for a great view of the bridge and skyscrapers. From here, loop back around and take the Queen's Bridge (Koninginnebrug) to the far side of the river, where you'll pedal south to the Erasmus Bridge. Cross it and follow the rest of the walk from there.

• *We'll begin inside the grand main arrivals hall of Rotterdam's...*

❶ Central Station

The city's sleek, futuristic, gigantic (430,000-square-foot) train station—opened by King Willem-Alexander in 2014—is a marvel in itself. A quick and easy ride from The Hague, Delft, Dordrecht, and many fine little bedroom communities, Rotterdam's station accommodates more than 100,000 daily commuters (and a few tourists). Stand under its soaring roof—which makes travelers seem like ants—and take it all in. The enormous football-field-long screen high on the wall plays video clips of Rotterdam life; below that sits the TI.

Head straight out the main doors, into the vast **plaza** in front of the station. Walk to the busy road and turn 180 degrees to appreciate the swoop of the station's roofline (which reminds me of the Starship *Enterprise*'s communicator badges). Shaped like an arrow, it marks Rotterdam as a city of the future—in strong contrast to Amsterdam, which revels in being a city of the past. The

angled glass pavilion to your left leads to an underground park-and-ride garage...not for cars, but for 5,000 bicycles (head here if you're renting a **bike**). You'll also see an entrance to what was the first metro stop in the country (from 1968). Tucked around the right side of the station are platforms for trams that fan out across the city (details earlier, under "Getting Around Rotterdam").

Turn back around (with the station at your back) and look left and right, up and down the busy cross-boulevard called **Weena**. After Rotterdam was leveled by Hitler's *Blitzkrieg* (see sidebar), city officials sent architects to Washington, D.C. for inspiration. This street (and others like it) feel more like American-style "downtown" zones than European streets. Some are even laid out according to specific American dimensions and proportions. While skyscrapers seem to be popping up all over Rotterdam like dandelions, in truth they're carefully zoned; this boulevard is one of four central axis streets where tall towers are permitted.

• *Cross Weena and head straight down Kruisplein (through the big, pedestrian-friendly median, with grassy parks on both sides) for two short blocks. After the second parking pavilion, angle left down the street in front of the red tower (Koninginnebrug; look for the* Stadhuis/City Hall *arrow). You'll emerge into one of many bold Rotterdam public spaces.*

❷ Schouwburgplein and Rotterdam's Central Shopping Zone

Named for the giant theater building (Schouwburg) that sits at its far end, **Schouwburgplein** is also ringed by a giant Pathé/IMAX theater and other entertainment venues. The adjustable, red crane-like lampposts evoke the busy port that made this city wealthy, and behind them are caged ventilation towers. Like the features of Paris' Pompidou Center, these adhere to the "form follows function" aesthetic of celebrating—rather than hiding—the inner guts of a working building. At night, the lights embedded in the square simulate floating through the Milky Way.

Continue straight ahead, and head down the pedestrian-only street called Korte Lijnbaan (under the big *Lijnbaan* sign, toward the copper-topped tower; cyclists must dismount and walk their bikes). This is just one leg of the **Lijnbaan**, a network of completely pedestrianized shopping streets that burrow through downtown Rotterdam. In the postwar boom of the 1960s and 1970s, several European cities pedestrianized downtown streets for shoppers—but Rotterdam's Lijnbaan was the first, created in 1953.

After one block, you reach a big intersection with a statue of rasslin' bears in the center. Our walk proceeds to the right from here (down Lijnbaan), but first, consider a brief detour straight ahead for a look at Rotterdam's **City Hall** (one block ahead and across the street). Dating from 1917, it's one of a handful of old Rotterdam structures that weren't destroyed in World War II. (The Germans, who knew they'd need a headquarters in the city, intentionally spared it—but if you look closely, you can still see bullet holes from the fighting.) Today it's a popular place for weddings, and it houses the office of Rotterdam's mayor. In keeping with the city's global demographics and progressive politics, the current mayor is a Moroccan immigrant and a practicing Muslim...a hard sell in just about any city stateside.

Back at the bears, head south down Lijnbaan. While not quite "charming," this zone is very user-friendly; daydream about doing your shopping here instead of at traffic-choked suburban malls. After two blocks, at Van Oldenbarneveltplaats (with the tram tracks), turn left and follow an even more enticing shopping zone called the **Beurstraverse**, where a swooping green canopy dips gracefully under a busy highway.

Continuing straight up the stairs after the tunnel, you'll wind up on **Hoogstraat**. This is known as Rotterdam's "High Street": It's a major shopping thoroughfare, and because it's literally high—it sits upon a dike. As you browse, keep in mind that this was the heart of Rotterdam's Old Town until 1940.

• *After crossing the wide canal, you'll see a church steeple on your left. Head up little Wijde Kerkstraat to reach the square in front of the church.*

❸ St. Lawrence Church (Laurenskerk)

This is the oldest surviving structure in Rotterdam (completed in 1525)—a rare survivor of the 1940 Nazi bombing campaign. The

church's nondescript exterior belies its vast, pristine interior. There's not much to see inside, but if you enter, be sure to look up to see a roof that was clearly built by a city of shipbuilders—it feels like you're huddled beneath an overturned boat (€1 to enter, €5 for exhibits, Tue-Sat 11:00-17:00, closed Sun-Mon).

Grotekerkplein, the "Great Church Square" in front of St. Lawrence, has a statue of Rotterdam native **Desiderius Erasmus** (1466-1536), who was born in a house nearby (now gone). This humanist philosopher and satirist grew nervous when his like-minded friend, Thomas More, was beheaded by the English king. So, to evade a similar fate, Erasmus traveled far and wide—to Italy, England, Belgium, Switzerland, and beyond. He forged the notion of being a European—a citizen of the world, not tied to a single nationality. In other words, Erasmus is the intellectual forebear of the European Union, which named its highly successful foreign study program after him. On the pedestal, in Dutch, a famous Erasmus quote is inscribed: "The entire world is your fatherland." (Several other major landmarks in this city are named for Erasmus, including Rotterdam's main university and its landmark bridge.)

• *Backtrack a short block to Hoogstraat and keep going. You'll pop out at Rotterdam's...*

❹ Binnenrotte Outdoor Market and Modern Architecture

On Tuesdays and Saturdays, **Binnenrotte** street is lively with an outdoor market: food, clothing, housewares, flowers, and so on. (A smaller market is on Sundays.) This is a good chance to shop around for a snack or meal. The market sits upon the original "Rotter-dam"—the dam on the Rotte River, which runs underground perpendicular to the Hoogstraat axis. (The name *Binnen-rotte* means "Rotte inside.") When you're done browsing, tune into these buildings:

First, on your right is Rotterdam's new **Market Hall** (Markthal). Created by local architecture firm MVRDV, it's designed as a market square turned inside-out: Inside, beneath the grandiose arch, is a bustling food market (conveniently protected from the elements, a plus in this very drizzly city). Wrapped around that are 230 apartments—some with an ideal view of what's fresh today, and others with terraces overlooking the city. Step inside this cathedral for shoppers and look up at the wildly colorful ceiling tiles.

Next, you'll see the top of the unmistakably pointy-topped tower that locals have dubbed **"The Pencil."** (There was really no other option.) The next stop on our walk is the blocks jutting out at its base.

But first, continue straight ahead to the **City Library** (the blocky white building with yellow tubes). The exterior is another

example of Pompidou-like "form follows function," while the interior reminds us that functionality is a very good thing for people using these buildings. Head inside (Mon 13:00-20:00, Tue-Fri 10:00-20:00, Sat 10:00-17:00, closed Sun except Oct and May 13:00-17:00, www.bibliotheek.rotterdam.nl). First, simply appreciate the space: Peering up into the atrium, see the many levels (with funky 1970s-style lampshades) that reach up through the structure, like a well-stocked warehouse of knowledge. But this is more than a library—it's a thriving and well-used community center. The information desk hands out brochures about local events, and you'll also find pay WCs, a handy café, and—behind the life-size chessboard busy with retirees—a huge map of Rotterdam that helps you get your bearings. (Start by finding the triangle-shaped old town, then work your way out to appreciate the stunning scope of the port area, with smaller and older harbors giving way to ever-larger ones on the outskirts.) Imagine funding a library like this with a levy in your hometown.

• *Exiting the library building, turn left and walk toward "The Pencil" building and the big industrial arch (which marks the busy Rotterdam Blaak tram-and-metro hub—nicknamed "The Manhole Cover" or "The UFO"). Walk up the gap between the library and "The Pencil," and follow the reddish ramp up into the...*

❺ Cube Houses (Kubuswoningen)

In the late 1970s, architect Piet Blom turned urban housing on its ear with this bold design: 39 identical yellow cubes, all tilted up on their corners, and each filled with the residence of a single family. Taken together, the Cube Houses look like dozens of dice in mid-toss. If Rotterdam has a single icon representing its bold approach to postwar architecture, this is it.

For a good look, follow the *museum* signs into the courtyard in the middle of the complex. Shops fill the gray boxes at the base, while people live in the yellow tops. The circle of angled cubes facing each other around this courtyard facilitates connections among neighbors. Inside each cube, the space is a bit awkward in places, but more functional than you might guess. Each cube has three floors: kitchen and living room downstairs; two bedrooms and one bathroom upstairs; and atop the ladderlike stairs in the summit, a cramped but relaxing sun lounge that feels made-to-order for reclining and gazing up at the stars. Everything is custom-designed to maximize efficient use of the odd space—cheap Ikea furniture just won't fit. To get a look inside one of the cubes, visit the **Kijk-Kubus Museum House** (at #70, €3, not covered by Museumkaart, daily 11:00-17:00, www.kubuswoning.nl).

• *From the main courtyard, carry on over the busy street (find the long corridor, passing the Stayokay hostel). At the far end, make your way to the overlook of Rotterdam's...*

❻ Old Harbor (Oudehaven)

This mostly modern re-creation is what's left of the harbor that was the basis for Rotterdam's early prosperity. Today it's a bustling so-cial zone, its embankments lined with inviting al fresco cafés and restaurants. You'll see a few houseboats, and a shipyard used for repairing historic vessels.

Directly across the har-bor is **The White House** (Het Witte Huis), a rare ex-ample of a surviving prewar building. When it was built in 1898, this structure was Europe's tallest building, at about 140 feet. It was inspired by Art Deco American skyscrapers of the time... with the addition of frilly Jugendstil (Art Nouveau) turrets. In the 1970s, there were plans to build a superhighway right through the Old Harbor area, but local Flower Power demonstrations kept this historic zone intact.

• *Follow the ramp down and curl around the left side of the Old Harbor, passing some enticing outdoor tables—handy if you're ready for a drink or snack. At the end of the harbor, pause at the little drawbridge to ap-preciate the great view of the harbor and White House. (The towers just beyond mark another harbor, Leuvehaven, where we'll be later.) Con-tinue straight ahead, cross the busy street, and duck under the bridge's flyover, then bear right to the boardwalk, with a great viewpoint of the...*

❼ Maas Riverfront

The Maas River begins in France (where it's called the Meuse) and flows through Belgium, merging with several other rivers (includ-ing the Rhine) on its way to the sea. As you face the river, to the left (upstream) are France, Belgium, Germany, and Switzerland, and to the right (downstream)—past ever-larger harbors—is the North Sea.

You're standing next to the big, red **Williams Bridge** (Wil-lemsbrug). In the distance, to the right, is the green, industrial-style bridge called **De Hef**. Before 1992, this rail drawbridge was part of the only train line through the city—so passengers would have to wait patiently while it went up and down.

Across the river is the island neighborhood called **Noorde-reiland**, whose low-lying buildings were largely spared the bombs of World War II, and retain a certain historic charm today. This evokes what much of Rotterdam's center might look like today, had Hitler not made an example of the city.

Panning right, you'll see several big towers surrounding the Erasmus Bridge—where we're headed next. If you're on a bike, now's the time for a long, scenic detour pedaling over this bridge and along Noordereiland. If you're tired and want to head back to the station, you can retrace your steps through the Cube Houses complex to the Blaak tram/metro hub (where you can take tram #21 in direction: Schiedam Woudhoek or #24 in direction: Holy to get back to Central Station).

But if you're on foot and ready to see more, turn right and head about a half-mile (15 minutes) south along the waterline. Much

of the stroll is through a fine, manicured park, with ever-changing views of the skyline across the river. Nearing the Erasmus Bridge, you'll see a towering **monument**. From the land side, it looks like a nondescript gray tower with a hole in the top. But circling around to the riverfront park, its symbolism is more apparent: It resembles a ship's prow, cutting through the water. Officially the National Monument for the Merchant Marine, but nicknamed "The Bow" (De Boeg), this honors all seamen from Al-

lied countries who were killed in World War II. If you find it a bit too abstract, you're not alone: The sailors lashed together at the bottom of the monument were added later to inject it with a bit more humanity.

• *At the monument, head inland to reach the drawbridge. Crossing it, turn left (toward the water) to head back down to the base of the bridge.*

❽ Erasmus Bridge (Erasmusbrug) and Rotterdam's Skyscraper Zone

Built in 1996, this icon of Rotterdam created an essential link between the north and south banks of the Maas River. Its huge, 450-foot-tall tower, at the south end, planted a flag for the then-underdeveloped part of the city—which has (thanks largely to the bridge) exploded into a new "downtown" zone of commerce.

Just past the base of the bridge, find the Spido boat dock, offering harbor tours (see page 412). From this point, take a visual

tour of Rotterdam's modern sky-line. (You can do this while waiting for your tour boat to depart, or in lieu of the cruise; if you're on foot, note that the views get better the farther down the embankment you go, with the best just before the Veerhaven harbor—a rare bit of Old World charm.)

At the far end of the bridge stands a lineup of creations by the top architects working on this planet today—most of them completed since 2000. Nicknamed "Manhattan on the Maas," many of these buildings are engineered to sit upon pylons driven deep into the marshy, riverfront soil. From left to right, find these buildings: First, behind the bridge (with the Deloitte logo), the **Maastoren** is the tallest building in Rotterdam (and in all of the Low Countries). The small cluster of buildings nearby are municipal and cultural institutions (court, customs, and theater)—placed here intentionally to spur development. Then comes the short, wavy **KPN Tower**, by Renzo Piano (best known for Paris' Pompidou Center). The dots embedded in the side can illuminate and display patterns for a lightshow. Then comes the **De Rotterdam** building—three independent towers with separate purposes (hotel, local government, and apartments) that share a unified base. This was designed by world-famous Rotterdam native Rem Koolhaas, who also created Rotterdam's Kunsthal, Porto's Casa de Música, and Seattle's Central Library. The tall, sandstone-colored **New Orleans** tower is by the Portuguese architect Álvaro Siza Vieira. In the next clump of two buildings, the gray, round **World Port Center** is by Lord Norman Foster (famous for Berlin's Reichstag dome; he also designed the plan for this entire peninsula, and renovated the low-lying cruise terminal), while the multicolored **Montevideo** is by the Delft-based Mecanoo firm. As you might guess, the real estate on this peninsula is 100 percent committed for future projects; architects are already trying to figure out ways to build new structures on the water itself. Stay tuned.

The much lower-lying building at the tip of land (with the copper-domed turrets) is the jarringly old-fashioned **Hotel New York.** This was built in 1901 as the world headquarters of Holland America Line—which, back then, catered primarily to immigrants seeking a better life in the New World. Passengers would undergo rigorous health screenings in this building, and if found to be contagious, they'd be quarantined in the shipyards. To commemorate the place where so many soon-to-be-former Europeans last set foot on their home soil, today the grassy park in front of the hotel is decorated with street names from New York City. (If you'd like a closer look, you can catch a water taxi across the river from the nearby Veerhaven harbor, or from the Leuvehaven harbor, which we'll visit next.)

Looking far to the right, you can see the beginnings of Rotterdam's busy **port**. The "Europoort" was the largest in the world until 2004, when it was surpassed by both Singapore's and Shanghai's. From the Erasmus Bridge, it's more than 20 miles to the North Sea—and virtually every inch is lined with heavy industry. Each year, 35,000 oceangoing ships stop here, hauling a total of 420 million tons of cargo. The plodding ships are weighted down with petroleum products, chemicals, and pharmaceuticals. This is also the biggest oil port on the planet, with five separate refineries.

• *If you're ready to return to the station from here, it's easiest to head for the Willemsplein tram stop, just above the Spido boat dock; as this is the end and start of the line, any tram from here will bring you back to the station.*

Or, to continue our walk to see more of Rotterdam, head back the way you came, and proceed straight past the drawbridge you crossed earlier, up Schiedamsedijk. You'll pass the top-heavy **Rotterdam Centre tower** *and the Leuvrehaven metro stop (another option for a quick return to the station). Just beyond, you'll be walking alongside the historic port area called...*

❾ Leuvehaven

When Antwerp was taken over by fiercely pro-Catholic Spanish invaders in the late 16th century, Rotterdam welcomed Protestant refugees seeking safe harbor.  And those refugees built this harbor—named for Leuven, Belgium. Today it's a strangely picturesque mix of old and new, with a few historic harbor buildings and a rash of glittering towers that try to keep to the footprints of the original street plan.

As you walk, notice the many fine cafés overlooking the harbor, as well as the **Harbor Museum** (Havenmuseum). While the collection is of most interest to sailors, you're free to walk down along the embankment, where you can peruse the open-air collection of historical ships and equipment. Near the end, a gangway crosses the harbor and passes a water taxi station. This is one of many stops in Rotterdam that let

you connect various waterfront areas (for example, from here you can ride over to the Hotel New York for a closer look at the skyscraper zone).

At the end of Leuvehaven is the big, drab **Maritime Museum,** offering an interesting look at Rotterdam's busy port, as well as some engaging children's exhibits (www.maritiemmuseum.nl). Sitting on the plaza up the stairs behind the Maritime Museum is the poignant statue **De Verwoeste Stad** (*The Destroyed City*), commemorating Rotterdam's

WWII destruction. An anguished figure—his heart pierced by a void—flails his arms, face frozen in a *Guernica* scream. This monument is an important symbol of this city, which is defined by the architecture built upon the blank canvas caused by that harrowing destruction.

• *Along the Leuvehaven embankment, near the tall cranes (just before the Maritime Museum), use the crosswalk to cross the busy street and head up Schilderstraat; after two blocks, the street angles left a bit and becomes...*

⑩ Witte de Withstraat

This lively, tree-lined street is an ideal place to browse boutiques, window-shop, or restaurant-hunt. It's funky but still accessible, with a rainbow of eateries: shwarma, döner kebab, Indonesian, burgers, hipster cafés, spit-and-sawdust pubs, and more. It also has sev-

eral art galleries and fashion boutiques. Relax, linger, and enjoy... our walk is almost finished.

• *You'll pop out at a canal, which marks the...*

⑪ Singel Belt

Singel means "moat," and this north-south stretch of grassy canals defines the edge of what was old Rotterdam. From here, you have several options.

Directly across the street (through the canal belt), on the left, is the city's top art collection at **Museum Boijmans Van Beuningen** (www.boijmans.nl). From this anchor, several additional museums sprawl south (back toward the river), surrounding Museumpark.

To return to the **train station**, you can hop on a tram (#7 or #20; the Museumpark stop is immediately to your left where Witte de Withstraat hits the Singel belt). Or, if your energy is still holding out, you can walk along these pleasant canals for about three-quarters of a mile to reach the station. After one long block, you'll reach the Eendrachtsplein metro stop, where you can hop on the metro out to the cute, cobbled Delfshaven zone (described later, under "More Sights in Rotterdam").

Farther along the Singel belt, you enter a small square called **Eendrachtsplein**. The Oude/Nieuwe Binnenweg cross-street is another good place to browse for restaurants, and is also known for its (sometimes outside-of-the-box) modern art and sculpture. For example, soon after the metro stop, in the square on the right, look for another Rotterdam landmark: Santa Claus holding what may be a misshapen Christmas tree, a giant ice-cream cone, or a sex toy? (The unofficial name of this 2001 creation by American sculptor Paul McCarthy is *The Butt-Plug Gnome*.) Originally designed for the Schouwburgplein—the square we saw near the start of this walk—the sculpture pushed the bounds even of Rotterdam residents' sense of tolerance and propriety. After hiding it away in a museum for a few years, they moved it here as a compromise.

• *With that image vivid in your mind, continue straight along the Singel belt. Before long, you'll see the unmistakable outline of Central Station, straight ahead.*

More Sights in Rotterdam

Most of the main sights in town are described along my self-guided walk. But here are some additional options.

▲Harbor Cruises

The **Spido** company runs 1.25-hour cruises that offer a good look

at part of Rotterdam's vast port. These sleek boats—with indoor and outdoor areas, a fully stocked bar, and WCs—broadcast a quadrilingual recorded commentary over the loudspeakers. Cruises depart from near Rotterdam's landmark Erasmus Bridge. You'll see the sprawling Staatspark (marked by the Euromast tower); several innovative waterfront housing blocks; and one small section of the bustling port, with stacks upon stacks of containers and a forest of busy cranes. While interesting, a little of this trip goes a long way, and the tour can get a bit boring. But if you view it as a nice chance to relax on a sunny boat deck while cruising through Europe's busiest port, it's fun and illuminating.

Cost and Hours: €11.25, April-Sept daily 10:15-17:00, departs about every 45 minutes, fewer departures off-season, confirm schedule at www.spido.nl, Willemsplein 85, tel. 010/275-9988.

Getting There: From the train station, you can either zip there directly on tram #7 (get off at the Willemsplein stop, at the end of the line), or follow my self-guided walk for a look at Rotterdam old and new en route to Spido's departure point.

▲Delfshaven

One of the few well-preserved bits of Rotterdam's Golden Age wasn't even part of Rotterdam—it was the port for the much smaller town of Delft (see the Delft chapter). Lacking its own outlet to the sea, Delft was given this harbor, which is still connected to Delft's town center by six miles of canals. Strolling along here, you can imagine the Pilgrims setting sail. You'd never know that modern Rotterdam is just around the corner.

Getting There: Delfshaven is on the outskirts of Rotterdam's center, but is easy to reach on the metro: Ride line A or B toward Schiedam Centrum or C toward De Akkers, and get off at the Delfshaven stop (from Central Station this requires a transfer at Beurs; you could instead ride tram #4 or #8, but it's less frequent).

Visiting Delfshaven: Exit the metro following signs for *Uitgang—Historisch Delfshaven*. You'll pop out in the middle of a busy immigrant neighborhood. Walk east on Schiedamsweg for about three blocks, and you'll emerge at the top of historic Delfshaven (on your right)—an idyllic canal pulled straight out of a Vermeer painting: old boats, a cantilevered drawbridge, and even a windmill still churning away in the distance. Wander and explore, going up and down Voorhaven canal and over the bridges. Next to the main drawbridge is the **Pilgrim Fathers Church** (Oude of Pelgrimvaderskerk), where the Pilgrims prayed the night before setting sail for the New World on August 1, 1620. (Their ship, the *Speedwell*, didn't...so they had to swap it out for the *Mayflower* in England before continuing to Plymouth Rock.) If it's open, step inside to catch some history (www.pelgrimvaderskerk.nl). For more on the Pilgrims' time in Holland, see the sidebar on page 96. The parallel Achtershaven canal, one block east, is half charming, half more modern.

Rotterdam Connections

Trains depart from Rotterdam's Central Station at least every 15 minutes and head north to **Delft** (15 minutes), **The Hague** (20 minutes), **Leiden** (35 minutes), **Haarlem** (1 hour, some with transfer in Amsterdam), and **Amsterdam** (1.25 hours on slower trains stopping at all of the above, or a speedy 45 minutes on express ICD train). Trains also head to **Utrecht** (4/hour, 40 minutes), where you can change to reach **Arnhem** (1.5 hours total). To reach **Antwerp**—where you can connect to other Belgian destinations—you can take the slower, cheaper IC train (hourly, 1.25 hours) or the speedy, expensive Thalys (hourly, 30 minutes).

By Cruise Ship

Rotterdam is used by Holland America (among others) as a starting point for many Northern European cruises. Ships use the Cruise Terminal Rotterdam, centrally located along the Wilhelmina Pier—the skyscraper-studded strip that juts out from the southern end of the Erasmus Bridge. The historic building, which was the home of Holland America Line in the days when Ellis Island-bound emigrants rather than hedonists departed from here, has been completely refurbished as a modern terminal with all of the amenities (www.cruiseportrotterdam.com).

Arriving at the Cruise Terminal: The metro easily connects the cruise terminal to Rotterdam's Central Station. Upon arrival, exit the terminal to the left onto Wilhelminakade and walk about five minutes. Just before the base of the big bridge, take the escalator down to the Wilhelminaplein metro station, and ride four stops to Rotterdam Centraal. (Trams #23 and #25 also connect Wilhelminaplein to Rotterdam Centraal.) From the station, you can follow my self-guided walk, or hop on a train to nearby towns (Delft, The Hague, Leiden, even Haarlem or Amsterdam—see connections details listed earlier).

Departing from the Cruise Terminal: If your cruise departs from Rotterdam, just reverse these directions: Ride the train to Rotterdam Central Station and hop on metro line D to Wilhelminaplein, then walk five minutes to the terminal. Taxis also stand by at the station (the ride shouldn't cost more than €10).

EAST OF AMSTERDAM

Most of this book's coverage hugs the western part of Holland. But some interesting sights lie to the east of Amsterdam. Near the German border, on the outskirts of Arnhem, are two very different, but equally fascinating, museums: one devoted to Dutch culture, and one to 20th-century art and sculpture. And halfway between Amsterdam and Arnhem is the hub city of Utrecht, with beautiful canals, lively student bustle, and several good museums.

Utrecht and Arnhem are on the same train line and complement each other well. But because Arnhem's two big sights are time-consuming to reach by public transportation, it's not practical to combine everything in one day. So it's smart to choose: Do both museums near Arnhem in one very long day from Amsterdam (see page 432); pick one Arnhem museum to focus on, then stop off in Utrecht on your way back to Amsterdam; visit only Utrecht; or spend the night in Otterlo, near the Kröller-Müller Museum, to buy yourself more time for this area.

DESTINATIONS
▲Utrecht
This medieval city located in the heart of the country is known for its lively downtown core, good museums (including the Netherlands' top railway museum), and double-decker canals with a particularly fun café scene.

Museums near Arnhem
Allow an extremely long day to visit the folk and modern-art museums (but not on Mon, when art museum is closed); you'll need to leave Amsterdam by 8:00. If you stay overnight near the art museum (in Otterlo), you'll have more time to fit in Utrecht's train museum on your return to Amsterdam.

▲▲**Netherlands Open-Air Folk Museum:** Holland's original and biggest open-air folk museum is also one of its best, sprinkling traditional buildings from around Holland across a delightful park, and populating them with chatty docents to give you a flavor of old-time lifestyles.

▲▲**Kröller-Müller Museum:** This superb modern-art museum has dozens of Van Goghs and a sculpture garden. It's located on the outskirts of the city of Arnhem, within the vast Hoge Veluwe National Park, which has free loaner bikes you can ride to the museum.

UTRECHT

The Netherlands' crossroads city, Utrecht has a thriving old center with unique and inviting canalside embankments, the towering remains of a half-ruined church, a variety of fun museums (including the country's best railroad museum, an endearing throwback candy shop, and a quirky collection of music-making machines), and a huge student population to keep things humming. Bigger and more bustling than Haarlem, Delft, or Leiden, but still exuding a small-town warmth along its gorgeous canalfront wharves, Utrecht feels at once packed with weighty history, and yet also fun to explore.

PLANNING YOUR TIME

Utrecht is a quick side-trip from Amsterdam (30 minutes away by train). You can see the downtown highlights in an easy two-hour stroll, following my self-guided walk. With more time, dip into some museums or climb the cathedral tower. The excellent Railway Museum, a bit farther out (but still an easy walk, or a train ride from Utrecht's Central Station), is also worth a visit, and demands an extra three hours or more.

Because it's on the same train line as **Arnhem**, it's tempting to combine a peek at Utrecht with a visit to Arnhem—but to fit everything in will take careful planning (see page 415 for suggestions).

Note: If you want to climb the 465 steps to the top of the cathedral tower, you'll need to pre-reserve online or by phone; for details, see page 426.

Orientation to Utrecht

With about 330,000 inhabitants, Utrecht (OO-tre*h*t) is the Netherlands' fourth-biggest city (after Amsterdam, Rotterdam, and The Hague). But it feels quite a bit smaller than those cities, thanks to its relatively central zone. Most of the sights are contained within or just outside the harp-shaped old town (Binnenstad)—which takes about 15 minutes to traverse on foot from end to end. This central zone is ringed by a moat *(singel)*—much of it now covered over with a ring road—and crisscrossed by two main canals, the Oudegracht (old canal) and Nieuwegracht (new canal).

TOURIST INFORMATION

The TI is on Cathedral (Dom) Square, facing the cathedral tower (whose ticket office is located inside; Sun-Mon 12:00-17:00, Tue-Sat 10:00-17:00, Domplein 9, tel. 030/236-0000).

ARRIVAL IN UTRECHT

By Train: Utrecht's train station is likely to be torn up for the next few years as they build a new terminal—but you should be able to find lockers (likely near the elevator to track 7). My self-guided walk, next, starts from your train platform, and leads you into town.

Utrecht Walk

This lazy, one-mile tour loops you from the train station into town, along Utrecht's most scenic canals, past a few of its worthwhile museums, and to its landmark cathedral tower. From there, you can head back to the station, or proceed across town to visit the excellent Railway Museum (adding about a half-mile of walking each way). The basic loop takes about an hour and a half, not including sightseeing stops; to add the Railway Museum, figure another three hours (including about two hours at the museum, and time to get there and back).

• *Step off your train into Utrecht—and, quite possibly, chaos. The Utrecht station is undergoing a years-long renovation (through at least 2017), so exactly what you'll see here may change. Find a quiet corner to read the following before making your way into town.*

Utrecht Central Station

Situated in the middle of the Netherlands, Utrecht is the country's primary transportation hub—with its biggest and busiest train station, the headquarters of the Dutch Railway, and the national rail museum (across town and described later).

The current train station was built in the 1970s, and wrapped inside a gigantic American-style shopping mall called Hoog Cath-

Utrecht History

While most of Holland flourished during the 17th-century Golden Age after the Reformation wars (Amsterdam, Haarlem, Delft, Leiden), or during the second half of the 20th century (Rotterdam, The Hague), Utrecht feels older. That's because it is: Utrecht was the biggest city in the Netherlands for centuries (from about 1100 until 1550), and still has the country's largest surviving medieval old town.

The Romans—eager to fortify the Rhine River, which marked their boundary with barbarian lands—built a *castellum* (fort) on today's Cathedral (Dom) Square in A.D. 47. They called their settlement Trajectum ("crossing point"), which later became U-trecht.

At the end of the seventh century, an English missionary named Willibrord traveled to the wilds of Holland. He built a church in the center of town (near today's cathedral). Later, to help cement Utrecht's standing as a seat of Church power, four churches were built at the endpoints of an imaginary city-sized cross—symbolically making Utrecht one gigantic mega-cathedral, with the actual cathedral at its center. To this day, Utrecht's nickname is Domstad ("Cathedral Town").

Strategically situated Utrecht—midway between seaside Dutch settlements and big Germanic cities farther inland—flourished as a trade crossroads, attaining city status in 1122. By its peak in 1500, Utrecht had around 25,000 inhabitants—more than Amsterdam (which soon eclipsed it).

The city's location made it pivotal not only for trade, but for defense. Looking at a map of Utrecht, you can still faintly see the outline of its moat and former star-shaped bastions ringing the Old Town. Utrecht was a critical fortress of the "Holland Waterline," a network of strategically linked canals and breakable dikes that served as a last-resort defense from the 17th through the 20th centuries. A band of low-lying land running through the middle of the country—from the Markermeer lake just east of Amsterdam, south through Utrecht, and all the way down to the broad river deltas near Belgium—could be quickly flooded at an ideal depth for thwarting would-be invaders: too deep to easily walk, but too shallow to maneuver large boats. Large fortified cities like Utrecht anchored the defense as militarized, high-and-dry bastions ideal for keeping an eye on approaching armies. Meanwhile, large population centers farther west—Amsterdam, Rotterdam, The Hague—could be isolated on what was effectively a giant island.

Over the centuries, Utrecht has soldiered on with the same historical roles: transportation hub (with a sprawling train station); spiritual center (as the official seat of the Catholic Church in the predominantly Protestant Netherlands); and center of learning (with the biggest university in the country). And yet, this old and young city also looks to the future, with ambitious plans to reverse some of the grim architectural choices of the postwar period, and make welcoming Utrecht even more so.

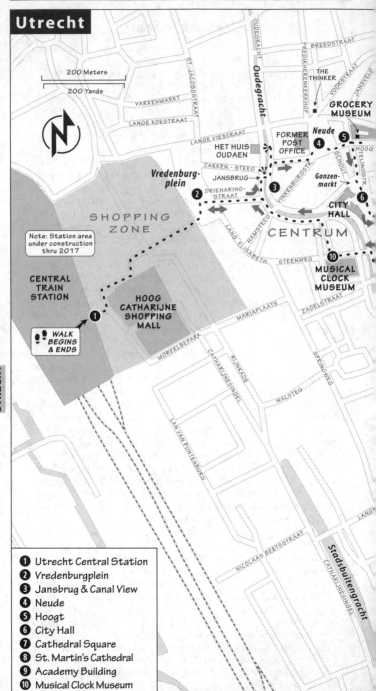

Utrecht

200 Meters
200 Yards

Note: Station area under construction thru 2017

SHOPPING ZONE

CENTRAL TRAIN STATION

HOOG CATHARIJNE SHOPPING MALL

WALK BEGINS & ENDS

OUDEGRACHT

BREEDSTRAAT

PREDIKHERENKERKHOF

VOORSTRAAT

JANSVELD

THE THINKER

GROCERY MUSEUM

St-JACOBSSTRAAT

VARKENMARKT

LANGE KOESTRAAT

LANGE VIESTRAAT

HET HUIS OUDAEN

Vredenburg-plein

ZAKKEN · STEEG

JANSBRUG

DRIEHARING· STRAAT

FORMER POST OFFICE

Neude

Oudegracht

VINKENBURGSTR.

Ganzen-markt

HOOG

HEELINGSTR.

SCHOUT

CITY HALL

LANG · ELISABETH

HAMSTEG

CENTRUM

STEENWEG

MUSICAL CLOCK MUSEUM

MARIAFLAATS

CATHARIJNESINGEL

RIJNKADE

WALSTEG

SPRINGWEG

ZADELSTRAAT

MOREELSEPARK

LAAN VAN PUNTENBURG

NICOLAAS BEETSSTRAAT

Stadsbuitengracht

CATHARIJNESINGEL

LANG

1 Utrecht Central Station
2 Vredenburgplein
3 Jansbrug & Canal View
4 Neude
5 Hoogt
6 City Hall
7 Cathedral Square
8 St. Martin's Cathedral
9 Academy Building
10 Musical Clock Museum

UTRECHT

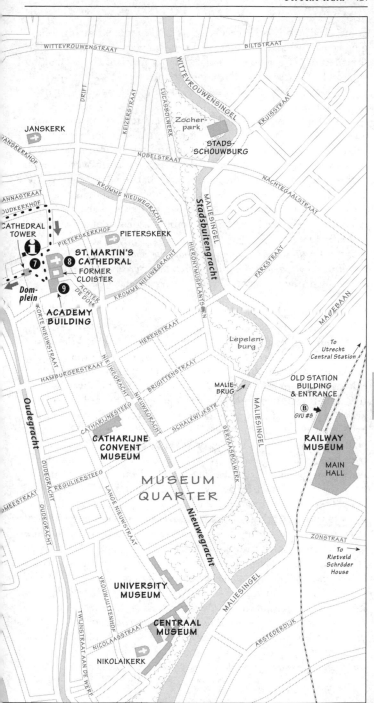

UTRECHT

arijne. And, while it succeeded at its goal of jump-starting a flag-ging economy, it's the opposite of user-friendly. The station seems designed to get arriving visitors lost in a maze of shops, making you feel like you're an overwhelmed toddler lost in a shopping mall in Anytown, USA. Inside and out, architecture like this earns its name: brutalist.

But now city planners are completely revamping the station area. They've also built a state-of-the-art convention center (be-hind the tracks), as well as the new TivoliVredenburg music center, which you may be able to see on the left as you cross over the busy highway on the glassed-in concourse. That highway follows the course of the former moat *(singel),* which was filled in as the town grew; part of Utrecht's long-range plan is to bring back that long-gone canal. (For the latest on this ambitious master plan, see www.cu2030.nl.)

• *Exit the train station through the shopping mall. While the route and markings may change with construction, look for signs to* Centrum *or* Binnenstad. *You'll emerge (hopefully) at the square called...*

Vredenburgplein

This historic market square (one of many in this trade crossroads) is still busy with an outdoor market every Wednesday, Friday, and Saturday. It's named for a long-gone-but-not-forgotten, deeply despised symbol of outsiders meddling in Utrecht's business. The original Vredenburg (ironically called "Peace Castle") was built by the Holy Roman Emperor Charles V after he annexed Utrecht. It kept the peace not by watching for invaders from the outside, but by keeping close tabs on the would-be enemies that lived inside the walls. Worse, during the Eighty Years' War, the castle was taken over by invading Spanish forces, who trained its cannons on the town's own people. After the siege was broken, the city wanted to keep the castle intact for its own defense...but people power took over. Trijn van Leemput led a cadre of local women in climbing up onto the fort and—in a dramatic event that looms large in local folklore—started pulling bricks off of the structure, inspiring their fellow townspeople to literally tear the building apart. (For a peek at the castle's foundation, curious archaeologists can duck into the bicycle parking garage at the left end of the square.)

• *From where you exited the train station, cut across the middle of the square and find the lane called Drieharingstraat. This street—crammed with café tables—offers one of many good opportunities in Utrecht to have a drink, snack, or meal. You'll emerge at the main canal, called Oudegracht. Turn left along the embankment, then head halfway across the first bridge you come to (Jansbrug), and survey the scene.*

Utrecht's Canals

While Dutch cities have no shortage of canals, Utrecht's are unique for their double-decker design: an upper walkway, lively with pe-

destrians and cyclists jostling in front of pretty townhouses; and a lower wharf, which was once the industrial zone where goods could be loaded off ships and directly into those houses' cellars. In the 1940s, these warehouses (no longer connected to the mansions above) were repurposed as restaurants and cafés.

Today the canal itself allows only leisure traffic (including touristy canal cruises and rental paddleboats), plus a few hardworking service barges: Look for the garbage-collection boat, and the red-and-white, city-operated "beer boats" that deliver kegs.

• *Let's head down for a better look. Continue the rest of the way across the bridge, turn left, and take the first set of steps down to the riverbank. Watch your step: The leafy trees provide nice shade, but their burly roots also bully up the pavement—and there are no barriers to keep you from stumbling into the canal.*

Look up across the canal, at the house marked **Het Huis Oudaen,** dating from around 1300. This is a typical, ritzy canal house (sometimes called "city castles")

from Utrecht's trading heyday. Scanning the building from left to right, identify the four parts: The tallest, skinny, turreted structure on the far left is the stair house (used for reaching the upper stories); next is the main house (with huge windows to let in maximum light and to show off residents' wealth); then, tucked on the right side, comes the shorter "side house" (where the cheapskate owners lived in the winter, since it's smaller and cheaper to heat); and finally, on the embankment down below, the warehouse cellars. This building was rebuilt after it was destroyed during the Spaniards' Vredenburg siege in 1577; the cannonballs embedded in the wall commemorate that dark history. Later, in the 18th century, the building became a home for seniors—notice the elderly couple decorating the stone entryway of the side house.

Before heading back up, look around and enjoy the canal's-eye view. While the walls rising up from the canals are uniform, you can gauge at a glance how wide each house is by the distance between the nose-high drainpipes that flank each foundation. Looking up to street level, notice the fine details carved into the square stone bases (called "corbels") of the wrought-iron lampposts. Each one of the 300-plus corbels in the city center is different, carved by local stonecutters since the 1950s. These whimsical sculptures usually have to do with the history of a nearby building, or may simply be biblical or mythological scenes.

• *Head back up the way you came to street level. At the top of the stairs, notice that the big building at the start of Drakenburgstraat is another typical canal house (and today houses a fun-to-browse design shop, Strandwest). Canal cruises depart from the bridge a block farther up the canal.*

Now head up Drakenburgstraat. Emerging into the big square, wade through hundreds of café tables to the middle.

Neude

This square is, clearly, one of Utrecht's main gathering points. The hulking building on your left as you entered the square is the **former Post Office** (labeled *Posteryen-Telegrafie*). The Dutch are extremely early adopters of new technology—and quick to abandon the old ways. (Have you noticed that your magnetic-swipe credit card is basically useless here?) In 2011, the Dutch mail system simply closed all of its post offices. Home delivery still exists, but

if you want to mail a package, you'll have to do it from a private shop. The closure of Dutch post offices left a big question mark for historic old buildings like this one, which is considered an important landmark of the architectural transition from the ornamented Jugendstil/Art Nouveau of the 1920s to the straightforward functionalism of the 1930s (a period collectively called the "Amsterdam School"). If it's open, step inside to peek at its far more impressive interior—with a swooping, parabolic roofline of shimmering yellow brick.

Past the end of the post office, just across the busy road, look for the sculpture of *The Thinker* as a hare, by Welsh sculptor Barry Flanagan. Between the buildings, look for a classic old **water tower**. These were built in cities throughout the Netherlands in the late 19th century, when scientists realized the importance of clean water in protecting public health. Overhead, look for the **red-and-white flag** of Utrecht. The city's coat of arms honors its patron saint, Martin, a Roman officer who famously cut off a piece of his mantle to share with a beggar: The red half represents what's left of the torn mantle, while the white half is St. Martin's underclothes peeking out.

• *As you face the former post office, exit the square down the lane that's over your left shoulder, Kintgenshaven. After one block, jog a few steps right, then left, onto a lane called Hoogt.*

Hoogt

Named for the gorgeous Dutch Renaissance building on your left, this sleepy part of town hides some fun surprises. Look for the  doorway with the *Cinema 't Hoogt* sign. Tucked inside this courtyard are a beloved art house cinema and the endearing **Grocery Museum**. First opened as an actual grocery store in 1873, today it's staffed by grannies selling traditional Dutch candies, and boasts an attic crammed with old bottles, soaps, matchboxes, ration coupons from World War II, and more. It's free to explore, but you'll get the hard sell to buy some hard candy (Museum voor het Kruideniersbedrijf, Tue-Sat 12:30-16:30, closed Sun-Mon, Hoogt 6, www.kruideniersmuseum.nl).

• *Exiting Hoogt lane, turn left down Telingstraat. You'll emerge into a square called Ganzenmarkt (also labeled* Korte Minrebroederstraat)*, dominated by the eclectic facade of...*

City Hall

Utrecht's seat of government is an architectural hodgepodge. It started out as several linked townhouses; later, in the 19th century, they slapped the stern Neoclassical facade on the front. More recently, in the early 2000s, renowned Catalan architect Enric Miralles added the modern extension. Notice that he left a jarring gap (the glass corridor) for future growth. Miralles' choices have been controversial on aesthetic grounds—although this is the main entrance of the building, it feels unfinished.

• *Walk to the far end of the square and turn left, following the pleasant, shop-lined Oudkerkhof, with lots of youthful fashion boutiques and other creative stores. At the end of the street, turn right down Domstraat, and head for those flying buttresses. Reaching the church, turn right and circle around to the square. Stand directly between the church and the tall tower. (If you're weary, rest at the base of the WWII monument.)*

Cathedral Square (Domplein)

Standing right here a few hundred years ago, you'd be in the middle of a massive cathedral's nave.

Several churches have stood on this spot, each marked today by a faint footprint of gray stones in the pavement. In the late sev-

enth century, the English missionary Willibrord built a chapel dedicated to St. Martin on this square. It was later replaced by a Romanesque version, then by a gigantic French-style Gothic structure, which was completed in the early 16th century. At the time of its completion, it was the biggest church in the Netherlands. But money ran out near the end of construction, causing the builders to skimp on the nave: Rather than weight-supporting flying buttresses (like the ones you just saw supporting the apse), it had a simple, flat wooden roof. On the hot summer evening of August 1, 1674, a violent tornado ripped through Utrecht, collapsing the nave of the church—exactly where you're standing now. Trying to salvage what they could of the hulking building, the townspeople sealed off the transept—enclosing a new, much smaller church—and let the jumble of ruins sit here for a century and a half, finally clearing out the rubble to create this square in 1826. Noticing how the outline of the nave is still visible in the wall of the surviving church, mentally resurrect what a mighty house of worship this once was.

Look up at the cathedral tower—368 feet tall, with 465 steps to the top, it's still the tallest one in the Netherlands. The openwork structure allows stiff breezes to blow right through, creating less wind resistance—and, some believe, preventing it from being toppled with the rest of the church. The carillon halfway up plays cheery jingles every quarter-hour, all day (and night), every day.

There are three activities relating to the church: climb the cathedral tower (buy tickets at the TI, to the right as you face the tower); tour the interior of the modern-day church (entrance to the right as you face the building); and descend underground, to see the fragments of earlier church structures embedded below the square (buy tickets a few doors to the right of the TI).

Cathedral Tower Climb: You can climb the tower only with a one-hour escorted tour, and you must reserve in advance by phone or online (€9 guided tour, €15 combo-ticket includes Musical Clock Museum; April-Sept Tue-Sat 11:00-16:00, Sun-Mon 12:00-16:00; Oct-March daily 12:00-16:00, tel. 030/236-0010, www.domtoren.nl). It's often possible to book ahead on the same day, but on summer weekends it's wise to reserve up to a few days

ahead. Pick up your ticket and meet your guide at the TI, across the square from the tower (free lockers for day bags). Your guide will lead you over to the tower, and up, up, up to the top. At each level, you can pause to catch your breath and see history exhibits. Just over halfway up, you'll get up close to the giant bells. Then you can proceed up another 80 feet to the viewpoint near the top. From here, more than 300 feet above the square, you can clearly see the outline of the once-massive cathedral—and pretty much everything else in Utrecht. There's no elevator, so count on lots of stair-climbing.

St. Martin's Cathedral Interior: Step inside the truncated church (€2.50 suggested donation, May-Sept Mon-Fri 10:00-

17:00, Sat 10:00-15:30, Sun 14:00-16:00, shorter hours Oct-April, www.domkerk.nl). The organ marks the point from which the nave once stretched much farther—all the way to the tower, now outside. Buried at the main altar isn't a saint, but an admiral and war hero, Jan van Gendt.

In the small chapel on the right as you face the main altar, find the poignant statues whose faces were ripped off from the 1560s through the 1580s. While originally Catholic, like many Dutch churches this became Protestant following the Reformation. But unlike in other churches, you can actually see the damaging effects of the iconoclasts that sought to destructively unclutter the worshippers' communion with God. The next chapel farther back has more such disfigured statues. These statues were later covered over by a wall, and only rediscovered in the 20th century.

DOMunder (Underground Church Foundations): The DOMunder experience lets you wander among giant old pillars in a subterranean visitors center 15 feet below the square. With a guide, you'll enter through the rusted entrance in the middle of the square, then follow the one-way route to learn about the history of the many churches and other buildings that have stood on this square. Point your innovative audioguide flashlight at items scattered around the ruins, and you'll hear about them on your headphones. Although it's well-presented and may interest armchair archaeologists, for most visitors it's less than thrilling (€10, same reservation system as tower, tours on the hour Tue-Sun 11:00-16:00, closed Mon, www.domunder.nl).

• *Facing the cathedral, head right, to the frilly building in the corner of the square.*

UTRECHT

Academy Building (Academiegebouw)

Originally the cathedral's chapterhouse, after the Reformation this gorgeous building became the main building of the Utrecht University. The Netherlands' biggest university—with an enrollment of about 30,000—the U.U. is also one of its oldest (founded in 1636). These days, the science faculties are neatly segregated at a modern campus called De Uithof, which was built on reclaimed polder land just east of town in the 1970s. But law and humanities are still in the city center, and students of all stripes still hang out downtown.

In the 19th century, architects celebrated the university's 250th birthday by dressing up this building with a stunning Neo-Renaissance facade. The U.U.'s symbol is the shining sun, represented both by the vivid sculpture on the gable above the main door (with the red-and-white crest of Utrecht) and by the giant sphere in the pavement in front. The building is usually open; if so, peek inside.

Facing the building, look for the ornately carved, stone, Gothic gateway just to the left. Step inside to enjoy a harmonious and peaceful space—the **former cloister** of the church, today used for special events for students. The carved triangles over the arches depict scenes from the life of the cathedral's namesake, St. Martin.

Leaving the cloister, look left down Korte Nieuwstraat. This street leads several blocks south through town to Utrecht's **museum quarter**—worth exploring if you have some extra time in town. Among the city's fine museums are the Centraal Museum (displaying art, design, fashion, and city history exhibits in a former monastery), the Museum Catharijneconvent (filling a medieval convent with religious art), and the University Museum (with a fine botanical garden and hands-on exhibits for children). And architecture students make a pilgrimage out to the Rietveld Schröder House, a famous Piet Mondrian-style single-family house in the suburbs just outside the center. For more details on any of these, ask at the TI.

The **Nieuwegracht**, a peaceful and scenic canal with the same double-checker construction as the Oudegracht, parallels Korte

Nieuwstraat one block to the left. The **Railway Museum** is a pleasant 15-minute walk from here: Head down Korte Nieuwstraat and, after a block, turn left down Hamburgerstraat, which becomes Herenstraat, and leads you to a park that traces the former city wall and moat. The museum is through the park and to the right.

• *Or, if you're ready to move on, you can head...*

Back to the Train Station

From Cathedral Square, go through the big tunnel at the base of the tower. In one block, you'll emerge at the main canal, Oudegracht.

Turn right and wander, simply enjoying the people-watching (but be careful of the bikes, which recklessly whiz along this embankment). After one short block, you'll reach a square covering the canal. At the far end of this, turn left up Hanengeschrei, which becomes Steenweg. The entrance for the **Musical Clock Museum** is on the left (described later, under "Sights in Utrecht").

You can follow the busy Steenweg shopping street all the way back to the station (it becomes Korte Elisabethstraat partway along). Or, for a more scenic stroll, turn right up the street just after the clock museum (Massegast), then turn left along the canal to follow Oudegracht for a few short-but-scenic blocks; just turn left on Drieharingstraat to return to the station.

UTRECHT

Sights in Utrecht

▲▲Railway Museum (Spoorwegmuseum)

The most interesting sight in town is Holland's biggest and best display of all things locomotive. It's full of vintage engines and cars (including the Dutch royal family's official train), model railways, and re-creations of historic scenes. Although primarily designed for Dutch families (with spotty English translations), it's easy for anyone to appreciate, and particularly fun for kids. Even the

most train-blasé will want to spend at least two hours here.

Cost and Hours: €16, Tue-Sun 10:00-17:00, closed Mon, at east edge of town in old-fashioned Maliebaanstation, tel. 030/230-6206, www.spoorwegmuseum.nl.

Getting There: From downtown (and the end of my self-guided walk), it's an easy 15-minute **walk** away—see directions earlier. Another option is to take the **train** from Utrecht's Central Station (departs about once hourly on weekdays, but times can change—confirm schedule for "Utrecht Maliebaan"; typically does not run Sat-Sun; 20 minutes, €2.20 one-way). While this sounds romantic, it uses a boring, middle-of-nowhere spur line; the walk through town to the museum is much more fun and takes about as long. (However, the train can be a nice option for a sweat-free return to Central Station—and your connecting Amsterdam-bound train—after touring the museum.) If you'd prefer the **bus**, hop the GVU bus #8 from Central Station (get off at Maliebaan stop).

Visiting the Museum: The ambitious, well-presented museum combines a remarkable collection of old train cars with a modest, Disney-style amusement park. You'll enter and buy your ticket in the fully restored Maliebaan train station, which evokes the genteel early days of rail travel (1874). Pick up a map, then cross the train tracks (passing the royal train, which is usually parked here) to reach the main hall and get oriented to the different areas. The main hall and train yard are filled with historic locomotives and carriages. Along the right side of the hall are several more engaging attractions: the Steel Monsters roller coaster for kids; an Orient Express exhibit with an original carriage from the train line that once connected Western Europe to Istanbul (as well as a small theater presenting a live show in Dutch several times a day); and a lavishly re-created mining village from 19th-century England (with a replica of the world's oldest passenger train car, from 1829). Outside is a picnic area, a mini-railroad that kids enjoy riding, and the prizewinning Trial by Fire ride—a jostling, nearly Disney-caliber simulator of a harrowing steampunk train ride, narrated by Dutch actor Rutger Hauer. (Unfortunately, the ride is entirely in Dutch, with no English translations—but it's still fun.) Be sure to explore the sprawling grounds, which include a giant playground, an enormous turntable for locomotives, an old shunting yard (used to supply steam locomotives), a thought-provoking exhibit on the use of railway cars in World War II and the Holocaust, and temporary exhibits.

Museum Speelklok (Musical Clock Museum)

This fun museum fills the cavernous hall of a former church with a fascinating array of self-playing instruments: musical clocks, calliopes, and street organs in all their clicking, clanking, and tooting glory. On the main floor, several soundproof rooms house hulking calliopes and player pianos, while upstairs in the gallery, smaller pieces overlook the former nave. Everything is explained in English, and some items are hands-on. But for the best experience, make a point to join the 40-minute included tour.

Cost and Hours: €11 includes tour, €15 combo-ticket includes cathedral tower (Domtoren), Tue-Sun 10:00-17:00, closed Mon, tours depart at :30 past each hour, last tour at 15:30, well-signed 10-minute walk from station, located on busy shopping street in city center at Steenweg 6, tel. 030/231-2789, www.museumspeelklok. nl.

Utrecht Connections

Utrecht is the crossroads of the Netherlands, with major lines running north to **Amsterdam** (5/hour, 30 minutes), where you can connect to **Haarlem** (50 minutes total); west to **The Hague** (at least 2/hour, 40 minutes); northwest to **Leiden** (2/hour, 45 minutes); southeast to **Rotterdam** (4/hour, 40 minutes), where you can connect to **Delft** (1 hour total) and **Antwerp**, Belgium (2 hours total); and east to **Arnhem** (4/hour, 40 minutes).

UTRECHT

MUSEUMS NEAR ARNHEM

Netherlands Open-Air Folk Museum • Kröller-Müller Museum

While the city of Arnhem itself is nothing special, it's close to a pair of fun and worthwhile side-trips: the Netherlands Open-Air Folk Museum and the exceptional Kröller-Müller Museum. Of all open-air folk museums in the Netherlands, Arnhem's—set just within the city limits—feels the most authentic. Its classically Dutch buildings sprawl across rolling hills, with rich details around every corner. Nearby, the Kröller-Müller Museum, located in the middle of Hoge Veluwe National Park, displays a world-class collection of modern art (including roomfuls of Van Goghs—they own 87 of them). It's also a delight to pedal through the park on free loaner bikes.

PLANNING YOUR TIME

Arnhem, an hour southeast of Amsterdam by train, is doable as a side-trip from Amsterdam. Unfortunately, its two museums are far from each other and far from Arnhem's Central Station. Both are superb and worth the time and effort, but if you want to see both, either spend the night in the town of Otterlo (recommended) or be prepared for a long day of somewhat rushed sightseeing. Note that the Kröller-Müller Museum is closed on Monday.

By Car: Drivers can visit both museums within a day...and might have time left to park the car and go for a pedal through the national park. Figure just over an hour's drive from Amsterdam to Arnhem, then about a 20-minute ride into the national park, and an hour back to Amsterdam. For driving directions, see the "Getting There" section for each museum.

By Public Transportation: You can day-trip to either museum by taking a train and bus ride; for specifics, see "Getting There" in the individual sight listings (see also the map on next page).

If you want to combine both museums in one long day of

Arnhem Area Transportation

sightseeing, weekends are easiest (with better bus options), but on any day you go, you must get an early start. Here's a basic outline: From Amsterdam Central Station, catch the train at about 8:00 for the one-hour ride to Arnhem. In Arnhem, hop a bus to the folk museum to arrive when it opens at 10:00. Leave the museum by 13:00, and catch a bus to Otterlo, near Hoge Veluwe National Park and the Kröller-Müller Museum. In the park, do the museum first (closes at 17:00), then the visitors center (closes at 18:00 in summer), then wind down your day by biking around the park. Plan on a late return train to Amsterdam from the Ede-Wageningen station (the station nearest the park).

On **weekends,** logistics are fairly simple, because a direct Syntus bus connects the Arnhem bus station (next to the train station), folk museum, Otterlo, and Kröller-Müller Museum. It takes about 40 minutes to get from the folk museum to the Kröller-Müller Museum.

On **weekdays**, there's no direct bus linking the museums, meaning you'll spend more time in transit (e.g., busing from the folk museum back to Arnhem, then catching a different bus to Otterlo) and less time sightseeing.

Saving on Bus Fares: Bus prices are high—each trip will cost between €2 and €6 (cheaper when using an OV-chipkaart; see page 490). If you're traveling with a companion on a weekday, ask for a

"Buzzer" day pass (€14, covers 2 adults and up to 3 children, buy from driver, good after 9:00 Mon-Fri or anytime weekends, www. connexxion.nl/buzzer_english/174). The Syntus bus offers a similar "Super Ticket" for weekends only (€15, covers 2 adults and up to 4 children, buy from driver, valid Sat-Sun, www.syntus.nl).

For Overnight Visitors: If you're spending the night in Otterlo, you can get a later start from Amsterdam, linger at the open-air folk museum (having left your things in a locker at Arnhem station), relax that evening in Otterlo, and tour the art museum and national park at a leisurely pace the next morning.

Orientation to Arnhem

Tourists view dreary Arnhem as a transit hub useful only for reaching the open-air folk museum on its outskirts and the nearby Kröller-Müller Museum and national park. A few hotels line up across from the train station, but I'd rather sleep in charming little Otterlo, near the park entrance (see "Sleeping in Otterlo" on page 444). Arnhem's old town—nowhere near as charming as similar towns in the Netherlands—is just across the busy ring road from the train and bus stations. Restaurants with outdoor seating cluster around the square called Korenmarkt and, a few steps deeper into the old town, around Jaansplaats.

Tourist Information: Arnhem's TI is across the street from the bus station (Mon-Fri 9:30-17:30, Sat 9:30-17:00, closed Sun, Stationsplein 13, tel. 0900-112-2344—€0.45/minute, www. vvvarnhem.nl). The TI provides a free city map and sells €2 city guides and a €6 tourist map that includes the national park and Kröller-Müller Museum (the park's visitors center sells a cheaper map).

ARRIVAL IN ARNHEM

By Train: Arnhem's train station is surrounded by a sea of construction and urban blight, as they're in the midst of a multiyear project to build a super-modern station complex. Expect changes to the following information.

The station has **WCs** (pay) and **lockers** (credit cards only). You'll also find a Rijwiel **bike-rental shop** (€7.50/day for 3-speed bike—you'll need all 3 gears to ride up to the open-air museum— plus €50 refundable deposit, open daily long hours). While the construction continues, the location of the shop changes—look for it near the front of the station.

The **bus station,** with connections to Otterlo, the Netherlands Open-Air Folk Museum, and the Kröller-Müller Museum and national park, is to the right as you exit the train station in a large parking garage along the busy street. Check the sign near the entry to the bus area to find the departure bay for your bus.

Arnhem Connections

From Arnhem by Train to: Amsterdam (3/hour, 1 hour, some with transfer in Utrecht), **The Hague** (4/hour, 1.5 hours, transfer in Utrecht; then another 15 minutes to **Delft**).

Netherlands Open-Air Folk Museum

Arnhem has the Netherlands' first and biggest folk museum, and it's also one of the best, rated ▲▲. You'll enjoy a huge park of windmills, old farmhouses and other buildings relocated from throughout the Netherlands, traditional crafts in action, and a

pleasant education-by-immersion in Dutch culture. It's great for families.

GETTING THERE

It's easiest to get to the museum (called "Nederlands Openluchtmuseum" in Dutch) on weekends, when Syntus bus #400 departs from Arnhem's bus station and runs right to the museum's entrance (leaves hourly around :19, 15 minutes, €3).

Weekday buses run more frequently, but leave you a few blocks from the museum: From the bus station, take either bus #8 (direction: *Arnhem Presikhaaf*) or bus #3 (direction: *Burgers Zoo/Nederlands Openluchtmuseum*—both buses run about 2/hour, 20 minutes, €3). If you take bus #8, get off at the Julius Rontgenweg stop: Walk a few steps west to the corner, turn right, and then left to reach the museum. Bus #3 drops you farther away, at the Het Duifje stop, a 10-minute walk from the museum entrance: Cross the street, head right, then left down the tree-lined avenue from the roundabout, then turn right (following signs for *Openluchtmuseum*).

From the Arnhem train station, you can also **walk** (30 minutes) or ride a **bike** (strenuous 20-minute uphill ride; bike-rental details on page 434). A **taxi** from the station costs about €20.

By **car** from Amsterdam, take A-2 south to Utrecht, then A-12 east to Arnhem. Just before Arnhem, take the Arnhem Nord exit (#26) and follow *Openluchtmuseum* signs to the museum (€5 parking, buy parking ticket when you buy entrance ticket). If driving from Haarlem, skirt Amsterdam to the south on A-9, take A-2 south to Utrecht, and then follow the previous instructions (via A-12).

ORIENTATION

Cost and Hours: Museum-€16, April-Oct daily 10:00-17:00, buildings closed Nov-March; in winter, the museum is open as a park only (€5 admission), Nov-mid-Jan daily, mid-Jan-March Sat-Sun only.

Information: Tel. 026/357-6111, www.openluchtmuseum.nl.

Getting Around: A free, old-fashioned tram does a lazy counterclockwise circle around the museum grounds, making six stops (well-marked on park maps).

Eating: The museum has several good budget restaurants and covered picnic areas. The **café** in the entrance pavilion is inexpensive but has limited choices (€5-6 sandwiches)—it's more enjoyable to eat inside the park. The rustic **Pancake House** (Pannekoeken Huis, a.k.a. "Restaurant de Hanekamp") serves hearty and sweet splittable Dutch flapjacks (€6-9 pancakes, soups, salads, and sandwiches). **Brabant Café,** in the "village" of Budel, resembles an old-fashioned farmhouse café and offers desserts and snacks. The **De Kasteelboerderij Café-Restaurant** at the Oud-Beijerland Manor serves a traditional €8 *dagmenu*—plate of the day (open daily July-Aug, otherwise Sun only).

⊙Self-Guided Tour

You could spend the whole day exploring this wonderful open-air museum. But to hit a few highlights, follow this tour. Because the layout of the grounds can be confusing, pick up the good free map at the entry—I've used the numbers on that map to help you navigate this tour. Don't hesitate to dip into any buildings that intrigue you, even if they're not on this tour—most have brief English explanations outside, and some have English-speaking docents inside. (Ask them questions...that's their job.) Especially with kids, it would be a shame to do this place in a rush—there's so much to experience.

• *Start in the...*

Entrance Pavilion: Consider buying the in-depth English guidebook, and ask about special events and activities, especially for kids. Downstairs are exhibits on traditional Dutch costumes and replicas of various storefronts. You'll also find Arnhem's effort to keep up with the Disneys: the high-tech **HollandRama** multimedia experience (inside the big copper blob you saw out front; runs about hourly—schedule posted by stairs). You'll sit on a giant platform that rotates inside a spherical theater to gradually reveal various Dutch dioramas: windmills, a snowy countryside, house and store interiors, and so on. Although the narration is in Dutch, the 20-minute presentation is an enjoyable rest.

• *To hit the park, exit the entrance pavilion and cross the tram tracks to walk up the path. You're likely to see animals in the pasture on your right—if so, take a closer look: They're rare Dutch breeds, not the high-yield animals used in modern farms. No longer cost-effective, these special animals are raised by the museum as part of its mission to preserve a piece of Dutch folk life.*

After a few buildings on the left, step inside the one-story...

Zuid-Scharwoude Farmhouse (#23, just before the pond): The cows lived on one side of this house from 1745, and the people on the other (notice the claustrophobic cupboard-beds). Along the cow stalls, see the patterns the farmwife would make with fresh sand and seashells each summer to show off family status.

• *Nearby, cross the...*

Yellow Drawbridge (#25): Dating from 1358, this double drawbridge takes you to perhaps the most scenic part of the park:

a pond surrounded by windmills and cabins (inspired by the Waterland area around Marken—described in the Edam, Volendam & Marken chapter). Pause on the bridge to look toward the sawmill. You might see kids playing with a small rope-pulled ferryboat.

Continue across the drawbridge into the little **village.** Along the way are some tempting shops where you can pick up an edible souvenir, including a well-stocked general store, a bakery, and a fragrant candy store.

• *At the center is the...*

Village Square: You can play here with toys from the 1800s. See if you can make the "flying Dutchman" fly, or try to ride an original "high-wheeled velocipede" without falling off. On the square is a restaurant specializing in *poffertjes* (puffy mini-pancakes dusted with powdered sugar).

• *Behind the* poffertje *shop, cross the little bridge toward the windmills, pass the boat workshop, and enter the...*

Fisherman's Cottage (#36): The black-tarred exterior hides a bright and colorful interior. Notice the rope-controlled smoke hatch, rather than a chimney. Wooden cottages like these were nicknamed "smokehouses." In front of the cottage is the boatyard, where vessels could be pulled out of the water to scrape off the barnacles.

• *Backtrack through the village square, then continue on to the...*

Laundry (#39, on the right): Inside, an industrial-strength agitator furiously pounds stubborn stains to smithereens. (There was no "delicate cycle" back then.) On nice days, the clean sheets are spread out on the lawn to dry.

• *For an optional detour (best for train buffs), hook around through the little cottages across the street, then turn right to reach the...*

Train Depot (#50): Inside, you can actually walk underneath a train to check out its undercarriage. The adjacent **goods shed** (#51) holds a virtual-reality postal carriage.

• *Head back past the laundry, then go beyond the cafeteria to reach the small, yellow windmill. Here, turn left and walk up the path, watching for the low-profile brown building through the trees on your right, near the bridge.*

Paper Mill (#90): At this building, dating from around 1850, you'll learn that farmers often made paper in their spare time to help make ends meet. Inside, you might see a demonstration of linen rags being turned into pulp, and then into paper. Peek upstairs at the finished paper hanging to dry.

• *Leaving the mill the way you came, walk straight ahead on the brick path, passing various buildings on your right until you reach the...*

Herb Garden (#65): This tranquil, hedge-lined garden is worth exploring. The map at the entry explains the various parts of the garden, each growing herbs for different purposes: dyes, food, medicine, and so on. Listen for the squeals of lively children from the playground behind the garden.

• *Continue past the garden and cross the tram tracks to the...*

Freia Steam-Dairy Factory (at #52, with the big smokestack): Named after Freia, the Norse goddess of agriculture, this was the Netherlands' first privately owned cheese and butter factory. Borrow the English explanations at the entry, sample some free cheese, and try to follow the huge belt of the steam engine as it whirls through the factory.

• *Leaving the factory, loop around to the right—past the little black-and-green windmill—then turn right again, down the path just before the brick-and-thatch forest hut. On the right, look for the...*

Peat Hut (#58): Humble little huts like these were used by day laborers and covered with the same turf that those laborers were paid so poorly to gather.

• *Continue to a big, thatched-roof...*

Farmhouse (#59): Step into the vast and rough 1700s interior, listen to recorded animal noises, and scope out the layout: grain stored up above, cows along the main room, and at the far end, a (no doubt smelly) residential zone for people.

• *Cross the tram tracks in front of the farmhouse to reach the tiny...*

Schoolhouse (#61): Aside from its brick construction (most were made of clay), this is typical of village schoolhouses from around 1730. Only kids from 6 to 12 years old, mostly boys, attended school, with an emphasis on reading and writing, with summers off to help on the farm. Imagine the schoolhouse back then, fragrant with smoke from the peat fire. Notice the slates used to follow along with lessons (stored in the wooden "lockers" on the walls). An underperforming student would have to wear the donkey picture around his neck.

Just beyond the schoolhouse is the **Pancake House** (#62; good for a snack or meal), with an adjacent playground.

• *Go back toward the school and cross the tram tracks to the right, down a forested path that leads to the...*

Dutch Reformed Chapel (#71): In the typical Dutch style, the church has an austere white interior, a central pulpit, and wooden pews. Wealthy parishioners paid to reserve a seat near the pulpit; the poor had to settle for a spot at the back or in the balcony.

• *Then continue along the tracks through the village, past the **Brabant Café** (#75), and follow the smell of hops to the modern, working **brewery** (#78, on the left), where you can duck inside for a free sample.*

Just beyond, on the left, look for the...

Four Laborers' Houses (#79): These houses offer a fascinating glimpse into the lifestyles of four generations of workers: from 1870, 1910, 1954, and 1970. See how home fashion and amenities—most interestingly, bathrooms—progressed from the rustic 1870s to the garish 1970s.

• *Continuing through the village, the **hospital** on the left (#83), from 1955, really does smell like a hospital. Next, the long **collection center** (#84) shows off a mind-numbing array of Dutch bric-a-brac, with futuristic exhibits about recycling and conservation. Just beyond it is a formal hedge garden. Finally, cross the tram tracks and walk to the big, white...*

Platform Windmill (#92): Hike up the steep steps of the park's centerpiece for an aerial view over the museum.

• *Our tour is over. Head back to the entrance, or continue exploring to your heart's content.*

Kröller-Müller Museum

The Kröller-Müller Museum of top-notch modern art, rated ▲▲, is located within Hoge Veluwe National Park, the Netherlands' largest at 13,000 acres. While the south end of the park is just outside Arnhem, the museum is buried deep in the forest close to the opposite end of the park, near the town of Otterlo. Because the museum is situated within the national park, you must buy a ticket for both the museum and the park.

This memorable museum shows off the collection of Helene Kröller-Müller (1869-1939), a wealthy fan of avant-garde art, and includes an outstanding collection of Van Goghs. The modern museum seamlessly blends artistic beauty and its own peaceful park setting. Stroll through the delightfully landscaped sculpture garden, and spend some time with virtually all the top artists of the late 19th and early 20th centuries.

Because it's difficult to get to, the Kröller-Müller Museum doesn't suffer from the hordes that descend on the Van Gogh Museum in Amsterdam. This is your best chance to get up close and personal with Vincent.

GETTING THERE

Visitors coming from Amsterdam can take the train to either Arnhem or the Ede-Wageningen station near Otterlo (4/hour, 1 hour, some transfer in Utrecht). If you're combining your visit here with the folk museum, definitely head to Arnhem.

On **weekends,** Arnhem is always the best choice (whether you're visiting the folk museum or not) because **Syntus buses** directly connect the Arnhem bus station with the park and museum (1/hour, 1 hour, €6).

On **weekdays,** getting from either station to the museum and park is more complicated. (Even the park's employees don't bother trying to commute by bus.) You'll need to go through the town of **Otterlo,** near the northwest entrance of the park, just over a mile from the museum. Its Rotonde bus stop is at a roundabout on the edge of town; its Centrum stop is in the center. Buses #105 from Arnhem and #106 to the park make both stops. Bus #108 from the Ede-Wageningen station stops only at the Rotonde stop. See specifics below and the map on page 433.

On Weekdays from Ede-Wageningen Station: Exit the station toward signs marked *Centrum* to find the bus stops, where you can catch **bus** #108 to Otterlo (bus marked *Apeldoorn,* runs hourly about :40 past the hour, or 2/hour on weekday mornings before 12:00, 20 minutes, €6). Hop off the bus at the Otterlo Rotonde roundabout, about a five-minute walk from the center (buses return from Rotonde to Ede-Wageningen station at :55 after each hour until 22:55). The #106 bus usually meets the #108 at this stop—making it an easy transition to the museum. When the #106 enters the park, the driver will stop at the ticket booth so that you can buy tickets for the park and the museum. Ask the driver to let you off at the museum; turn right at the giant blue trowel and follow the road for a few minutes past the parking lot with all the white bikes; the museum entrance is on the left.

If you miss the #106, **walk** five minutes into the town center, and then hang a left to the park entrance (about 20 minutes total), where you can buy your combo-ticket and hop on a free white bike to ride to the Kröller-Müller Museum or the park's visitors center. A **taxi** from the Ede-Wageningen station to the museum costs about €40 one-way.

On Weekdays from Arnhem Central Station: During the week, there's no direct bus to the museum, so you'll go via Otterlo: From Arnhem's bus station (right next to the train station), take **bus** #105 marked *Barneveld/Syntus,* and get off at Otterlo Centrum (1-2/hour, 20 minutes, €5). Once in Otterlo, you can take bus #106 or **walk** to the park (both options described above). You can hire a **taxi** from Arnhem's station (about €45).

By Car: From Amsterdam, take A-1 southeast, then exit on N-310 to Otterlo. From Arnhem, take A-12 north, then pick up N-310 to Otterlo. Parking inside the park costs €8.40, or you can pay €3 to park at the entrance and bike or walk in.

GETTING AROUND HOGE VELUWE NATIONAL PARK

Once at Hoge Veluwe, you have various options for connecting the attractions. My favorite plan: Bus from Otterlo directly to the Kröller-Müller Museum and view the collection, then pick up a free white bike to pedal to the park's visitors center, then bike back to the park entrance (or, with more time, bike around the park).

By Bike: The park has 1,700 loaner bikes—an endearing remnant of Holland's hippie past—that you're free to use to make your explorations more fun. The one-speed bikes, with no hand brakes (just pedal brakes), are good enough to get around on, but not good enough to get stolen. Just pick one up (or drop one off) wherever you see a bike rack, including at park entrances or at any attraction. While riding through the vast green woods, make a point of getting off your bike to climb an inland sand dune.

By Bus: Bus #106 does a convenient circuit around the park, connecting the Otterlo Rotonde stop (at the edge of town), the Otterlo Centrum stop (in the town center), the Otterlo entrance to the park, a stop 200 yards from the Kröller-Müller Museum, and the park's visitors center. Unfortunately, its frequency isn't ideal (hourly on weekdays, 2/hour on weekends until 19:00; last bus at 20:00

May-Aug, earlier in off-season). But it can be a handy way to connect the dots if you're tired or in a hurry.

ORIENTATION

Cost: €16.80 combo-ticket includes national park entry.

Hours: Tue-Sun 10:00-17:00, sculpture garden closes at 16:30, closed Mon, Houtkampweg 6, tel. 031/859-6157, www.kmm.nl.

Eating at the Kröller-Müller Museum: Consider the self-service restaurant Monsieur Jacques (€6 soups and sandwiches, €11 salads, Tue-Sun 10:00-16:30, closed Mon).

VISITING THE MUSEUM

A stern-looking statue of Monsieur Jacques (the museum's mascot) greets you on the entry path. Once inside, pick up the informative booklet-guide and drop your bag at the mandatory bag check. Computers near the entry let you tailor a self-guided tour to your interests. Each work is labeled (but not described) in English, and there is no audioguide.

There are two parts to the museum: the outside sculpture garden and the interior art collection.

The **sculpture garden** shows off more than a hundred sculptures, displayed on 60 rolling acres of lawn. You can appreciate works by Auguste Rodin, Barbara Hepworth, Claes Oldenburg, Christo, and others—or just enjoy this excuse for a walk in a pretty park with something fun to look at. Look for Jean Dubuffet's beloved *Garden of Enamel*, a giant, psychedelic, black-and-white roller rink you can climb around on. Since the garden closes at 16:30, head here first if you're arriving later in the day.

Inside, the permanent **art collection** is like a *Who's Who* of modern art. The works are displayed chronologically and grouped by movement, in keeping with Helene Kröller-Müller's wishes to foster understanding and appreciation of new art styles. You'll go from the hazy landscapes of the Impressionists (Monet, Manet, Renoir), to the intricate compositions

of the Pointillists (Seurat, Pissarro), to the bold innovations of the Post-Impressionists (Gauguin, Van Gogh), to the slinky scenes of Art Nouveau (Toulouse-Lautrec), to the shattered-glass canvases of the Cubists (Picasso, Braque, Gris), and, finally, to the colorful grids of Dutchman Piet Mondrian.

The museum's highlight is its Vincent van Gogh collection, the second largest in the world (after Amsterdam's Van Gogh Museum; Kröller-Müller usually displays about 50 of their 87 Vincent canvases). Look for some famous pieces, including various self-portraits; some *Sunflowers*—including one with a blue background; and *Café de Nuit,* the famous scene of an al fresco café on a floodlit Arles square. Notice how thickly the paint is caked on to create the almost-3-D lamp, the work's focal point.

VISITING HOGE VELUWE NATIONAL PARK

The Netherlands' biggest national park, rated ▲▲, is a delight to explore. On a quick visit, a short pedal and a visit to the Kröller-Müller Museum are enough; with more time, also swing by the visitors center and bike to your heart's content. The hunting lodge within the park, the former residence of the Kröller-Müller family, makes a fun destination. If you head deeper into the park, you'll find a surprising diversity of terrain, from inland sand dunes to lakes to peat bogs to moorland. Get advice, maps, and brochures at the park entrances or at the visitors center.

Cost and Hours: Park entry-€8.70, €16.80 combo-ticket includes the Kröller-Müller Museum. The park is open daily June-July 8:00-22:00, May and Aug 8:00-21:00, April 8:00-20:00, Sept 9:00-20:00, Oct 9:00-19:00, Nov-March 9:00-18:00, last entry one hour before closing (tel. 055/378-8100, www.hogeveluwe.nl).

Visitors Center (Bezoekerscentrum)

This is a good place to get your bearings in the park, with a helpful information desk, a nature exhibit, WCs, a playground, a restaurant, and a hub for free loaner bikes (daily April-Oct 9:30-18:00, Nov-March 9:30-17:00). Browse the collection of brochures and maps, including the good €2.50 map of the park, and the €1 self-guided bike tour in English, with commentary on the main stops.

The **nature exhibit** features interactive, kid-oriented exhibits, well-explained in English. It's divided into two parts: An above-ground section focuses on the parks' various landscapes and the animals that live above ground; then you'll go through a tunnel to reach the second section, called the "Museonder," which shows life underground (animals, fossils, the water table), with conservation-themed displays. Ask for an English showing of the nature films when you enter (a favorite is the 30-minute movie about park deer).

Eating at the Visitors Center: The good **Restaurant de Koperen Kop** serves up surprisingly tasty self-service cafeteria food, with indoor or outdoor seating (€8-12 plates, same hours as visitors center).

St. Hubertus Lodge

This dramatic hunting lodge, at the north end of the park, is another popular excuse for a bike ride. Once the countryside residence  of the modern art-collecting Kröller-Müller family, it's perched on the edge of a lake with a tower looming overhead. Designed to resemble the antlers of a stag, this structure evokes the story of St. Hubert, who supposedly discovered a crucifix miraculously dangling between a deer's antlers (sporadic tours, in Dutch only). The 45-minute walk around the adjacent lake is dotted with sculptures. Combining this lodge, the Kröller-Müller Museum, and the visitors center makes for a fun 6.5-mile biking loop.

OTTERLO

The tiny village of Otterlo is located just outside the northwest entrance to the park, which is the closest one to the Kröller-Müller Museum. Though not exciting, it's a good place to spend the night near the park. The town has tandem-bike tourists zipping through on their way to the park, cafés, and a meager **TI** (in the middle of the town center, Mon-Thu 8:00-18:00, Fri 8:00-20:00, Sat 8:00-17:00, closed Sun, Dorpsstraat 9, tel. 0318/614-444, www.otterlo.nl).

Sleeping in Otterlo: Both of these accommodations are on the road between Otterlo and the northwest entrance to the park; Sterrenberg is about a half-mile from the park entrance, and Kruller is closer to the town center.

$$ Boutique Hotel Sterrenberg is a Dutch designer's take on a traditional hunting lodge. With woodsy touches and modern flair in its 33 rooms, it's a pleasant splurge (Sb-€123-138, Db-€145-195, price depends on season and room size, pricier "luxury" rooms, great Sunday-night deals include dinner, elevator, Wi-Fi, restaurant with terrace, swimming pool, sauna, 6 rentable bikes for guests—€8.50/day—or use free white bikes within nearby park gates, about 1.5 miles to Kröller-Müller Museum, Houtkampweg 1, tel. 0318/591-228, www.sterrenberg.nl, info@sterrenberg.nl).

$ Hotel Kruller has 30 stylishly simple rooms over a busy restaurant (small Sb-€59, mid-size Sb-€79, small Db-€79, mid-size Db-€99, large Db-€119, cheaper for 2 or more nights, no elevator, Wi-Fi, Dorpsstraat 19, tel. 0318/591-231, www.kruller.nl, info@kruller.nl).

HISTORY

Twenty Centuries in Nine Pages

Born from the mud of a river delta that spills into the North Sea, the Dutch provinces united to become a global force of hardy seafarers, clever merchants, and freethinkers.

ROMANS AND INVASIONS (A.D. 1-1300)

When Rome falls (c. 400), the Low Countries shatter into a patchwork of local dukedoms that are ravaged by Viking raids. It's a poor, agricultural, and feudal landscape ruled loosely by the Counts of Holland. Holland's first major city is Utrecht—a former Roman fort that becomes a crossroads of trade and bulwark of Christianity.

Around 1250, fishermen in Amsterdam build a dike (dam) where the Amstel River flows into the North Sea, creating a prime trading port. Soon the town gains independence and trading privileges from the local count and bishop.

Sights
- Amsterdam's Dam Square
- Exhibits in Amsterdam Museum
- Haarlem's Grote Markt
- The Hague's Ridderzaal and Binnenhof

BOOMING TRADE TOWNS (1300-1500)

Amsterdam becomes a bustling little port, trading its signature salt-cured herring for German beer, all financed with a budding capitalism: banking, loans, and speculation in stock and futures. The city attracts religious pilgrims when a communion wafer mysteriously survives a fire, and subsequently causes a rash of miraculous healings. But Amsterdam is only one among several trade towns in this land of businessmen—Haarlem, Delft, Edam. By 1500, it's Leiden that's the region's biggest city.

Politically, the Netherlands is ruled by the cultured empire of the Dukes of Burgundy (centered in the southern provinces—today's Belgium).

Tiny Holland's future changes forever in the year 1492, when Columbus' voyage hints at the potential wealth awaiting hardy seafarers...like the Dutch.

Sights

- Churches: Amsterdam's Old Church (Oude Kerk) and New Church (Nieuwe Kerk), Delft's New Church (Nieuwe Kerk, see photo), and Haarlem's Grote Kerk
- Amsterdam's Mint Tower from the original city wall, and the wooden house at Begijnhof 34

PROTESTANTS VS. CATHOLICS, FREEDOM FIGHTERS VS. SPANISH RULERS (1500s)

Protestantism spreads through the Low Countries. Thanks to royal marriages, the Low Countries are now ruled from afar by the very Catholic Habsburg family in Spain. In 1566, angry Protestants rise up against Spain and Catholicism, vandalizing Catholic

churches ("iconoclasm") and deposing Spanish governors. William of Orange rallies the Dutch, becoming the father of his country and establishing his family—and their heraldic color—as national institutions; see the sidebar. (The current king is distantly descended from William.) When Spain sends troops to restore order and brutally punish the rebel-heretics, it begins the Eighty Years' War, also known as the Dutch War of Independence (1568-1648).

During the war, the Dutch stand strong in the brave Alamo-like stand in the siege of Haarlem (1572-1573). In 1574, they flood South Holland and sail flat-bottomed ships against the Spanish to save Leiden. When the thriving (Belgian) city of Antwerp falls to Spanish troops (1585), Antwerp's best and brightest flee to the Netherlands. Other refugees of religious persecution, including Calvinists and Anabaptists, find a home in tolerant Amsterdam. The influx of talented immigrants would spur the coming Golden Age.

William of Orange (1533-1584)

A wealthy noble who was the confidant of the Holy Roman Emperor; a sensual aristocrat who had four wives and many mistresses; a religious chameleon who was born a Lutheran, became a Catholic, and ended up a Calvinist—William of Orange sounds like the hero of a romantic novel. But to the Dutch, he will always be the George Washington of the Netherlands—the leader of their war of independence against Spain. They call him *De Vader des Vaderlands*, "Father of the Fatherland," and when they sing the Dutch national anthem (the *Wilhelmus*, the oldest national anthem in the world), the text is actual 16th-century propaganda justifying William's stand.

Born into Lutheran German nobility, as a teenager William inherited the French principality of Orange and several domains in the Low Countries. He was invited to serve in the court of Holy Roman Emperor Charles V—provided he become a Catholic, which he did. Mixing with the ruling elite of his era, William was set to live a life of ease, but he embraced religious tolerance in an era when people were often murdered for their beliefs.

Those beliefs would clash with Spanish King Philip II, who began a crusade against Protestants after inheriting the Low Countries from his father. At the same time Philip weakened the rights and privileges of the local nobility. William was *stadholder* (sort of a governor-general) of two Dutch provinces, and other nobles looked to him to lead the resistance against the Spanish. During a meeting of the Council of State, he is supposed to have

Within a few years, most Spanish troops are driven south into Belgium. Belgium remains under Spanish control while Holland's towns and nobles form a Protestant military alliance (the United Provinces) to keep the Spaniards at bay.

Sights

- Various churches (e.g., Amsterdam's New Church and Delft's New Church) that were stripped bare of decoration during the iconoclasm
- Civic Guard portraits in Amsterdam Museum
- Mementos of the Siege of Haarlem in Haarlem's Grote Kerk
- Delft's Prinsenhof and Tomb of William of Orange

HOLLAND'S GOLDEN AGE... AND FALL (1600s)

By 1600, Holland gains its independence from the Habsburgs (officially in 1648) and emerges stronger and more energized than ever. When England defeats the Spanish Armada (navy, in 1588), Spain's monopoly on overseas trade is broken, and Holland is poised to leap in.

HISTORY

declared, "I cannot approve of monarchs who want to rule over the conscience of the people, and take away their freedom of choice and religion."

Accused of aiding Protestant rebels, William was summoned before the Spanish governor, but he fled to Germany instead. From 1568 onward, he led several military campaigns against Spanish forces in the Low Countries—which initially failed (just as most of George Washington's battles ended in defeat). But the rebellion persevered, William eventually became a Calvinist, and in 1576 seven Dutch provinces signed a treaty to become the United Provinces of the Netherlands—the forerunner to the Dutch Republic.

Philip detested William—calling him a religious opportunist, bigamist, and drunkard. To stop the rebellion, he put a price of 25,000 guilders on William's head. In 1582, an assassin almost succeeded in killing William in Antwerp, but he eventually re-covered. William's final days were spent in Delft's Prinsenhof. A French assassin managed to sneak in, and shot William at close range with two pistols—the first head of state in the world to be assassinated by handguns. The Dutch leader's last words, spoken in French, were: "My God, my God, have pity on me and these poor people."

When he died the rebellion was still in doubt, but less than 25 years later, the Dutch provinces had become a thriving republic—with William of Orange as its founding father.

Amsterdam invents the global economy, as its hardy sailors ply the open seas, trading in Indonesian spices, South American sugar,

and African slaves. The government-subsidized Dutch East and West India Companies establish colonies all over the world. (Henry Hudson sails up America's Hudson River to what would become New Amsterdam.) The Dutch people's nautical and capitalist skills combine to make Amsterdam—population 100,000—the world's wealthiest city. It's home to the painter Rembrandt, philosopher René ("I think, therefore I am") Descartes, plus many different religious sects and a bustling Jewish Quarter.

The Golden Age is not confined to Amsterdam. Delft is a thriving market town of textiles and export beer, and home to painter Vermeer and microscope-maker Van Leeuwenhoek. In

Haarlem, Frans Hals paints humanist portraits. Leiden's prestigious university welcomes scholars, and the tolerant town welcomes the persecuted Pilgrims (Protestants from England), who would eventually leave (in 1620) for the New World.

In 1648, the Eighty Years' War officially ends, and the United Provinces (today's Netherlands) are now an independent and prosperous republic.

Even at Holland's Golden Age peak (c. 1650), forces are at work that would eventually drag it down. In 1637, after several years of insanely lucrative trade in tulip bulbs ("tulip mania"), the market crashes. As the century progresses, the harbors of Edam and Marken begin silting up.

Holland is overtaken by the rise of the new superpowers on the block—England and France. In 1652, Holland goes to war with England over control of the seas, the first of three wars that would sap Holland's wealth. In 1689, Holland's *stadholder*—William III of Orange—is invited by England's Parliament to rule (with his wife Mary) as King William III of England. Meanwhile, Louis XIV of France invades Holland and gets to within 15 miles of Amsterdam before being stopped when the citizens open the Amstel locks and flood the city. By century's end, France and England control the seas, and Holland has been drained by costly wars.

Sights

- Amsterdam's Rijksmuseum and Haarlem's Frans Hals Museum—paintings by Rembrandt, Hals, Vermeer, and Steen. There are still more in The Hague's Mauritshuis
- Old townhouses and gables in Amsterdam's Jordaan neighborhood and Red Light District
- Amsterdam's Begijnhof, Royal Palace, Westerkerk, and Rembrandt's House
- Hoorn's Westfries Museum of period rooms
- The Hague's Mauritshuis Royal Picture Gallery—paintings by Vermeer, Rembrandt, and Rubens
- Edam's Grote Kerk
- Leiden's American Pilgrim and Lakenhal museums

ELEGANT DECLINE (1700s)

The Dutch survive as bankers, small manufacturers, and craftsmen in luxury goods—but on a small scale fitting their geographical size. They cruise along on exploited wealth from their colonies in Indonesia and Suriname. Delft continues to crank out Delftware, but the quality declines.

The Netherlands hits rock bottom in 1795, when French troops occupy the Low Countries (1795-1815) and Napoleon Bonaparte proclaims his brother, Louis Napoleon, to be King of Holland.

Sights
- Amsterdam's Amstelkring Museum (hidden church), Willet-Holthuysen Museum (Herengracht Canal Mansion), and Jewish Historical Museum synagogue
- Indonesian foods from the colonial era
- Delftware porcelain
- Amsterdam's Royal Palace

REVIVAL (1800s)

After Napoleon's defeat, Europe's nobles decide that the Low Countries should be a monarchy, ruled jointly by a Dutch prince, who becomes King William I. (Today's King Willem-Alexander is descended from him.) When Belgian patriots revolt against the Dutch-born king and form their own nation, the two countries—the Netherlands and Belgium—officially split. The Netherlands soon becomes a constitutional monarchy with a parliament.

Though slow to join the Industrial Revolution, Holland picks up speed by century's end. In 1876, the North Sea Canal opens after 52 years of construction, revitalizing Amsterdam's port. In the next decade, the city builds Central Station, the Rijksmuseum, and Concertgebouw, and hosts a World Exhibition (1883) that attracts three million visitors. Progressive thinkers are questioning the country's repressive colonial tradition in Indonesia.

Sights
- Amsterdam's Central Station (see photo), Rijksmuseum, Stadsschouwburg theater, Concertgebouw music hall, and Magna Plaza
- Van Gogh paintings at the Van Gogh Museum

INVASIONS BY GERMANS, HIPPIES, AND IMMIGRANTS (1900s)

The 20th century starts off badly, with World War I, though neutral Holland was spared the worst of it.

In 1932, the Dutch Zuiderzee dike is completed, creating many square miles of reclaimed land (including today's Flevoland). On the downside, the project closes off access to the North Sea, reducing once-thriving harbor towns like Enkhuizen and Marken to their role as cutesy time-passed villages.

In World War II, Holland suffers a brutal occupation by Nazi

Islam and the Netherlands Today

The hottest hot-button issue in the Netherlands today is the culture clash between secular, multicultural Netherlands and its recent Muslim immigrants. Many Muslims arrived in the last half of the 20th century after Indonesia (a Dutch colony) gained independence. Guest workers from Turkey and Morocco—drawn by economic incentives—swelled the ranks. Today, one in ten Amsterdammers is Muslim. The Muslim cultures have not meshed seamlessly with the Netherlands' Western, secular, and liberal culture.

Several events have colored the discussion of Islam in the Netherlands:

During the Bosnian War of the 1990s, 400 Dutch soldiers were stationed in Srebrenica, charged by the UN with keeping peace. In July 1995 the town was overrun by Bosnian Serbs. While the outnumbered Dutch soldiers huddled helplessly in their compound, the Serbs rounded up 8,000 Muslim men and boys and massacred them. To this day, many Dutch people are haunted by why the troops didn't do more to help, and discussions of current events still tend to mention this episode.

In spring of 2002, a charismatic Dutch politician named Pim Fortuyn—socially liberal but strongly anti-immigration—campaigned for Parliament on a platform that Islam posed a threat to Dutch tolerance. On May 6, he was gunned down in a parking lot by a mentally troubled man (whose full motives remain unclear).

Germany. Queen Wilhelmina (1880-1962) flees to England and Anne Frank goes into hiding. Rotterdam is utterly destroyed by German bombs. After the war, the city is ultimately rebuilt in a modern style and becomes Europe's busiest port.

In Amsterdam, postwar prosperity and a tolerant atmosphere in the 1960s and 1970s make it a global magnet for hippies...and your co-authors.

ANNE FRANK
TAGEBUCH

In the 1970s and 1980s, the city is flooded with immigrants from former colonies (especially Indonesia and Suriname), causing friction and bringing a degree of ethnic diversity to the population.

Holland continues its eternal battle with the sea. Major floods kill almost 2,000 people (in 1953) and a billion dollars in damage (in 1995), prompting more dams and storm barriers. Facing global warming, the "Low Countries"—with much of their territory below sea level—keep a close watch on rising seas.

The Netherlands is an active participant in the international community. In 1957, it helps found the Common Market, and joins the BeNeLux economic union (in 1960). In 1992, the Nether-

Dutch people were stunned by the violence, the kind of thing they thought happened only in America.

On the morning of November 2, 2004, the great-grandnephew of Vincent van Gogh was bicycling past Amsterdam's Oosterpark on his way to work. Theo van Gogh was a well-known filmmaker who'd recently released a controversial film about women and Islam. A Muslim Dutch citizen of Moroccan descent shot Van Gogh, then stabbed a letter into his dead body threatening to harm the film's female screenwriter as well.

The screenwriter, Ayaan Hirsi Ali, has become a lightning rod for Western/Muslim controversy. Born a Muslim in Somalia, she emigrated to the Netherlands, where she became a member of Parliament and an outspoken critic of Islam and its treatment of women. She currently lives (under a 24-hour security watch) and teaches in the US, where she became a citizen in 2013.

Lately, Dutch politician Geert Wilders has taken up Fortuyn's mantle, advocating the banning of the Quran and an end to Muslim immigration. His party won 15 percent of the votes in 2010 (but lost nine seats in 2012).

Whatever happened to peaceful, tolerant, quaint old Holland? That's what the Dutch want to know. The Muslim immigration issue has forced the Dutch to confront a difficult paradox—how to be tolerant of what they perceive to be an intolerant culture.

lands—along with 11 other countries—signs the Treaty of Maastricht (in southern Holland), becoming a founding member of the European Union. The Hague is home to the world court.

Sights

- Amsterdam's Beurs, Tuschinski Theater, and National Monument on Dam Square
- Enkhuizen's Zuiderzee Museum
- Amsterdam's Anne Frank House and Dutch Resistance Museum
- Amsterdam's Heineken Brewery, rock-and-roll clubs Paradiso and Melkweg, and the Stopera opera house
- Rotterdam's striking modern architecture
- Haarlem's Corrie ten Boom House
- The Hague's Peace Palace
- Flevoland's Schokland Museum

HISTORY

THE NETHERLANDS TODAY (2000-PRESENT)

The assassinations of Pim Fortuyn and Theo van Gogh cause a backlash against immigration and a move to the right (see sidebar).

In 2008, the mayor of Amsterdam announces a plan to "clean up" parts of the Red Light District, reducing the number of window brothels by almost half. A few years later, Maastricht and other southern Dutch cities restrict marijuana purchases to Dutch citizens only. But in 2014, the mayors of Amsterdam and other cities ask the national government to start licensing and regulating pot growers and sellers—just like states such as Alaska, Colorado, Oregon, and Washington do.

In 2013, King Willem-Alexander (b. 1967) becomes ruler of the Netherlands, the first male on the Dutch throne in 123 years—heralding a new era. Today, the Netherlands is peaceful, prosperous, and forward-thinking—waiting for you to arrive and make your own history.

Sights

- Amsterdam's metro, EYE Film Institute Netherlands, and Muziekgebouw performance hall
- Rotterdam's Central Station and Market Hall

For more on Dutch history, consider *Europe 101: History and Art for the Traveler,* written by Rick Steves and Gene Openshaw (available at www.ricksteves.com).

PRACTICALITIES

Contents

This chapter covers the practical skills of European travel: how to get tourist information, pay for purchases, sightsee efficiently, find good-value accommodations, eat affordably but well, use technology wisely, and get between destinations smoothly. To study ahead and round out your knowledge, check out "Resources" for a summary of recommended books and films.

Tourist Information

The Netherlands' national tourist office **in the US** can be a wealth of information (tel. 212/370-7360, www.holland.com). Its website has trip-planning advice, festival schedules, downloadable city maps, and much more. Another useful website is www.iamsterdam. com (Amsterdam Tourism Board).

In the **Netherlands,** the tourist information office (abbreviated **TI** in this book) is generally your best first stop in any new town (although Amsterdam's TIs are so crowded that you're better off visiting the airport TI, or the TIs in Haarlem or Delft).

TIs are good places to get a city map and information on public transit (including bus and train schedules), walking tours, special events, and nightlife. Many TIs have information on the entire country or at least the region, so try to pick up maps for destinations you'll be visiting later in your trip. If you're arriving in town after the TI closes, call ahead or pick up a map in a neighboring town.

While TIs are eager to book you a room, steer clear of their room-finding services (bloated prices, booking fees, and they take a sizeable cut from your host). Even if there's no "fee," you'll save yourself and your host money by going direct with the listings in this book.

Travel Tips

Emergency and Medical Help: Dial 112 for police or medical emergencies in the Netherlands. If you get sick, do as the Dutch do and go to a pharmacist for advice. Or ask at your hotel for help—they'll know the nearest medical and emergency services.

Theft or Loss: To replace a passport, you'll need to go in person to an embassy or consulate (see page 503). If your credit and debit cards disappear, cancel and replace them (see "Damage Control for Lost Cards" on page 461). File a police report, either on the spot or within a day or two; you'll need it to submit an insurance claim for lost or stolen rail passes or travel gear, and it can help with replacing your passport or credit and debit cards. For more information, see www.ricksteves.com/help. Precautionary measures can minimize the effects of loss—back up your photos and other files frequently.

Time Zones: The Netherlands, like most of continental Europe, is generally six/nine hours ahead of the East/West Coasts of the US. The exceptions are the beginning and end of Daylight Saving Time: Europe "springs forward" the last Sunday in March (two weeks after most of North America) and "falls back" the last Sunday in October (one week before North America). For a handy online time converter, see www.timeanddate.com/worldclock.

Business Hours: Most stores throughout the Netherlands are open from about 9:00 until 18:00-20:00 on weekdays, but close early on Saturday (generally between 12:00 and 17:00, depending on whether you're in a town or a big city). In the Netherlands, the first Sunday of every month is "shopping Sunday" *(koopzondag),* when many stores are open. Otherwise, Sundays here have the same pros and cons as they do for travelers in the US: Sights are generally open, while banks and many shops are closed, public transportation options are fewer, and there's no rush hour). Popular destinations are even more crowded on weekends. Rowdy evenings are rare on Sundays. Many museums and sights are closed on Monday.

Watt's Up? Europe's electrical system is 220 volts, instead of North America's 110 volts. Most newer electronics (such as laptops, battery chargers, and hair dryers) convert automatically, so you won't need a converter, but you will need an adapter plug with two round prongs, sold inexpensively at travel stores in the US. Avoid bringing older appliances that don't automatically convert voltage; instead, buy a cheap replacement in Europe.

Discounts: Discounts aren't listed in this book. However, many sights offer discounts for children under 18, seniors, groups of 10 or more, families, and students or teachers with proper identification cards (www.isic.org). Always ask. Some discounts are available only for citizens of the European Union (EU).

Online Translation Tip: You can use Google's Chrome browser (available free at www.google.com/chrome) to instantly translate websites. With one click, the page appears in (very rough) English translation. You can also paste the URL of the site into the translation window at www.google.com/translate.

Money

This section offers advice on how to pay for purchases on your trip (including getting cash from ATMs and paying with plastic), dealing with lost or stolen cards, VAT (sales tax) refunds, and tipping.

WHAT TO BRING

Bring both a credit card and a debit card. You'll use the debit card at cash machines (ATMs) to withdraw euros for most purchases, and the credit card to pay for larger items. Some travelers carry a third card as a backup, in case one gets demagnetized or eaten by a temperamental machine.

For an emergency stash, bring several hundred dollars in hard cash in $20 bills. If you need to exchange the bills, go to a bank; avoid using currency exchange booths because of their lousy rates and/or outrageous fees.

CASH

Cash is just as desirable in the Netherlands as it is at home. Small businesses (B&Bs, mom-and-pop cafés, shops, etc.) prefer that you pay your bills with cash. Some vendors will charge you extra for using a credit card, and some won't take foreign credit cards at all. Cash is the best—and sometimes only—way to pay for cheap food, bus fare, taxis, and local guides.

Exchange Rate

1 euro (€) = about $1.40

To convert prices in euros to dollars, add about 40 percent: €20 = about $28, €50 = about $70. (Check www.oanda.com for the latest exchange rates.) Just like the dollar, one euro (€) is broken down into 100 cents. Coins range from €0.01 to €2, and bills from €5 to €500.

So those €65 wooden clogs are about $90, and the €90 taxi ride through Amsterdam is...uh-oh.

Throughout Europe, ATMs are the standard for travelers to get cash. To withdraw money from an ATM (known as a *geld-automaat* in Dutch), you'll need a debit card (ideally with a Visa or MasterCard logo for maximum usability), plus a PIN code. Know your PIN code in numbers; there are only numbers—no letters—on European keypads. For increased security, shield the keypad when entering your PIN code, and don't use an ATM if anything on the front of the machine looks loose or damaged (a sign that someone may have attached a "skimming" device to capture account information). Try to withdraw large sums of money to reduce the number of per-transaction bank fees you'll pay.

When possible, use ATMs located outside banks—a thief is less likely to target a cash machine near surveillance cameras, and if your card is munched by a machine, you can go inside for help. Stay away from "independent" ATMs such as Travelex, Euronet, Moneybox, Cardpoint, and Cashzone, which charge huge commissions, have terrible exchange rates, and may try to trick users with "dynamic currency conversion" (described at the end of "Credit and Debit Cards," next).

Although you can use a credit card for an ATM transaction, it only makes sense in an emergency, because it's considered a cash advance (borrowed at a high interest rate) rather than a withdrawal.

While traveling, if you want to monitor your accounts online to detect any unauthorized transactions, be sure to use a secure connection (see page 487).

Pickpockets target tourists. To safeguard your cash, wear a money belt—a pouch with a strap that you buckle around your waist like a belt and tuck under your clothes. Keep your cash, credit cards, and passport secure in your money belt, and carry only a day's spending money in your front pocket.

CREDIT AND DEBIT CARDS

Credit cards are not as readily accepted in the Netherlands as they are in other European countries: Be prepared to use cash for many transactions. While Dutch hotels, souvenir shops, and most restaurants will take US and Canadian credit cards, some stores only accept Dutch credit cards. The main Dutch grocery chain—Albert Heijn—only takes Dutch cards. Dutch train stations will not accept foreign credit cards unless they have a chip, and most automated machines will only take a chip-and-PIN card (described later) or cash. In general, Visa and MasterCard are more commonly accepted than American Express.

When I do use my credit card here, it's only in a few specific situations: to book hotel reservations by phone, to cover major expenses (such as car rentals, plane tickets, and long hotel stays), and to pay for things near the end of my trip (to avoid another visit to the ATM). While you could use a debit card to make most large purchases, using a credit card offers a greater degree of fraud protection (because debit cards draw funds directly from your account).

Ask Your Credit- or Debit-Card Company: Before your trip, contact the company that issued your debit or credit cards.

• Confirm that your **card will work overseas,** and alert them that you'll be using it in Europe; otherwise, they may deny transactions if they perceive unusual spending patterns.

• Ask for the specifics on transaction **fees.** When you use your credit or debit card—either for purchases or ATM withdrawals—you'll typically be charged additional "international transaction" fees of up to 3 percent (1 percent is normal) plus $5 per transaction. If your card's fees seem high, consider getting a different card just for your trip: Capital One (www.capitalone.com) and most credit unions have low-to-no international fees.

• If you plan to withdraw cash from ATMs, confirm your **daily withdrawal limit** (€300 is usually about the maximum), and if necessary, ask your bank to adjust it. Some travelers prefer a high limit that allows them to take out more cash at each ATM stop (saving on bank fees), while others prefer to set a lower limit in case their card is stolen. Note that foreign banks also set maximum withdrawal amounts for their ATMs. Also, remember that you're withdrawing euros, not dollars—so if your daily limit is $300, withdraw just €200. Many frustrated travelers walk away from ATMs thinking their cards have been rejected, when actually they were asking for more cash in euros than their daily limit allowed.

• Get your bank's emergency **phone number** in the US (but not its 800 number, which isn't accessible from overseas) to call collect if you have a problem.

• Ask for your credit card's **PIN** in case you need to make an emergency cash withdrawal or encounter Europe's "chip-and-PIN" system; the bank won't tell you your PIN over the phone, so allow time for it to be mailed to you.

Chip and PIN: Europeans are increasingly using chip-and-PIN cards, which are embedded with an electronic chip (in addition to the magnetic stripe found on American-style cards). To make a purchase with a chip-and-PIN card, the cardholder inserts the card into a slot in the payment machine, then enters a PIN (like using a debit card in the US) while the card stays in the slot. The chip inside the card authorizes the transaction; the cardholder doesn't sign a receipt. Your American-style card might not work at payment machines using this system, such as those at train and subway stations, toll roads, parking garages, luggage lockers, bike-rental kiosks, and self-serve gas pumps.

If you have problems using your American card in a chip-and-PIN machine, here are some suggestions: For either a debit card or a credit card, try entering that card's PIN when prompted. (Note that your credit-card PIN may not be the same as your debit-card PIN; you'll need to ask your bank for your credit-card PIN.) If your cards still don't work, look for a machine that takes cash, seek out a clerk who might be able to process the transaction manually, or ask a local if you can pay them cash to run the transaction on their card.

And don't panic. Many travelers who use only magnetic-stripe cards don't run into problems. Still, it pays to carry plenty of euros; remember that you can always use an ATM to withdraw cash with your magnetic-stripe debit card.

If you're still concerned, you can apply for a chip card in the US (though I think it's overkill). One option is the no-annual-fee GlobeTrek Visa, a true chip-and-PIN card offered by Andrews Federal Credit Union in Maryland (open to all US residents; see www.andrewsfcu.org). In the future, chip cards should become standard issue in the US: Visa and MasterCard have asked US banks and merchants to use chip-based cards by late 2015. But the majority of these are "chip-and-signature" cards, for which your signature verifies your identity, not the "chip-and-PIN" cards being used in Europe. In most cases, "chip-and-signature" cards will work in the Netherlands, but make sure you know your PIN.

Dynamic Currency Conversion: If merchants offer to convert your purchase price into dollars (called dynamic currency conversion), refuse this "service." You'll pay even more in fees for the expensive convenience of seeing your charge in dollars. "Independent" ATMs (such as Travelex and Moneybox) may try to confuse customers by presenting DCC in misleading terms. If an ATM offers to "lock in" or "guarantee" your conversion rate, choose "proceed without conversion." Other prompts might state, "You can be charged in dollars: Press YES for dollars, NO for euros." Always choose the local currency in these situations.

Damage Control for Lost Cards

If you lose your credit, debit, or ATM card, you can stop people from using your card by reporting the loss immediately to the respective global customer-assistance centers. Call these 24-hour US numbers collect: Visa (tel. 303/967-1096), MasterCard (tel. 636/722-7111), and American Express (tel. 336/393-1111). In the Netherlands, to make a collect call to the US, dial 0800-022-9111. Press zero or stay on the line for an English-speaking operator. European toll-free numbers (listed by country) can be found at the websites for Visa and MasterCard.

Providing the following information will allow for a quicker cancellation of your missing card: full card number, whether you are the primary or secondary cardholder, the cardholder's name exactly as printed on the card, billing address, home phone number, circumstances of the loss or theft, and identification verification (your birth date, your mother's maiden name, or your Social Security number—memorize this, don't carry a copy). If you are the secondary cardholder, you'll also need to provide the primary cardholder's identification-verification details. You can generally receive a temporary card within two or three business days in Europe (see www.ricksteves.com/help for more).

If you report your loss within two days, you typically won't be responsible for any unauthorized transactions on your account, although many banks charge a liability fee of $50.

TIPPING

Tipping in the Netherlands isn't as automatic and generous as it is in the US. For special service, tips are appreciated, but not expected. As in the US, the proper amount depends on your resources, tipping philosophy, and the circumstances, but some general guidelines apply.

Restaurants: Tipping is an issue only at restaurants that have table service. If you order your food at a counter, don't tip.

At Dutch restaurants that have waitstaff, service is included, although it's common to round up the bill after a good meal (usually 5-10 percent; so, for an €18.50 meal, pay €20).

Taxis: For a typical ride, round up your fare a bit (for instance, if the fare is €4.50, pay €5; or for a €28 fare, give €30). If the cabbie hauls your bags and zips you to the airport to help you catch your flight, you might want to toss in a little more. But if you feel like you're being driven in circles or otherwise ripped off, skip the tip.

Services: In general, if someone in the service industry does a super job for you, a small tip of a euro or two is appropriate...but not required. If you're not sure whether (or how much) to tip for a service, ask your hotelier or the TI.

GETTING A VAT REFUND

Wrapped into the purchase price of your souvenirs is a Value-Added Tax (VAT) of about 21 percent in the Netherlands. You're entitled to get most of that tax back if you purchase more than €50 (about $70) in the Netherlands worth of goods at a store that participates in the VAT-refund scheme. Typically, you must ring up the minimum at a single retailer—you can't add up your purchases from various shops to reach the required amount.

Getting your refund is usually straightforward and, if you buy a substantial amount of souvenirs, well worth the hassle. If you're lucky, the merchant will subtract the tax when you make your purchase. (This is more likely to occur if the store ships the goods to your home.) Otherwise, you'll need to:

Get the paperwork. Have the merchant completely fill out the necessary refund document, called a "Tax-Free Shopping Cheque." You'll have to present your passport. Get the paperwork done before you leave the store to ensure you'll have everything you need (including your original sales receipt).

Get your stamp at the border or airport. Process your VAT document at your last stop in the European Union (such as at the airport) with the customs agent who deals with VAT refunds. Arrive an additional hour before you need to check in for your flight to allow time to find the local customs office—and to stand in line. It's best to keep your purchases in your carry-on. If they're too large or dangerous to carry on (such as knives), pack them in your checked bags and alert the check-in agent. You'll be sent (with your tagged bag) to a customs desk outside security, where an official will examine your bag, stamp your paperwork, and put your bag on the belt. You're not supposed to use your purchased goods before you leave. If you show up at customs wearing your new wooden clogs, officials might look the other way—or deny you a refund.

Collect your refund. You'll need to return your stamped document to the retailer or its representative. Many merchants work with a service, such as Global Blue or Premier Tax Free, that has offices at major airports, ports, or border crossings (either before or after security, probably strategically located near a duty-free shop). These services, which extract a 4 percent fee, can refund your money immediately in cash or credit your card (within two billing cycles). If the retailer handles VAT refunds directly, it's up to you to contact the merchant for your refund. You can mail the documents from home, or more quickly, from your point of departure (using an envelope you've prepared in advance or one that's been provided by the merchant). Then you'll have to wait—it can take months.

CUSTOMS FOR AMERICAN SHOPPERS

You are allowed to take home $800 worth of items per person duty-free, once every 30 days. You can take home many processed and packaged foods: vacuum-packed cheeses, dried herbs, jams, baked goods, candy, chocolate, oil, vinegar, mustard, and honey. Fresh fruits and vegetables and most meats are not allowed, with exceptions for some canned items. As for alcohol, you can bring in one liter duty-free (it can be packed securely in your checked luggage, along with any other liquid-containing items).

To bring alcohol (or liquid-packed foods) in your carry-on bag on your flight home, buy it at a duty-free shop at the airport. You'll increase your odds of getting it onto a connecting flight if it's packaged in a "STEB"—a secure, tamper-evident bag. But stay away from liquids in opaque, ceramic, or metallic containers, which usually cannot be successfully screened (STEB or no STEB).

For details on allowable goods, customs rules, and duty rates, visit www.cbp.gov.

Sightseeing

Sightseeing can be hard work. Use these tips to make your visits to the Netherlands' finest sights meaningful, fun, efficient, and painless.

PLAN AHEAD

Set up an itinerary that allows you to fit in all your must-see sights. For a one-stop look at opening hours in Amsterdam, see the "At a Glance" sidebar (page 52). Most sights keep stable hours, but you can easily confirm the latest by checking with the TI or visiting museum websites.

Don't put off visiting a must-see sight—you never know when a place will close unexpectedly for a holiday, strike, or restoration. On holidays (see page 503), expect reduced hours or closures. In summer, some sights may stay open late. Off-season, many museums have shorter hours.

Going at the right time helps avoid crowds. This book offers tips on the best times to see specific sights. Try visiting popular sights very early, at lunch, or very late. Evening visits (when possible) are usually peaceful, with fewer crowds.

Study up. To get the most out of the self-guided tours and sight descriptions in this book, read them before you visit. The Rijksmuseum is much more entertaining if you've boned up on ruffs and Dutch Masters the night before.

AT SIGHTS

Here's what you can typically expect:

Entering: If you arrive 30 to 60 minutes before closing time, you may not be allowed to enter. And guards start ushering people out well before the actual closing time, so don't save the best for last.

Some important sights have a security check, where you must open your bag or send it through a metal detector. Some sights require you to check daypacks and coats. (If you'd rather not check your daypack, try carrying it tucked under your arm like a purse as you enter.)

Photography: If the museum's photo policy isn't clearly posted, ask a guard. Generally, taking photos without a flash or tripod is allowed. Some sights ban photos altogether.

Temporary Exhibits: Museums may show special exhibits in addition to their permanent collection. Some exhibits are included in the entry price, while others come at an extra cost (which you may have to pay even if you don't want to see the exhibit).

Expect Changes: Artwork can be on tour, on loan, out sick, or shifted at the whim of the curator. To adapt, pick up a floor plan as you enter, and ask museum staff if you can't find a particular item.

Audioguides: Some sights rent audioguides, which generally offer excellent recorded descriptions of the art in English. If you bring your own earbuds, you can enjoy better sound and avoid holding the device to your ear. To save money, bring a Y-jack and share one audioguide with your travel partner. Increasingly, museums are offering apps and audio tours (often free) that you can download to your mobile device. I've produced free downloadable audio tours of the major sights in Amsterdam; see page 10.

Services: Important sights may have an on-site café or cafeteria (usually a handy place to rejuvenate during a long visit). The WCs at sights are free and generally clean.

Before Leaving: At the gift shop, scan the postcard rack or thumb through a guidebook to be sure that you haven't overlooked something that you'd like to see.

Every sight or museum offers more than what is covered in this book. Use the information in this book as an introduction—not the final word.

Sleeping

I favor hotels and restaurants that are handy to your sightseeing activities. Rather than list hotels scattered throughout a city, I choose  two or three favorite neighborhoods and recommend the best accommodations values in each, from dorm beds to fancy doubles with all of the comforts.

A major feature of this book is its extensive and opinionated listing of good-value rooms. I like places that are clean, central, relatively quiet at night, reasonably priced, friendly, small enough to have a hands-on owner and stable staff, run with a respect for Dutch traditions, and not listed in other guidebooks. (In the Netherlands, for me, meeting six out of these eight criteria means it's a keeper.) I'm more impressed by a convenient location and a fun-loving philosophy than flat-screen TVs and a pricey laundry service.

Book your accommodations well in advance, especially if you'll be traveling during busy times. See page 503 for a list of major holidays and festivals in the Netherlands; for tips on making reservations, see page 468.

Some people make reservations as they travel, calling hotels a few days to a week before their arrival. If you'd rather travel without any reservations at all, you'll have greater success snaring rooms if you arrive at your destination early in the day. If you anticipate crowds (weekends are worst), on the day you want to check in, call hotels at about 9:00 or 10:00, when the receptionist knows who'll be checking out and which rooms will be available. If you encounter a language barrier, ask the fluent receptionist at your current hotel to call for you.

RATES AND DEALS

I've described my recommended accommodations using a Sleep Code (see sidebar). Prices listed are for one-night stays in peak season, generally include breakfast, and assume you're booking directly with the hotel (not through an online hotel-booking engine or TI). Booking services extract a commission from the hotel, which logically closes the door on special deals. Book direct.

My recommended hotels each have a website (often with a built-in booking form) and an email address; you can expect a response in English within a day (and often sooner).

If you're on a budget, it's smart to email several hotels to ask for their best price. Comparison-shop and make your choice. This is especially helpful when dealing with the larger hotels that use

Sleep Code

(€1 = about $1.40)

Price Rankings

To help you easily sort through my listings, I've divided the accommodations into three categories, based on the highest price for a standard double room with bath during high season:

$$$	**Higher Priced**
$$	**Moderately Priced**
$	**Lower Priced**

I always rate hostels as $, whether or not they have double rooms, because they have the cheapest beds in town.

Prices can change without notice; verify the hotel's current rates online or by email. For the best prices, always book directly with the hotel.

Abbreviations

To pack maximum information into minimum space, I use the following code to describe accommodations in this book. Prices listed are per room, not per person. When a price range is given for a type of room (such as double rooms listing for "Db-€80-120"), it means the price fluctuates with the season, size of room, or length of stay; expect to pay the upper end for peak-season stays.

S = Single room (or price for one person in a double).

D = Double or twin. "Double beds" can be two twins sheeted together and are usually big enough for nonromantic couples.

T = Triple (generally a double bed with a single).

Q = Quad (usually two double beds; adding an extra child's bed to a T is usually cheaper).

b = Private bathroom with toilet and shower or tub.

s = Private shower or tub only (the toilet is down the hall).

According to this code, a couple staying at a "Db-€90" hotel would pay a total of €90 (about $126) for a double room with a private bathroom. Unless otherwise noted, breakfast is included, hotel staff speak basic English, and credit cards are accepted.

There's almost always Wi-Fi and/or a guest computer available, either free or for a fee.

"dynamic pricing," a computer-generated system that predicts the demand for particular days and sets prices accordingly: High-demand days will often be more than double the price of low-demand days. This makes it impossible for a guidebook to list anything more accurate than a wide range of prices. I regret this trend. While you can assume that hotels listed in this book are good, it's very difficult to say which ones are the better value unless you email to confirm the price.

As you look over the listings, you'll notice that some accommodations promise special prices to Rick Steves readers. To get these rates, you must book direct (that is, not through a booking site like TripAdvisor or Booking.com), mention this book when you reserve, and then show the book upon arrival. Rick Steves discounts apply to readers with ebooks as well as printed books. Because I trust hotels to honor this, please let me know if you don't receive a listed discount. Note, though, that discounts understandably may not be applied to promotional rates.

In general, prices can soften if you do any of the following: offer to pay cash, stay at least three nights, or mention this book. You can also try asking for a cheaper room or a discount, or offer to skip breakfast.

TYPES OF ACCOMMODATIONS
Hotels
In this book, the price for a double room ranges from $70 (very simple, toilet and shower down the hall) to $300 (maximum plumbing and more), with most clustering at about $140. You'll pay more at Amsterdam hotels, less at small-town B&Bs. There is often a city room tax, which may not be included in the prices I list.

Most hotels have lots of doubles and a few singles, triples, and quads. And though groups sleep cheap, traveling alone can be expensive. Singles (except for the rare closet-type rooms that fit only a twin bed) are simply doubles used by one person, so they often cost nearly the same as a double.

A hearty breakfast with cereal, meats, local cheeses, fresh bread, yogurt, juice, and coffee or tea is standard in hotels.

For environmental reasons, towels are often replaced in hotels only when you leave them on the floor. (In cheaper places, they aren't replaced at all, so hang them up to dry and reuse.) Hotel elevators, while becoming more common, are often very small, forcing you to send your bags up separately—pack light.

If you're arriving early in the morning, your room probably won't be ready. You can drop your bag safely at the hotel and dive right into sightseeing.

Hoteliers can be a great help and source of advice. Most know their city well, and can assist you with everything from public tran-

PRACTICALITIES

Making Hotel Reservations

Reserve your rooms several weeks in advance—or as soon as you've pinned down your travel dates. Note that some national holidays merit your making reservations far in advance (see page 503).

Requesting a Reservation: It's easiest to book your room through the hotel's website. (For the best rates, always use the hotel's official site and not a booking agency's site.) If there's no reservation form, or for complicated requests, send an email (see below for a sample request). Most recommended hotels take reservations in English.

The hotelier wants to know:
- the number and type of rooms you need
- the number of nights you'll stay
- your date of arrival (use the European style for writing dates: day/month/year)
- your date of departure
- any special needs (such as bathroom in the room or down the hall, cheapest room, twin beds vs. double bed, and so on)

Mention any discounts—for Rick Steves readers or otherwise—when you make the reservation.

Confirming a Reservation: Most places will request a credit-card number to hold your room. If they don't have a secure online reservation form—look for the *https*—you can email it (I do), but it's safer to share that confidential info via a phone call or two emails (splitting your number between them).

Canceling a Reservation: If you must cancel, it's courteous—and smart—to do so with as much notice as possible, especially

sit and airport connections to finding a good restaurant, the nearest launderette, or a Wi-Fi hotspot.

Even at the best hotels, mechanical breakdowns occur: Air-conditioning malfunctions, sinks leak, hot water turns cold, and toilets gurgle and smell. Report your concerns clearly and calmly at the front desk. For more complicated problems, don't expect instant results.

If you suspect night noise will be a problem (if, for instance, your room is over a bar), ask for a quiet room in the back or on an upper floor. To guard against theft in your room, keep valuables out of sight. Some rooms come with a safe, and other hotels have safes at the front desk. I've never bothered using one.

Checkout can pose problems if surprise charges pop up on your bill. If you settle your bill the afternoon before you leave, you'll have time to discuss and address any points of contention (before 19:00, when the night shift usually arrives).

From: rick@ricksteves.com
Sent: Today
To: info@hotelcentral.com
Subject: Reservation request for 19-22 July

Dear Hotel Central,

I would like to reserve a room for 2 people for 3 nights, arriving 19 July and departing 22 July. If possible, I would like a quiet room with a double bed and a bathroom inside the room.

Please let me know if you have a room available and the price.

Thank you!
Rick Steves

for smaller family-run places. Be warned that cancellation policies can be strict; read the fine print or ask about these before you book. Internet deals may require prepayment, with no refunds for cancellations.

Reconfirming a Reservation: Always call to reconfirm your room reservation a few days in advance. For smaller hotels and B&Bs, I call again on my day of arrival to tell my host what time I expect to get there (especially important if arriving late—after 17:00).

Phoning: For tips on how to call hotels overseas, see page 478.

Above all, keep a positive attitude. After all, you're on vacation. If your hotel is a disappointment, spend more time out enjoying the city you came to see.

Bed-and-Breakfasts

B&Bs offer double the cultural intimacy and—often—nicer rooms for a good deal less than most hotel rooms. Hosts usually speak English and are interesting conversationalists.

In the Netherlands, B&Bs are common in well-touristed areas outside the big cities. Amsterdam has some B&Bs; I've listed the better-value ones). Local TIs have lists of B&Bs and can book a room for you, but you'll save money by booking direct with the B&Bs listed in this book.

Hostels

You'll pay about $30 per bed to stay at a hostel. Travelers of any age

The Good and Bad of Online Reviews

User-generated travel review websites—such as TripAdvisor, Booking.com, and Yelp—have quickly become a huge player in the travel industry. These sites give you access to actual reports—good and bad—from travelers who have experienced the hotel, restaurant, tour, or attraction.

My hotelier friends in Europe are in awe of these sites' influence. Small hoteliers who want to stay in business have no choice but to work with review sites—which often charge fees for good placement or photos, and tack on commissions if users book through the site instead of directly with the hotel.

While these sites work hard to weed out bogus users, my hunch is that a significant percentage of reviews are posted by friends or enemies of the business being reviewed. I've even seen hotels "bribe" guests (for example, offer a free breakfast) in exchange for a positive review. Also, review sites can become an echo chamber, with one or two flashy businesses camped out atop the ratings, while better, more affordable, and more authentic alternatives sit ignored farther down the list. (For example, I find review sites' restaurant recommendations skew to very touristy, obvious options.)

Remember that a user-generated review is based on the experience of one person. That person likely stayed at one hotel and ate at a few restaurants, and doesn't have much of a basis for comparison. A guidebook is the work of a trained researcher who has exhaustively visited many alternatives to assess their relative value. I recently checked out some top-rated TripAdvisor listings in various towns; when stacked up against their competitors, some are gems, while just as many are duds.

Both types of information have their place, and in many ways, they're complementary. If a hotel or restaurant is well-reviewed in a guidebook or two, and also gets good ratings on one of these sites, it's likely a winner.

are welcome if they don't mind dorm-style accommodations and meeting other travelers. Most hostels offer kitchen facilities, guest computers, Wi-Fi, and a self-service laundry. Nowadays, concerned about bedbugs, hostels are likely to provide all bedding, including sheets. Family and private rooms may be available on request.

Independent hostels tend to be easygoing, colorful, and informal (no membership required); www.hostelworld.com is the standard way backpackers search and book hostels, but also try www.hostelz.com and www.hostels.com.

Official hostels are part of Hostelling International (HI) and share an online booking site (www.hihostels.com). HI hostels typically require that you either have a membership card or pay extra per night.

OTHER ACCOMMODATION OPTIONS

Whether you're in a city or the countryside, renting an apartment, house, or villa can be a fun and cost-effective way to go local. Websites such as HomeAway and its sister sites VRBO and GreatRentals let you correspond directly with European property owners or managers.

Airbnb and Roomorama make it reasonably easy to find a place to sleep in someone's home. Beds range from air-mattress-in-living-room basic to plush-B&B-suite posh. If you want a place to sleep that's free, Couchsurfing.org is a vagabond's alternative to Airbnb. It lists millions of outgoing members, who host fellow "surfers" in their homes.

Eating

Traditional Dutch food is basic and hearty, with lots of bread, soup, and fish. Dutch treats include cheese, pancakes *(pannenkoeken)*, and "syrup waffles" *(stroopwafels)*. Popular drinks are light, pilsner-type beer and gin *(jenever)*.

Treat your tongue to some new experiences in Holland. Try a pickled herring at an outdoor herring stand, linger over coffee in a "brown café," sample a variety of cheeses at a cheese market, sip an old *jenever* with a new friend, and consume an Indonesian feast—a *rijsttafel*.

When restaurant-hunting, choose a spot filled with locals, not the place with the big neon signs boasting, "We Speak English and Accept Credit Cards." Venturing even a block or two off the main drag leads to higher-quality food for less than half the price of the tourist-oriented places. Locals eat better at lower-rent locales.

Lunch and dinner are served at typical American times (roughly 12:00-14:00 and 18:00-21:00). At restaurants, tipping is not necessary (15 percent service is usually included in the menu price), but a tip of about 5-10 percent is a nice reward for good service. In bars, rounding up to the next euro ("keep the change") is appropriate if you get table service, rather than ordering at the bar.

When ordering drinks in a café or bar, you can just pay as you go (especially if the bar is crowded), or wait until the end to settle up, as many locals do. If you get table service, take the cue from your waiter. Cafés with outdoor tables generally charge the same whether you sit inside or out.

Waiters constantly say, *"Alstublieft"* (AHL-stoo-bleeft). It's a useful, catchall polite word meaning, "please," "here's your order," "enjoy," and "you're welcome." You can respond with a thank you by saying, *"Dank u wel"* (dahnk oo vehl).

If you enjoy your meal, use the Dutch word for "yummy!":

Dutch Cheeses

The Dutch—who eat about 40 pounds of cheese per person each year—are famous for their cheese. In fact, worldwide, some small Dutch towns (like Gouda or Edam) are synonymous with cheese.

Traditionally, the Dutch produced mostly cow's milk chees-es—including most of the types described below—but recently goat cheese is becoming more popu-lar. Some Dutch goat cheese is fresh and soft, while other types are hard and aged in big Gouda-like rounds. You can tell the difference by color: Cow's milk cheese is yellow or orange (from the carotene in the roots of the grass), while goat cheese is white (goats only eat the top of the grass).

Young (*jong*) cheeses are mel-low: smooth, buttery, and mild. Ma-ture or "old" (*oude*) cheeses are aged—traditionally in wooden warehouses, with hatches that can be opened and closed to adjust the heat and humidity. Aging brings out a salty, crumbly, and pungent qualities—the longer, the stronger. Look for the terms *jonge* (1 month old), *jong belegen* (2 months), *belegen* (4 months), *extra belegen* (7 months), *oude* (10 months), and *over-jarig* ("over a year"). Old cheese has no more salt content than new cheese—but the salt is more concentrated, so you taste it more. What look like "crystals" (little, white, crunchy specks) are concentrated pockets of protein. Either new or old, cheese may be seasoned with cumin, cloves, pepper, and other spices—even nettles.

Half of all Dutch cheeses are **Gouda** (*H*OW-dah)—a term that refers not to a particular cheese, but to the way it is produced and packaged: in giant, wax-covered, 30-pound, tire-sized rounds that could be rolled along streets and wharves for easier trans-port. Gouda (which was traditionally traded—not necessarily made—in the town it's named for) is typically cow's milk cheese, and the flavor varies dramatically with how long it ages. *Graskaas*

Lecker! (LEH-ker). When a Dutch person really enjoys the food, he or she waves one hand to the side of their head.

DUTCH SPECIALTIES

Cheeses: The Dutch are probably better known for their cheese than for any other food. For more on this quintessential Dutch specialty, see the sidebar.

French Fries: Commonly served with mayon-naise (ketchup, curry sauce, hot peanut sauce, and various flavored mayonnaises

is a special kind of Gouda that's made with the first harvest of milk after the cows return to the pasture each spring.

Edammer comes in smaller rounds (like an oversized softball), is covered with red wax, and travels well without refrigeration. Its portability made it popular during the Age of Exploration, when it was widely exported, which explains its worldwide appeal today: It turns up in national specialties as far away as Latin America and Pacific islands. Young Edam is extremely mild, but it gets firmer and more flavorful with age.

Cheeses that are not as well-known—but still worth trying—include the following: *Leidse kaas* ("Leyden cheese") is a hard cow's cheese flavored with cumin. *Boerenkaas* ("farmer cheese") is farm-produced in small batches with raw (unpasteurized) milk. *Limburger* is a famously fragrant, semi-soft cow's cheese. *Leerdammer* and *Maasdammer* resemble what we'd call "Swiss cheese" (with big holes and a pungent bouquet). *Nagelkaas* ("nail cheese," from Friesland in the far north of Holland) is a firm cow's milk cheese flavored with cumin and cloves. And *Parrano* and *Prima Donna* are Italian-style cheeses—with a Parmesan flavor, but a smoother texture. Blue cheeses are not traditional, but are catching on (look for the brand names Delfts Blauw and Bastiaanse Blauw). Other names you may see—such as Beemster, Old Amsterdam, or Reypenaer—are name brands rather than types of cheese.

To sample some Dutch cheese, drop into any cheese shop; tourist-oriented stores in Amsterdam and other Dutch cities are particularly generous with samples. For a better selection at a top-quality cheese shop with a staff that's knowledgeable and passionate about their cheese, visit De Kaaskamer van Amsterdam, in the Nine Little Streets district (see page 244). You can also do a guided cheese tasting at the Reypenaer shop in Amsterdam (see page 61). Or, for the full Dutch cheese experience, hop on a train to Alkmaar on a Friday morning in spring or summer to experience a traditional cheese market in action (see the Alkmaar and Zaanse Schans chapter).

are often available) on a paper tray or in a newspaper cone. Flemish *(Vlaamse) friets* are made from whole potatoes, not pulp.

Pannenkoeken: Dutch pancakes are typically halfway between a fluffy, American-style pancake and a thin French crêpe. They come with either savory or sweet toppings.

Haring (herring): Pickled herring, always served with chopped raw onions and sometimes also with pickles. You can eat them straight, or tucked into a thick, soft, white bun. For more on herring, see page 218.

Hutspot: Hearty meat stew with mashed potatoes, onions, and car-
rots, especially popular on winter days.

Stamppot: Hearty side dish—a mash of potatoes and other ingredients—originally designed to fortify farm workers for a
busy day in the fields. The basic *stamppot* mixes potatoes with
stewed meat and cabbage, but you'll also see *andijviestamppot*
(with endive and bacon), *zuurkoolstamppot* (with sauerkraut),
and *boerenkoolstamppot* (kale and potatoes with smoked sau-
sage).

Snert: Thick pea soup.

Gehaktbal: Giant meatball. A *slavink* is a meatball wrapped in
bacon.

Balkenbrij: Meatloaf made with organ meat and blood mixed with
grains.

Kibbeling/Lekkerbekje: Little chunks/filets of deep-fried fish,
dipped into mayonnaise or other flavored sauces (like fish-
and-chips, but without the chips).

Hapjes (bar snacks): The Dutch enjoy lingering in bars and brown
cafés, while nibbling a variety of (mostly deep-fried) bar
snacks. Popular options include *kroketten* (not quite "croquettes"—log-shaped rolls of meats and vegetables that are
breaded and deep-fried, kind of like corn dogs), *bitterballen*
(smaller, deep-fried balls of meat ragù—named not for the flavor, but for the "bitters"-based drinks typically consumed with
them), *frikandellen* (minced-meat, uncased sausages, usually
deep-fried rather than grilled), *loempia* or *vlammetjes* (spring
rolls), and *bamihap* or *bamischijf* (deep-fried, Indonesian-
spiced fried rice). Vegetarians can look for *kaassoufflé*, a deep-
fried pastry filled with cheese.

TYPICAL MEALS

Breakfast: Breakfasts are big by continental standards: bread,
meat, cheese, and maybe an egg or omelet. Hotels generally
put out a buffet spread, including juice and cereal.

Lunch: Simple sandwiches are called *broodjes* (most commonly
made with cheese and/or ham). An open-face sandwich of
ham and cheese topped with two fried eggs is an *uitsmijter*
(OUTS-mi-ter). Soup is popular for lunch, including *snert* or
erwtensoep, a thick, hearty pea soup.

Snacks and Take-Out Food: Small stands sell *friets* (french·fries)
with mayonnaise, pickled herring, falafels (fried chickpea balls
in pita bread), *shoarmas* (lamb tucked in pita bread), and *döner
kebabs* (Turkish version of a *shoarma*). Delis have deep-fried
meat-and-veggie snacks *(kroketten)*. Although less rigid about
"teatime" than their British cousins, the Dutch also enjoy an

afternoon cup of tea with a snack. Cafés serve a pricey afternoon tea around 16:00.

Dinner: It's the biggest meal of the day, consisting of meat or seafood with boiled potatoes, cooked vegetables, and a salad. Hearty stews are served in winter. These days, many people eat more vegetarian fare.

Sweets: The Dutch work hard to satisfy their sweet tooth. The quintessential Dutch treat is a *stroopwafel*—syrup sandwiched between two crispy, thin waffles. Prepackaged stacks of *stroopwafels* are sold in grocery stores, but a fresh, hot *stroopwafel* from a street vendor is a revelation. Pancake variations include *pannenkoeken* (skinny pancakes with fruit and cream), *poffertjes* (bite-sized, sugared puffy pancakes), and *wentelteefjes* (french toast). A bottle of *stroop* (sweet syrup—but not as flavorful as North American maple syrup) is on the table for drizzling. *Oliebollen* ("oil balls") are deep-fried dough balls dusted with powdered sugar. A *zeeuwse bolus* is like a cinnamon roll. And while we like to say "as American as apple pie," the Dutch are also renowned for their *appelgebak* or *appeltaart*. Another favorite dessert is *spekkoek*, a flavorful spice cake (with very thin, alternating layers of strong spice flavors including clove, cinnamon, nutmeg, and anise) that originated in Indonesia. The Dutch also have an appreciation for licorice *(drop)*, including salty licorice *(zoute drop)*—usually sold in small pellets (hence the name).

ETHNIC FOODS

If you're not in the mood for meat and potatoes, sample some of Amsterdam's abundant ethnic offerings.

Indonesian *(Indisch):* The tastiest "Dutch" food is Indonesian, from the former colony. Find any *Indisch* restaurant and experience a *rijsttafel* (literally, "rice table"). The spread usually includes many spicy dishes (ranging from small sides to entrée-sized plates) and a big bowl of rice (or noodles). A *rijsttafel* can be split and still fill two hungry tourists. Vegetarian versions are yours for the asking. For a smaller version, order *nasi rames* (several tiny portions on one plate). For more on Indonesian food, see the sidebar on page 214.

Middle Eastern: Try *shoarma* (roasted lamb with garlic in pita bread, served with bowls of different sauces), falafel, gyros, or a *döner kebab*. Some shops sell a kitchen-sink gut-bomb called a *kapsalon* ("hair salon"): *friets*, *shoarma* meat, and melted cheese, with salad on top.

Surinamese *(Surinaamse):* Surinamese cuisine is a mix of Caribbean and Indonesian influences, featuring *roti* (spiced chicken wrapped in a tortilla) and rice (white or fried) served with meats in sauces (curry and spices). Why Surinamese food in Amsterdam? In 1667, Holland traded New York City ("New Amsterdam") to Britain in exchange for the small country of Suriname (which borders Guyana on the northeast coast of South America). For the next three centuries, Suriname (renamed Dutch Guyana) was a Dutch colony, which is why it has indigenous Indians, Creoles, and Indonesian immigrants who all speak Dutch. When Suriname gained independence in 1975, 100,000 Surinamese immigrated to Amsterdam, sparking a rash of Surinamese fast-food outlets.

More Ethnic Cuisine: In addition to the types listed here, you'll also find plenty of Thai, Greek, Italian, and other foods.

TYPES OF EATERIES

Any place labeled "restaurant" will serve full sit-down meals for lunch or dinner. But there are other places to fill the tank.

A *café* or *eetcafé* is a simple restaurant serving basic soups, salads, sandwiches, as well as traditional meat-and-potatoes meals in a generally comfortable but no-nonsense setting.

A *salon de thé* serves tea and coffee, but also croissants, pastries, and sandwiches for a light brunch, a lunch, or an afternoon snack. *Bruin* cafés ("brown cafés") are named for their nicotine-stained walls—until smoking was banned indoors in 2008, they were filled with tobacco smoke. These places are usually a little more bar-like, with dimmer lighting and wood paneling.

A *proeflokaal* is a bar (with snacks) offering wine, spirits, or beer. "Coffeeshop" is the code word for an establishment where marijuana is sold and consumed, though most offer drinks and munchies, too (for details, see the Smoking chapter).

There's no shortage of stand-up, take-out places serving fast food, sandwiches, and all kinds of quick ethnic fare.

No matter what type of establishment you choose, expect it to be *gezellig*—a much-prized Dutch virtue, meaning an atmosphere of relaxed coziness.

DUTCH DRINKS

Beer: Order "a beer," and you'll get a *pils,* a light lager/pilsner-type beer in a 10-ounce glass with a thick head leveled off with a stick. Typical brands are Heineken, Grolsch, Oranjeboom, Amstel, and the misnamed Bavaria (brewed in Holland). Another common tap beer is Palm Speciale, an amber ale served in a stemmed, wide-mouth glass. *Witte* (white) beer is light-colored and summery, sometimes served with a lemon slice (it's like Hefeweizen, but yeastier). *Bruin* ("brown," or dark) beers are also available; one popular brew is Imperator, made by the Brand brewery. Belgian beers—which, most aficionados would insist, are superior to Dutch beers—are quite popular; because many Belgian specialty beers are bottle-fermented, some of the best come in bottles, though others may be available on tap.

Jenever (yah-NAY-ver)*:* Try this Dutch gin made from juniper berries. *Jong* (young) is sharper; *oude* (old) is mellow. These terms refer not to how long the *jenever* ages (although some are aged), but to whether they use an older or newer distilling technique. I prefer *oude jenever,* which is smooth and soft, with a more mature flavor—like a good whiskey. It's served at room temperature, while *jonge jenever* is served chilled. *Jenever* is meant to be chugged with a *pils* chaser (this combination is called a *kopstoot*—head-butt). Typically bartenders will fill your small, tulip-shaped *jenever* glass to the very brim. Wasting *jenever* is frowned upon, so lean over to sip a bit off the top before picking it up.

Liqueur: You'll find a variety of local fruit brandies *(brandewijn)* and cognacs. If you have a sweet tooth, try *advocaat*—a super-rich, eggnog-like cocktail of brandy, eggs, and sugar.

Wine: Dutch people drink a lot of fine wine, but it's almost all imported.

Coffee: The Dutch love their coffee, enjoying many of the same drinks (espresso, cappuccino) served in American or Italian coffee shops. Coffee usually comes with a small spice cookie. A *koffie verkeerd* (KOH-fee fer-KEERT, "coffee wrong") is an espresso with a lot of steamed milk—the closest thing to our latte.

Soft Drinks: You'll find the full array.

Orange Juice: Many cafés/bars have a juicer for making fresh-squeezed orange juice.

Water: The Dutch drink tap water with meals, but many prefer mineral water, still or sparkling (Spa brand is popular). At restaurants, you can get tap water—*kraanwater* (KRAHN-vah-ter)—free for the asking.

Communicating

"How can I stay connected in Europe?"—by phone and online—may be the most common question I hear from travelers. You have three basic options:

1. "Roam" with your US mobile device. This is the easiest option, but likely the most expensive. It works best for people who won't be making very many calls, and who value the convenience of sticking with what's familiar (and their own phone number). In recent years, as data roaming fees have dropped and free Wi-Fi has become easier to find, the majority of travelers are finding this to be the best all-around option.

2. Use an unlocked mobile phone with European SIM cards. This is a much more affordable option if you'll be making lots of calls, since it gives you 24/7 access to low European rates. Although remarkably cheap, this option does require a bit of shopping around for the right phone and a prepaid SIM card. Savvy travelers who routinely buy European SIM cards swear by this tactic.

3. Use public phones, and get online with your hotel's guest computer and/or at Internet cafés. These options work particularly well for travelers who simply don't want to hassle with the technology, or want to be (mostly) untethered from their home life while on the road.

Each of these options is explained in greater detail in the following pages. Mixing and matching works well. For example, I routinely bring along my smartphone for Internet chores and Skyping on Wi-Fi, but also carry an unlocked phone and buy SIM cards for affordable calls on the go.

For an even more in-depth explanation of this complicated topic, see www.ricksteves.com/phoning.

How to Dial

Many Americans are intimidated by dialing European phone numbers. You needn't be. It's simple, once you break the code.

Dialing Within the Netherlands

The following instructions apply whether you're dialing from a Dutch mobile phone or a landline (such as a pay phone or your hotel-room phone). If you're roaming with a US phone number, follow the "Dialing Internationally" directions described later.

The Netherlands, like much of the US, uses an area-code dialing system. If you're dialing within an area code, you just dial the local number to be connected—but if you're calling outside your area code, you have to dial both the area code (which starts with a 0) and the local number. For example, the number of a recommended hotel in Haarlem is 023/532-4530. To call it within Haarlem, dial 532-4530. To call it from Amsterdam, dial 023/532-4530.

Dialing Internationally to or from the Netherlands

Always start with the **international access code**—011 if you're calling from the US or Canada, 00 from anywhere in Europe. If you're dialing from a mobile phone, simply insert a + instead (by holding the 0 key).

• Dial the **country code** of the country you're calling (31 for the Netherlands or 1 for the US or Canada).

What Language Barrier?

People speak Dutch in Amsterdam. But you'll find almost no language barrier in the Netherlands, as all well-educated folks, nearly all young people, and almost everyone in the tourist trade also speak English. (When asked if they speak English, the Dutch reply, *"Natuurlijk"*—"naturally.") Regardless, it's polite to use some Dutch pleasantries (see pages 509 and 510).

• Then dial the area code (without its initial 0) and the local number. The European calling chart on the next page lists specifics per country.

Calling from the US to the Netherlands: To call a Haarlem hotel from the US, dial 011 (US access code), 31 (the Netherlands' country code), 23 (Haarlem's area code without the initial 0), and then the hotel's phone number (e.g., 532-4530).

Calling from any European country to the US: To call my office in Edmonds, Washington, from anywhere in Europe, I dial 00 (Europe's access code), 1 (US country code), 425 (Edmonds' area code), and 771-8303.

More Dialing Tips

The chart on the next page shows how to dial per country. For online instructions, see www.countrycallingcodes.com or www.howtocallabroad.com.

Remember, if you're using a mobile phone, dial as if you're in that phone's country of origin. So, when roaming with your US phone number in the Netherlands, dial as if you're calling from the US. But if you're using a European SIM card, dial as you would from that European country.

Note that calls to a European mobile phone are substantially more expensive than calls to a fixed line. Off-hour calls are generally cheaper.

USING YOUR SMARTPHONE IN EUROPE

Even in this age of email, texting, and near-universal Internet access, smart travelers still use the telephone. I call TIs to smooth out sightseeing plans, hotels to get driving directions, museums to confirm tour schedules, restaurants to check open hours or to book a table, and so on.

Most people enjoy the convenience of bringing their own smartphone. Horror stories about sky-high roaming fees are dated and exaggerated, and major service providers work hard to avoid surprising you with an exorbitant bill. With a little planning, you

PRACTICALITIES

European Calling Chart

Just smile and dial, using this key:
AC = Area Code, LN = Local Number.

European Country	Calling long distance within ...	Calling from the US or Canada to ...	Calling from a European country to ...
Austria	AC + LN	011 + 43 + AC (without initial zero) + LN	00 + 43 + AC (without initial zero) + LN
Belgium	LN	011 + 32 + LN (without initial zero)	00 + 32 + LN (without initial zero)
Bosnia-Herzegovina	AC + LN	011 + 387 + AC (without initial zero) + LN	00 + 387 + AC (without initial zero) + LN
Croatia	AC + LN	011 + 385 + AC (without initial zero) + LN	00 + 385 + AC (without initial zero) + LN
Czech Republic	LN	011 + 420 + LN	00 + 420 + LN
Denmark	LN	011 + 45 + LN	00 + 45 + LN
Estonia	LN	011 + 372 + LN	00 + 372 + LN
Finland	AC + LN	011 + 358 + AC (without initial zero) + LN	999 (or other 900 number) + 358 + AC (without initial zero) + LN
France	LN	011 + 33 + LN (without initial zero)	00 + 33 + LN (without initial zero)
Germany	AC + LN	011 + 49 + AC (without initial zero) + LN	00 + 49 + AC (without initial zero) + LN
Gibraltar	LN	011 + 350 + LN	00 + 350 + LN
Great Britain & N. Ireland	AC + LN	011 + 44 + AC (without initial zero) + LN	00 + 44 + AC (without initial zero) + LN
Greece	LN	011 + 30 + LN	00 + 30 + LN
Hungary	06 + AC + LN	011 + 36 + AC + LN	00 + 36 + AC + LN
Ireland	AC + LN	011 + 353 + AC (without initial zero) + LN	00 + 353 + AC (without initial zero) + LN
Italy	LN	011 + 39 + LN	00 + 39 + LN

European Country	Calling long distance within ...	Calling from the US or Canada to ...	Calling from a European country to ...
Latvia	LN	011 + 371 + LN	00 + 371 + LN
Montenegro	AC + LN	011 + 382 + AC (without initial zero) + LN	00 + 382 + AC (without initial zero) + LN
Morocco	LN	011 + 212 + LN (without initial zero)	00 + 212 + LN (without initial zero)
Netherlands	AC + LN	011 + 31 + AC (without initial zero) + LN	00 + 31 + AC (without initial zero) + LN
Norway	LN	011 + 47 + LN	00 + 47 + LN
Poland	LN	011 + 48 + LN	00 + 48 + LN
Portugal	LN	011 + 351 + LN	00 + 351 + LN
Russia	8 + AC + LN	011 + 7 + AC + LN	00 + 7 + AC + LN
Slovakia	AC + LN	011 + 421 + AC (without initial zero) + LN	00 + 421 + AC (without initial zero) + LN
Slovenia	AC + LN	011 + 386 + AC (without initial zero) + LN	00 + 386 + AC (without initial zero) + LN
Spain	LN	011 + 34 + LN	00 + 34 + LN
Sweden	AC + LN	011 + 46 + AC (without initial zero) + LN	00 + 46 + AC (without initial zero) + LN
Switzerland	LN	011 + 41 + LN (without initial zero)	00 + 41 + LN (without initial zero)
Turkey	AC (if there's no initial zero, add one) + LN	011 + 90 + AC (without initial zero) + LN	00 + 90 + AC (without initial zero) + LN

- The instructions above apply whether you're calling to or from a European landline or mobile phone.
- If calling from any mobile phone, you can replace the international access code with "+" (press and hold 0 to insert it).
- The international access code is 011 if you're calling from the US or Canada.
- To call the US or Canada from Europe, dial 00, then 1 (country code for US and Canada), then the area code and number. In short, 00 + 1 + AC + LN = Hi, Mom!

PRACTICALITIES

can use your phone—for voice calls, messaging, and Internet access—without breaking the bank.

Start by figuring out whether your phone works in Europe. Most phones purchased through AT&T and T-Mobile (which use the same technology as Europe) work abroad, while only some phones from Verizon or Sprint do—check your operating manual (look for "tri-band," "quad-band," or "GSM"). If you're not sure, ask your service provider.

Roaming Costs

"Roaming" with your phone—that is, using it outside its home region, such as in Europe—generally comes with extra charges, whether you are making voice calls, sending texts, or reading your email. The fees listed here are for the three major American providers—Verizon, AT&T, and T-Mobile; Sprint's roaming rates tend to be much higher. But policies change fast, so get the latest details before your trip. For example, as of mid-2014, T-Mobile waived voice, texting, and data roaming fees for some plans.

Voice calls are the most expensive. Most US providers charge from $1.29 to $1.99 per minute to make or receive calls in Europe. (As you cross each border, you'll typically get a text message explaining the rates in the new country.) If you plan to make multiple calls, look into a global calling plan to lower the per-minute cost, or buy a package of minutes at a discounted price (such as 30 minutes for $30). Note that you'll be charged for incoming calls whether or not you answer them; to save money ask your friends to stay in contact by texting, and to call you only in case of an emergency.

Text messaging costs 20 to 50 cents per text. To cut that cost, you could sign up for an international messaging plan (for example, $10 for 100 texts). Or consider apps that let you text for free (iMessage for Apple, Google Hangouts for Android, or WhatsApp for any device); however, these require you to use Wi-Fi or data roaming. Be aware that Europeans use the term "SMS" ("short message service") to describe text messaging.

Data roaming means accessing data services via a cellular network other than your home carrier's. Prices have dropped dramatically in recent years, making this an affordable way for travelers to bridge gaps between Wi-Fi hotspots. You'll pay far less if you set up an international data roaming plan. Most providers charge $25-30 for 100-120 megabytes of data. That's plenty for basic Internet tasks—100 megabytes lets you view 100 websites or send/receive 1,000 text-based emails—but you'll burn through that amount quickly by streaming videos or music. If your data use exceeds your plan amount, most providers will automatically kick in an additional 100- or 120-megabyte block for the same price. (For more, see "Using Wi-Fi and Data Roaming," later.)

Setting Up (or Disabling) International Service

With most service providers, international roaming (voice, text, and data) is disabled on your account unless you activate it. Before your trip, call your provider (or navigate their website), and cover the following topics:

• Confirm that your phone will work in Europe.

• Verify global roaming rates for voice calls, text messaging, and data.

• Tell them which of those services you'd like to activate.

• Consider add-on plans to bring down the cost of international calls, texts, or data roaming.

When you get home from Europe, be sure to cancel any add-on plans that you activated for your trip.

Some people would rather use their smartphone exclusively on Wi-Fi, and not worry about either voice or data charges. If that's you, call your provider to be sure that international roaming options are deactivated on your account. To be double-sure, put your phone in "airplane mode," then turn your Wi-Fi back on.

Using Wi-Fi and Data Roaming

A good approach is to use free Wi-Fi wherever possible, and fill in the gaps with data roaming.

Wi-Fi is readily available throughout Europe. At accommodations, access is usually free, but you may have to pay a fee, especially at expensive hotels. At hotels with thick stone walls, the Wi-Fi signal from the lobby may not reach every room. If Wi-Fi is important to you, ask about it when you book—and be specific ("In the rooms?"). Get the password and network name at the front desk when you check in.

When you're out and about, your best bet for finding free Wi-Fi is often at a café. They'll usually tell you the password if you buy something. Or you can stroll down a café-lined street, smartphone in hand, checking for unsecured networks every few steps until you find one that works. Some towns have free public Wi-Fi in highly trafficked parks or piazzas. You may have to register before using it, or get a password at the TI.

Data roaming is handy when you can't find Wi-Fi. Because you'll pay by the megabyte (explained earlier), it's best to limit how much data you use. Save bandwidth-gobbling tasks like Skyping, watching videos, or downloading apps or emails with large attachments until you're on Wi-Fi. Switch your phone's email settings from "push" to "fetch." This means that you can choose to "fetch" (download) your messages when you're on Wi-Fi rather than having them continuously "pushed" to your device. And be aware of apps—such as news, weather, and sports tickers—that automati-

Internet Calling

To make totally free voice and video calls over the Internet, all you need are a smartphone, tablet, or laptop; a strong Wi-Fi signal; and an account with one of the major Internet calling providers: Skype (www.skype.com), FaceTime (preloaded on most Apple devices), or Google+ Hangouts (www.google.com/hangouts). If the Wi-Fi signal isn't strong enough for video, try sticking with an audio-only call. Or...wait for your next hotel. Many Internet calling programs also work for making calls from your computer to telephones worldwide for a very reasonable fee—generally just a few cents per minute (you'll have to buy some credit before you make your first call).

cally update. Check your phone's settings to be sure that none of your apps are set to "use cellular data."

I like the safeguard of manually turning off data roaming on my phone whenever I'm not actively using it. To turn off data and voice roaming, look in your phone's settings menu—try checking under "cellular" or "network," or ask your service provider how to do it. If you need to get online but can't find Wi-Fi, simply turn on data roaming long enough for the task at hand, then turn it off again.

Figure out how to keep track of how much data you've used (in your phone's menu, look for "cellular data usage"; you may have to reset the counter at the start of your trip). Some companies automatically send you a text message warning if you approach or exceed your limit.

There's yet another option: If you're traveling with an unlocked smartphone (explained later), you can buy a SIM card that also includes data; this can be far cheaper than data roaming through your home provider.

USING EUROPEAN SIM CARDS

While using your American phone in Europe is easy, it's not always cheap. And unreliable Wi-Fi can make keeping in touch frustrating. If you're reasonably technology-savvy, and would like to have the option of making lots of affordable calls, it's worth getting comfortable with European SIM cards.

Here's the basic idea: With an unlocked phone (which works with different carriers; described next), get a SIM card—the microchip that stores data about your phone—once you get to Europe. Slip in the SIM, turn on the phone, and bingo! You've got a European phone number (and access to cheaper European rates).

Getting an Unlocked Phone

Your basic options are getting your existing phone unlocked, or buying a phone (either at home or in Europe).

Some phones are electronically "locked" so that you can't switch SIM cards (keeping you loyal to your carrier). But in some circumstances it's possible to unlock your phone—allowing you to replace the original SIM card with one that will work with a European provider. Note that some US carriers are beginning to offer phones/tablets whose SIM card can't be swapped out in the US but will accept a European SIM without any unlocking process.

You may already have an old, unused mobile phone in a drawer somewhere. Call your service provider and ask if they'll send you the unlock code. Otherwise, you can buy one: Search an online shopping site for an "unlocked quad-band phone," or buy one at a mobile-phone shop in Europe. Either way, a basic model typically costs $40 or less.

Buying and Using SIM Cards

Once you have an unlocked phone, you'll need to buy a SIM card (note that a smaller variation called "micro-SIM" or "nano-SIM"—

used in most iPhones—is less widely available.)

SIM cards are sold at mobile-phone shops, department-store electronics counters, and newsstands for $5–10, and usually include about that much prepaid calling credit (making the card itself virtually free). Because SIM cards are prepaid, there's no contract and no commitment; I routinely buy one even if I'm in a country for only a few days.

An increasing number of countries—including the Netherlands—require you to register the SIM card with your passport (an antiterrorism measure). This takes only a few minutes: The shop clerk will ask you to fill out a form, then submit it to the service provider. Sometimes you can register your own SIM card online. Either way, an hour or two after submitting the information, you'll get a text welcoming you to that network.

When using a SIM card in its home country, it's free to receive calls and texts, and it's cheap to make calls—domestic calls average 20 cents per minute. You can also use SIM cards to call the US—sometimes very affordably: (Lebara and Lycamobile, which operate in multiple European countries, let you call a US number for less than 10 cents a minute). Rates are higher if you're roaming in another country. But if you bought the SIM card within the European Union, roaming fees are capped no matter where you travel throughout the EU (about 25 cents/minute to make calls, 7 cents/minute to receive calls, and 8 cents for a text message).

While you can buy SIM cards just about anywhere, I like to seek out a mobile-phone shop, where an English-speaking clerk can help explain my options, get my SIM card inserted and set up, and show me how to use it. When you buy your SIM card, ask about rates for domestic and international calls and texting, and about roaming fees. Also find out how to check your credit balance (usually you'll key in a few digits and hit "Send"). You can top up your credit at any newsstand, tobacco shop, mobile-phone shop, or many other businesses (look for the SIM card's logo in the window).

To insert your SIM card into the phone, locate the slot, which is usually on the side of the phone or behind the battery. Turning on the phone, you'll be prompted to enter the "SIM PIN" (a code number that came with your card).

If you have an unlocked smartphone, you can look for a European SIM card that covers both voice and data. This is often much cheaper than paying for data roaming through your home provider.

LANDLINE TELEPHONES AND INTERNET CAFÉS

If you prefer to travel without a smartphone or tablet, you can still stay in touch using landline telephones, hotel guest computers, and Internet cafés.

Landline Telephones

Phones in your **hotel room** can be great for local calls and for calls using cheap international phone cards (described in the sidebar). Many hotels charge a fee for local and "toll-free" as well as long-distance or international calls—always ask for the rates before you dial. Since you'll never be charged for receiving calls, it can be more affordable to have someone from the US call you in your room.

While **public pay phones** are on the endangered species list, you'll still see them on the street and at train stations. Pay phones generally come with multilingual instructions. Most public phones work with insertable phone cards (described in the sidebar). Be aware that pay phones in train stations may require a different card than phones at other locations.

You'll see many cheap **call shops** that advertise low rates to faraway lands, often in train-station neighborhoods. While these target immigrants who want to call home cheaply, tourists can use them, too. Before making your call, be completely clear on the rates.

Types of Telephone Cards

Europe uses two different types of telephone cards. Both types are sold at newsstands, street kiosks, tobacco shops, and train stations.

Insertable Phone Cards: These cards can only be used at pay phones: Simply take the phone off the hook, insert the card, wait for a dial tone, and dial away. The phone displays your credit ticking down as you talk. Each European country has its own insertable phone card—so your Dutch card won't work in a Belgian phone.

International Phone Cards: These prepaid cards can be used to make inexpensive calls—within Europe, or to the US, for pennies a minute—from nearly any phone, including the one in your hotel room. The cards come with a toll-free number and a scratch-to-reveal PIN code. If the voice prompts aren't in English, experiment: Dial your code, followed by the pound sign (#), then the phone number, then pound again, and so on, until it works. Some international phone cards work in multiple countries—if traveling to both the Netherlands and Belgium, try to buy a card that will work in both places.

Internet Cafés and Public Internet Terminals

Finding public Internet terminals in Europe is no problem. Many hotels have a computer in the lobby for guests to use. Otherwise, head for an Internet café, or ask the TI or your hotelier for the nearest place to access the Internet.

European computers typically use non-American keyboards. A few letters are switched around, and command keys are labeled in the local language. Many European keyboards have an "Alt Gr" key (for "Alternate Graphics") to the right of the space bar; press this to insert the extra symbol that appears on some keys. Europeans have different names for, and different ways to type, the @ symbol. In Dutch, it's called the *apenstaartje* ("little monkey tail"). If you can't locate a special character (such as the @ symbol), simply copy it from a Web page and paste it into your email message.

Internet Security

Whether you're accessing the Internet with your own device or at a public terminal, using a shared network or computer comes with the potential for increased security risks. Ask the hotel or café for the specific name of their Wi-Fi network, and make sure you log on to that exact one; hackers sometimes create a bogus hotspot with a similar or vague name (such as "Hotel Europa Free Wi-Fi"). It's better if a network uses a password (especially a hard-to-guess one) rather than being open to the world.

While traveling, you may want to check your online banking

or credit-card statements, or to take care of other personal-finance chores, but Internet security experts advise against accessing these sites entirely while traveling. Even if you're using your own computer at a password-protected hotspot, any hacker who's logged on to the same network can see what you're up to. If you need to log on to a banking website, try to do so on a hard-wired connection (i.e., using an Ethernet cable in your hotel room), or if that's not possible, use a secure banking app on a cellular telephone connection.

If using a credit card online, make sure that the site is secure. Most browsers display a little padlock icon, and the URL begins with *https* instead of *http*. Never send a credit-card number over a website that doesn't begin with *https*.

If you're not convinced a connection is secure, avoid accessing any sites (such as your bank's) that could be vulnerable to fraud.

MAIL

You can mail one package per day to yourself worth up to $200 duty-free from Europe to the US (mark it "personal purchases"). If you're sending a gift to someone, mark it "unsolicited gift." For details, visit www.cbp.gov and search for "Know Before You Go."

The Netherlands closed its last post office in 2011. You can still buy stamps or mail packages at any newsstand, book store, or grocery store with an orange *TNT* logo. To send a package in a smaller town, ask your hotelier for assistance, but for quick transatlantic delivery (in either direction), consider services such as DHL (www.dhl.com).

Transportation

Because of the short distances and excellent public transportation systems in the Netherlands, I recommend traveling by train. Hourly trains connect each of these towns faster and easier than you could by driving. But for other destinations, a car could be a good alternative. In the Netherlands, cars are best for three or more traveling together (especially families with small kids), those packing heavy, and those scouring the countryside.

TRAINS

The easiest way to reach nearly any Dutch destination is by train. Connections are fast and frequent. The Dutch train system—Nederlandse Spoorwegen—is usually identified by its initials NS. InterCity (IC) trains are speedy for connecting big cities, and the high-speed Thalys is the fastest (the speed comes at a price; see "Reservations for Rail Pass Holders," later). InterRegio (IR) and *sneltreins* connect smaller towns; *stoptreins* are pokey milk-run trains that stop at every station; and the Netherlands' misnamed

Train Lines in the Low Countries

100 Kilometers

50 Miles

North
Sea

See detail map in
Day Trips chapter

Leeuwarden

Groningen

To
Hamburg

Den
Helder

NETHERLANDS

Medemblik

Alkmaar

Enkhuizen

To
Berlin

Haarlem

Amsterdam

Deventer

Hengelo

The
Hague

Delft

Utrecht

Rotterdam

Gouda

Arnhem

Rhine

Roosendaal

Eindhoven

Oostend

Bruges

Antwerp

GERMANY

Bus

Flanders

Ghent

Brussels

Cologne

Ypres

Maastricht

Rhine

To
London

Kortrijk

BELGIUM

Aachen

Lille

Liège

Mons

Namur

Koblenz

W a l l o n i e

Bastogne

FRANCE

LUX.

Trier

To
Paris

Luxembourg
City

"Sprinter" trains are actually slow *stoptreins*. Throughout the Netherlands, smoking is prohibited in trains and train stations.

Schedules

To get train schedules in advance, use the German Rail (Deutsche Bahn) website, which has comprehensive schedules for almost anywhere in Europe (www.bahn.com). Or try the Dutch Rail site (www.nshighspeed.nl for international trains, www.ns.nl for domestic trains). For a slick website that combines information on Dutch trains, buses, and trams (and even includes walking directions to get to the bus stop), visit www.9292.nl. In the Netherlands dial toll tel. 0900-202-1163.

OV-Chipkaart

The Netherlands has integrated its local and intercity public transportation into a single payment system, called the OV-chipkaart (www.ov-chipkaart.nl). Cards come in three options: disposable one-time paper tickets (called a single-use or disposable OV-chipkaart), the Anonymous OV-chipkaart, and the Personal OV-chipkaart (not useful for tourists, as it must be linked to a Dutch bank account).

To use this microchip-embedded pass, just touch it against the pink-and-gray box to "check in" and "check out" as you enter and exit any form of transportation or a train platform. The cost of your journey is automatically deducted.

If you are staying for more than three days, an Anonymous OV-chipkaart may save you some money. Trams in cities like Amsterdam or The Hague are much cheaper—usually about half-price—with an OV-chipkaart comparable to buying a flat-fee disposable ticket. For train rides, you avoid a €1 surcharge on single-use tickets.

To get an OV-chipkaart, you'll pay a nonrefundable €7.50 fee, then load it with credit. Cards must have a minimum balance of €4 for you to use it to ride a tram, and €20 (plus the cost of your ticket) to ride a train. Go under that amount, and the card won't work the next time you use it. Forget to "check out" when you leave the tram or train, and you'll lose your entire deposit.

You can buy an Anonymous OV-chipkaart at train and bus station ticket windows and at some blue ticket machines at the airport and train stations. The card comes with €10 of credit (so you'll pay €17.50 to start). To reload, you must be at a train station or Amsterdam metro station—and you'll need coins or a credit card with a chip to reload at a machine. Think carefully about how much credit you'll need: Any balance under €30 can be refunded at a ticket office, but you'll pay a €2.50 fee to get it back.

Bottom Line: You'll save roughly €1 per trip using the OV-chipkaart, but you'll pay a total of €10 to buy the card and cash it out at the end of your vacation. You'll also spend time loading credit and waiting in line to get a refund. But if you take 10 or more bus, tram, or train trips in the Netherlands, the OV-chipkaart may be worth it.

To find schedules at train stations, check the yellow schedule posters, or look for TV screens listing upcoming departures. The direction of the train is identified by its final station. If you can't find your train, or are unclear on departure details, visit an information booth or enlist the help of any official-looking employee.

Buying Tickets

The Dutch did away with paper tickets for domestic trains in 2014; instead travelers use smartcards that are part of its OV-chipkaart system (see sidebar). While this system works fine if you're Dutch, it is confusing and cumbersome for foreigners.

If you are going to take just three or four train trips in the Netherlands, it's easiest to buy a "single-use chipcard"—a paper ticket with that contains a chip inside—each time you travel. You can only purchase these single-use tickets on the day you are traveling, and you'll pay a €1 surcharge for each ticket. So if you are making a day trip from Amsterdam to Haarlem, you'll pay the price for a round-trip ticket (€8), plus the €1 surcharge.

Most Americans will have to use cash to buy these tickets. The Dutch train system won't take US credit cards unless they have a chip—and even some US cards with chips may not work; see page 459. If your card won't work at ticket machines, some of them also take coins—so it's smart to stock up before you get to the station. To find a machine that takes coins, look for a coin slot above the upper right corner of the video screen. Otherwise you'll have to wait in line at the ticket window, where they charge a €0.50 service fee.

Online purchases are possible but tricky. While you can buy international tickets with a US credit card at the www.nshighspeed.nl website, you can't buy a ticket on the domestic website unless you have a Dutch bank account. However, you can buy tickets for domestic Dutch trains at the Belgian rail website—www.b-europe.com—which charges the same price, takes US credit cards, and doesn't have extra fees. Print your tickets at home before you leave or ask if you can use your hotel's printer. Unfortunately, the Belgian website only works if your travel starts or ends at Amsterdam, Schiphol Airport, The Hague, Rotterdam, Utrecht, or Arnhem.

If you are going to take many train trips and also plan to use buses and trams frequently, it may be better to purchase an Anonymous OV-chipkaart (see sidebar), but for train travel you'll need to have €20 plus the cost of your ticket loaded on the card before each trip.

At the Station

If you have a single-use ticket or Anonymous OV-chipkaart, you must "check in" and "check out" as you enter and exit the train plat-

PRACTICALITIES

form by swiping your card at a card reader. Printed tickets bought online have a bar code that can be scanned if there is a gate, or travelers can show a printed ticket or a rail pass to an employee and be let through.

Bikes on Trains

If you're traveling with a bike, you'll pay extra to bring it on the train. In the Netherlands, bikes are only allowed during off-peak hours (all day on weekends, and weekdays only after 9:00) and require a "Bicycle Day Travel Card" (€6, no matter the destination).

Rail Passes

Most visits to the Netherlands don't cover enough miles to justify a rail pass, but if your trip includes other countries, a rail pass could save you money. For instance, good rail pass options exist for those traveling between Benelux (Belgium, the Netherlands, and Luxembourg) and either France or Germany; Eurail Select Passes (or a Global Pass) make sense if you're touring the Netherlands and Belgium as part of a larger trip (see sidebar).

Reservations for Rail Pass Holders: Regional and InterCity trains do not require reservations, allowing you plenty of flexibility as you explore Benelux. Between Amsterdam-Brussels or Brussels-Cologne, fast Thalys trains cost more (for point-to-point tickets) or require expensive reservations with a rail pass, so I'd choose an IC train if going to Brussels or an ICE train if going to Cologne (reservation optional). Direct service from Amsterdam to Paris is by Thalys, with reservations costing €25-60 in addition to a pass that covers Benelux and France. Note that you can buy a Thalys ticket if you don't have a rail pass; you'll simply pay more for it.

For more detailed advice on figuring out the smartest rail pass options for your train trip, visit the Trains & Rail Passes section of my website at www.ricksteves.com/rail.

BUSES

While you'll mostly use trains to travel in this region, a few destinations (for example, the tulip gardens of Keukenhof, the flower auction in Aalsmeer, or the Kröller-Müller Museum near Arnhem) are reachable only by bus.

Confusingly, there's no unified national bus company for the Netherlands—various destinations are served by different companies. Arriva (www.arriva.nl) and Connexxion (www.connexxion.nl) are the main companies serving the Netherlands. The best public transit website in the Netherlands for bus schedules is www.9292.nl.

Rail Passes

Prices listed are for 2014 and are subject to change. For the latest prices, details, and train schedules (and easy online ordering), see www.ricksteves.com/rail.

Benelux = Belgium, Netherlands and Luxembourg. "Saver" prices are per person for two or more people traveling together. "Youth" means under age 26. The fare for children 4–11 is half the adult individual fare or Saver fare. Kids under age 4 travel free.

BENELUX PASS

	Individual 1st Class	Individual 2nd Class	Saver 1st Class	Saver 2nd Class	Youth 2nd Class
3 days in 1 month	$298	$240	$254	$204	$157
5 days in 1 month	$408	$327	$347	$278	$214

Valid on Thalys trains within Benelux (with paid seat reservation), but not to/from Paris.

BENELUX–FRANCE PASS

	Individual 1st Class	Individual 2nd Class	Saver 1st Class	Saver 2nd Class	Youth 2nd Class
5 days in 2 months	$458	$390	$390	$332	$299
6 days in 2 months	$502	$427	$427	$372	$327
8 days in 2 months	$581	$506	$495	$443	$379
10 days in 2 months	$656	$578	$558	$503	$434

BENELUX–GERMANY PASS

	Individual 1st Class	Individual 2nd Class	Saver 1st Class	Saver 2nd Class	Youth 2nd Class
5 days in 2 months	$446	$336	$336	$271	$271
6 days in 2 months	$493	$372	$372	$297	$297
8 days in 2 months	$583	$436	$436	$351	$351
10 days in 2 months	$678	$508	$508	$406	$406

SELECTPASS

This pass covers travel in three adjacent countries, such as Benelux-Germany-Switzerland, but not including France. Please visit **www.ricksteves.com/rail** for four- and five-country options.

	Individual 1st Class	Saver 1st Class	Youth 2nd Class
5 days in 2 months	$524	$446	$342
6 days in 2 months	$572	$487	$373
8 days in 2 months	$666	$567	$434
10 days in 2 months	$762	$468	$497

RENTING A CAR

If you're renting a car in the Netherlands, bring your driver's license. In the Netherlands, you're also required to have an International Driving Permit—an official translation of your driver's license (sold at your local AAA office for $15 plus the cost of two passport-type photos; see www.aaa.com). While that's the letter of the law, I've often rented cars without having this permit. If all goes well, you'll likely never be asked to show this permit—but it's a must if you end up dealing with the police.

Rental companies require you to be at least 21 years old and to have held your license for one year. Drivers under the age of 25 may incur a young-driver surcharge, and some rental companies do not rent to anyone 75 or older. If you're considered too young or old, look into leasing (covered later), which has less-stringent age restrictions.

Research car rentals before you go. It's cheaper to arrange most car rentals from the US. Call several companies or look online to compare rates.

Most of the major US rental agencies (including Avis, Budget, Enterprise, Hertz, and Thrifty) have offices throughout Europe. Also consider the two major Europe-based agencies, Europcar and Sixt. It can be cheaper to use a consolidator, such as Auto Europe/Kemwel (www.autoeurope.com) or Europe by Car (www.europebycar.com), which compares rates at several companies to get you the best deal—but because you're working with a middleman, it's especially important to ask in advance about add-on fees and restrictions.

Regardless of the car-rental company you choose, always read the fine print carefully for add-on charges—such as one-way drop-off fees, airport surcharges, or mandatory insurance policies—that aren't included in the "total price." You may need to query rental agents pointedly to find out your actual cost.

For the best deal, rent by the week with unlimited mileage. To save money on fuel, ask for a diesel car. I normally rent the smallest, least-expensive model with a stick shift (generally much cheaper than an automatic). Almost all rentals are manual by default, so if you need an automatic, request one in advance; be aware that these cars are usually larger models (not as maneuverable on narrow, winding roads).

Figure on paying roughly $200 for a one-week rental. Allow extra for supplemental insurance, fuel, tolls, and parking. For trips of three weeks or more, look into leasing; you'll save money on insurance and taxes. Be warned that international trips—say, picking up in Amsterdam and dropping off in Paris—can be expensive (it depends partly on distance).

As a rule, always tell your car-rental company up front exactly which countries you'll be entering. Some companies levy extra insurance fees for trips taken in certain countries with certain types of cars (such as BMWs, Mercedes, and convertibles). Double-check with your rental agent that you have all the documentation you need before you drive off (especially if you're crossing borders into non-Schengen countries, such as Croatia, where you might need to present proof of insurance).

Big companies have offices in most cities; ask whether they can pick you up at your hotel. Small local rental companies can be cheaper but aren't as flexible.

Compare pickup costs (downtown can be less expensive than the airport) and explore drop-off options. Always check the hours of the location you choose: Many rental offices close from midday Saturday until Monday morning and, in smaller towns, at lunchtime.

When selecting a location, don't trust the agency's description of "downtown" or "city center." In some cases, a "downtown" branch can be on the outskirts of the city—a long, costly taxi ride from the center. Before choosing, plug the addresses into a mapping website. You may find that the "train station" location is handier. But returning a car at a big-city train station or downtown agency can be tricky; get precise details on the car drop-off location and hours, and allow ample time to find it.

When you pick up the rental car, check it thoroughly and make sure any damage is noted on your rental agreement. Find out how your car's lights, turn signals, wipers, radio, and fuel cap function, and know what kind of fuel the car takes (diesel vs. unleaded). When you return the car, make sure the agent verifies its condition with you. Some drivers take pictures of the returned vehicle as proof of its condition.

Navigation Options

When renting a car in Europe, you have several alternatives for your digital navigator: Use your smartphone's online mapping app, download an offline map app, or rent a GPS device with your rental car (or bring your own GPS device from home).

Online mapping apps used to be prohibitively expensive for overseas travelers—but that was before most carriers started offering affordable international data plans. If you're already getting a data plan for your trip, this is probably the way to go (see "Using Your Smartphone in Europe," earlier).

A number of well-designed apps allow you much of the convenience of online maps without any costly demands on your data plan. City Maps 2Go is one of the most popular of these; OffMaps, Google Maps, and Navfree also all offer good, zoomable offline maps for much of Europe (some are better for driving, while others are better for navigating cities).

Some drivers prefer using a dedicated GPS unit—not only to avoid the data-roaming fees, but because a stand-alone GPS can be easier to operate (important if you're driving solo). The major downside: It's expensive—around $10-30 per day. Your car's GPS unit may only come loaded with maps for its home country—if you need additional maps, ask. Make sure your device's language is set to English before you drive off. If you have a portable GPS device at home, you can take that instead. Many American GPS devices come loaded with US maps only—you'll need to buy and download European maps before your trip. This option is far less expensive than renting.

Car Insurance Options

When you rent a car, you are liable for a very high deductible, sometimes equal to the entire value of the car. Limit your financial risk by choosing one of these options: Buy Collision Damage Waiver (CDW) coverage from the car-rental company, get coverage through your credit card (free, if your card automatically includes zero-deductible coverage), or get collision insurance as part of a larger travel-insurance policy.

CDW includes a very high deductible (typically $1,000-1,500). Though each rental company has its own variation, basic CDW costs $10-30 a day (figure roughly 30 percent extra) and reduces your liability, but does not eliminate it. When you pick up the car, you'll be offered the chance to "buy down" the basic deductible to zero (for an additional $10-30/day; this is sometimes called "super CDW" or "zero-deductible coverage").

If you opt for **credit-card coverage,** there's a catch. You'll technically have to decline all coverage offered by the car-rental company, which means they can place a hold on your card (which can be up to the full value of the car). In case of damage, it can be time-consuming to resolve the charges with your credit-card company. Before you decide on this option, quiz your credit-card company about how it works.

If you're already purchasing a **travel-insurance policy** for your trip, adding collision coverage is an option. For example, Travel Guard (www.travelguard.com) sells affordable renter's collision insurance as an add-on to its other policies; it's valid everywhere in Europe except the Republic of Ireland, and some Italian car-rental companies refuse to honor it, as it doesn't cover you in case of theft.

For more on car-rental insurance, see www.ricksteves.com/cdw.

PRACTICALITIES

Leasing

For trips of three weeks or more, consider leasing (which automatically includes zero-deductible collision and theft insurance). By technically buying and then selling back the car, you save lots of money on tax and insurance. Leasing provides you a brand-new car with unlimited mileage and a 24-hour emergency assistance program. You can lease for as little as 21 days to as long as five and a half months. Car leases must be arranged from the US. One of many companies offering affordable lease packages is Europe by Car (www.europebycar.com).

DRIVING

Road Rules: Traffic cameras are everywhere in the Netherlands; speeding tickets for even a few kilometers over the limit are common. Kids under age 12 (or less than about 5 feet tall) must ride in an appropriate child-safety seat. Seat belts are mandatory for all, and two beers under those belts are enough to land you in jail. Be aware of other typical European road rules; for example, many countries require headlights to be turned on at all times, and it's generally illegal to drive while using your mobile phone without a hands-free headset. In Europe, you're not allowed to turn right on a red light, unless there is a sign or signal specifically authorizing it, and on expressways it's illegal to pass drivers on the right. Ask your car-rental company about these rules, or check the US State Department website (www.travel.state.gov, search for your country in the "Learn about your destination" box, then click on "Travel and Transportation").

Fuel: Gas (*benzine* in Dutch) is expensive—about $8-9 per gallon. Diesel (*diesel or dieselolie* in Dutch) is less—about $7 per gallon—and diesel cars get better mileage, so try to rent a diesel to save money. Be sure you know what type of fuel your car takes before you fill up. Gas is most expensive on freeways and cheapest at big supermarkets. About 30 percent of the filling stations in the Netherlands are unmanned, and your US credit and debit cards may not work at self-service gas pumps unless they have a chip. Look for stations with an attendant or be sure to carry sufficient cash in euros.

Parking: Finding a parking place can be a headache in larger cities. Ask your hotelier for ideas, and pay to park at well-patrolled lots (blue *P* signs direct you to parking lots). Parking structures usually require that you take a ticket with you and pay at a machine on your way back to the car. US credit cards without a chip may not work in these automated machines but euro coins (and sometimes bills) will.

FLIGHTS

The best comparison search engine for both international and intra-European flights is www.kayak.com. For inexpensive flights within Europe, try www.skyscanner.com or www.hipmunk.com; for inexpensive international flights, try www.vayama.com.

Flying to Europe: Start looking for international flights four to five months before your trip, especially for peak-season travel. Off-season tickets can be purchased a month or so in advance. Depending on your itinerary, it can be efficient to fly into one city and out of another. If your flight requires a connection in Europe, see our hints on navigating Europe's top hub airports at www.ricksteves.com/hub-airports.

Flying within Europe: If you're considering a train ride that's more than five hours long, a flight may save you both time and money. When comparing your options, factor in the time it takes to get to the airport and how early you'll need to arrive to check in.

Well-known cheapo airlines include easyJet (www.easyjet.com) and Ryanair (www.ryanair.com), along with Amsterdam-based Transavia (www.transavia.com).

Be aware of the potential drawbacks of flying on the cheap: nonrefundable and nonchangeable tickets, minimal or nonexistent customer service, treks to airports far outside town, and stingy baggage allowances with steep overage fees. If you're traveling with lots of luggage, a cheap flight can quickly become a bad deal. To avoid unpleasant surprises, read the small print before you book.

Resources

RESOURCES FROM RICK STEVES

Rick Steves Amsterdam and the Netherlands is one of many books in my series on European travel, which includes country guidebooks, city and regional guidebooks (Rome, Florence, Paris, London, etc.), Snapshot guides (excerpted chapters from my country guides), Pocket guides (full-color little books on big cities, such as Amsterdam), and my budget-travel skills handbook, *Rick Steves Europe Through the Back Door.* Most of my titles are available as ebooks. My phrase books—for German, French, Italian, Spanish, and Portuguese—are practical and budget-oriented. My other books include *Europe 101* (a crash course on art and history designed for travelers); *Mediterranean Cruise Ports* and *Northern European Cruise Ports* (how to make the most of your time in port);

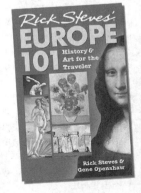

Begin Your Trip at
www.RickSteves.com

My **website** is *the* place to explore Europe. You'll find thousands of fun articles, videos, photos, and radio interviews on European destinations; money-saving tips for planning your dream trip; monthly travel news; my travel talks and travel blog; my latest guidebook updates (www.ricksteves.com/update); and my free Rick Steves Audio Europe app. You can also follow me on Facebook and Twitter.

Our **Travel Forum** is an immense, yet well-groomed collection of message boards, where our travel-savvy community answers questions and shares their personal travel experiences (www.ricksteves.com/forums).

Our **online Travel Store** offers travel bags and accessories that I've designed specifically to help you travel smarter and lighter. These include my popular bags (rolling carry-on and backpack versions), money belts, totes, toiletries kits, adapters, other accessories, and a wide selection of guidebooks, journals, planning maps, and DVDs.

Choosing the right **rail pass** for your trip—amidst hundreds of options—can drive you nutty. Our website will help you find the perfect fit for your itinerary and your budget: We offer easy, one-stop shopping for rail passes, seat reservations, and point-to-point tickets.

Want to travel with greater efficiency and less stress? We organize **tours** with more than three dozen itineraries and 800 departures reaching the best destinations in this book... and beyond. We offer an 11-day Heart of Belgium and Holland tour that includes Amsterdam and Delft, and a 21-day tour of Europe that begins in Haarlem and Amsterdam. You'll enjoy great guides, a fun bunch of travel partners (with small groups of 24 to 28 travelers), and plenty of room to spread out in a big, comfy bus when touring between towns. You'll find European adventures to fit every vacation length. For all the details, and to get our Tour Catalog and a free Rick Steves Tour Experience DVD (filmed on location during an actual tour), visit www.ricksteves.com or call our Tour Department at 425/608-4217.

and *Travel as a Political Act* (a travelogue sprinkled with tips for bringing home a global perspective). A more complete list of my titles appears near the end of this book.

Video: My public television series, *Rick Steves' Europe*, covers European destinations in 100 shows, with two shows on the Netherlands. To watch full episodes online for free, see www.ricksteves.com/tv. Or to raise your travel I.Q. with video versions of our popular classes, see www.ricksteves.com/travel-talks.

Audio: My weekly public radio show, *Travel with Rick Steves*,

features interviews with travel experts from around the world. I've also produced free, self-guided **audio tours** of the top walks in Amsterdam. All of this audio content is available for free at Rick Steves Audio Europe, an extensive online library organized by destination. Choose whatever interests you, and download it for free via the Rick Steves Audio Europe smartphone app, www.ricksteves.com/audioeurope, iTunes, or Google Play.

MAPS

The black-and-white maps in this book are concise and simple. They're designed to help you locate recommended places and get to local TIs, where you can pick up more in-depth maps of cities and regions (usually free). Better maps are sold at newsstands and bookstores. Before you buy a map, look at it to be sure it has the level of detail you want. Everything in this book is covered by the excellent, detailed *ANWB Wegenkaart Nederland midden* map (1:200,000, sold at bookstores). Map apps for your smartphone or tablet are also handy (see "Navigation Options," earlier).

RECOMMENDED BOOKS AND MOVIES

To learn more about the Netherlands past and present, check out some of these books and films.

Nonfiction

Amsterdam (Geert Mak, 1999). Academic but engaging and thorough look at centuries of the city's history.

A Bridge Too Far (Cornelius Ryan, 1974). A gripping account of Operation Market Garden, a failed attempt by the Allies to sweep across the Netherlands in the fall of 1944.

Daily Life in Rembrandt's Holland (Paul Zumthor, 1994). Focuses on the everyday concerns of Dutch society in the 17th century, covering art, history, culture, sports, holidays, and more.

Dear Theo: The Autobiography of Vincent van Gogh (edited by Irving Stone, 1995). A look into the psyche of Vincent van Gogh through letters to his brother.

The Diary of a Young Girl (Anne Frank, 1952). Remarkable diary of a young Jewish girl hiding out from the Nazis in Amsterdam.

The Embarrassment of Riches: An Interpretation of Dutch Culture in the Golden Age (Simon Schama, 1997). A comprehensive overview of Dutch culture and the attitudes of Dutch citizens, from their early beginnings to their most famous struggles.

The Hiding Place (Corrie ten Boom, 1971). The story of a Christian family caught hiding Jews and resistance fighters in Haarlem.

My 'Dam Life: Three Years in Holland (Sean Condon, 2003). An Australian writer's humorous account of his time in the Low Countries.

Nathaniel's Nutmeg: Or the True and Incredible Adventures of the Spice Trader Who Changed the Course of History (Giles Milton, 1999). The Netherlands and England struggle to harness the world supply of nutmeg in the 1600s.

Spice: The History of a Temptation (Jack Turner, 2005). Holland at the center of the spice trade, back when a pinch of cinnamon was worth its weight in gold.

Tulipmania: The Story of the World's Most Coveted Flower & the Extraordinary Passions It Aroused (Mike Dash, 2001). The Golden Age tulip craze of the 1600s.

The UnDutchables: An Observation of the Netherlands, Its Culture and Its Inhabitants (Colin White and Laurie Boucke, 2013). Irreverent guide to modern Dutch culture.

Fiction

The Black Tulip (Alexandre Dumas, 1850). A classic swashbuckling tale of fortunes won and lost.

Confessions of an Ugly Stepsister (Gregory Maguire, 1999). A twist on the classic tale of Cinderella, set in Haarlem.

Girl in Hyacinth Blue (Susan Vreeland, 1999). A professor traces the history of a secret, long-lost Vermeer painting.

Girl with a Pearl Earring (Tracy Chevalier, 1999). Historical portrait of artist Johannes Vermeer and his maiden servant in 17th-century Delft (also a fine film).

Max Havelaar: Or the Coffee Auctions of the Dutch Trading Company (Multatuli, 1860). Satirical novel denouncing the injustices of the Dutch colonial system in Indonesia.

Tulip Fever (Deborah Moggach, 1999). A love-triangle drama set in 17th century Amsterdam.

Films

Antonia's Line (1995). A portrait of five generations of Dutch women.

Black Book (2006). A sexy blonde bombshell fights for the Dutch Resistance.

The Diary of Anne Frank (1959). A moving version of Anne's story.

Girl with a Pearl Earring (2003). A fictionalized Vermeer paints—and falls in love with—his servant in Delft.

Ocean's Twelve (2004). Heist sequel to *Ocean's Eleven*, with scenes set in Amsterdam's Jordaan neighborhood.

Soldier of Orange (1977). Epic tale about the Nazi occupation and Dutch Resistance during World War II (and a good book).

Vincent and Theo (1990). Captures the relationship between the great artist and his brother.

APPENDIX

Contents

Useful Contacts
Emergency Needs
Police, Ambulance, or Fire: 112

Embassies and Consulates
US Embassies and Consulates: Amsterdam—tel. 020/575-5309 during normal office hours, otherwise in case of emergency call after-duty officer at tel. 070/310-2209 (Museumplein 19, http://amsterdam.usconsulate.gov). Online appointments are mandatory for all public services.

The Hague—tel. 070/310-2209, visits by appointment only (Lange Voorhout 102, http://netherlands.usembassy.gov).
Canadian Embassy: The Hague—tel. 070/311-1600 (Sophialaan 7, Mon-Fri 9:00-13:00 & 14:00-17:30, closed Sat-Sun; consular services Mon-Fri 9:30-13:00, closed Sat-Sun; www.canada.nl).

Holidays and Festivals

This list includes selected festivals in major cities, plus national holidays. Many sights and banks close on national holidays—keep this in mind when planning your itinerary. Before planning a trip around a festival, verify its dates by checking the festival's website or TI sites (www.holland.com).

Here are some major holidays:

Jan 1	New Year's Day
Feb	Carnival (Mardi Gras)
March-May	Keukenhof flower show, Lisse (check opening dates at www.keukenhof.nl)
Easter	Sunday and Monday (April 5-6 in 2015, March 27-28 in 2016)
April	Flower Parade (April 25 in 2015, www.bloemencorso-bollenstreek.nl), Noordwijk to Haarlem
April 27	King's Day (Koningsdag), King Willem-Alexander's birthday, party in the streets of Amsterdam
May 4	Remembrance of WWII Dead (Dodenherdenking)
May 5	Liberation Day (Bevrijdingsdag)
May	Art Amsterdam—contemporary-art exhibition (May 27-31 in 2015, www.kunstrai.nl)
May or June	Ascension (May 14 in 2015, May 5 in 2016)
May or June	Pentecost and Whit Monday (May 24-25 in 2015, May 15-16 in 2016)
Late June	Grachtenloop run around canals, www.grachtenloop.nl), Haarlem
June	Holland Arts Festival (concerts, theater, etc., www.hollandfestival.nl), Amsterdam
June	Amsterdam Roots Festival—Oosterpark (ethnic food, music, world culture; www.amsterdamroots.nl)
June	The Hague Festivals—three weeks of music festivals: Festival Classique, Parkpop, and The Hague jazz (www.thehaguefestivals.com)
Mid-July	North Sea Jazz Festival (www.northseajazz.nl), The Hague
Late July-Early Aug	Gay Pride (www.amsterdamgaypride.nl), Amsterdam
Early-mid-Aug	Pluk de Nacht—outdoor film festival on the site of an old harbor (www.plukdenacht.nl), Amsterdam

Aug 15	Assumption Day
Mid-Aug	SAIL Amsterdam, held every five years (Aug 19–23 in 2015, tall ships and other historic boats, www.sail.nl)
Mid-Aug	Prinsengracht canal concert on barges—music and other festivities (Aug 14-23 in 2015, www.grachtenfestival.nl), Amsterdam
Late Aug	Haarlem Jazz—free jazz festival held on Grote Markt (third weekend of August, www.haarlemjazzstad.nl)
Sept (first week)	Flower parade on canals, Aalsmeer to Amsterdam
Mid-Sept	Jordaan Festival—neighborhood street party (www.jordaanfestival.nl), Amsterdam
Sept or Oct	Yom Kippur (Sept 22-23 in 2015, Oct 11-12 in 2016, Jewish holiday, some closures, including Anne Frank House and Jewish Historical Museum in Amsterdam)
Nov 1	All Saints' Day
Mid-Nov	Sinterklaas ("Santa Claus") procession, Amsterdam
Dec 5	St. Nicholas' Eve (Sinterklaasavond, when Sinterklaas and Zwarte Piet arrive), procession and presents
Dec 25	Christmas
Dec 26	"Second Day" of Christmas (Tweede Kerstdag)

Conversions and Climate

NUMBERS AND STUMBLERS

- Europeans write a few of their numbers differently than we do. 1 = 1, 4 = 4, 7 = 7.
- In Europe, dates appear as day/month/year, so Christmas 2016 is 25/12/16.
- Commas are decimal points and decimal are commas. A dollar and a half is $1,50, one thousand is 1.000, and there are 5.280 feet in a mile.
- When counting with fingers, start with your thumb. If you hold up your first finger to request one item, you'll probably get two.
- What Americans call the second floor of a building is the first floor in Europe.

- On escalators and moving sidewalks, Europeans keep the left "lane" open for passing. Keep to the right.

METRIC CONVERSIONS

A kilogram is 2.2 pounds, and l liter is about a quart, or almost four to a gallon. A kilometer is six-tenths of a mile. I figure kilometers to miles by cutting them in half and adding back 10 percent of the original (120 km: 60 + 12 = 72 miles, 300 km: 150 + 30 = 180 miles).

1 foot = 0.3 meter	1 square yard = 0.8 square meter
1 yard = 0.9 meter	1 square mile = 2.6 square kilometers
1 mile = 1.6 kilometers	1 ounce = 28 grams
1 centimeter = 0.4 inch	1 quart = 0.95 liter
1 meter = 39.4 inches	1 kilogram = 2.2 pounds
1 kilometer = 0.62 mile	32°F = 0°C

CLOTHING SIZES

When shopping for clothing, use these US-to-European comparisons as general guidelines (but note that no conversion is perfect).

- Women's dresses and blouses: Add 30
  (US size 10 = European size 40)
- Men's suits and jackets: Add 10
  (US size 40 regular = European size 50)
- Men's shirts: Multiply by 2 and add about 8
  (US size 15 collar = European size 38)
- Women's shoes: Add about 30
  (US size 8 = European size 38-39)
- Men's shoes: Add 32-34
  (US size 9 = European size 41; US size 11 = European size 45)

THE NETHERLANDS CLIMATE

First line, average daily high; second line, average daily low; third line, average days without rain. For more detailed weather statistics for destinations in this book (as well as the rest of the world), check www.wunderground.com.

J	F	M	A	M	J	J	A	S	O	N	D
41°	42°	49°	55°	64°	70°	72°	71°	66°	56°	48°	41°
30°	31°	35°	40°	45°	52°	55°	55°	51°	43°	37°	33°
8		9	16	14	16	16	14	12	11	11	10

APPENDIX

FAHRENHEIT AND CELSIUS CONVERSION

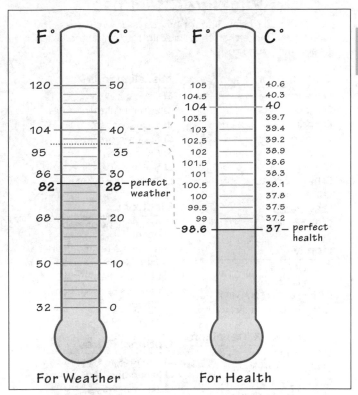

For Weather

For Health

Europe takes its temperature using the Celsius scale, while we opt for Fahrenheit. For a rough conversion from Celsius to Fahrenheit, double the number and add 30. For weather, remember that 28°C is 82°F—perfect. For health, 37°C is just right. At a launderette, 30°C is cold, 40°C is warm (usually the default setting), 60°C is hot, and 95°C is boiling.

Packing Checklist

Whether you're traveling for five days or five weeks, you won't need more than this. Pack light to enjoy the sweet freedom of true mobility.

Clothing

- ❑ 5 shirts: long- & short-sleeve
- ❑ 2 pairs pants or skirt
- ❑ 1 pair shorts or capris
- ❑ 5 pairs underwear & socks
- ❑ 1 pair walking shoes
- ❑ Sweater or fleece top
- ❑ Rainproof jacket with hood
- ❑ Tie or scarf
- ❑ Swimsuit
- ❑ Sleepwear

Money

- ❑ Debit card
- ❑ Credit card(s)
- ❑ Hard cash ($20 bills)
- ❑ Money belt or neck wallet

Documents & Travel Info

- ❑ Passport
- ❑ Airline reservations
- ❑ Rail pass/train reservations
- ❑ Car-rental voucher
- ❑ Driver's license
- ❑ Student ID, hostel card, etc.
- ❑ Photocopies of all the above
- ❑ Hotel confirmations
- ❑ Insurance details
- ❑ Guidebooks & maps
- ❑ Notepad & pen
- ❑ Journal

Toiletries Kit

- ❑ Toiletries
- ❑ Medicines & vitamins
- ❑ First-aid kit
- ❑ Glasses/contacts/sunglasses (with prescriptions)
- ❑ Earplugs
- ❑ Packet of tissues (for WC)

Miscellaneous

- ❑ Daypack
- ❑ Sealable plastic baggies
- ❑ Laundry soap
- ❑ Spot remover
- ❑ Clothesline
- ❑ Sewing kit
- ❑ Travel alarm/watch

Electronics

- ❑ Smartphone or mobile phone
- ❑ Camera & related gear
- ❑ Tablet/ereader/media player
- ❑ Laptop & flash drive
- ❑ Earbuds or headphones
- ❑ Chargers
- ❑ Plug adapters

Optional Extras

- ❑ Flipflops or slippers
- ❑ Mini-umbrella or poncho
- ❑ Travel hairdryer
- ❑ Belt
- ❑ Hat (for sun or cold)
- ❑ Picnic supplies
- ❑ Water bottle
- ❑ Fold-up tote bag
- ❑ Small flashlight
- ❑ Small binoculars
- ❑ Insect repellent
- ❑ Small towel or washcloth
- ❑ Inflatable pillow
- ❑ Some duct tape (for repairs)
- ❑ Tiny lock
- ❑ Address list (to mail postcards)
- ❑ Postcards/photos from home
- ❑ Extra passport photos
- ❑ Good book

Dutch Survival Phrases

Most people speak English, but if you learn the pleasantries and key phrases, you'll connect better with the locals. To pronounce the guttural Dutch "g" (indicated in phonetics by *h*), make a clear-your-throat sound, similar to the "ch" in the Scottish word "loch."

English	Dutch	Pronunciation
Hello.	*Hallo.*	**hah**-loh
Good day.	*Dag.*	da*h*
Good morning.	*Goedemorgen.*	**hoo**-deh-mor-*h*ehn
Good afternoon.	*Goedemiddag.*	**hoo**-deh-mid-da*h*
Good evening.	*Goedenavond.*	**hoo**-dehn-ah-fohnd
Do you speak English?	*Spreekt u Engels?*	shpraykt oo **eng**-ehls
Yes. / No.	*Ja. / Nee.*	yah / nay
I (don't) understand.	*Ik begrijp (het niet).*	ik beh-**hripe** (heht neet)
Please. (can also mean "You're welcome")	*Alstublieft.*	**ahl**-stoo-bleeft
Thank you.	*Dank u wel.*	dahnk oo vehl
I'm sorry.	*Het spijt me.*	heht spite meh
Excuse me.	*Pardon.*	**par**-dohn
(No) problem.	*(Geen) probleem.*	(hayn) **proh**-blaym
Good.	*Goede.*	**hoo**-deh
Goodbye.	*Tot ziens.*	toht zeens
one / two	*een / twee*	ayn / t'vay
three / four	*drie / vier*	dree / feer
five / six	*vijf / zes*	fife / zehs
seven / eight	*zeven / acht*	**zay**-fehn / aht
nine / ten	*negen / tien*	**nay**-hehn / teen
What does it cost?	*Wat kost het?*	vaht kohst heht
Is it free?	*Is het vrij?*	is heht fry
Is it included?	*Is het inclusief?*	is heht in-**kloo**-seev
Can you please help me?	*Kunt u alstublieft helpen?*	koont oo **ahl**-stoo-bleeft **hehl**-pehn
Where can I buy / find...?	*Waar kan ik kopen / vinden...?*	var kahn ik **koh**-pehn / **fin**-dehn
I'd like / We'd like...	*Ik wil graag / Wij willen graag...*	ik vil *h*rah / vy **vil**-lehn *h*rah
...a room.	*...een kamer.*	ayn **kah**-mer
...a train / bus ticket to ____.	*...een trein / bus kaartje naar ____.*	ayn trayn / boos **kart**-yeh nar ____
...to rent a bike.	*...een fiets huren.*	ayn feets **hoo**-rehn
Where is...?	*Waar is...?*	var is
...the train / bus station	*...het trein / bus station*	heht trayn / boos **staht**-see-ohn
...the tourist info office	*...de VVV*	deh fay fay fay
...the toilet	*...het toilet*	heht **twah**-leht
men / women	*mannen / vrouwen*	**mah**-nehn / **frow**-ehn
left / right	*links / rechts*	links / reh*h*ts
straight ahead	*rechtdoor*	**reh***h*-dor
What time does it open / close?	*Hoe laat gaat het open / dicht?*	hoo laht *h*aht heht **oh**-pehn / di*h*t
now / soon / later	*nu / straks / later*	noo / strahks / **lah**-ter
today / tomorrow	*vandaag / morgen*	**fahn**-da*h* / **mor**-*h*ehn

In the Restaurant

The all-purpose Dutch word *alstublieft* (**ahl**-stoo-bleeft) means "please," but it can also mean "here you are" (when the server hands you something), "thanks" (when taking payment from you), or "you're welcome" (when handing you change). Here are other words that might come in handy at restaurants:

English	Dutch	Pronunciation
I'd like / We'd like...	*Ik will graag / Wij willen graag...*	ik vil *hrah* / vy **vil**-lehn *hrah*
...a table for one / two.	*...een tafel voor een / twee.*	ayn **tah**-fehl for ayn / t'vay
...to reserve a table.	*...een tafel reserveren.*	ayn **tah**-fehl **ray**-zehr-feh-rehn
...the menu (in English).	*...het menu (in het Engels).*	heht meh-**noo** (in heht **eng**-ehls)
Is this table free?	*Is deze tafel vrij?*	is **day**-zeh **tah**-fehl fry
to go	*om mee te nemen*	ohm may teh **nay**-mehn
with / without	*met / zonder*	meht / **zohn**-der
and / or	*en / of*	ehn / of
special of the day	*dagschotel*	**dahs**-hoh-tehl
specialty of the house	*huisspecialiteit*	**hows**-shpeh-shah-lee-tite
breakfast	*ontbijt*	**ohnt**-bite
lunch	*middagmaal*	**mid**-da*h*-mahl
dinner	*avondmaal*	**ah**-fohnd-mahl
appetizers	*hapjes*	**hahp**-yehs
main courses	*hoofdgerechten*	**hohfd**-heh-reh-tehn
side dishes	*bijgerechten*	**bye**-heh-reh-tehn
bread / cheese	*brood / kaas*	brohd / kahs
sandwich	*sandwich*	**sand**-vich
soup / salad	*soep / sla*	soop / slah
meat / chicken / fish	*vlees / kip / vis*	flays / kip / fis
fruit / vegetables	*vrucht / groenten*	fruht / **hroon**-tehn
dessert / pastries	*gebak*	heh-**bahk**
I am vegetarian.	*Ik ben vegetarisch.*	ik behn vay-*h*eh-**tah**-rish
mineral water / tap water	*mineraalwater / kraanwater*	min-eh-rahl-**vah**-ter / **krahn**-vah-ter
milk / (orange) juice	*melk / (sinaasappel) sap*	mehlk / **see**-nahs-ah-pehl (sahp)
coffee / tea	*koffie / thee*	**koh**-fee / tay
wine / beer	*wijn / bier*	vine / beer
red / white	*rode / witte*	**roh**-deh / **vit**-teh
glass / bottle	*glas / fles*	*h*lahs / flehs
Cheers!	*Proost!*	prohst
More. / Another.	*Meer. / Nog een.*	mayr / noh ayn
The same.	*Het zelfde.*	heht **zehlf**-deh
The bill, please.	*De rekening, alstublieft.*	deh **ray**-keh-neeng **ahl**-stoo-bleeft
Do you accept credit cards?	*Accepteert u kredietkaarten?*	**ahk**-shehp-tayrt oo kray-deet-**kar**-tehn
Is service included?	*Is bediening inbegrepen?*	is beh-**dee**-neeng in-beh-*hray*-pehn
tip	*fooi*	foy
Tasty.	*Lekker.*	**leh**-ker
Enjoy!	*Smakelijk!*	**smah**-keh-like

INDEX

MAP INDEX

Our website enhances this book and turns

Explore Europe

At ricksteves.com you can browse through thousands of articles, videos, photos and radio interviews, plus find a wealth of money-saving travel tips for planning your dream trip. And with our mobile-friendly website, you can easily access all this great travel information anywhere you go.

TV Shows

Preview the places you'll visit by watching entire half-hour episodes of Rick Steves' Europe (choose from all 100 shows) on-demand, for free.

ricksteves.com

your travel dreams into affordable reality

Radio Interviews

Enjoy ready access to Rick's vast library of radio interviews covering travel

tips and cultural insights that relate specifically to your Europe travel plans.

Travel Forums

Learn, ask, share! Our online community of savvy travelers is a great resource

for first-time travelers to Europe, as well as seasoned pros. You'll find forums on each country, plus travel tips and restaurant/hotel reviews. You can even ask one of our well-traveled staff to chime in with an opinion.

Travel News

Subscribe to our free Travel News e-newsletter, and get monthly updates from Rick on what's happening in Europe.

Audio Europe™

Pack Light and Right

Gear up for your next adventure at ricksteves.com

Light Luggage

Pack light and right with Rick Steves' affordable, custom-designed rolling carry-on bags, backpacks, day packs and shoulder bags.

Accessories

From packing cubes to moneybelts and beyond, Rick has personally selected the travel goodies that will help your trip go smoother.

Rick Steves has

Save time and energy

This guidebook is your independent-travel toolkit. But for all it delivers, it's still up to you to devote the time and energy it takes to manage the preparation and logistics that are essential for a happy trip. If that's a hassle, there's a solution.

Rick Steves Tours

A Rick Steves tour takes you to Europe's most interesting places with great

great tours, too!

with minimum stress

guides and small groups of 28 or less. We follow Rick's favorite itineraries, ride in comfy buses, stay in family-run hotels, and bring you intimately close to the Europe you've traveled so far to see. Most importantly, we take away the logistical headaches so you can focus on the fun.

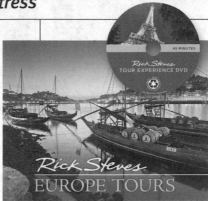

customers—along with us on 40 different itineraries, from Ireland to Italy to Istanbul. Is a Rick Steves tour the right fit for your travel dreams? Find out at ricksteves.com, where you can also get Rick's latest tour catalog and free Tour Experience DVD.

Join the fun

This year we'll take 18,000 free-spirited travelers— nearly half of them repeat

Europe is best experienced with happy travel partners. We hope you can join us.

See our itineraries at ricksteves.com

Rick Steves®

EUROPE GUIDES

Best of Europe
Eastern Europe
Europe Through the Back Door
Mediterranean Cruise Ports
Northern European Cruise Ports

COUNTRY GUIDES

Croatia & Slovenia
England
France
Germany
Great Britain
Ireland
Italy
Portugal
Scandinavia
Spain
Switzerland

CITY & REGIONAL GUIDES

Amsterdam, Bruges & Brussels
Barcelona
Budapest
Florence & Tuscany
Greece: Athens & the Peloponnese
Istanbul
London
Paris
Prague & the Czech Republic
Provence & the French Riviera
Rome
Venice
Vienna, Salzburg & Tirol

SNAPSHOT GUIDES

Basque Country: Spain & France
Berlin
Bruges & Brussels
Copenhagen & the Best of
   Denmark
Dublin
Dubrovnik
Hill Towns of Central Italy
Italy's Cinque Terre
Krakow, Warsaw & Gdansk
Lisbon
Madrid & Toledo
Milan & the Italian Lakes District
Munich, Bavaria & Salzburg
Naples & the Amalfi Coast
Northern Ireland
Norway
Scotland
Sevilla, Granada & Southern Spain
Stockholm

POCKET GUIDES

Amsterdam
Athens
Barcelona
Florence
London
Paris
Rome
Venice

Rick Steves guidebooks are published by Avalon Travel,
a member of the Perseus Books Group.

NOW AVAILABLE:
eBOOKS, DVD & BLU-RAY

Credits

For help with this edition, Rick and Gene relied on...

RESEARCHERS

Cameron Hewitt

Cameron writes and edits guidebooks for Rick Steves, specializing in Eastern Europe. For this book, he enjoyed speedy visits to Rotterdam, Delft, Leiden, and Utrecht, and explored the dining and shopping scene in Amsterdam. When he's not traveling, Cameron lives in Seattle with his wife, Shawna.

Amanda Zurita

Amanda caught the travel bug early—she's been flying since before she could walk. When she's not hovering over a bowl of mussels in Bruges, checking out vintage shops in Antwerp, or dodging cyclists in Amsterdam, she lives in Seattle with her beloved Labrador, Hadrian.

Avalon Travel
a member of the Perseus Books Group
1700 Fourth Street
Berkeley, CA 94710, USA

Printed in Canada by Friesens.
First printing March 2015.

ISBN 978-1-63121-066-2
ISSN 2376-5666

For the latest on Rick's lectures, guidebooks, tours, public radio show, and public television series, contact Rick Steves' Europe, 130 Fourth Avenue North, Edmonds, WA 98020, tel. 425/771-8303, www.ricksteves.com, rick@ricksteves.com.

Rick Steves' Europe

Managing Editor: Risa Laib
Editorial & Production Manager: Jennifer Madison Davis
Editors: Glenn Eriksen, Tom Griffin, Cameron Hewitt, Suzanne Kotz, Cathy Lu, Carrie Shepherd
Editorial & Production Assistant: Jessica Shaw
Editorial Interns: Stacie Larsen, Mallory Presho-Dunne
Researchers: Cameron Hewitt, Amanda Zurita
Maps & Graphics: David C. Hoerlein, Sandra Hundacker, Lauren Mills, Mary Rostad

Avalon Travel

Senior Editor & Series Manager: Madhu Prasher
Editor: Jamie Andrade
Associate Editor: Maggie Ryan
Copy Editor: Denise Silva
Proofreader: Megan Mulholland
Indexer: Stephen Callahan
Production & Typesetting: Tabitha Lahr
Cover Design: Kimberly Glyder Design
Maps & Graphics: Kat Bennett, Mike Morgenfeld

Photo Credits

Front Cover: Keizersgracht, Amsterdam © Fraser Hall/Getty Images
Title Page: p.i, Amsterdam at night © Rick Steves, p. xii, Amsterdam © Rick Steves
Full-page Photos: p. 15, Edam; p. 23, Amsterdam Canal; p. 261, Haarlem Hofje; p. 303, Delft Canal; p. 329, Enkhuizen/Historic Triangle
Additional Photography: Dominic Arizona Bonuccelli, Rich Earl, Tom Griffin, Jennifer Hauseman, Cameron Hewitt, Gene Openshaw, Rick Steves, Gretchen Strauch, Laura VanDeventer, Wikimedia Commons—PD-Art/PD-US (photos are used by permission and are the property of the original copyright owners)

More for your trip!
Maximize the experience with Rick Steves as your guide

Guidebooks
Dozens of European city and country guidebooks

Planning Maps
Use the map that's in sync with your guidebook

Rick's TV Shows
Preview Amsterdam with Rick's TV shows

Free! Rick's Audio Europe™ App
Get free audio tours for Amsterdam's top sights

Small Group Tours
Including the Heart of Belgium and Holland

For all the details, visit ricksteves.com